ESSENTIAL PSYCHOLOGY

ESSENTIAL PSYCHOLOGY

A CONCISE INTRODUCTION

EDITED BY **PHILIP BANYARD, MARK N.O. DAVIES, CHRISTINE NORMAN** & BELINDA WINDER

Los Angeles | London | New Delhi
Singapore | Washington DC

First published 2010

SAGE Publications Ltd
1 Oliver's Yard
55 City Road
London EC1Y 1SP

SAGE Publications Inc.
2455 Teller Road
Thousand Oaks, California 91320

SAGE Publications India Pvt Ltd
B 1/I 1 Mohan Cooperative Industrial Area
Mathura Road
New Delhi 110 044

SAGE Publications Asia-Pacific Pte Ltd
33 Pekin Street #02-01
Far East Square
Singapore 048763

Library of Congress Control Number: 2009933629

British Library Cataloguing in Publication data

A catalogue record for this book is available from the British Library

ISBN 978-1-84787-537-2
ISBN 978-1-84787-538-9 (pbk)

Typeset by C&M Digitals (P) Ltd, Chennai, India
Printed and bound in Great Britain by Ashford Colour Press Ltd
Printed on paper from sustainable resources

CONTENTS

**Section F   HOW WE KNOW AND MEASURE OUR INDIVIDUALITY
The Psychology of Individual Differences   315**

ABOUT THE BOOK

What is psychology? Everyone seems to have a good idea about what it is, but those ideas often don't match what is studied at university. If you ask someone what a psychologist does then they are most likely to suggest that they

- read minds
- tell you how to improve your love life
- study body language
- sit you on a couch and talk to you about your mother
- chase serial killers.

Sadly, none of these are true. Take the first one, for example. Psychologists cannot read minds and neither can anyone else. If someone tells you that they can read minds then they are lying, deluded or both. In fact the complexities of your own mind are so great that you can't even read it that well yourself. We may not be able to read minds but we can certainly study how the mind works and influences the world around us. The truth is far more exciting than the fiction. Psychology is the scientific study of mind and experience; we leave the myth-making and psychobabble to entertainers.

Psychology, we believe, is an amazing subject. Whether you want to know if a baby smiles because it recognises its mother, or how a cricketer manages to strike a ball with his bat, psychology offers you a way of exploring these questions. Studying psychology will encourage you to challenge the way you think about yourself and your place in the world.

Our text is aimed at A level students and first year undergraduates. We do not assume too much prior knowledge of the subject. Nevertheless, our philosophy in writing the book is that you are introduced to some of the big questions in psychology. These are questions like: who am I? And why am I here? And why do I feel annoyed when Nottingham Forest loses a game? From big questions to small questions there is so much we don't know about the way that people tick. To be a psychologist is to be an explorer, discovering new information to help those that follow. We invite you to join us on this big adventure.

An example of one of the big questions in psychology concerns the distinction between sensation and perception. Various things hit our senses: for example, light enters our eyes, and changes in air pressure are detected by our ears. We detect these changes in the environment, but the psychological miracle is that our brain processes the information our senses detect to produce the fantastic images and sounds that we perceive. If you have studied biology at school you'll probably know that we detect light on the flat screen of our retinas at the back of our eyes, but had you wondered how we manage to see in 3D? Our brains turn that flat image into the 3D world we experience. Our brains are sophisticated perceptual detectives. They take in a range of sensory cues to generate a plausible account of the world we experience – the perceived 3D world we are all familiar with.

When you read this book you'll find it full of the information that you might expect in a textbook, but try to keep these bigger questions in mind. The way that we experience the world, interact with people, problem solve and reflect on our own behaviour is a miracle that psychology is only just starting to explore.

THE TEXT

The text is designed around the six areas that make up the core of any undergraduate curriculum in the UK. We start with the difficult stuff, which comprises the areas commonly referred to as CHIPS by psychologists (conceptual and historical issues in psychology). Our journey begins with an evolutionary explanation to questions about how we came to be as we are in Chapter 1. This stretches from the cave to the computer and we consider one possible future for human evolution. We go on in Chapters 2 and 3 to look at the history of psychology and the modern ways that we describe what it means to be alive, to be conscious. We have introduced these concepts at the beginning not to put you off or try to impress you but because we think that these are the ideas that infuse the whole of modern psychology.

The following sections each have three chapters about cognitive psychology, biological psychology, social psychology, developmental psychology and the psychology of individual differences. In the space available we aim to provide you with enough material to understand and explore the basic concepts in these fields. We also hope to arouse your interest and provide you with enough questions so that you feel the urge to go on to further study in one or more of the areas.

The text has a number of features that have been chosen to help your understanding of the material and make it interesting to read. These include key studies on particular topics, short biographies of key contemporary researchers, exercises, suggestions for further reading and some lame attempts at humour.

THE AUTHORS

The book has contributions from 36 academic staff in the Division of Psychology at Nottingham Trent University. It has been edited by four of these staff and we hope that we have created a text that reads as if it has one author rather than many. We were going to include a picture of all the authors but modesty and, frankly, good taste prevailed. Maybe we will put one up on the website for the curious to marvel at.

One of the most striking aspects of being an editor is to watch your colleagues adopt the behaviour of students. Much of this is very positive but some of the negative aspects also crept in. At the university we have strict deadlines and word limits for student work and it is part of the corridor culture for staff to throw their eyebrows to the ceiling when these basic rules are not met by their students. Lecturers commonly think that it is easy to keep to deadlines and word limits.

Imagine our surprise to find that these same staff used the worst excuses to explain their own lateness. Bargaining for an extension accompanied by the lamest of excuses became a daily event for the editors. Avoidance, denial and emotional blackmail became part of the daily discourse on the corridor. And as for word limits ... you'd think it could not get more simple than to say 7500–8000 words, but only a handful of chapters were submitted around the word limit. The most extreme was 15,000 words, which also included a note to say that they still needed to add another section. Most inexplicable was the 8500-word chapter that was sent back to the author to reduce it a bit and came back at 9500 words.

Students, take heart from this. If these authors had been students at this university most of them would have had their work failed for lateness, marked down for being overlength and derided for the poor quality of their excuses. It must be harder being a student than we remember, and that is a key lesson we'll take from this process.

ACKNOWLEDGEMENTS

The editors would like to acknowledge their students at Nottingham Trent University who have put up with our weak attempts at humour over the years and have engaged with us in a positive and productive way. Learning is not something that stops when you get your degree, and our students help us to keep looking at material afresh and keep learning ourselves.

The editors would also like to acknowledge the positive and supportive working environment that they enjoy with their colleagues at Nottingham Trent University. We would like to thank Tim Clack, Eleanor Davey, Mark Thomas, Kathy Bach, Jemma Underwood, Sheilah Han, Tim Wells, Aarti Kotecha, Danni Mayes and Leah James for their help with this project. Michael Carmichael and the staff at SAGE have been very supportive and shown remarkable confidence in, and tolerance of the editors. Finally, the editors would like to namecheck The Bread and Bitter, psychexchange, Amy Jailbird Harris, Somnium the Tortoise and Clifford the Wise.

The editors and publishers would like to thank the many academic peer reviewers who have provided useful comments at various points throughout the project. Specific thanks goes to those who took the time to read the proofs at the final stages before going to press, including Professor S. Alexander Hallam, Professor Peter K. Smith, Professor Rom Harré, Professor Rick Hanley, Dr Suzanne Higgs, Dr Harriet E.S. Rosenthal and Dr Dawn Watling.

GUIDED TOUR

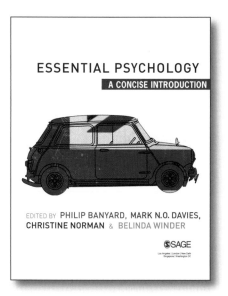

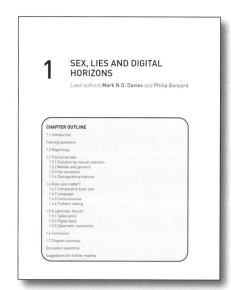

Chapter Outline: The first page of all chapters includes the list of contents.

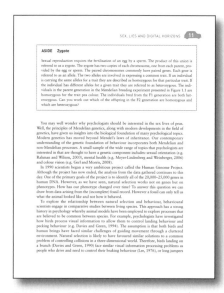

Introduction and Framing Questions: Each chapter begins with an introduction that provides you with the overall framework of the chapter. It gives you a map of the journey you are about to undertake with each topic area, the key ideas, and the contexts in which these ideas developed. The framing questions provide key questions which will emerge in the chapter.

Aside: Not all of the interesting things we want to tell you about fit into the narratives we create in each chapter. We have added some asides which are descriptons of a relevant idea or piece of research. You might like to explore them further once you've read the main body text.

Key Researcher: Every field in psychology has thousands of researchers. We've selected a number of mainly current researchers to highlight their work and also to give a flavour of the range of interests that psychologists have. You might find that you want to follow up their work, if so then Google them. It's amazing what you can find out.

Key Study: Psychology is mainly led by research studies. These are the basic evidence that is at the heart of any theory. To emphasise this we have included an outline of one important piece of research which has been carried out and which relates to the topics in the chapter.

Exercise: We all learn best by doing. With this in mind we have made some suggestions of things you can do which will clarify or extend your learning. We include group and individual-based exercises which are designed to provide practical and reflective learning on key issues, concepts and phenomena covered in each chapter.

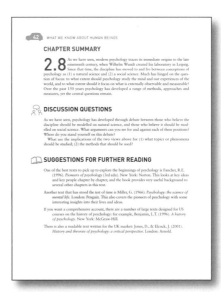

Chapter Summaries: A review of the main concepts and issues covered in the chapter to reinforce the key points. These are followed by **Discussion Questions** to explore with friends on your course or individually and **Suggestions for Further Reading** which point you towards more material to explore relating to the chapter.

COMPANION WEBSITE

For the cyber-hungry of you, or for those who are more inclined to read in pixels than in print, this textbook comes with an accompanying website (www.sagepub.co.uk/banyard) providing lecturers and students with a suite of materials written by the editors and authors.

Naturally, being the *Essential Psychology* website, we believe it consists of the *essential* materials needed for lecturers to help them teach from the textbook and for students to prepare for assignments or exams on a foundation course. Below is the top half of the rather funky homepage image for the website including, of course, the Mini image that you're probably all pondering about … Well, we think that this textbook is compact, affordable, stylish and gives you what you need for your journey without all the redundant extras – just like the eponymous Mini! Get it? Well, we like it anyway.

Anyway, we digress. Here's an image of the website and a list of its features:

- A **test bank of multiple choice questions** (30 per chapter), a set of **teaching notes** and a full set of **PowerPoint slides** per chapter for lecturers available on a password restricted basis. These are wrapped up ready in a cartridge for importing into any VLE (Virtual Learning Environment).

- An **online multiple choice quiz** (10 per chapter), a **flashcard glossary quiz** per chapter for students freely available to all, plus a list of interesting and selective **web links** related to discussions throughout the textbook.

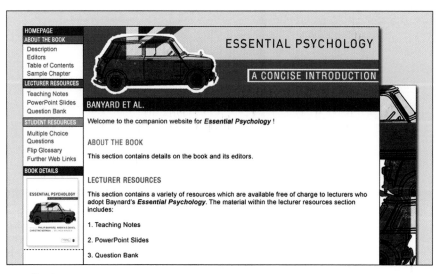

Happy surfing!

WHAT WE KNOW ABOUT HUMAN BEINGS

The Foundations of Psychology

If I have seen further it is by standing on the shoulders of Giants.

Isaac Newton, 1676

Human beings are remarkable creatures. Most remarkable is our ability and almost obsession to pass our knowledge on from one generation to another. We have studied our world and recorded the data for thousands of years and from this study we know a lot about the world and also about ourselves.

Modern psychology is commonly dated to the middle of the nineteenth century but our interest in who and what we are dates back to early civilisations. There are writings from ancient Egypt, China, India and Greece that speculate on what a person is and how we came to be. The way that we think about ourselves today has been developed over generations, and to understand modern psychology it is important to know about the history of the subject. This is often placed at the end of psychology courses and texts but we have started our book with this section because we think it presents ideas that will help you understand what follows in later sections.

The distinguishing feature of modern psychology is its position in the sciences, and the key feature of science is the way that it gathers and interprets its evidence. The scientific approach is to be *empirical*, which means that we gather evidence that is open to scrutiny, is preferably replicable (we can repeat the study to check our findings) and is falsifiable. This last point sounds strange at first glance but is actually very important.

Science moves on in small steps. The quote above from Isaac Newton, probably the UK's greatest scientist, shows how even the most eminent scientists are aware of this. The common view of science is that we are able to prove things and discover once and for all how things work. This is not the case, however: we are not able to prove anything, but can only come up with theories that offer the best explanation of the phenomena we observe. If we obtain new information in the future we might well find that there is a better explanation and so we then discard our original theory.

Knowledge is provisional. This means that we are not uncovering the truth but inching our way to new understandings. What we 'know' today will be the chip paper of tomorrow. Newton's law of gravity is an example of this. The shock of being hit on the head by an apple helped Newton devise his law, which stood for more than 200 years until a better understanding of the movement of objects in the universe was devised by Einstein in his theory of general relativity. Our psychological theories cannot expect to last as long as Newton's laws.

If we want psychology to progress then we have to accept that what we believe to be true today might well be shown to be not true tomorrow. Our theories therefore have to allow for the possibility of disproof.

The foundation of psychology is based on traditions from philosophy, biology, medicine and literature. It is among a number of new sciences like economics that try to analyse and explain the ways that people behave in their world. The section gives the background to the development of this science of behaviour and experience.

ASIDE   Are we as clever as we think?

The excellent *Hitch hiker's guide to the galaxy* by Douglas Adams suggests that dolphins are more intelligent than humans:

> For instance, on the planet Earth, man had always assumed that he was more intelligent than dolphins because he had achieved so much – the wheel, New York, wars and so on – whilst all the dolphins had ever done was muck about in the water having a good time. But conversely, the dolphins had always believed that they were far more intelligent than man – for precisely the same reasons. (Adams, 1979)

KEY ISSUES

One of the key issues for psychologists looking into the history of the subject is to define exactly what the subject is about. The perspective we take to looking at people affects what we see. If we take an evolutionary perspective, then we will see much of human behaviour as being motivated by the drive to reproduce. If we take a physiological perspective, we will see people as biological machines and their actions as largely mechanical responses to changes in their environment. The perspective is important because it will affect not only how we see people but also how we treat them.

THIS SECTION

In this section we have three chapters looking at the development of psychological ideas. We start off in Chapter 1 by looking at how Darwin's theory of evolution shapes modern psychology and we speculate about what the next big jump will be in the development of humanity. In Chapter 2, we look at the early psychologists and how they have framed the debate about who we are and what we are, and devised the methods to explore these questions. In Chapter 3 we look at some philosophical issues that have puzzled and continue to puzzle psychologists concerning our consciousness and our identity.

1 SEX, LIES AND DIGITAL HORIZONS

Lead authors **Mark N.O. Davies** and **Philip Banyard**

INTRODUCTION

1.1 Psychology asks the big questions, and among the biggest are questions about why people think, feel and behave in the way that they do. How did we come to look like this, be like this and behave like this? One part of the answer comes from our understanding of evolution and genetics. From single-celled swamp organisms we have evolved into the complex creatures we are today. In this chapter we will consider how this development has taken place, what effect our ancestry has on us today and where we may be heading in the future. Don't expect all the answers, but do expect to think differently about some of the questions. What better place to start a psychology book than to ask what are human beings, and how did they come to be?

> **? FRAMING QUESTIONS**
>
> Did Darwin invent evolution?
> What does the term *Homo sapiens* mean and why is it used?
> Is there any attribute that is uniquely human?
> What is the future of psychology?

BEGINNINGS

1.2 How we became the animal known as *Homo sapiens* (Greek meaning 'wise man') is a fascinating story that requires us to draw on the thinking of two giants of the natural sciences: **Charles Darwin** (1809–1882) and **Gregor Mendel** (1822–1884). Through meticulous description and systematic empirical investigation, both men developed world-changing theories to explain how we evolved. It is clear that as life evolved on earth the physical form of species changed, though it is not only physical characteristics that are affected by evolution. Behaviour can also be an identifiable feature of a species and can evolve over time.

In psychology the emphasis is placed on causal explanations: that is, we look at what has caused a behaviour to occur. This is an important question, but we also need to look at the 'why' question. In an evolutionary context this question becomes 'What use is that behaviour?' or 'What function does it serve?' To illustrate this we can look at the syndrome we know as **schizophrenia**. Quite naturally, as the condition is seen as causing

Schizophrenia   Schizophrenia is not a single condition but is best described as a syndrome. The typical symptoms include difficulties in organising behaviour (including speech) as well as detachment from reality which may involve delusion and/or hallucinations. Schizophrenia is often misrepresented in the popular media as a case of split or multiple personalities.

distress to people, the emphasis has been on identifying and resolving the causes of the negative consequences of schizophrenia. These causes are sometimes identified as chemical imbalances in the individual or something in the social world of the person. Without dismissing this very important approach, it is also helpful to ask whether there is a function to the syndrome within our species. This might give us some clues as to why the behaviour developed and continues to occur. If we have a clearer understanding of the origins and function of a particular behaviour or psychology then we will have a more effective means of responding to its expression. In the case of schizophrenia the answer may not be a direct one, though there is evidence that schizotypy is positively correlated with creativity and mating success (Nettle and Clegg, 2006); so a by-product of evolving creativity in our species might have been to also evolve a chance that some individuals will develop schizophrenia.

The 'how' questions concerned with mechanisms sit alongside the 'why' questions which are concerned with function. As we can see by the example of schizophrenia and creativity, a functional explanation begins to unravel what function the underlying mechanisms may play in our species, while the causal explanation aims to understand how the syndrome appears in individuals and therefore how it may be managed using various forms of treatment.

In this chapter a functional perspective is going to be implicit in a lot of what is covered. In particular, it will come to the fore when we consider the question of how we evolved and why we have such big brains. We will consider whether there is a correlation between brain size, our ability to communicate with each other via language and our ability to communicate with the environment via our tool use. Finally you will be presented with a glimpse of a cybernetic future – a future that might be the next big jump in our evolution.

THE HUMAN APE

1.3 What are we? This has been a question that has stimulated intellectual debate for centuries. In the fifteenth century the debate was dominated by a view that placed humans at the centre of the universe. Therefore the philosophers of the day, in line with the European religious doctrine of the time, had the earth at the centre of the universe with all the other planets, including the sun, revolving around the 'seat of man'. This began to change when Copernicus, a Polish astronomer and mathematician, using empirical data, disproved the geocentric theory of the universe. His work, published in *De revolutionibus orbium coelestium* in 1543, challenged the religious thinking of the time by demonstrating that the earth revolved around the sun. The work of Copernicus is seen as the start of the **scientific revolution**.

> **Scientific revolution**   In the sixteenth and seventeenth centuries there was a period of rapid change in the intellectual endeavour of making sense of the world that people lived in. Medieval philosophy was replaced by scientific principles of observation, measurement and experimentation. These developments are linked with Bacon (1561–1626), Galileo (1564–1642), Descartes (1596–1650), and Newton (1642–1727).

Growing out of the scientific revolution that is epitomised by Copernicus's achievements was a commitment to the scientific ideals of observation, analysis and experimentation. Over the centuries science has progressed our understanding (and control) of the world around us. For psychologists, even more significant than the ideas of Copernicus was the contribution in the nineteenth century of Darwin, which changed the way we see ourselves in relation to life on earth. From his careful observations on his voyage aboard the *Beagle* and through his experiments involving selective breeding of domestic animals such as dogs and cattle, he developed his theory of evolution by natural selection (we cover more about the development of science in the next chapter).

1.3.1 EVOLUTION BY NATURAL SELECTION

Evolution as a concept was not invented by Darwin. Evolution describes a process whereby there is change in the features of some body or system over time. The key question is by what processes these changes occur. In 1859 Charles Darwin published a book entitled *On the origin of species*. A key idea outlined in the book was that human beings share a common ancestor with other contemporary primates such as chimpanzees and gorillas. Darwin proposed that the way in which organisms changed over time (evolved) was through a process of natural selection. This provided the basis of the explanation of how a common ancestor could evolve into more than one species.

We can summarise three key factors that are required for natural selection to have a differential impact as a mechanism of evolution:

1   Natural selection requires variation in the individuals of each generation. If they were all the same then there would be no possibility for change.

2   If everything that was required to successfully promote offspring into the next generation was available without limit (such as food, water and safe environments with respect to predators or disease) then selection would not operate. In reality, access to resources is limited, which enables selection to work.

3   As resources are limited, this creates competition. Individuals and groups will compete within and between species for desirable resources. Those able to compete successfully will be in a good position to breed and contribute to the next generation.

Living creatures have evolved under the influence of the environment to become more able to fit into that environment. This leads to the survival of the fittest. Darwin, however, did not specify the crucial element that allowed natural selection to have an impact so that successful characteristics were maintained across generations. It was an Austrian monk who revealed the nature of this crucial element.

1.3.2 MENDEL AND GENETICS

In the mid nineteenth century an Austrian monk called Gregor Mendel was busy growing peas. Like any good farmer he selectively bred his peas to promote certain characteristics such as flower colour, smoothness of the pea, mushiness etc. The selective breeding was done systematically and records were carefully taken so that the lineage of his peas could be clearly specified. Through careful study Mendel was able to demonstrate that the transmission of the physical characteristics of his peas across generations obeyed certain laws, sometimes referred to as the basic laws of inheritance. We now refer to these laws as Mendelian laws of genetics. The basic element involved in the transfer was called a **gene** and this has become part of our everyday language. Mendel published his work in 1866 and is seen as the father of genetics. There is no evidence that Darwin was aware of Mendel's work, which was rediscovered at the turn of the century. The gene, however, is the discrete element of inheritance that Darwin attempted to grapple with in his account of the impact of evolution through natural selection.

> **Gene**　A discrete portion (sequence) of DNA (deoxyribonucleic acid). DNA is the building block of our chromosomes. In *Homo sapiens* there are 23 pairs of chromosomes contained in the nucleus of each cell. For each pair, one of the chromosomes is inherited from the mother and one from the father. We have around 20,000 to 25,000 genes.

Our understanding has moved on a lot since the nineteenth century. We now appreciate that it is not only physical characteristics that are influenced by genes. The modern field of behavioural genetics (for example see Plomin et al., 2005) attracts scientists interested in the expression of genes (how they affect us). We need to bear in mind, however, that you can't directly inherit a behaviour (which is something you do): you can only inherit the biological structures that influence your behaviour.

Let's consider the laws of inheritance that Mendel developed from his work with peas. For example he chose to cross two strains of garden pea. Strain 1 was a pea that was yellow in colour and had a smooth skin. In contrast strain 2 was green in colour with a wrinkled surface. This initial pairing of strain 1 and strain 2 is referred to as the parent generation. The seedlings (offspring) that arise from this parent generation are called the F1 generation. By pairing plants from the F1 generation it is then possible to generate a second (F2) generation.

The simplified example presented in Figure 1.1 focuses on the characteristic of colour. Two strains are involved, a yellow pea and a green pea. The left-hand side of the figure represents the expressed characteristic (**phenotype**) of colour in each generation. On the right-hand side the genes (**genotype**) that underlie the phenotype in each generation are presented. Genes usually come in pairs, referred to as alleles (one on each chromosome of a pair of chromosomes). The allele that represents yellow is represented by a capital Y and the allele for green is represented by a small y. The reason for this form of representation will become clear later.

When we look at the pea phenotype we see that the green characteristic appears to be lost amongst the F1 generation. However, looking at the gene we can see

> **Genotype**　Genes that make up the genetic code for an individual are described as the genotype. In humans the genotype comprises approximately 25,000 genes. Genes mostly come in pairs. Each member of a pair of genes is referred to as an allele.
>
> **Phenotype**　The characteristics of an organism resulting from the interaction between its genetic makeup and the environment. These characteristics can be biological or behavioural.

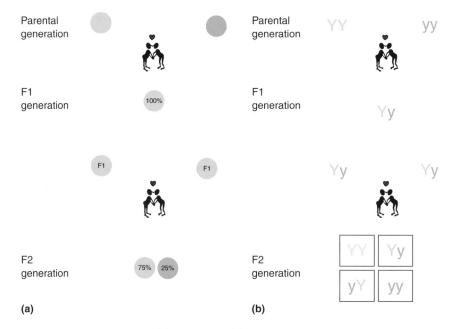

FIGURE 1.1 Mendelian genetics: (a) phenotype, (b) genotype

that alleles for both yellow and green are present in individuals in the F1 generation. We can conclude, therefore, that there is differential expression of the genes. The Y gene is described as dominant and the y gene is **recessive**. Therefore when they come together in an individual the Y allele will dominate the expression of the characteristic. So in this case all Yy individuals in the F1 generation will express the yellow characteristic. The fact that the green allele is not lost within the gene pool (even if not expressed within a particular generation) is demonstrated by cross-breeding individuals from the F1 generation. The F2 generation shows a different pattern from the F1 generation. The green characteristic appears in the F2 generation at a ratio of one in four offspring. We can see the reason for the reappearance of green peas if we look at the pairing of the dominant (Y) and recessive (y) genes on the right-hand side of Figure 1.1. All individual peas that carry a Y version of the pea colour gene will be yellow since Y is dominant. However a small proportion of individual peas will have inherited two y alleles, referred to as double recessive, and therefore will express the colour green.

In summary, the relationship between an individual's genetic profile (genotype) and how these genes are expressed in any given environment (phenotype) is critical to the operation of evolution by natural selection. Natural selection impacts differentially on phenotype, which differentially impacts on the frequency of genes available to be replicated in future generations.

ASIDE   Zygote

Sexual reproduction requires the fertilisation of an egg by a sperm. The product of this union is referred to as a zygote. The zygote has two copies of each chromosome, one from each parent, provided by the egg or sperm. The paired chromosomes commonly have paired genes. Each gene is referred to as an allele. The two alleles are involved in expressing a common trait. If an individual is carrying the same alleles for a trait they are described as homozygous for that particular trait. If the individual has different alleles for a given trait they are referred to as heterozygous. The individuals in the parent generation in the Mendelian breeding experiment presented in Figure 1.1 are homozygous for the trait pea colour. The individuals bred from the F1 generation are both heterozygous. Can you work out which of the offspring in the F2 generation are homozygous and which are heterozygous?

You may well wonder why psychologists should be interested in the sex lives of peas. Well, the principles of Mendelian genetics, along with modern developments in the field of genetics, have given us insights into the biological foundation of many psychological topics. Modern genetics has moved beyond Mendel's laws of inheritance. Our contemporary understanding of the genetic foundation of behaviour incorporates both Mendelian and non-Mendelian processes. A small sample of the wide range of topics that psychologists are interested in that are thought to have a genetic component includes: sexual orientation (e.g. Rahman and Wilson, 2003), mental health (e.g. Meyer-Lindenberg and Weinberger, 2006) and colour vision (e.g. Gerl and Morris, 2008).

In 1990 scientists began a very ambitious project called the Human Genome Project. Although the project has now ended, the analysis from the data gathered continues to this day. One of the primary goals of the project is to identify all of the 20,000–25,000 genes in human DNA. However, as we have seen, natural selection works not on genes but on phenotypes. How has our phenotype changed over time? To answer this question we can draw from data arising from the (incomplete) fossil record. However a fossil can only tell us what the animal looked like and not how it behaved.

To explore the relationship between natural selection and behaviour, behavioural scientists engage in comparative studies between living species. This approach has a strong history in psychology whereby animal models have been employed to explore processes that are believed to be common between species. For example, psychologists have investigated how birds process visual information to allow them to control landing behaviour and pecking behaviour (e.g. Davies and Green, 1994). The assumption is that both birds and human beings have faced similar challenges of guiding movement through a cluttered environment. Natural selection is likely to have favoured similar solutions to a common problem of controlling collisions in a three-dimensional world. Therefore, birds landing on a branch (Davies and Green, 1990) face similar visual information processing problems as people who drive and need to control their braking behaviour (Lee, 1976), or long jumpers

FIGURE 1.2 The evolution of human beings
By permission of the artist, Mark Thomas.

wishing to optimally strike the takeoff board (Lee et al., 1982). The goal in each case is to control the collision in an adaptive, functional manner.

1.3.3 OUR ANCESTORS

Human beings belong to the animal kingdom. Our closest relatives amongst living animals are the primates. Within the primates we have most in common with apes. In this chapter we do not have space to go into the details of how we have evolved from the same ancestors as modern day monkeys. As psychologists, however, it is useful to consider the recent history (in evolutionary terms) of our species.

The evolution of hominids begins around 2.5 million years ago. The origin of the **genus** is open to debate, but in general what we see is change in a number of key features. The changes of interest are an increase in overall size, greater emphasis on bipedalism (walking on two legs) and an increase in brain size (Figure 1.2). From around 1.5 million years ago our ancestors had similar anatomical features to ourselves, although they had smaller brains. The later **species** in the hominid line portrayed increased brain size. *Homo sapiens* is associated with language development, social organisation (culture) and sophisticated problem solving (tool use).

The earliest stone tools are dated around 2.5 million years ago. We know that other species do use and manufacture tools, but it is clear that hominids developed this skill in a sophisticated manner. The ability to manipulate and manufacture tools has been associated with increased dexterity (opposing thumb and fingers of the hands) and increased brain size. However, we should also recognise that cultural transmission of knowledge is important in maintaining the manufacture and use of tools across generations. Therefore language and social organisation became important too. Let's

Genus A class, group or category that possesses common attributes. Our own species exists in the genus *Homo* alongside other species (all of which are now extinct).

Species A group that exists within a genus. Members of a species in the same or in different populations are able to interbreed under natural conditions to produce viable offspring. Species are defined by reproductive isolation. There is one hominid species which we all belong to called *Homo sapiens*.

look at these key characteristics that are a feature of hominid evolution. As individual characteristics they are not unique to hominids, but as a cluster they are important in defining our genus.

1.3.4 DISTINGUISHING FEATURES

First, let us consider the early ancestor of the hominid line. It is generally accepted that the early common ancestor was small in stature and able to engage (in part) in bipedal locomotion. This commitment to bipedal locomotion increased over time and therefore freed the forelimbs to be used in tasks other than locomotion and basic grasping activities. For example, there was greater freedom for the hands to be used in early and rudimentary forms of non-verbal language, the remnants of which we still see in our communication. Gestures of the shoulders, arms and hands all help to convey emotion or emphasise the verbal points we wish to make in a conversation. The arms (or forelimbs) could also be used to develop and use tools. An increase in cranial capacity (brain size) is also seen as the hominid line evolved.

If we take a comparative perspective we can see that contemporary species of apes, such as the chimpanzee, are able to use their forelimbs to move, grasp, communicate and make rudimentary tools to solve particular problems they face in their environment. Chimpanzees are also organised in complex social groups that have **social hierarchies**. The need to navigate the complex political world of the social group and also to be engaged in cultural transmission of useful information requires advanced cognitive capabilities. These abilities are only possible if the brain is able to process complex and detailed information with the intention of planning sophisticated actions – all of which needs to be recorded and maintained over time. In other words, to be a successful tool-using social animal, sophisticated information processing capabilities are required. This is achieved in vertebrates by the evolution of the brain and in particular the cortical area of the brain.

> **Social hierarchies**   Classic research describes a pecking order which determines the dominant and subordinate positions of individuals. This is a pyramid-like form of organisation that has at its head the most dominant individual, while others will be at various levels of dominance or influence.

1.4 DOES SIZE MATTER?

1.4.1 COMPARATIVE BRAIN SIZE

The above provides an account of how our hominid ancestors evolved, but what evidence is there to support this view? Although we certainly do not have space here to look at all the evidence, we can at least begin to test the hypothesis that social organisations and problem-solving co-evolved. To do this we will look at the evidence that brain size in mammals is associated with increased social complexity and cognitive function. Dunbar (1998) describes how the group size of non-human primates, our close relatives in evolutionary terms, is related to the volume of the neocortex (the clever bit of the brain). In other words, as the typical group size of a given species increases you also see a comparable increase in neocortical volume. Taking this as a starting point we can predict, from the statistical analysis of the pattern of data, the typical group size for *Homo sapiens* based on the typical neocortical volume in our species. Interestingly the group size that is predicted for humans is 150 and this equates to the size of group that has been recorded in hunter-gatherer societies and traditional farming societies. Bailey and Geary (2009) support the claim that social competition is correlated with an increase in brain size. The social environment can be thought of as a complex, changeable world which individuals cope with by solving complex social problems such as knowing which individuals have power as a direct result of either their own physique and/or cognitive capabilities or the social relationships they can call on. The ability to recognise individuals and remember cheats or those who helped you in the past requires an increase in cognitive capabilities.

1.4.2 LANGUAGE

In terms of recent history, human society has not been organised consistently around relatively small groups. In small groups, especially in non-human primate species, social contact and **social grooming** or **allogrooming** between individuals creates a stable social network within the group. Dunbar proposes that in humans, as the group size increased, the physical contact became an inefficient means of maintaining social group cohesion. One function of language communication is therefore thought to be a means of promoting social cohesion in large groups. In primates social grooming is a key means of maintaining functional social bonds, but in human beings language now achieves the same goals. Around 60 per cent of our communication tends to be 'small talk' which is seen as equating to social bonding through verbal grooming (Dunbar, 1996).

> **Social grooming** or **allogrooming**   A behaviour seen in many social species including our own. It involves an individual or individuals assisting others to keep clean and in good condition. In addition to the obvious health benefits, the behaviour has also taken on a significant social function.

Having established that brain size matters, now let's consider the evidence concerning the evolution of brain size and associated psychology. The first thing to make clear is that size by and of itself is not the critical issue. Bigger animals have bigger brains but that doesn't mean their brains are more complex. A more useful measure is brain size relative to the body. Again this alone tells us only so much. If we consider the hominids, the species that has had the largest brain is *Homo neanderthalensis* with a brain capacity of 1450cm^3. This compares with our own species which has an average brain capacity of 1350cm^3. However, *Homo neanderthalensis* was large in build: it would be difficult to find anyone who would argue that its psychology was more advanced than our own.

The picture becomes more confusing when we note that our species is thought to have come into being around 150,000 years ago, but some of the things we see as critical to being human were not displayed in an advanced form until 50,000 years ago. William Calvin (2002) talks of 'The Mind's Big Bang' between 150,000 and 50,000 years ago. Something seems to have happened during this period to have changed the manner in which information was processed, stored and used by our ancestors to result in an explosion of creativity and cultural transmission. In some respects it is around 150,000 years ago that we can envisage human psychology having burst onto the stage of life.

1.4.3 CONSCIOUSNESS

The social brain hypothesis (outlined above) is a compelling account of how brain size and social complexity evolved alongside each other. When it comes to primates (particularly apes and human beings), the ability to interpret our own actions and the actions of others in the context of a social group and with reference to past actions (along with their consequences) is important in the evolution of primate psychology. **Consciousness** (awareness of self and others) gives us the ability to place our actions in a social and historical context. It is seen as assisting an individual in identifying group members, their motives and how best to operate within the social world of the group. In terms of human psychology there is considerable interest in the nature of consciousness, particularly when applied to children or other individuals who demonstrate conscious states different from our own. This begins to lead us towards **theory of mind** which explores how we develop an idea of another person's thoughts and feelings (see Chapter 14).

An important aspect of being part of a complex social group is to be able to read the behaviours and feelings of other members of the group. Recognising when someone is angry, happy or scared is an important skill. One way to study this ability is through the recently developed psychometric concept of **emotional intelligence**. Although the validity of the concept is debated, there are common strands of argument associated with the idea of emotional intelligence, the evolution of consciousness and the social brain hypothesis. For example, Shevlin et al. (2003) have shown that people are able to recognise psychopathy in the face. In evolutionary terms this means that humans can recognise whether someone is a risk-taker.

> **Consciousness** Often used in everyday speech to describe being awake or aware in contrast to being asleep or in a coma. In psychology, the term has a more precise meaning concerning the way in which humans are mentally aware so that they distinguish clearly between themselves and all other things and events.
>
> **Emotional intelligence** An ability to identify, assess and manage the emotions of yourself, other individuals and groups.

1.4.4 PROBLEM SOLVING

The emphasis so far has been on the role of social factors. However, the cognitive aspects of psychological evolution should not be overlooked. It is evident that within the period of 'The Mind's Big Bang' around 50,000 years ago there was an explosion of creativity. Calvin (2002) emphasises that the creativity was not mindless hit-or-miss behaviour but was useful for everyday activities. He also proposes a very interesting hypothesis to explain what change in the environment brought about this rise in creativity. There is evidence that at around 50,000 years ago there was major and rapid fluctuation in climate. This would make the environment more difficult to predict, and accessing the resources within the environment more challenging. It is therefore possible that these environmental challenges brought about by climate fluctuation acted as natural selection pressures to promote more effective social organisation, communication and cultural transmission. What is clear is that creative tool-making is seen to explode at this time. The first carved bone tools appear (although raw bone material would have been available prior to 50,000 years ago). Bead jewellery and incision carving also appear soon afterwards. By 50,000 years ago *Homo sapiens* had become a proficient and skilled tool-maker and tool-user.

A CYBERNETIC FUTURE?

1.5

We started this chapter with Copernicus's challenge to the view that we are the centre of the universe. People instinctively like to consider our species and, by extrapolation, themselves to be special. Is this the wrong thing to do? We are not special if what is meant by this is that we sit outside the natural processes that have enabled life to evolve. Nor are we special if we refer to a list of separate features used to describe our species such as language, relative brain size or tool use, as other species express these individual traits. What makes us special is the manner in which these traits have come together to facilitate the development of creativity in our expression of social relationships and our problem solving capabilities.

We all naturally identify ourselves through group membership, which is expressed by our involvement with different aspects of shared culture. Alongside this 'cultural bonding' is our species' exceptional ability to manufacture and use tools of all kinds. Has such exceptional tool manufacture and tool use led us to the pinnacle of evolution? The answer is no. By definition there is no pinnacle to the process as it is defined by change over time. Evolution is not purposeful; there is no predetermined goal or pinnacle to be reached. Although we see ourselves as distant from the natural world and operating within a sophisticated, technologically dominated environment, it is still an environment.

A moment's reflection will confirm that the basic selection pressures remain in place. We all face competition of some kind for resources, and something drives the majority of the population (though not all) to have children and support people with similar genes to themselves in social groups we like to call families. However, as modern, sophisticated human beings operating advanced technologies, maybe we have broken free from these basic biological mechanisms. We will reflect on this question when we consider the involvement of digital technology in our modern lives.

1.5.1 CYBERNETICS

We have seen how our species has evolved and how our psychology, in terms of social and cognitive capabilities, has its foundation in our evolution. It is also evident from our modern lives that language, culture and technology are dominant themes. So how should we make sense of our evolutionary past with respect to our unchartered future? Of course there is no right or wrong answer to this question, but we would like to offer you a view of one possible way forward. The approach we are going to take is to embed psychology in a cybernetic framework.

Cybernetics has Greek origins and means 'steersman'. It emphasises functionality and stresses the importance of feedback and self-organising systems, enabling a goal to be achieved through action. Knowledge of whether you have reached the goal (or not) is achieved through feedback. This concept is well established. Norbert Wiener in 1948 wrote a book entitled *Cybernetics: or control and communication in the animal and the machine*. It is interesting to note that the action and communication are seen as companion concepts which nicely parallel the proposed importance of these activities in hominid evolution around 150,000 years ago.

1.5.2 DIGITAL TOOLS

When scientists describe tool use in human beings it is usually in terms of mechical tools. This may apply to tools such as a sharpened flint blade or an electric drill. The key point is that the tool is thought of as passive (inert without human involvement) and with a small number of predetermined uses. The digital revolution has begun to change this landscape in a significant way. Tools are now being developed along cybernetic principles so that they are set a general function (goal) but are not predetermined in their operations. As a result it is not possible to predict the outcome of their use (what solutions they will arrive at to problems they encounter).

For example, the personal computer is designed with the general function (goal) of handling and processing information, but exactly how the PC is used is not predetermined. Therefore for some it may offer a means of communication, for others a sophisticated means of managing accounts, and for yet others an entertainment platform. In reality all these functions will be used to greater or lesser extent while new ones will be 'invented'. Contrast this with the TV. The TV has one purpose: to display visual and auditory information. The latest developments in digital TV (interactive choice etc.) rely on other systems that exist beyond the TV. The standard TV is a closed predetermined system while the PC is the reverse.

This is also a pretty good description of how humans operate as problem solving organisms. Our genetic makeup is predetermined, but how our genome will appear as a phenotype is not predetermined. So even twins with the same geneotype can grow up to look different and behave differently. We are facing a new world in which the tools we build are able to operate outside the limits of what they were developed for. This may be because the tools themselves act as adaptive, evolving systems or because the users of the tools are able to see different functions associated with the tools beyond their original purpose. Both scenarios illustrate the self-organising principle that is part of the cybernetic framework. In the following we outline some examples of this brave new world.

KEY STUDY   Griffiths, M.D., Davies, M.N.O., & Chappell, D. (2003). Breaking the stereotype: the case of online gaming. *Cyberpsychology and Behavior,* *6*: 81–91.

The field called cyberspychology is a relatively new area for psychologists. However, the interplay between human behaviour and the use of digital technologies is becoming increasingly important. This can be in relation to information sharing, education, commerce and finding partners, to name but a few activities. A key area of human activity is entertainment, which has seen an explosion of interest in terms of computer gaming; this industry now generates more money than films. One aspect of the growing importance of computer gaming is the development of shared virtual worlds over the world wide web. Such a development provides a rich opportunity for psychologists to monitor the formation of new behaviours as well as old behaviours in new environments.

The freedom for people to switch identities, explore new roles in social groups, and be judged on their ability in the virtual world rather than on sex, social class or age offers alternative forms of reinforcement and learning opportunities. In 2003 a group of psychologists at Nottingham Trent University undertook a study of secondary data looking at one of the leading online games at the time. The game still runs today and is called EverQuest. The paper is one of the first academic papers to be published in psychology aiming to describe the natural history of the psychology of online players. The data were taken from the leading fan sites and the analysis applied was straightforward descriptive statistics.

The data clearly showed some surprising results. Contrary to common belief the study found that a significant proportion of women played the game. The age range also suggested that the stereotypical view of only teenagers being engaged in playing was also incorrect. The reasons for playing were also diverse in nature. In summary, the data confirmed that EverQuest supported a diverse community of people with complex psychologies that reflected those seen outside the game.

At Queen's University, Belfast, a European Union funded research project based in the School of Psychology and going by the title HUMAINE was established to bring together academics across Europe to explore and understand more clearly the interface between humans and the computers they design. Such work suggests that the development of emotionally sensitive computers, able to express and respond to emotions, will by definition enable us to move beyond the deterministic programming that currently dominates contemporary applications. One of the outcomes from the project was an award winning website for the HUMAINE Association (http://emotion-research.net/).

Other groups such as the Fluid Interfaces Group at MIT's Media Lab are looking to redesign how information delivery is aware of the user and responsive to their actions. For example, would you like to be able to check your email by drawing a @ sign with your finger against a blank surface? Information delivery becomes an extension of our everyday living rather than an adjunct to it. You may like to visit their website to get a flavour of the exciting work they are involved in: http://ambient.media.mit.edu/.

In addition, a group of researchers in Spain have brought biopsychology and music together to produce a Multimodal Brain Orchestra. The performers in the orchestra produce music by their brain waves via an electroencephalogram (EEG). The premiere performance was held in April 2009. You can visit their website at http://specs.upf.edu/ to find out more about this project.

These developments are exciting applications that are looking to expand the relationship between the technology involved and the human using the tool. However, we now turn to one of the recent phenomena that has seen an explosion of activity in terms of the use of technology for communication. The origins of the world wide web exist in the work of British physicists at CERN (the giant science facility in Europe) in 1989. The initial aim was to assist communication amongst the scientific community. However, it soon became apparent that others saw different uses, which has led to the phenomenon we now know as the world wide web. At the same time other digital technologies were being developed that also facilitated ease of communication. Mobile phones made a cultural impact in the 1980s, but it soon became apparent that a use associated with mobile phones that was not envisaged as a primary function, namely the small message system (SMS), exploded in popularity. In 2008 it was estimated that 1.4 billion text messages were sent every week in the UK! A parallel can be drawn between Dunbar's (1996) proposal that verbal grooming is important in humans and this technological form of social grooming, as most of the information contained in the messages is of little intrinsic value but helps to maintain social bonds.

A recent development associated with the world wide web is Web 2.0. It is envisaged as the second generation of the web, promoting information sharing and communication. This development has proved phenomenally successful in the rise of social network sites such as Facebook and the real-time social messaging services such as Twitter. If you strip away the technology you have the common process of maintaining and strengthening social bonds (social grooming), but there are also some interesting new developments. It is only through the world wide web that individuals from special interest groups (such as the Blancmange Mould Society) can find similar individuals with relative ease. The web therefore has the ability to reduce the sense of social isolation. The role of digital technology in educating young people is growing, in terms of both formal processes and informal activity (Underwood et al., 2007b).

As a place to store information the cyberworld gives us easy access to more information more of the time, and this is likely to impact on the type and rate of cultural change and cultural transmission of information. This may have implications for the species in the future. When we look at the potential impact on individuals we can see that the cyberworld offers a means of exploring different aspects of one's personality. There are opportunities to enter virtual environments such as Second Life or what are called massively multiplayer online role-playing games (MMORPGs) as virtual avatars.

It is a common perception that people who play computer games are adolescent boys who lack social skills. However, a ground-breaking study by Griffiths et al. (2003) showed

FIGURE 1.3   By day you are Diane Dibley from accounts but in cyberspace you are Street Boy avatar, ready to hang out with some cool dudes in your online game of skateboarding and kebab eating
© Dex Image/Corbis

this was not the case when it came to MMORPGs. As an avatar you control how others perceive you (Figure 1.3). For example, you can project to others that you are opposite to your real sex or you are non-human. Of course the cyberworld is an environment that some individuals may try and exploit (like any other environment), so the importance of suitable safeguards is not to be ignored. Interestingly many of the safeguards are driven by individual users themselves. For example, in MMORPGs, although exploration of different play styles is encouraged, players are often actively involved in moderating the environments.

1.5.3 CYBERNETIC COEVOLUTION

Finally, returning to Calvin's (2002) point about 'The Mind's Big Bang' between 150,000 and 50,000 years ago, can we see any parallels here? We would like to suggest an idea for you to think over. A part of Calvin's argument was that significant and frequent change in the climate led to explosions of creativity. Perhaps a similar situation exists here. We are seeing rapid and significant change in the way that social processes are supported, the information that is available to us, and how that information is accessed. Is the brain about to go through a major evolutionary change? This new cyberworld creates new challenges and new areas of competition between people. Will the people best adapted to this world prosper and be the parents of a new generation of cyberchildren? Perhaps this is a bit fanciful, but our culture and our individual behaviours are likely to change rapidly as people operate in the cyberspace as much as in the organic world. It is already noticeable that students use 'text speak' in communicating with lecturers, not something the latter always welcome!

CONCLUSION

1.6 As psychologists, should we be ready to hand over our subject to computer scientists or biologists? We could, but everyone would lose out. The interface between the organic system of *Homo sapiens* and how it forms and responds to the digital world it is creating is most effectively addressed by psychologists who are knowledgeable about the natural sciences and digital technologies. It is how we as biological creatures *psychologically* experience the environment, including the digital world, that defines the human condition. It is a brave new world. Whether we consider our ancestors or those to follow us, it is clear that social communication and social bonds will remain at the heart of who we are and how we function in the world. The world may radically change and the mode of social communication may change along with it, but the function to be achieved remains. The global village is becoming something of a reality as people form social bonds of varying kinds with different subsets of people. This has all been achieved through our exceptional talent as a species to creatively see solutions to problems by developing and using tools to our benefit. The brave new world affords an opportunity whereby the tools may creatively present their own solutions to problems we did not know existed.

CHAPTER SUMMARY

1.7 We have seen how the development of science enabled people to explain the world around them, drawing upon empirical data and therefore largely forgoing belief without evidence as a suitable means of tackling questions in the natural sciences. Psychology has at its heart a commitment to empiricism. It also draws significantly from the sister biological disciplines of palaeoanthropology, neo-Darwinian evolutionary theory and behavioural genetics. The story of human evolution is the story of how our brain and our psychology have evolved alongside each other. Communication, problem solving and tool-making are yoked abilities within our species. They were critical for 'The Mind's Big Bang' and they are central to the cybernetic future that emphasises the merging of human psychology and new technologies – what some psychologists refer to as cyberpsychology.

 ## DISCUSSION QUESTIONS

Can you think of examples of our own, contemporary behaviour that may be explained from an evolutionary point of view? To help, think of what men tend to stress in their partners if they are attracted to the opposite sex, and contrast this with the signals women use to select men. To what extent do both sexes rate features in the same way? If not much, is this a case of different natural selection pressures applying to the sexes in making a mate choice?

Do you think that cyberpsychology is a fad? You may wish to reflect on the following points before arriving at your conclusion. Consider the digital technologies that exist in your everyday life and how they interplay with your own behaviour and psychology. For example, if you were to have your mobile phone removed or if you could not access a personal computer, would this affect your quality of life? If it would, why would it? Do you think your family and friends would have a similar reaction to yourself or a different one? Can you identify what, if anything, would be affected in terms of your psychology if these items were not available?

SUGGESTIONS FOR FURTHER READING

Dawkins, R. (1989). *The selfish gene* (3rd edn). Oxford University Press. The modern evolutionary approach continues to have a significant impact on how behavioural scientists, including psychologists, think about the function and maintenance of behaviour. This is a classic and very readable text that helped promote the importance of neo-Darwinian thinking in relation to behaviour.

Buss, D. (2008). *Evolutionary psychology: the new science of the mind* (3rd edn). Pearson Higher Education. David Buss is one of the key people in the field of evolutionary psychology. The book is written in a style that engages you to consider the argument as an active reader. You are not told what to think but are invited to apply what you are reading to a range of questions that arise from the work he covers.

Pickering, A. (2002). Cybernetics and the mangle: Ashby, Beer and Pask. *Social Studies of Science, 32,* 413–437. This paper gives an overview of how cybernetics can be conceived in terms of human endeavour. The author is a sociologist and therefore the language can be a little unfamiliar, but it is well worth persevering to the end.

http://www.apa.org/science/genetics/. If you are interested in exploring further the relationship between genetics and behaviour, we recommend you visit the very helpful website hosted by the American Psychological Association.

2 HOW PSYCHOLOGY BECAME A SCIENCE

Lead author **Simon Watts**

CHAPTER OUTLINE

2.1 Introduction

Framing questions

2.2 Key moments in the emergence of modern psychology
    2.2.1 Determinism
    2.2.2 The riddle of our selves
    2.2.3 An important decision for psychology

2.3 Psychology as a study of the conscious mind: Helmholtz, Fechner, Wundt and a 'natural science of the mental'
    2.3.1 Quantification
    2.3.2 The introspective method

2.4 Two alternative ways of founding psychology: Sigmund Freud and the unconscious, William James and functionalism
    2.4.1 And in the USA ...

2.5 Conditioning: Watson, Pavlov, Skinner and the study of behaviour
    2.5.1 Man and brute

2.6 Modern psychology: cognitive science, humanism and the return of the social sciences

2.7 Conclusion

2.8 Chapter summary

Discussion questions

Suggestions for further reading

INTRODUCTION

2.1 The history of psychology is not a straightforward tale. In fact, history is by no means an exact science: this means that the important stuff is inevitably a matter for interpretation and debate. What follows, therefore, is not *the* history of psychology, but *a* history. It's a history of psychology designed especially to introduce you to the main issues, concepts, people and debates that have helped to shape and define a fascinating and multifaceted discipline.

FRAMING QUESTIONS

How has the discipline of psychology developed? What have been the main stages in its development?

To what extent has psychology developed as a natural science and to what extent as a social science?

How have questions about what *type* of discipline psychology is been related to questions of what it should take as its subject matter?

KEY MOMENTS IN THE EMERGENCE OF MODERN PSYCHOLOGY

2.2 The beginnings of modern psychology are usually traced to the year 1879. That's when Wilhelm Wundt (1832–1920) established the first dedicated psychological laboratory at Leipzig. The selection of this date is somewhat arbitrary. Wundt himself had, for example, highlighted the possibility of a distinct psychological discipline as early as 1862 (in his book *Contributions to the theory of sensory perception*). Yet the key events which led Wundt and others to this distinct discipline occurred even earlier.

Such events lie at the very heart of modern science, in the work of such great scientists as Isaac Newton (1642–1727) and Charles Darwin (1809–1882). Newton's work in physics had a profound influence on psychology. First, he developed a scientific 'method' consisting of observation, the formulation of hypotheses designed to predict events and outcomes, and the subsequent testing of these hypotheses through further observation. In this way, the scientific method worked toward the revelation of ever more general explanatory laws (Cushing, 1998). Such principles remain central to the scientific method that is used in psychology.

Second, and crucially, Newton had great success in applying these methods. He was able to offer an explanation of the entire physical universe based upon a limited number of basic laws (describing a limited number of basic 'forces'), each of which was expressed in a purely mathematical or quantitative form. In principle, it was thought that if you knew where all the physical bodies in the universe were at time *A*, Newton's laws would allow you to predict their future movements and hence to know (in advance) their respective locations at time *B*. Though this is a simplification, the basic point is that the behaviour of all physical bodies was shown to be lawful and knowledge of the laws appeared to make the subsequent trajectories and relative positions of these bodies entirely predictable. According to this theory, everything behaved in a mechanistic or machine-like fashion because the behaviour of everything was determined by the impact of the same set of basic forces.

> **Determinism** The idea that every event including human thought and behaviour is causally determined by an unbroken chain of prior events. According to this idea there are no mysterious miracles and no random events.

2.2.1 DETERMINISM

This theory of mechanical **determinism** has been a strong influence on psychology. Newton's ideas also impacted on people in general. The pre-Newtonian worldview was characterized by its **anthropocentrism**. That is, people considered themselves to have a central and fundamental place in the universe. Newton's work brought this anthropocentrism into question. The universe was mechanical and its behaviour predetermined: it was 'as it was', regardless of us and our existence. Far from being central, people and their opinions and viewpoints appeared superfluous. The sense of alienation that resulted from this view was the key that opened the door to psychology. Alexander Koyré captures this nicely:

> **Anthropocentrism or anthrocentrism** The belief that people (*anthro*) are the most important thing in the universe rather than the worthless pile of brown stuff that we really are.

> modern science ... united and unified the universe ... But ... it did this by substituting for our world of quality and sense perception, the world in which we live, and love, and die, another world ... the world of quantity ... a world in which though there is a place for everything, there is no place for man. Thus the world of science – the real world – became estranged and utterly divorced from the world of life. (cited in Prigogine & Stengers, 1984: 35–36)

The point here is that Newton and his scientific methods – the modern mind at its best – solved the riddle of the universe, but in so doing produced a dramatic (and tragic) side effect. They appeared to separate us from the universe. Serious questions followed about 'mind' itself, about where humans, and the qualities and perceptions of the everyday human world, fitted in. Our place in the bigger scheme of things was under threat. And, vitally for psychology, this threat made 'us' the next scientific riddle to be solved.

2.2.2 THE RIDDLE OF OUR SELVES

The 'riddle of our selves' became even more pressing following the publication of Darwin's *On the origin of species* in 1859. As we have seen, Newton had 'decentred' us and lessened

FIGURE 2.1 The riddle of our selves. On the ceiling of the Sistine Chapel in Rome is a picture that shows one view of where people come from: God reaches out and creates the first man – Adam. Darwin's version would have Adam reaching back to touch his past – a monkey
© Jim Zuckerman/Corbis and Frans Lanting/Corbis

our apparent importance. However, at least the principles of mechanical determinism remained and these were widely held to be 'consonant with the generally accepted theological belief in an omnipresent, omniscient God' (Cushing, 1998: 168). Newton himself stayed true to the belief that 'the mechanical universe required the active intervention of God, not just to create and order it, but also to maintain it' (1998: 168).

Darwin's theory of evolution by natural selection (see Chapter 1), on the other hand, sat far less comfortably with conventional religious ideas. In fact, it directly challenged them. Human beings, which Christian religion saw as the 'closest thing to God', became the 'nearest thing to apes' in the blink of a scientific eye (Figure 2.1). This was a bitter pill to swallow and one which Sigmund Freud (1856–1939) called 'the second great blow to the human ego' (following the Newtonian blow described earlier). Darwin's theory reignited debates about humans' fundamental nature. It was in the midst of this debate that Wundt's psychological laboratory was founded, just eight years after Darwin's publication of *The descent of man, and selection in relation to sex* (in 1871).

2.2.3 AN IMPORTANT DECISION FOR PSYCHOLOGY

The previous section suggests that psychology emerged in order to solve the 'riddle of our selves'. Thanks to Newton, the discipline also appeared at a time when its most immediate subject matter (the human world of life, quality and sense perception) had been 'estranged and utterly divorced' from the *real* world that Newtonian science had begun to reveal. Our scientific approach has given us answers to many questions about how things work. We know something about how the planets move (the theory of gravity) and we know something about how our senses work (see Chapter 5). What is much more puzzling, however, is our own existence on this world and how we make sense of it. The contrasts in what we know and what we are still puzzling over is shown in Table 2.1.

The word *psychology* means 'a science of mind or soul', and the psychological world (psychology's most immediate subject matter) appears on the right of Table 2.1. It is worth

TABLE 2.1 The big riddles. The universe that Newtonian science dealt with is on the left. The universe it missed out is on the right. Consider the opposing categories carefully. The dualism they represent has been fundamental to psychology and to Western thought and culture more generally

The riddle of the universe	The riddle of our selves
The world of *science*	The world of *life*
The *real* world	The *perceived* world
The *objective* world	The *subjective* world
The world of *quantity*	The world of *quality*
The *physical* world	The *psychological* world
The *somatic* world	The *semantic* world
The world *as it is*?	The world *as it is experienc*ed?
A science of *matter*	A science of *mind* (and of things *that matter*?)

remembering both these points as we proceed. For the moment, however, psychologists had to decide how best to study this subject matter. Two basic models presented themselves. On the one hand, there was Newton's natural science model which employed **quantitative** research methods and pursued nomothetic knowledge as a priority (i.e. objective and lawful knowledge which is considered to be generally applicable). This system had triumphed in the physical world.

On the other hand, a social science model was also a possibility. This approach predominated in the humanities and was embodied by the German word *Geisteswissenschaft* (which means 'science of the spirit'). Under this model, the aim was to study humans, human life and human events by re-creating their meaning for the actors involved, in order to find out their *reasons* for doing what they were doing. To achieve this goal, **qualitative** research methods were generally employed and idiographic knowledge was pursued as a priority (i.e. subjective and specific

> **Qualitative data** Describe meaning and experience rather than providing numerical values for behaviour such as frequency counts.
>
> **Quantitative data** Focus on numbers and frequencies rather than on meaning or experience.

knowledge of a person, event or situation which reveals that person, event or situation in its uniqueness).

This distinction (between the social and natural sciences) was popularised by the historian Wilhelm Dilthey (1833–1911). Dilthey offered clear advice to psychology. First, he acknowledged that humans and human events both possess important physical properties. As an example, your brain is a physical object and its physical properties are going to be pretty important if you want to think. I'm sure you'd realised that (see 'Aside' over the page). This simple observation nonetheless creates a serious complication for psychology, because it means that our status as physical and material 'objects' has a massive effect on our capacity to be psychological. In other words, in order to fully grasp the psychological world (captured on the right of Table 2.1), the discipline of psychology must also engage with aspects of the physical world (captured on the left of Table 2.1). This latter task demands a natural scientific approach. But whilst psychology cannot avoid our physical or somatic properties (the latter means 'of the body'), Dilthey also warned that:

> explaining human actions is fundamentally different from explaining physical events. A woman shooting a man is a physical event. However, understanding the event in human terms involves more than tracing the path of the bullet and showing how the bullet caused the man's death. We need to know why she shot the man, not just how she did so. (Leahey, 2004: 248)

ASIDE

Had you realised that 'thinking' (biologically speaking) involves the passage of electrical impulses through the nerve cells of the brain and the chemical transmission of those impulses across lots of tiny 'gaps' between the nerve cells called **synapses**? If you were to start counting the synapses now, at a rate of one per second, you would finish in approximately *30 million* years time. The brain is extraordinary. The number of possible pathways available to the brain's electrical impulses (and hence the possibilities for thought) are *greater than the number of atoms in the known universe.*

'Why' questions are central to psychology. The brain, for example, is a good way of explaining *how* we think but not *why* we do it. It doesn't cause us to think, any more than having legs causes us to run. In the same way, any rigorous psychological explanation of running would require, as a matter of precedence, that we understand *why* the running is taking place and not just how it is taking place (the latter presumably involving a series of neuronal signals leading to a more or less rapid movement of the legs).

Dilthey wanted psychology to remember that its primary subject matter was the subjective or psychological world itself, not just the physical properties that made this world possible. Dilthey suggested that if we want to find out 'why', priority must be given to the psychological world – the ways that people make sense of their experience and the meanings they attach to them. In other words, to understand why I am running, you will first need to understand my experience of the current situation and the meanings I assign to it, because only in this way can you find out my motives and reasons for acting. This task demands a social scientific approach.

So what should psychology do? If the psychological world was its proper subject matter, then surely psychology was a humanitarian discipline? For this reason, Dilthey felt a social scientific approach was preferable. But the psychological world can only exist through the physical world. If I don't have a physical body I can't see or hear, for example. Psychology couldn't ignore this either. It needed to study the physical world as well and the natural scientific model dominated in this domain.

This double-edged nature of psychology was (and remains) both a challenge and an opportunity. Psychology had the chance to bridge the divide between the natural and social sciences and it could do so by retaining a foot in both camps (Danziger, 1990). **Nomothetic** and **idiographic** knowledge, quantitative and qualitative methods, could all be embraced. It needed to study its subject matter from both perspectives. Wilhelm Wundt tried to support this vision (as did other early psychologists), but it was not a vision that psychology would ultimately sustain. As we're about to see, psychology was intent on becoming a natural science.

> **Nomothetic** and **idiographic** measures   Nomothetic approaches look for laws of behaviour and collect measures that can be observed and verified and quantified. They are concerned with averages and norms. By contrast, idiographic approaches look for unique and individual experiences.
>
> The term 'nomothetic fallacy' refers to the common belief that if you can name a problem then you have solved it. For example, if you feel very upset and someone says you have post-traumatic stress, you still feel upset.

PSYCHOLOGY AS A STUDY OF THE CONSCIOUS MIND: HELMHOLTZ, FECHNER, WUNDT AND A 'NATURAL SCIENCE OF THE MENTAL'

2.3 All things being equal, psychology in the late nineteenth century is probably best categorised as one of the humanities (Windelband, 1894/1998). And the subject matter left to it by the natural sciences – the psychological and inherently subjective world of perception, quality and experience – probably required the application of methods traditionally associated with the social sciences. But all things were not equal. The unprecedented success of the natural science model had a big influence on the emergence of psychology. It also established the view that natural scientific methods were 'the only reliable methods for securing useful and reliable knowledge about anything' (Danziger, 1990: 41). In order to flourish, psychology *had* to align itself with the methods of the natural sciences.

This conclusion was nonetheless complicated by a long-standing philosophical belief that subjective, mental phenomena were not amenable to natural scientific analysis. Immanuel Kant (1724–1804), for example, had rejected the possibility of a 'science of mind' on the grounds that mental phenomena (1) had no spatial dimension, (2) were too transient to observe, and (3) could not be experimentally manipulated in a controlled fashion. Overall, Kant concluded that mental phenomena couldn't be mathematically analysed or described (Fancher, 1996). Such phenomena, he felt, could only ever support a qualitative and philosophical analysis.

To overcome this barrier, psychology exploited the fact that our psychological world is connected to our physical properties. Earlier, we suggested (as a means of explaining Dilthey's arguments) that the brain does not cause us to think. But if the brain doesn't cause us to think, then what does? So psychology went along with the idea that all mental phenomena could, in fact, be explained in terms of physiological causes. This double whammy of **reductionism** and **materialism** reduced the psychological world to a by-product of the physiological properties which produced it. It also neatly sidestepped Kant's objections. As a by-product, subjective mental phenomena were no longer psychology's primary subject matter; physiology was. And natural scientific methods operated very comfortably in this physical domain. As Leahey puts it:

> **Reductionism** and **materialism** Curt describes reductionism as 'the attempt to reduce or "boil down" any complex phenomenon into the simple elements which are thought to constitute it or cause it' (1994: 241). Philosophically speaking, materialism encapsulates the view that the world/universe is entirely constituted of matter. This view leaves little room for the psychological world. Materialism is sometimes also known as 'physicalism'.

by insisting that the nervous system is the basis of all mentality, and by defining psychology as the investigation of the physiological conditions of conscious events, the new field ... could establish itself as a [natural] science. (2004: 235)

But defining psychology in this way was not enough. Establishing psychology as a natural science also demanded that psychological experimentation be carried out in the same way as the natural sciences, and this in turn demanded that psychological phenomena be mathematically measured and described. This was now to involve the 'investigation of the physiological conditions of conscious events' (rather than the events themselves), yet those conditions would still have to be counted and measured.

2.3.1 QUANTIFICATION

The first attempts at counting and measuring in psychology, otherwise known as quantification, were developed by a number of people in a number of different ways. In 1850 Hermann von Helmholtz (1821–1894), an eminent natural scientist, demonstrated that nerve impulses travelled at finite speeds which could be measured in terms of *reaction times*. He did this by passing electric currents through the severed leg of a frog. He also established the psychological principle that human perception (by which he implied the psychological reality we experience) was not a simple replication of the physical reality captured by our senses. Helmholtz proposed instead that sensations were *transformed* into perceptions in a mechanical and lawful fashion by the physiological machinery of our minds.

F.C. Donders (1818–1889) built upon Helmholtz's reaction-time work. Donders realised that the time between the presentation of a stimulus and a person's response to it could be used as a quantifiable measure of the speed of physiological and mental processes (processes which could not otherwise be observed). It was even possible, by making a person choose between two stimuli, to ascertain the exact duration of a mental judgement. This act of quantification (which became known as *mental chronometry*) was exactly what psychology needed if it was to distinguish itself as a natural science.

Gustav Fechner (1801–1887) quantified psychological phenomena in a different way. Like Helmholtz, Fechner had noticed that the information gathered by our senses was processed and transformed *before* it reaches conscious awareness. In particular, he observed that the perceived intensity of a physical stimulus did not perfectly reflect its physical intensity. A lighted match would, for example, appear to be brighter when it was placed against a dark background. If, Fechner surmised, we could somehow measure the physical *and* the perceived intensity of the stimulus, it might become possible to mathematically determine their relationship (and hence to mathematically connect the psychological and physical worlds).

But how could we measure the perceived intensity? Fechner realised that you couldn't quantify it directly or as an absolute value. What you could do, however, was quantify the smallest *perceptual discrimination* people are capable of making, and you could do this as a function of changes in the physical intensity itself. Let's say, for example, that I put a weight in your right hand and its physical intensity is 100 grams. What is its perceived intensity? There is of course no pure mathematical answer. So suppose I start putting weights into your left hand, one by one – 101 grams, 102, 103 and so on. The question becomes, 'At what weight can you perceive a difference (or discriminate) between the two weights?' And, thanks to Fechner, we know the answer. On average it's when the weight in your left hand is 1/30th (or 3.33 per cent) heavier or lighter than the weight in your right (or, in our example, when the weight in your left hand is 103.33 grams or more). Fechner called this perceived change in intensity a 'just noticeable difference' (or JND) and it constituted a quantitative measure of perceived intensity.

EXERCISE Sensation and perception

Take a box of matches. Light one of the matches and hold it up in front of a light background. How bright does it look? Try and put a number on your judgement of brightness (your perception). Now light another match in front of a different coloured background. How bright does that look?

The amount of light from the two matches will be the same (sensation) but your judgement might well be different. Try this out with a number of backgrounds and explore the factors that change your perception. By the way, try not to burn down your house during this study.

Fechner was able to measure the JND across a range of sensory functions and to graphically represent the relationship between physical and perceived stimulus intensities in each case. He also demonstrated that the relationship between physical and perceived intensity could *always* be expressed via a single mathematical formula. In truth this law was anything but perfect. Nonetheless, Fechner's psychophysical experiments had clearly shown that: (1) the content of the psychological world could be manipulated by controlling the stimuli presented to it; (2) whilst such content might actually represent a subjective 'distortion' of the physical world, such distortion was nevertheless carried out (by our physiology) in a mechanical and lawful fashion; and (3) as a result, the content of the psychological world could be shown to have a lawful and quantifiable relationship with the content of the physical world.

Other important work on counting and measuring psychological qualities was occurring at roughly the same time. Perhaps the most notable was the development of mental and intelligence testing procedures, via the work of Francis Galton (1822–1911) in Britain, Alfred Binet (1857–1911) in France (see Chapter 17) and America, and latterly William Stern (1871–1938) in Germany. The truth is then that the new discipline's desire to become a 'natural science of the mental' was already well established before Wundt's laboratory ever appeared.

Wundt had indeed called his first taught course in psychology 'Psychology as a natural science' (in 1862), and both mental chronometry and Fechner-like experiments quickly characterised the work of Wundt's laboratory at Leipzig. Yet, in common with most German academics, Wundt remained a strong advocate of the distinction between the *Natur-* and *Geisteswissenschaften* (natural and social sciences) and his general approach recognised that psychology stood at the point of transition between the two. This is not surprising because Wundt had been employed at Leipzig to teach philosophy and to teach psychology as a part of that humanitarian discipline (Leahey, 2004). His methodological approach duly combined the new methods of quantification described above with a more traditional method called *introspection*, which had been employed by the 'old-fashioned philosophical psychology … to reveal the contents and workings of the mind' (2004: 237).

2.3.2 THE INTROSPECTIVE METHOD

In 1873, Wundt's *Principles of physiological psychology* described the emerging discipline of psychology. It combined physiology, which 'informs us about those life phenomena that we perceive by our external senses', with a psychological and introspective approach in which 'the person looks upon himself from within' (1873: 157). The introspective method, which relied on a process of self-report about the 'goings-on' in one's psychological world, had previously been dismissed by scientists and philosophers alike because of its unreliability and inherent subjectivity. Wundt himself doubted its effectiveness. He had responded, however, by trying to transform this unreliable act of internal perception into something akin to scientific observation (Danziger, 1990).

To do this, Wundt restricted his so-called physiological psychology to the study of processes that were simultaneously accessible to both internal and external acts of observation. In practice, a stimulus was presented to a participant and quantified response measures were gathered at the same time as subjective reports of the conscious content elicited by the stimulus (Figure 2.2). In this way, the introspective data always appeared alongside the more important objective measures. In order to control the style of the introspective reports they were only collected from trained researchers. This move was clever in as much as it gave introspection a new status as a special skill. Only a trained scientist could carry out these scientific observations with sufficient reliability. Despite this, the qualitative data introspection produced were still not accepted as a basis for knowledge claims. Only quantitative data could do that.

FIGURE 2.2   Wundt (right) in his laboratory in Leipzig: the team are shown taking part in a joke telling experiment

These many restrictions limited Wundt to the study of psychological processes on the edge of conscious experience: basically, sensation, perception and motor responses. But this did not concern Wundt, for he considered these to be the only processes properly accessible to natural scientific analysis and the only ones directly and mechanistically caused by physiological processes. Higher-order mental processes (complex thought, memory, voluntary effort, creativity etc.) were, for Wundt, part of a distinct psychic causality, and they were caused, not by physiology, but by an underlying layer of unconscious psychological mechanisms. These mechanisms were said to be qualitative in nature and for this reason Wundt felt they would always resist experimental or natural scientific analysis. Non-experimental approaches would also be required.

Wundt spent the last 20 years of his life developing his *Völkerpsychologie*, that is a kind of historical and comparative psychology which looked at people as part of a collective and which tried to understand them within their social, cultural and communal context. Wundt believed these historical, qualitative and distinctly social scientific analyses were a very necessary addition to experimental studies of individual people in the laboratory. He felt strongly that the 'experimental method plus *Völkerpsychologie* would furnish a complete, albeit not completely natural-scientific, psychology' (Leahey, 2004: 239).

Few agreed: Wundt's desire for psychology to retain links with the humanities was at odds with the prevailing vision. Psychology wanted to be a natural science. Completely.

Hermann Ebbinghaus (1850–1909) had already demonstrated (in 1879) that the higher-order mental process of memory could potentially be made accessible to experiment (Fancher, 1996) and Wundt's influence was waning. He died in 1920 along with many of his ideas.

Introspection, meanwhile, was to flourish in the work of two of Wundt's students, Oswald Külpe (1862–1915) and Edward Titchener (1867–1927). Both the 'Würzburg School' of systematic introspection established by Külpe and Titchener's 'structural psychology' relieved introspection of its restrictions. Memory, thinking and complex feelings became legitimate topics for introspective analysis and the resulting qualitative data took centre stage. Titchener described these changes in 1912:

> The experimenter of the early nineties trusted, first of all, in his instruments … [which were] of more importance than the observer … There were still vast reaches of mental life which experiment had not touched … Now … we have changed all that. The movement towards qualitative analysis has culminated in what is called … the method of 'systematic experimental introspection'. (cited in Danziger, 1990: 43)

Yet this was ultimately a backward step. Simply calling introspection 'systematic' and 'experimental' could not hide the fact that psychology's subject matter had once again drawn the discipline away from the natural sciences and back toward the humanities. As Titchener's experimental psychology explored the 'vast reaches of mental life', so a qualitative analysis along the lines of the old philosophical psychology had reappeared. The first attempts to establish a natural science of the mental had reached a dead end. Alternatives were required.

TWO ALTERNATIVE WAYS OF FOUNDING PSYCHOLOGY: SIGMUND FREUD AND THE UNCONSCIOUS, WILLIAM JAMES AND FUNCTIONALISM

2.4 In truth, the work of Sigmund Freud is something of a distraction in a chapter about psychological science. Had Freud's work developed differently, this might not have been the case: when in 1894/5 Freud was writing his *Project for a scientific psychology* he 'defined his Newtonian "intention … to furnish a psychology that shall be a natural science: that is, to represent psychical processes as quantitatively determinate states of specifiable material particles"' (cited in Leahey, 2004: 267). This statement, early in Freud's work, was reminiscent of Wundt's view. Yet Freud was to depart dramatically from these intentions.

Freud's work in psychology began with an interest in **hysteria**, a complaint in which physical symptoms appeared in the absence of any obvious physical cause, and his psychoanalytic approach emerged as a therapy to deal with this problem. He believed the physical symptoms were caused by unconscious (and potentially damaging) psychological memories, needs or desires, as they made themselves manifest in the hysteric's behaviour.

Psychoanalysis itself was a 'talking cure' in which patients voiced their problems and feelings under the guidance of a therapist, with the aim of bringing the hitherto unconscious desires into conscious awareness.

ASIDE

Hysteria is a condition in which physical symptoms appear in the absence of any obvious physical cause.

Today, hysteria would be called a dissociative disorder. In Freud's time, only women were thought to be hysterical. Nice. This is a prime example of the masculine bias which has long afflicted psychology.

In fact, Freud initially proposed (*very* controversially) that all hysterics had suffered sexual abuse in childhood. He later retracted this 'seduction theory' of hysteria. He nonetheless retained the belief that many of the hysteric's 'potentially damaging' ideas and desires were of a sexual nature and that much of *everybody's* behaviour was driven by the repression of such sexual desires.

On the basis of just six case studies of psychoanalytic therapy (of which only two were claimed as successes) and a process of self-analysis, Freud came to the conclusion that all human behaviour was caused by psychological drives and events occurring in the unconscious mind (and were of a primarily sexual and pleasure-seeking nature). In non-hysterics, Freud saw dreams as the primary means of uncovering and interpreting this unconscious content (and he regarded his 1900 publication *The interpretation of dreams* as his master work).

Freud undoubtedly wanted psychoanalysis to be a science. Yet most of his claims about the nature and influence of the unconscious mind have never been substantiated by scientific evidence. He did not try 'to create an experimental psychology of the unconscious, nor did he welcome attempts to scientifically verify his ideas' (Leahey, 2004: 265). As a result, Freud's ideas have generally been vilified by a psychological discipline intent on emulating the natural sciences (Eysenck, 2004).

It is nonetheless important to acknowledge the huge popularity of psychoanalysis. Freud's ideas and concepts have also greatly influenced 'contemporary ways of thinking about human feelings and conduct' (Gay, 1989: xii). It may not be science, but Freud's conceptual scheme clearly remains a compelling means of reading and interpreting human behaviour. Psychology was also affected by Freud in two further ways. First, his ideas led the way into abnormal psychology (and studies of mental health); and second, they showed that psychology was not just an academic discipline, but also an *applied* and therapeutic one. The psychologist could be a scientist and/or the practitioner.

2.4.1 AND IN THE USA …

This tension between academic and applied psychology was first noted by William James (1842–1910). James was to American psychology what Wundt had been in Europe: a founding father for the new discipline. He was initially impressed by the work of Wundt and the German physiological psychologists. The mechanical, causal explanations they offered and the idea that psychology might be based upon natural scientific principles excited him intellectually. On the other hand, he found its implications quite distressing from a spiritual perspective. And you can see his point. Are we really so mechanical and predictable? Are we really so controlled by our physiology? For James, such explanations left little room for the expression of human choice, creativity and free will.

James's resolution of this personal conflict is ultimately central to understanding his later work. He decided that it was useful to accept mechanistic explanations in a scientific context. He even accepted that psychology had little choice but to progress in this direction. But this didn't mean he had to think and behave in a predictable and determined fashion. In this personal context, he would live creatively and with free will. This course of action, which rested on the principle that an idea may be true or have utility only in a specific context, was to become a central feature of James's later career in philosophy.

This personal accent on free will and his ultimate preference for philosophy also hint at James's subsequent attitude to psychology. In his much acclaimed *Principles of psychology* (1890), James strongly criticised the experimental and structural approach to psychology he associated with Wundt and Titchener. This approach was, for James, both very reductive and a bore! Its pursuit of basic mental structures or elements involved a wholly artificial and barbaric dissection of mental life. In contrast, James emphasised the continuous, indivisible and ever-changing nature of mental life via his concept of the stream of consciousness. He saw consciousness as both selective and functional. It was selective in so far as it evolved in order to help people choose (between various courses of action) and it was functional in as much as these choices were vital in helping the individual adapt to their environment.

EXERCISE   Do you have free will?

The free will versus determinism debate remains a key argument for psychologists. Is our behaviour determined by physiology, unconscious forces or even environmental influences? Or are we free to act according to our own free will? It's a tricky one, but in everyday life we tend to fall down on the free will side of the debate.

Try this one out on family and friends. Try using determinist arguments to get yourself out of tricky situations like crashing your mum's car. For example, try saying 'I couldn't help myself, I was born that way', or 'I was just responding to the flux of neurochemicals washing around my brain.' If you get a response that is anything other than a two-word sentence where the second word is 'off', then let us know. That's how much people don't believe in determinism.

European psychology had founded itself on the principles of Newtonian science and this allegiance created a focus on mental structures and underlying explanatory mechanisms. James's emphasis on the functional and adaptive significance of consciousness demonstrates the alternative but 'powerful influence of Darwin on early U.S. scientific psychology' (Hergenhahn, 2005: 313). From around 1900, American psychology steadily moved away 'from the traditional psychology of conscious content … toward a psychology of mental adjustment inspired by evolutionary theory' (Leahey, 2004: 341–342).

This movement inspired important changes in the view of psychology and its subject matter. First, the conscious mind came to be understood as just another biological adaptation. It existed because it served an evolutionary function, and that function was to enable people to adapt their behaviour in relation to their current circumstances. Given this association of mind with biology, it is not surprising to find that mind and body, and particularly mind and behaviour, were increasingly viewed as inseparable and synonymous entities. Mind was an 'outgrowth of conduct, a superior and more direct means of adjusting the organism to the environment' (Bolton, 1902, cited in Leahey, 2004: 343). In a very real sense, mind *became* action.

This theoretical shift initially showed itself in renewed attempts by psychologists to make psychology useful in an applied and therapeutic way. Psychology, it was felt, had to have a practical *function*. And it could achieve this by bringing about improvements in education and learning, by intervening in matters of abnormal psychology (now increasingly defined as maladaptive behaviour), and by bringing about human and societal betterment through these interventions. If mind involved mental adjustment, psychology could help us adjust more profitably. The Great War (1914–1918), so damaging in so many ways, actually gave applied psychology a tremendous boost. The mental testing procedures of Galton and Binet, exploited most famously in America by James McKeen Cattell (1860–1944), thrived in this sort of applied environment. And they have done so ever since. These methods have formed the basis of an individual differences tradition in psychology. Section F in this text will tell you all you need to know.

But this applied success, whilst welcome, still failed to satisfy the natural scientific and experimental ideal that the academic discipline held so dear. This needed to be remedied. If mind *is* action, the argument went, then a person's psychological world was freely observable and accessible in the physical world by simple reference to what they do. Experimental psychology was about to start a new life, most 'satisfactorily defined as the science of human behaviour' (Pillsbury, 1911: 1).

CONDITIONING: WATSON, PAVLOV, SKINNER AND THE STUDY OF BEHAVIOUR

2.5 In 1913, John B. Watson (1878–1958) laid out an aggressive manifesto for this science of human behaviour in a paper entitled 'Psychology as the behaviourist views it':

Psychology as the behaviourist views it is a purely objective branch of natural science. Its … goal is the prediction and control of behaviour. Introspection forms no essential part of its methods, nor is the scientific value of its data dependent on the readiness with which they lend themselves to interpretation in terms of consciousness. The behaviourist … recognizes no dividing line between man and brute. (1913: 158)

This all seems quite straightforward. Introspection had reached a scientific impasse and the functionalists had begun to see mind as synonymous with behaviour. As one might predict, therefore, Watson's rejection of introspection caused little argument. Watson's technology of behaviour also set out to ignore the facts of consciousness, and for this reason even Titchener (the undisputed champion of introspection) did not see it as competition. It just wasn't psychology. Yet most psychologists trained in the ways of **functionalism** were quite happy to accept a form of methodological behaviourism which allowed them to acknowledge the presence of conscious experience, but also to ignore it as something hopelessly unsuited to scientific analyses.

But behind Watson's words lay radical change. He strongly advocated a strict or radical behaviourism in which the very existence of consciousness was brought into question. Psychology, he proposed, should henceforth 'discard all reference to consciousness'.

The use of mentalistic terminology such as 'the mind' or 'consciousness' did indeed become more and more problematic for psychologists over the next decade or so. For the strict behaviourist, consciousness had no place in the discipline or in human life more generally. Behavioural adaptation was not a function of consciousness; it was instead a function of our capacity to learn.

This principle had already been demonstrated by Edward Thorndike (1874–1949) and perhaps more famously by Ivan Pavlov (1849–1936). Pavlov received a Nobel Prize for work which exploited the (delightful) fact that dogs salivate at the merest expectation of food. Pavlov demonstrated, by repeatedly pairing a particular stimulus (the food) with a sound (famously a bell but more probably a metronome), that his dogs would eventually salivate in response to the sound alone. They had, in other words, learned to connect the food (known as the unconditioned stimulus) with the sound (or conditioned stimulus). This form of learning, in which new stimulus–response connections were created, became known as classical conditioning. Thorndike, on the other hand, showed through a series of clever 'puzzle box' experiments that animals could be trained to produce a specific behavioural response more frequently if that response elicited a tangible reward. This form of learning, which could be used to strengthen (or weaken) pre-existing response tendencies, became known as operant conditioning.

2.5.1 MAN AND BRUTE

These animal studies nonetheless became directly applicable to psychology only when Watson, in true Darwinian style, forcefully pointed out that 'man and brute' were no longer seen as divided. Watson argued that, because we are animals, so the study of other, simpler, animals could shed light on the way humans function. Following this emphasis on learning, Watson was also able to argue that 'instinct' was another concept that psychology could do without. We began life as a blank slate (with no personality, no intelligence – just a mental blank canvas) and everything we subsequently did, all our knowledge and skills, was the result of processes of learning or deliberate training. And the latter, the training and ultimate control of behaviour, was now the central aim of the psychologist. As Watson (1930) put it, we 'can build any man, starting at birth, into any kind of social or a-social being upon order' (cited in Leahey, 2004: 377).

Behaviourism reached its height between 1930 and 1950 and is now most prominently associated with the work of B.F. Skinner (1904–1990). Skinner developed Thorndike's ideas. Using similar apparatus he focused on *contingencies of reinforcement*: in other words, the nature and specific patterns of reward-giving through which spontaneously emitted and random behaviours (or operants) could best be 'shaped' into direct, learned (or conditioned) responses. Theoretically, Skinner shared Watson's radical behaviourism: he stressed the determining influence of environmental influences on behaviour, whilst excluding all reference to mental states (Hergenhahn, 2005).

In two philosophical publications (*Walden two* published in 1948, and *Beyond freedom and dignity* in 1971), Skinner also explored the ultimate behaviourist vision of a utopian society in which people 'were conditioned into socially admirable ways of acting' (Harré, 2006: 18). In this brave new world, people would be rewarded for good behaviour and the society would be ordered, productive and calm. Crime would be low and happiness would be everywhere. It's easy to mock this ambition, but if we could create a better and happier world by engineering the rewards that people got for their behaviour, then at first glance this might appear to be a good idea. Further reflection however reveals a serious flaw with this ambition in that someone has to decide what constitutes a 'better' or 'happier' world and also what behaviours are worthy of reward. We could end up with a Ministry of Happiness run by psychologists in a world with no dissent and no challenge to authority.

Skinner and behaviourism were both enormously important. Skinner was voted the most influential psychologist of the twentieth century (Dittman, 2002). The methodological approach associated with behaviourism, which promoted 'a causal metaphysics, an experimental methodology based upon independent and dependent variables applied to a population and the use of statistics as the main analytical tool', is still used by the discipline as *the* benchmark for 'what a scientific psychology should be' (Harré, 2006: 8). The classes in research methods that you attend will no doubt confirm that this methodology is still very much alive and well in psychology.

Eventually, however, the influence of behaviourism itself began to give way. In Europe in particular, work in a more traditional psychological vein (with a focus on active mental processes) had continued throughout the period of behaviourist domination. Frederic Bartlett's (1886–1969) work on *Remembering* (1932) and Jean Piaget's (1896–1980) approach to cognitive development are good examples, as is the work of the **Gestalt psychologists**. Even in the midst of American behaviourism, influential theorists like Edward Chace Tolman (1886–1959) and Clark Leonard Hull (1884–1952) also promoted the idea that mental processes played a fundamental role in the determination of behaviour. Both acknowledged these processes as 'intervening variables' (so called because they intervened between the stimulus and response) in their respective behaviourist theories.

In the end, the demise of behaviourism was almost inevitable. It had always been problematic to draw conclusions about humans on the basis of animal studies. Animals often behaved in an apparently mindless fashion, but this needn't mean that humans were similarly without minds. The image of humans as pawns in the environment also seemed unnecessarily negative. It is a depressing view of humanity if we think of ourselves as being puppets that are manipulated by changes in our environment.

The most damning indictment of behaviourism was nonetheless painfully straightforward: it wasn't psychology. Psychology, after all, means the study of mind, so abandoning that concept really did create a problem and limit the areas that psychology could investigate. We have seen throughout this chapter that psychology has tended (for mainly methodological reasons) to sidestep what may be its key subject matter: the subjective world of mental phenomena. But behaviourism took this avoidance to its logical conclusion. In the final section we will briefly consider modern attempts to put this right.

MODERN PSYCHOLOGY: COGNITIVE SCIENCE, HUMANISM AND THE RETURN OF THE SOCIAL SCIENCES

2.6 In the middle of the last century behaviourism ran out of steam, and it became obvious that we needed to look at the thought processes that intervene between stimulus and response. It was no longer enough to see us as puppets just responding to whatever stimulus came our way. Cognitive science (the study of mental processes) took over from behaviourism as the dominant paradigm in psychology around 1960 and it remains dominant to this day. A benefit of this is that cognitive science's tendency to exploit the behaviourist experimental model, combined with a focus on information processing, has made psychology look like a 'natural science of the mental' once again. It has made a significant contribution to the discipline's progress in recent years (the cognitive approach is dealt with in Section B).

On the downside, many psychologists would argue that cognitive science has again avoided the psychological world of subjective, mental phenomena in order to study a whole host of supposedly more permanent mental and causal structures which are said to lie beneath. These structures have various names – traits, attitudes, schemas, personalities, and so on: the list is very long. And unlike the subjective, mental phenomena themselves, these entities are hypothesised to have an enduring existence, to be experimentally manipulable in a controlled fashion, and hence to possess a substance which allows mathematical analysis and description. The problem is that nobody has ever proved their existence. Harré launches a critique along precisely these lines:

> People, for the purposes of psychology, are not internally complex. They have no parts ... There are no mental states other than the private thoughts and feelings people are aware of from time to time. There are no mental mechanisms by which a person's powers and skills are implemented, except the occasional private rehearsals for action in which we sometimes engage. The whole top heavy apparatus of ... cognitive psychology is at worst a fantasy and at best a metaphor. (1998: 15)

A related critique focuses on methods. Clearly, natural science has progressed a long way since Newton; yet despite its long-held desire to emulate these disciplines, psychology has not moved with it (Harré, 1999). The experimental methodology based upon independent and dependent variables we described earlier is, in truth, an invention of psychology (Harré, 2006) which is not properly reflective of any natural science model.

Psychologists are nonetheless resourceful creatures and two distinct responses to this situation are now discernible. The experimental and quantitative tradition in psychology has, for example, developed a number of statistics and techniques which are closely related to modern developments in physics and chemistry (Gelman & Hill, 2007). Huge advances in both structural and functional brain scanning technology have also allowed *cognitive neuroscience* to link subjective mental phenomena to brain function (and physiology) in ways that would have amazed Wundt and James (Frith, 2007).

A second response has involved the re-emergence of more 'humanitarian' values and methods within psychology. This began with the humanist movement in the 1960s, which offered itself as a 'third force' in psychology. It aimed to provide an antidote to the negativity which seemed to characterise behaviourism and Freudian psychoanalysis. Most associated with **Abraham Maslow** (1908–1970) and **Carl Rogers** (1902–1987), humanism suggested that the subjective mental phenomena (or 'reality') which psychology had so often ignored were actually the primary guide for human behaviour. Behaviour was not *caused*: rather, it was motivated by each individual's desire to *self-actualise* and reach their full potential. Humanism stalled, however, primarily because it failed to come up with a method of collecting data about people and ultimately because its uncritical and positive assessment of humans felt more like a form of wishful thinking than a serious scientific endeavour.

In the last 30 years, the social scientific model has nonetheless returned to psychology in a more rigorous fashion. To a large extent, this movement continues to be inspired by suspicions that natural science may be inappropriate as a model for psychology. There is a renewed belief that the subjective world of meaningful human experience (look at Table 2.1 again!) really *is* psychology's rightful subject matter. And a proliferation of qualitative research methods has duly emerged to interrogate particular aspects of this extraordinarily diverse, and very human, world of life (see Willig & Stainton Rogers, 2007).

CONCLUSION

2.7 This is an exciting time to be studying psychology. As we've just discussed, the natural and social scientific models are showing marked signs of convergence. Psychologists are connecting human meaning-making and creativity to brain function in ever greater detail (Edelman, 2006). Psychology is now armed with a range of quantitative and qualitative methods, as well as some very advanced technologies, which all satisfy the scientific ideal (in a range of different ways). Research which deliberately 'mixes' methods traditionally associated with the natural and social sciences has also become very fashionable (Creswell & Plano Clark, 2007). Psychology finally seems to be accepting its position at the divide between the natural and social sciences, and acknowledging that to take full advantage of this position it really *has to* retain a foot in both these (increasingly connected) camps. Now comes your chance to contribute …

CHAPTER SUMMARY

2.8 As we have seen, modern psychology traces its immediate origins to the late nineteenth century, when Wilhelm Wundt created his laboratory in Leipzig. Since that time, the discipline has moved to and fro between conceptions of psychology as (1) a natural science and (2) a social science. Much has hinged on the question of focus: to what extent should psychology study the mind and our experiences of the world, and to what extent should it focus on what is externally observable and measurable? Over the past 150 years psychology has developed a range of methods, approaches and measures, yet the central questions remain.

DISCUSSION QUESTIONS

As we have seen, psychology has developed through debate between those who believe the discipline should be modelled on natural science, and those who believe it should be modelled on social science. What arguments can you see for and against each of these positions? Where do you stand yourself on this debate?

What are the implications of the two views above for (1) what topics or phenomena should be studied; (2) the methods that should be used?

SUGGESTIONS FOR FURTHER READING

One of the best texts to pick up to explore the beginnings of psychology is Fancher, R.E. (1996). *Pioneers of psychology* (3rd edn). New York: Norton. This looks at key ideas and key people chapter by chapter, and the book provides very useful background to several other chapters in this text.

Another text that has stood the test of time is Miller, G. (1966). *Psychology: the science of mental life*. London: Penguin. This also covers the pioneers of psychology with some interesting insights into their lives and ideas.

If you want a comprehensive account, there are a number of large texts designed for US courses on the history of psychology: for example, Benjamin, L.T. (1996). *A history of psychology*. New York: McGraw-Hill.

There is also a readable text written for the UK market: Jones, D., & Elcock, J. (2001). *History and theories of psychology: a critical perspective*. London: Arnold.

3

ISSUES AND DEBATES IN PSYCHOLOGY

Lead author **Garry Young**

CHAPTER OUTLINE

INTRODUCTION

3.1

Who am I? What am I doing? What's it all for? Why are we here? These are the questions that come up when we have time to ponder the wonder of our existence. Staring at the night sky on a summer evening, we can only wonder at it all. Such questions also tend to come up at weak moments as we struggle through the events of daily life: for example, when we confront our own mortality or when we lose someone close to us or even when things just seem to be going against us. Alternatively, these questions can be induced by alcohol or by dropping your choc-ice.

In this chapter we are going to consider some of the thinking around the above questions. We will examine ideas about consciousness and the mind–body problem. We will also explore some of the tensions in psychological thinking that arise from the clash between two approaches to psychology, namely (1) reductionism and (2) folk psychology. Though these terms may not be familiar to you yet, they will be explained below.

In developing our thinking on these questions, we will explore some areas where two disciplines – namely, psychology and philosophy – frequently overlap or interact with each other.

? FRAMING QUESTIONS

What is consciousness?

What, if any, is the distinction between my mind and my body?

Is it possible to explain everything by reducing phenomena to their constituent parts?

How do our everyday explanations of what we do and why we do it compare to what science tells us about human behaviour and experience?

To what extent is psychology a natural science?

THE MIND–BODY PROBLEM

3.2

Imagine that you are having a confidential conversation with a friend, who says to you, 'I may look happy, but inside I am crying.' This statement is not difficult to understand. A straightforward interpretation might be that your friend is hiding the fact that he or she is feeling sad. The statement refers both to what we might call an overt behavioural expression (looking happy) and an emotional state (feeling sad) – and the two clearly do not correspond.

Typically, we don't expect these statements to be literally true (for example, we don't take the word 'crying' to mean that tears are literally welling up inside the person). The use of 'inside' here is metaphorical. This metaphor is revealing: it indicates that there is both a private and a public component to our being.

Note that when we use the word 'private' here, we don't mean simply that there are some things we would prefer to keep to ourselves (because they are personal, might be embarrassing, and so on). Instead, in this context we are using the word 'private' to mean that there are some things we *cannot* make public. Each person has direct access only to his or her *own* experiential content: only *you* can directly access the inner world of *your* own thoughts and feelings. In this sense, when we say 'You don't know how I feel', we are being 100 per cent accurate.

If we accept that as humans we have both a private (experiential) and a public (behavioural and physiological) component to our being, we can ask how this affects the way we explain our existence and how we investigate it. It is useful here to introduce two contrasting terms, namely, 'mental states' and 'brain states'. In everyday usage, talk of thoughts and feelings, or **mental states**, is often assumed to refer to the mind. Mental states are private in the sense already mentioned. Brain states, on the other hand, are public. That is to say, whilst they are not typically on display or observed, they are nevertheless directly observable in principle, and in a way that mental states are not. We can, for example, monitor brain activity by using scanning devices such as positron emission tomography (PET) or functional magnetic resonance imaging (fMRI), or even by employing more invasive techniques such as direct electrode stimulation (see Chapter 7). This latter technique was famously employed by Wilder Penfield.

Penfield (1958; 1975) stimulated regions of the exposed brain of a conscious patient who then reported what he experienced. During this research, Penfield stood perhaps as close as anyone could do to what is regarded by most as the vessel that 'houses' the mind – the living brain. The brain was clearly observable; the mind was not. When Penfield stimulated the brain, the effect this had on the individual – in terms of what that person *experienced* – could only be recorded indirectly. To illustrate, when Penfield stimulated one particular region of the patient's brain, the patient's arm moved

> **Mental states**   In the philosophy of mind, a mental state is unique to thinking and feeling beings, and forms part of our cognitive processes. These processes include our beliefs and attitudes as well as our perceptions and sensations, such as the taste of wine or the pain of a headache.
>
> **Volition**   The act of deciding to do something. It is also referred to as 'will'.

and he began to clench his fist. The patient was unable to resist performing this action. However, when asked to move his arm voluntarily, what the patient experienced was different. The movement stimulated by Penfield lacked the latter's accompanying sense of **volition**. What Penfield was unable to observe directly was the presence or absence of this *sense* of volition (the experience of willing the movement to occur).

We can summarise this point by saying that the patient has first-person access to the content of their own mind, whereas Penfield (and anyone else) must be satisfied with third-person access only. This third-person access is gained indirectly, through observation of the patient's behaviour, through measures of their (neuro) physiological states, and, of course, what they tell us about their experience.

There is, then, a discrepancy between how I gain knowledge of my own mental states (acquired through first-person access) and how I gain knowledge of someone else's (acquired through third-person access); or even a discrepancy between how I come to know states of my own mind (first person) and states of my brain (third person). As we will see, this discrepancy has direct bearing on the study of psychology.

ASIDE

The study of what we know and how we know it is called epistemology. It is one of those topics, like 'thinking about thinking', that most people find mentally extremely taxing. Elsewhere in this book we consider similar issues: for example, Jean Piaget (see Chapter 14) examined how children develop their thinking and come to know the world they live in. In this text we have tried to deal with these issues as fully as we can whilst using accessible language.

3.2.1 CARTESIAN DUALISM

Does this difference between *how* I come to know my mental states and *how* I come to know my brain states mean that these states come from two different things, my mind and my brain?

Someone who drew precisely this conclusion (that the mind and the brain are different things) was the philosopher René Descartes (1596–1650). Descartes established a way of thinking about the mind and the body that has become known as **Cartesian dualism.** This is the view that the mind is **immaterial** (i.e. not made up of material things), and therefore distinct and independent from the **material** body (including the brain). In other words, we are made up of a mind (which we can't see) and a body (which we can). You can also think of this model in terms of 'a ghost in the machine'.

Descartes famously arrived at this idea after thinking about the problem using his 'method of doubt'. This was a method of argument that involved doubting anything he could not prove to be true. Descartes argued that, though he could doubt that his body actually existed, he could not doubt that he himself existed. His argument was that the very fact that he was able to doubt something showed that he must exist: if he didn't, he would not be able to doubt or to think at all. Descartes summarised this argument in the Latin phrase *cogito, ergo sum* ('I think, therefore I am').

This conclusion is drawn from the discrepancy noted earlier concerning how we receive information about ourselves. How I come to know my body, and whether it exists, occurs indirectly – through the senses – and is therefore open to error, and its validity is questionable. However, I come to know my mind directly, and my knowledge of its existence is resistant to even the most extreme scepticism.

Descartes argued that since he could not doubt that he existed but could doubt that his body existed, then (1) he and his body (hereafter, 'body' includes the brain unless otherwise stated) must be distinct, and (2)

Cartesian dualism   The idea that we are made up of two parts, a mind and a body. The body is like all other material objects and can be examined using the material sciences, whereas the mind is not physical and cannot be measured.

Material and **immaterial**   If something is material it is made up of the atoms and molecules that are building blocks of our world, whereas if it is immaterial it is not made up of these things. We cannot measure or see immaterial things such as 'mind', which challenges their existence. The existence of immaterial things is a matter of belief rather than evidence.

he could not be his body: rather he must be something other than his body. Descartes further argued that because he was not an extended and therefore physical thing (or, to use the Latin phrase, a *res extensa*) he must be a thinking and therefore immaterial thing (*res cogitans*).

In short, Descartes attempted to draw a conclusion about the nature of his being from the discrepancy that exists between how he came to know his body and how he came to know his mind. He also employed what is known as Leibniz's law in support of this distinction. This law relates to what it means when two things are exactly the same (sometimes referred to as the *indiscernibility of identical*). The law states that for A and B to be identical, all properties of A must be identical to all properties of B, and vice versa. Applying Leibniz's law, Descartes concluded that A (the mind) and B (the body) cannot be identical because they have different properties. The body can be doubted and so has the property of doubtability. The mind cannot be doubted and so does not have this property. To reiterate, if the mind and body have different properties, they cannot be the same.

ASIDE   Hope for students

René Descartes was a frail individual, and he usually spent most of his mornings in bed, where he did most of his thinking, fresh from dreams in which he often had his revelations. In his latter years, Descartes moved to Sweden to give Queen Christina lessons in philosophy. Unfortunately for Descartes, the Queen was an early riser who wanted her lessons at 5.00 in the morning. This new schedule did no favours to Descartes's fragile health, and he contracted pneumonia, from which he died on 11 February 1650 at the age of 54. There is a lesson here for all of us: get up later!

Despite concluding that he was his mind (and thus distinct from his body), Descartes did recognise (because he experienced it as such) that he was intimately related to *his* body like no other. This ambiguity – that I (as a mind) am distinct from the physical body, yet intimately related to one body in particular, which I call mine – can be seen in the English language. For example, think about the statement 'I hate my body.' Here, the 'I' doing the hating appears distinct from the body which is hated. There does, however, appear to be a relationship between them: one of ownership (the body somehow belongs to the 'I'). But this still indicates a difference. If they were the same – that is, referring to the same thing – then you should be able to turn this around. Yet it does not seem to make sense to say 'My body hates I' or even 'My body hates my body.' There is clearly some ambiguity here – an ambiguity made all the more apparent in the two examples that follow.

Consider here the statements: 'I hate my body' and 'I hate myself'. Are they equivalent? If so, in what way? If not, why not? What extra ingredient is contained within the reference to my *self* that is absent in the case of my body? Next, consider this example: 'I am envious of my body'. Whilst it makes sense (so to speak) to be envious of someone else's body, it makes no sense to be envious of one's own. Here the 'I' and 'my body' seem to be too closely related for the statement to be meaningful. It could be argued that these examples simply reflect a limitation in the English language. Perhaps. Nonetheless, they do illustrate a dualism in our expression of self.

3.2.2 AN EXPLANATORY PROBLEM: HOW DOES THE MIND INTERACT WITH THE BODY?

There are many problems with Cartesian dualism (too many for us to discuss all of them here). Perhaps the most damning is the problem of explaining how the ghost can work the machine (Figure 3.1). This problem is known as the problem of interaction. To explain: if, as Descartes maintains, the mind and the body are distinct – one being immaterial and the other material – then how do such utterly different and incompatible substances interact? In other words, how can the mind have an effect on the body (or how can the ghost work the machine)?

Descartes's solution, incidentally, was to claim that the interaction occurred at the pineal gland within the brain. Even if this were true, which it is not (more contemporary research has established that the pineal gland serves a function unknown to Descartes in his day), and the pineal gland were indeed the seat of mind–body interaction, there is a problem: knowing *where* something occurs is not an explanation of *how* it occurs. When pushed on this matter, Descartes's response was to claim that the interaction is *sui generis* (unique). This is possible, of course, but unlikely; and, philosophically, it is a weak position to adopt. He might as well have said 'It's magic.'

EXERCISE   Get your mind and body to interact

Carry out a small test to show that your mind and body can interact.

First let's demonstrate that your mind can affect your body. You can do this by using your mind to think about the person you most dislike in all the world. Keep thinking about them and imagine that they win the lottery. This will probably make you feel angry and you will notice changes in your body and even your behaviour brought about by these thoughts. You can create different changes in your body by thinking about the person you most fancy in the world. Leave that for later.

Now see how your body can affect your thoughts. Take in a small amount of a psychoactive food (for example, a pint of lager, an energy drink or a cup of coffee) and observe how your thoughts can change as a result. The use of alcohol is the most obvious example: it is common for people who have drunk a lot of alcohol to have 'beer goggles' and think about the world and people in a very different way, and to change their assessment of risk.

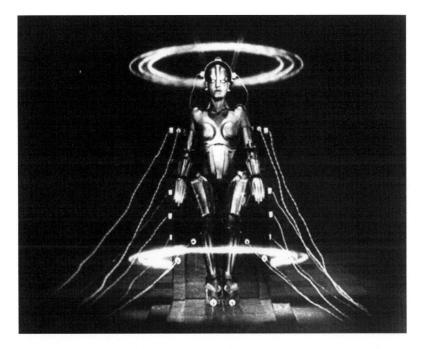

FIGURE 3.1   The mind–body problem is the key idea behind many science fiction films. One of the first was the silent classic *Metropolis* by Fritz Lang (1927). The female robot is used by the callous factory owner to take the place of the saintly Maria and create chaos amongst the workers. The key question concerns how we can distinguish between the machine and the person (the machine with a soul)
© Bettmann/Corbis

What is appealing about Descartes's dualism, however, is the causal role it gives to the mind. It seems intuitively the case that my thoughts cause my actions, at least some of the time. So according to Descartes the mind can be the cause of some behaviours and experiences and this prevents it from being regarded as having no effect on the body. Under Descartes, then, the mind is found at the centre of explanations of human action.

Despite its intuitive appeal, the Cartesian 'problem of interaction' remains a major challenge to overcome when attempting to explain the causal connection between mind and body. To illustrate: suppose I claim that with the power of my (Cartesian) mind alone I can move a small physical object on the table in front of me – a pen, say. Would you bet against me? Jedi mind tricks aside, would you believe that it is something I could do? If I did manage to do this, I suspect you would be very impressed. However, consider how totally unimpressed you would be if I claimed, instead, that with the power of my mind alone I could raise my arm in the air! Why is it that this latter feat is so underwhelming? The raising of arms in the air is, I suppose, something that is often witnessed, whereas the movement of a pen by the power of one's mind is not.

Yet, according to Cartesian dualism, the same interaction of immaterial mind with material object, necessary to move the pen, is required every time we engage in deliberate behaviour, even when it is as mundane as raising one's arm in the air. Therefore, no matter how detailed the description, and no matter how complete our understanding of the underlying neurophysiology of the behaviour, if the desire to move the arm is generated by a Cartesian self, then this desire must ultimately have stemmed from an immaterial mind. Consequently, at some point, our detailed explanation of the action, which includes a description of the neurophysiology involved in raising a hand in the air, must also explain how the mind, and the desire it generates, caused this change in neurophysiology to occur.

KEY STUDY Hofstadter, R.D., and Dennett, D.C. (1981). *The mind's I: fantasies and reflections on self and soul.* Brighton: Harvester.

The study of the relationship between mind and body doesn't offer much opportunity for traditional experiments in psychology. One of the techniques that has been developed to test out ideas is the *Gedankenexperiment* (thought experiment). The fabulous advantage of this technique is that you can do a *Gedankenexperiment* while sitting in your chair with a cup of hot chocolate on the table. The disadvantage is that you have to think very hard and very long.

One of the most entertaining thought experiments was devised by Dennett (Hofstadter & Dennett, 1981), and is particularly applicable to Section 3.2.3. Imagine having your brain removed by keyhole surgery, keeping it alive in a glass container and replacing all the severed nerve connections with nanotechnology radio transmitters. This is the stuff of nightmares and many science fiction films. Your have now separated your brain from your body. Imagine your body moving to the other side of the room and looking at your brain (which it can still see because your eyes have been reconnected via the radio transmitters). Now ask yourself the question, 'Where am I?' Are you over there, or over here, and who, in any case, is doing the asking?

Go one step further and watch the body carry out a murder. Now which bit of you should be locked up, your body or your brain?

The example in the key study illustrates the difficulty faced by Cartesian dualism. For although it is true that within our everyday language we often distinguish mind from body, it seems there is a limit to how far this distinction can be taken. In turning the mind and the body (and therefore the mind and the *brain*) into two distinct substances, Descartes's theory therefore entails the problem of interaction.

Cartesian dualism also raises an important methodological question, namely: what role would there be for scientific psychology in the study of an entity (the mind) that exists outside the realm of the physical sciences? If we are our minds and scientific psychology's role is to help solve the 'riddle of our selves', then scientific psychology faces a problem, namely: how can the material sciences and therefore scientific psychology study an immaterial, non-physical mind?

3.2.3 MIND–BRAIN IDENTITY THEORY: REMOVING THE NEED FOR INTERACTION

Perhaps the solution is to alter the status of the mind, and with it its relation to the body (including, of course, the brain). Mind–brain identity theory (hereafter, identity theory) (Lewis, 1966; Place, 1956; Smart, 1959), in contrast to Descartes, holds that the mind and the brain are one; or, more specifically, that a particular mental state (call it M_1) is identical to a particular neurological state (call it N_1). There is no interaction between the mind and the brain, nor does there need to be, for they are one and the same thing.

KEY RESEARCHER   Susan Blackmore

FIGURE 3.2   Susan Blackmore

Susan Blackmore is a freelance writer, lecturer and broadcaster, and a Visiting Professor at the University of Plymouth. She has a degree in psychology and physiology from Oxford University (1973) and a PhD in parapsychology from the University of Surrey (1980). Her research interests include memes, evolutionary theory, consciousness and meditation. She practises Zen and campaigns for drug legalisation.

She writes for several magazines and newspapers, blogs for *The Guardian* newspaper and *Psychology Today*, and is a frequent contributor and presenter on radio and television. She is author of over 60 academic articles, about 50 book contributions, and many book reviews. Her books include *Dying to live* (on near-death experiences, 1993), *The meme machine* (1999, now translated into 13 other languages), *Consciousness: an introduction* (a textbook, 2003), *Conversations on consciousness* (2005) and *Ten Zen questions* (2009).

Mind–brain identity theory is based on the idea that there is nothing above or beyond the physical. It reduces mental states to the level of neurological states. It does not deny that mental states exist, but rather argues that they are identical to brain states. Identity theory therefore employs a **reductionist** explanation (see Section 3.3) when accounting for how mental states cause human action. Such actions and interactions are explained using the same language as the natural sciences. The cause of an action is described in terms of the neurophysiological state of the person: a descriptive state that can be explained at (and therefore reduced to) the level of physics.

Identity theory also uses a reductive methodology. The relationship between mind and brain can only be discovered after the event (*a posteriori*, to use the Latin phrase). This means that knowledge about which mental state is identical to which brain state can only be discovered through the use of brain scanning techniques, or other more intrusive methods used to record localised brain activity, or through the study of corresponding behaviour or reported subjective experience. In short, in order to explain changes in a person's mental states we give explanations involving changes in brain states.

There is one further important idea to consider here. According to identity theory, the changes or damage to states of the brain do not *cause* changes in the person's mental states, in the sense of A causing B. Instead any change to a given brain state *equates* to differences in the subject's experience (because the mind and brain are one and the same thing). Therefore, understanding what caused differences in a person's mental states requires us to understand what caused differences in the same person's neural states: to understand one is to understand the other. When we give an explanation of a person's action in terms of mental states such as beliefs and desires, then according to identity theory we are actually explaining that behaviour in terms of the changes in the person's neurophysiology. Why? Because mental states and brain states are one and the same.

> **Reductionism**   The idea that a complex system is nothing more than the sum of its parts, and that a description of a system can be reduced to descriptions of the individual components.
>
> **Parsimony**   The idea that 'less is better' and, in particular, that a complicated explanation is not needed when a simple one is sufficient.

Identity theory has a number of points in its favour. As a theory of mind–body relations, it is certainly **parsimonious**. For some, it may even appear intuitively sound. Certainly it is compatible with evidence introduced as a result of advances in brain imaging equipment. Functional MRI (magnetic resonance imaging) scans, for example, allow the anatomical structure and function of a living brain to be studied. With such equipment we can observe and record those areas of the brain that exhibit increased (or even decreased) activity when an individual performs a particular mental task. We can even examine patients suffering injury or disease in order to identify which parts of the brain, when damaged, correspond to deficits in mental function and/or experiential content. Francis Crick, one of the co-discoverers of the structure of DNA, once famously remarked that our joys and sorrows, our memories and ambitions, are nothing more than a vast assembly of nerves cells and molecules (Crick, 1994).

Identity theory, with its idea that mind and brain are one and the same, is able to sidestep the problem of how the mind interacts with the brain. The mind can bring about changes in the brain, but as the mind is the brain there is no problem of interaction to explain. Talk of thoughts causing behaviour is, then, nothing but talk of neurological states causing behaviour. In reality, the mind has no causal power independent of the brain because it is not independent of the brain. As a result, explanations of why we do things do not need to use the language of the psychological (the mental).

There is, however, a difficulty here. To remove reference to mental states such as beliefs or desires from our explanations of actions is to ignore an important component: the rational nature of reasons. We make sense of our lives through our beliefs and desires. In fact we explain our behaviour in these terms, so to ignore them and just describe behaviour in terms of chemical changes in the brain fails to capture why we do things and what we hope to achieve. Without these important mental states we cannot hope to provide a full picture of human behaviour.

3.2.4 HOW TO CAPTURE RATIONAL RELATIONS: INTRODUCING FOLK PSYCHOLOGY

Suppose you know (from some previous conversation) that I do not enjoy spending time in crowded places and that I try to avoid them whenever possible. Suppose further that one day you see me enter a café you know to be crowded, and then, seconds later, leave. You might conclude that because I have a desire to avoid crowded places (whenever possible), and because the café is crowded and I have come to the belief that the café is crowded (after entering the premises), I decide to leave.

If this is your conclusion then it amounts to what is sometimes referred to as a **folk psychology** account of my actions (Stitch & Ravenscroft, 1994). Put simply, you explain my actions in terms of the beliefs and desires you have attributed to me: that I have a desire to avoid crowded places and a belief that the café is crowded. Part of this explanation is your assumption that my beliefs and desires *caused* my behaviour.

This simple folk psychology explanation is clearly intended to be a causal explanation (explaining why it happened). Now, this in itself is not a problem for identity theory because what is really being stated here is that a neural state (identical to my desire to avoid crowded places) and another neural state (identical to my belief that the café was crowded)

> **Folk psychology**   Ways of thinking about the mind that are implicit in how we make everyday attributions of mental states to ourselves and others.

caused me to leave the café. However, folk psychology here provides not only a causal explanation, but also a reason-giving explanation. The reason I left the café was because I have a desire to avoid crowded places, and the café was crowded. As well as citing the cause of my behaviour, then, this explanation shows my behaviour to be rational, or at least reasonable under the circumstances, based as it is on my beliefs and desires.

Beliefs and desires, generally speaking, are connected to each other. They form a network of interrelated structures that express themselves through behaviour deemed reasonable within a given context. Such rational relations seem appropriate when talking about beliefs and desires. What is less clear is how appropriate it is to talk about neurological states being connected rationally to each other.

What the crowded café example illustrates is that there are essentially two types of explanation, one causal and the other reason-giving. Folk psychology explanations are explicitly reason-giving and implicitly causal: we imply that the reasons given for our actions are at the same time the cause of our actions. In contrast, neurological explanations are predominantly causal, and no attempt to capture reason-giving explanations at the level of electrochemical excitation and inhibition of neurons seems possible. If identity theory is to provide a valid explanation of the relationship between mind and brain, then it must be able to capture at the level of neuronal interaction the rational connections that so clearly exist at the psychological level. In short, what we need is a theory that is able to explain how lumpy grey matter can be rational. As it stands, identity theory is unable to do this.

Identity theory involves reducing the mental to the physical, such that the mind is nothing but the brain. Perhaps a closer look at reductionism and objections to it, particularly regarding the functional and irreducible nature of mind, will go some way toward untangling the puzzle that is the mind–body problem.

REDUCTIONISM

3.3

In scientific psychology, reductionism is the view that any complex phenomenon is simply the sum of the components that make it up. So feeling happy, for example, is best described as a series of physical changes (such as smiling) and chemical changes in the brain that create a sensation we call happiness (Figure 3.3). Thus, according to reductionism, psychological phenomena are nothing but physical phenomena which can be explained using physical facts and studied using methods appropriate to measuring this more fundamental level of reality.

We have already seen this viewpoint expressed in the context of identity theory. In the rest of this chapter, we will look more closely at reductionism in general within scientific psychology, and at the challenges that arise when trying to reduce psychological states to states of the brain.

Reductionism has been successfully applied to physics, and to the other natural sciences of chemistry and biology. After Newton (1642–1727) and later Darwin (1809–1882), our view of our place in the universe changed: instead of seeing ourselves as the centre of the universe and the reason the universe exists, humans began to see themselves as part of a continuum of

FIGURE 3.3 Reductionism: Wallace and Gromitt (shown here with creator Nick Park) appear to be alive when we watch them on film but we know that their actions are created step by step by animators moving bits of plasticine. The reductionist argument is that when we learn more about people we will be able to see that our actions can be explained in a very similar way. For example, a behaviourist might see our behaviour as being a series of small steps that are caused by rewards and punishments
© Louis Quail/Corbis

organic life. According to the fundamental laws of physics, it would seem that organic life itself forms part of a continuum with the inorganic. For though, at this fundamental level, organic life differs from inorganic material in terms of its complexity, it does not do so in terms of its substance. It would seem we are all fundamentally made of the same stuff (ashes to ashes and dust to dust: we start as particles of dust and we end up the same way).

If, however, we are all made of the same stuff, and if the same laws of physics that apply to the inorganic likewise apply to us, it would seem to be logical that the same principles used to study and explain the inorganic should be used to study and explain us. This is certainly an argument proposed in support of reductionism. However, an important objection to this idea is that we differ from objects in one important aspect: our minds.

Once again, the problem of explaining the mind within a physical universe needs to be dealt with. To argue, much as Descartes did, that the mind is distinct is to reject reductionism and to claim that what exists is more than just the physical. Few psychologists support this position, preferring instead to champion *substance monism* – the view that there is only one substance, which is physical.

3.3.1 PROBLEMS WITH REDUCTION IN PSYCHOLOGY

Yet there is dissatisfaction with reductionism in psychology. Let us consider some of the reasons. According to Burwood et al. (1999), when we use a reductionist analysis we must be able to explain all the phenomena in the higher property by the lower property we are reducing it to, so that there is no distinct role for the higher property to be playing independently of the lower-level ones. In our example of happiness, we must be able to explain all the features we experience in happiness by the physical and chemical changes in our body. When it comes to psychological phenomena like this, we have already identified a potential problem for reductionist explanations, namely how to capture the reason-giving explanations that exist between psychological states at the more fundamental neurological level. With happiness, sometimes we feel happy because we think of happy thoughts, and so our higher processes have created the physical changes that we associate with happiness.

Neurological explanations do have a role to play in explaining human action, however, and can be seen as *compatible* with higher-level psychology. Importantly, what they are not capable of doing is capturing the nature of the relation that exists between psychological phenomena. A useful way to illustrate this is by demonstrating the difference between a *movement* and an *action*.

What is the difference between your signature and a squiggle? To the unknowing eye they may look the same, but one of them means something and the other one does not. If you think about the processes in your brain that created the squiggle and the signature, what would be the difference between them? Even if they originated in two different regions of the brain, it seems reasonable to ask why that should be. What is it about them that makes one originate in one area and the other in a different one? Similarly, when tracing the neural route through the body – from brain to muscles in the arm and hand – what would be the difference between the two actions? There may be slight variations in muscle movement, but these variations would be there when comparing the movement involved in the same person writing their signature on two separate occasions (no two signatures are ever exactly the same).

A signature on a document, for example, is likely to mean that I am authorising something – possibly a transaction. A squiggle, by comparison, is fairly meaningless, though it might suggest I was bored and doodling. The neurological explanation provides a detailed account of the movement in each case (it explains *how* the behaviour occurred), but each movement is only differentiated at the level of action ('What sort of action is it?', 'What does it mean?'), and this is a psychological differentiation that cannot be captured at the lower level.

To appreciate the value of a psychological level of explanation, think about life and death. At the biological level, you can clearly distinguish between life and death. At this level, you might even draw a distinction between a natural death and a non-natural, intentional act of killing (by observing that a foreign object had entered the system – a bullet or poison, say – or even that the organism's head had been removed from its body). However, at *purely* the biological level, you cannot distinguish between killing and murder: that is, between legal execution and unauthorised death. It is only possible to make this distinction by incorporating into your thinking differences that occur only at the *psychological* level: for it is only at this level that you are able to differentiate between killing that is judged to be legal and that deemed illegal. Even if you were to argue that all intentional killing is murder, such an argument is only meaningful *as an argument* at the psychological level.

3.3.2 MOVING AWAY FROM REDUCTIONISM

Those who oppose a reductionist approach to psychology argue that a methodology that tries to give explanations of human action at the neurological level alone is impoverished. This is because such a methodology is capable of supporting explanations only of movement; and critically, as humans, we do not engage in movement *per se*. Rather, our *movements* form the basis for our *actions*; and as the signature and killing examples illustrate, an action is something more than just a movement; it is something that cannot be explained fully at the level of interconnecting neurons. For a fuller explanation of behaviour, we need to draw too on higher-level psychological terms such as beliefs and desires, or to incorporate the symbolic nature of the movement into the explanation (murder or sanctioned execution). Psychological explanation transforms the movement into a meaningful act within a social context.

The signature and killing examples above help to illustrate that explanatory reductionism is not without its problems. However, as Hull and Van Regenmortel (2002) note, reductionism is not to be despised: rather it must be placed in its proper context. As an alternative, **explanatory pluralism** holds that different levels of description, like the psychological and the neurophysiological, can coevolve, and mutually influence each other, without the higher-level theory being replaced by, or reduced to, the lower-level one (Bem, 2001; Looren de Jong, 2001). The properties of the higher-level explanation are often described in terms of their function – in terms of what it is the function of the lower level to do. Importantly, though, the higher-level, functional property cannot be reduced to this lower level.

An often used example to illustrate this irreducibility is a 'timepiece'. Over the years, there have been many different ways to record the passage of time: sundials, candles, sand pouring through an hourglass, the hands of a clock, and most recently digital watches. At the physical level, each is very different to the other. What they all have in common, however, is their function. Despite being physically distinct, they each serve the same function: to record the passage of time. Yet this functional property cannot be reduced to any one physical state. The functional property 'timepiece' is not identical to any one particular physical structure; rather it is realised by them all. The descriptive term used to group together these disparate physical structures is, at the same time, the functional state of each physical system. Perhaps, then, a functional explanation of mind provides a way of understanding the relationship between mental states and neurological states of the brain.

> **Explanatory pluralism**　Holds that different levels of description, like the psychological and the neurophysiological, can coevolve, and mutually influence each other, without the higher-level theory being replaced by, or reduced to, the lower-level one.

3.4 CONCLUSION

3.4.1 FOLK PSYCHOLOGY VERSUS SCIENTIFIC PSYCHOLOGY

The purpose of this chapter has been to outline some of the challenges involved in trying to answer the fundamental questions (for example, 'Who am I?') that make up the 'riddle of our selves'. These challenges arise from differences that are said to exist between a scientific approach to the study of our selves and the qualities that make up our experience of being alive: in particular, the way we can reflect on our selves and our very existence. This reflective experience lies at the heart of everyday folk psychology accounts of *why* we do what we do.

As we have seen, folk psychology explanations give a reason-giving role to psychological states such as beliefs, or desires, or hopes, and see them as the *cause* of our actions. I left the crowded café *because* I want to avoid crowds and believe the café to be crowded. The word 'because' in that last sentence indicates that the *want* and the *belief* are the cause of the subsequent action because they are rationally related to each other and to the behaviour that follows. It makes sense, given the person's belief and wants, that he should exit the café within moments of entering it.

The challenge faced by scientific psychology is twofold. First, it must be capable of providing a scientific explanation of behaviour that captures the rational relations that exist between our psychological states and our subsequent behaviour. Second, it must do this without violating the principles of physicalism.

An immediate objection to this challenge might be to claim that scientific psychology should replace, rather than respect, folk psychology explanations. The question here is what we could replace folk psychology with. As we have seen, scientific attempts to reduce psychological explanation to questions of neurophysiology encounter difficulties. A scientific psychology that reduces the psychological to the level of neuronal interactions thus seems self-defeating. In short, if we were to reduce the rational relations characteristic of psychological states to the neuronal level, psychology would become nothing more than a science of the brain. How then could we differentiate psychology from, say, neurobiology?

This chapter has illustrated the challenges that reductionist accounts face when trying to capture the psychological at the level of neuronal interactions. A promising, though by no means problem-free, approach has been to recognise the irreducible nature of psychological states and their interdependent rational relations, and to suggest a non-reducible relation between them and the physical system.

Such an approach maintains the spirit of folk psychology explanations, but also tries to adopt the rigours of science, at least when trying to provide an account of how the lower-level states of the brain work. Within such an account of mind–brain relations, the discipline of psychology is able to maintain its independence from a pure *science of the brain*. It does, however, raise a fresh question for you to consider: if psychology gains its independence as a discipline through focusing on the study of states and properties that are not reducible to lower-level explanations, can it rightly still be called a science?

3.4.2 A NOTE OF CAUTION

We will end this chapter on a cautionary note. Whilst folk psychology is not itself infallible as a means of explaining human action – we can, after all, be mistaken about the reasons we attribute to a given action (as research on attribution theory shows: see Chapter 12) – it does nevertheless remind us about a fundamental component of our behaviour, its meaningfulness. If, therefore, we adopt the view that such behaviour *can* and *should* be studied using the natural scientific methods, then we must resolve the problem of mind. However, if we rely on a model of mind that is reducible to the natural sciences, this is likely to result in the reduction of psychology itself to the natural sciences. Psychology therefore risks becoming a science of the brain. If, on the other hand, the explanation of mind adopted by psychology cannot be reduced to the natural sciences then, although its independent status may be preserved, its recognition as a science may be challenged. It may be that psychology is guilty of *scientism*: 'the borrowing of methods and a characteristic vocabulary from the natural sciences in order to discover causal mechanisms that explain psychological phenomena' (Van Langenhove, 1995: 14).

A psychology that at its heart embraces the philosophy and methodology of the natural sciences, whilst maintaining its independence as a distinct discipline, must face the challenge of bridging the explanatory gap that exists between mind and brain, between the reducible and the irreducible. The problem, then, is one of accommodation: how to accommodate the mental within the physical, and psychology within the natural sciences.

CHAPTER SUMMARY

3.5

This chapter has looked at the ways we try and explain who and what we are and has considered the problems with these explanations. On a basic level, if we are made up of exactly the same substance as a blancmange, then what is it that gives us our ability (maybe curse?) to be able to think about ourselves and act in the world? Does a blancmange know that it is a blancmange? Of course not, but you know that you are a person and different from all other people. The gap between our knowledge of the material world (the stuff that makes up blancmanges) and our experience of the mental world (thinking about ourselves and worrying if people think we are stupid) is what psychology has to try and bridge. Easier said than done!

DISCUSSION QUESTIONS

If a psychological theory is said to be reductionist, does that necessarily make it a bad theory?

Consider the case of love. Is the love you have for your family or partner, or even for psychology, nothing but the workings of a vast assembly of neurons?

Instead of *explaining* important aspects of who you are – your beliefs, hopes, aspirations – does reductionism *explain them away*, by describing them as nothing but the intricate processes of lumpy grey matter?

If you yourself and your hopes are not just the workings of lumpy grey matter, then what else are these phenomena? How should psychologists set about studying these phenomena?

SUGGESTIONS FOR FURTHER READING

Valentine, E. (1992). *Conceptual issues in psychology* (2nd edn). London: Routledge. This book expands on the topics and issues raised in this chapter in an accessible way.

Bem, S., & de Jong, H.B. (2006). *Theoretical issues in psychology: an introduction* (2nd edn). London: Sage. This book tackles some of the issues and topics raised in this chapter in much more depth. It provides a good opportunity to develop your understanding further.

Dietrich, A. (2007). *Introduction to consciousness: neuroscience, cognitive science, and philosophy*. London: Palgrave Macmillan. This book enables you to engage with the topic of consciousness in a much more detailed and in-depth way. It provides an accessible way into what is often referred to as the 'hard problem' of the philosophy of mind.

HOW WE THINK AND MAKE SENSE OF THE WORLD

Cognitive Psychology

Our senses are bombarded with information and we do something very special with it: we use it to create our perceptions of the world. There is a big gap between what we sense and what we perceive and that gap is what cognitive psychology is most interested in. We study how we see the world, how we store and recall information, how we communicate and how we think.

It is commonly reported that the first psychology laboratory was set up by Wilhelm Wundt (1832–1920) in Leipzig, Germany in 1879. Wundt's view was that psychology is the study of immediate experience – which does not include any issues of culture or social interaction. About half the work in the laboratory dealt with the topics of sensory processes and perception, though they also looked at reaction time, learning, attention and emotion. During the first half of the twentieth century, cognitive psychology was not as prominent as it is today, but we still draw on work from psychologists in that time, for example, Jean Piaget and Frederic Bartlett.

THE COGNITIVE REVOLUTION

Cognitive psychology became prominent in psychology in the middle of the twentieth century. George Miller hosted a seminar in the USA in 1956 where Newell and Simon presented a paper on computer logic, Noam Chomsky presented a paper on language, and Miller presented his famous paper on 'The magical number seven, plus or minus two'. Each of these presentations defined their field and modern cognitive psychology was born.

The models of cognitive psychology reflect the technology of the time. So the early models of human information processing (for example Broadbent, 1958) were based on the way that a telephone exchange works. As technology has developed, the models of cognitive psychology have developed with it. The models are now based on computer processes. This brings up a question about whether cognitive psychology is studying the cognitive processes of people or the cognitive processes of computers. It also brings up a much deeper question about what it means to be human and be alive. Can a computer think? Can it be aware of itself? Can it have a theory of mind? These are questions that the material discussed in this section of the book and also in Section A will enable you to think about.

Artificial intelligence (AI) is one of the key strands of modern cognitive psychology. This is the science of making intelligent machines, especially intelligent computer programs. The origins of AI can be seen in the work of British scientist Alan Turing in the 1950s on intelligent machines. Turing believed that eventually computers will be programmed to acquire abilities that rival human intelligence. He created an 'imitation game', in which a human being and a computer can be questioned under conditions where the questioner would not know which was which. This is possible if the communication is entirely by written messages. Turing argued that if the questioner cannot distinguish them, then we should see the computer as being intelligent. Turing's 'imitation game' is now usually called 'the Turing test'. If you want to see an example of a computer that appears to be intelligent, then type 'eliza' into Google and check out the therapy she offers.

Science fiction films often have robot characters that appear human and make us think about what is the difference between people and machines
© Sav Scatola/Illustration Works/Corbis

KEY ISSUES

One of the key issues for cognitive psychologists concerns the mechanical models it uses. On the plus side these models have told us a lot more about how the brain processes information and also the limitations of that processing. On the down side, the focus on thought has sometimes neglected the emotional side of our life. It has also concentrated on logical thinking (the way a computer works) rather than intuitive thinking (the way people often work).

THIS SECTION

In this section we have three chapters looking at various aspects of cognition. Chapter 4 looks at memory: are there different types of memory; how does memory work; and how can we apply such knowledge in practice, for example in exam revision? Chapter 5 looks at how information from the outside world gets to our brains (via our senses), how we attend to that information and how we interpret it. Chapter 6 looks at how we solve problems and to what extent we think logically when drawing conclusions about events.

4 MEMORY

Lead authors **Thom Baguley** and **Andrew Edmonds**

INTRODUCTION

4.1

We tend to think about our memory only when it lets us down (when we fail to remember something) or when it surprises us by giving us an obscure answer to a quiz question, but our memories are central to what makes us human. Without memories we wouldn't know where we are, what we are or even who we are. This is the wonder of memory, and psychologists have studied it for over 150 years. This chapter looks at some of that research.

One obvious characteristic of humans, both individually and collectively, is that they collect information. This information allows us to become skilled, for example, in essential areas such as sailing, farming and tool use. When we use our memory and expertise in particular circumstances we find new learning opportunities *in those circumstances*: the more you know, the more you learn about what you know. This crudely explains why individuals develop highly specialised skills and why we hear of extraordinary individuals with great knowledge in areas as diverse as chess, European train timetables or 1980s pop trivia. Coupled with language skills, and another basic characteristic – that humans live in communities as social animals – this accumulation of knowledge has been transmitted across society and generations to sum to what we might call civilisation.

What follows from this is a vastness of human knowledge. Most of us get to learn and need to remember a great deal of information to get by. Memory is key to everyday behaviour and experience and we are only just starting to find out how it works.

? FRAMING QUESTIONS

Why do people forget?

If memory is so central to human functioning and survival, why is so much information apparently discarded?

Why is recent information better remembered than information from the distant past?

Why does wanting or needing to remember something have so little impact on subsequent memory?

THEORETICAL FOUNDATIONS

4.2

A first step is to understand some of the core principles of memory that psychological research has revealed, or perhaps more accurately, begun to reveal. In this section we set out some of the theoretical foundations of research on human memory. The section will begin, however, with an overview of the 'anatomy' of a memory experiment.

Like much of psychology, memory research has a lot of technical terms ('jargon') that, although useful for experts, can be an obstacle for newcomers. Understanding the technical terms may also help you see how some theoretical research relates very directly to applied research.

4.2.1 THE ANATOMY OF A MEMORY EXPERIMENT

Let's begin with the 'bare bones' of an experiment on human memory. All memory experiments start with a simple distinction between **presentation** and **test**:

$$\text{presentation} \rightarrow \text{test}$$

At *presentation* the experimenter will expose participants to the to-be-remembered material (e.g. a list of words, a set of faces or odours). At *test* the experimenter will attempt to measure participants' memory for the material that was presented.

From this simple beginning there are many ways to manipulate the structure of the experiment. A good researcher will not pick these manipulations at random, but will usually be guided by their knowledge of memory theory in general, and often by a particular theory. This usually leads to one or more hypotheses about what will happen. We can get a richer appreciation of how this is done by considering a very basic general theory of memory. Such a simple view might break down memory processing into three stages: **encoding, storage** and **retrieval**. In this account, encoding occurs at presentation, retrieval occurs at test and storage occurs between presentation and test.

> **Encoding**   The stage of memory involving interpreting and transforming incoming information in order to 'lay down' memories.
>
> **Storage**   The stage of memory between encoding and retrieval.
>
> **Retrieval**   The stage of memory where information is brought back into mind to be used or reported.

Encoding

It follows that a researcher can learn about encoding by manipulating the conditions under which presentation occurs. They can manipulate the quantity, duration, order or timing of presentations to influence encoding (not to mention manipulating the to-be-remembered material itself). A very common manipulation is whether or not to tell participants that they will be tested. If participants are not told they are to be tested this is referred to as **incidental** learning or memory. If participants are told they are going to be tested it is an **intentional** learning or memory experiment. Often, incidental memory is markedly worse than intentional memory, but this is not always the case, and this is an interesting puzzle for memory research. Hyde and Jenkins (1969) found that asking participants to rate the pleasantness of words produced levels of incidental memory that were as good as or better than intentional learning of words. This is a striking example of the phenomenon that merely having the intention or desire to remember something won't necessarily result in good memory (Anderson & Schooler, 2000).

Storage

Manipulating how encoded material might be stored is less straightforward. These manipulations tend to be indirect. It is possible to manipulate the duration of storage by increasing the **retention interval** (the gap between presentation and test). Researchers can investigate what factors might be important for storage (and hence subsequent forgetting) by manipulating the activities that take place prior to testing (e.g. sleeping versus staying awake: Jenkins & Dallenbach, 1924).

Retrieval

Retrieval processes can be investigated by manipulating the way memory is tested. One of the most important decisions to consider in testing memory is how to measure it; a key distinction is between **recognition** and **recall**.

Recognition

Involves re-presenting the original material and asking participants to determine if it occurred in the experiment. Although recognition appears to be a very simple procedure, it is surprisingly complex. For example, in an **old–new recognition** test only one item is presented at a time and a 'new' (unrecognised) or an 'old' (recognised) response is required. In a **two-alternative forced-choice** recognition test the 'new' and 'old' items are presented together and the recognised item is selected. Researchers often manipulate other factors such as the proportion of 'new' and 'old' items or their similarity to those originally presented.

Recall

Involves prompting participants to remember material that was originally presented. Here the main options are **free recall**, where the prompt is general and retrieval undirected (e.g. 'remember as many words as you can from the list'), and **cued recall**, where specific prompts or cues are used to direct or constrain recall (e.g. 'try to recall the first word on the list'). A good example of cued recall is paired-associate learning (PAL). In PAL participants are presented with **word pairs** such as 'Dentist–Smug'. At test they are given one half of the word pair (e.g. 'Smug') as a cue to retrieve the other. All sorts of things can act as recall cues: indeed, applied memory research often looks to reproduce the kinds of memory cues that occur in everyday life (e.g. someone's face acts as a cue to retrieve their name).

Most memory research uses what are known as **explicit memory tests** where the participant is told that they are being tested. However, it is also possible to have an **implicit memory test**. An implicit test involves performing an activity apparently unrelated to memory at test (e.g. asking people to complete the word stem 'BA___' with the first word that comes to mind). Participants' responses are then examined to determine if material presented earlier has influenced the implicit memory task (e.g. a participant who encoded BATTLE might respond with that word more often than a control participant exposed to the word CATTLE). It is tempting to conclude from these studies that implicit memory tests tap into unconscious memory processes whilst explicit memory tests tap into conscious processing, but the issue of whether there is a separate, unconscious 'implicit' memory system is controversial.

What if only part of the stimulus was encoded? Such a fragment might make it more likely that a word stem was completed with the original item, yet might not be sufficient to produce explicit recall (Whittlesea & Dorken, 1993). Furthermore, it seems unlikely that any measure of memory is purely explicit or implicit (e.g. participants are probably aware that some of their responses on the word stem completion task were also on the earlier word list). The implicit–explicit dichotomy is one of many proposed distinctions in memory.

4.2.2 SHORT-TERM AND LONG-TERM MEMORY

> **EXERCISE   Memory for films, part 1**
>
> Take a blank sheet of paper and a pen. Give yourself three minutes. Think about films you have seen at the cinema and write down the names of as many of the films as you can.
>   We will return to this exercise later in order to reflect on it.

One of the best known of such distinctions is between **short-term memory** and **long-term memory**. These are terms that we use in everyday speech and they seem to fit with our experience. Some things can be remembered from years ago but at the same time you will be unable to recall some of the things you wanted when you set off to the Co-op just five minutes ago. Researchers tend to use short-term or immediate memory to describe experiments where tests closely follow presentation, and long-term memory where there is a delay between presentation and test (Neath & Suprenant, 2003).

It turns out that there are important differences in short-term and long-term memory experiments. For instance, Postman and Phillips (1965) looked at free recall for 10-, 20- or 30-word lists with either no delay between presentation and test or a short delay of 15 or 30 seconds. They looked at what happens as the serial position (order of presentation) of an item changes. The results for the 20-word list are shown in Figure 4.1 in the form of a **serial position curve**. With immediate testing, recall shows a characteristic bow-shaped serial position effect, with good recall for both the first few items – the **primacy effect** – and the last few items – the **recency effect**. Recall for the middle serial positions is poor. The primacy effect is unaffected by delay. In contrast, the recency effect is dramatically reduced by the 15 second delay, and after 30 seconds disappears altogether. These and other findings led to an intuitively appealing explanation: that of separate short-term and long-term memory stores.

According to this view, participants rehearse (e.g. by repeating them silently or out loud) the items in the order they are presented. If we assume, as most psychologists do, that **primary memory** has a limited capacity, then the first few items will rapidly exceed this capacity. As more items are presented, participants abandon rehearsal of the early items and switch to rehearsing middle and later items. On balance, however, early items benefit from more rehearsal than later items. Assuming that rehearsal increases the chance of an item entering a **long-term store** (LTS) then this accounts for the primacy effect. A separate **short-term store**

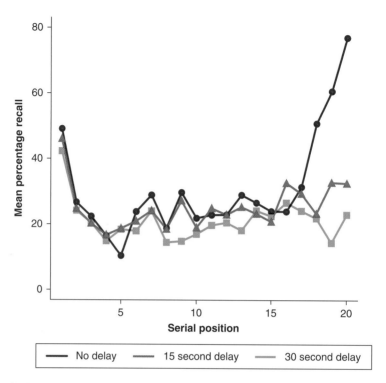

FIGURE 4.1 Serial position curves plotting percentage recall against order of presentation for 20-word lists with no delay, 15 second filled delay or 30 second filled delay (adapted from Postman & Phillips, 1965). For the delay conditions the retention interval is filled with a counting task to prevent rehearsal

(STS) can account for the recency effect: immediate testing allows a participant to output the contents of the STS first. However, even a short delay involving a cognitively demanding activity (e.g. Postman and Phillips's counting task) seems to eliminate these items from the STS and disrupts the recency effect. Consistent with this, Waugh (1970) showed that recalls from later serial positions (recent items) are faster than those for earlier ones.

The concept of separate long-term and short-term stores was incorporated into a number of models of short-term memory in the 1960s and 1970s (e.g. Atkinson & Shiffrin, 1968; Waugh & Norman, 1965). The best known of these, Atkinson and Shiffrin (1968), has become known as the **modal model** of short-term memory. This model is set out in Figure 4.2. In this simple version of the model (which does not include sensory memory, added in later versions) items enter the short-term store as a consequence of attention to environmental input. The STS has a limited capacity and items in the store **decay** rapidly or are displaced by new input unless maintained by rehearsal. The longer an item spends in the STS, the more likely it is to enter the LTS, which has unlimited capacity. Rundus (1971) tested the model by asking participants to rehearse out loud. The number of times an item was

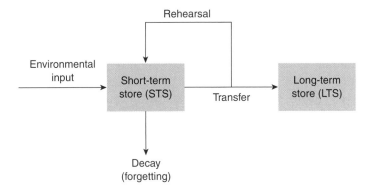

FIGURE 4.2   The Atkinson and Shiffrin (1968) modal model of short-term memory

rehearsed predicted recall, except for the most recent items: just as predicted by the modal model.

Despite its intuitive appeal, the modal model rapidly became untenable as an account of short-term memory. Studies of brain damaged patients (originally taken as support for separate STS and LTS) suggested that impaired short-term memory did not disrupt long-term memory (Shallice & Warrington, 1970) as it should do if items only enter the LTS via the STS. Studies by Bjork and Whitten (1974) and Tzeng (1973) showed that engaging in an activity such as arithmetic for a short period after presenting a list of word pairs eliminated the recency effect, but not if the activity took place after each word pair. This makes no sense in the modal model because in neither case should participants be able to access recent words from the STS. More generally, **long-term recency** effects have also been found. For example, Baddeley and Hitch (1977) found that rugby players showed recency effects for the last few matches they had played.

EXERCISE   Memory for films, part 2

Now look back at the list of films you made in the previous exercise.

Are the last three or four films you have seen on the list? Is there any evidence of a long-term recency effect?

Are more recent films recalled earlier or later in the list?

Baddeley and Hitch (1974) responded to the shortcomings of the modal model by proposing a multiple component **working memory model**. This model dominated short-term memory research in the 1980s and 1990s (but a full discussion is beyond our scope here). In many ways the working memory model is an extension of earlier two-store memory models. But is it necessary to propose distinct STS and LTS at all?

An increasingly popular view is that there may only be a single memory system. Is it possible to explain long-term recency and short-term recency effects with the same mechanism? The most likely candidate is *temporal distinctiveness* (Bjork & Whitten, 1974; Glenberg & Swanson, 1986). This suggests that what makes memories easier to retrieve is their recency in time. According to this explanation, remembering involves discriminating between various competing memory traces. This discrimination is a perceptual process and, just as it is easier to detect a large item among a set of small objects, so it should be easier to detect a recent memory among a set of old memories. Research on perception suggests that such discrimination depends on the ratio of the time interval between the encoding and retrieval of items (not on the absolute difference in times). Retrieving something presented 5 seconds ago is much easier than something presented 10 seconds ago (a ratio of 1:2). But there will not be much difference in the ease of retrieving items presented 105 and 110 seconds ago (a ratio of 21:22).

4.2.3 FROM ENCODING PROCESSES TO RETRIEVAL PROCESSES

Although a lot of research on memory has focused on the distinction between memory structures such as the STS and the LTS, this can distract from a more fundamental issue: how does memory operate? The beginnings of the answer to this question lie in considering the processing that occurs when items are encoded and retrieved.

The way we process material at encoding influences whether it will be retrieved. Craik and Lockhart (1972) proposed that how well we remember material was determined by the extent to which we extract meaning from it (which they term 'depth'). Their **levels of processing theory** argues that shallow, **perceptual processing** leads to worse retention than deep, **semantic processing**. Many studies have found that perceptual tasks (e.g. counting the number of times the letter 'E' appears in a word) result in poorer memory than tasks that involve the semantics of a word (e.g. deciding whether it completes a sentence).

> **Semantic processing** Processing of material that extracts meaning from it.
> **Perceptual processing** Processing of material to extract superficial sensory characteristics such as shape or colour.

Levels of processing theory sparked enormous interest in the way processing influences later memory performance. There is evidence that the quantity of processing (Johnson-Laird et al., 1978), the distinctiveness of processing (Eysenck, 1979) and the extent to which processing elaborates or links items (Anderson & Reder, 1979; Marschark & Surian, 1989) all influence memory performance.

Levels of processing theory has had mixed fortunes. Many researchers (e.g. Baddeley, 1978) were unhappy with the focus on depth rather than other aspects of processing. A critical problem is the difficulty of determining depth independently of later memory performance: it is tempting to explain poor performance as resulting from 'shallow' processing because it is difficult to determine precisely how much meaning participants have extracted during encoding. Last, but not least, it neglects the role of retrieval processes.

KEY STUDY   Morris, C.D., Bransford, J.D., & Franks, J.J. (1977). Levels of processing versus transfer appropriate processing. *Journal of Verbal Learning and Verbal Behaviour*, 16, 519–533.

This important study contrasted perceptual and semantic processing. For the former a participant might hear the sentence 'BLANK rhymes with legal' followed by the word 'Eagle' or 'Train'. For the latter they might hear 'The BLANK had a silver engine' followed by the word 'Eagle' or 'Train'. In each case they had to make a 'Yes' or 'No' decision about whether the target word filled the BLANK.

   The big difference between this and levels of processing experiments is the inclusion of a rhyme recognition test. In this test participants were presented with a list of words such as 'Regal' or 'Plane' and were asked to decide whether the word rhymed with a word that had previously been presented.

   Using a standard recognition test, a depth of processing effect was observed: semantic processing produced better memory than perceptual processing. This effect was reversed with the rhyme recognition test: words learned with the perceptual (rhyming) task were recognised better than words learned with the semantic (sentence completion) task.

   Morris et al. (1977) interpreted this in terms of **transfer-appropriate processing**. What matters is the overlap in processing between encoding and retrieval, rather than just encoding processes. Processing the sound of the word when it is encoded (which must happen if you have to decide whether it rhymes with another word) makes it possible to associate the sound of the word with aspects of the *context* at encoding. If you are subsequently prompted with those sounds at test, this cues the retrieval of the associated context.

The importance of the relationship between encoding and retrieval is captured by what Tulving and Thomson termed the **encoding specificity principle**:

> Specific encoding operations ... determine what is stored, and what is stored determines what retrieval cues are effective. (1973: 369)

Our memories can be triggered by all manner of things. Sometimes we remember a childhood event when we hear a song that was playing at the time. This song is an example of a **retrieval cue**, but it could just as easily be something that you see, smell or touch. Retrieval cues

> **Retrieval cue**   Any stimulus that helps us recall information, for example a picture, an odour or a sound.

are effective because they are part of what was encoded. The principle is important because it helps remind us of the interrelationship of encoding and retrieval, but it is not very useful as a theoretical statement. After all, in its most general form it does not predict what cues are effective: it only implies that, once found, an effective cue must overlap with what was encoded. Nevertheless, encoding specificity is useful in understanding a number of well-known and sometimes puzzling effects in the literature. For instance, a number of studies have shown that reinstating at test the original context in which something was presented improves memory. One striking demonstration of this **context-dependent memory** is Godden and Baddeley (1975), who showed that if a word list is learned under water, it is better remembered if testing also takes place under water (rather than on dry land). Of course you might ask what possible use there is to learning a list of words under water, and the answer is something to do with counting fish (and you probably do not want to know any more than that).

4.2.4 FORGETTING

Studying forgetting turns out to be especially tricky. We can measure what is remembered in different ways (e.g. recognition or recall) and we can influence what is retrieved by the effectiveness of the cues used at test. Even so, there are two particular issues in forgetting that have been widely debated in the literature and which are worth exploring here. These are the form of the **forgetting function,** and the question of what causes us to forget.

Forgetting function   The mathematical equation that determines the precise rate of forgetting as a function of time.

It is important in research on forgetting to be sure that the material was ever in memory at all. Otherwise it cannot be forgotten. This is usually achieved by ensuring items are learned to criterion (e.g. repeating items until accuracy on an immediate test is 100 per cent).

We also need to consider that just because material has not been retrieved does not mean that it has been permanently lost. As Tulving and Pearlstone note: 'it is useful to draw a distinction between what information or what traces are *available* in [memory] and what are *accessible*' (1966: 381–382). Any time memory is tested, the relationship between retrieval cues and what was encoded means that only a subset of what is potentially accessible is available. One explanation of the loss of information between presentation and test is therefore *cue-dependent forgetting*. Cue-dependent forgetting is undoubtedly a major source of everyday forgetting. However, it is incomplete as an explanation of forgetting because it fails to address the fundamental observation that memory performance declines over time.

An explanation of forgetting therefore requires us to consider the deceptively simple problem of why memory gets worse over time. The two main rival explanations of time-based forgetting are **decay** and **interference**. Decay can be considered the 'deterioration of the organic correlate' of learning (McGeoch, 1942: 455). That physical damage of brain tissue (e.g. via brain injury) can result in memory loss is indisputable. Thus, if we suppose that brain tissue suffers 'wear and tear' over time then decay is a plausible explanation of forgetting. However McGeoch (1932; 1942) is widely regarded

Decay   An explanation of forgetting that suggests memories fade or deteriorate over time.

Interference   An explanation of forgetting in which other learning (old or new) can disrupt or prevent retrieval.

as having killed off decay as a popular explanation of forgetting in long-term memory, his crucial argument being:

> *that* forgetting is found to vary with the character of the events which fill a constant interval and with the conditions obtaining at the time of measuring retention. (1942: 455)

McGeoch's account is supported by Jenkins and Dallenbach (1924) in which two participants learned word lists and were tested at delays of 1, 2, 4 or 8 hours. Each participant was tested twice: once after sleeping, and once after staying awake during the retention interval. At test they recalled fewer words if they had stayed awake than if they had slept. An obvious explanation of this, favoured by McGeoch, is that during sleep the participants were not exposed to material that might interfere with what they had learned.

McGeoch's explanation appeals to what is now termed *retroactive inhibition* (RI). In RI, learning new material during the retention interval interferes with older learning (e.g. learning dog–bone would interfere with an earlier dog–cat association). Experiments have also shown that *proactive inhibition* (PI) can occur (e.g. a prior dog–cat association makes it harder to learn dog–bone). Much of the subsequent research on interference has focused on PI. PI is relatively easy to demonstrate in laboratory experiments (e.g. Underwood, 1957), whereas psychologists have struggled to show consistent evidence of RI in the laboratory.

Wixted (2004a) has argued that research in experimental psychology (wrongly) focused on PI as a source of forgetting and largely rejected the leading account of RI: **consolidation theory**. This was the idea that memories are fragile and easily disrupted immediately after encoding and require time to consolidate before storage in long-term memory. Wixted also notes that most laboratory experiments that suggest PI causes forgetting used massed learning: several lists presented in a short space of time. Indeed, Underwood (1957) excluded studies without massed learning from his analysis. In contrast, everyday memory usually involves learning information spread out over long periods of time. This point is vital because PI pretty much disappears if learning is spread over a longer period (Underwood & Ekstrand, 1967).

A more plausible account of the results of laboratory and everyday experiments on forgetting, which was anticipated by Keppel (1968), is that forgetting is caused by non-specific RI. In other words, prior learning may interfere with new learning only when items are similar (PI), but new learning interferes with all old learning (RI). Wixted (2004a; 2005) argues that formation of new memories interferes with old memories – possibly because of some processing bottleneck (e.g. because consolidation and encoding share processing resources). If so, RI did not occur in studies using massed learning because participants are learning new information at a high rate throughout the study (and therefore RI is more or less constant). Wixted's account of forgetting is rather elegant and has also been proposed as an explanation of the mathematical form of the forgetting curve: in particular, a phenomenon known as *Jost's law of forgetting* (Wixted, 2004b).

According to Jost's law, if two memories are equally likely to be recalled at some point in time, the younger of the two memories will be forgotten more quickly (see Figure 4.3). Wixted suggests that this is because of consolidation: the older memory is less vulnerable to RI than the younger memory.

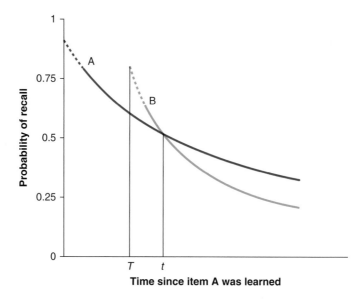

FIGURE 4.3 An illustration of Jost's (1897) law of forgetting. Item A receives more learning than item B, but is learned earlier than time *T*. According to Jost's law the probability of recalling the more recent item (B) decreases faster than the older item (A) and therefore the two forgetting curves meet at time *t*

This work has coincided with (and probably sparked) a renewed interest in theoretical analysis of the causes of forgetting. Lansdale and Baguley (2008) proposed an alternative explanation of forgetting that can also account for the mathematical form of the forgetting function (and hence also Jost's law). Their explanation, known as the *population dilution model*, starts with the simple idea that remembering can be considered as a process of sampling a memory trace from a population of traces (rather like drawing cards at random from a deck). This population contains correct traces (ones that contain relevant details of whatever a person is trying to remember), null traces (memories that are not relevant and produce no recall) and errors. The probability of a correct response in a memory experiment therefore depends on the proportion of correct traces in the total population (e.g. if there are 100 traces, and 82 of them are correct, the probability of a correct response is 82 per cent). In this model it is possible to explain forgetting simply by assuming that the overall population of traces is diluted (by null traces) at a steady rate over time.

Lansdale and Baguley suggest that this dilution occurs because the original event becomes less temporally distinctive. This is potentially intriguing because it links long-term forgetting to mechanisms introduced to explain recency effects in both long- and short-term memory (Bjork & Whitten, 1974; Glenberg & Swanson, 1986). Brown et al. (2007) have also argued that forgetting in both the long and the short term may be accounted for by common mechanisms such as temporal distinctiveness, though they doubt that a single explanation for the form of the forgetting function exists.

4.2.5 MEMORY AS A RECONSTRUCTIVE PROCESS

Most experimental research on memory has focused on memory for 'impoverished' material such as word lists. Everyday memory typically involves richer, structured material such as conversations, pictures or events. Research with such 'real-world' material suggests that memory works in a constructive or reconstructive way. The best known example is Bartlett's (1932) 'War of the ghosts' study. Bartlett gave participants stories including the American Indian folk tale 'War of the ghosts' and asked them to reproduce them after a 15 minute retention interval and again one or more times at retention intervals of weeks, months or years (six years being the longest interval).

Bartlett found that the reproductions often contained rationalisations of parts of the story participants did not understand, as well as intrusions or distortions (adding or changing details of the stories). Participants tended to reconstruct a story that made sense to them, filling in missing elements that made sense to them even if it meant including details that were not in the original. A particular emphasis of Bartlett's work is that social and cultural factors will influence recall: the rationalisations and errors in memory are not random, and inaccurate recall is rather more common than some might suppose. Bartlett's findings are usually explained in terms of **schema** theory – the key ideas of which are found in Bartlett's (1932) own theory of remembering.

> **Schema**   A mental representation of some aspect of the world built from experience and into which new experiences are fitted.

There are a number of striking demonstrations of schematic effects in the memory literature. Anderson and Pichert (1978) have shown that schemata can operate both at encoding and at retrieval. They asked participants to read a description of a house whilst adopting one of two perspectives: that of a home buyer or that of a burglar. At test they asked people either to adopt the same perspective or to switch perspective. Participants tended to remember details appropriate to the perspective they adopted (e.g. valuable items for the burglar), and switching perspective after an initial attempt to recall allowed people to retrieve information that had not previously been reported.

Although schema theory was a popular account of how memory is influenced by prior knowledge, it has somewhat fallen out of favour. There are probably two main reasons for this. While many of the phenomena predicted by schema theory can be demonstrated in laboratory and real-world settings, the concept of a schema is not necessary to account for them (Hintzman, 1986).

A second reason is that some of the phenomena reported by Bartlett, notably rationalisation and distortions, do not occur as extensively as in his original studies (e.g. Gauld & Stephenson, 1967). Only relatively recently have Bartlett's repeated reproduction studies been fully replicated (Bergman & Roediger, 1999). Bergman and Roediger suggest that the spacing of tests (including the 15 minute delay for the first tests) and the subsequent retests are probably important contributors to Bartlett's original findings and conclusions. An immediate test may protect against some of the distortions and rationalisations. This is relatively easy to understand in terms of a multiple trace memory model. Any errors from earlier tests are part of the population of traces to be recalled in later tests, while omissions create gaps that encourage or require rationalisations from the participants. Successful correct recall increases the population of correct traces and makes subsequent retests more accurate, as well as leaving fewer opportunities for rationalisation or distortion. Indeed it is well known that successful retrieval improves later accuracy and reduces forgetting (e.g. Ballard, 1913; Roediger & Karpicke, 2006).

MEMORY IN ACTION

4.3

This section considers how some of the theoretical work discussed above has practical consequences. Our particular focus will be on two domains, eyewitness memory and exam revision, that are likely to be relevant for many readers.

4.3.1 EYEWITNESS MEMORY

Eyewitness testimony is an interesting testing ground for many of the core ideas in memory research. In many real-world cases of eyewitness memory, people don't know that they will later be interrogated about an event. As with laboratory studies of incidental memory, the nature of the event and how people respond to it will have important consequences for later retrieval. Work by Memon et al. (2003) reported that young participants were 29 per cent accurate at picking faces from a line-up after a 12 second exposure compared to 95 per cent accurate after a 45 second exposure. It might be tempting to conclude that this just confirms common sense, but bear in mind that an applied researcher might be interested in the precise relationship between exposure times and accuracy. In addition, Memon et al. (2003) looked at factors such as the age of the participant and how exposure influences participants' confidence in their responses.

Research by Loftus and colleagues has focused on reconstructive processes in memory. A famous study by Loftus et al. (1978) showed participants a series of slides depicting a red Datsun car making a turn at an intersection and hitting a pedestrian. Half the participants were shown slides depicting a 'stop' sign at the intersection and half were shown a 'yield' sign. Participants were later asked a series of questions, one of which took the form: 'Did another car pass the red Datsun while it was stopped at the _____ sign?' They were then asked which of two photographs corresponded to what they had originally seen. For half the participants the blank was filled with a word consistent with what they'd seen, and for half it was inconsistent (e.g. 'stop' if they had seen a slide with a 'yield' sign). For the consistent group the accuracy was around 75 per cent, while for the inconsistent group it was only about 40 per cent.

Many subsequent experiments have confirmed that this kind of post-event information can distort people's eyewitness testimony (e.g. Wright & Loftus, 2008). Exactly what is going on in these studies is still a matter of some debate (and there may be more than one factor contributing to this *misinformation effect*). One relatively simple explanation is again in terms of a multiple trace model of memory. Traces for both the original event and the post-event information may compete for recall. Factors such as recency, or the similarity of the testing context with the context in which the post-event information was presented, may explain why the post-event information rather than the correct information is retrieved.

Loftus has gone beyond these simple tasks and demonstrated the much more perplexing phenomena of creating false memories for people. At an amusing level she has been able to create a memory of meeting Bugs Bunny at Disneyland (in fact, he doesn't live there because he is a Warner Brothers character), and at a more serious level to implant a memory of being lost in a shopping mall as a child (Loftus & Pickrell, 1995). Most controversially she has challenged the role of therapists using hypnosis and guided imagery to 'discover' memories of childhood abuse. It has subsequently been shown that some of these memories have been created during the therapy.

KEY RESEARCHER   Elizabeth Loftus (1944 – present day)

FIGURE 4.4   Elizabeth Loftus

Professor Elizabeth Loftus is a hugely influential figure in memory research. A 2002 list in the *Review of General Psychology* ranked Loftus 58th on the list of the 100 most eminent psychologists of the twentieth century (the highest-placed woman on the list). As well as making major theoretical contributions to the study of human memory, she is also widely recognised as a leading pioneer of applied memory research and eyewitness memory in particular.

Her major contributions have included research into false memories and the accuracy of memory in real-world settings. Her work on the misinformation effect (see text) has shown how people can 'remember' specific details about events (when in reality the detail did not occur), simply by being given misleading or suggestive information. Her work on the potential unreliability of eyewitness testimonies has also been hugely influential in the field, and she has acted as an expert witness in a number of high-profile criminal trials (Haggbloom et al., 2002).

So far we've considered examples of factors such as exposure duration that can influence eyewitness memory prior to retrieval. It is also possible to manipulate conditions at test to influence memory. Geiselman et al. (1986) did exactly this when they developed the *cognitive interview* to enhance the accuracy of eyewitness memory. This involves a number of different components, but one of the most important seems to be context reinstatement: witnesses are asked to imagine themselves back in the original context prior to recall (this draws on ideas such as transfer-appropriate processing discussed earlier). The effects of the cognitive interview can be quite striking, with several studies showing 40–50 per cent increases in the quantity of information recalled. Not only can memory research help us to understand how memory works in everyday life, but we can also apply our theoretical understanding to important real-world problems.

4.3.2 REVISING FOR AN EXAM

While, with any luck, most people will only very rarely be witnesses of a crime, we can apply an understanding of memory theory in at least one far more common situation: revising for an exam or a test. Much of what we have covered in this chapter can be used to design an effective revision strategy. While there are lots of factors to consider, there are also many constraints imposed by what someone is learning and how they will be tested. In a traditional examination the material to be learned, the environmental context at retrieval and the time of testing are likely to be fixed. On the other hand, the way material is presented, the environment in which learning takes place and the time course of presentation are usually easy to manipulate. Organising a study environment so it is similar to the testing environment (e.g. sitting at a desk in a quiet room) is probably a good starting point. If this isn't possible, imagining the context in which you learned (i.e. context reinstatement) when you to try to retrieve information may help. However, there are far simpler revision strategies that are known to have a very powerful effect on learning.

Ample research has shown that what people do with the material they are trying to learn has an enormous impact on what is remembered (e.g. Craik & Lockhart, 1972; Hyde & Jenkins, 1969). It also matters what you are trying to learn. If you are trying to understand the content of a text (as opposed to remembering the exact wording) it is a good idea to write a summary of it (Schmalhofer & Glavanov, 1986). Given that many (but not all) exams involve understanding the meaning of material, both depth of processing and transfer-appropriate processing would suggest that extracting meaning from the material to be learned is a good idea. In addition, it will be easier to retrieve material that is more distinctive or has more links to other material. One of the best ways to learn material is therefore to structure or organise it in some way. Mandler (1967) asked one group of participants to learn a set of words and one group simply to sort them into semantic categories (without instructions to learn them). The categorisation group learned as well as the intentional learning group.

> **Mnemonics**   Strategies for helping people to remember information, usually involving cues such as rhyme or imagery.

Organisation provides a structure that can be used to deliberately cue memory, to reconstruct the original material, as well as to make links that increase the opportunities for spontaneous cueing to occur. These principles can be recruited to construct **mnemonics** (e.g. the colours of the rainbow are often remembered as 'Richard Of York Gave Battle In Vain', representing the colours red, orange, yellow, green, blue, indigo and violet). Stories and rhymes (or even songs!) also make excellent recall structures.

Two further principles are particularly important in planning a revision strategy. The first is that spaced learning is very much more efficient and more durable than massed learning (this is sometimes termed the *distributed practice effect*). So, four hours of revision spread out over four days is more effective than if it is crammed into one afternoon. This may seem counter-intuitive. 'Cramming' just before a test can be effective – but such material is forgotten rapidly (Cepeda et al., 2006; Neath & Suprenant, 2003). Furthermore, if you have a lot to learn, the material encoded at the start of your cramming session may experience interference from the most recently learned material (Wixted, 2005). Spaced learning is a particularly good strategy for university students because the learned material is more resistant to forgetting; this is essential if what you learn early on is important for your later studies. Retrieving information from memory is itself an excellent way to learn material. Roediger and Karpicke (2006) have shown that this testing effect is not simply because tests offer opportunities for relearning, and other researchers (e.g. Lansdale & Baguley, 2008) have suggested that testing memory for an item has a bigger impact than re-presenting an item.

Although revising for an exam involves many other factors (e.g. **motivation**, anxiety, fatigue), a good understanding of memory can help someone design a revision strategy that will be both effective and relatively painless to implement.

CHAPTER SUMMARY

4.4

Early theorists divided memory into short- and long-term stores (Atkinson & Shiffrin, 1968) based on evidence of seemingly different properties. For example, short-term memory was theorised to be affected by recency and long-term memory by primacy effects. Later models refined this modal model to produce a working memory model (Baddeley & Hitch, 1974), although more recent theories favour a single memory system.

Although lots of research has focused on the distinction between memory structures such as STS and LTS, the more fundamental issue is how memory operates. Several factors at encoding have been proposed to influence whether material will be retrieved. The levels of processing model suggests that it is the depth of processing (in particular processing meaning) that influences how well material is remembered. The phenomenon of context-dependent memory demonstrates that the cues available at encoding aid retrieval; it is thought this is because they are stored along with the material being encoded.

What causes us to forget has been examined, and there is relatively little evidence that memory is discarded *per se*. Although decay may occur and memory loss may result from what McGeoch called 'deterioration of the organic correlate', we can explain most (possibly all) of forgetting in terms of the effects of interference or the matching of retrieval cues to what was originally encoded. If memories compete for recall – the essence of most interference theories – then learning new information inevitably carries a cost. Forgetting thus occurs because it is necessary to keep memory efficient (e.g. see Anderson & Schooler, 2000).

Memory is unreliable. It is a reconstructive process in which we interpret what has been experienced in light of our expectations, which in turn are based on existing mental representations (schemata) about the world. Memory has also been demonstrated to be influenced by later events that interfere with earlier memory traces. Psychological investigation of such misinformation effects has been influential in our understanding of the accuracy of memory and has made a significant contribution to real-world issues like eyewitness testimony and the phenomenon of false memory.

Anderson and Schooler suggest that it is puzzling, in evolutionary terms, why intention to learn has so little effect on what we remember. But this finding is less puzzling if we think of memory in terms of transfer-appropriate processing. People are probably only rarely aware that they'll need to know something in future (or what retrieval cues will be available when they try to remember it). A logical consequence of transfer-appropriate processing is that it is probably unwise to think of memory as separate from other aspects of cognition. The processing involved in interacting with and thinking about the world, from perception through to reasoning or problem solving, probably produces memory as a by-product (e.g. Crowder, 1993; Lansdale, 2005; Payne & Baguley, 2006). Of course, it is somewhat ironic to end a chapter on memory by noting that memory shouldn't just be considered in isolation from the rest of cognition – or indeed the rest of psychology.

DISCUSSION QUESTIONS: FORGETTING

Recent work on forgetting suggests that forgetting is largely (or possibly entirely) an issue of trace discrimination. Does this mean that once something is learned it is never truly lost from memory?

In this chapter we focused strongly on forgetting in long-term memory. What account of forgetting is most strongly supported for short-term memory? What does this tell us (if anything) about the difference between short-term and long-term memory?

SUGGESTIONS FOR FURTHER READING

Cohen, G., & Conway, M.A. (2008). *Memory in the real world* (3rd edn). Hove: Psychology. This text provides an excellent overview of research on everyday memory (both inside and outside the laboratory).

Kelley, M.R. (Ed.) (2009). *Applied memory*. Hauppauge, NY: Nova Science. This is an interesting edited volume showing how research grounded in theories of memory can be applied in a surprising range of domains.

Gluck, M.A., Mercado, E., & Myers, C.E. (2008). *Learning and memory: from brain to behavior*. Basingstoke: Palgrave Macmillan. This provides an overview of learning and memory from a neuroscience perspective, looking at findings in both animals and humans.

Neath, I., & Suprenant, A.M. (2003). *Human memory: an introduction to research, data, and theory* (2nd edn). Belmont, CA: Wadsworth. This gives an excellent review of the history of memory research with particular emphasis on major models and theories of memory.

5

AN INTRODUCTION TO SENSATION, PERCEPTION AND ATTENTION

Lead authors **Andrew K. Dunn** and **Paula Stacey**

INTRODUCTION

5.1 Perception is one of the wonders of being alive. We tend to take it for granted, but a little thought reveals just how remarkable it is. William James, in his *Principles of psychology* written in 1890, described the perceptual world of the newborn baby as 'one great blooming, buzzing confusion' (1890: 488). The wonder is how we manage to organise that blooming, buzzing confusion into the meaningful sounds and shapes that we experience every day when we wake. These perceptual experiences are at the very core of human experience, but how exactly do we use them to make sense of the world? How do we encode and represent what we see, hear, smell, taste or touch?

In this chapter we will first explain how we deal with incoming sensory information and then consider how our brain decodes this information in order to perceive the world around us. We will go on to examine a phenomenon known as attentional processing. What we 'pay attention' to determines, to a large extent, what aspects of the environment we perceive in the first place and which sensory inputs get further processing.

Finally, we will consider some of the problems that occur when our perceptual and attentional systems go wrong. But first we will begin by outlining what we mean by sensation, perception and attention, and provide some idea of the issues involved.

> **?**
>
> ### FRAMING QUESTIONS
>
> How do we encode and represent what we see and hear?
> How do we make sense of our perceptions? From the bottom up or from the top down?
> At what point in the process of attention is auditory information filtered?
> Is our attention to visual scenes object based or space based?

SENSATION, PERCEPTION AND ATTENTION

5.2 Psychologists often use everyday language, but in more precise ways. A good example is 'sensation'. For psychologists, **sensation** is the initial stimulation of our sensory systems (sight, hearing, touch, taste and smell); it is the sequence of physiological events that causes our nervous system to send electrical impulses to our brain. The stimulation of our senses is the first step on the road to our mental representation of the external world, and is in some respects the first step on the road to mental life.

Perception is the apparently holistic experience of the external world. That is, perception seems to provide us with experience of a reality that is integrated and complete when, for example, we look around us, watch television, talk or eat. Yet, intriguingly, perception does not produce an exact copy of the physical world: rather, perception involves a mental re-creation. It is not an *accurate* representation of our environment but an *adequate* one.

Perception is in effect a best guess, derived from an endless stream of external information (such as light and sound), and influenced by our arousal states (for example, whether we are alert, distracted or sleepy) and past experience (for example, we may interpret situations differently according to whether they are novel or familiar to us). Sensing and perceiving the world around us is a monumentally complex task that we do not fully understand, and yet somehow we do it, for the most part, effortlessly.

Attention plays a critical role in making sense of our sensations. The world is a complex place, and at any one time there are multiple sources of information that we could process. Since we do not have limitless cognitive resources, we limit what we process by focusing on what is important (*selective attention*), but this is only one aspect of attention. Attention is a multifaceted phenomenon that is difficult to define. Perhaps the best way to define it is to ask not what it consists of, but rather what it is *for* and what it *does*. Ultimately, attention directs, filters and controls how we process the vast amount of external information bombarding our senses and produce internal responses to it.

Sensing, perceiving and attending to the world around us are complex. The aim of this chapter is to introduce you to these interrelated processes in more detail. Here we will focus our discussion on the primary senses of vision and audition in particular. We begin with sensation.

5.3 THE SENSES

5.3.1 AUDITION (HEARING)

Although hearing is sometimes described as our second most important sense, it is clear that our ears provide us with an abundant source of information. Human communication systems rely heavily on the ability to hear, and adults who lose their hearing often suffer from social isolation. Hearing is by no means a minor sense.

5.3.2 THE EAR

The ears are specialised for detecting **sound waves**. Sounds differ along three key dimensions: amplitude, frequency and complexity. These dimensions correspond to people's perception of sound, which can be characterised according to loudness, pitch and timbre.

We can divide the auditory sensory apparatus (the ear) into three interdependent portions (Figure 5.1):

1   The **outer ear**: comprising the **pinna** (the bendy bit on the side of your head), the **auditory canal**, and the **tympanic membrane** (the ear drum).

2   The **middle ear**: comprising the **ossicles** – made up from three connected bones called the malleus (hammer), the incus (anvil) and the stapes (stirrup) – and the **Eustachian tube** (which helps regulate air pressure).

3   The **inner ear**: comprising the **cochlea**.

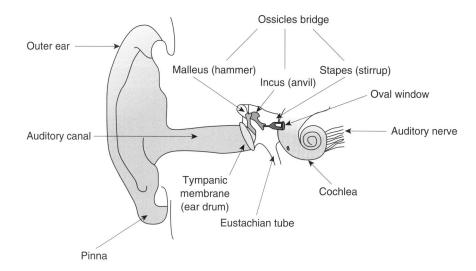

FIGURE 5.1   Peripheral auditory system   (Andrew Dunn)

The process of audition begins when sound waves enter the ear and travel down the audi-tory canal, causing the oval-shaped tympanic membrane to vibrate. The tympanic mem-brane (surface area ≈ 68 mm² in humans) is exquisitely sensitive and works with remarkable efficiency even when perforated. It is sensitive to vibrations that displace the membrane by only 1/100,000,000 of a centimetre – the width of a single hydrogen atom.

Tympanic vibrations are transmitted through the air-filled middle ear by the three tiny bones of the ossicles. These three bones (malleus, incus and stapes) are connected and so the vibration passes between them and to the inner ear where the stapes makes contact with the oval window – a covered opening in the bony wall of the fluid-filled cochlea that is about 1/20th the size of the tympanic membrane.

The cochlea (meaning snail) is a spiral-shaped structure about the size of a garden pea, and is divided into three chambers (**vestibular canal**, **tympanic canal** and **cochlear duct**) by two flexible membranes called the **basilar membrane** and **Reissner's membrane**. When the stapes makes contact with the oval window, vibrations are sent down the length of the basilar membrane, much like the cracking of a whip. The basilar membrane is **tonotopic**, i.e. the tones are ordered spatially adjacent to each other according to similarity in frequency, with high tones at one end through to low tones at the other. High-frequency sounds (a flute, for instance) cause large displacements at the narrow *basal* end (near the oval window); low-frequency sounds (such as a double bass) cause large displacements at the broad *apical* end (the tip). The frequency that gives maximum response at a particular place on the basilar membrane is known as the characteristic frequency of that place.

> **Tonotopic**   The spatial organisation of responses to different sound frequencies, with low-frequency sounds being represented at one loca-tion and high frequencies at another.

Just above the basilar membrane in the cochlear duct is the **organ of Corti**. It is responsible for converting the movement of the basilar membrane into electrical brain activity. It does this using hair cells sandwiched between two membranes, the basilar and the tectorial. Movement of the basilar membrane in relation to the **tectorial membrane** disturbs the **inner hair cells,** causing electrical signals to be sent towards the brain.

5.3.3 EAR TO BRAIN

Signals from the ear are sent to the auditory cortex of the brain via the auditory nerve along the **ascending auditory pathway.** There are between 10 and 20 auditory nerve fibres connected to each inner hair cell, which means the response of each nerve fibre is determined by a very small section of the basilar membrane (Moore, 2003). As the hair cells are selective for particular sound frequencies, the responses in the auditory nerve fibres are highly *frequency selective.*

Auditory signals reaching the brain are subject to increasingly complex processing in different brain regions. Following processing by the brain stem, mid brain and thalamus, signals reach the **primary auditory cortex,** situated in the temporal lobes. The primary auditory cortex is tonotopic: low-frequency sounds are positioned at the front (anterior) portion, and high-frequency sounds at the rear (posterior). Additionally, the cells of the primary auditory cortex are arranged in columns according to frequency. Together these two arrangements of tone and frequency, in conjunction with higher functions of the auditory cortex, play a very important role in signalling what a sound is so that we can identify it (Moore, 2003).

Generally the cells here are stimulated by information from both ears (binaural summation); however, some are stimulated by information from one ear and inhibited by information from the other ear and are arranged in excitatory or inhibitory rows. This inhibitory–excitatory mechanism appears to be important in signalling sound location (Hackney, 2002; Moore, 2003).

Beyond the primary auditory cortex is the highly interconnected auditory association area. The cells here respond to complex features of the incoming auditory signals including temporal information (differences in the time between sound arriving in one ear or the other, used to locate sounds), object identity and speech processing (Hackney, 2002; Moore, 2003). Projecting from here are two important cortical streams (see Clarke et al., 2002; Rauschecker & Tian, 2000): an auditory ventral stream that terminates in the orbitofrontal cortex, and an auditory dorsal stream that terminates in the dorsolateral prefrontal cortex (both in the frontal lobes). The ventral stream has been labelled the 'what' pathway of audition, since damage to this stream leads to deficits in identifying different sounds (*auditory agnosia*) but leaves sound location processing intact. The dorsal stream has been labelled the auditory 'where' pathway, since damage to this stream leads to deficits in locating sounds (*auditory neglect*) but leaves sound differentiation processing intact. A similar sort of **double dissociation** (complementary deficits) has been identified in vision (Goodale & Milner, 1992).

Double dissociation A term used in brain sciences to indicate that two cognitive processes are distinct, such that damage to a particular brain region affects one of those processes but not the other. For example, damage to Broca's area of the brain means a patient cannot speak but can still understand speech, whereas damage to Wernicke's area means a patient cannot understand speech but can still speak.

5.3.4 VISION (SEEING)

Vision dominates the human experience and we rely heavily upon it in our day-to-day inter-actions. It is thought that vision evolved to support motor action (Milner & Goodale, 1995) and, for typically developing humans, vision is the most immediate and commanding sense. It is commonly reported that over 80 per cent of all information about our external world comes through vision and about 50 per cent of the cortex is given over to visual processing alone – as compared with about 10 per cent for audition (Snowden et al., 2006).

5.3.5 THE EYE

The eye has an amazingly complex anatomical structure (Figure 5.2) specialised for detect-ing light energy. Vision begins when light enters the eye through the **cornea**, a transparent protective layer on the surface of the eye. It then passes through to the **pupil** and is focused on to the back of the eye (the **retina**) by the **lens**. The retina contains a number of different types of cell that convert light energy into electrochemical signals, so that they can be trans-mitted to and interpreted by the brain. Of prime concern here are the **photoreceptor cells**. Put simply, their chemical structure changes when they encounter light energy. Human pho-toreceptor cells come in two types, **rods** and **cones**, so called because of their shape.

There are approximately 125 million rods in the human eye, which are distributed throughout the retina except at the location of the **blind spot** where the **optic nerve** (which carries information to the brain) is formed. There are approximately 6 million cones, mostly concentrated in the centre of the retina in a tiny area (approximately 0.3 mm) called the

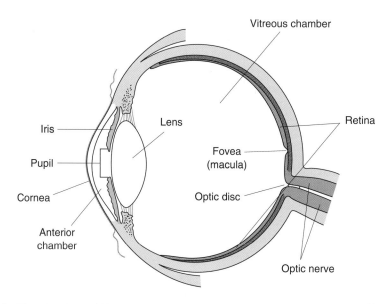

FIGURE 5.2 The structure of the eye   (Andrew Dunn)

fovea. This tiny area of retina (via its cones) is responsible for most of what we think of as vision: fine detailed information (this is referred to as having high visual acuity) and colour vision. Rods (and some cones) are distributed in the periphery of the retina (i.e. outside the fovea). Rods are extremely sensitive to movement, as they have good temporal resolution, but not to colour, and they do not carry fine detailed information (they have poor visual acuity).

EXERCISE   Find your blind spot

+   **O**

Close your left eye and stare at the cross. Now move your head towards the page and the circle will at some point disappear. This is the point at which it enters the blind spot on the retina. Keep moving closer and it will magically reappear.

Chemical changes in the rods and cones are detected by the **bipolar cells,** which respond by either depolarising or hyperpolarising (see Chapter 8 for a description of how neuronal cells conduct information) in response to changes in the rods and cones. Such changes in the bipolar cells trigger action potentials in the **retinal ganglion cells.** There are approximately 1 million retinal ganglion cells, some of which condense information from the rods (ratio 120:1), whilst others receive more or less uncondensed information from the cones (ratio between 1:1 and 6:1).

5.3.6 EYE TO BRAIN

The axons of the retinal ganglion cells form the optic nerve which carries information to the brain. There are two significant visual pathways to the brain: the *primary visual pathway* and the evolutionarily older *retino-tectal pathway.* In normal visual processing these pathways work in parallel.

The primary visual pathway (Figure 5.3) goes from the eye, via the optic nerve, across the optic chiasm (where there is a partial crossover of axons projecting from each eye) to the dorsal part of the **lateral geniculate nucleus** (LGN). The precise function of the LGN is poorly understood but it seems to play an important role in regulating information flow (Blake & Sekular, 2006). From here, information is projected along the optic radiations to the primary visual cortex in the occipital lobe.

The visual cortex is the primary site for processing visual information in the brain. It comprises five main areas, V1–V5. Each area has a specialised function and is characterised by different connections to other parts of the brain. Beyond here, information travels along two large cortical pathways: a ventral stream that terminates in the temporal lobes, and a

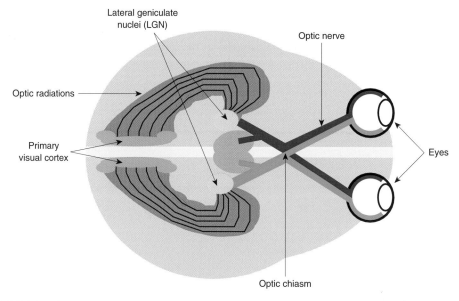

FIGURE 5.3   The primary visual pathway   (Andrew Dunn)

dorsal stream that terminates in the parietal lobes. Goodale and Milner (1992) argue that the ventral stream is specialised for processing visual information for perceptual purposes ('what' processing) whilst the dorsal stream processes visual information for visual motor purposes ('how' processing). However, it should be stressed that whilst these two streams perform functionally different tasks, in normal everyday processing they are complementary, working together such that one informs the other.

PERCEIVING THE WORLD

5.4 So far we have focused on how our perceptual systems encode and transform incoming sensory information. However, perception is more than this: it is about making sense of the incoming information. With perception we are able to turn a series of changes in air pressure into the glory of music and enjoy '*These Arms of Mine*' by Otis Reading (clearly the greatest song ever written). Also with perception we can turn a series of electrical changes in our eyes into an image that can bring tears to those eyes. So how might we do this?

5.4.1 TOP-DOWN VERSUS BOTTOM-UP PROCESSING

There is no single theory of perception. However, a key question for perceptual scientists concerns the extent to which **bottom-up** and **top-down** processes contribute to our perceptual experiences. People who place more importance on bottom-up processing (e.g. Gibson, 1950; 1966) argue that low-level sensory information is the most important determinant of what we perceive. In contrast, top-down theorists such as Gregory (1970; 1997) posit that higher-level cognitive processes are the important determinants of perception. The truth, as usual, is somewhere in between.

> **Bottom-up processing** A cognitive process that starts with simple (low-level) processes and builds up to the more complex higher levels. It doesn't depend on prior knowledge.
>
> **Top-down processing** A way of explaining a cognitive process in which higher-level processes, such as prior knowledge, influence the processing of lower-level input.

5.4.2 BOTTOM-UP APPROACHES

The best known theory emphasising the importance of bottom-up processing was proposed by J.J. Gibson (1966), and is known as a theory of *direct perception*. Gibson argued that what we perceive is directly determined by the information in the visual scene, and that no higher-level cognitive processing is necessary. He proposed that movement through the environment is crucial for generating information, and that *action* is key to perceiving the world around us. Accordingly, the distribution of light energy in the environment, the so-called *optic array*, provides a rich and immediate source of information. Movement in the environment causes the information in the optic array to change and we directly perceive this change through our eyes (what he terms the *ecological optics*). The perception of visual change is influenced by *invariants* – sources of information in the visual field which remain constant. A comparison of the changing (variant) versus unchanging (invariant) aspects of the visual scene provides direct information about the visual environment. For example, when you are driving down an open road the horizon remains constant. However, as you speed towards your destination, there is variance in the rate at which cars pass you (this movement of objects is called **optic flow**) and in the apparent size of the cars in front of you (of course, real size is invariant). Thus you can gauge the relative speed at which you and others are travelling from changes in the rate of optic flow, or from the increase/decrease in apparent car size.

Another important aspect in Gibson's theory is the notion of **affordances**. According to Gibson, the purpose of objects can be directly perceived, without any prior knowledge. For example, the function of a chair (to be sat upon) is directly perceived because it *affords* sitting upon. Likewise, the function of a ladder can be directly ascertained because the structure of the object affords climbing.

Gibson's theory has been highly influential, particularly since it encourages visual scientists to think about perception in the real world rather than in an artificial lab-based environment where natural sources of visual information are stripped away. Gibson's work shows that natural visual scenes are information rich, that the visual scene is dynamic not static, and that to underestimate these factors is to limit our understanding of perception. He also highlights the importance of action and movement in perception, something which had (has) been largely overlooked in other theories.

However, the theory is problematic and has been subject to quite harsh criticisms. In particular, critics raise concern with the apparently contrived notion of affordances. Is it really plausible that we can always directly perceive the function of an object, even if we have no prior knowledge of that object? For example, how would we know that an apple was for eating and not for playing cricket if we had no experience of apples?

5.4.3 TOP-DOWN APPROACHES

Top-down theories assume that higher-level processes such as knowledge and memory have important influences on perception. Theorists such as Richard Gregory (1970; 1997) have provided **constructivist** accounts. These are accounts based on the idea that our perceptual experiences are constructed from the imposition of high-level processing on sensory perceptions. Such theories have been around for a long time. And whilst there is no one unifying theory, all constructivist accounts have three things in common (Eysenck & Keane, 2005). They all take perception to be:

1   not just sensation, but an active and constructive process

2   a direct by-product of sensations and hypotheses about the world and how it works

3   influenced by individual differences and personal experiences.

Accordingly Gregory (1970; 1997) argues, in contrast to Gibson, that sensory input is impoverished, and that we have to interpret the information provided by our senses in order to make sense of what is going on. The existence of **perceptual constancies** (cognitive assumptions about the world) and the effects of visual **illusions** provide support for a constructivist approach.

As we navigate our way around the world, the image falling on the retina is constantly changing. Thus, if the image falling on our retina was the sole determinant of what we perceived, then visual objects would appear to change shape and size as our position changed. But because of perceptual constancies, perceptual experience remains stable. In the earlier example, the size of the image of a car on the retina changes as we move nearer to it. However, rather than perceiving the object as changing in actual size, we perceive a change in viewing distance (*size constancy*: see Figure 5.4). This is because the brain applies *constancy scaling* and scales up or down the mental image of the car to take into account our relative movement.

Likewise, the image of the shape of a door changes on the retina (or in a photograph) depending on whether it is open or closed, but we easily recognise that these differently shaped images are the same object (Figure 5.5). This is because the brain applies constancy scaling.

Visual illusions illustrate that perception is an active interpretive process. They work because we are trying to make sense of the visual information, even though the specific cause is different from one illusion to another and there may be more than one mechanism at play. The Müller–Lyer illusion (see Figure 5.6) is a classic example. Here the line with the outward-facing fins appears to be longer than the line with the inward-facing fins. Gregory (1963; 1997) proposed that this is because the fins imply depth. The inward-facing fins

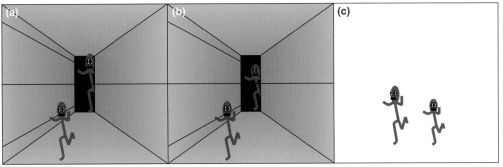

(Andrew Dunn)

FIGURE 5.4 An example of size constancy: (a) The stick person in the front appears to be smaller than the stick person at the back. In fact they are the same size. (b) The stick people appear to be the same size but in fact the one at the back is smaller. (c) Measure them and see

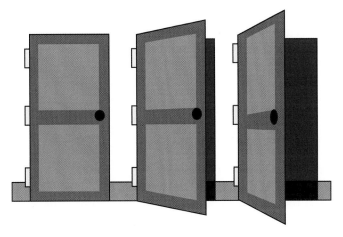

(Andrew Dunn)

FIGURE 5.5 Constancy scaling. Although the shape and dimensions of the door change on the retina (right edge of the door increases in size as the width decreases) the door does not appear to change in physical size. Rather it is scaled in a manner consistent with a door opening towards the viewer

imply the front of an object that recedes from us (e.g. the front corner of two walls), and the outward fins imply the far inside corner of an object that advances towards us (e.g. the far corner of a room). Gregory calls this *misapplied scaling constancy*, and similar processes are thought to underlie some other visual illusions.

The constructivist approach is important in showing that knowledge and memory *can* and *do* influence perception. However, critics (e.g. Gibson, 1950; Morgan & Casco, 1990) argue that too much emphasis is placed on the importance of visual illusions, which are frequently artificial two-dimensional stimuli. After all, how could you possibly hope to understand how a machine works if you only consider what it is doing wrong or what happens when it is broken? Nevertheless, the constructivists' basic point remains: top-down processes influence perception.

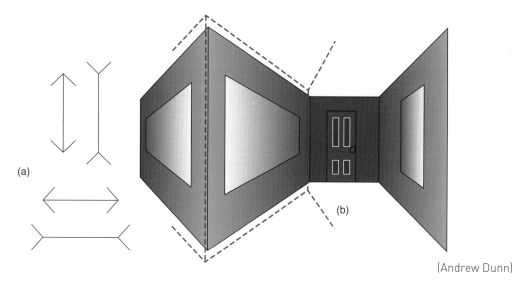

(Andrew Dunn)

FIGURE 5.6 The Müller-Lyer illusion: a) The line above appears to be shorter than the line below; b) an example of how receding or advancing objects have the shapes seen in the Müller-Lyer illusion (in this case, rotated through 90°)

5.4.4 PERCEPTUAL ORGANISATION

You've probably never really thought about it, but we tend to perceive our environment as a whole (albeit containing distinct objects) as opposed to lots of different parts. This is surprising given that the sensory systems break down the incoming sensory information into basic constituents (e.g. wavelength, spatial frequency etc). The **Gestalt psychologists** (e.g. Max Wertheimer, 1880–1943; Wolfgang Kohler, 1887–1967; and Kurt Koffka, 1886–1941) sought to understand how we organise and piece together perceptual experience of the world. They argued that perception involves much more than the incoming signal and that what is experienced (the whole) is much more than the parts it comprises. They sought to identify principles (*Gestalt laws*) that explained how elements in a scene are put together perceptually. Some of the laws along with visual examples (these principles *do not only* apply to vision) are shown in Figure 5.7. For example, closure is where our minds complete and perceive a whole object even if part of it cannot be seen or does not exist. Although here we have listed these principles independently, in the real world they can work independently or together and sometimes they may interfere with each other (Quinlan & Wilton, 1998).

> **Gestalt psychology** A school of psychology that began in Germany in the first half of the twentieth century. It proposed that an experience or behaviour can only be understood as a whole, not by understanding the individual constituent parts.

Law/Principle	Explanation
Similarity	Items that are similar in type (e.g. colour or shape) tend to be grouped together
Proximity	Items that are close together tend to be grouped together
Continuity	We tend to perceive lines as continuing in their established direction (for example, in (c) we tend to perceive a truck
Closure	The mind tends to 'complete' 'objects' in order to perceive regular figures

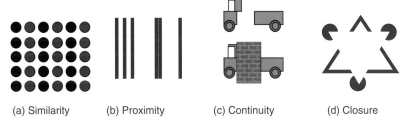

(a) Similarity   (b) Proximity   (c) Continuity   (d) Closure

FIGURE 5.7   Gestalt laws and explanations   (Andrew Dunn)

5.4.5 SUMMARY

At present there is no single general theory of perception. Matlin and Foley (1992) argue that perception works because (1) the sensory world is rich in information (there's lots of information out there), (2) human sensory systems are good at gathering information, and (3) high-level concepts shape (impose constraints on and determine) what we experience. Ultimately the brain and the rest of the nervous system have evolved to create a system that is best suited to extracting and filtering out what it needs to sense and perceive what is in the stimulus-rich world around us.

KEY RESEARCHER   Peter Thompson

FIGURE 5.8   Peter Thompson

Visual scientist Peter Thompson is a Senior Lecturer at the University of York, where he teaches and researches in visual perception. Peter graduated from the University of Reading with a BSc in Psychology (1972) and a PGCE (1973). He then studied for his PhD at the University of Cambridge (1976). He is the Executive Editor of the journal *Perception* and the co-creator of Viperlib (htpp:/viperlib.york.ac.uk, an online resource for visual perception). Peter has worked in

(Cont'd)

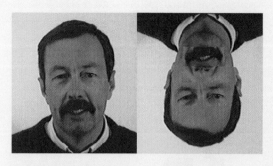

FIGURE 5.9   The Thatcher illusion

the USA and spent 6 months at NASA's Ames Research Center in California (1990). He is a Royal Society and British Association Millennium Fellow and received an HEA National Teaching Fellowship in 2006. He also happens to be the creator of the solar system. No, seriously: look it up at http://www.solar.york.ac.uk.

Peter's primary research interest is in movement perception (e.g. Thompson, 1982), though he has broader interests in visual sciences and has published a wide range of articles in this area. He is perhaps best known (at least outside academic circles) for the Thompson illusion (also called the Thatcher illusion: Thompson, 1980). Faces convey all manner of social, emotional and personality information, and they are a special kind of visual object for humans. We are especially sensitive to the eyes and mouth, but only when the face is the right way up. The Thompson illusion illustrates this beautifully. Look at the images in Figure 5.9. They appear to be perfectly normal. Now turn the page round urgk! Interestingly, newborns do not show this effect, which suggests that the effect is learnt (we usually see faces upright, but newborns have never seen a face). A dynamic illustration of the illusion can be found at OUP Thatcher illusion on YouTube: http://www.youtube.com/watch?v=jdADSx8JpfI.

ATTENTION

5.5

Attention plays an important role in sensation and perception, though these are by no means the only aspects of cognition in which it operates (e.g. memory, learning, planning). When people talk about attention they are often talking about different kinds of attention. For example, selective attention involves attending to one thing whilst ignoring everything else (e.g. reading this page whilst ignoring the television); divided attention involves processing several inputs simultaneously (reading this page whilst also watching television); sustained attention concerns maintaining our attention for long periods of time (e.g. getting through to the end of this chapter); and conflict resolution involves inhibiting automatic responses (e.g. falling asleep whilst reading this chapter). It is not surprising then, given its broad mediating role, that attention is so varied or that there is no one single mechanism at work (Allport, 1993).

Attention is involved in both choice and awareness, and operates both explicitly (overtly and intentionally) and implicitly (covertly and without intent). So, when choosing to read this chapter, you stop overtly attending to the music playing behind you or the chair you are sitting on, though you *know* they are both there (did you suddenly feel your chair?). But if the music stopped or the chair broke you would be immediately aware, so you must be attending to them at some level (covertly). Chalmers (1996) has suggested that conscious attention allows us to process objects for action (e.g. open the book to read) and that unconscious attention sustains automatic reactions (e.g. reaching out to stop or cushion your fall when the chair breaks). Attention is operating all the time, though you may not be aware of everything.

In due course we will see intriguing examples of what happens when attention is faulty (*neglect*), how attention does not work the way you might think it should (*change blindness* and *inattentional blindness*), and what all this says about attentional processing. But first we will look at the development of attention research, beginning with auditory attention.

5.5.1 AUDITORY ATTENTION

Interest in auditory attention was sparked following Cherry's (1953) research into the *cocktail party effect*. This is the problem of how we can follow what one person is saying when there are several people speaking in the same room. If you tape recorded the sound it would be hard to pick out individual conversations in the recording, but when you are there in person you can filter out some of the conversations while listening to others. In fact you can even switch when you are suddenly aware of something interesting in a conversation that you are not listening to. To investigate this phenomenon experimentally, Cherry devised the *shadowing (dichotic listening) task*. In this task, different messages were presented to the left and right ears, and participants were asked to 'shadow' (repeat out loud) the message presented to one of the ears. Cherry found that people had very little memory for the meaning of the *unattended message* in the non-shadowed ear. Listeners even failed to notice when the unattended message was in a foreign language, or in reversed speech. Participants in such experiments have even failed to notice when words in the unattended message were repeated 35 times (Moray, 1959). However, physical characteristics of the unattended message, such as the sex of the speaker, could almost always be remembered.

Various theories of auditory attention have been proposed to explain these and subsequent findings. Of particular concern here is the seminal work of Broadbent (1958), his student's later work (Treisman, 1964) and an alternative theory by Deutsch and Deutsch (1963). Common to all these accounts is the notion of a *bottleneck* which acts as an information **filter** that affects what is and isn't attended to. The key different between them is where this filter lies. For both Broadbent (1958) and Treisman (1964) the filter appears early, and in Treisman's scheme it is more flexible. For Deutsch and Deutsch (1963) the filter occurs much later. A summary of all three models can be seen in Figure 5.10.

Filter In the context of attentional processing, a filter serves the purpose of allowing some sensations of stimuli through to be processed whilst screening out others. This is based on the theoretical approach that we can only cope with a limited amount of information and so select which stimuli to process.

Broadbent's early filter theory

Broadbent's (1958) work on attention paved the way for much of what we know today and remains hugely important. According to him, information first enters a *sensory buffer* where it is held for a very short time. The selective filter then identifies one of the messages on the basis of its physical properties (e.g. location, intensity, sex of speaker). Only one message makes it through this filter; the unattended message receives no further processing while the attended message receives semantic analysis by a *limited capacity processor*. Capacity limitation is a key aspect of Broadbent's theory. He assumed that since our cognitive resources are finite, we cannot process everything at the same time; hence there must be some constraints on what is or is not processed.

Broadbent was able to explain Cherry's main findings. However, more of the unshadowed message is processed than Broadbent had predicted; and his model does not explain why, for example, one-third of participants could hear their own name if it was presented in the unattended message (Moray, 1959). This is because Broadbent took little account of message meaningfulness (he used strings of meaningless numbers) or message context. Taking these into account, Gray and Wedderburn (1960) demonstrated that when a meaningful message is split across the two streams of sound (part of the message is delivered to one ear, e.g. '7, fire, 1', and the other part is simultaneously delivered to the other ear, e.g. 'red, 1, engine') listeners report the meaningful message (i.e. 'red fire engine') but ignore the meaningless material. People also automatically switch between messages: on about 6 per cent of trials people automatically switched ears and began to repeat the previously unshadowed ear message if it was contextually relevant (Treisman, 1960). Thus listeners are not constrained by the physical properties of the stimulus but are able to switch and divide their attention using meaning and context. Treisman's (1964) model provides an explanation of why.

Treisman's attenuator model

Treisman's (1964) work built on Broadbent's earlier model, and she has been highly influential in attention research. There are similarities between her model and Broadbent's. The key difference between them lies in the location of filter. Specifically Treisman replaced Broadbent's selective filter with an **attenuator** which acts to turn down the processing of the incoming unattended message. Treisman (1964) argued that the processing of unattended messages is not halted completely. Unattended messages are processed but to a lesser degree because there is reduced capacity in the unattended channel. Accordingly the processing of auditory information proceeds in a hierarchy, beginning with physical cues and ending with semantic analysis. In essence the early bottleneck becomes more flexible. Usually there are only sufficient resources for the physical properties of unattended stimuli to be extracted. However, some stimuli (e.g. names and context-relevant messages like 'FIRE!') have a *low threshold* for identification (they are easy to identify and take priority), especially if they are primed on the basis of information in the attended channel ('matches, petrol, flame'). Thus Treisman was able to explain why physical properties of a message are almost always remembered, and why some information is able to 'break through' from the unattended message. Consequently her work has remained hugely influential. However, the concept of the attenuator is poorly specified. How does it actually work, and how can there be attenuated processing of meaning?

Deutsch and Deutsch's late selection model

Deutsch and Deutsch's (1963) model of attention is somewhat different from other earlier models. According to them, all incoming stimuli are *fully* analysed, but it is only the

Broadbent: selective filter model

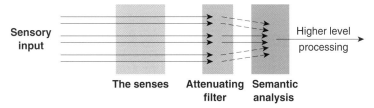

Treisman: attenuating filter model

Deutsch and Deutsch: late filter model

FIGURE 5.10   The three main theories of auditory attention   (Andrew Dunn)

most important or relevant stimulus that determines how we respond. Accordingly their filter occurs at the response stage, rather than at the analysis stage. This notion is highly counter-intuitive, and for a long time Deutsch and Deutsch's work seemed at odds with what appears to be happening with attention.

Like Treisman, Deutsch and Deutsch can explain why the physical properties of messages can be reliably reported, why 'breakthrough' occurs, and how meaning can be extracted from unattended messages. In fact, distinguishing between Deutsch and Deutsch's and Treisman's theories is difficult since both make very similar predictions experimentally. However, two sources of evidence suggest that Treisman's account might be more accurate than Deutsch and Deutsch's. First, the rate of message 'breakthrough' is low; if both messages were fully analysed, the rate of breakthrough should be much higher. Second, neuropsychological evidence indicates that there are differences between attended and unattended messages much earlier on in processing than would be predicted by Deutsch and Deutsch (e.g. Woldorff et al., 1993). This suggests that attention modulates the early parts of our sensory systems (Umiltà, 2001). However, it is clear that attention can also operate at a much higher level before the object of concern becomes consciously reported (see Lamme, 2003). One mediating factor is *perceptual load*: essentially, how much there is to perceive and how busy perception is (Lavie,

1995). When perceptual load is high, the processing resources are allocated to the main task and selection occurs early. When perceptual load is lower, we have more cognitive resources available and late selection tends to occur (Lavie, 1995).

In summary, auditory attention operates with a filter or an attenuator that extracts the attended message using both physical properties of the message and/or meaning. Attention may operate early, using physical properties of the message; or late, depending upon context, importance of the message and demands on cognitive resources.

Although these principles are generally true, particularly limitations on available resources, this does not necessarily mean that attention operates in the same way in other sensory modalities (e.g. vision). Our next section will consider visual attention.

5.5.2 VISUAL ATTENTION

Theories of selective visual attention fall within two main categories: *space-based* and *object-based* theories. Space-based (attentional spotlight and zoom lens) theories assume that we direct our attention to discrete regions of space within the visual field. Object-based theories assume that we direct our attention to the object, rather than its location *per se*.

Space-based attention – spotlight and zoom lens theory

Early accounts of visual attention (e.g. Eriksen & Eriksen, 1974) used a *spotlight* analogy. They assumed that everything within a small region of space – within the radius of the attentional spotlight – enters conscious awareness, whilst everything else receives only a cursory degree of processing. Indeed, decision response times about a target are relatively faster or slower if attention is directed towards (valid cue) or away from (invalid cue) the target location before it appears (Posner, 1980). This is because in the valid-cue condition, attention is already at the location when the target arrives, which saves processing time. But in the invalid-cue condition, attention must move to the true target location, which costs processing time.

Zoom lens models (e.g. Eriksen & Yeh, 1985) also assume that people attend to a particular area of space. However, unlike spotlight theory, the zoom lens model assumes that the area of focus can be increased or decreased according to task demands. This can have a significant (sometimes disastrous) influence on our processing of the world. For example, as the 'Think Bike' campaigns illustrate all too clearly, we are slower to process objects (e.g. a bicycle) that appear outside our attention focus (e.g. the car in front) but relatively unaffected if we are spreading our attention across a wider area (e.g. the traffic around us). Why? Well, when our attentional spotlight is focused (e.g. on the car in front) it has to expand the focus of the spotlight (zoom out), which takes time. Thus attentional focus can vary according to task demands. Hold this in mind, as it relates to change blindness and inattention which will be discussed later.

Object-based attention

Attention does not have to be space based. First, the focus of attention can be split over multiple locations (e.g. Awh & Pashler, 2000; Castiello & Umiltà, 1992); for example, we could be attending to more than one member of Take That at once. Second, we can pay attention to visual (Rock & Gutman, 1981; Watson & Kramer, 1999) or auditory (Dyson & Ishfaq, 2008) objects as well as the space they occupy (e.g. Mark Owen's voice, as well as the beautiful space he and Gary occupy). Memory for unattended objects in the same spatial location can be very poor (what roadie?: Rock & Gutman, 1981), and reaction times to properties of one object (e.g. shape or colour) can be faster than responses to the same properties in another object that occupies the same spatial location (Dyson & Ishfaq, 2008; Watson & Kramer, 1999), e.g. the colour of the lovely Mark's T-shirt as opposed to the roadie's.

So which account – space based or object based – is correct? The answer is, 'Both!': object-based attention appears to operate *within* the attended spatial region (*spatial spotlight*). Certainly, participants are better at spotting two object properties if both properties appear on the same object, but if participants only attend to a small region of space, then the object bias disappears (Lavie & Driver, 1996).

ARE WE AWARE OF EVERYTHING?

5.6 It feels to us that we are aware of everything around us, and yet object-based attention illustrates that under normal operating conditions we do not in fact attend to everything we thought we were attending to. Our brain has incredibly powerful processing capacity but it is a finite resource. Consequently, there are limitations to what we can process and we literally miss huge chunks of information. Two quite remarkable examples of how much we actually miss are change blindness and inattentional blindness (excellent examples of these can be found at: http://viscog.beckman.illinois.edu/djs_lab/demos.html/).

5.6.1 CHANGE BLINDNESS AND INATTENTION BLINDNESS

Change blindness (CB) refers to when people fail to perceive (big or small) changes in the very thing they are attending to. A simple (static) illustration of this can be found in traditional 'spot the difference' games. However, CB also occurs in dynamic scenes (e.g. change in object colour, or features being added or taken away) as they are being attended to. Take a look at the key study for a remarkable illustration of change blindness.

In *inattentional blindness* (IB) observers miss changes or events in the visual scene whilst they are attending to something else. These changes may be quite small (e.g. a briefly presented shape or word) but they can also be quite dramatic. For example, Simons and Chabris (1999) showed naive participants a video event in which two teams were playing a game of basketball. The viewers were asked to concentrate on just one of the teams and to count the number of passes they made. During this event (and unexpected by the viewers), either a woman holding an umbrella or a man in a gorilla suit walked fairly slowly in front of the game. Unbelievably, high numbers of people did not see the unexpected event: in one condition only 8 per cent saw the gorilla! The video shown to participants can be found at http://viscog.beckman.illinois.edu/flashmovie/15.php.

KEY STUDY   Simons, D.J., & Levin, D.T. (1998). Failure to detect changes to people during a real-world interaction. *Psychonomic Bulletin and Review,* **5: 644–649.**

How much do we notice in our day-to-day interactions? Surprisingly little, it seems. Simons and Levin first demonstrated this in their now famous change blindness studies. In the first of these they had an experimenter dressed as a workman (in hard hat and tool belt) stop and ask passers-by for directions. During the conversation two other workmen (who were actually fellow experimenters) walked straight between the two people, carrying a large door that obscured the passer-by's view of the person asking for directions. At the same time, the workman asking for directions swapped places with one of the two men carrying the door, who then continued the conversation about directions. Remarkably, 8 out of the 12 passers-by reported noticing no change and carried on giving directions, even though the change was quite dramatic (i.e. the workmen wore different coloured clothes and generally looked and sounded nothing like each other). Three passers-by retrospectively claimed to have noticed. Even if these are taken into account, this still leaves almost half not noticing at all. It seems incredible but it's absolutely true.

Simon's research group has repeated this basic experiment in many different forms. You can see one of Simon's experiments in action at http://www.youtube.com/watch?v=mAn Kvo-fPs0.

5.6.2 SO WHAT DOES IT ALL MEAN?

Clearly we do not attend to everything we think we do, and most examples of these absences go unnoticed in our day-to-day interactions. Focused attention results in generation of a specific representation relating to the task being engaged in. But it is not a complete general purpose representation of the attended scene (Rensink, 2002). The examples of CB and IB are intriguing and amusing, but it should be remembered that these are phenomena which occur as part of the way attention works when it is doing its job properly! Consequently everyday acts involving focused attention, like driving, operating machines or flying aeroplanes, are potentially fraught with danger. Imagine just how much more dangerous things become when we are dividing our attention across tasks, like using a mobile phone or talking with your friends whilst driving. You have been warned.

CHAPTER SUMMARY

5.7 This chapter's aim was to introduce themes and issues in sensation, perception and attention. In doing so we have discussed how we manage to detect, process and manage information from the noisy, information-rich environment in which we live. We have shown how we construct a representation of the world through a combination of bottom-up and top-down processes, and highlighted the role of experience and context. Our sensory, perceptual and attention systems are powerful tools that work together, but our resources are finite. It feels as though we experience and represent everything. In fact we do not do this. Instead we have evolved systems that extract what is necessary to interact with our world, and at best our representation of the world is adequate, even if it is not accurate. Human perception is not perfect and we do not fully understand it, but it works just fine ... well, most of the time!

DISCUSSION QUESTIONS

Why might our representation of the world not be entirely accurate?

Now that you have seen evidence that what we perceive of the world does not equate with what is 'out there' and that perception requires us to construct and interpret the world, how trustworthy would you say our perceptions are?

How might the matters we have discussed in this chapter relate to such phenomena as delusions and hallucinations? To what extent is the above account adequate for explaining them?

SUGGESTIONS FOR FURTHER READING

Mather, G. (2009). *Perception*. Psychology Press. For more on sensation and perception, this is a useful and accessible text.

Snowden, R., Thompson, P., and Tronscianko, T. (2006). *Basic vision*. Oxford University Press. This is a good starting point for those primarily interested in visual sensation and perception. It is engaging, colourful and often funny.

Styles, E. (2006). *The psychology of attention*. Psychology Press. For pure attention-related material, this book is hard to beat. It's comprehensive, informative and readable.

Johnson, A., and Proctor, I.W. (2004). *Attention: theory and practice*. Sage. This book is very readable and has some nice practical applications.

Quinlan, P., & Dyson, B. (2008). *Cognitive psychology*. Prentice Hall. A general cognitive psychology text, but relevant chapters here are 5, 6, 8, 9 and 13. A punchy, colourful, humorous but informative text.

6 THINKING AND PROBLEM SOLVING

Lead author **Gary Jones**

CHAPTER OUTLINE

INTRODUCTION

6.1

Two children were sat in front of me on the bus the other day. It was a cold and rainy day and the two boys noticed that the inside windows of the bus were full of condensation. One boy said to the other, 'These windows are wet because it's wet outside'. The other, noticing that blowing on the window caused further condensation, said, 'No, it's because my breath is wet!' (while quickly drawing a smiley face in the condensation, naturally). In a sense, both of them were correct: condensation in this instance is caused because our breath contains water vapour, which on contact with a cold surface (the windows of the bus on a cold day) causes condensation.

This simple example shows our thought processes at work; the two boys were wondering why there was condensation on the windows and their thoughts produced two possible solutions to their question. Because we use thought in everyday situations, as in the above example, there is a danger that we take it for granted. However, thought is a crucial attribute that humans possess. Without it, we would not be able to reason about the world. In this chapter we examine this broad area, discovering that, though we may be inclined to take it for granted, thought is actually rather difficult to explain. We will examine two important areas in the process of thinking: problem solving and reasoning.

FRAMING QUESTIONS

Do humans solve problems in the same way as computers?
Are there different ways to solve problems?
What is reasoning?
How logical are we in our thinking?
What is insight, and can I have some?

PROBLEM SOLVING

6.2

A problem occurs when we are faced with a particular state of the world that we want to change or to explain but there is no obvious way to accomplish this. Problems may take many different forms: for example, needing to discover how to find the quickest route by car from Nottingham to London, how sunlight creates a rainbow, or how to change your profile on a website.

Problem solving is an area that is interlinked to many other domains in cognitive psychology. For example, to solve a problem we may need to memorise certain aspects of the area concerned, or use our visual capabilities to examine the characteristics of a problem. In this case, a theory of problem solving cannot consider only the processes governing the actual problem solving, because some of these processes may well lie outside problem solving *per se*. For example, if the problem we are facing is performing an

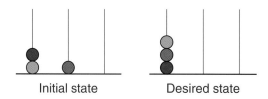

FIGURE 6.1   Example of initial and desired states for the Tower of London problem

arithmetic sum in our heads, then part of the constraint on how well we are able to solve the problem is how long we can keep numbers in memory when we are doing the arithmetic sum, which therefore encompasses aspects of memory. This should be borne in mind when examining theories of problem solving. This section will mainly cover Newell and Simon's (1972) theory of problem solving, because as we will see, most subsequent theories of problem solving and related areas are derived from it.

Let us first consider the common elements that are involved in basic problem solving. A problem must have an initial starting state; a given goal (or desired) state; and some constraints. For example, in finding a route the initial starting state may be, say, Nottingham; the given goal (i.e. the destination) may be London; and the constraint may be the need to find the quickest route. There may also be states other than the starting state or the goal state, as we manipulate the problem and work towards the solution (e.g. being on the M1 heading south towards London). Let us use a well-known problem solving scenario, the Tower of London problem, to illustrate these concepts.

The Tower of London problem (Shallice, 1982) consists of a number of coloured balls placed on pegs. The goal is to arrange the balls on the pegs in a specific way. Our example scenario (shown in Figure 6.1) has three coloured balls (red, blue and green) and three pegs, and the goal is to have all three balls on the first peg in the order red, blue, green, from bottom to top. Therefore we have an initial state where the green and red balls are on the first peg (green at the bottom) and the blue ball is on the second peg, and we have a desired state where the red, blue and green balls are all on the first peg, in that order from the bottom. Two constraints are specified in the Tower of London problem: balls can only be moved one at a time; and any move must place a ball on a peg (i.e. balls can't be set aside).

If we were mindless problem solvers who did not know anything about the problem domain, then the simplest way of trying to solve it would be by **trial-and-error**. Trial-and-error means trying every possible move until – if we're lucky – we finally reach the desired (goal) state. This would mean continually moving balls and comparing the new state of the problem (i.e. the current state of balls on pegs) to the desired state to see if it matched. A diagram of all the possible moves could be produced, and this would illustrate every state that could be created (i.e. all possible configurations of balls on pegs). Such a diagram might look a little like that in Figure 6.2. At the top is the initial state, and below this are all the possible states that arise from applying all the possible first moves to the initial state. Below each of these new states are all the possible moves that can be made (excluding the move that was made to get to the state in the first place!); and so on.

In problem solving, this type of diagram is called the **search space** or problem space, and it represents all the possible states that can be achieved in a given problem. This is important

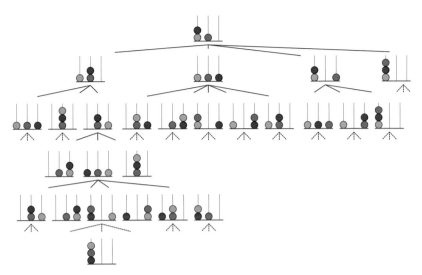

FIGURE 6.2 States that could be reached in the Tower of London problem by applying all possible moves to the initial starting state (note that due to space limitations not all moves are shown)

because it means that by necessity the search space must contain the desired (goal) state. Even a mindless problem solver could therefore work their way through this search space by continually moving balls onto pegs (in this example, a move from one state to the next is achieved by moving a ball from one peg to another) until they reach a state that matches the desired state.

Obviously, the search space for all the possible states that can be visited in the problem will be huge. However, with a little bit of memory, the search space can be cut down a great deal (e.g. by never making a move that would result in a state that had been encountered before). There are also other things that can be done to cut down the search space: for example, the problem solver could impose some kind of structure to their problem solving. Let's think what we would do when trying to solve this problem. One possibility is that we might try and break the problem down into smaller, more achievable goals: for example, setting a goal of moving the green ball from the bottom of the first peg. Applying some form of structure to our problem solving could help to cut down the amount of search that we are likely to have to do. All these things should be borne in mind when we look at Newell and Simon's (1972) theory of problem solving, for they consider and explain many of them.

ASIDE   Using problem solving tasks to solve the problem of the brain

The Tower of London problem was originally devised by Shallice (1982) to study problem solving in patients with damage to the frontal lobes of the brain. Shallice found that patients with damage to the left anterior frontal lobe demonstrated impaired planning (i.e. a greater number of moves was required for solution). Patients with damage to the right anterior and the left or right posterior areas of the frontal lobes were not impaired. This gives us some clues about the parts of the brain crucial to problem solving.

6.2.1 THEORIES OF PROBLEM SOLVING

Newell and Simon's (1972) theory of problem solving derives from their earlier work (e.g. Newell et al., 1958). Their belief is that a theory of problem solving can be implemented as a computer program, although they stress that this should not be seen as analogous to the way the human brain accomplishes problem solving. What they argue is that the necessary mechanisms and processes can be implemented as a program, but this is not absolutely necessary because the processes and mechanisms can be described and worked through using paper and pencil; it is simply that a computer program can work through them more quickly.

KEY RESEARCHER   Herbert Alexander Simon (1916–2001)

Simon was a US social scientist who carried out research across a range of disciplines including cognitive psychology and computer science. He is regarded as one of the founding fathers of modern scientific areas such as artificial intelligence and decision making in economics. He is described as a uniquely innovative thinker and his achievements are evidenced by the number of awards he received during his life, most notably the Nobel Prize for Economics in 1978 for 'pioneering research into the decision-making process within economic organizations'; the US National Medal of Science in 1986; and an American Psychological Association Award for Outstanding Lifetime Contributions to Psychology in 1993.

FIGURE 6.3   Herbert Simon

A notable quotation from Simon is:

What information consumes is rather obvious: it consumes the attention of its recipients. *Hence a wealth of information creates a poverty of attention*, and a need to allocate that attention efficiently among the overabundance of information sources that might consume it. (Simons, 1971, emphasis added)

The basic idea of the theory is that, as with all problems, there is an initial state and a desired state. Of primary importance in terms of the theory is the setting of a goal to transform the initial state into the desired state. This goal is then broken down into further subgoals, which need to be achieved in order to accomplish the main goal. The whole process of breaking down a problem into subgoals and further subgoals is termed **means–ends analysis**, and is short for 'accomplishing a means to an end'. It really just means setting subgoals (and further subgoals, or sub-subgoals if you like) that help to achieve the overall goal.

Providing some structure to the problem by the use of means–ends analysis obviously means that the search space is narrowed down so that only the most relevant states are likely to be visited. In the Tower of London example in Figure 6.1, the first subgoal might be to remove the green ball from the leftmost peg, so that the red ball can be the lowest on that peg. This would immediately rule out initial moves that did not involve removal of the green ball in the search space that was outlined above (e.g. initial moves involving the blue ball).

> **Means–ends analysis** Setting a goal and then breaking it down to produce subgoals which need to be achieved.

In order to work out what aspects of the problem the goals and subgoals should involve, Newell and Simon suggest the problem solver compares problem states to see what the differences between states are, and then sets goals and subgoals to remove those differences. For example, in the Tower of London problem, the initial state is the green and red balls on the left peg and the blue ball on the middle peg; the **desired state** is the red ball, then blue ball, then green ball on the left peg. Newell and Simon suggest that these two states will be compared, and some difference will be found to set a subgoal to attain. For example, it may be noticed that the green ball is the first ball on the left peg; a subgoal will thus be set to move the green ball to another peg (say the right peg).

So the combination of means–ends analysis and comparing the differences between the current state of the problem and the desired state means that a problem can be structured somewhat so that problem solving does not progress in a simple trial-and-error fashion. Note that with each subgoal, there is a slightly different desired state to the initial one: for example, the desired state for moving the green ball to the right peg is a state whereby the green ball is actually on the right peg. For this reason, the desired states for subgoals are often called **goal states**, so as not to confuse them with the overall desired state, which is the ultimate goal of the problem.

> **Desired state** The ultimate state, i.e. when the problem is solved.
>
> **Goal state** A desired state for a subgoal of the problem solving process.

Further to means–ends analysis, Newell and Simon also put forward the idea that a problem is constrained by operators – the mechanisms and processes that can act upon the initial state (and each subsequent state) in order to attempt to change it to the desired state. In the Tower of London example, there was really only one operator: moving a ball from one peg to another. Other problems may have many possible operators though. For example, given the starting equation $2X = 6$ (the initial state) with a desired state to find X, a goal state can be set to have X by itself on one side of the equation. The set of operators for this problem would be the set of mathematical processes which can change the current state of the problem. For example, an operator could be based around knowledge such as the fact that adding the same number to both sides of an equation (i.e. to both sides of the equal sign) keeps the equation equal. These operators can continually be applied to the problem to change the state of the problem and thus try and solve subgoals or goals. So in the example, the problem solver would eventually divide both sides of the equation by 2 in order to get X by itself on one side, leading to the solution $X = 3$, as follows:

$$2x = 6$$
$$2x/2 = 6/2$$
$$x = 3$$

One type of problem examined in detail by Newell and Simon was that of **cryptarithmetic**. This is where a sum is made from letters of the alphabet, with the goal being to find the numeric values of all of the letters so as to make the sum correct. Take the problem shown in Figure 6.4. Each letter is assigned a number from 0 through 9, with no number being assigned to more than one letter. A head start has been given by informing the problem solver that $D = 5$.

DONALD
+ GERALD $D = 5$
ROBERT

FIGURE 6.4   An example of a cryptarithmetic problem. The answer is at the end of the chapter

Remember that Newell and Simon implemented their theory as a computer program – which they called the **general problem solver** (GPS). The GPS began with four basic operators for cryptarithmetic: (1) to process a column in order to infer something about it; (2) to generate possible values of a letter; (3) to assign a value to a letter; (4) to test if a letter could take a specified value.

Using these operators together with means–ends analysis as a method for breaking down the problem into goals and subgoals, in conjunction with comparing the current state of the problem with the desired state (the identification of all of the letters in terms of what numerical values they are assigned), the GPS is able to solve the problem.

General problem solver (GPS)   A computer program created in 1957 by Herbert Simon and Allen Newell to build a universal problem solving machine.

The way in which the GPS solved cryptarithmetic problems compared favourably to verbal protocols of people solving problems. A verbal protocol is the transcript produced when someone 'thinks aloud' when they are performing something. Newell and Simon analysed the verbal protocols from problem solvers in order to identify the types of goals, subgoals and operators that they were trying to apply at different situations in a problem. This would then give them some idea as to whether their theory carried out problem solving in a similar way to humans. In general, they found that there was a great deal of overlap between how the GPS solved cryptarithmetic problems and how human participants solved them.

However, although the theory does predict some human problem solving behaviour, it does not predict all. For example, novice problem solvers may solve problems like the GPS does (using means–ends analysis) but experts do not. For example, Larkin (1983) studied physics problems using students and professional physicists. The students, who had little knowledge of physics, would solve the problems in a similar fashion to the GPS. The professional physicists, however, would solve the problem in a completely different way: they would classify the problem as being similar to a set of problems they knew of already, and then apply the methods and processes that would be used for this class of problem. This process is called analogy, and it is something we will come to later. Nevertheless, Newell and Simon's theory of problem solving has provided a basis for much of the more contemporary theories of problem solving.

More recent theories of problem solving have retained several elements of Newell and Simon's theory, particularly the goal-oriented aspects and the idea of representing the theory as a computer program. The main current theory is adaptive character of thought–rational, (ACT–R) (Anderson, 1993). ACT–R is intended as a general theory of human intelligence, of which problem solving is only a part. ACT–R is implemented in the form of a production system (e.g. Anderson, 1993). Rather than covering ACT–R in detail here, we will briefly cover production systems so that you have some idea of how contemporary ideas of problem solving are implemented.

Production systems hold two types of knowledge: factual knowledge and **procedural knowledge**. Factual knowledge is statements about what we know: for example, I like football. Procedural knowledge is represented by the rules of the game. A rule is an *if …then* construct. For example, *if* I like football, and I know a football match is on the television, *then* stay in and watch the football. **Declarative knowledge** is used to see if any of the *if* parts of rules can be matched, and if this is the case, then that rule is put forward as a possible rule to be used.

Take the following pieces of declarative knowledge: I like football, I like rugby, I want to play football, I want to play rugby. Now take the following rules: *if* I like football, and I want to play football, *then* go outside and play football; *if* I like rugby, and I want to play rugby, *then* go outside and play rugby. If all of this knowledge was in the production system, then both rules could be used (the first would suggest playing football and the second would suggest playing rugby). How would we select which rule should be used at a given moment in time?

> **Production system**   A system that uses facts and rules about those facts to govern its behaviour. The term arises because rules are also known as productions.

When more than one rule can be used at any given time, the system is said to be in conflict – in which case **conflict resolution** will be utilised to decide which rule should be used. There are a variety of methods for resolving conflict: in the example above, the most obvious method is to place weightings on the rules, so that (for example) a preference for playing football over rugby could be reflected by that rule having a higher weighting. There are also alternative ways of resolving conflict: the rule that was used most recently could be selected, or the rule which uses the most recently added knowledge to declarative memory.

Behaviour in production systems proceeds in the manner of selecting which rules can be used for the given set of declarative knowledge, selecting a rule from this set using conflict resolution, and then applying the rule. Note that the *then* part of the rule can change declarative knowledge, which would mean that the next time the system examined which rules can be used, a completely different set of rules might appear. For example, given the rule '*if* I like Radiohead's new single *then* buy it as a download', together with a liking for Radiohead's new single, the fact that we want to buy it as a download is placed in declarative knowledge. Other rules would then act upon this knowledge (e.g. going onto the internet etc.). More detailed explanations of production systems can be found in Anderson (1993; 2000).

The **Tower of Hanoi** is a problem solving puzzle consisting of three rods. On one of the rods are placed a number of disks of various sizes (placed in order of size from large to small). The aim is to move all disks onto another rod in the correct order of size. The constraints are that only one disk can be removed at a time and may not be placed on top of a smaller disk. The aim is to use the smallest possible number of moves to achieve the goal.

Using production systems as a basis for intelligent behaviour, ACT–R has simulated problem solving behaviour in the **Tower of Hanoi** problem, transfer problems, and geometry problem solving. ACT–R also provides a timing estimate of how long a rule takes to be executed. Comparisons with human data have been very favourable, illustrating how ACT–R compares well to human problem solving in terms of not only timing data but also general problem solving behaviour.

6.2.2 INSIGHT PROBLEM SOLVING

However, not all of human problem solving fits neatly into the idea that we apply rules based on certain facts about the world. Have you ever given up on a problem, only for its solution to suddenly appear out of the blue in what can be described as a 'flash of **insight**'? These are the types of problem we discuss in this section.

Consider the anecdote of King Hiero asking Archimedes to prove that the amount of gold in his newly made crown equalled the amount of gold given to the goldsmiths. Archimedes considers the problem for some time, and becomes stuck in an **impasse**: he simply cannot see a solution. Some days later when taking a bath, he notices that his body displaces the water in the bath tub. Immediately, he has his flash of insight and runs naked through the streets, crying out 'Eureka! I have found it!' (Gruber, 1995). This is the essence of insight – a situation where the solution to a problem seems impossible until suddenly it appears as if from nowhere. The **Gestalt psychologists** were the first to illustrate insight in the early 1900s, though relatively recently insight has had a resurgence of interest, with two theories being proposed as to why insight occurs.

The Gestalt psychologists (e.g. Köhler, 1925; Scheerer, 1963) argued that insight was a process of restructuring: the problem solver needs to restructure the problem in a different way than that originally thought of. One of the first studies of insight actually involved chimpanzees. Köhler (1925) set up a problem situation where a banana was hanging out of reach in a chimpanzee's cage. On the floor was a set of crates, the idea being that the chimpanzee should stack the crates in such a way as to create a set of steps leading to the banana. Köhler found that this solution came to the chimpanzees quite suddenly, and was normally preceded by a period of intense thought.

Insight   This is when we reach a dead end in problem solving, until suddenly – 'aha!' – we realise the solution. A rare phenomenon.

This confirmed the two states we have met: *impasse* (where the problem solver becomes stuck on the problem and either keeps repeating problem solving moves, or stops and thinks about the problem for a while) and *insight* (where the solution to the problem suddenly appears). Of course, just being in an impasse does not necessarily mean insight will subsequently follow. If only it did!

Taking Köhler's lead, Maier (1931) examined insight in humans, setting up a room where two pieces of string hung from the ceiling, each out of arm's reach from the other (an example of the room is given in Figure 6.5). The goal was to tie the two pieces together. Various implements (e.g. scissors) were given to help. The correct solution was to tie one of the implements to one of the pieces of string and set it in a pendulum motion so that both pieces could then be held. Participants in this problem had great difficulty in solving it, often needing a hint (the experimenter 'accidentally' brushing against one of the pieces of string and setting it into motion). Previously the implements were seen in terms of their function, a concept the Gestalt psychologists called **functional fixedness** – an early recognition that insight problems might be difficult because of prior experience. After the hint, for example, the scissors might be seen not in terms of their usual function (cutting things) but rather in terms of what else they could be used for (a pendulum weight). Today we might refer to this as 'thinking outside the box' where we try to come up with new solutions to a problem. In this case we look for new uses for all the objects at our disposal and see that the scissors can help create a pendulum.

One recent theory of insight uses these Gestalt ideas. The representational change theory (Knoblich et al., 1999; 2001) suggests that, because of prior experience, the problem solver begins with a representation of the problem that is incorrect for its solution. Only by changing this representation can the problem be solved. This is done in one of two ways: **constraint relaxation** and/or **chunk decomposition**. Constraint relaxation involves relaxing constraints that the problem solver unnecessarily imposes on the problem (e.g. thinking of the function of scissors as being only to cut

> **Gestalt psychology** A school of psychology that began in Germany in the first half of the twentieth century. It proposed that an experience or behaviour can only be understood as a whole, not by understanding the individual constituent parts.

things). Chunk decomposition involves realising that certain components of the problem can be broken down further (e.g. the Roman numeral for 4, IV, can be broken down into an I and a V).

Knoblich and colleagues used a Roman numeral matchstick arithmetic domain to illustrate the theory. In Roman numeral matchstick arithmetic, an incorrect equation is written out in Roman numerals using matchsticks, with the goal being to move one and only one matchstick to make the equation correct. Figure 6.6 shows an example problem.

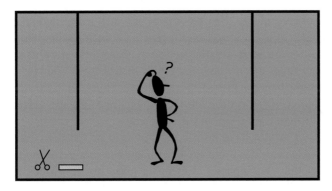

FIGURE 6.5 Maier's (1931) two-string problem

FIGURE 6.6   An example matchstick problem. (The solution can be found at the end of this chapter.)

The problem outlined in Figure 6.6 requires the relaxation of the constraint that numerical values in equations cannot be arbitrarily changed without some corresponding change to the other side of the equation (i.e. you would not normally change a 4 into a 6 on one side of the equation without also adding 2 to the other side of the equation). The problem also requires decomposing the chunk IV into the components I and V (i.e. thinking of the I as a matchstick that can be moved and not thinking of it as having to be part of the IV).

Sets of matchstick problems were created and predictions were made by the theory as to the difficulty of each, based on what constraints needed to be relaxed and what chunks needed to be decomposed. The predictions of the theory were borne out, with participants quickly solving arithmetic equations that the theory predicted should be easy, and taking a long time to solve equations that the theory predicted to be difficult.

However, there is an alternative theory of insight, the constraint for satisfactory progress theory (MacGregor et al., 2001), which is based on Newell and Simon's problem solving theory. If we think of an insight problem in terms of a search space, where all possible moves to be made in the problem are outlined, then it seems strange that people have difficulty solving insight problems, because surely they should just search this space of possible states in the problem to find the solution. MacGregor and colleagues suggest that this is in fact what people do, but their search space does not contain *all* of the possible moves. Only when people have tried all of the available (but fruitless) moves will they realise that the problem space requires expanding.

Ormerod et al. (2002) examined the theory using the eight-coin problem. In this problem, a set of eight coins is laid on a table; the task is to move two coins such that each coin touches three and only three others. Two initial configurations of coins were given (see Figure 6.7). The idea was that if people searched their space of possible moves, a configuration that offered plenty of initial moves in which a coin would touch three others would lead to people taking a long time to reach a solution: they would feel they were satisfying subgoals of moving a coin to touch three others. On the other hand, a configuration where there are no obvious initial moves for a coin to touch three others should result in insight being achieved more quickly. This is exactly what the researchers found, with the configuration on the left side of Figure 6.7 being solved more often and more quickly than the configuration on the right side.

The two theories of insight have both been shown to be effective, but in the context of different insight problems. It has therefore been suggested that perhaps the best explanation of insight is a theory that encompasses elements of both theories (Jones, 2003).

(a)

(b)

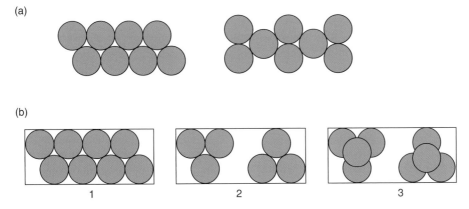

FIGURE 6.7 a) Two initial configurations for the eight-coin problem. b) The solution is to stack coins. Using the left side configuration as an example (1), a solution would be to move the upper coin in the third column (2) on top of the triangle of coins in columns one and two (3), and to move the lower coin in the second column on top of the triangle of coins in columns four and five (3) as illustrated

---

ASIDE Thinking about thinking

Insights are remarkable things. We sometimes have lightbulb moments when a solution to a problem suddenly appears. Fortunately most of us don't decide to suddenly run down the street naked like Archimedes (see text), as this would create a whole set of new problems to solve. When we look back at where the answer came from, it can sometimes appear almost mystical. Suddenly it all became clear and we got a sense that we understood the puzzle we were thinking about. Sometimes the puzzle can be like those described here, and sometimes they can be human problems like why your partner dumped you. Something happens in our thinking and we dramatically restructure our thoughts and see the world in a different way. Most remarkably, this restructuring often happens when we are not thinking about the problem. A famous example of this is the discovery of the benzene ring by German chemist Friedrich Kekulé in 1890 after a dream about a snake eating its own tail.

REASONING

6.3

Reasoning is the process of drawing conclusions through logical thinking. It tends to be considered part of problem solving but also part of thinking in general. There are a variety of forms of reasoning, such as **probabilistic reasoning**, **inductive reasoning** and **deductive reasoning**, all of which will be briefly covered here.

6.3.1 PROBABILISTIC REASONING

Probabilistic reasoning is how we reason under varying degrees of uncertainty. This has links with everyday reasoning, because often problems and situations may involve a variety of factors which are uncertain, e.g. when you leave your house to go to the shops, you may consider how likely it is to rain so that you can determine whether or not to take a coat with you. The weakness of this sort of reasoning can be seen in the observation that it usually rains when you leave your coat at home and is very sunny when you wrap up against the weather.

Uncertainty is usually represented by a probability measure, which is a number between 0 and 1 (0 being no chance of something happening, 1 being certainty that something will happen, and 0.5 representing a 50/50 chance that something will happen). Probability can be influenced by frequency (how often something has happened in the past) and belief (your own belief in whether something will happen).

There is a way of calculating probability taking into account frequency and belief. This is **Bayes theorem,** which outlines how frequency information can be used when calculating probability. Try the exercise on probabilistic reasoning. Also if you feel up to the challenge (not for the faint-hearted) there is an optional detailed explanation of Bayes theorem in the 'Nerds' corner' aside, once you have worked through the exercise.

EXERCISE   Probabilistic reasoning

You are a fashionista of cool as well as a psychologist (the two often go together). A man comes to see you for advice, very distressed because he has been told by several 'so-called' friends that he is unstylish. He has always considered himself the height of fashion and is worried that he may be suffering from Howard Moon Syndrome (HMS), a distressing condition in which the person believes that they are stylish whilst continuing to wear tweed safari suits and listening to trad jazz!

On the basis of your experience, 1 in 10 (i.e. 10 per cent) of people in a similar situation have HMS. In order to diagnose him you administer the HMS battery of tests. You know that the HMS diagnostic test is not 100 per cent reliable. In fact, you know that for people who do have HMS, it only identifies them 90 per cent of the time. For people who do not have HMS, it incorrectly identifies them as having the syndrome 20 per cent of the time. The test results diagnose HMS.

What are the chances that the man actually has HMS?

To work out an answer to the exercise, we can consider 100 people in the same situation as that outlined. We know that 10 of these will have HMS and 90 will not, because your fashionista experience tells us this. Of the 10 who have HMS, the tests will identify 90 per cent (i.e. nine people) correctly as having it, and incorrectly identify 10 per cent (i.e. one person) as not having it. Of the 90 who do not have HMS, the tests will correctly identify

80 per cent (72 people) as not having it, but will incorrectly identify 20 per cent (18 people) as having it. The man in the exercise had test results that came out positive, so he must be either one of the nine people who have been correctly identified as having HMS, or one of the 18 who have been incorrectly diagnosed. Therefore the chances that he actually has HMS are 9/(9 + 18) which is 9/27 or 33 per cent. (For a more formal explanation, see the 'nerds' corner' aside.)

ASIDE   Nerds' corner: Bayes theorem

Bayes theorem is a method by which probabilistic information can be outlined. Bayes theorem is basically a probability of a hypothesis being true given some factual evidence (or data) related to the hypothesis. Let us use the example in the exercise to outline the theorem. The hypothesis H is that a man has HMS. The data D are that the test result has come out positive.

There are some values that we can fill in based on the probabilities given in the exercise. The probability of the hypothesis H being correct is 0.1 (10 per cent). This can be written as $p(H) = 0.1$. The probability of the evidence being correct assuming the hypothesis is correct is 90 per cent (i.e. for those who have HMS, the test identifies it 90 per cent of the time). This can be written as $p(D|H) = 0.9$ (the | means 'given', i.e. this is the probability of the data occurring given that the hypothesis is correct). The probability of the evidence being correct assuming the hypothesis is incorrect is 20 per cent (i.e. for those who do not have HMS, there is a 20 per cent chance that the tests will incorrectly identify them as having HMS). This can be written as $p(D|\neg H) = 0.2$ (the $\neg$ means 'not', i.e. this is the probability of the data occurring given that the hypothesis is not correct). What we want to find is $p(H|D)$, or the probability of the hypothesis being correct (i.e. that the man has HMS) given that the data are true. The formula for Bayes theorem is:

$$p(H|D) = \frac{p(D|H) \times p(H)}{[p(D|H) \times p(H)] + [p(D|\neg H) \times p(\neg H)]}$$

The top line of the formula is 0.9×0.1, which is also the first part of the bottom line. The second part of the bottom line is 0.2×0.9. So the top line is 0.09 and the bottom line is $0.09 + 0.18$. This gives $p(H|D)$ as 0.09/0.27 or 0.33 (33 per cent).

If people always used Bayes theorem, their probabilistic reasoning would be error-free; but let's face it, the theorem uses quite a scary formula! Not surprisingly, people rarely use anything like Bayes theorem when dealing with probabilistic information. Therefore the reality is that people are relatively poor at working with probabilities. This is partly because people do not use theorems like the one outlined by Bayes, but partly for various other reasons. Tversky and Kahneman have played a major role in identifying those reasons (e.g. Kahneman & Tversky, 1972; Tversky & Kahneman, 1974; 1980; 1983). Details of some of the reasons are given in the following.

EXERCISE Logical fallacies

Before you read on, try and solve this problem.

A taxi-cab was involved in a hit and run accident one night. Two cab companies, Green and Blue, operate in the city. You are given the following information:

1 In the study, 85 per cent of the cabs are Green, 15 per cent are Blue.
2 In a court, a witness identified the cab as being Blue.

The witness's ability to identify the colours of cabs was tested, and it was shown that the witness was able to correctly identify the colour of a cab 80 per cent of the time and was wrong 20 per cent of the time.

What is the probability that the cab involved in the accident was Blue rather than Green?

One reason that we often get it wrong in calculating probability is due to the **base rate fallacy**. This is where people fail to take into account the base rate when calculating the probability of an event occurring. The base rate is the prior probability of a certain event occurring when the data related to the event are *not* taken into account (this is $p(H)$ in Bayes theorem). Take the example shown in the cab exercise (from Tversky & Kahneman, 1980). Most individuals state that the probability of the taxi being Blue is 80 per cent; however, this answer completely ignores the base rate of a taxi being Blue, which is only 15 per cent. Bayes theorem can be used to compute the correct probabilities, and would actually show that the chances of the cab being Blue are 0.41 (41 per cent), meaning that there is in fact more chance of the taxi being Green.

Another reason for our poor probability calculations is the *availability heuristic*. This applies where more emphasis is placed on information that is readily available to us. For example, Tversky and Kahneman (1974) asked questions of the form:

If a word of three letters or more is chosen at random from a dictionary, is there more chance of it beginning with a K or more chance that the third letter is a K?

The majority of participants get this question wrong. People are likely to say there is more chance of the word beginning with a K, when in fact there is more chance of a K being the third letter. The reason they do this is that we can quickly think of words that begin with K, and it is more difficult to think of words which have a K as their third letter; that is, words beginning with a K are more *available*. This type of fallacy occurs for many things, such as people thinking certain causes of death (e.g. murder) are more common than other less publicised causes (e.g. suicide) (Lichtenstein et al., 1978).

The *representativeness heuristic* applies where people often become misled by instances that they believe to be representative of a category. It's easier to think of such representative instances (e.g. that people studying English would go on to become journalists) than instances which tend not to be representative of a category (e.g. that people who study English would go on to be footballers: Tversky and Kahneman, 1983).

The *gambler's fallacy* is where people become completely misled in their belief of what is likely to happen by chance. For example, when tossing a coin six times, people believe a sequence of heads and tails of THHTHT to be much more likely to happen than a sequence of TTTHHH, even though both are equally as likely (Kahneman & Tversky, 1972). See also the TV programme 'Deal or No Deal', where people believe that there is a strategy in their actions to guess which box has the most money.

> **Heuristic** A mental shortcut (or rule of thumb) that represents a 'best guess', allowing people to make solution attempts or make decisions quickly and efficiently (though not always correctly).

6.3.2 DEDUCTIVE REASONING

Another type of reasoning is deductive reasoning. This is reasoning which involves deducing a conclusion from a set of given premises. Take the example shown in Figure 6.8.

```
All S are M.
All M are P.

Therefore:

A   All S are P.
B   All S are not P.
C   Some S are P.
D   Some S are not P.
E   None of the above.
```

FIGURE 6.8 Example of deductive reasoning: the correct conclusion from the premises is option A

Deductive reasoning is usually examined in the form given in Figure 6.8 – that is, using **syllogisms**. A syllogism has two *premises* (e.g. all S are M; all M are P) and a *conclusion* (therefore, all S are P). As we will see, people tend to find deductive reasoning difficult, particularly when the premises and conclusion involve items or things that are unfamiliar to them, or contradict their real-world beliefs. Take the following two syllogisms:

> War times are prosperous times, and prosperity is highly desirable; therefore, wars are much to be desired.

> Philosophers are all human, and all human beings are fallible; therefore, all philosophers are fallible, too.

Both of the conclusions to these statements are true based on the premises; however, people are much happier to accept the second as true, and less happy to accept the first as true. This illustrates how our prior knowledge can affect our deductive reasoning, something which is

> **Syllogisms** A form of deductive reasoning consisting of a major premise, a minor premise, and a conclusion. For example, all Liverpool players are divers; Steven Gerrard is a Liverpool player; therefore Steven Gerrard is a diver.

called *belief bias* (e.g., Evans et al., 1983), where believable conclusions are much easier to accept than unbelievable ones.

There are other factors that also affect our ability to interpret syllogisms. For example, the way in which the premises and conclusions are ordered (called the *figure* of the syllogism) can hamper the reasoning process, as illustrated in the following statements:

> Some people eat cake, and some cake eaters believe in ghosts; therefore, some people believe in ghosts.

> Some cake eaters are people, and some people who believe in ghosts eat cake; therefore, some people believe in ghosts.

The two statements are exactly the same, but they are ordered differently. In the first, the standard format is used, whereby the first statement begins with people and specifies a relationship to cake eaters, and then the second begins with cake eaters and specifies a relationship to believers in ghosts. This is called an A–B, B–C format, and it is the easier format for people to interpret. In the example, the A represents people, the B cake eaters, and the C believers in ghosts. The second has an order of B–A, C–B, because the first part begins with cake eaters and specifies their relationship to people, and the second part begins with believers in ghosts and specifies their relationship to cake eaters. People tend to find the first version much easier to interpret than the second (e.g. Dickstein, 1978).

Finally, the *mood* of the syllogism can also affect performance (e.g. Evans et al., 1993). The mood describes the terms used to illustrate the relationships in the syllogism, e.g. *some, all, some ... are not*. For example, the inclusion of 'not' in the first syllogism below seems to make the interpretation of the syllogism more difficult than the second one:

> Some artists are not painters, and some painters are rich; therefore, some artists are not rich.

> Some artists are painters, and some painters are rich; therefore, some artists are rich.

Belief bias, mood and figure combine to affect our reasoning. For example, people find A–B, B–C premises easier, *but* find them harder for unbelievable conclusions (Newstead et al., 1992). For example, the first syllogism below is easier to interpret than the second even though it does not follow the A–B, B–C format, because the second one contains information that contradicts prior beliefs:

> Some animals are not cats, and milk drinkers are cats; therefore, some animals drink milk.

> Some canaries are not birds, and some birds drink coffee; therefore, some canaries drink coffee.

What we see from deductive reasoning is that interpreting syllogisms is based on a variety of factors that combine to make the syllogism either easy or hard to interpret. There are some explanations of deductive reasoning, in particular mental models (e.g. Johnson-Laird & Byrne, 1991). We do not have space to go into this theory, but you should be aware of its existence – and if you want to read about it further, you should seek out Johnson-Laird (1983; 1999).

6.3.3 INDUCTIVE REASONING

Inductive reasoning involves working from the specific to the general (as opposed to deductive reasoning where we apply general rules to specific instances). What we mean by this is that in inductive reasoning we form a general conclusion based on certain instances or facts. For example, if it has rained for the last three Wednesdays, then it will rain the following Wednesday. That is, based on evidence (it has rained for the last three Wednesdays), a hypothesis has been derived (it rains on Wednesdays). Of course, in this simple example we know from prior experience that the hypothesis is unlikely to be true; even though the weather is bad in the UK, it never usually rains every single Wednesday! Nevertheless, inductive reasoning is a key process, particularly in science, where hypotheses are often derived from sets of factual evidence.

However, much of our inductive reasoning is based on evidence that confirms our hypothesis: for example, we derived the hypothesis that it rains on Wednesdays based on evidence that confirmed this hypothesis (that it had rained the last three Wednesdays). Popper (1968) argued that it is not enough to conclude hypotheses based on confirmatory evidence alone; one must also seek to find any evidence that disconfirms the hypotheses (and therefore the hypotheses are no longer valid). If no disconfirming evidence can be found, then this indicates a high likelihood that the hypotheses are true.

Unfortunately, people tend to show a confirmation bias: that is, they derive hypotheses from supporting facts and don't often look for disconfirming evidence. This is illustrated in a classic study by Peter Wason – the 2–4–6 task. Wason's (1960) 2–4–6 task was created with the intention of investigating the significance of Popper's claims regarding falsification. The outline of the task is as follows:

> I have a rule in mind that specifies how a sequence of three numbers (triples) can be ordered. Your task is to discover what my rule is. To start you off, I can tell you that '2-4-6' is a triple that fits my rule. In order to discover the rule, you should produce number triples, and I will tell you whether your number triple fits my rule or not. You can try as many or as few triples as you wish, and once you feel you have discovered the rule, then you can state it aloud to me.

Wason was interested in the types of triples that people would generate. His idea was that people would hypothesise a rule and would then test this rule using triples. His main interest was in seeing whether people would produce triples to confirm their hypothesised rule, and/or whether they would produce triples that attempted to disconfirm their hypothesised rule. The correct answer is 'any ascending sequence', but people rarely manage to derive this rule (only around 20 per cent of people arrive at this answer). The vast majority of people produce an overly restrictive rule, such as 'numbers increasing by two'.

Wason found that people who solved the task produced not only more triples but triples with more variation. Non-solvers of the task tended to produce fewer triples, and their triples did not vary as much in terms of what they tested. For example, they might suggest triples of 12–14–16 and 20–22–24 if they hypothesised a rule along the lines of 'ascending numbers increasing by two'. If they tried a triple of (for example) 8–21–52 they would find that such a triple also received positive feedback; but they would be less likely to try it because it would invalidate their hypothesised rule. The majority of people seek to confirm their hypotheses and fail to look for evidence that might disconfirm their hypotheses, thereby showing 'confirmation bias'.

Confirmation bias is very strong and has been found in a variety of research related to the 2–4–6 task (e.g. Mynatt et al., 1977). Even when participants are given explicit instructions to use a non-confirmatory strategy to test their rules, performance does not seem to improve (Tweney et al., 1980). However, it seems that the confirmation bias can be removed, in the 2–4–6 task at least, by altering the instructions. In the final study of Tweney et al. (1980), participants were given a 'dual-goal' task – being asked to discover two rules rather than one. The first rule was called the Dax rule and was the same as that in the Wason task (triples containing an ascending sequence of numbers) and the second rule was called the Med rule (all other triples). They were given an example of a triple that fitted the Dax rule (2–4–6). Even though this task was much the same as that of Wason (1960), success rates rose dramatically. Why should this be the case? Various reasons have been put forward, but this is a question that is arguably still unanswered in the reasoning literature. Nevertheless, these studies show that under normal circumstances people do not seek to disconfirm their hypotheses, yet they can do when circumstances are presented that encourage them to do so.

CHAPTER SUMMARY

6.4 We have now covered a variety of perspectives on thought. In the problem solving section we looked at Newell and Simon's (1972) influential theory of problem solving and then saw how this theory has influenced subsequent ones, not only the ACT–R theory (e.g. Anderson, 1993) but also contemporary theories of insight problem solving. We also looked at different types of reasoning (probabilistic, deductive, inductive) and illustrated how and why we can find reasoning about the world difficult. You have been provided with many fundamental areas of thought, and knowledge of these areas will be invaluable to you not only for comprehending the basics but also if you now seek to explore further information in these areas.

 ## DISCUSSION QUESTIONS: CONFIRMATORY BIAS

If we have a bias towards confirming our hunches and beliefs, then this bias might well affect the ways that people carry out their work.

Consider the way you study. See whether you can identify examples of where you have unwittingly been influenced by the confirmatory bias.

Consider also one or more of the following: (1) how doctors make a diagnosis; (2) the way police investigate crime; and (3) the way psychologists collect evidence. How do you think confirmatory bias might affect these practices? How could confirmatory bias be challenged or prevented?

 # SUGGESTIONS FOR FURTHER READING

Anderson, J.R. (2000). *Cognitive psychology and its implications* (5th edn). New York: Worth. A good cognitive psychology text that has chapters on problem solving and reasoning.

Eysenck, M.W., & Keane, M.T. (2005). *Cognitive psychology: a student's handbook* (5th edn). Hove: Psychology Press. Comprehensive text on cognitive psychology that includes problem solving and reasoning. A good source of material for the beginner wishing to learn more about cognitive psychology.

Mayer, R.E. (2005). *Thinking, problem solving, cognition* (3rd edn). New York: Freeman. A comprehensive review of the literature that covers most of the topics in this chapter in great depth plus related areas such as analogical problem solving.

Parkin, A.J. (2000). *Essential cognitive psychology*. Hove: Psychology Press. An easy to read book that covers all of the fundamental areas of cognitive psychology including problem solving and reasoning.

Robertson, S.I. (2001). *Problem solving*. Hove: Psychology Press. An in-depth examination of problem solving, covering search spaces, heuristics, insight and much more.

✓ ANSWERS TO PROBLEMS

Cryptarithmetic

G=1, O=2, B=3, A=4, D=5, N=6, R=7, L=8, E=9, T=0

Matchstick algebra

VI=III+III

Eight coin

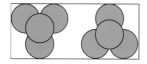

HOW OUR BRAINS AFFECT OUR BEHAVIOUR

Biological Psychology

My brain ... that's my second favourite organ!' says Woody Allen (in *Sleeper*, 1973), and who can disagree with him? What a fantastic thing the brain is. It creates for us an amazing array of sounds, smells and tastes. It thinks, it remembers, it feels and it communicates. The more you think about it, the more remarkable it becomes. Roger Sperry, who was awarded a Nobel Prize for his work on brains, commented:

> Prior to the advent of brain, there was no color and no sound in the universe, nor was there any flavor or aroma and probably rather little sense and no feeling or emotion. Before brains the universe was also free of pain and anxiety. (1964: 2)

This is a remarkable quote, and one that is quite hard to digest. One of the things he is saying is that there is no such thing as sound. What happens is that there are changes in air pressure caused by movement. Over the course of evolution we have developed a sense to detect very small changes in air pressure. This is useful because the creatures that can detect movement are most likely to be able to run away from bigger and hungrier creatures. We detect these changes through our ears, and our brains have transformed changes in air pressure into the phenomenon we call sound. You might think that Susan Boyle ('Britain's Got Talent' contestant, probably long forgotten before this book hits the shelves) is making the music, but really she is just creating changes in air pressure and your brain is doing most of the work converting it into sound.

The discovery that the brain is the main controller of behaviour and experience was relatively recent. It is commonly dated to Franz Josef Gall (1758–1828) who was a pioneer in the field. Unfortunately he blotted his copybook, and these days is remembered more for inventing the bogus pseudoscience of phrenology (studying bumps on the head). After Gall it was clear that the brain could control our movements and our bodily functions. The next big breakthrough for our understanding came with the work of Paul Broca (1824–1880) who was able to show that a small area of the brain is responsible for the production of speech. Damage to this area renders a person speechless even though they can still understand the spoken word. This area is still referred to as Broca's area. The striking discovery here is that the brain is also clearly important in cognitive functions such as thought and language, which seems obvious to us but was a major breakthrough.

Since then the brain has been enthusiastically studied and we can now connect a number of cognitive processes to specific parts of the brain. However, some of the work has been surprisingly disappointing: for example, the attempt by Karl Lashley (1890–1959) to look for the part of the brain responsible for memory. Despite decades of work with rats in which he systematically removed parts of their brains to observe the effects on their memory, he was unable to find a specific site. He eventually proposed the law of mass action, which states that the decline in performance of the animal is related to the amount of brain tissue that is removed rather than which bit is removed. This shows that although we talk about having a memory, there is no evidence that such a thing exists in the brain. We have found parts of the brain that affect our ability to recall faces or events or maps, but we have not been able to find a part of the brain that would correspond to a computer hard drive. In other words, we remember things but we don't have a part of the brain that we can identify as the memory store.

A brain looking at a brain
© Hill Street Studios/Blend Images/Corbis

The past hundred years has seen an explosion in brain research and we now know a lot more about how the brain is wired and how it influences our behaviour. Most recently the development of a range of scanning techniques has allowed us to observe the brain while it is actually working. Despite all this research, the big questions still remain unanswered. In particular, what makes the collection of chemicals and cells in the brain become the reflective, thinking, feeling organism that is aware of itself and able to act and make choices? We have discovered many remarkable things about our brains – and this itself is one of the most remarkable phenomena. When we study the brain, who and what is studying who and what? At one level we might suggest that the brain is studying the brain. This is very puzzling, and we recommend you don't spend too long thinking about it.

KEY ISSUES

Biological psychology has an underlying assumption that people are biological machines. These biological machines are made up of chemicals and cells which control our thoughts, feelings and behaviour. This assumption allows us to research the brain and develop models of the effect it has on our behaviour and experience. The main problem with the model is that it does not match our experience of being alive. We might say 'I love you' to someone, but never 'my attachment neurons fire more strongly when I see you'.

The machine model leads us to some strange contradictions. Look at the following quote from physiological psychologist Peter Milner:

> I am interested in organisms as pieces of machinery, and I would like to know much the same about them as I once wanted to know about the gadgets I saw around me: first, what happens when the controls or inputs are manipulated and, a little later, how it happens. (1970: 1)

If I went to my doctor and said, 'I feel like a machine. I am a gadget. One of my bits is going wrong, could you fix it please', the doctor might regard this statement as a sign of my mental instability and immediately send for the straightjacket. If, on the other hand, I make this statement to a conference of psychologists, and make it not about myself but about 'people', then I can be hailed as a scientific genius.

THIS SECTION

In this section we have three chapters looking at the biology of the brain. Chapter 7 presents an overview of how the human brain is organised in terms of its different structures and their various functions. Chapter 8 describes how information is processed within the brain to enable it to function. Chapter 9 discusses how the brain interacts with behaviour, using sex as an example.

7 THE HUMAN NERVOUS SYSTEM: FUNCTIONAL ANATOMY

Lead authors **Antonio Castro** and **Mark J.T. Sergeant**

CHAPTER OUTLINE

7.1 Introduction

Framing questions

7.2 Overview of the nervous system
    7.2.1 General divisions within the nervous system
    7.2.2 Neuroanatomical directions and planes

7.3 Central nervous system
    7.3.1 The brain
    7.3.2 Telencephalon (division 1)
    7.3.3 Diencephalon (division 2)
    7.3.4 Midbrain (division 3)
    7.3.5 Metencephalon (division 4)
    7.3.6 Myelencephalon (division 5)
    7.3.7 Spinal cord
    7.3.8 Protection of the central nervous system

7.4 Peripheral nervous system
    7.4.1 Somatic nervous system
    7.4.2 Autonomic nervous system

7.5 Chapter summary

Discussion questions

Suggestions for further reading

Answers to problems

INTRODUCTION

7.1

The remarkable organ at the top of our necks is responsible for giving us the rich experience that we call consciousness. This sense of consciousness involves thoughts, feelings, memories and perceptions. Some of these experiences of the world come from direct contact with the environment. For example, if someone stands on your toe, a message is passed from your toe to your brain and you have a sensation of pain.

The way the message is passed to your brain, and the way that you process that message and respond to it, are of interest to biological psychologists. Not all processes in the brain involve contact with the environment: for example, we can happily sit with our eyes closed creating a visual scene from our imagination and having a strong emotional response to it. The organ that allows us to do this is the brain. The brain also sorts out the complicated stuff of staying alive without us having to worry about it: we are able to breathe, maintain our heart rate, get about in the world and eat, for example, without having to be taught how to do it or think much about it.

The more you think about the brain and its processes, the more remarkable it appears. All these processes require some biological basis for them to exist and this is what biological psychologists study. The structure of the nervous system has evolved over millions of years and it has developed some remarkable specialisations. What started out as a collection of cells in a simple creature has evolved into the complex human brain made up of 100 billion neurones each connected to hundreds of other cells, as well as trillions of support cells. The part of the nervous system that processes information and takes decisions is anatomically quite different from the part that interacts with the outside world.

This chapter covers the basics of biological psychology and focuses in particular on the physical layout of neuroanatomical structures as well as on their functions. To help you achieve an understanding of the biological bases of behaviour, the next section provides an overview outlining the general layout of the nervous system and some key neuroanatomical terms, which are particularly useful in describing the location of various structures within the nervous system.

Equipped with this knowledge, it will be easier for you to gain an insight about the five major divisions of the brain and an appreciation for the spinal cord. You will also learn about the four ways in which the central nervous system is protected from hazard. And the chapter will end with an account of the somatic and autonomic divisions of the peripheral nervous system with which we regulate the functioning of internal organs and interrelate with the external environment.

? FRAMING QUESTIONS

How can you find your way around the nervous system?
Which brain regions control which behaviours?
How well protected is the central nervous system?
What systems allow the brain to interact with the environment?

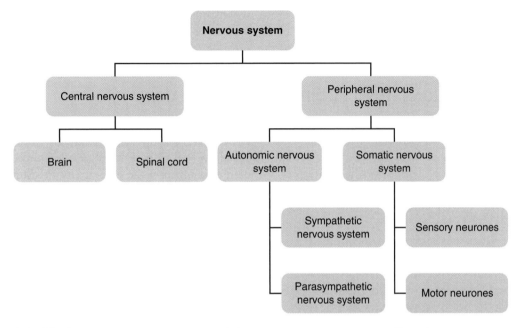

FIGURE 7.1 The hierarchical structure of the nervous system: a system of 'twos'

7.2 OVERVIEW OF THE NERVOUS SYSTEM

7.2.1 GENERAL DIVISIONS WITHIN THE NERVOUS SYSTEM

The human nervous system is largely considered to be a system of twos as it is composed of two divisions: the central nervous system (CNS) and the peripheral nervous system (PNS) (Figure 7.1). The central nervous system itself can be subdivided into the brain and spinal cord. The peripheral nervous system, which conveys messages to and from the central nervous system, has two parts as well: the somatic division and the autonomic division.

Furthermore, the somatic nervous system consists of cranial nerves and spinal nerves that can be either sensory or motor, and the autonomic nervous system has sympathetic nerves and parasympathetic nerves.

The brain is the part of the central nervous system located within the skull. It processes information received by the spinal cord and cranial nerves, thinks, takes decisions and is capable of experiencing emotions. It also sends action commands to the peripheral nervous system which may or may not travel through the spinal cord.

The spinal cord is the part of the central nervous system located within the spinal or vertebral column. It passes on the motor commands received from the brain to the muscles, transmits sensory information received from receptors to the brain, and is also capable of responding directly to sensory stimuli by means of spinal reflexes.

The peripheral nervous system is the means by which human beings are able to interact with the world. Thanks to the somatic nervous system we can act on and be influenced by the external environment, and thanks to the autonomic nervous system we are able to regulate the internal environment (i.e. glandular activity and internal organ functioning).

7.2.2 NEUROANATOMICAL DIRECTIONS AND PLANES

Neuroanatomy is much easier to understand when you know some basic terminology used to describe the position of areas, structures, nuclei and nerves in the nervous system. These terms are as useful as the terminology that would allow you to find the student union in your university campus or the location of the main post office in the nearest city to your home. Hence, learning neuroanatomy is much like finding your way when you are out and about. Once you become familiar with these terms, you will find it easier to understand and remember how the nervous system is arranged.

When describing the location of a particular area of brain, we will be using the terminology described in Table 7.1. All these terms are used in a relative sense. For example, the brain structure called the hypothalamus is said to be ventral to the thalamus but dorsal to the pituitary gland. Now see whether you can work out where these three structures are in relation to each other (answer at end of this chapter).

The direction in which the information flows is also important in neuroanatomy as it gives you an idea about the sort of information that is being carried and the type of nerve that is being used. Nerves or tracts that carry messages towards a given structure are said to be *afferent*; those that carry messages away from the structure are said to be *efferent*; and if the structure is not mentioned, you should assume that the statement is made in reference to the central nervous system. For example, afferent projections or neurons carry information to the central nervous system, so these are potentially sensory nerves; and efferent projections or neurons carry information from the central nervous system, which makes them potentially motor nerves. We can have sensory neurons and motor neurons in the same nerve and this would make it a mixed nerve.

TABLE 7.1   Terms for anatomical directions and locations

Term	Meaning
Dorsal	Towards the top or above for brain Back for brain stem and spinal cord
Ventral	Towards the bottom or below for brain Front for brain stem and spinal cord
Medial	Towards the middle
Lateral	Towards one side
Ipsilateral	Towards the same side
Contralateral	Towards the opposite side
Bilateral	On both sides
Proximal	Close together
Distal	Far apart
Anterior	Towards front
Posterior	Towards back

ASIDE   Making sense of terms, or, why do I have to learn all this?

As perhaps you are discovering, there is a good deal of specialist terminology in biological psychology. To enable scientists of all nationalities to communicate there needs to be a common set of terms. It just so happens that the terminology was developed in the days when Greek and Latin dominated the language of science. The names for brain areas were often simple descriptions of their appearance: for example, the brain region called the **hippocampus** was so named because it resembles a seahorse in appearance (from *hippo,* the Greek for 'horse' and *kampus,* the Greek for 'sea monster'). Without these common terms there would be little communication possible. For example, two students observing slices of rat brains under a microscope were overheard. One was suggesting that they start their investigation at the 'pepperami' and stop at the 'dickie bow'. These terms may have provided an accurate pictorial description of the areas being examined, but it is unlikely that if these students had written down their method using these terms, everyone would understand them.

It is difficult for students not familiar with ancient Greek or Latin to learn these terms because we don't know the references that would have originally made sense. There is no easy way around this; you just have to learn them. For some words you can take an educated guess, for example 'subcortical' means below the cortex in the same way that 'submarine' means under the sea and 'subway' means under the road. You can guess where the hypothalamus is because 'hypo' also means below, so it is below the thalamus, in the way that 'hypodermic' means below the skin.

When it comes to observing particular brain structures it is common practice, in order to keep matters simple, for most neuroanatomists to convert three-dimensional parts of the nervous system (the dimensions being height, width and depth) into two-dimensional images (e.g. just height and width). This seems like a sensible thing to do if you want to make something more practically manageable. In effect, this practice provides us with an anatomical map: that is, a limited, two-dimensional representation of a three-dimensional world. Anatomical planes can be as useful as geographical maps when you are trying to find your way around. The neuroanatomical planes are illustrated in Figure 7.2.

Different neuroanatomical planes denote different orientations or perspectives of the nervous system, and there are three main planes: the sagittal plane, the coronal plane and the horizontal plane. A sagittal plane cuts the brain vertically, perpendicularly to the long axis of the body, and divides it into left and right parts. Using this type of plane, it is possible to see anterior and posterior areas as well as dorsal and ventral areas, but it is not feasible to see both **cerebral hemispheres** of the brain at once. All but one of the sagittal sections are actually parasagittal sections; they cut through just one hemisphere. The sagittal section that severs the brain between the two hemispheres is called a midsagittal section. Hence, to see and compare both hemispheres, one would have to look at more than one sagittal image or apply one of the other two main planes.

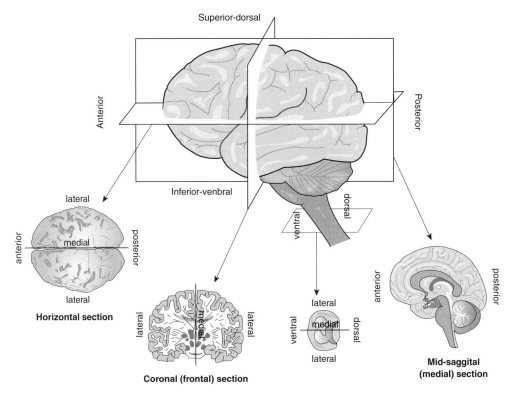

FIGURE 7.2 Neuroanatomical directions and planes. Adapted from www.homepage. smc.edu/russell_richard/Psychz/Graphics/human_brain_directions.htm

Cerebral hemispheres The right and left halves of the most anterior part of the brain. They play a primary role in most of our mental abilities, such as language, attention and perception. This is another example of the nervous system being a system of twos.

Choosing which plane to look at depends on the structure you want to see. For example a coronal plane cuts the nervous system vertically, perpendicularly to the sagittal plane, and produces an anterior or a posterior section. Using a coronal plane it is possible to see dorsal and ventral areas as well as medial and lateral areas, but it is not possible to see anterior and posterior areas of the brain in the same coronal section. To view anterior and posterior areas, it would be necessary to look at a succession of coronal sections or choose one of the other two main planes.

Finally, a horizontal plane cuts the brain at a right angle to the spinal cord and produces an upper and lower part. Using this type of plane it is possible to see anterior and posterior areas as well as medial and lateral areas, but not dorsal (top) and ventral (bottom) areas. To see these areas of the brain, one would have to look at more than one horizontal image or apply one of the other two main planes. You cannot lose a dimension and expect no drawbacks; simplicity has its price and its advantages.

7.3 CENTRAL NERVOUS SYSTEM

7.3.1 THE BRAIN

To understand how the brain is divided into five divisions, it helps to look at brain development from conception. In the fourth week after conception, the neural tube which will later become the human brain develops three swellings (also known as **vesicles**). These primary swellings are the **forebrain, midbrain** and **hindbrain** (Figure 7.3). A week later, week 5 of gestation, two of these divisions subdivide into two other subdivisions. The forebrain gives rise to the telencephalon and diencephalon, the midbrain remains undivided, and the hindbrain gives rise to the metencephalon and myelencephalon – resulting in five divisions altogether. This section will outline these five divisions and their functions.

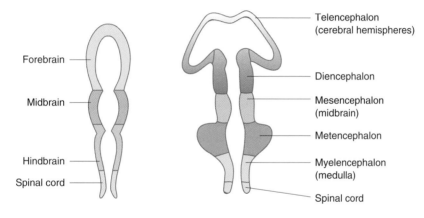

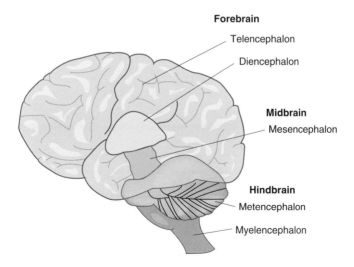

FIGURE 7.3 Divisions within the brain   (Dr Worm)

It is worth noting that the higher in the brain a structure is positioned in terms of brain divisions, the more complex is its function. The more complex brain processes are often referred to as higher-order functions (such as problem solving, planning and using language) as opposed to basic functions (such as breathing or moving).

7.3.2 TELENCEPHALON (DIVISION 1)

The telencephalon is the most anterior (furthest forward) of the five divisions within the brain and one of the two divisions of the forebrain. It includes the cerebral cortex, the limbic system and the basal ganglia.

Cerebral cortex

The **cerebral cortex** surrounds the telencephalon and is deeply convoluted or wrinkled. These convolutions considerably enlarge the surface area of the cortex, which is approximately 2500 cm². However, it is these very wrinkles that are responsible for higher mental processes. In this context, deep clefts or grooves are called fissures and shallower clefts are known as *sulci* (singular 'sulcus'). Ridges or bulges between grooves are called *gyri* (singular 'gyrus'). One of the most prominent fissures in the cerebral cortex, the longitudinal fissure, separates the left hemisphere from the right hemisphere. The two hemispheres are nearly, but not completely, symmetrical. They are connected by axons and these neuronal axons are grouped into bundles called *commissures*.

The largest commissure in the brain is the **corpus callosum**, connecting the two hemispheres (Figure 7.4). This makes it possible for each of the hemispheres to know what

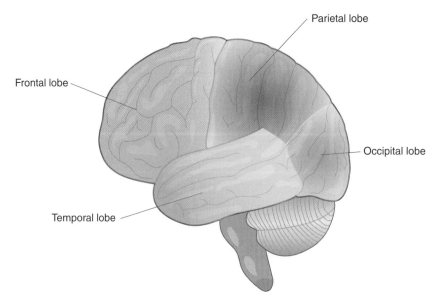

FIGURE 7.4 Lobes of the cerebral cortex   (Dr Worm)

the other hemisphere is up to and for the two hemispheres to cooperate with each other. However, some functions are located primarily in one side of the brain (and this is referred to as functional laterality). For example, in most people the left hemisphere specialises in language functions and the right hemisphere is better in visual-spatial functions. Because cell bodies predominate in the cerebral cortex, the outer surface of both hemispheres has a greyish appearance: hence the term 'grey matter'. Beneath the cerebral cortex, it is a quite different story; there, fast-conducting myelinated axons with their characteristic opaque white appearance outnumber cell bodies: hence the term 'white matter'.

KEY STUDY Bryden, M.P., & MacRae, L. (1989). Dichotic laterality effects obtained with emotional words. *Neuropsychiatry, Neuropsychology, and Behavioral Neurology, 1* (3), 171–176.

Bryden and MacRae in 1989 published a neat research study that illustrates a body of research that has investigated the hemispheric lateralisation of language and emotion in the normal human brain. The authors used a behavioural technique known as the dichotic listening task, which involves presenting different stimuli (such as words) simultaneously to each ear via headphones. In this case the experimental stimuli consisted of four similar sounding words (power, bower, dower and tower) each spoken in four different emotional tones (happy, sad, angry and neutral). For example, the word 'power' spoken in a happy voice was presented to the left ear while the word 'bower' spoken in a sad voice was presented to the right ear. Participants were asked to detect either a specific word or a specific emotion.

Results revealed that when words were the target, there was a significantly greater level of accuracy if the word in question was presented to the right ear (i.e. right ear advantage for words), whereas when emotions were the target, they were more accurately detected in the left ear (i.e. left ear advantage for emotions).

Given that the auditory system is anatomically crossed, although not as completely crossed as the visual system, these results confirm that the left hemisphere is dominant for language whereas the right hemisphere is dominant or superior for emotional material.

The research also shows that the idea of functional specialisation by our cerebral hemispheres is something that, with ingenuity on the part of the researcher, can be studied in the general population using relatively inexpensive means. You may like to consider how you could explore this topic further through your studies.

The two hemispheres are each described as having four lobes: the frontal lobe, the parietal lobe, the temporal lobe and the occipital lobe. They are named after the bones of the skull that cover them. The frontal lobe is separated from the parietal lobe by the central sulcus. The temporal lobe is also clearly separated from the frontal and parietal lobes by the lateral fissure. However, the anatomical boundary between the occipital lobe and the parietal and temporal lobes is not as clearly defined.

The frontal is the largest of the four lobes and is mostly involved in planning and movement. Just anterior to the central sulcus is the precentral gyrus, which is occupied mainly by the primary motor cortex. The primary motor cortex is somatotopically organised and is involved in the initiation of voluntary movements. The fact that it is **somatotopically organised** was described beautifully by Penfield and Jasper in 1954 from their experiments during brain surgery. Patients who required surgery for medical reasons gave permission for areas of the cortex to be electrically stimulated and the resulting sensations recorded. From these experiments Penfield produced his homunculus: a cartoon representation of the localisation of areas of cortex to body parts, in which the drawn size of body part represents the amount of cortex dedicated to it rather than its physical size.

> **Somatotopical organisation** The arrangement of brain structures whereby regions of brain represent particular parts of the body. For example, when the hand area in the primary motor cortex is activated, the hand moves.

The primary motor cortex is also contralaterally organised (or cross-wired) so that we are able to move the right side of the body voluntarily thanks to the left primary motor cortex, and vice versa. In addition, those parts of the body with which we can conduct fine movements, such as with our fingers, are overrepresented in the primary motor cortex. The premotor area and the supplementary motor area, known as secondary motor areas and also located in the frontal lobe, are functionally related to the programming of specific patterns of movements.

The frontal lobe is also where Broca's area is located. This area is implicated in the production of written and spoken language. Finally, the prefrontal cortex of the frontal lobe is involved with personality and formulating plans and strategies. These functions and a change in personality were precisely those impaired in the case of a famous patient called Phineas Gage, who had his prefrontal cortex seriously damaged as a result of sustaining a penetrating brain injury caused by a tamping rod in the course of a job-related accident (Damasio et al., 1994). Medical reports at the time described a change of personality from a respectable, hardworking and energetic businessman to a profane, disrespecting, capricious and impulsive type (Harlow, 1894, in Neylan, 1999).

REASONS TO BE SCEPTICAL

Given what we know about the functions of the prefrontal cortex today, the attribution of a change in the personality of Phineas Gage to brain damage seems a sensible conclusion to draw. However, we should remember that there is only anecdotal evidence of the character of Gage prior to his injury (i.e. no reliable baseline measure) for comparison. Also, who knows what effect a near death experience might have on one's **motivation** to work hard and be a productive member of society!

The parietal lobe is posterior to the central sulcus and anterior to the occipital lobe (Figure 7.4). The postcentral gyrus in this lobe corresponds to the primary somatosensory cortex, which is where information about touch, pain, pressure, temperature and body position is initially processed in the cortex. In a similar way to the primary motor cortex, the primary somatosensory cortex is also organised somatotopically, and parts of the body where we have a very fine sense of touch, such as the hands and the mouth, are overrepresented. The parietal lobe, usually that of the left hemisphere, is also concerned with language comprehension. In addition, the posterior area of this lobe receives projections from the occipital lobe carrying visual information and is involved in spatial orientation and perception.

The temporal lobe is where the primary auditory cortex is located. This area receives auditory information from a subcortical structure, the thalamus, which will be explained later in the chapter, and it is in the primary auditory cortex that auditory information is processed for the first time in the cerebral cortex. Destruction of this area of the temporal lobe leads to cortical deafness, an inability to recognise sound despite an intact auditory system within the ear.

The posterior portion of the superior temporal gyrus, usually in the left hemisphere, is where Wernicke's area is located. This area is known to play a fundamental role in the comprehension of language. The medial part of the temporal lobe is concerned with intricate aspects of learning and memory. The ventral surface of the temporal lobe is a visual association area implicated in higher-order processing of optical information.

The main function of the occipital lobe is the analysis of visual information. The primary visual cortex, located in this lobe, receives visual information from the thalamus and is where visual information is processed for the first time in the cerebral cortex. Damage to the primary visual cortex or brain regions that project to it causes 'blindsight' – that is, an ability to see some features of the visual environment but unconsciously. Patients with blindsight will report being unable to see visual stimuli in the area of the visual field that is damaged, and yet if asked to make a guess where a stimulus is they can accurately pinpoint it 99 per cent of the time (Weiskrantz et al., 1974); this is because the more primitive visual area responsible for location (the superior colliculus in the brain stem) remains intact.

It is a pity that Weiskrantz et al. made their discoveries too late to save the injured soldiers who during the First World War (1914–1918) reported blindness but were 'found out' by neurosurgeons (and subsequently shot) because they caught a ball that was thrown towards them. It is likely that many of these poor individuals were genuinely suffering from blindsight as a result of brain injury.

The rest of the occipital lobe is referred to as the visual association cortex and is concerned with more complex analysis of visual information.

KEY RESEARCHER   Vilayanur S. Ramachandran

Ramachandran is Director of the Centre for Brain and Cognition and Professor in the Psychology Department and Neurosciences Programme at the University of California in the United States. He studied for an MD at Stanley Medical College in India, where he was

(Cont'd)

FIGURE 7.5 Vilayanur
S. Ramachandran

born, and subsequently moved to England where he obtained a PhD from Trinity College at the University of Cambridge. Before becoming Professor at the University of California, he also spent some time as a postdoctoral fellow at Oxford University.

Most of his academic life has been dedicated to the study of visual perception and neurological syndromes such as phantom limbs, synesthesia and autism. For example, in the area of phantom limbs he is credited with introducing the use of visual feedback as a treatment for the pain that is often associated with this condition. The way in which he went about doing this was theoretically well informed and quite ingenious.

Ramachandran hypothesised that the paralysis experienced by patients with phantom limbs is due to visual and proprioception feedback received by the brain when trying to move the phantom limb. Basically, the brain gives repeated orders to move but the phantom limb refuses. To resolve this learned paralysis, he invented a mirror box (yes, just a box with a mirror inside) and asked patients to move their able arm in front of the mirror. Of course patients did so without any difficulty, and the interesting thing is that by looking at the reflection produced by the mirror box they saw and felt as if their phantom limb was back alive. The even more striking thing was that by being able to experience the imaginary limb move many of these patients stopped feeling phantom pain.

The results of this line of research and many of his other research projects have been published in over 180 scientific papers, several of them in high-impact journals such as *Nature* and *Science*. He also wrote *Phantoms in the brain* (1998) with Sandra Blakeslee and is the editor of the *Encyclopaedia of the human brain*. In 2003 he gave the BBC Reith Lectures, entitled 'The Emerging Mind' (http://www.bbc.co.uk/radio4/reith2003/) and in 2007 was conferred with the title of Padma Bhushan by the President of India. It is no surprise then that he has been called 'the Marco Polo of neuroscience' by Richard Dawkins and 'the modern Paul Broca' by Eric Kandel.

If you want to see a few of the visual illusions he discovered as part of his research on visual perception, visit http://cbc.ucsd.edu/ramaillusions.html. You can also find more about him by searching for his Facebook website. Do you think he is a researcher role model?

Limbic system

The **limbic system** is also part of the first brain division (the telencephalon) and plays a major role in emotions and memory. It includes the hippocampus, the amygdala and the cingulate gyrus. The **hippocampus**, a long and curved structure (the seahorse, remember), and the **amygdala**, a much smaller and rounded structure, are located at the base of a large cerebral cavity in the temporal lobe of both hemispheres; the amygdala is anterior to the

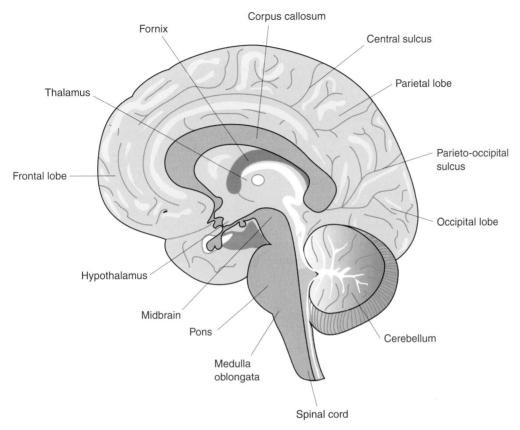

FIGURE 7.6   Sagittal section of the brain   (Dr Worm)

hippocampus. The cingulate gyrus, instead, can be found at the medial edge of the cerebral hemispheres, surrounding the corpus callosum dorsally.

The amygdala is concerned with emotional memories and emotional feelings such as fear or anger. For example, in post-traumatic stress disorder, where following trauma fear arousal is easily triggered, there is evidence of increased reactivity of the amygdala (van der Kolk & Fisler, 1995). The hippocampus plays a major role in learning and memory, particularly spatial memory. Most famously a study by Maguire et al. (2000) showed that London taxi drivers, who have to study for years to learn 'The Knowledge' of the London street plan, have enlarged areas of their hippocampus compared to other drivers. The cingulate gyrus, which has an important role in attention, is also involved in the experience of emotions.

Basal ganglia

The **basal ganglia** consist of three large hemispheric nuclei located beneath the anterior regions of the cerebral cortex. They are the caudate nucleus, the putamen and the globus pallidus. Together, the caudate nucleus and the putamen form the dorsal striatum; but the putamen and the globus pallidus form the lenticular nucleus. No, the caudate nucleus and the globus pallidus do not form any other nucleus (there is no need to complicate matters unnecessarily!), but all three nuclei form a circuit with the cortex and another brain section, the midbrain. This provides an example of how a structure can form part of more than one brain system. It demonstrates that we have imposed an order onto brain structures that suits our understanding, often based on function. Functionally, the basal ganglia are involved in the control of movement and in habit learning. They play a crucial role in the sequencing of movements and in maintaining posture and muscle tone. Degeneration of neurons in the basal ganglia is seen in Huntington's disease (Walker, 2007), a hereditary disorder of motor and intellectual function that eventually becomes terminal.

7.3.3 DIENCEPHALON (DIVISION 2)

The second division of the forebrain is the **diencephalon,** which is located between the telencephalon and the midbrain. It includes two main structures: the thalamus, a subcortical relay station, and the **hypothalamus,** a collection of nuclei that regulate the **endocrine system** and control many aspects of behaviour (Figure 7.6).

Thalamus

The **thalamus** is an oval structure in the diencephalon that is composed of many nuclei. There is one thalamus in each cerebral hemisphere, and they tend to be fused in many but not all human brains by the interthalamic adhesion or massa intermedia. As neuroanatomists do not yet know or cannot agree on what purpose this adhesion serves (it is absent in some brains), the first reader to discover its advantageous or disadvantageous function gets a prize! The nuclei of the thalamus relay sensory and motor information to different parts of the cerebral cortex. All sensory information except olfactory (smell) information reaches the cerebral cortex through the thalamus. The thalamus also relays information between cortical areas.

> **Endocrine system**   A series of small organs responsible for producing hormones that regulate a variety of processes including growth and development, metabolism and puberty.

Hypothalamus

The hypothalamus is a relatively small structure that lies under the thalamus, forming the ventral part of the diencephalon. Despite its small size, its activity has far-reaching implications across the body. The hypothalamus is involved in regulating the functioning of internal organs and takes part in many crucial aspects of motivated behaviour such as eating, drinking, sleeping and having sex. It is also involved in temperature regulation and emotional behaviour. It controls the production of hormones produced by a gland that sits just beneath it, the **pituitary gland,** and thanks to this direct influence it is able to regulate the endocrine system.

7.3.4 MIDBRAIN (DIVISION 3)

The midbrain (sometimes called **mesencephalon**) consists of two main divisions: the **tectum** and the **tegmentum.** The tectum is situated in the dorsal part of the midbrain and contains the **superior** and **inferior colliculi**. The superior colliculi, of which there are two, are part of the visual system and are primarily involved in visual reflexes such as blinking. The inferior colliculi, of which nature has also produced two, are part of the auditory system and mediate hearing-related behaviours.

Ventral to (below) the tectum is the tegmentum, the second division of the midbrain. This division is larger than the tectum and it also contains a greater number of structures, too numerous to mention here, but involved in basic behaviours such as pain perception, voluntary movement and postural adjustments. One important structure within the tegmentum is the **reticular formation**, a diffuse and interconnected network of neurons which extends beyond the tegmentum into posterior parts of the brain. Functionally, it maintains consciousness and is involved in sleep, attention and arousal.

7.3.5 METENCEPHALON (DIVISION 4)

The metencephalon is the most anterior division of the hindbrain. It consists of the **cerebellum** and the **pons**. The cerebellum is the dorsal part of the metencephalon and looks like a cauliflower. It has two hemispheres, which although much smaller than the cerebral hemispheres also present a somewhat convoluted cortex and subcortical nuclei; it is this appearance of a small cerebrum that gives its name (cerebellum).

Functionally, the cerebellum is involved in equilibrium, postural control and muscle tone as well as coordination, learning and planning of movements. It may even play a part in cognitive tasks such as attention. However, one of its main functions is the adjustment of ongoing movements. It does this by comparing the visual, auditory, vestibular and somatosensory information it receives from sense organs about movements that are being conducted with information about movements that are being intended, allowing it to make appropriate changes in real time. Damage to the cerebellum is known to result in postural defects, impaired walking and poor coordination of movements (Konczak and Timmann, 2007).

Next to the cerebellum is the pons, the second part of the metencephalon. This large bulge contains a section

> **Brain stem**   The part of the brain that regulates vital reflexes such as heart rate and respiration; it consists of the midbrain, the pons and the medulla. It is activity or the lack of it in this region that is used by medics to establish if a patient is 'brain dead'.

of the reticular formation and relays information from the cerebral cortex to the cerebellum. Many neural messages from cranial nerves and the spinal cord also pass through this hindbrain structure.

7.3.6 MYELENCEPHALON (DIVISION 5)

Finally, the most posterior part of the hindbrain and hence also the most posterior part of the brain is the myelencephalon. This is where the **brain stem** and the reticular formation end and the spinal cord begins. The myelencephalon, often called **medulla oblongata** or just medulla, is involved in fundamental functions that are essential for life: for example, respiration and the regulation of the cardiovascular system. The medulla also intervenes in reflexive responses such as coughing, salivating and vomiting, and relays sensory information received from some of the cranial nerves. It also acts as a passageway and synaptic area for some neural tracts carrying afferent information toward the brain and efferent information toward the spinal cord.

7.3.7 SPINAL CORD

The **spinal cord** is the most posterior part of the central nervous system. In adult human beings, it is about 42 to 45 cm long and about 1 cm in diameter. It consists of 31 segments systematically related to areas of skin and muscles. Sensory information from receptors enters these segments through the dorsal roots, whereas motor information destined to muscles leaves them through the ventral roots. This is known as the Bell–Magendie law.

The main function of the spinal cord is to carry sensory information to brain structures such as the thalamus, the cerebellum and the brain stem, and to carry motor information from the cerebral cortex and various brain stem nuclei towards the periphery. It may help here to think of the spinal cord as the central nervous system's motorway. However, the spinal cord is also capable of acting without the involvement of the brain. It achieves this degree of autonomy thanks to spinal reflexes such as the patellar reflex or knee-jerk reflex. These stereotyped responses to sensory input allow quick reactions without conscious analysis, leaving the brain free to concentrate on other tasks.

The ascending and descending myelinated tracts (see Chapter 8) form the spinal cord's white matter. The neuronal cell bodies and short, unmyelinated axons form the spinal cord's grey matter. So the spinal cord, as the brain, has grey and white matter. However, whereas the grey matter is on the outer part and the white matter is on the inner part of the brain, in the spinal cord the white matter is on the outer side and the grey matter is in the inner side. This grey matter looks like a butterfly in a cross-section of the spinal cord.

Damage to this part of the central nervous system can cause tetraplegia or paraplegia depending on where in the spinal cord the lesion is located (Castro et al., 2007). If the lesion is localised in any of the eight cervical segments then the diagnosis will be that of **tetraplegia**; if it is localised in any of the thoracic, lumbar or sacral segments it will be a case of **paraplegia**. The damage to the spinal cord can also be complete (when no sensory or motor signals cross the injured area) or incomplete (when some neural signals are able to pass through). The degree of functional impairment is greater in cases where the damage is complete and located in any of the eight cervical segments.

Tetraplegia   Paralysis characterised by inability to move and/or feel the lower part and most of the upper part of the body, secondary to damage in the cervical segments of the spinal cord.

Paraplegia   Paralysis characterised by failure to move and/or feel the lower part of the body due to damage in the thoracic, lumbar or sacral segments of the spinal cord.

7.3.8 PROTECTION OF THE CENTRAL NERVOUS SYSTEM

Owing to their crucial importance for normal life, the brain and spinal cord are the most preciously protected divisions of the nervous system. They are encased in bone, surrounded by three membranes and washed in **cerebrospinal fluid**; the brain is further protected by the **blood–brain barrier**. These means, which defend the central nervous system from injury and infection, are explained below in greater detail.

The brain is protected from injury by the skull or cranium, a bony structure resulting from the fusion of a number of bones. The spinal cord is enclosed in the spinal column or backbone. This protective and long formation consists of 24 interlocking bones called vertebrae as well as the fused bones of the sacral and coccygeal areas.

Between the skull and the brain, and between the spinal column and the spinal cord, there are three layers of connective tissue which offer a second level of protection to the central nervous system. These protective sheaths or membranes are called **meninges**. The outermost meninx is the dura matter, which is thick, tough and flexible but non-stretchable; it encloses the central nervous system in a somewhat loose sack. The middle meninx, soft and spongy, is the arachnoid. And between the arachnoid and the pia mater, which is the innermost meninx, lies the **subarachnoid space**, which is filled with cerebrospinal fluid. The pia mater, thin and delicate, is the membrane that adheres closely to the surface of the brain and spinal cord.

The inflammation or infection of any or all of these meninges is called meningitis. This condition is caused by bacteria, viruses, fungi or parasites and may include symptoms such as severe headache, stiff neck, fever and intense sensitivity to light (Chávez-Bueno & McCracken, 2005). It can be life threatening if not treated promptly with appropriate medication.

An additional level of protection in the central nervous system is provided by the ventricular system and cerebrospinal fluid. The ventricular system consists of four **ventricles**, which are a series of interconnected chambers within the brain. All four ventricles are filled with cerebrospinal fluid. This fluid is a colourless solution extracted from the blood that resembles blood plasma in its composition. It is produced continuously by the choroid plexus of each ventricle and flows through the ventricular system, the subarachnoid space and the central canal of the spinal cord until it is finally reabsorbed by the blood supply.

From a functional point of view, the cerebrospinal fluid plays a mechanically supportive role and acts as a shock absorber. It may also constitute a medium for the exchange of materials, such as nutrients and metabolic waste, between blood vessels and the brain, and for neuroactive hormones to flow within the nervous system.

Finally, blood vessel walls in the brain are much more tightly packed than in the rest of the body. Additionally a type of glial cell called an astrocyte sends out fatty protrusions that wrap around the capillaries and neurones, preventing substances from diffusing across the cell membrane. This is what is known as the blood–brain barrier. This barrier mechanism prevents the passage of many molecules from the blood into the brain and hence protects the brain from many chemical substances, some of which would be toxic to the brain. Because of the fatty composition of the glial protrusions, lipid soluble molecules, such as nicotine and caffeine, are able to pass through the barrier relatively easily, whereas water soluble molecules such as sodium and potassium ions find it much more difficult.

PERIPHERAL NERVOUS SYSTEM

7.4

The second major division of the nervous system is the peripheral nervous system, through which human beings interact with the environment by conveying messages to and from the central nervous system. It consists of the somatic nervous system and the autonomic nervous system.

7.4.1 SOMATIC NERVOUS SYSTEM

The **somatic nervous system** receives input in the form of sensory information from receptors and sends output in the form of motor commands to skeletal muscles; it comprises cranial nerves and spinal nerves.

Cranial nerves

Twelve pairs of nerves enter or leave the human brain through small openings in the skull or cranium and can be found on the ventral surface of the brain; they are the **cranial nerves**. All but the vagus nerve (or cranial nerve X as it is sometimes mysteriously called) serve sensory and/or motor functions of the head and neck. The vagus nerve, instead, wanders around the body and carries information to and from thoracic and abdominal organs including the heart, liver and intestines.

Spinal nerves

As described earlier in the chapter, dorsal and ventral roots emerge from spinal cord segments. The ventral roots are formed by axons of neurons whose cell bodies are contained within the grey matter of the spinal cord, whereas the dorsal roots are formed by axons of neurons whose cell bodies are grouped outside the spinal cord, in the dorsal root ganglia. It is the merger of these dorsal and ventral roots that gives rise to the 31 pairs of **spinal nerves** present in the human body. Each one of these pairs leaves the vertebral column at regularly spaced intervals through the intervertebral foramen of the spinal column, with one of the members destined to the right side of the body and the other destined to the left side of the body. Afferent axons bundled in them carry information to the brain from sensory receptors found in areas of the body covered by strips of skin called dermatomes, whereas efferent axons carry information from the brain, innervating muscles and glands, also in a systematic way.

> ### EXERCISE   How sensitive are you?
>
> Skin contains many sensory receptors such as pain, touch, pressure and heat receptors. They convey sensation via peripheral sensory nerves to the cortex to enable behavioural response to environmental stimuli. These sensory receptors are present in varying concentrations: for example, areas such as hands and face have far more touch receptors per square centimetre than areas such as arms or legs. This is of course

related to the function of body areas (for example, we explore fine detail with our finger-tips, not elbows).

You can demonstrate this using a two-point discrimination test on a friend. Bend a paperclip into the shape of a U with the tips about 2 cm apart and level with each other. Get your participant to close their eyes (or blindfold them if you don't trust them not to peep). *Lightly* touch the two ends of the paper clip to the back of their hand, making sure both tips touch the skin at the same time. Ask how many points they can feel. If they report feeling two points, then gradually decrease the distance between the points until they report one point. Record this distance. Conversely if the participant could only feel one point at 2 cm apart, then widen the points and repeat the touch test until they can feel two. Comparing various areas of skin, you can work out which areas are most sensitive and therefore have most touch receptors.

7.4.2 AUTONOMIC NERVOUS SYSTEM

The **autonomic nervous system** regulates glandular activity and the functioning of internal organs. It consists of a **parasympathetic division** and a **sympathetic division**.

Parasympathetic nervous system

The parasympathetic division of the autonomic nervous system is generally involved in activities of rest or recovery that preserve or increase energy levels in the body. These activities include salivation, gastric and intestinal motility, decreased cardiac output and blood pressure, as well as constriction of the pupils and bladder contraction.

Sympathetic nervous system

Sympathetic nerves are more widely distributed than parasympathetic nerves and generally (but not exclusively) have the opposite function, in that the sympathetic nervous system is involved in activities that require expenditure of energy. These activities can be triggered by conditions that promote arousal and many of them prepare the organism to respond to situations perceived as dangerous – what is often called the 'fight or flight' response. For example, when you are in actual or perceived danger, your sympathetic nervous system will generate an increase in heart rate and respiration, dilate your pupils and divert blood from the skin and gut to skeletal muscles (so that you can leg it or fight if necessary). The sympathetic nervous system is involved in all kinds of arousal, not just fear, and so you may recognise many of these symptoms for example when you are physically attracted to someone.

CHAPTER SUMMARY

7.5

The two divisions of the human nervous system are the central nervous system and the peripheral nervous system. The central nervous system consists of the brain and spinal cord. The brain enables us to think, take decisions, experience emotions and move voluntarily. It consists of the telencephalon, which includes the cerebral cortex, the limbic system and the basal ganglia; the diencephalon, which comprises the thalamus and hypothalamus; the midbrain or mesencephalon, which contains the tectum and tegmentum; the metencephalon, which includes the pons and the cerebellum; and the myelencephalon. The spinal cord, which is divided into segments each representing an area of skin (dermatome), conveys motor commands from the brain to the muscles and transmits sensory information from receptors to the brain.

The brain and spinal cord are the most protected divisions of the nervous system. They are encased in the skull and the spinal column; are covered by three membranes called meninges and are washed in cerebrospinal fluid. The brain is further protected by the blood–brain barrier.

The second division of the human nervous system, the peripheral nervous system, conveys messages to and from the central nervous system. It consists of the somatic nervous system with which we interact with the external environment, and the autonomic nervous system with which we regulate the functioning of internal organs. The somatic nervous system consists of 12 pairs of cranial nerves and 31 pairs of spinal nerves, whereas the autonomic nervous system has a parasympathetic division, which is largely involved in building up energy levels and preserving energy, and a sympathetic division, which is generally involved in expending energy.

DISCUSSION QUESTIONS

During this chapter we have examined the structure and function of various brain systems: for example, the limbic system is involved in emotion. How far do you think that knowledge takes us in understanding our behaviour and emotions? What other information would we need to consider? When you feel happy, for example, at one level that could be described as activity in regions of the brain involved in reward, but what other levels of explanation might come into play?

SUGGESTIONS FOR FURTHER READING

Carlson, N.R. (2007). *Physiology of behavior.* Boston: Pearson. Chapter 3. This text uses easily accessible language and explanations.

Haines, D.E. (1991). *Neuroanatomy: an atlas of structures, sections and systems* (3rd edn). Baltimore: Urban & Schwarzenberg. This atlas contains illustrations of brain structures and pictures of brain scans in full colour.

Kolb, B., & Whishaw, I.Q. (2003). *Fundamentals of human neuropsychology.* New York: Worth. Chapter 3. This text is more detailed than most of the introductory biological psychology texts.

Nolte, J. (1999). *The human brain: an introduction to its functional anatomy.* St Louis: Mosby. This whole book is devoted to anatomy and so is far more detailed than the general texts.

Pinel, J.P.J. (2006). *Biopsychology.* Boston: Pearson. Chapter 3. Of the introductory biological psychology texts, this one is particularly good on anatomy.

Rosenzweig, M.R., Breedlove, S.M., & Watson, N.V. (2005). *Biological psychology: an introduction to behavioral and cognitive neuroscience.* Sunderland, MA: Sinauer. Chapter 2. This text is rich on detail.

Witelson, S.F., Kigar, D.L., & Harvey, T. (1999). The exceptional brain of Albert Einstein. *Lancet, 353,* 2149–2153. An interesting article on the great man.

✓ ANSWERS TO PROBLEMS

The hypothalamus is below the thalamus and above the pituitary gland, i.e. it is between the two.

8 COMMUNICATION WITHIN THE BRAIN

Lead authors **Rachel R. Horsley** and **Christine Norman**

INTRODUCTION

8.1

When you are awake, your brain generates 25 watts of power – which is enough to power a light bulb. That energy comes from all the activity of sending and receiving messages between the 100,000,000,000 cells that make up your brain. In the previous chapter we took a brief tour of the main structures of the nervous system. Now it is time to examine how information is transported around those systems in order to achieve their various functions.

At its most basic, the brain's purpose is to monitor and respond to the environment. It receives information from its surroundings, processes it and signals the body to respond; but how does the nervous system communicate this information? In this chapter we will find out, by examining the processes of communication of information within and between neurones (brain cells). In addition, we will outline the major neurotransmitter (brain chemical) systems and examples of how drugs can produce their effects by acting on these processes.

FRAMING QUESTIONS

What types of cells make up the nervous system?
How is information handled within and between cells in the nervous system?
How do drugs interact with the natural chemistry of the brain?
Will you be the same person after reading this chapter?

8.2 CELLS IN THE NERVOUS SYSTEM

8.2.1 NEURONAL CELLS

The mature brain is composed of approximately 100 billion individual neurones (specialised brain cells). The function of the neurone is to transmit information, in the form of electrochemical signals, around the brain. It receives the signal at one end, conducts the signal along its length and transmits it to the next neurone from the other end. These processes will be described in detail, but first it is helpful to look at the anatomical and functional characteristics of two different types of cells found in the brain: neurones and glial cells.

All **neurones** follow the same basic design (see Figure 8.1). The five gross components of a typical neurone are dendrites, soma, axon, axonal branches and synaptic buttons. Here we will consider each of these in turn.

Dendrites form a major receiving part of neurones: they can be thought of as extensions of the soma (cell body) because the soma itself is also capable of receiving input from other neurones. Dendrites most likely evolved to increase the receptive surface of the soma, so

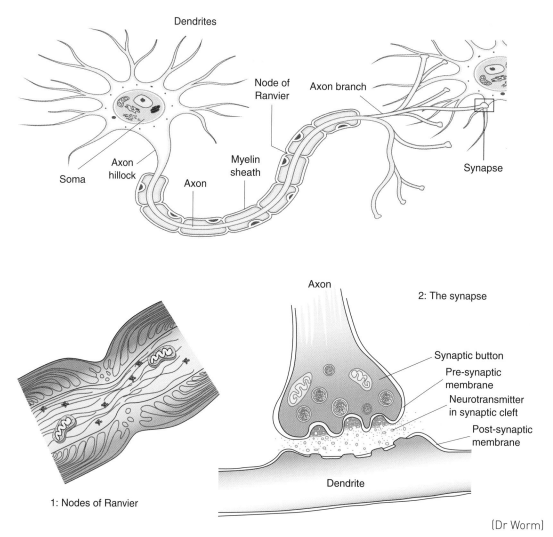

(Dr Worm)

FIGURE 8.1   The neurone. Dendrites are branch-like structures that emanate from the soma (cell body). Their role is to receive information from other neurones in the form of chemical messages, convert these chemical messages into electrical impulses and convey them towards the soma. The axon then conveys electrical information away from the soma towards the axonal branches and synaptic buttons. When the electrical information reaches these, it triggers the release of chemical messages (neurotransmitters) to be received by dendrites on other neurones. Inset 1: Nodes of Ranvier: unmyelinated sections of myelinated axons. Action potentials happen only at these nodes. Inset 2: The synapse: consists of the pre-synaptic membrane, the synaptic cleft and the post-synaptic membrane

neurones can receive many more synaptic inputs from other neurones than they could receive to the soma alone. In this way, a given neurone is able to integrate information from many different sources.

The **soma** is the factory of the neurone and is filled with a potassium-rich salty fluid called **cytoplasm** which contains little structures called **organelles** (little 'organs'). Each type of organelle has a specialised role, but together they provide energy, manufacture parts and form a production line to assemble the parts into completed products.

Overseeing and controlling these processes is the **nucleus**. Within the nucleus are genes consisting of **deoxyribonucleic acid** (**DNA**). Their function is to hold the cell history and the basic information to manufacture all the proteins characteristic of that cell. Such proteins are necessary for the formation and maintenance of dendrites, axons etc.

The **axon** conducts information in the form of an electrical impulse (**action potential**) that flows away from the soma towards the synaptic buttons. Axons can be very long (in some cases over a metre in length) and can carry impulses at a speed of up to 100 metres per second or more. The greater the diameter of the axon, the faster the electrical impulses will travel along it.

Another very important factor determines the speed with which axons are able to conduct impulses, namely **myelin**. Myelin is insulation around the axon deposited by specific glial cells known as **oligodendrocytes** (in the peripheral nervous system (PNS) the same job is done by **Schwann cells**). Oligodendrocytes send out flat, paddle-like processes which wrap themselves around an axon, forming a many-layered fatty sheath as an insulator. The myelin sheath is interrupted every millimetre or so by small regions of unmyelinated axon: these are known as **nodes of Ranvier** (see Figure 8.1, node of Ravier inset). The insulation of axons has three consequences: saving time, energy and space. It speeds up the conduction of nerve impulses, through a mechanism that does not require large amounts of additional space or energy. A non-myelinated axon would need to have a diameter of several centimetres in order to conduct nerve impulses as rapidly as a myelinated fibre with a diameter of just a few **micrometres**.

Synaptic buttons are located at the end of the **axonal branches** and are the terminal points of the neurone. Together the membrane of the synaptic button and that of the receiving part on the dendrite or soma of the next cell form the **synapse** (see Figure 8.1, synapse inset). The synapse is the unit of communication from one neurone to the next, but that's jumping ahead. We will look at the synapse in the next section on the transfer of information between neurones.

8.2.2 GLIAL CELLS

Glia means 'glue', and for many years scientists thought that **glial cells** performed the humble task of holding the brain together. However, they are a lot more interesting than that! Over time, it has emerged that they perform a wide variety of vital tasks in the central nervous system (CNS), having roles in providing nutrients, in managing waste, in the formation and maintenance of synapses and even in the transmission of electrical signals.

There are three main types of glial cell in the CNS. You recall oligodendrocytes that provide the myelin for neurons in the CNS. In addition, there are **astrocytes** (so called because they are star shaped). One role of astrocytes is to provide a physical support matrix – so they are the glue – but astrocytes also have a very important role in protecting the brain from toxic substances that can be found in the blood. They achieve this by the formation of the **blood–brain barrier**. Astrocytes send out processes known as glial feet to form a fatty layer of insulation around blood vessels in the brain. This fatty layer means that only substances that are fat soluble can cross into the brain. Some astrocytes are **phagocytes** and maintain the extracellular environment by clearing away debris.

Blood–brain barrier   Protective barrier between the brain and blood vessels, providing a mechanism by which certain substances are prevented from entering the brain.

Phagocytes   Cells which are able to 'swallow' and break down unwanted materials such as pathogens and cell debris.

Astrocytes also support neurons in other important ways such as supplying them with nutrients, keeping the chemical environment around them clean and healthy by absorbing waste products, and enhancing transmission of the signal from one neurone to another by surrounding and isolating synapses so that they work more effectively. **Microglia** are the in-house immune system for the CNS, e.g. they cause inflammatory response when the brain is injured. Like astrocytes, they can also be phagocytes.

ASIDE   (Bad) Biopsychology joke

How do you know when a glial cell is happy?
When its myelin.

COMMUNICATION WITHIN THE NEURONE

8.3 Here we consider how information is handled within individual neurones. The transmission of information along the neurone is a function of its structure, and so the anatomy of the neuronal membrane and the physical forces acting upon it will be described. This will show how the electrical state of the neurone membrane is maintained when it is at rest and then what happens when the resting electrical state of the neurone is disturbed. It is this change in electrical state that leads to transmission of a signal by producing an action potential.

All neurones are bounded by a membrane known as the **neurone membrane** (the external boundary to the cell, or 'skin' if you like). This is a crucial structure in determining the electrical state of the neurone. All neurones carry an electrical charge called a membrane potential. Essentially we are interested in three types of membrane potential in neurones: the resting potential, post-synaptic potentials and the action potential. To understand how the neurone membrane is involved in these potentials it is necessary to look at the anatomy of the membrane itself.

8.3.1 ANATOMY OF THE NEURONE MEMBRANE

The neurone membrane contains tiny pores known as **ion channels**. Three **ions** are central to producing resting and action potentials: two positively charged ions, **sodium** and **potassium**, and one negatively charged ion, **chloride.** Each ion has its own specialised channels, that is, potassium passes through potassium channels, chloride through chloride channels and so on. However, sodium is small enough to leak through potassium channels, the consequences of which we shall see later. Ion channels can be in one of two states: open or closed. The resting potential of the neurone membrane is largely determined by ions passing freely in and out of the neurone through permanently open channels. However, other ion channels are gated, that is, they can open and close depending on the state of the neurone membrane.

> **Ion channels**   Pores (formed by proteins) found in cell membranes that allow or restrict the passage of ions in and out of the cell.

8.3.2 MEMBRANE POTENTIALS

First we will examine the processes involved in maintaining the resting **membrane potential** (electrical charge). In a neurone at rest, the inside of the cell is −70 **millivolts (mV)** compared to the outside. This difference in voltage is what constitutes the membrane potential. The inside of the cell is more negative than the outside because the neurone contains protein molecules that are negatively charged and are too large to pass out of the cell. However, the resting potential is also dependent on the passage of ions such as sodium and potassium, in and out of the cell via the ion channels. This movement is constant and results in a **dynamic equilibrium** between positively and negatively charged elements produced by the forces of **diffusion** and **electrostatic pressure** acting on the cell. To understand the processes involved in maintaining resting potentials and in the production of action potentials, we must first understand these physical forces.

> **Dynamic equilibrium**   When two opposing processes operate at equivalent rates.

Diffusion involves the natural movement of molecules. Here the laws of physics determine that molecules are redistributed from areas of high concentration to areas of low concentration. For example, if there were a lot of sodium ions outside the neurone, and few sodium ions inside the neurone, diffusional forces would move sodium ions into the neurone. Electrostatic pressure is the second force that moves ions around; in this case it is the electrical charge of the ion that is important. All ions have an electrical charge, either positive or negative. Positive and negative (opposite) charges are attracted to each other, whereas the same charge repels. This means that a balance of positive and negative charges will be present inside and outside the neurone. For example, if too many ions with a positive charge are present inside the neurone compared to outside, electrostatic pressure will result in some of the positively charged ions leaving the neurone or some negatively charged ions entering. Figure 8.2 shows how diffusion and electrostatic pressure act on the neurone membrane to maintain the resting potential at −70 mV.

As we saw above, potassium, sodium and chloride ions play a role in maintaining the resting potential at −70 mV. This is because potassium cannot pass entirely freely as some of the ion channels are closed by gates (chloride can cross only half as freely, and sodium 1/20th as freely, but both of these ions play only a small role in determining the resting

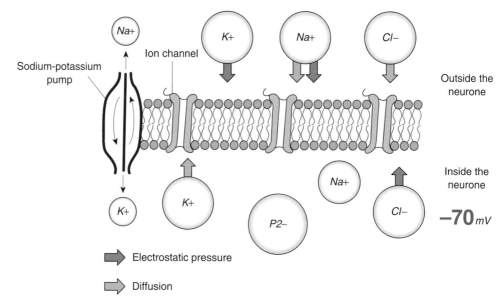

FIGURE 8.2 Physical forces acting on the membrane of the neurone (Dr Worm)

potential). At the same time as electrostatic pressure is attracting potassium into the cell (because of its positive charge), diffusion is acting in opposition; diffusion demands that potassium be evenly distributed and pulls potassium back out of the cell. Restrictions on free movement result in more potassium inside the cell and more chloride outside, producing the potential difference of −70 mV. The potential difference of −70 mV will remain constant providing ion concentrations remain steady. However, ion concentrations do not remain steady.

Remember that we said earlier that sodium is small enough to pass through potassium ion channels? Sodium slowly leaks into the cell due to strong diffusional and electrostatic pressure and forces potassium back out of the cell to compensate. This leads to an imbalance in ion concentrations. In order to deal with this there is a *sodium-potassium pump* in the membrane to pump sodium out of the cell and potassium back in to restore ion concentrations.

8.3.3 ACTION POTENTIALS

The neurone conducts information along its length in the form of a rapid, transient change in voltage. These changes in voltage or potential are a result of the ability of positively and negatively charged ions to move in and out of the neurone quickly. Thus an **action potential** is a discrete region of voltage change that is conducted along the axon from soma to synaptic buttons like a bead sliding down a wire.

The action potential is originally triggered at the **axon hillock**, located at the point at which the axon leaves the soma (Figure 8.1). Charge builds up here as a result of input from other cells via dendrites and soma. An action potential develops when the input from other

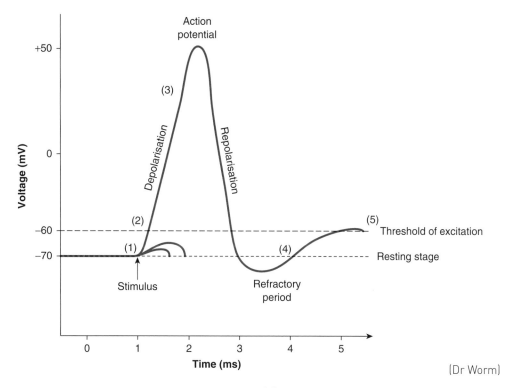

FIGURE 8.3 The five stages of an action potential: (1) electrical charge builds at the axon hillock; (2) threshold of excitation is reached; (3) depolarisation of the membrane occurs (action potential); (4) equilibrium returns with the restoration of the original electrical charge (membrane potential); (5) the message (this change in membrane potential) is triggered in the next section of axon; and so on

cells results in a build-up of charge such that the threshold of excitation is exceeded; this is when the membrane changes from its resting −70 mV to approximately −60 mV.

When the threshold of excitation is reached, it causes sodium channels to open, allowing sodium to enter the cell by diffusion and electrostatic pressure, until the voltage reaches +50 mV. The voltage does not exceed this as it has reached its **equilibrium potential**. Shortly after sodium channels open, so do voltage-gated potassium channels. The voltage at this stage, due to the influx of sodium, is positive and so potassium begins to move out, resulting in restoration of the resting potential. However, potassium ion channels are slow to close, resulting in an 'overshoot' beyond −70 mV. In terms of ion distribution, there is by this stage more potassium outside the neurone and more sodium inside the neurone than in the resting state, so a specialised sodium-potassium pump in the cell membrane helps to restore levels by moving potassium and sodium out of the neurone. It is this 'reset' process that results in the action potential only ever travelling in one direction, i.e. from axon hillock to synaptic buttons. In principle, action potentials could travel either way on an axon, but the time taken to 'reset' the voltage level within the neurone to −70 mV (the *refractory period*) prevents this. The processes involved in an action potential are summarised in Figure 8.3.

Equilibrium potential Each type of ion has its own equilibrium potential, which is the voltage at which the net effect of the passage of a given ion in and out of the cell is zero.

The above account describes the events that underpin the action potential at any given point on the axon. Now we will examine how the action potential moves along an unmyelinated axon. Once the action potential is triggered, sodium moves into the axon at the site of the action potential and the adjacent axon membrane depolarises (becomes less negative than −70 mV). The influx of sodium depolarises the membrane because positive charge builds up on the interior of the membrane near open gates and does so until the charge reaches the threshold (−60 mV) for adjacent sodium channels to open. Sodium enters, an action potential occurs there, and so the cycle repeats itself, propagating the action potential along the length of the axon. In other words the axon potential is regenerated at every point along the entire length of the unmyelinated axon.

In myelinated axons, things are a little different. Recall that the myelin sheaths enveloping axons are interrupted by small regions of axon that are unmyelinated: nodes of Ranvier. Myelin is an insulator, so charge cannot cross the membrane anywhere else on the axon other than at these unmyelinated nodes. Fortunately the **axoplasm** (fluid inside the axon) is a good conductor, so current can be conducted quite rapidly along the interior of the axon between nodes. Positive charge accumulates at a node until the threshold for sodium gates to open is reached and the action potential is regenerated at that node. This provides sufficient charge to be conducted down the interior of the axon to the next node. Thus in myelinated axons, the action potential is regenerated at the nodes of Ranvier.

This method is termed *saltatory conduction* and is faster than in unmyelinated axons because the charge does not need to be regenerated at every point; this kind of conduction saves time, energy and space. In that case, why not myelinate the entire length of the axon and do away with nodes of Ranvier altogether? Although axoplasm is a good conductor, the strength of the action potential diminishes with distance; thus nodes are necessary in order that the action potential can regenerate and not 'die out' as it travels along the axon.

Ultimately, the action potential, once it has passed down the axon and along the axonal branches, arrives at the synaptic buttons. Here it triggers the release of a chemical transmitter that diffuses across the gap to affect the next neurone. We will discuss this important process in detail later, in Section 8.4. For now it is enough to know that when the chemical transmitters reach the next neurone, they produce changes in the electrical state of that neurone known as post-synaptic potentials. It is also useful at this point to introduce some terminology: the neurone sending information (from the synaptic buttons) is the **pre-synaptic neurone** and the one receiving that information is the **post-synaptic neurone**.

8.3.4 POST-SYNAPTIC POTENTIALS

The processes involved in producing an action potential follow the laws of axonal conduction. An action potential either happens or not, depending on whether the threshold of excitation has been reached: there are no half measures. This is the **all-or-none law**. Regeneration of the signal at the nodes of Ranvier also means that action potentials are always the same strength, no matter how long or branching the axon is. This has consequences for indicating the strength of a signal as it cannot rely on differing strengths of the action potential. Instead it depends on the rate at which action potentials are fired (**rate law**). In the CNS, a single input from a single synapse is not usually sufficient to trigger an action potential in a post-synaptic neurone; instead, the frequency of inputs is added up. This is known as *temporal summation* (number of inputs over time). Additionally, inputs from several pre-synaptic neurones are typically needed and these are also summed. As these come in from various locations, this is known as *spatial summation*. Therefore both frequency and location of inputs determine the size of the signal received by the post-synaptic neurone.

To further complicate matters (hang on in here), inputs from pre-synaptic neurones can have excitatory or inhibitory effects, respectively increasing or decreasing the likelihood that the post-synaptic cell will produce an action potential. These inputs are called **post-synaptic potentials** and congregate at the axon hillock. **Excitatory post-synaptic potentials** (EPSPs) make an action potential more likely because they depolarise the membrane, opening potassium and sodium channels and triggering the axon potential. Importantly this means that EPSPs (unlike action potentials themselves) are graded: that is, the more excitatory synapses activated, the bigger the total EPSP will be and the more likely it is that an action potential will develop. In principle, **inhibitory post-synaptic potentials** (IPSPs) work in a similar fashion to EPSPs, except that they open chloride and potassium ion channels, not sodium channels. The influx of chloride into the neurone and the efflux of potassium make the neurone more negative (hyperpolarised) than usual and so less likely to fire an action potential, as a greater number and/or rate of excitatory inputs is needed to reach the threshold of excitation.

In summary, what determines whether an action potential will fire is the net activity produced by both excitatory and inhibitory inputs summed over space and time.

COMMUNICATION BETWEEN NEURONES

8.4 So far we have looked at how information travels along a neurone. This section will focus on how information is conveyed from one neurone to another. Charles Sherrington (1897) was the first to introduce the synapse as the mechanism that accounted for communication between individual nerve cells. There are at least 10 trillion synapses (connections) between neurones in the brain, and a given neurone might have several thousand synaptic connections with other neurones. Thus synaptic transmission of information is the critical event that underpins all the 'doings' of the nervous system, from blinking to ballet and beyond.

ASIDE

There are at least 10 trillion connections between neurones in your brain. If you started to count them at one every second it would take you over 300,000 years to get them all.

Until the 1930s it was not known whether communication between neurones in the CNS was electrical or chemical. However we now know that there are both chemical and electrical synapses distributed throughout the brain (Furshpan & Potter, 1959). Here we will concentrate on the dominant method of communication between neurones: chemical transmission. However, if you would like to find out more about **electrical synapses**, please see the suggestions for further reading at the end of this chapter.

To understand how information is communicated between neurones with **chemical synapses** we will need to look in greater detail at **pre-synaptic events** (how neurotransmitters are released), at how the pre-synaptic neurone forms a synapse with a post-synaptic neurone at receptors, and at **post-synaptic events** (how neurotransmitters affect the post-synaptic neurone).

8.4.1 THE CHEMICAL SYNAPSE AND PRE-SYNAPTIC EVENTS

Synapses are junctions between neurones that involve parts of two different neurones being in very close proximity to one another (see Figure 8.1). Usually this involves the synaptic button of a pre-synaptic neurone (the *sending* neurone) synapsing onto a dendrite or soma of the post-synaptic (receiving) neurone. Where two neurones synapse, they do not actually touch; instead the **pre-synaptic membrane** and **post-synaptic membrane** are separated by a tiny 20 nanometer gap (the **synaptic cleft**). Communication occurs when neurotransmitter is released from the synaptic button of the pre-synaptic neurone into the synaptic cleft, where it diffuses across and activates receptors on the post-synaptic neurone.

The process of neurotransmission is straightforward: the action potential travels down the axon of a neurone to the synaptic button. In the same way that there are sodium and potassium ion channels in the axon membrane, there are voltage-dependent calcium ion channels in the membrane of the synaptic button. As the action potential reaches them, the change in voltage causes voltage-gated calcium ion channels to open. Consequently calcium rushes into the cell, attracted in by diffusional forces because there is a higher calcium concentration outside the cell than inside. Within the synaptic button, **vesicles** containing neurotransmitter congregate around the release zone and some are already docked onto the membrane via protein bonds. The arrival of calcium into the synaptic button causes the vesicles to open, releasing neurotransmitter into the synaptic cleft by a process called **exocytosis** (see Figure 8.1, synapse insert). During exocytosis, calcium binds with the protein bonds that join the vesicle to the membrane. This binding causes the vesicle membrane to fuse with and so become part of the pre-synaptic button membrane. This results in the vesicle contents (neurotransmitter molecules) being released into the synaptic cleft (Almers, 1990).

ASIDE

The theory of how chemical synapses work is based on observations made of transmission of the neurotransmitter acetylcholine. However, this is actually a description of communication in the PNS, not the CNS, and between muscular synapses, not neuronal ones. Whilst the mechanisms described are widely accepted as applying to neuronal synapses and there is no reason to assume that they are different, neither can we assume they are the same.

8.4.2 RECEPTOR ACTIVATION AND POST-SYNAPTIC EVENTS

Neurones can do one of two things to influence another cell: they can make the other cell more excitable or less excitable (remember excitatory and inhibitory post-synaptic potentials). Using the fast excitatory neurotransmitter **acetylcholine** (ACh) as an example, unsurprisingly the action is to excite the post-synaptic cell. Here, ACh diffuses across the synaptic cleft and attaches to **receptors** (protein molecules: see Figure 8.1, synapse insert) on the post-synaptic membrane. In turn, this causes sodium channels to open in the post-synaptic cell. Note that the sodium ion channels in the post-synaptic membrane are chemically gated (opened by ACh rather than a change in membrane potential, as is the case with voltage-gated channels involved in the action potential).

Sodium enters (due to diffusional and electrostatic pressure) and the post-synaptic cell becomes slightly depolarised. The entrance of sodium produces an EPSP that is then conducted towards the axon hillock, making an action potential *more* likely to be triggered in the post-synaptic cell than before because the cell's electrical charge has become more positive.

> **Receptors** Proteins embedded in cell membranes that respond to ligands (specific chemical substances, e.g. neurotransmitters).

Neurotransmitters and receptors are somewhat specific to each other; usually only one type of neurotransmitter can dock onto a given type of receptor (although this is perhaps not always the case). The molecular structure of the neurotransmitter fits into the receptor like a lock and key (Fischer, 1894). As we shall see later, it is the ability of some drugs to 'mimic' the structure of a neurotransmitter in this way that allows them to have psychoactive effects. Additionally there are subtypes of each receptor. These all bind the neurotransmitter concerned but are structurally different, resulting in differing effects of binding. When we get on to specific neurotransmitters and drugs you will see that these subtypes are important.

8.4.3 TERMINATION OF THE SIGNAL

Neurotransmitter released into the synaptic cleft will continue to affect the post-synaptic neurone as long as it is present. How then does the process of neurotransmission stop? Excess neurotransmitter must be removed from the synaptic cleft. For most neurotransmitters the signal is terminated by reuptake of the neurotransmitter into the pre-synaptic button it was released from by **reuptake** transporters. These are proteins in the pre-synaptic membrane specific to the neurotransmitter and actively carry molecules of neurotransmitter back into the cell. This process is discrete, controllable and rapid but requires lots of energy. A less common method of termination of the signal is by **enzymatic degradation**. Neurotransmitters are complex chemicals made up of simpler components. Proteins known as enzymes are involved in the processes of both building them from simple proteins (amino acids) and breaking them down again. For ACh, for example, an enzyme known as **acetylcholineresterase** (AChE) cleaves to ACh and breaks it down into its two constituent parts, choline and acetate, rendering it inactive at the receptors.

Once neurotransmitter has been taken back into the synaptic button it is not wasted, but is recycled into vesicles ready to be used again. Recall that the release of neurotransmitter from the pre-synaptic membrane involves the membrane of the vesicle becoming part of the pre-synaptic membrane (Figure 8.1, synaptic insert). As a result the pre-synaptic membrane gets bigger and would continue to do so if not for this recycling process. Sections of membrane are pinched off into vesicles within the synaptic button and repackaged with neurotransmitter. This process is conducted by organelles called **cisternae** (Heuser and Reese, 1973).

EXERCISE   Virtual neurophysiology

This exercise involves using the Howard Hughes Virtual Neurophysiology Lab. Access this resource:

http://www.hhmi.org/biointeractive/vlabs/neurophysiology/index.html

Investigate the nervous system of the leech using the virtual dissection of the leech followed by use of fluorescent dyes to visualise the anatomy of different **sensory neurones**. Record electrical activities of individual neurones when they are stimulated. Identify the neurones based on their morphology and their response to different mechanical stimuli.

NEUROTRANSMITTERS AND DRUGS

8.5

Neurotransmitters work in circuits or systems and these interact to produce cognition, experience and behaviour. A given neurotransmitter or neurotransmitter circuit may be involved in producing many different psychological and behavioural phenomena. Rather than look here at all of the many, many neurotransmitters in the brain, we will focus on a few examples to equip you with basic knowledge. This will enable you to do further reading on other neurotransmitters. We will then look at examples of how drugs that are active in the brain (*psychoactive*) exert their effects.

Lipids   Substances that are fat soluble.

Ligand   Any substance (e.g. neurotransmitter or drug) with the capacity to bind to a receptor.

8.5.1 NEUROTRANSMITTERS

There are many **neurotransmitters** in the brain and they are grouped into classes based on their structure. There are four major neurotransmitters in the CNS that are important to know about: acetylcholine (ACh), dopamine (DA), norepinephrine (NE) and serotonin (5-HT). For a brief overview of their roles see Table 8.1.

ASIDE

Soluble gases are one of the most unusual transmitter substances because they can 'walk through walls'. Rather than travelling across synapses in the regular way, they pass from one cell to another as soon as they are produced, activate an enzyme for a **second messenger**, then degrade immediately.

Neurotransmitters are complex chemicals built up from simple proteins by the action of **enzymes**. The basic building blocks that make up neurotransmitters are called **precursors** and are obtained from our diet in the form of essential amino acids. For example, the neurotransmitter serotonin is made from the precursor tryptophan, an amino acid found in bananas amongst other foods (which is why bananas allegedly help recovery from a hangover by aiding the replacement of depleted serotonin). These precursors are acted upon by particular enzymes in the body, which lead to addition and/or subtraction of molecular components in a step-by-step fashion. For example, the neurotransmitters dopamine and norepinephrine are built from the amino acid tyrosine (obtained from food) that is converted to L-DOPA by an enzyme called tyrosine hydroxylase. This L-DOPA is converted to dopamine by the enzyme DOPA decarboxylase. Dopamine is a neurotransmitter in its own right, but if it is in the presence of an enzyme called dopamine β-hydroxylase then it can be converted into norepinephrine.

Neurotransmitters work in systems made up of a collection of neurones (although some neurones contain more than one neurotransmitter). Typically the cell bodies congregate together into what are called nuclei. These are often situated in a lower part the brain, from where the axons project forward (in a bundle) to terminate onto other structures they connect with (synapse onto).

> **Precursor** In biochemistry, a substance from which more complex compounds are made.

Again let's look at the neurotransmitter dopamine as an example of this. There are four dopaminergic systems with differing functions, but we will look at one of them, the nigro-striatal system, to illustrate how neurotransmitter systems are organised (see Figure 8.4). The nigro-striatal system starts with the nuclei of cell bodies in an area of the brain called the substantia nigra (in the midbrain). The bundle of axons project forward as part of a structure made up of many axons called the medial forebrain bundle and synapse onto the dorsal striatum (made up of two brain regions, the caudate and putamen). So when action potentials are activated in the substantia nigra the signal passes down the axons to the dorsal striatum, where dopamine is released and activates the dorsal striatum.

This particular dopaminergic system is involved in the control of movement. If it is damaged then too little dopamine gets through to the dorsal striatum and movement is impaired. This is what happens in the disease known as *Parkinson's disease*, resulting in muscular rigidity, tremors, and problems with balance and with the initiation of movement. Interestingly, Parkinson's disease has been a focus of research using *stem cells* (undifferentiated

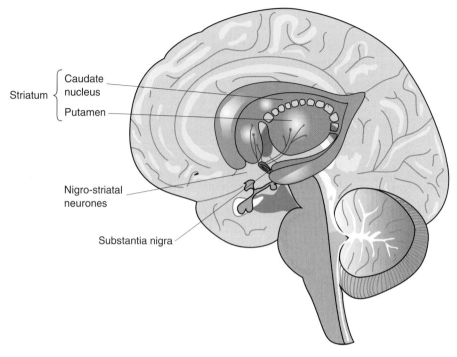

FIGURE 8.4   The anatomy of the nigro-striatal system   (Dr Worm)

cells that are special because they have the potential to develop into any type of cell depending on the environment that they are in). Parkinson's disease is an ideal candidate for stem cell therapy because the deficiency is specific (dopaminergic cells are lost) and discrete (in a small area, the substantia nigra) compared to the complex and widespread loss in most other brain diseases. Stem cells have been implanted into the substantia nigra of Parkinsonian patients in an attempt to regenerate dopaminergic cells and so restore normal function, but to date with limited success.

KEY RESEARCHER   Arvid Carlsson

Professor Arvid Carlsson (born 1923) has had an extensive and illustrious career in biological science, and in particular in the field of pharmacology for which he is most well known. Carlsson (with Paul Greengard and Eric Kandel) received the Nobel Prize in Physiology or Medicine in 2000 for ground-breaking work on signal transduction in the nervous system.

Carlsson's famous discovery was that dopamine is an active neurotransmitter substance in its own right; it had been thought that dopamine was a precursor (building

block) for another neurotransmitter, norepinephrine. He then went on to discover the role of dopamine in movement. Reducing dopamine in animals disrupted motor control, and when Carlsson restored dopamine levels by administering a dopamine precursor, control of movement returned.

Carlsson's findings have had far-reaching implications for our understanding of certain neuropsychiatric disorders. The discovery that dopamine plays a key role in movement led to the development already discussed of L-DOPA as a treatment for Parkinson's disease. The startling effects of dopamine depletion and reinstatement as discovered by Carlsson in animals are dramatically illustrated in humans in the book *Awakenings* by Oliver Sacks (1973). This is an account of his treatment of survivors of a disease called encephalitic lethargica who 'awake' from their catatonic state when treated with L-DOPA. It was later made into a film of the same name, well worth a watch, but be warned about the sad ending.

FIGURE 8.5 Arvid Carlsson

8.5.2 DRUGS AND THE BRAIN

Until now we have looked only at the process of synaptic transmission involving naturally occurring substances originating within the body (**endogenous** substances) like neurotransmitters. Now we will look at how substances from outside the body (**exogenous** substances) such as **drugs** affect the nervous system.

Any substance which binds to a receptor is a **ligand**. Ligands therefore include both endogenous neurotransmitters and exogenous drugs that 'mimic' the structure of a certain neurotransmitter. Drugs can have functionally **agonist** effects (facilitating the effects of neurotransmitters on the post-synaptic neurone) or can have functionally **antagonist** effects (inhibiting the effects of neurotransmitters on the post-synaptic neurone). There are many ways that agonist and antagonist effects can be produced by drugs. Recall the processes involved in synaptic transmission (Figure 8.1, synapse insert); drugs can affect any of the steps involved. Table 8.1 has some examples of how drugs exert their effects.

A drug could prevent or facilitate the synthesis of neurotransmitter, causing more or less to be produced. For example, a drug that has an agonist effect at this stage is L-DOPA, a treatment for Parkinson's disease. You recall that Parkinson's disease is a result of depleted dopamine. L-DOPA improves the condition because it is a precursor (building block) of dopamine. Its presence facilitates the production of dopamine and so treats the symptoms. Interestingly, if you have high levels of dopamine (in a brain system called the mesolimbic system) this has been found to be related to psychiatric conditions such as schizophrenia (see below and the key study). The antipsychotic drugs used to reduce the symptoms of these conditions block the transmission of dopamine and sometimes create the symptoms of Parkinson's disease.

TABLE 8.1　Major neurotransmitters, their function in brain and examples of drug effects

Neurotransmitter		Examples of drugs		
Neurotransmitter	Function	Drug	Mechanism	Effect
Acetylcholine (ACh)	Role in REM sleep, attention, learning and memory	Curare	Post-synaptic receptor blocker (of nicotinic type of ACh receptor)	Antagonist
		Black widow venom	Stimulates release of ACh	Agonist
Dopamine (DA)	Role in movement, memory, planning, problem solving, emotion, attention, reinforcement and motivation	Chlorpromazine (antipsychotic)	Post-synaptic receptor blocker (of D2 type of receptor)	Antagonist
		Amphetamine	Reverses action of reuptake transporter	Agonist
Serotonin (5-HT)	Role in sleep, mood, sex, anxiety, feeding, pain	Ritanserin (antipsychotic, but also used for insomnia)	Post-synaptic receptor blocker (of 5-HT 2 type of receptor)	Antagonist
		Fluoxetine (Prozac)	Reuptake transporter blocker	Agonist
Norepinephrine (NE)	Role in attentional focus, mood, arousal and sexual behaviour	Clonidine (used to treat Tourette syndrome)	Stimulates pre-synaptic autoreceptor resulting in feedback to slow down NE production	Antagonist
		Venlafaxine (antidepressant)	Reuptake transporter blocker	Agonist

Neurotransmitter release itself might be affected by a drug. Remember, an action potential is necessary to trigger neurotransmitter release, so a drug could interfere with the action potential directly, e.g. by affecting ions like sodium. The infamous Japanese delicacy, pufferfish, contains a poison that does exactly that. The flesh itself is safe to eat, but within the liver is a compound called tetrodotoxin that binds to the sodium channels on neurones in muscles. This prevents the channels from opening and so prevents action potentials, resulting in paralysis of muscles – to deadly effect as respiratory muscles are affected. No wonder chefs need a licence to prepare pufferfish!

Alternatively, drugs could affect neurotransmitter release by helping or hindering the release of neurotransmitter (exocytosis). For example *botox* (botulinum toxin), the compound well loved by Hollywood stars for its ability to immobilise facial muscles (although expressing that delight is difficult for them), works by preventing vesicular release of ACh from the pre-synaptic button. Remember that ACh signals contraction of skeletal muscles and so prevention of release will result in inability to move muscles.

Another stage of neurotransmission that could be affected relates to events that take place within the synaptic cleft. Drugs binding to receptors on the post-synaptic membrane can agonise or antagonise. An agonist here might bind to the post-synaptic receptor if its structure is close enough to that of the neurotransmitter to 'fool' the receptor (remember the lock and key analogy). Alternatively an antagonist might fit the receptor but not activate it, thus blocking post-synaptic receptors and preventing neurotransmitter from binding. In this case, the drug may have no direct effect on the post-synaptic cell itself, that is, it might simply occupy the receptor sites like a dog in a manger. An example of this is antipsychotic drugs used to treat schizophrenia (see the key study). Almost without exception, antipsychotics are dopamine antagonists that block the D2 receptor (a specific type of dopamine receptor), thus preventing naturally produced dopamine from binding to these sites and reducing dopamine transmission.

KEY STUDY   Henri Laborit and the discovery of anti-psychotics

Pena Trevino, R. (1955). Introduction of Dr Henri Laborit from France at the meeting of the Academy on 8 March 1955. *Cirugia y Cirujanos, 23*(4), 181–182.

Schizophrenia, characterised by disordered thought, emotions and perception, is treated largely by the use of antipsychotic drugs. These drugs exert their effect predominantly by decreasing dopamine transmission in a dopaminergic system known as the mesolimbic system. The drugs were first discovered by surgeon Henri Laborit in 1952, who noted that a drug he used to reduce anxiety prior to surgery produced what he described as indifference and relaxation but without loss of consciousness. Laborit's suggestion that it might be useful for psychiatric disorders was revolutionary at the time and not well received, but persistence paid off. Eventually the drug, chlorpromazine, was tried out on any and all psychiatric disorders (in the days before ethics committees). It had little effect on most disorders but a profound effect on symptoms of schizophrenia. So effective was this drug that many other similar compounds followed; antipsychotics became the most common treatment for schizophrenia, and remain so today.

Antipsychotics have been through several generations of drug type. The most recent third generation includes exciting 'smart' drugs that can alter the level of dopamine turnover either up or down depending on the basal level and so reduce side effects to a minimum.

Whatever the controversies around drug treatments for psychiatric disorders (now there's a fascinating discussion), there is no doubt that this discovery revolutionised (for good or ill) the way schizophrenics were treated from then on, resulting in many people being allowed out of psychiatric institutes and having a far-reaching influence on the field of psychiatry.

The final stage of neurotransmission that drugs could affect is the termination of the signal. Here the processes of reuptake or enzymatic degradation could be facilitated or inhibited. If reuptake of excess neurotransmitter was prevented (for example because a drug was blocking reuptake transporters), the neurotransmitter would remain in the synaptic cleft and continue to affect the post-synaptic neurone. This would be an agonist effect. Prozac, the well-known treatment for depression, works in this way by blocking serotonin reuptake transporters (hence it is known as a selective serotonin reuptake inhibitor or SSRI). Interestingly amphetamines put the reuptake transporters into reverse, moving dopamine back out of the synaptic button and so having an agonistic effect. It should be noted that many drugs have effects at more than one of these stages or on more than one neurotransmitter at once.

CHAPTER SUMMARY

8.6 Neurones have three basic functions: sending sensory information to the brain, sending motor commands from the brain, and shuttling information around the brain itself. Information is handled *within* the neurone as electrical charges triggered by neurotransmitters received from other (pre-synaptic) neurones. Any resulting action potential (a small region of voltage change that exists as a result of the rapid movement of ions in and out of the neurone) travels down the axon to the synaptic buttons, where it triggers the release of neurotransmitters which in turn produce changes in electrical charge on the post-synaptic neurone.

Communication *between* neurones occurs when neurotransmitter is released from the synaptic button of the pre-synaptic neurone into the synaptic cleft, where it diffuses across and binds to receptors on the post-synaptic neurone. The signal, for most neurotransmitters, is terminated by reuptake of neurotransmitter into the pre-synaptic neurone.

Neurotransmitters work in circuits or systems and these interact to produce cognition, experience and behaviour. Drugs can affect the functioning of neurones by 'mimicking' the structure of neurotransmitters, and can have agonist or antagonist effects at any of the various stages of synaptic transmission to produce change.

 ## DISCUSSION QUESTIONS: NEURAL PLASTICITY AND LEARNING. ARE YOU THE SAME PERSON AFTER READING THIS CHAPTER?

Neurones undergo changes as a consequence of being activated by our experiences; synaptic connections can be formed or 'die away', or receptor numbers can increase or decrease. This enables our brains to remain 'plastic' (basically, the capacity of the nervous system to change in response to events).

This ability to change raises an interesting philosophical debate. In his inspiring book *Into the silent lands*, Paul Broks (2004) retells the story of a philosophical debate that centres on the nature of identity. In the story it is possible to teleport, which is achieved by reassembling an exact copy of the person at their desired location out of locally available materials, whilst simultaneously destroying the 'original'. There is a law against duplicates, so destruction of one duplicate must happen. Broks tells the tale of a man whose 'original' is not destroyed due to a malfunction in the teleportation device. The question is, which duplicate should be destroyed: the 'copy' or the 'original'? Moreover, at what point do the experiences (and consequent structure and function of their brains) of the two duplicates diverge such that they are no longer copies of one another and are essentially *different* people?

In the time that it has taken you to read this chapter, there has been a lot going on in your brain (hopefully!). You will have at least had the experience of reading this chapter, which leads to a memory of having read this chapter. It might be an emotional memory, depending on whether you found the experience exciting or traumatic! If you have managed to retain any information, then you will have learned something. All of these processes and experiences involve changes to, or formation of, synaptic connections in the brain. Thus, the structure and function of your brain have altered subtly during the time it has taken you to read this chapter. Therefore, you are no longer exactly the same person that you were before you began.

 ## SUGGESTIONS FOR FURTHER READING

Breedlove, S.M., Rosenzweig, M.R., & Watson, N.V. (2009). *Biological psychology* (5th edn). Sunderland, MA: Sinauer. Relevant chapters are 2, 3 and 4. This text is strong in detail on communication within the neurone (Chapter 3).

Carlson, N.R. (2009). *Physiology of behaviour* (10th edn). Boston: Pearson. Relevant chapters are 2, 3 and 4. This text is strong in detail on neurotransmitters and drugs (Chapter 4).

Grilly, D.M. (2006). *Drugs and human behavior*. Boston: Pearson. For more depth than the general biological psychology texts.

McKim, W.A. (2007). *Drugs and behavior: an introduction to behavioral pharmacology*. London: Prentice Hall. For more depth than the general biological psychology texts.

Shepherd, G.M. (1991). *Foundations of the neuronal doctrine*. Oxford: Oxford University Press. An interesting text giving the history of the discovery of the anatomy and function of neurones. Gives insight into the scientific process. Also describes electrical synaptic transmission (alluded to in this chapter).

9 BRAIN AND BEHAVIOUR: SEX DIFFERENCES

Lead authors **Mark J.T. Sergeant** and **Antonio Castro**

CHAPTER OUTLINE

INTRODUCTION

9.1

When describing another person, one of the first things likely to be mentioned is whether they are male or female. This is not only because males and females tend to look different, but also because we tend to make a number of assumptions about an individual's temperament and behaviour based on their sex. As our perception of what it means to be male and female has varied over time, and varies enormously between cultures, some have assumed that any differences between the sexes are socially created rather than **innate**. There are some obvious exceptions to this, however, such as the ability of females to become pregnant and bear children.

Yet what do we mean by the term *sex*, what are the differences between males and females, and what is the difference between sex and *gender*? This chapter will examine these questions, looking in particular at how differences between males and females begin at the genetic level, at the process of sexual differentiation in the womb, and at sex differences in brain and behaviour. In doing so, the chapter builds on the base of the biological knowledge established in the previous two chapters. We will also examine what happens when individuals undergo an atypical process of sexual differentiation and provide an overview of research into the biological basis for an individual's sexual orientation.

FRAMING QUESTIONS

What makes someone male or female?
What is the difference between sex and gender?
Are males really better than females at maths?
What are intersex conditions?
Is there a biological basis to homosexuality?
What are the implications of any biological basis to homosexuality?

ASIDE   Sex or gender?

The terms 'sex' and 'gender' are not interchangeable. 'Sex' refers to the biological characteristics used to differentiate individuals and identify them as either male or female. Sex can be measured by examining an individual's chromosomes (whether they possess XY or XX sex chromosomes), gonads (whether they possess testes or ovaries) and external reproductive organs (whether they possess a penis and testes or a vagina).

'Gender' refers to the sociocultural characteristics that are associated with a biological sex. The concept of gender is frequently subdivided into (1) gender identity and (2) gender role. Gender identity refers to an individual's own perception of whether they are male or female. Usually this is concordant with an individual's sex chromosomes and reproductive organs, but transsexual

(Cont'd)

individuals, for example, feel that their sense of gender identity is incompatible with their biological sex. Gender role refers to the behaviours that society deems appropriate or acceptable to be expressed by a particular sex, for example mowing the lawn versus changing nappies (no prizes for guessing which role is attached to which gender).

With sex we refer to individuals as being male or female, whereas with gender we talk about people being masculine or feminine.

9.2 THE PROCESS OF SEXUAL DIFFERENTIATION

9.2.1 GENETIC SEXUAL DIFFERENTIATION

Human cells contain 46 **chromosomes** arranged into 23 pairs. Twenty-two of these pairs of chromosomes are autosomes (non-sex chromosomes), and do not differ between males and females. They are not significantly involved in the process of sexual differentiation, which is the process by which an individual begins to develop into either a male or a female.

The final pair of chromosomes, known as sex chromosomes, differs between males and females. The sperm (male reproductive cell) and the egg (female reproductive cell) both only contain one copy of the 23 chromosome pairs common to humans. Once the sperm reaches the nucleus of the egg they fuse together to form a complete set of 23 chromosomal pairs (fertilisation).

In humans, eggs always contain an X sex chromosome while sperm can potentially carry either an X or a Y sex chromosome. If the sperm contains an X sex chromosome then the embryo will eventually develop into a female, as two X chromosomes (XX) are present. If the sperm contains a Y sex chromosome then the embryo will develop into a male, as X and Y chromosomes (XY) are present.

Hormones   From the Greek *horman,* 'to excite' or 'impetus'. Hormones are chemical messengers, released by the endocrine system, that are carried to other areas of the body through the bloodstream. Once they have reached a specific area of the body, they bind to certain receptor sites within tissues or organs and induce physiological change. Hormones have powerful effects on physiology and behaviour.

9.2.2 ORGANISATIONAL HORMONES

After the two sex chromosomes have combined during fertilisation, the process of prenatal sexual differentiation begins (see Figure 9.1). Following conception the egg begins to divide, first becoming a two-celled organism, then a four-celled organism, then an eight-celled organism and so on. After 28 days the embryo has divided numerous times and reached a length of approximately 1 cm.

Twins occur either when a fertilised egg divides into two identical copies (identical or *monozygotic twins,*

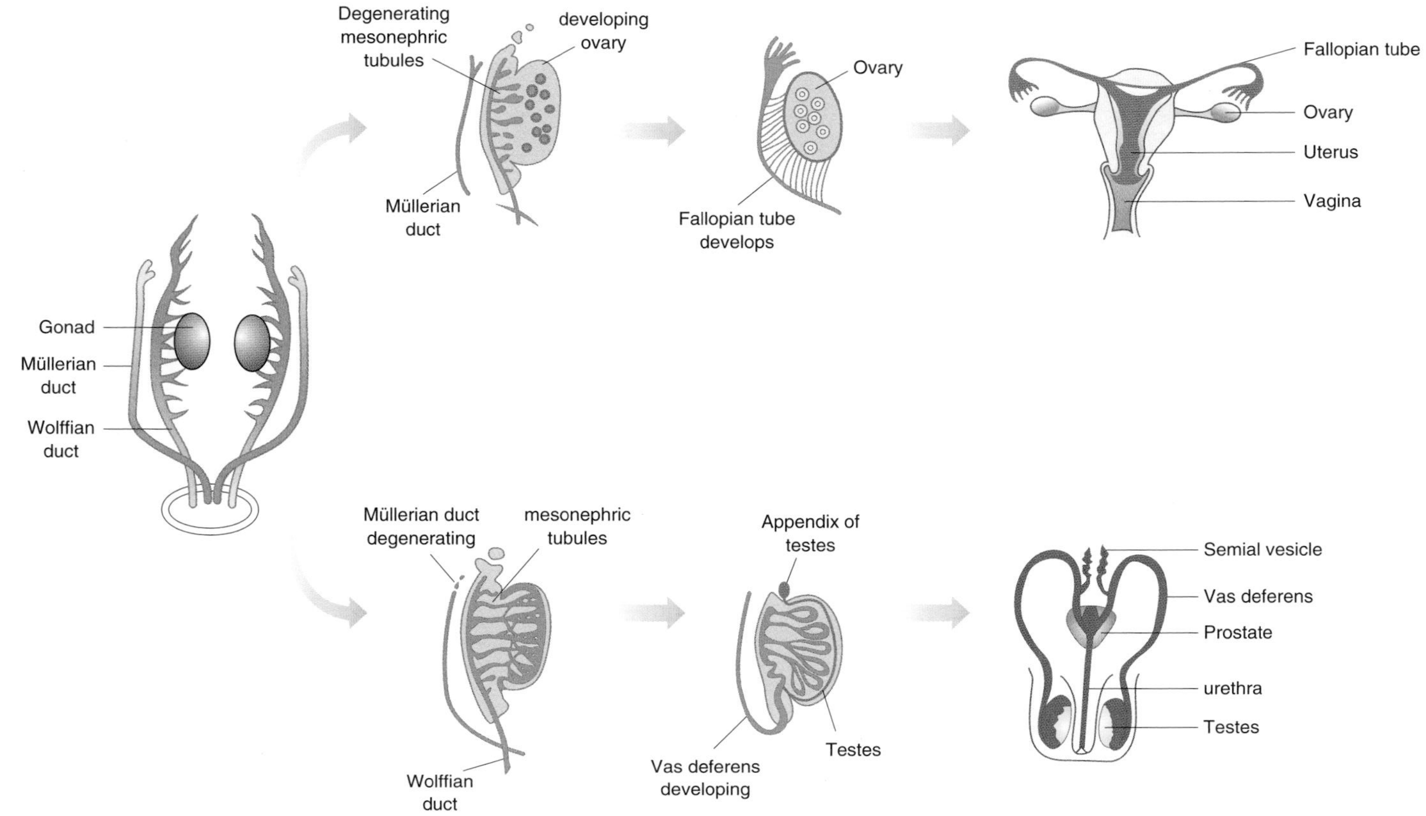

FIGURE 9.1 Development of the male and female reproductive organs. Adapted from www.medscape.com

(Dr Worm)

who share 100 per cent of their genes) or when two different eggs are fertilised by two different sperm (fraternal or *dizygotic twins*, who share 50 per cent of their genes).

For up to 28 days after conception there is no discernible difference between a male and a female foetus: the foetus remains in an undifferentiated state. By the seventh week after conception some basic structures have emerged in the foetus, which are the precursors to either the male or the female reproductive systems. The foetus possesses gonads and undeveloped external genitalia (the urethral fold, the genital swelling and the genital tubercle). At this time both male and female foetuses also possess two sets of ducts – the Müllerian ducts and the Wolffian ducts.

> **SRY gene** The 'sex determining region of the Y chromosome' (Haqq et al., 1994). This is part of a group of genes referred to as testes determining factor (TDF).

In females, the gonads develop into the ovaries and the Müllerian ducts develop into parts of the female reproductive system (the uterus, inner vagina and fallopian tubes specifically). The urethral fold develops into the inner labia, the genital swellings develop into the outer labia and the genital tubercle develops into the clitoris. In females, the Wolffian ducts do not develop and are reabsorbed into the foetus.

Among males, this development is different. The short arm of the Y chromosome contains the **SRY gene**. If the foetus possesses a Y chromosome then the undifferentiated gonads do not develop into ovaries, but instead begin to produce the SRY protein, causing the gonads to develop into testes. The testes then begin to secrete the anti-Müllerian hormone that causes the Müllerian ducts to cease development and be reabsorbed into the body (Vainio et al., 1999). The testes also begin to produce **testosterone** which masculinises the foetus, and the Wolffian ducts begin to develop into parts of the male reproductive system (the ejaculatory duct, vas deferens and epididymis). Testosterone also causes the tissue around the urethra to form into the prostate gland. **Dihydrotestosterone** causes the external genitals to develop; the urethral fold develops into the shaft of the penis, the genital swellings develop into the scrotum and the genital tubercle develops into the glans of the penis.

> **Androgen** A class of male sex hormones responsible for the maintenance and development of male characteristics.
>
> **Testosterone** The primary type of androgen, involved in the development of male characteristics and sexual functioning.
>
> **Dihydrotestosterone** An androgen converted from testosterone by the actions of the enzyme 5-alpha reductase.

In many instances, male and female reproductive organs are homologous, which means that they develop from the same embryonic tissue. The timing of this development, however, differs between males and females. The undifferentiated gonads develop into testes around seven weeks after conception, while the ovaries develop slightly later, around week 13 or 14. Approximately 16 weeks after conception, the external genitals of the foetus clearly indicate its sex.

At this point it is worth highlighting that two kinds of hormones are discussed in this chapter. The first kind, involved in foetal development (such as testosterone and dihydrotestosterone), is referred to as **organisational hormones**. These hormones affect the structure of the developing foetal brain and their effects are set in place for life. The other type of hormones is referred to as **activational hormones**. These hormones can vary enormously over the course of an individual's lifespan and are linked to a variety of behaviours. For example, the physiological changes that individuals go through at puberty have been linked to a sudden surge in activational hormone levels (see Section 9.3.2).

9.2.3 ATYPICALITY DURING SEXUAL DIFFERENTIATION

Although the process of sexual differentiation *usually* causes the development of either male-typical or female-typical characteristics, for some individuals this process is not so straightforward. Individuals who are born with both male and female sexual characteristics have historically been labelled **hermaphrodites.** They have both ovarian and testicular tissue. Such individuals are extremely uncommon (Blackless et al., 2000). However, much more common, occurring in approximately 1 in 2000 births, are individuals known as **pseudohermaphrodites** (Colapinto, 2000). These individuals have gonads that are consistent with their sex chromosomes (ovaries in females and testes in males) but have ambiguous internal and external genitalia.

The term 'hermaphrodite' has fallen out of favour in recent years, and is being replaced by a newer term **intersex**, which refers to an individual who has undergone atypical sexual differentiation, and has external genitalia that appear to be between those of a typical female and a typical male (Morris et al., 2004). Intersex conditions can result from either atypicality in the combination of sex chromosomes an individual receives, or from some form of atypicality in the effects of organisational hormones. We will look at these in turn. By studying the atypical development of intersex individuals we gain greater insight into how the process of sexual differentiation functions.

> **Hermaphrodite**   A term derived from Hermaphroditus, a Greek deity believed to possess both male and female attributes. Such individuals possess both testicular and ovarian tissue.
>
> **Pseudohermaphrodites**   These individuals have gonads that are consistent with their sex chromosomes (ovaries in females and testes in males) but have ambiguous internal and external genitalia.

Sex chromosome atypicality

More than 70 atypical conditions resulting from sex chromosomes have been documented. Detailed below are four of the most well-known conditions: Klinefelter's syndrome, Turner's syndrome, XYY syndrome and XXX syndrome.

Males typically receive X and Y chromosomes during conception, but individuals with **Klinefelter's syndrome** have XXY sex chromosomes. As a result of the additional X chromosome, male-typical development is altered, resulting in the emergence of an undersized penis and abnormal testes that are incapable of producing sperm (Winter & Couch, 1995). This condition occurs in approximately 1 in 500 to 1 in 1000 live male births. Although there is considerable variation in expression, males with Klinefelter's syndrome also tend to be more feminine, having a more rounded body shape, narrower shoulders, less body hair and possibly breasts. Individuals with Klinefelter's syndrome also tend to express reduced, and sometimes absent, sexual **motivation** and tend to be tall in stature. Treatment with testosterone can aid in the development of male-typical secondary sexual characteristics and sexual motivation.

Although females typically inherit two X chromosomes, individuals with **Turner's syndrome** only inherit a single X chromosome (signified as XO). This syndrome is rare, occurring in around 1 in 2000 live female births (Blackless et al., 2000). Such females have underdeveloped or absent ovaries although, as no SRY gene is present, they develop as females. Due to their underdeveloped or absent ovaries, females with Turner's syndrome do not menstruate, are unable to become pregnant, do not develop breasts during puberty and are generally short in stature (Gravholt et al., 1998). However, females with Turner's syndrome do not differ from typical females in terms of their behaviour and interests (Kagan-Krieger, 1998).

Human males can sometimes receive an additional Y sex chromosome during sexual differentiation, referred to as **XYY syndrome**. Given the overwhelming function of the Y chromosome in the development of testes, possessing an additional Y chromosome is not necessarily debilitating. Such individuals are virtually indistinguishable from typical (XY) males, though XYY males tend to be slightly taller in stature and have larger canine teeth. Most XYY males also experience male-typical sexual development and are able to father children. There is some evidence, however, that such individuals have an increased risk of learning difficulties and delayed language skills. This is not an inherited condition, but instead usually occurs as an error during sperm production. This syndrome is quite rare, occurring in around 1 in 1000 live male births.

Also known as X trisomy or super X syndrome, **XXX syndrome** occurs when a female inherits an additional X chromosome during sexual differentiation. Ordinarily only one X chromosome is needed for normal function in a woman (one X chromosome is active and the other dormant). As a result, XXX females simply carry two inactive X chromosomes rather than the one inactive chromosome typical of XX females. XXX females do not have any distinguishing features and are virtually impossible to tell apart from typical XX females, though they tend to be taller in stature and more at risk of developing learning difficulties. Such individuals go through female-typical sexual development, though they may begin menstruation prematurely, and are able to conceive without problem. As with XYY syndrome, this is not an inherited condition, but is instead caused by an error during the formation of either sperm or eggs. This syndrome is quite rare, occurring in around 1 in 1000 live female births.

Organisational hormone atypicality

In addition to possible atypicality resulting from sex chromosomes, a variety of conditions have been linked to the actions of organisational hormones. Three such conditions are described below. The first two of these affect individuals who are genetically male: androgen insensitivity syndrome and 5-alpha reductase syndrome. Both conditions are associated with a decreased sensitivity to the masculinising effects of organisational hormones. The third condition, congenital adrenal hyperplasia, affects individuals who are genetically female, and is the consequence of female foetuses being exposed to an excess of androgens, or androgen-like substances, in the womb.

Although individuals with XY sex chromosomes develop as males, the process of sexual differentiation is dependent upon the masculinising effects of androgens in the womb. With complete **androgen insensitivity syndrome**, a male produces typical levels of androgens in the womb but is unresponsive to their masculinising effects; the individual does not produce androgen receptors for the androgens to bind to. This syndrome develops due to a mutation in the gene responsible for creating androgen receptors, located on the X chromosome. As a result, individuals who are genetically male and born with two testes (due to the presence of the SRY gene) are also born with the external genitalia of females. With no obvious sign of atypicality, such individuals are typically raised as girls and fully adopt a feminine gender identity. However, as these individuals possess testes rather than ovaries they do not menstruate and are incapable of becoming pregnant. Individuals with androgen insensitivity syndrome also tend to have fair complexions and well-developed breasts.

KEY STUDY   Money, J. (1975). Ablatio penis: normal male infant sex-assigned as a girl. *Archives of Sexual Behavior*, 4, 65–71.

FIGURE 9.2   David Reimer

Many parents of children born with ambiguous genitalia decide their child should undergo sex reassignment surgery. In the majority of cases this involves surgically altering babies with more masculinised ambiguous genitalia into boys and more feminised ambiguous genitalia into girls, regardless of what sex they actually are. John Money argued that this process was successful and that children could be brought up to be comfortable in whatever gender was chosen for them. This view was challenged by, among others, Milton Diamond.

Around the time of their academic debate, two six-month-old twin boys were taken into hospital to have circumcision operations. Unfortunately one boy, David Reimer, had his penis severed beyond repair. Some months later the family saw John Money on television describing his theory and made contact with him. He advised them to reassign the boy into a girl. This provided a perfect test of his theory as the boy had a twin to compare with as they grew up. The decision was made at 17 months of age to raise David as a girl. His testes were removed and surgery was soon performed to make his features more typical of a female. Oestrogen treatment was used to encourage the development of female-typical characteristics.

The psychologist John Money advised David's parents that their son would adopt a female gender identity later in life following his surgery. In numerous follow-up studies, Money reported Brenda (the new name given by his parents) was successfully

(Cont'd)

developing as a female, and was interested in a number of sex-typical activities (Money, 1975).

Money, however, did not allow access to the case files or the family and the full story did not emerge for over 20 years. Diamond finally made contact with the family and spoke to the boy who had been brought up as a girl. He was by this time living as a man and was unaware of the celebrity of his story. His childhood had been one of continual struggle with his identity and he had been unable to live successfully as a girl. The story is recorded in brief in the reports by Diamond (Diamond, 1997; Diamond & Sigmundson, 1997) and more fully in a text by a US journalist (Colapinto, 2000).

Individuals with **5-alpha reductase syndrome** are genetically male (they possess XY sex chromosomes) but they appear to be female at birth. They possess a small penis, approximately the same size as the clitoris, and a vaginal pouch in place of a scrotum. The syndrome is caused by a rare recessive genetic mutation that reduces the production of 5-alpha reductase. Given their female appearance, such individuals are typically raised as girls and adopt a feminine gender identity. However, during puberty, when testosterone production accelerates (see Section 9.3.2), their penises fully develop and their body develops a muscular build and narrow hips. Such individuals are known as guevodoces (meaning 'eggs [testes] at 12 [years]'). Interestingly there is evidence that this change in external genitalia is accompanied by a change in gender identity. Among the 18 documented cases of guevodoces reported by Imperato-McGinley et al. (1979), 17 expressed a male gender identity, with the majority of these individuals forming romantic relationships with females.

Congenital adrenal hyperplasia can affect individuals who are genetically female (they possess XX sex chromosomes) and possess ovaries which have developed in a sex-typical fashion. During development, however, the adrenal glands do not produce corticosteroids (a type of hormone) as normal but instead begin to produce large amounts of androgens. The cause of this atypicality is a recessive genetic condition. Due to the excess of androgens present during prenatal sexual differentiation, a number of characteristics do not develop in a female-typical fashion. The clitoris is enlarged and often resembles a penis, while the labia often fuse together so there is no vaginal opening. Some parents choose for their daughter to have reconstructive surgery to give the external genitals a more feminine appearance, increasing the size of the vaginal opening and reducing the size of the clitoris. Corticosteroids are prescribed to reduce the levels of circulating androgens that are still being produced.

However, it is possible that the degree of masculinisation may be more pronounced, and in such cases the parents may decide to enhance the masculine appearance of the external genitals, by fully closing the fused labia to create a scrotum and inserting artificial testes. In such instances the child is raised as a boy (the ethics of this type of surgery are discussed below). Females with congenital adrenal hyperplasia demonstrate elevated levels of masculine behaviour during childhood play, and several studies have also documented elevated levels of homosexuality among these individuals.

9.3 SEX DIFFERENCES

9.3.1 SEX DIFFERENCES IN THE BRAIN

In addition to influencing the development of genitals, organisational hormones also affect the brain of the developing foetus, possibly resulting in sex differences in the structure and function of the brain. As equipment designed to measure brain development in the foetus has not yet been developed, much of what we know about this process comes from the study of non-human animals (Morris et al., 2004). The study of differences in brain function between the sexes has, as I am sure you can imagine, been extremely controversial over the years. Only a few centuries ago it was thought that a woman's brain would overheat if she attempted to do anything as complex as read!!

The simplest way to compare the brains of adult males and females is to look at the overall size and volume of the brain. Human males have an overall brain size approximately 15 per cent larger than human females (Gibbons, 1991). Based on this size difference, some people have concluded that males are usually more intelligent than females, working on the assumption that bigger brain equals more intelligent. Such an approach is too simplistic. Instead what should be considered is the overall ratio between brain and body size, which is comparable in both males and females (remember, human females are on average smaller than human males). Note that we do not use the entire brain for every action we perform. Parts of the brain are specialised to perform specific tasks (see below), so if we are interested in looking at how males and females may differ on these tasks it is important to study the specific brain area in question.

Although several areas of the brain appear to differ in size between males and females (such as the corpus callosum which connects the right and left hemispheres of the brain), one of the most widely studied structures is the hypothalamus, which controls the actions of the pituitary gland and as such controls hormone production in the human body (see Chapter 7 for more information on its whereabouts and function). Amongst many other functions the hypothalamus has been linked to sexual behaviour: for example, human males have shown increased activation in the hypothalamus when sexually aroused (Arnow et al., 2002).

As discussed above, the actions of organisational hormones are dependent upon receptor sites. If testosterone is present in the womb, then specialised receptor cells in the hypothalamus do not respond to oestrogen (as in males). Alternatively if oestrogen is present, the receptor cells become sensitive to oestrogen later on (as in females). A specific region of the hypothalamus showing differences between males and females is the preoptic area (Swaab et al., 1995), a part of the brain involved in regulating body temperature. One tiny portion of the hypothalamus, the bed nucleus of the stria terminalis (believed to be linked to stress and anxiety responses), also shows a difference between males and females, with a posterior section of this area being approximately twice as large in males (Allen & Gorski, 1990). However, it has been argued that this difference may emerge due to the behaviour of males and females differing over the course of the lifespan rather than being innate.

9.3.2 PUBERTY

The second important time for the development of sex differences, after the prenatal one, is **puberty**, the physiological process resulting in sexual maturity. The precise mechanisms behind puberty are not completely understood, but it appears that between 8 and 14 years of age large amounts of gonadotropins (a type of hormone) are released into the body. In males the gonadotropins cause the testes to produce large amounts of testosterone, while in females they cause the ovaries to begin producing large amounts of oestrogen. This process is marked in males by the onset of sperm production (spermarche) while in females it triggers the onset of the menstrual cycle (menarche), approximately two years after which ovulation begins. The specific age at which menarche occurs has been falling since the start of the twentieth century (Anderson et al., 2003) and is linked to a variety of factors such as general health, the percentage of body fat a girl has and even altitude. Psychologically, the most important event associated with puberty is often the first menstruation for females and the first ejaculation for males.

There are notable sex differences in the timing that puberty begins, as well as there being substantial individual variability in the onset and length of puberty. In Western countries boys typically begin puberty between the ages of 10 and 14, while for girls this process occurs roughly two years before. Similarly, while boys often do not reach their full height until the age of 18, or even later, girls normally reach their full height by the age of 16.

During puberty, secondary sexual characteristics also develop. These are characteristics other than sperm and egg production that indicate sexual maturity. For example, males get facial hair and a deepening of their voice (due to changes in the larynx); females experience the development of their breasts and hips; and both sexes experience the development of pubic and underarm hair as well as sebaceous gland development (linked to the onset of acne). External genitalia also develop further, with the penis and testes increasing in size among males and the labia and clitoris increasing in size among females. After puberty, males are statistically larger than females, with greater bone mass and less body fat.

As with prenatal sexual differentiation, atypicality can also occur during pubertal development. Sexual maturity has been previously documented in young children, some less than one year of age. Such development (referred to as precocious puberty) can be the result of disease or abnormal hormone exposure, or may simply reflect variation in normal development. While the effects of such a precocious puberty are not dangerous in themselves, sexual maturity at such a young age can profoundly affect development and may make the child a target for unwanted sexual advances. Alternatively, puberty can also be delayed for several years after the usual age of onset as a result of poor nutrition, stress, ill-health and a variety of medical complaints such as glandular tumours. If the child in question is otherwise healthy, medical intervention is usually unnecessary; it is simply a case of waiting for pubertal development. However, hormone treatment (with testosterone for males, and estradiol and progesterone for females) is possible to speed up the process.

9.3.3 COGNITIVE AND BEHAVIOURAL SEX DIFFERENCES

Given that there are certain differences between male and female brains, researchers have been curious about how behaviour differs between the sexes. In a review of over 2000 studies, Maccoby and Jacklin (1974) concluded that there are four robust sex differences; males are more aggressive than females; males perform better on visual-spatial tasks; males demonstrate greater mathematical abilities; and females have superior verbal skills. Many popular beliefs of the time, such as the belief that males were superior at higher-level cognitive functions and girls were better at simpler cognitive tasks, were not supported.

Before we examine these findings in more detail, as well as more recent research, it is important to consider the nature of these sex differences. Are observed sex differences based on an innate difference between males and females, or do they result from a process of socialisation? Adults often treat boys and girls very differently based on societal gender roles, usually encouraging boys to express more masculine traits and girls to express more feminine traits. It is possible that this type of socialisation could alter the expression of behaviour over time, and explain any adult sex differences that are observed. For example, although Maccoby and Jacklin (1974) reported that males show greater mathematical ability than females, this difference has decreased noticeably in recent years, possibly as a consequence of greater equality in education (Fausto-Sterling, 2000). Indeed some feminist authors have suggested that sex differences are used as a means of maintaining established gender norms and inequality between the sexes (e.g. Fausto-Sterling, 2000).

A number of feminist authors, however, acknowledge and celebrate the innate differences between males and females, believing that a possible sex difference in characteristics such as mathematical ability or emotional reasoning does not make one sex 'better' or 'worse' than the other (e.g. Fisher, 1999).

Hyde (2005) has conducted a review of 46 meta-analyses on research investigating possible sex differences. A total of six categories of possible differences were examined: cognitive variables (such as mathematical ability), motor behaviour (such as throwing velocity), social or personality variables (such as aggression), verbal or non-verbal communication, psychological wellbeing (such as self-esteem) and miscellaneous behaviour (such as moral reasoning).

Of all the characteristics considered, 78 per cent showed little or no difference between males and females, suggesting that the sexes are more similar than different in many regards. However, large sex differences were noted for certain motor behaviours such as throwing velocity (particularly after puberty when males generally have greater muscle mass than females), levels of physical aggression, and certain aspects of sexual behaviour such as an interest in uncommitted sex. For each of these characteristics males scored, on average, higher than females.

When considering reported differences between males and females, we should remember that we are dealing here only with averages and that there can be considerable overlap between the sexes. For example, female boxers are likely to be more aggressive than the average male person. In addition, it is important always to be very specific about the nature of the characteristic being discussed. For example, although the evidence strongly suggests that males show more physical aggression than females, the differences for other types of aggression (such as verbal aggression) can be virtually non-existent (Archer, 2004). Similarly, when considering sex differences in verbal abilities, females tend to score significantly higher than males for tasks of verbal fluency, but not for specific abilities such as reading comprehension or vocabulary (Eagly, 1995).

EXERCISE   Men are better at map reading: fact or fiction?

Make a list of abilities that show a difference between men and women. Do a quick survey of family or friends to include their views in the list. What do you think are the implications of such sex differences for the way society sees men and women? Also, do you think it matters whether these differences are real or perceived?

SEXUAL ORIENTATION

9.4

Psychosocial theories typically see an individual's sexual orientation as the result of various environmental factors or 'life incidents', such as the child-rearing strategies employed by an individual's parents. Such theories tend to produce rather vague predictions about how homosexuality actually develops and generally lack substantial empirical support (see Wilson & Rahman, 2005). An alternative approach is to examine the possible biological underpinnings of an individual's sexual orientation, focusing on genetic factors and the influence of organisational hormones.

9.4.1 THE SEARCH FOR GAY GENES

The first real indication that an individual's sexual orientation may have a heritable component came from a series of twin studies.

ASIDE

Twin studies indicate the relative contribution of genetic factors to the formation of specific characteristics. This is calculated by comparing the similarities found in identical or monozygotic (MZ) twins to those found in fraternal or dizygotic (DZ) twins. Since both types of twin are likely to share the same environment during early development, any trait which MZ twins share more frequently than DZ twins implies a greater influence of genetic factors.

Bailey and Pillard (1991) recruited a large sample of homosexual individuals who had a twin. Fifty-two per cent of male MZ twins and 48 per cent of female MZ twins had the same sexual orientation, compared to 22 per cent of male DZ twins and 16 per cent of female DZ twins. Although precise rates of homosexuality differ between the studies that have followed, and some methodological criticisms have been made of earlier studies in this area, a number of researchers have reported significantly higher similarity for sexual orientation among MZ compared to DZ twins (e.g. Bailey et al., 2000; Kendler et al., 2000). This strongly suggests a genetic influence on both male and female homosexuality. Although initial work to identify genes linked to the development of homosexuality in males has begun (see below), there has been no substantial work on the specific genes involved in female homosexuality.

Researchers have also studied rates of homosexuality within close family groups, following the logic that a potentially heritable trait such as homosexuality would tend to be more common in families where at least one member was homosexual. In an analysis of 7321 individuals, Blanchard (1997) revealed that adult homosexuality in males was specifically associated with having a large number of older brothers (known as the **fraternal birth order effect**, FBOE). There was no significant relationship between having a homosexual orientation and the number of older sisters, younger brothers and younger sisters, or the mother's age. To date there is no evidence for such a birth order effect among homosexual females, suggesting this is a phenomenon unique to male homosexuality. Cantor et al. (2002) estimated that each male foetus a mother has after the first raises the chance of homosexuality by 33 per cent, equating to a 2 per cent chance of homosexuality among first-born sons, rising to 6 per cent among fifth-born sons. The influence of the fraternal birth order effect is not mediated by a male growing up with older stepbrothers but is influenced by them having biological brothers (who share the same mother) regardless of whether they are raised together or apart (Bogaert, 2006). Blanchard and Bogaert (1996) proposed that this prenatal origin of the FBOE was specifically due to the mother's immune system reacting to certain antigens that are only carried by male foetuses.

Hamer et al. (1993) reported that homosexual males had a larger number of homosexual relatives on their mother's side, particularly maternal uncles and cousins. As mothers pass on an X chromosome to their sons, the high rates of homosexuality among maternal relatives was an indication that genes associated with homosexuality may be present on the X chromosome. Hamer et al. (1993) looked at the X chromosome in 40 pairs of homosexual male brothers and found that 33 of the pairs (82 per cent of the sample) had co-inherited the same region of the X chromosome, labelled Xq28. Although this was the first attempt to identify a so-called 'gay gene', the results were far from conclusive: 18 per cent of the sample did not co-inherit the same region of the X chromosome, and subsequent research on Xq28 and homosexuality has been contradictory (e.g. Rice et al., 1999).

The most recent and comprehensive study of the genes contributing to male homosexuality was conducted by Mustanski et al. (2005) and involved a full genome scan of 456 homosexual males from 146 families. Three regions of interest emerged: 7q36 on the seventh chromosome, 8p12 on the eighth chromosome and 10q26 on the tenth chromosome. Although the precise function of each of these genes is yet to be determined, it is interesting that 7q36 contains two genes that potentially relate to the development of the supra-chiasmatic nucleus, an area that is enlarged in homosexual males (see later), while 8p12 contains genes involved in the creation, regulation and release of certain hormones.

9.4.2 THE ROLE OF ORGANISATIONAL HORMONES

As described above, organisational hormones are crucial to the process of sexual differentiation and have marked effects on the sex-typical development of an individual's brain and body. Given that homosexual individuals are attracted to sex-atypical romantic partners (i.e. members of the same sex), researchers have questioned whether organisational hormones may be involved in the formation of a homosexual orientation. The key principle of Ellis and Ames's (1987) prenatal androgen theory is that male homosexuality results from underexposure to prenatal androgens during sexual differentiation compared to male-typical levels. Female homosexuality is seen to result from exposure to an excess of androgens during this period. Such thinking was based in part on a number of studies demonstrating a connection between organisational and activational hormones on sex-atypical mating behaviour in non-human animals (e.g. Pheonix et al., 1959).

Empirically testing Ellis and Ames's (1987) theory is problematic. It would be highly unethical to conduct experiments where we directly manipulate the levels of organisational hormones that a foetus is exposed to in order to see the resulting effects on their adult sexual orientation. However, there are other ways of evaluating this theory. The first is to examine the sexual orientation of individuals who were exposed to unusually high or low levels of organisational hormones. One such group is females with congenital adrenal hyperplasia (see earlier). In addition to elevated levels of masculine behaviour during childhood play, a number of studies have reported significantly elevated levels of homosexual preference among females with congenital adrenal hyperplasia (reviewed in Meyer-Bahlburg et al., 2008).

A second means of evaluating the effects of organisational hormones on sexual orientation is to look at certain proxy markers – physical characteristics believed to reflect the hormone levels a foetus was exposed to. One such characteristic is the length of certain bones in the arms and hands. Among adults, these bones tend to be longer in heterosexual males compared to heterosexual females. Research by Martin and Nguyen (2004) suggests heterosexual males and homosexual females experience greater bone growth, consistent with exposure to higher levels of organisational androgens, than both homosexual males and heterosexual females.

However, the findings for these proxy markers are often not unidirectional: that is, homosexual males do not always display feminised traits, while homosexual females do not always display masculinised ones. For example, Bogaert and Hershberger (1999) report penis size, which covaries with organisational hormone levels, to be larger (i.e. more masculinised) among homosexual males than heterosexual males. It may therefore be more accurate to say that homosexual individuals possess a mosaic of masculinised, feminised and sex-typical traits (reviewed in Rahman & Wilson, 2003).

9.4.3 SEXUAL ORIENTATION AND THE BRAIN

Researchers have attempted to identify areas of the brain that may differ between heterosexual and homosexual individuals. Given the sex atypicality that homosexual individuals often show, most of the initial studies on the brain have focused on areas showing sex differences, particularly the hypothalamus (see earlier). One of the first differences documented between the brains of homosexual and heterosexual males was the size of the supra-chiasmatic nucleus, an area of hypothalamus involved in the regulation of circadian rhythms. Compared to heterosexual males, this area of the brain was found to be significantly larger and elongated in homosexual males, a pattern consistent with the brains of heterosexual females (Swaab & Hofman, 1990).

REASONS TO BE SCEPTICAL

So far we have only discussed two types of sexual orientation – heterosexuality and homosexuality. Do you think that everyone's sexual orientation fits into these two discrete groups, or do you think that it is expressed on a continuum, with numerous intermediate stages (i.e. varying degrees of bisexuality)? Do you think this is the same for both males and females? Why do you think researchers tend to focus on heterosexual and homosexual, rather than on bisexual, participants?

Perhaps the best known report of a difference between the brains of heterosexual and homosexual males concerns another area of the hypothalamus called INAH-3 (the third interstitial nucleus of the anterior hypothalamus). This is an area of the brain that is significantly larger in heterosexual males compared to heterosexual females (Allen et al., 1989) and in non-human animals it plays a role in sexual behaviour. LeVay (1991) not only documented this sex difference, but also reported that INAH-3 was significantly smaller in homosexual males compared to heterosexual males, a pattern again consistent with the brains of heterosexual females. In more recent research on INAH-3, Byne et al. (2000) confirmed a significant sex difference in this area, but only recorded a non-significant trend for INAH-3 to be smaller among homosexual males. Although the above studies imply that sexual orientation in males does relate to the size of INAH-3, further research is needed to substantiate the strength of this relationship.

Two final differences have been observed between heterosexual and homosexual males in areas of the brain connecting the two cerebral hemispheres. Allen and Gorski (1992) report that one of these areas, the anterior commissure, was larger in homosexual males and heterosexual females compared to heterosexual males. However, a replication of this study by Lasco et al. (2002) did not find any significant differences based on either sex or sexual orientation. Witelson et al. (in press) recently reported that right-handed homosexual males also show a larger isthmus of the corpus callosum, a bundle of fibres that carries information between the two hemispheres of the brain, than heterosexual males.

9.4.4 SEXUAL ORIENTATION AND BEHAVIOUR

Based on the differences in both neuroanatomy and other physical characteristics between heterosexual and homosexual individuals, a number of researchers have questioned if there are also behavioural differences between these groups. Many of these studies have focused on characteristics and abilities that usually show marked sex differences (see earlier). Given the sex atypicality that homosexual individuals often show, homosexual males are usually predicted to respond or score in a way more characteristic of heterosexual females, while homosexual females would score or respond in a way more characteristic of heterosexual males. There is certainly some evidence to support this, with homosexual males as a group performing worse on mental rotation tasks and better on verbal fluency tasks compared to heterosexual males (e.g. McCormick & Witelson, 1991; Rahman et al., 2005; Sanders & Wright, 1997). This is a pattern consistent with findings for heterosexual females. The trend for homosexual females is not as consistent (e.g. Rahman et al., 2003b) but does indicate that for some tasks homosexual females perform in a heterosexual male-typical direction (e.g. Rahman et al., 2003a).

KEY RESEARCHER   Qazi Rahman

FIGURE 9.3   Qazi Raham

Qazi Rahman is currently a lecturer in cognitive biology at Queen Mary, University of London. Dr Rahman obtained his BSc (Hons) in Psychology at the University of Staffordshire and his PhD at the Institute of Psychiatry (King's College, London) where he examined the neurodevelopmental, sensorimotor and neurocognitive basis of human sexual orientation. He has held lectureships at the University of East London, The Institute of Psychiatry and Guy's, King's and St Thomas's Schools (King's College, London).

Rahman's research focuses on the psychobiology of human sexual orientation and sex differences in cognition. His projects include the investigation of:

- sexual-orientation-related differences in basic spatial abilities (such as the manipulation of spatial relations)

- spatial memory (involving navigating and finding important objects in the environment)

- linguistic ability

- social or emotional cognition (e.g. 'reading' emotions in another person's face or eyes)

- the genetic basis of sexual orientation using twin modelling and molecular genetics

- the role of sexual orientation in human mating tactics and partner preferences

- the utility of proxy somatic markers (e.g. finger length ratios, handedness, and hair whorl patterning) as windows on the prenatal development of sexual orientation.

According to Hyde's (2005) meta-analysis (see earlier), two of the largest sex differences were noted for certain motor behaviours, such as throwing velocity and levels of physical aggression. How then are these characteristics expressed in homosexual individuals? With regard to throwing *accuracy*, the pattern of findings is remarkably consistent. Hall and Kimura (1995) report heterosexual males have significantly greater throwing accuracy than heterosexual females. Furthermore, homosexual males were not as accurate as heterosexual males and in fact tended to perform in a similar fashion to heterosexual females. Homosexual females were more accurate than heterosexual females and tended to perform in a similar fashion to heterosexual males. With regard to physical aggression, the findings are not so consistent. Homosexual males have been reported to show lower levels of physical aggression than heterosexual males (Gladue & Bailey, 1995; Sergeant et al., 2006), a pattern that is consistent with heterosexual females. The findings for homosexual females however are more inconsistent, with some studies suggesting *lower* levels of physical aggression than heterosexual females (Gladue, 1991), contrary to the predicted pattern, while other studies find no difference between these two groups (Gladue & Bailey, 1995).

CHAPTER SUMMARY

9.5 Sex describes the biological characteristics used to identify individuals as either male or female, and can be measured by examining an individual's sex chromosomes, gonads and external reproductive organs. Gender refers to the sociocultural characteristics associated with being either male or female, and is frequently divided into gender identity and gender role.

The sex chromosomes that an individual possesses (usually XX among females and XY among males) begin the process of sexual differentiation. Among females the Müllerian duct system develops into the female reproductive system, whereas in males the presence of the SRY gene causes the development of the Wolffian duct system, which in turn develops into the male reproductive system. Organisational hormones in the womb influence the developing foetal brain and body, usually causing the foetus to develop in a male-typical or female-typical fashion.

The process of sexual differentiation does not always proceed in a typical manner. A number of conditions can arise due to sex chromosome atypicality, such as Klinefelter's syndrome or Turner's syndrome. Alternatively, a variety of atypical conditions, such as 5-alpha reductase syndrome or congenital adrenal hyperplasia, can arise due to the action of organisational hormones. The appropriate course of treatment for many individuals born with such conditions is contentious.

The second important time for the development of sex differences, after the prenatal one, is puberty. During this time an individual sexually matures and secondary sexual characteristics develop. Although many people believe there are large-scale behavioural and psychological differences between the sexes, current research suggests that only a limited number of these differences, such as levels of physical aggression, are large in magnitude.

The current research suggests there is a biological basis to homosexuality. A number of studies have identified a heritable component to both male and female homosexuality, and research is currently under way to identify so-called 'gay genes'. Organisational hormones also appear to play a prominent role in the development of homosexuality. Research has identified areas of the brain and certain cognitive and behavioural tasks that appear to vary based on an individual's sexual orientation, particularly among males.

 # DISCUSSION QUESTIONS

Sex testing at the Olympics

Most humans can be classified as male or female, with their sex chromosomes, gonads and external genitalia all developing in either male-typical or female-typical fashion. However for some individuals one or more of these components may be inconsistent with the others, leading to difficulty in establishing an individual's biological sex.

Problems with sex typing at international sporting events are recurrent in the twentieth century. In the 1936 Olympic Games Helen Stephens was accused of being a man in disguise after winning the women's 100 metre race. Following a number of controversial articles about her in the press, Stephens took a sex test to clear her name and it confirmed her status as a female. The process of determining an athlete's sex by examination of their sex chromosomes was initiated by the International Olympic Committee (IOC) in 1968. Such a move was motivated by fears that male athletes were disguising themselves and entering competitions established for female athletes.

One recent case of note is that of Caster Semenya, a female South African runner who was required by the International Association of Athletics Federations (IAAF) to take a sex test before she was allowed to run (and subsequently win) the women's 800 metre race at the World championships in Berlin in August 2009. The tests demonstrated that she had an intersex condition, having internal testicles and no ovaries or uterus. As this book goes to press, her exact condition is unknown and the IAAF are yet to decide if she can keep her gold medal.

Sex chromosome testing is largely discontinued by the IOC but has been used recently by the IAAF. How far do you agree with these decisions and on what grounds? From your research beyond this chapter, what alternative methods would you say are available?

Sexual orientation

Research suggests that homosexuality is not a learnt behaviour but an innate characteristic. It has been argued that, if an individual's sexual orientation is innate and not a matter of personal choice, then society should be more accepting of homosexuality. How far do you agree with this proposition?

Some feel that research into the biological basis of homosexuality is wrong as it is seen as endorsing homosexuality as some form of aberrant medical condition. How far do you agree with this position?

SUGGESTIONS FOR FURTHER READING

Archer, J., & Lloyd, B. (2002). *Sex and gender* (2nd edn). Cambridge: Cambridge University Press. A very good book discussing research into sex differences and highlighting the distinction between sex and gender.

Breedlove, S.M., Rosenzweig, M.R., & Watson, N.V. (2007). *Biological psychology* (5th edn). London: Sinauer. A classic biological psychology textbook. Chapter 12 provides additional material on the process of sexual differentiation in human and non-human species.

Crooks, R., & Baur, K. (2007). *Our sexuality* (10th edn). London: Thomson. An easily accessible textbook, aimed at undergraduate students, with provides further information on a variety of biological and social topics connected with sex and sexuality.

Wilson, G., & Rahman, Q. (2005). *Born gay: the psychobiology of sexual orientation*. London: Owen. An excellent book providing a comprehensive and insightful review of research into the psychobiology of homosexuality.

HOW WE INTERACT WITH EACH OTHER

Social Psychology

Social psychology is about the phenomena of social behaviour. It attracts a lot of attention because it is about the events and processes that make up our daily lives. It looks at our feelings, our thoughts and our behaviour, and tries to describe and explain aspects of the human condition such as love and hate, happiness and sadness, pride and prejudice, comedy and tragedy. More than any other field of psychology, it is directly about me and you.

We live in a world that is awash with psychological analysis. We are looking to explain why someone is a good contestant on 'Big Brother' or a good prime minister, and we commonly look to their character and their relationships with other people. This analysis is carried out with varying degrees of scientific rigour and, to be fair, it rarely rises above the level of speculation and gossip. The field of scientific social psychology, however, has over 100 years of research findings to inform our understanding of social behaviour.

The start of social psychology is sometimes dated to 1897 and the experimental work of Norman Triplett into the effects of cooperation and competition on performance. Triplett observed that racing cyclists achieved better times on a circuit when they had someone pacing them. In a ride of 25 miles, the average times per mile were 20 per cent quicker when using a pace-maker on practice runs and even quicker in real competition. He went on to observe this improved performance in other tasks and found, for example, that children wound fishing reels faster when there were other children also winding fishing reels in the same room.

Triplett showed that cyclists achieve better times when cycling with someone rather than alone
© Hulton-Deutsch Collection/Corbis

The main concerns of social psychology commonly reflect the concerns of the time. For example, at the end of the nineteenth century there were social concerns about the behaviour of crowds. In particular, there was increasing unrest on the part of working people against repressive social conditions, and the emergence of strategies of collective political action, such as mass strikes and demonstrations. These demonstrations frequently led to violence as police and army forces attempted to suppress them. It was during this time that LeBon (1895) carried out his research and proposed that the source of this violence lay in a kind of 'mob psychology'. When people were in a crowd, their individual conscience and autonomy were suppressed, and they reverted to what LeBon described as a primeval, animalistic state in which they would commit acts for aggression which were unthinkable to the same people when acting as individuals. These ideas have been challenged and developed by modern psychologists and we cover some of them in this section.

During the middle of the twentieth century, social psychologists carried out some of the great studies that have defined the field for generations of students. The Milgram study on obedience, the Seligman study of cult membership and the Sherif study on prejudice are just some of the many investigations that had a wide scope and have challenged the ways that we think about ourselves. For many years following these studies, social psychology largely withdrew to the laboratory and carried out clever but very narrow research. More recently, the field has been looking outwards again and dealing directly with real-life behaviour, and sometimes carrying out large-scale studies (for example Reicher & Haslam, 2006). There is also a strong focus on applied work looking at health behaviours and crime, for example.

KEY ISSUES

One of the key issues for social psychology concerns the way it carries out its studies. If we carry out a study in chemistry, for example, we look at some chemicals in a flask and do stuff to them. We are in control of most of what is happening. This is not the case in psychology because the things we are studying (i.e. people) are thinking about what is going on and changing their behaviour accordingly. Every social psychology experiment is a social situation, and the objects of the experiment (the people) are responding to the demands of that situation. So we can never be sure whether their behaviour is due to the variables we are investigating in the study or the social situation of the experiment itself.

THIS SECTION

In this section, we have three chapters looking at the work of social psychologists. In Chapter 10 we explore how being in a group can affect an individual's behaviour and decision making. Commonly these influences are positive and are part of daily social interaction, but sometimes the group can lead us into poor decisions. In Chapter 11 we look at how groups behave towards each other and how we categorise and respond to people from various groups. One of the issues here concerns the nature of prejudice and racism. Finally in Chapter 12 we explore how we make judgements about other people and how we try to explain their behaviour.

10 BEHAVIOUR WITHIN GROUPS

Lead authors **Susan Hansen, Paige Wilcoxson**
and Don Bysouth

CHAPTER OUTLINE

INTRODUCTION

10.1 We take very few decisions in life entirely in isolation. We nearly always take into account the needs, opinions and expectations of other people. In some ways we are always part of a group, and being part of a group has an effect on us. Being a member of a group can affect our opinions, our decisions and even our behaviour. In this chapter, we will consider behaviour *within* groups, and we will discover some of the striking findings made by social psychologists in their research on how groups operate. We investigate the way that your performance on a task can be helped or hindered by the mere presence of others: that is, we investigate the concepts known as 'social facilitation' and 'social inhibition'.

We will also look at how working in teams can sometimes lead individuals to *decrease* their efforts, as a form of social loafing. We will explore too how it is that groups make decisions, and how groupthink might pose problems. We will consider how individual behaviour may change dramatically when an individual is part of a group, and how deindividuation may occur, with individuals giving up or losing their 'sense of self' when part of a group. Finally, we will consider the phenomena of group polarisation and of individual influence on group behaviour.

?

FRAMING QUESTIONS

Does performing in front of an audience help or hinder individual performance?
Do people work harder, or do they become lazier, when working in groups?
How do crowds influence individual behaviour?
How do groups make decisions?
Does being in a group change who we are?
What exactly *is* a group, anyway?

WHAT IS A GROUP?

10.2 The question 'What is a group?' is deceptively simple. It is a question that has occupied social psychologists for much of the last century. Social psychologists have long recognised the distinction between 'a group defined by outsiders' that has no social reality for its members, and groups that have social and psychological reality. We all belong to countless groups, but not all of these represent social psychologically meaningful group memberships. For example, you probably identify as a student and as a fan of (insert the name of your favourite band or team here!), but you may be less likely to find some of the sociodemographic groups that technically you are a member of (e.g. double-income family in urban area) to be meaningful social categories in your everyday life. The European social psychologist Henri Tajfel (1982) pointed out that there are two distinct theoretical senses of the term *group*:

1 objective collections of similar individuals as defined by outside observers, that is, objectively defined groupings that may not be subjectively significant for their members, e.g. some demographic or sociological category such as single-income families in rural areas (Turner, 1996: 28)

2 shared representations, that is, a dynamic social psychological process in which the capacity of people to (re)present themselves as members of social categories is part of the process by which sociological categories may become meaningful social psychological groups.

So, the first question we need to ask about a group that we might be interested in studying is whether this group is meaningful as a group, for its members. Indeed Tajfel, proponent of the famous social identity theory (see Chapter 11), argued that:

> Social groups are not 'things'; they are processes ... the existence of a group for its members is a complex sequence of appearances and disappearances, of looming large and vanishing into thin air ... In the static conception, the groups are seen as 'being there' side by side, almost like herrings packed in a box, coming to life to 'perceive' each other whenever prodded into doing so by the researchers. In the dynamic conception, groups (and intergroup relations) come to life when their potential designations as such have acquired a psychological and behavioural reality. (1982: 485)

Thus, as social psychologists, we should be interested in the relations *between* and *within* groups only in so far as these groups have a psychological and behavioural 'reality' – or life – for their members. That is, the groups we study should ideally be meaningful, *as groups*, for the people who belong to them – as well as to the scientists studying them!

Entitativity is a concept that has helped social psychologists explain the extent to which we regard groups as coherent and 'group-like'. For example, a queue at a city café may be regarded as less 'group-like' than a family Christmas gathering. 'Real' groups have what social psychologists call 'high entitativity'; this phenomenon occurs when the group in question is regarded as important by, and to, its members, and when there is a high frequency of interaction between group members. Other factors that predict high entitativity include group members regarding each other as similar in significant ways, and as sharing common goals and ways of making sense of the world. Conversely, groups with low entitativity are those which are regarded as less 'real'; there may be a low frequency of interaction between group members, and members may regard each other as having little in common.

> **Entitativity** Refers to how coherent and connected a group is, that is, how much the people in the group can be seen as being a part of the group rather than being a collection of individuals.

The extent to which groups are regarded as 'real' by their members is crucial in determining the extent to which group membership exerts an influence on our behaviour.

This behaviour can be mundane and inconsequential – such as whether you like (or admit to liking) a particular band – or it can be more serious and far-reaching in its consequences. Gupta (2001) points out that group membership can exert a powerful influence on individual behaviour in 'crimes of obedience', where group members behave in morally problematic ways. Research into such crimes of obedience is grounded in an interest in better understanding how some of the more horrific crimes of obedience in human history came to pass. These crimes include unthinkable acts of genocide, such as the Holocaust.

10.2.1 BENEFITS AND COSTS OF GROUP MEMBERSHIP

Being a member of a group can provide us with rewarding benefits: group membership can contribute to our senses of self and self-worth. Through our group memberships we can feel a sense of pride or achievement in accomplishments that we have not directly contributed to, yet feel a part of. Think of the last time you said, 'We won!'. It is quite likely (unless you play sports) that you made no active contribution to this victory, but yet such accomplishments can enhance our sense of self-worth and pride. In the case of the Olympics, you may even feel a further sense of accomplishment and pride at the achievements of your nation – when the medal tally is favourable, at least!

Group membership can also provide us with a vital sense of belonging and of being understood. That is, being a member of a group can give us a significant sense of meaningful connection to the social world. Indeed, this sense of belonging to a larger social world is a key potential benefit of group membership. Knowles and Gardner (2008) examined the consequences for this sense of belonging when participants experienced social rejection. They found that, after experiencing rejection, people experienced a heightened sense of group membership, and regarded the groups they belonged to as being more entitative (or group-like) than other groups. Knowles and Gardner (2008) regard this as a protective benefit of group membership, that when we feel rejected, we remind ourselves that there are groups we value that we belong to.

One particularly important and very common type of group is a team. Teams refer to groups of people who are united in the pursuit of a common goal or achievement – whether that be an in-class presentation or winning a football match. Team members work interdependently together to achieve shared performance goals, and team members hold each other responsible for their work towards these goals.

WATCHING YOU, WATCHING ME: AHA!

10.3
What is the effect of the presence of other people on an individual's behaviour or performance on a task? Think about some of the activities that you engage in, and how the mere presence of others might influence your behaviour. For example, do you think your performance in singing is better when alone or when in front of a group? How about writing an essay or driving a car or asking someone on a date? In short, does having an audience help or hinder individual performance?

10.3.1 PERFORMANCE ANXIETY OR PERFORMANCE BOOST?

The term **social facilitation** was first used by Floyd Allport (1920) to describe the phenomenon that many people seem to perform better when in front of an audience. This phenomenon was first reported (in what some have suggested represents the first social psychological experiment) by Norman Triplett (1898), who observed that people cycled faster when provided with pacing than they did when cycling alone, and faster still when engaged in competition than with pacing. Now, while the notion that people perform better when engaged in competition was hardly novel, Allport's suggestion that it was the mere presence of other persons that influenced performance certainly was.

Indeed, Allport suggested that this phenomenon was not unique to human beings, but might extend to members of other species when they were engaged in the same behaviours as each other (though not interacting) or as passive observers of each other's behaviour.

> **Social facilitation**   Refers to the effect that the presence of one or more people can have to boost our performance.
> **Social inhibition**   Refers to how the presence of one or more people can have a detrimental effect on our performance.

This led to an explosion in research on the effect during the 1920s and 1930s, with research conducted not only on humans but also on chickens, fish and even cockroaches!

KEY STUDY   Zajonc, R.B., Heingartner, A., & Herman, E.M. (1969). Social enhancement and impairment of performance in the cockroach. *Journal of Personality and Social Psychology, 13,* 83–92.

In this study, Zajonc and colleagues demonstrated that even the performance of cockroaches can be affected by the presence of other cockroaches. Given an easy maze to run, the visible presence of other cockroaches 'watching' made the cockroach in the maze run faster, but when cockroaches were given a more difficult maze to solve, they actually ran slower when other cockroaches were 'watching' them! The audience was a little unusual, in that cockroaches don't normally sit down to watch another cockroach run a maze, so the researchers kept them in place by fixing them to the grandstands with nails. Don't try this at home.

What this research indicated, perhaps counter-intuitively, was that the presence of others can lead to a decrease or detriment in task performance, and this became known as **social inhibition.**

Why does the presence of others sometimes facilitate performance, and at other times inhibit performance? One explanation offered by Robert Zajonc (1965) was that when individuals are in the presence of others they experience an increase in drive or **motivation.** In short, they experience increased arousal; this arousal tends to enhance whatever the 'dominant' response is likely to be. Thus, if the task is relatively easy, and the responses are well learned or dominant, then there is likely to be an *increase* in performance in the

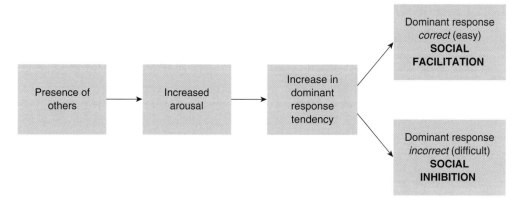

FIGURE 10.1   Pathway to social facilitation or social inhibition

presence of others. However, if the task is difficult, novel or poorly learned, then the increase in arousal from having others around is likely to *impair* performance.

One result of such research into social facilitation and inhibition was findings that suggested that, while the presence of others often improves performance on simple tasks, performance on more complex tasks is inhibited, as shown in Figure 10.1.

10.3.2 CROWDING: BEING IN THE PRESENCE OF TOO MANY OTHERS?

The magnitude with which the presence of other people can affect individuals is amplified with greater numbers (Freedman et al., 1971). For example, consider the difference if you had to present a student project in a small tutorial room or a large and crowded lecture theatre (Jackson & Latané, 1981). While performance may be increased with an audience, a large audience may interfere with even the most well-learned behaviours (e.g. speaking) and, in certain situations, individuals may suffer 'choking'. For example, learning lines for a speech may present no real difficulties when practising in a small group; however, when giving the speech in a packed lecture theatre the lines may be completely forgotten.

Further, it is important to consider that being in a crowd can intensify positive or negative reactions (Figure 10.2). For example, consider seeing your favourite performer in an almost empty auditorium as opposed to a packed and crowded venue. Studies have also shown that when individuals are in close physical proximity, friendly people are liked more and unfriendly people are disliked more (Storms & Thomas, 1977). One well-studied issue is the well-known effect of the 'home advantage' in competitive sports, with a team more likely to win playing at their home field than away (Schlenker et al., 1995). This has usually been explained as the result of playing in front of a larger supportive audience as opposed to a larger, less supportive or even overtly hostile audience!

So, on to a question we have not considered yet: *why* does the presence of others arouse or motivate individuals? Beyond the reason of an **innate** tendency to become aroused

FIGURE 10.2 Although many of the theories of groups focus on the negative aspects of the groups, our common experience of being in large groups is very positive. For example, people at Glastonbury get together in a large, lively and relatively unhygienic group and behave in very positive ways towards each other
© Luke Macgregor/Corbis

physiologically by the mere presence of other individuals (e.g. Zajonc, 1965) we can consider three explanations: evaluation apprehension, distraction conflict and challenge–threat.

Consider how you feel just before a big exam, on match day or before a first date. Are you motivated to do well and give a good impression? One theory is that people want to make a good impression and are concerned about how they will be evaluated, which is known as *evaluation apprehension*. Judgements and evaluations given by others when we engage in simple tasks can encourage us and boost our performance; on complex tasks the pressure of being evaluated can impair performance. In one classic study, participants involved in the preparation of a perception experiment were given blindfolds (condition 1) or allowed to observe other participants (condition 2). The mere presence of blindfolded participants did not boost dominant responses (Cottrell et al., 1968): that is, when confederates were blindfolded, participants' performance was similar to that of participants working alone. Only participants working in front of 'seeing' confederates were more likely to produce dominant responses.

Another explanation is that the presence of others is distracting. In short, there is a conflict between attending to others and how they are evaluating us, and how we perform on a particular task – a *distraction conflict*. On easy tasks, we compensate for the distraction with increased concentration, and may well perform better; however, on difficult tasks this distraction impairs performance (Baron, 1986).

A more recent theory is that of *challenge–threat* (Blascovich et al., 1999) which suggests that the presence of others evokes one of two distinct physiological responses. When an individual has the resources to undertake the task, a challenge response occurs – similar to the changes that occur during aerobic exercise. However, when the individual does not have the resources to meet the task, a threat response occurs which may impede performance.

ARE GROUPS ELECTRIC?

10.4

Now, you might assume that when people undertake various tasks in teams, the presence of others might lead individual members of the team to work harder and perform better. However, in the 1880s, the French agricultural engineer Max Ringelmann asked student volunteers to pull as hard as they could on a rope in a tug-of-war (see Kravitz & Martin, 1986). In what has come to be termed the *Ringelmann effect*, Ringelmann observed that as more people helped to pull on the rope, the total force exerted by the group overall increased (so the rope was pulled harder); however, the average force exerted by each group member (i.e. the efforts of each individual) actually declined.

In a later replication of this study, participants pulling on the rope were blindfolded; the results showed that they pulled 18 per cent harder when they could see that they were pulling alone than when they were blindfolded and told that up to five others were helping them to pull the rope (Ingham et al., 1974). Subsequent researchers have found that, in teamwork, individual persons often work less hard and put in less effort – a phenomenon termed **social loafing** (Latané et al., 1979).

10.4.1 SOCIAL LOAFING

Social loafing appears to occur remarkably consistently (Karau & Williams, 1993) and has been found in studies of clapping, shouting, sports participation, making clinical ratings, navigating mazes and even generating ideas.

Social loafing   The reduction in individual effort that can occur in tasks when only group performance is measured (not each person individually).

Diffusion of responsibility   The phenomenon of individuals taking less responsibility for events when there are other people present because they feel less personally responsible for what is happening.

Remember, in our discussion of social facilitation and inhibition, the effect that task type has on performance in the presence of others: social facilitation occurs with simple and easy tasks and social inhibition with more complex and demanding tasks. So, the question is, does engaging in a complex task in a group result in poorer performance? One explanation is that when people work in groups they feel personally less responsible for their own contribution, and there is a **diffusion of responsibility** (Comer, 1995).

Another possible explanation is that individuals 'loaf' in groups as they believe that this is what people *do* in groups, and to maintain equity of effort between group members, they loaf themselves (Jackson & Harkins, 1985).

In this regard, it is important to draw a distinction here between social facilitation or inhibition and social loafing. With social facilitation or inhibition the focus is on an individual's specific performance or behaviour as evaluated by others, while the focus with social loafing is on the evaluation of group performance. In short, social loafing seems to occur when an individual's contribution to a group is pooled. Consider also that 'what people *can* do' (maximal performance) may be different to 'what people *will* do' (typical performance) when examining social loafing.

10.4.2 HOW TO SPOT A SOCIAL LOAFER – AND WHAT TO DO ABOUT IT WHEN YOU FIND ONE

Before we come down too hard on social loafers (ourselves included), it is important to note that individuals may *not* be consciously aware that they are getting a free ride on the efforts of their group (Frohlich & Oppenheimer, 1970). Indeed, studies show that individuals often report that they believe they make equal contributions in situations in which tasks are performed alone or in a group. In other words, social loafers may well believe that they are contributing to the group effort as much as they are able to, and certainly as much as the next person; they may be shocked at the idea that they are exploiting the group for individual gain.

So, how can social loafers be identified, and what kinds of things can be done to minimise the effect they have on the group's performance? One finding that appears consistent across studies (Karau & Williams, 1993) is that social loafing experiments seem to demonstrate the importance of evaluation apprehension. That is, in situations in which *group* performance is evaluated, rather than the unique contribution of each individual, there is a decrease in evaluation apprehension, and social loafing ensues. However, when individuals undertake tasks in which their individual performance may be explicitly evaluated, there is an increase in evaluation apprehension and social facilitation occurs. So, one strategy for reducing social loafing in group-based activities is to ensure that there is explicit observation, not just of group performance, but of individual performances within the groups.

ASIDE

As a student, you may be asked to work in small groups to prepare a poster for one of your psychology modules; the mark you get for this piece of work may be split between an overall mark for the group's poster, and a mark based on your personal contribution to the poster, as evidenced by a log of individual actions and efforts that you prepared. Lecturers choose to assess you in this way because they realise that, if students know they are also going to be individually assessed, they are less likely to act as social loafers! Sneaky, eh?

Karau and Williams (1993) noted in their meta-analysis of social loafing studies that two key factors appear important in the reduction of social loafing in groups. The first is the importance of the task, and the second is the significance that the group has for the individual (see Figure 10.3).

Indeed, individuals may actually increase efforts and work harder in groups, an effect called *social compensation* (Williams & Karau, 1991; Zaccaro, 1984). This occurs in circumstances where greater value is placed on the group itself as opposed to the individual (see, for example, the Star Trek extract in the aside), and/or when group members are expected to be effective in achieving goals that are important to both the individuals and the group (Guzzo & Dickson, 1996). In the Star Trek film 'The Wrath of Khan', one of the crew, Spock, sacrifices himself in order to save the rest of the crew. Sometimes, we will put a lot of

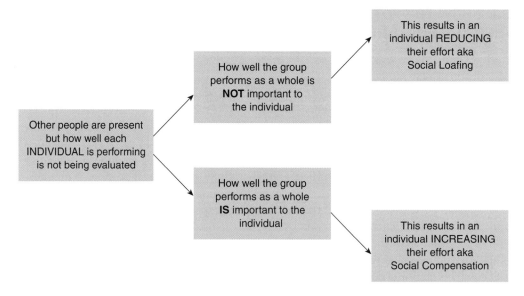

FIGURE 10.3 Pathway to social loafing or social compensation

effort into a group that we are part of, as demonstrated in the aside box below; in such circumstances, the performance or well being of the group is so important to the individual (i.e. the crew of the Starship Enterprise to Spock in this instance), that they will contribute over and above anything that could be expected of an individual – in this Star Trek film, Spock actually sacrifices his own life to ensure the survival of the group that he has bonded with.

ASIDE   The needs of the many

In the film *Star Trek II: The Wrath of Khan* (1982, Paramount Pictures), Mr Spock, having sacrificed himself to save the starship *Enterprise*, is dying.

Kirk: Spock!
Spock: The ship ... out of danger?
Kirk: Yes.
Spock: Don't grieve, Admiral. It is logical. The needs of the many outweigh ...
Kirk: ... the needs of the few ...
Spock: ... or the one. I never took the Kobayashi Maru test until now. What do you think of my solution?
Kirk: Spock ...
Spock: I have been and always shall be your friend.
[Holds up his hand in the Vulcan salute]
Spock: Live long and prosper.
[Audience of Trekkies quietly sob]

In summary, while diffusion of responsibility might explain why on simple tasks social loafing occurs, and evaluation apprehension may impair performance on more complex tasks, these seem to cancel each other out when people carry out complex tasks in settings in which group performance rather than individual performance is evaluated.

To conclude this section, we have considered how the presence of others can lead to changes in individual behaviour. We have considered how this can lead to improvements in performance (as social facilitation) and to declines in performance (as social inhibition). Further, we examined the surprising counter-intuitive finding of social loafing – that often people work less when part of a team or group than when alone. We also considered some factors that facilitate individuals to work harder when they are working in a group, such as task complexity, the importance of the task, and even the manner in which individual or group performance is evaluated. We will now consider how the presence of others can have profound effects on individual behaviour, specifically when it comes to making decisions in groups.

DECISION MAKING WITHIN GROUPS

10.5

Think of the last time you had to make an important decision alone, perhaps about going to university. How did you make this decision? Did you talk to other people about it? Did you weigh up the pros and cons and think about the impact of the decision on your future? Now think about the last time you had to make an important decision within a group. How was that different? Did you feel pressure? Were you comfortable voicing your opinion if it differed from other people's opinions? The next part of this chapter will look at how groups make decisions. In particular, we will be examining the concept of groupthink, a term coined by Irving Janis in 1972.

> **Groupthink** A style of thinking shown by group members who try to minimise conflict and reach a consensus without critically testing and evaluating ideas.

10.5.1 GROUPTHINK

Janis (1972; 1982) conducted case studies analysing US government groups that had made important decisions under stressful conditions. He found that on a number of occasions when groups made poor decisions he was able to identify several variables that were present and appeared to have affected the decision making. He termed this **groupthink**:

> a mode of thinking that people engage in when they are deeply involved in a cohesive in-group, when the members' strivings for unanimity override their motivation to realistically appraise alternative courses of action ... *Groupthink* refers to a deterioration of mental efficiency, reality testing, and moral judgment that results from in-group pressures. (1972: 9)

FIGURE 10.4 Tony Blair visits British troops in Iraq when he was the British Prime Minister. The Butler report into the decision to invade Iraq in 2003 suggested that the UK intelligence service had developed a groupthink about the issues. This analysis has also been applied to the way that Tony Blair looked for advice and took the final decision to go to war
© Corbis

Janis cites a number of examples, most famously the disastrous decision in 1961 by the USA to support an invasion of Cuba by Cuban exiles trying to overthrow Fidel Castro. The President at the time (John Kennedy) took advice from a close group, and together they came to the conclusion that the invasion was a good idea and would enhance the influence of the USA in the area. In fact, the invasion was a disaster and the involvement of the USA with the rebels led to other countries being more suspicious of them (Janis, 1972). The issue that Janis raises is about how a group of people who usually make good decisions end up making one that is so disastrous (Figure 10.4). Janis explicitly differentiated between group-think and a group making a *poor* decision. Groupthink is where group members seek agreement, such that this leads to an inadequate consideration of alternative courses of action, which in turn may result in a poor decision (McCauley, 1989). Thus, when the necessary factors are in place for groupthink to occur, it is possible that a poor decision will be made, but this is not always the result. Likewise, groups that do *not* engage in groupthink do not always make good decisions.

Indeed, most important decisions that affect our lives are made not by individuals but by groups, such as Parliament, government committees and businesses (Neck & Moorhead,

1995). Therefore, it is important to know how groups function and how to spot circumstances that may occur in groups that increase the likelihood of groupthink.

10.5.2 HOW TO SPOT GROUPTHINK

So what conditions are necessary for groupthink to occur? To put it simply, groups who engage in groupthink are more concerned with reaching agreement within the group and keeping the group cohesive (i.e. strong, positive and together) than with the quality of the decision they will make (Jones & Roelofsma, 2000). Janis and Mann (1977) set forth a model for groupthink that includes antecedents, symptoms and defects of groupthink. The antecedents are the conditions that lay the groundwork for groupthink to occur. When these conditions are present, the group is likely to have a tendency to seek agreement. Symptoms of this behaviour include self-censorship and the belief that the group is invulnerable, and these symptoms lead to factors that contribute to defective decision making and make it more likely that a poor decision will result.

10.5.3 CRITICISMS OF GROUPTHINK

Whilst groupthink continues to be a useful model that aids our understanding of group decision making, it is not without criticism. Researchers have questioned the robustness of the retrospective case study approach used by Janis (Tetlock, 1979) and empirical research has evidenced mixed results for support of Janis's theory. Supporting evidence has been put forward by Moorhead and Montanari (1986), who found that the insulation of group members from external influences most affects group decision making. Callaway and Esser (1984) found that highly cohesive groups made the poorest decisions, and groupthink was characterised by a lack of disagreement and a high level of confidence in group decisions. However, other researchers have criticised the model as ignoring several factors that have been shown to contribute to group decision making, such as: group norms, or what is acceptable behaviour within the group (Moorhead, 1982); the style and amount of power held by the group leader (McCauley, 1989); and the stage of group development, that is, whether the group had been together and making decisions for a long time, or whether there were new group members (Leana, 1985). Furthermore, other researchers question whether the concept of groupthink is generalisable, since Janis identified the phenomenon in highly cohesive groups in political and military contexts (Jones & Roelofsma, 2000).

It is clear that while the groupthink model has its critics, it has illuminated our understanding of the processes that can occur when small groups are tasked with making important decisions under pressure. Whilst the model is not without criticism, it has shown that level of cohesion, leadership style, members' self-censorship, their refusal to look at alternatives, and their unwillingness to engage in dissent, are important variables to examine when groups engage in decision making tasks.

> **EXERCISE   Reflect on the following questions:**
>
> - Have you ever been in a situation where groupthink has occurred?
> - In light of what you have learned in this chapter, what could you do to prevent faulty decision making?

DEINDIVIDUATION

10.6 Have you ever been in a group and done something you would not usually do? Have you observed this behaviour in others? Incidents of mob violence, such as football hooliganism have long been a topic of inquiry in the field of social psychology. This phenomenon was first examined by LeBon (1895), who theorised that when an individual is in a crowd, a sense of anonymity, suggestibility and the influence of others combine to overcome the individual, resulting in loss of self-control and violations of personal and/or social norms (Postmes & Spears, 1998). Here we need to examine the concept of **deindividuation**, a term first used by Festinger et al. in 1952 to describe the process that occurs when an individual is in a group and feels less identifiable and accountable for his or her behaviour than they usually would (Crisp & Turner, 2007).

The theory of deindividuation has evolved since its conception. Zimbardo's (1969) model of deindividuation specified the process through which deindividuation occurs, beginning with what he termed input variables. These are factors that encourage deindividuation to occur, such as feelings of anonymity, altered responsibility, substance use, group size and unstructured situations. According to Zimbardo, when these factors are present, subjective changes in an individual could occur; for example, an individual may become less observant and evaluative of his/her behaviour and there may be a weakening of controls that regulate their normal behaviour, leading to output behaviour that may be impulsive, emotional and regressive. Zimbardo believed this behaviour could be prosocial as well as antisocial, but he stressed the antisocial elements of the model (Postmes & Spears, 1998).

> **Deindividuation**   A process whereby the presence of others leads an individual to lose their sense of personal identity and to feel anonymous, becoming less socially responsible and guided by moral principles.

Other theorists have focused solely on the individual's internal process. Diener (1977) reviewed much of the research literature on deindividuation and found a lack of empirical support for the concept as put forth by Festinger et al. (1952) and Zimbardo (1969). He found that variables associated with deindividuation, such as anonymity, altered responsibility and group size, did not always disinhibit behaviour (Postmes & Spears, 1998). Wicklund (1975) theorised that attention must be focused either inward to the self or outward to the environment. Diener (1980) borrowed from this model and theorised that deindividuation is the result of decreased self-awareness and occurs when the individual focuses attention away from the self and therefore loses some capacity to evaluate his or her actions and plan behaviour. However, empirical support for this model has been lacking and, furthermore, the variable of decreased self-awareness has proven difficult to isolate and therefore its impact on deindividuation is difficult to determine (Postmes & Spears, 1998).

10.6.1 CRITICISMS OF DEINDIVIDUATION

Postmes and Spears (1998) conducted a meta-analysis of 60 studies that examined deindividuation, and some of the studies showed results opposite to those that deindividuation theory would predict. Overall, there was only a small effect of deindividuation on the transgression of social norms, with decreases in the accountability of individuals more likely to increase anti-normative behaviour. According to Postmes and Spears's (1998) research, there is small but consistent support for the theory of deindividuation as originally conceptualised by Festinger et al. (1952) and Zimbardo (1969), but no support for Diener's (1980) and Prentice-Dunn and Rogers's (1982) conceptualisations.

GROUP POLARISATION

10.7
Do groups make better decisions than individuals? Can being a member of a group change your opinion on important issues? In this section we explore group polarisation, or the finding that groups sometimes make decisions that are more extreme than the combination of individual group members' opinions would suggest.

10.7.1 THE 'RISKY SHIFT'

The **risky shift** refers to the counter-intuitive finding that groups may sometimes make riskier decisions than individuals. We often assume that groups are more conservative in their decisions than individuals – and that a group's position will be some sort of average of each individual group members' position. However, Moscovici and Zavalloni (1969) demonstrated that when individual group members all favoured a relatively risky course of action prior to group discussion, the decision made after group discussion was significantly more risky than the average of individual positions would have predicted.

Subsequent research has demonstrated the same amplification when group members were all relatively cautious as individuals prior to group discussion (Manstead & Hewstone, 1996). Stated simply, a group of individuals favouring a risky course of action will decide as a group on an even riskier course of action; a group of individuals favouring a cautious course of action will decide as a group on an even more cautious course of action. This phenomenon is known as group polarisation – the tendency for groups, after discussion, to lean towards decisions that significantly exceed the mean of individual group members' opinions, in the direction suggested by that mean (Hogg, 1996).

Risky shift   When individual group members all favour a relatively risky course of action prior to group discussion, the decision made after group discussion is more risky than the average of individual positions would have predicted.

This is a finding that obviously has clear consequences for groups that are charged with important decision making tasks. Indeed, social psychological research on decision making processes in juries has found some evidence of group polarisation (e.g. Bray & Noble, 1978; MacCoun & Kerr, 1988).

10.7.2 HOW DOES GROUP POLARISATION HAPPEN?

A great deal of literature has been devoted to generating theories that might help to explain the social psychological processes underlying group polarisation. These theories can be grouped according to three major perspectives. These relate to the relative importance of persuasive argument, social comparison processes and social categorisation processes (Hinsz & Davis, 1984; Sanders & Baron, 1977; Tajfel, 1982; Turner, 1991). Theories that emphasise the role of *persuasive argument* assert that group polarisation is the result of the more novel and persuasive arguments that a collection of individuals who lean in a particular direction will generate in support of their initial positions (Burnstein & Vinokur, 1977). These arguments, theorists argue, will be more novel and persuasive than any opposing arguments which group members might attempt during discussion. As a result, group members will become even more strongly convinced of their position (e.g. Hinsz & Davis, 1984).

Theories that emphasise **social comparison** processes (e.g. Sanders & Baron, 1977) argue that group polarisation is the result of individuals acting according to a desire to follow socially desirable courses of action and to avoid group censure. That is, group members will strive to publicly adhere to the cultural norms of the group and will thus shift their opinions in the direction expressed by the group.

Theories based on **social categorisation** processes (e.g. **self-categorisation theory**, Turner, 1991; social identity theory, Tajfel, 1982) draw attention to the role of group members' identification with the group, and to their active construction of identity-relevant group norms which they will adhere to, as part of their self-categorisation as group members.

INDIVIDUAL INFLUENCE ON GROUPS

10.8

It seems that groups can exert a powerful influence on us as individuals. But can we as individuals, or minority groups, hope to exert any kind of influence on the majority? Studies on minority influence and leadership can tell us about the circumstances under which such an influence may be possible.

10.8.1 MINORITY INFLUENCE (OR, AND THE LITTLE ONE SAID 'MOVE OVER')

Can small or minority groups exert an influence on the majority? For much of this century, the research focus for social psychologists was on the influence of majority groups over minority groups. But in the late 1960s, this focus shifted to consider the potential influence of minority groups on majority opinions (Moscovici & Zavalloni, 1969). This represented an important shift away from the exclusive focus at that time which, in the tradition of research on conformity, was very much restricted to considering the powerful influence of the dominant majority on less powerful minorities. Moscovici put forth the challenging argument that minority influence, far from being inconsequential, was actually a crucial factor in social change and innovation. That is, while minorities may not have the power of majority groups in terms of available resources, they may exert an influence via the creative and challenging ideas they espouse. However, minority influence can only occur under certain conditions. These include the relative size of the majority, in that the larger the majority, the less the influence of the minority (Latané & Wolf, 1981); various situational factors, such as one's position relative to other group members around a table (Maass & Clark, 1984); behavioural style and consistency (Moscovici & Nemeth, 1974); and the **snowball effect** (Nemeth et al., 1974).

> **Snowball effect**   Refers to the processes by which the opinions of the majority shift in order to agree with the position of the minority, which is then, strictly speaking, no longer a minority.

Minority groups are more likely to exert successful influence on majority opinion if they can maintain a consistent position over time (Moscovici & Nemeth, 1974). This is crucial in terms of maintaining the credibility of the minority group's position, and thus the potential to exert a meaningful influence on the majority.

10.8.2 LEADERSHIP

One final area of social psychology related to the ability of individuals to exert an influence on groups is that pertaining to leadership. Leadership is a positively regarded characteristic, and indeed, most people regard themselves as average or above average as leaders. The earliest social psychological research failed to get to grips with analysis of what qualities or attributes are shown by successful leaders and simply reflected commonsensical views of the time: that some people are, simply, 'born' to be leaders. This 'great person' theory of leadership is no longer in favour, and contemporary social psychological research focuses on the role of a range of behavioural, group and environmental factors in effective leadership.

The contemporary literature on leadership is large and diverse. However, most researchers agree that leadership is 'a process of social influence through which an individual enlists and mobilises the aid of others in the attainment of a collective goal' (Chemers, 2002: 204). Thus, the focus is more on what an individual can get others to accomplish and the social processes that are involved than leadership as an aspect of individual psychology. By this definition, leadership is not simply a matter of being 'the boss': that is, leadership involves not coercion but the enlistment and encouragement of the active support of group members. Think about the difference between a manager and a leader: most of us would think of a manager as someone who tells us what to do, whereas a leader is someone we would willingly do things for.

Social psychological research on leadership demonstrates that leaders may have characteristic behavioural styles (Weissenberg & Kavanaugh, 1972). These include task-oriented style, which involves 'getting the job done'. Alternatively, leaders may demonstrate a person-oriented style of leadership (Judge et al., 2004): this refers to the focus of leaders on establishing and maintaining harmonious and positive relations with their group. Other key dimensions identified in the literature include the extent to which leaders are autocratic-participative and directive-participative (Muczyk & Reimann, 1987). These refer to the extent to which leaders share participation with group members, and the extent to which the conduct of group members is directed.

Different styles can be effective in different environments. In a high-stress working environment, where critical decisions must be made with haste (e.g. an operating theatre), an autocratic leadership style may be the most effective; in a less stressful workplace, people may prefer a more participative style. Similarly, a leader may vary the extent of direction or permissiveness they exhibit according to the relative status of an employee or apprentice, with established workers being treated with more permissiveness than those who may need more direction in order to 'learn the ropes'.

Finally, transformational or charismatic leaders – like Martin Luther King – may exert considerable influence on entire societies. Researchers regard such influence as being due to a confluence of factors, including a charismatic personal style, the adoption of a clear and consistent vision, and successfully magnifying the significance and importance of their goals with reference to group and societal goals. In contrast, transactional leaders operate within an existing system, rather than attempting to change it.

CHAPTER SUMMARY

10.9

This chapter has introduced some important areas in the study of within-group behaviour. We have learned how being a member of a group can affect our opinions, our decisions and even our behaviour. We have considered behaviour within groups, and have explored some of the striking findings made by psychologists in their investigations of how groups work. We examined social facilitation and social inhibition – the way that an individual's performance on a task can be helped or hindered by the mere presence of others. We then considered how, perhaps counter-intuitively, working in teams might lead individuals to decrease their efforts as a form of social loafing. Importantly, we considered that the manner by which measures of task performance are obtained for individual and group tasks appears linked to whether social loafing or social facilitation occurs. We then turned our attention to how groups make decisions, and how groupthink might pose problems. We then explored how individual behaviour may change dramatically when an individual is part of a group, and considered how deindividuation may occur, with individuals giving up or losing an individual 'sense of self' when part of a group. In the following chapter, we extend our focus on groups to consider the equally important topic of intergroup behaviour, or how it is that groups behave in the context of other groups.

DISCUSSION QUESTIONS

So, how do psychologists define what counts as a 'group'? If groups can more or less comprise any collection of members for an infinite range of reasons and activities, how do findings from one particular setting relate to findings in another? Can psychologists really study such groups outside the laboratory? That is to say, perhaps one of the greatest challenges facing this kind of research is that while measures of various group outcome processes are collected and analysed (e.g. measures of task performance, rating scales), psychologists know very little about the actual interactional practices that real social groups engage with.

SUGGESTIONS FOR FURTHER READING

If you are interested in issues around decision making, and in particular groupthink, then go to the work of Janis, for example: Janis, I.L. (1972). *Victims of groupthink*. Boston: Houghton Mifflin.

Deindividuation and our behaviour in public and private space is interestingly dealt with in Prentice-Dunn, S., & Rogers, R.W. (1982). Effects of public and private self-awareness of deindividuation and aggression. *Journal of Personality and Social Psychology*, 43, 503–513.

On a similar theme, it is worth checking out the darkroom study by Gergen which gives a surprising take on the deindividuation story: Gergen, K.J., Gergen, M.M., & Barton, W.H. (1973). Deviance in the dark. *Psychology Today*, October, 129–130.

Finally, one of the great studies of social psychology is the robber's cave by Sherif, which you can read in its journal form or on the internet at the 'classic studies in the history of psychology' site: Sherif, M. (1956). Experiments in group conflict. *Scientific American*, 195, 54–58.

11 BEHAVIOUR BETWEEN GROUPS

Lead authors **Mick Gregson, Rowena Hill** and **Nicholas Blagden**

CHAPTER OUTLINE

INTRODUCTION

11.1
Barack Obama's inauguration as the first black President of the USA was witnessed by veterans of the US Civil Rights movement who 40 years ago fought for basic rights denied to black people in some parts of the USA. In his inaugural speech, President Obama emphasised the USA's diversity as 'a nation of Christians and Muslims, Jews and Hindus, and nonbelievers … shaped by every language and culture'.

President Obama's election is remarkable partly because of the prejudice and discrimination against black people that have contributed to social inequality. Psychological analysis should be relevant to such examples of behaviour between groups. Before reading on, consider the following. While still at school, you may have witnessed, or even taken part in, verbal or physical conflict between pupils from different areas or different schools. Pupils with a 'different' appearance and lifestyle may have been targets of rumour and gossip, verbal abuse or physical threats. What similarities can you see between this kind of conflict and the kind of political and social divisions that may lead in the most extreme cases to genocide – or are they completely different?

FRAMING QUESTIONS

How have social psychologists explained behaviour between groups?
To what extent are prejudice and discrimination inevitable?
How have psychological approaches been influenced by the social context?
How can conflict between groups be reduced?

11.2 FUNDAMENTAL CONCEPTS

11.2.1 INTERPERSONAL VERSUS INTERGROUP BEHAVIOUR

Intergroup relations can only exist when we have groups. In everyday life we have no problem in using the word 'group' and knowing what we mean by this, so it should be straightforward to discuss intergroup relations. A classic definition, provided by Sherif, suggests that this is the case:

whenever individuals belonging to one group interact, collectively or individually, with another group or its members in terms of their group identifications we have an instance of intergroup behaviour. (1966: 12)

Though this seems clear, defining the meaning of 'group' more precisely is problematic. Different criteria have been employed by different psychologists at different times. Psychologists interested in behaviour in small groups focus on factors such as face-to-face interaction, group norms and interdependence (e.g. Johnson & Johnson, 1987). The behaviour of very large groups may differ. Thus we would be interested in looking not so much at individual, face-to-face interactions, but rather at interactions on the group level, and the 'us versus them' scenarios that arise as groups confront each other.

To encompass large-scale social conflict and to avoid some of the problems associated with defining groups in more specific ways, Tajfel (1978) proposed that a group is essentially a set of people who feel that they are a group. This can be applied to anything from a small 'gang' of friends to very broad groupings such as a religious grouping or a nation. According to Tajfel, the salience of a group membership for us will depend on the context. For example, many people become more conscious of their nationality at times of conflict or major sporting competition.

Tajfel proposed that there is a continuum of behaviour between acting purely in terms of self and acting purely in terms of group. These extremes are 'ideal' in the sense that we can never act completely independently of our group memberships or of our own personal characteristics and relationships. Rather, we may be acting more or less in terms of self or group, and this will vary according to changes in the context. Changes from the interpersonal to the intergroup may occur quite suddenly.

EXERCISE   Are you talking about ME?

Imagine two students, new to university, who have just met. They find each other attractive and both seem to be enjoying chatting away happily on quite a personal level. They begin talking about the different parts of the country where they come from, and then one makes a sarcastic comment about people from the other's region based on a well-known stereotype.

Consider a spectrum of behaviour running from 'acting in terms of self' at one end to 'acting in terms of group' at the other. Analyse the above example in terms of this spectrum. At different stages of the interaction, where would you place the behaviour of the two students on this continuum? Would you expect any change to follow from the sarcastic comment? What would this depend on?

Now reflect on how you imagined the scenario. For example, did you imagine the two students to be of the same or different sex; of similar or different ages or ethnic backgrounds? What difference would it have made if you'd imagined them differently?

11.2.2 SOCIAL CATEGORISATION AND STEREOTYPING

In everyday life, we can categorise objects as being similar to some other objects (e.g. cars and vans are similar) and different from others (e.g. pedestrians are 'different' from cars).

Similarly for intergroup behaviour, we can distinguish between members of one group (e.g. fellow students) and another (e.g. lecturers). A failure to perceive group similarities and differences can lead to social embarrassment and could even put us in danger. Without this process of social categorisation, intergroup behaviour cannot occur.

> **Stereotype** An oversimplified, generalised impression of someone or something.

Social categorisation is partly a *cognitive* process, and early approaches rested on a view that prejudice results from inflexible and faulty cognitive processing (Allport, 1954). Central to this is the concept of **stereotyping**. The term was popularised by Lippman who claimed that 'stereotypes … preconceptions … mark out certain objects as familiar or strange, emphasising the difference, so that the slightly familiar is seen as very familiar, and the somewhat strange as sharply alien' (1922: 55).

This accentuation of difference between categories (e.g. the familiar and the strange) may result from categorisation itself (Tajfel & Wilkes, 1963). Further, Tajfel (1981) argued that *social* categorisation can similarly lead to overestimation of intergroup differences, just as Lippman had argued concerning stereotypes.

The potential disadvantages of stereotyping (i.e. crude oversimplifications and over-generalisations) do not seem to stop people making use of stereotypes. One reason for this is that they act as 'mental shortcuts', simplifying our environment for us and allowing us to make sense of the world without too much effort (Hamilton & Crump, 2004). Another is that important stereotypes are not developed by isolated individuals but are *shared* with other group members and thus serve a function for the group (Oakes et al., 1994; Snyder & Miene, 1994; Stangor & Schaller, 1996). Stereotypes of a minority group may allow a powerful majority to blame them for societal problems or to justify acting in an exploitative way towards them.

KEY STUDY   Burt, M.R. (1980). Cultural myths and supports for rape. *Journal of Personality and Social Psychology, 38* (2), 217–230.

In 1980, Martha Burt published what became a very influential paper on how rape myths served to justify rape. She defined rape myths as 'prejudicial, stereotyped, or false beliefs about rape, rape victims, and rapists' (1980: 217). Such myths include the beliefs that 'only bad girls get raped' and 'women ask for it', as well as common myths and stereotypes about rapists as 'sex starved' or 'insane' (or both).

Burt devised a rape myth acceptance (RMA) scale incorporating 19 rape myths, and was the first to operationalise the concept of rape myths. Items on the scale included: 'If a woman gets drunk at a party and has intercourse with a man she's just met there, she should be considered 'fair game' to other males at the party who want to have sex with her, whether she wants to or not.'

(Cont'd)

She demonstrated that many people in the USA do subscribe to rape myths and that such beliefs are related to sex role stereotyping, a belief that sexual relationships are fundamentally exploitative, distrust of the opposite sex, an acceptance of interpersonal violence, and a relative lack of education. Rape myth acceptance can be seen as a way of justifying and legitimising the rapist's behaviour while shifting blame onto the victim. This has significant implications for the criminal justice system as it is notoriously difficult to secure a conviction for rape.

These examples take us from a simple focus on stereotyped *beliefs* about other groups to matters of **prejudice** and **discrimination**. Stereotypes matter because they have *effects*. Lyons and Kashima (2003) showed that, when accounts are passed on from one person to another, information that does not conform to stereotyped expectations tends gradually to be dropped. In their research, they showed that in later versions of a story about football players, the story tended to retain information about their beer drinking (stereotypical behaviour) but lose information about their listening to classical music (non-stereotypical behaviour). Lyons and Kashima (2003) showed that the emphasis on stereotypical information was strongest when the story teller and their audience shared the same stereotypes. Communication processes thus help maintain stereotypes of other groups as people may just omit or ignore information which does not 'fit' a stereotype.

Prejudice   An unreasonable or unfair dislike of something, or more usually someone – typically because they belong to a specific race, religion or group.

Discrimination   The consideration or treatment of others based on general factors (e.g. their race, religion or some other grouping), rather than on individual merit.

Memories also reflect stereotypes (e.g. Belleza & Bower, 1981; McRae et al., 1993). Fiske (1998) concludes that the tendency for memories to match stereotyped expectations is greatest in complex social environments, in which stereotypes are strong, and where people do not, because of time pressure or for some other reason, have the mental resources to focus on information which is not in line with the stereotype. The bias for remembering in line with expectations can have important practical consequences in eyewitness testimony (Boon & Davies, 1987; Loftus, 1996).

What effects does stereotyping have on those who are stereotyped? In an important development, Steele (1997; Steele et al., 2002) introduced the concept of **stereotype threat**. Steele argues that when an individual is aware that they could be the target of a negative or demeaning stereotype, their performance may be impaired on tasks relevant to that stereotype. Yeung and von Hippel (2008) examined this in relation to driving. Female participants took part in a realistic driving simulation during which pedestrians unexpectedly appeared in the road. Among participants reminded beforehand of the stereotype that women are poor drivers, 59 per cent struck the pedestrians, compared with 25 per cent of participants who were not so reminded.

Steele argues that the 'threat in the air' of low expectations of black students' abilities in terms of academic performance can lead to distracting thoughts and anxiety in test situations. Steele and Aronson (1995) compared the performance of black and white undergraduates at Stanford University (one of the top universities in the USA) on a very difficult standardised verbal ability test. Before taking it, the students were all told that the task was very difficult and either that the test measured intellectual ability or that it was simply a laboratory task to examine how people solve problems. The prediction was that black students told they were taking a test of intellectual ability would experience stereotype threat and would thus perform less well. The results confirmed this finding. There were no differences between the performance of black and white students when they had not been told the test was a measure of ability, but the black students performed significantly worse than the white students when they thought the test was measuring intellectual ability. Similar findings have been obtained in other studies involving a range of different groups in different situations (Kassin et al., 2008).

ASIDE   Intergroup relations jokes

Q: How many psychologists does it take to change a lightbulb?
A: Only one, but the lightbulb really has to want to change!

There are thousands of lightbulb jokes, and most of them exemplify the pervasiveness of intergroup relations. Our example is slightly different from the norm, but the general form of the joke is:

Q: How many [of some group] does it take to change a lightbulb?
A: *N* [any number] ... [followed by some derogatory comment about the group in question].

Thus:

Q: How many students does it take to change a lightbulb?
A: Two: one to hold the bulb, and the other to drink until the room spins!

As a student, you may or may not find that joke amusing. You may enjoy or be offended by the stereotype of students on which it is based. It doesn't take much imagination, or web searching, to find variants of the joke which are very unlikely to be amusing to the targets of the joke, who may be accused of being stupid (*A*: Five: one to hold the bulb and four others to turn the ladder); criminally violent (*A*: Two: one to take the bulb out and another to glass a random stranger's face with it); or lazy and exploitive of others (*A*: None, they expect us to do it for them). From an intergroup relations perspective, then, jokes are not simply a laughing matter, even when they are funny, because many of them rely on the expression of negative stereotypes of other groups and may further serve a function of making other expressions of prejudice more acceptable. See Ford et al. (2008) and Billig (2001) for two very different studies of the importance of humour in the maintenance of **sexism** and racism respectively.

11.2.3 PREJUDICE, DISCRIMINATION AND ETHNOCENTRISM

In the previous section we were focusing on stereotyped beliefs about groups and their members. Stereotyped beliefs may be associated with negative or prejudiced attitudes or feelings about another group and with discriminatory behaviour towards them. Prejudice is typically defined as being a biased (usually negative) *attitude* towards another group and its members, while discrimination refers to unfair or unequal *behaviour* towards others on the basis of their group membership (Dion, 2003). Prejudice from this perspective involves both negative thoughts and feelings about another group, which may or may not be expressed as discriminatory behaviour. This will depend on the circumstances and other factors governing social behaviour. For example, fear of legal consequences may constrain even the most prejudiced individual from acting completely in line with their hatred of another group.

> **Ethnocentrism**   A stance in which an individual believes that their own race or ethnic group (or aspects of it, e.g. its culture) is superior to other groups.

Ethnocentrism is a concept introduced by Sumner (1906) in relation to cultural identity and intercultural relations. As well as encompassing people's attitudes and behaviours towards groups to which they do not belong (i.e. **outgroups**) it emphasises the importance of their attachment and identification with the group to which they do belong (i.e. the **ingroup**) and has underpinned much thinking on intergroup behaviour ever since (Brewer, 1999). Sumner argued that 'one's own group is at the centre of everything' (1906: 13); whilst Brewer, writing about Sumner's concept of ethnocentrism, declared that ethnocentrism engenders 'positive sentiments toward the ingroup: pride, loyalty, and perceived superiority. However, Sumner also believed that these positive sentiments towards the ingroup were directly correlated with contempt, hatred and hostility toward outgroups' (1999: 430).

Brewer (1999) questions whether strong positive feelings about one's own group are necessarily accompanied by hostility and strong negative feelings about other groups but, as she points out, Sumner's proposal has been reflected in the social psychological literature. Several approaches associate overidealisation of the ingroup with strong prejudice against outgroups, and key historical examples include the Nazi idealisation of the pure Aryan type and their dehumanisation and genocide of Jews, homosexuals, occultists, people with learning difficulties or mental health problems, and other minority groups.

EXPLAINING PREJUDICE AND DISCRIMINATION

11.3

Here we describe some theories of prejudice and discrimination chosen for their importance in psychology's attempts to confront these issues and because they illustrate different levels or kinds of explanation. Prejudice, discrimination and intergroup relations have been at the heart of social psychology for many decades (Duckitt, 1992). Any brief account of the theory and research developed in that time must be selective. For a more comprehensive view see the further reading at the end of this chapter.

11.3.1 FRUSTRATED AND PREJUDICED INDIVIDUALS

The idea that we may 'take out' our frustrations on someone or something innocent is a commonplace in everyday life. A refereeing decision may cause an angry football manager to kick out at whatever inanimate object happens to be nearby, or the TV commentator may refer (metaphorically) to the manager's cat 'getting a kicking tonight'. For some reason it seems acceptable in the UK to refer to kicking cats, but there would be more concern if the commentator referred to the manager's dog instead; and any commentator foolish enough to confuse family members and cats would be looking for a new job in the morning! Some expressions of annoyance are more socially acceptable than others, and the restraint required to meet norms of social acceptability in relation to aggression is a basis of theories derived from Freud's ideas.

11.3.2 FRUSTRATION AND AGGRESSION

The **frustration-aggression hypothesis** (FAH) was developed by Dollard et al. (1939). The basic propositions of the original FAH were that individuals frustrated (or thwarted) in their pursuit of a goal will become aggressive and that all acts of aggression are preceded by such frustration. The small child who screams and hits its parent who has just stopped it having a sweet would be a straightforward example of this.

However, just as our angry football manager did not run on to the pitch and attack the referee, the cause of his frustration, then so children learn that hitting their parents is neither acceptable nor likely to be successful. They learn to suppress their immediate urge to be aggressive. However, in line with Freudian thinking, the FAH proposes that an unreleased urge to aggress causes an unpleasant build-up of psychic energy which needs to be released in some way, a process known as **catharsis**. If aggression cannot be expressed against the source of the frustration (the parent in our example) then it needs to be released in some other way (e.g. through sport) or *displaced* on to another target against which it is safer or more acceptable to aggress. The child may hit another child or a doll rather than its parents.

What has this got to do with intergroup relations and discrimination? The argument is that widely experienced frustrations resulting from social, economic or political factors may not be expressed against those responsible (governments, elites, the military etc.) who may be too powerful. Instead, minority groups may be **scapegoated**. For example, Hovland and Sears (1940) investigated whether the number of lynchings of black people in the southern states of the USA over a 50 year period up to 1930 was related to economic conditions. They found a negative cor-relation between the number of lynchings and the price of cotton (a key crop in those states); thus, as the price of cotton went up, the number of lynchings went down. Hovland and Sears claimed that the lynchings (killings) were a consequence of displaced aggression resulting from the frustrations associated with economic hardship.

Catharsis   The release of built-up emotional energy. The term is generally used to typify a healthy and restorative outpouring of such energy.

Scapegoat   Someone who is (often unfairly) made to take the blame for something.

The above explanation cannot be the complete one (it says nothing, for example, about the form of aggression), and later work (Green et al., 1998) casts doubt on the relationship between economic conditions and collective violence. The FAH has been modified considerably, with frustration now recognised as only one possible instigator of aggression (along with pain, discomfort etc.) and aggression being just one possible response to frustration (Berkowitz, 1993). Bandura (1977), in his influential social learning theory, convincingly argued that the expression of aggression, rather than being cathartic, may increase the likelihood of future aggressive acts. Nevertheless, the notion that frustration lies behind some aggression and that collective violence is a response to economic conditions remains very influential, and Staub (2000) includes it as an important instigator of 'ethnic cleansing' and genocide.

11.3.3 PERSONALITY AND PREJUDICE

Published just after the Second World War, *The authoritarian personality* (Adorno et al., 1950) was a major attempt to understand the psychological dynamics involved in the anti-Semitism and wider ethnocentrism of the prewar and war years. Carried out in the USA, the research involved a 'widening circle of covariation' (Brown, 1965). The researchers started by developing a scale to measure the extent to which individuals agreed with anti-Semitic statements (e.g. 'I can hardly imagine myself marrying a Jew') and then gradually broadened out the work to include other attitudes, beliefs and personality characteristics which were shown to covary (i.e. cluster together). As well as questionnaires, the research utilised projective tests and in-depth clinical interviews, reflecting the psychoanalytic basis of the theory that the authors developed.

The first stages of the work showed that anti-Semitism among those sampled (mostly white, non-Jewish and middle class individuals) was associated with a more general ethnocentrism in which various outgroups other than the Jews were also disparaged and in which the 'American Way' of life and family was viewed very positively. Ethnocentrism (E) was then shown to be related to political and economic conservatism (PEC) or the extent to which the person 'liked things as they are'. Clinical interviews and projective test results with a group who scored highly on the E-scale led the researchers to believe that a personality syndrome lay beneath this cluster of prejudiced and conservative attitudes. People with this kind of personality were seen to be potentially fascist. The F-scale (Potential for Fascism scale) was developed as a measure of this personality syndrome. It was designed to measure nine aspects of what came to be known as **authoritarianism**.

Any approach that focuses on individuals may underestimate the power of situations and social and political circumstances, and people may do things that they would be unlikely to do without this added pressure (e.g. Milgram, 1974). Conforming to society's norms may lead people to act in discriminatory ways irrespective of their personality. While authoritarianism may be associated with individual differences in prejudice *within* a society or group, differences *between* groups result more from social norms (Pettigrew, 1958). Changes in attitudes to particular groups occurring in response to world events may happen too quickly to be explicable in terms of changes in child-rearing practices (Brown, 1995).

Nevertheless, the concept of authoritarianism remains an important one. Better measuring instruments have been devised, including Altemeyer's (1998) Right Wing Authoritarianism (RWA) scale, leading to a renewed interest in this field. Some research indicates that authoritarian values and behaviour may increase as a response to external threats, for example after terrorist attacks (Perrin, 2005), or to changes in the social context such as increased unemployment (Doty et al., 1991), rather than resulting from upbringing.

11.3.4 REALISTIC CONFLICT THEORY

Sherif (1966) advocated a completely different group-level approach to intergroup conflict. He argued that discrimination and psychological constructs like prejudice and negative stereotyping of outgroups have their basis in competition for scarce resources. In his view, psychological processes followed from 'material relations' and thus the psychological relations between groups follow from their objective relations. For example, in a time of increased competition for jobs, 'immigrants' may be blamed by more established groups for taking away 'our jobs'.

Sherif and his co-workers carried out three famous studies between 1949 and 1954 to test out his ideas. Unlike many studies in social psychology, these did not take place in controlled laboratory conditions. Instead they were field experiments, each carried out over several weeks. The participants in the studies were 11- to 12-year-old boys attending a camp for the summer holiday. They were unaware that they were there for the purpose of research. The researchers played various roles in running the camp (and thus perhaps had to work a lot harder than many psychologists do when collecting data!). Great care was taken in selecting the boys attending the camps to ensure they were similar in terms of factors such as religion (they were all from Protestant families) and family background. None of the boys knew each other before they arrived at the camp. The reason for all of these checks was to try and ensure that the behaviour of the boys could not be explained in terms of prior friendships or problems in the family.

Of the three studies, the first two sought to test Sherif's ideas about the development of intergroup conflict. The third study, known as the 'robber's cave' study, was slightly different in that an additional goal was to test ideas on the resolution of intergroup conflict. We discuss this famous study further below. The experiments were each carried out in three stages. The first two studies contained the following stages, whilst the final study omitted the first stage:

1 *Friendship development*: The boys arrived at the camp and spent a few days getting to know each other, taking part in the camp's activities and forming friendships.

2 *Group formation*: Two groups were formed. Boys who had become friends during the first stage were split up and put in separate groups as far as possible. The groups were kept isolated from each other, living in separate areas and taking part in different activities.

3 *Intergroup competition*: After a week of being observed separately, the groups were brought together to compete against each other for prizes in a tournament or series of sports and games.

During the second stage the groups developed group structures with leaders, norms of behaviour, group names and insignias. Friendships were now with the members of their own groups. Once the competitions started the initial good sportsmanship disappeared quite quickly, to be replaced by intergroup hostility (Figure 11.1). Name calling, fights and insults became common and 'raids' on the other group's camp took place. As well as hostility towards the outgroup, ingroup solidarity increased during this stage. When the boys were asked to estimate performance in games, the performance of ingroup members tended to be overestimated while that of the other group's members was underestimated.

What Sherif and his colleagues had demonstrated was that the introduction of real conflict of interest between the groups had led to manifestations of ethnocentrism, including negative stereotypes of the outgroup, prejudice, discrimination, aggression and greater valuing of the ingroup. The effect was so strong that the first two studies ended with the two groups still exhibiting animosity to each other. However, as you'll see below in the section on conflict reduction, there was a happy ending to the third summer camp study!

Blake and Mouton (1961) showed that it is not just young boys who behave in this way. They studied business executives on management training courses and also examined established management and union relations in industry. They found that intergroup competition affected ingroup relations (groups becoming more cohesive), perceptions of the outgroup (stereotypes) and relations between the groups when it came to negotiating solutions to problems. For example, in the training context, group representatives strongly tended to see their own group's solutions to problems as superior to those of the competing group, even when, in the eyes of objective judges, one group had produced a clearly better solution than the other. Studies in other contexts and other cultures have also provided support for **realistic conflict theory** (RCT) (Jackson, 1993). If you watch the TV programme 'The Apprentice' you may find it interesting to analyse it in terms of group and intergroup processes.

11.3.5 SOCIAL CATEGORISATION TO SOCIAL CHANGE: SOCIAL IDENTITY THEORY

One key question asked about RCT is whether competition is necessary for group conflict to occur. In Sherif's work there were indications that skirmishes between the groups took place before the stage of competition was introduced, and other studies (e.g. Ferguson & Kelley, 1964) showed that groups may adopt a competitive approach to each other even when there is no objective reason for them to do so. These observations led to the development by Tajfel and his colleagues of a series of experiments designed to explore the minimum conditions under which intergroup discrimination would take place.

In the first of these **minimal intergroup** studies, Tajfel et al. (1971) attempted to set up an experiment in which, apart from the social categorisation between one group and another (ingroup and outgroup), there were none of the usual factors influencing group behaviour,

In-group	19	18	17	16	15	14	13	12	11	10	9	8	7
Out-group	1	3	5	7	9	11	13	15	17	19	21	23	25

MIP   Fair   MJP
MD

In-group	7	8	9	10	11	12	13	14	15	16	17	18	19
Out-group	1	3	5	7	9	11	13	15	17	19	21	23	25

MIP   Fair   MJP
MD

MD=maximise difference in favour of in-group
MIP=maximise in-group profit
MJP=maximise joint profit

FIGURE 11.1 *Examples of Payoff Matrices used by Tajfel et al. (1971)*

i.e. there was no previous hostility between the groups, no interaction and no explicit competition, and all actions were anonymous. The participants were schoolboys who were told they were taking part in a study of decision making. Each participant was randomly assigned to one of two groups (though they were told that this was based on preference for paintings by either Klee or Kandinsky) and their task was to assign points (which were worth money) to other participants in the study.

The task involved the participants making a series of choices in each of which they allocated points to two other boys who were identified only in terms of a code number and the group they belonged to (e.g. 'member 52, Klee group'). The choice 'matrices' were carefully constructed to examine the strategies used by the boys in making their decisions (see Figure 11.1 for examples of the kinds of matrices used). The participants would indicate their choice by circling one of the columns.

Several strategies were available to them including:

1   *MJP*: To give away as many points as possible irrespective of whom they were giving them to. In the matrices in Figure 11.1 this would be done by choosing one of the columns to the right of the matrix.

2   *Fair*: To allocate points as equally as possible. In the examples given this would be done by choosing an option near the centre of the matrix.

3 *MIP*: To give as much money as possible to the member of the ingroup. In the first matrix this would be done by choosing a column to the left, and in the second matrix by choosing one to the right.

4 *MD*: To maximise the difference in favour of the ingroup. In both matrices shown, the column at the left end would be the favoured choice if using this strategy. Note that in the second matrix, if this approach was adopted the ingroup member would actually receive less money than with any other choice.

The unexpected finding was that, while fairness did play a part in determining the allocations made, the preferred strategy was one which favoured ingroup members over outgroup members. In other words, the preferred strategy was to discriminate in favour of the ingroup. Given the 'emptiness' of the situation, this raises many questions about why discrimination was taking place. One possibility is that the boys thought that their friends would probably share their views on painting and thus thought that they were in the ingroup. However, Billig and Tajfel (1973) found the same effect even when the participants were explicitly told they had been randomly allocated to groups.

This finding of 'intergroup discrimination in minimal group settings has proved to be a remarkably robust phenomenon' (Brown, 1995: 47) and has been replicated many times. If you now think back to the distinction between 'acting as self' and 'acting as part of a group', it seems that, in these studies, a simple and arbitrary social categorisation leads the participants to act in terms of group. Does this mean that ethnocentrism is an inevitable consequence of social categorisation? Turner (1975) showed that if participants could 'act in terms of self' and allocate money to themselves then group membership did not influence allocations to others unless group membership was made more salient to the participants. Grieve and Hogg (1999) showed that 'subjective uncertainty' influenced allocations: participants given more confidence in the use of the matrices displayed less intergroup bias. Thus it seems that social categorisation may be necessary for intergroup discrimination, but may not be sufficient.

Though it is perhaps surprising that one of the most influential of intergroup theories should have its roots in these simple experiments, **social identity theory** (Tajfel, 1978; Tajfel and Turner, 1979) has 'perhaps become the pre-eminent contemporary social psychological analysis of ... intergroup relations' (Hogg & Vaughan, 2008: 407). The theory rests on the distinction made earlier between acting in terms of self and acting in terms of group, and on the idea that we have multiple and shifting social identities related to our various group memberships. The theory proposes that people want to belong to groups about which they feel positive and which provide them with a positive social identity. This happens when group members feel their group is positively distinct from other relevant groups in terms of some valued characteristics. For example, inhabitants of a rural region may feel proud of the relative friendliness and generosity they believe people from their region display, compared to people from a nearby city. The city dwellers in turn may look down on what they see as a lack of sophistication in the rural population. In this case, both groups can be said to have a positive social identity, as each values the characteristics they see themselves as having superiority in.

Having a positive social identity, then, involves a process of social comparison with another group or groups from which the ingroup is seen as positively distinct. What if a group's members do not have a positive social identity? There are several possibilities:

1   In some cases, individual group members may simply try to exit the group and develop other social identities. This kind of **social mobility** may not be possible. In many situations, passing from one group to another is very difficult to achieve.

2   Alternatively they may 'accept' their inadequate social identity because there is a belief within the group that the differences between them and other groups are legitimate or that there are no achievable alternatives to the existing situation. Group members may focus instead on within-group social comparison.

3   When potential alternatives are seen to be appropriate and achievable, then a group may act to try to achieve **social change** through collective action. This may involve:

   (a)   attempts to directly challenge other groups and engage in social conflict; or
   (b)   more creative approaches such as adopting new positive characteristics or redefining existing negative group characteristics so that they come to be seen as positive.

For example, parents of young children may be proud of the school their children attend and have a positive social identity as a consequence. If this is not the case, though, and there are few constraints on changing schools, they may just leave. If changing schools is not an option and they see few possibilities for change at the current school, parents may simply focus on getting the best for their own individual child. Alternatively they may seek to change the school's image by making a virtue out of its existing characteristics or by helping the school to develop new valued characteristics (perhaps a summer camp for all the children?!). Finally, if they believe the school to be unfairly under-resourced compared to other schools and they see the possibility for changing this, they may take collective action to lobby the local authority for a reallocation of funds.

The theory is an ambitious attempt to combine social psychological processes and societal factors to account for social change, and some writers (Hogg, 2006; Reicher, 2004; Rubin & Hewstone, 2004) argue that its scope and complexity have been underestimated by critics. These writers argue that, though there are problems with and large gaps in the research that has been conducted on social identity theory, the theory is sound in most respects. While this is not the point they are making, it is useful to consider to what extent the kinds of laboratory experiments done can illuminate real-life attempts at social change.

11.3.6 SOCIAL PSYCHOLOGY, RACISM AND PREJUDICE

Duckitt's (1992) historical overview of the psychological study of prejudice analyses the changes in the explanations put forward by psychologists over the last 100 years or so. At different times, theories have focused on individual psychopathology, situational forces or sociocultural factors. Some of these changes may be seen as attempts to remedy inadequacies or limitations in older approaches, but Duckitt argues that this is not the complete story. Older approaches are not usually replaced; rather there are shifts in the nature of the questions being asked or the issues being addressed. This may partly be a response to topical events, but Duckitt argues that historical circumstances affect not just topic choice but also the questions that are asked which, in turn, influence the kinds of theories and research methods that are developed.

In terms of racism, Duckitt argues that conceiving of prejudice as a problem requiring psychological study did not occur in the USA until the 1920s. Before then, the white majority simply assumed that they were superior, and thus the work of psychologists in this area was in mapping the different characteristics and abilities of 'inferior peoples'. This is an approach which continued through the 1930s and 1940s, especially in Nazi Germany (Billig, 1978), and which re-emerges periodically. In mainstream psychology in the USA a number of social changes during the 1920s led to the beginnings of questioning the inferior status of minority groups and their level of deprivation relative to white people. This was the initial period of research on racial prejudice. Duckitt outlines seven stages (up to the early 1990s) in the 'historical evolution' of psychology's understanding of prejudice.

The key points here are as follows:

1   Psychology as a discipline does not stand outside the wider social context in which inequalities between social groups exist. Social and political events may change the questions that psychologists ask, the methods that they adopt, and the answers that they provide. There has been a tendency for Western psychologists to assume that the processes they have identified are 'universal' (i.e. they apply across cultures). This belief may not be warranted.

2   The uses to which psychological research is put may result from political or other forces. Psychology has been used to justify exploitation as well as to combat it (Billig, 1978).

3   Psychology is only one of a number of disciplines being applied to these issues. A full understanding requires a multi-disciplinary approach.

REDUCING INTERGROUP CONFLICT

11.4
Up to this point, the research that we have discussed has provided little that could be deemed positive. However, we will now consider whether and how conflicts between groups can be resolved through psychological intervention.

11.4.1 CONTACT

The **contact hypothesis** proposes that if contact between groups is encouraged (under appropriate conditions) then prejudice between groups will reduce. The initial hypothesis (Allport, 1954) suggested that contact between groups should be encouraged if four conditions are satisfied. First, social conditions, like education, housing and law, should be equal for both groups. Second, the groups should share common goals that, third, they cooperate to achieve. Fourth, the officials and authorities of those groups must support the contact. Subsequently, there have been a number of additions to those conditions. These include the need for contact to be rewarding (Amir, 1969), close and for a sustained period of time (Cook, 1978). These two additions allow potential for friendship to grow between members of the different groups. Friendships between individuals from different groups can improve intergroup relations directly (Pettigrew, 1997) and also indirectly, as other group members come to know of these friendships (Wright et al., 1977).

Thus contact has the potential to reduce intergroup conflict, but providing the required conditions is very difficult. For example, people from different cultures may live in the same area but have little contact and, when they do, it may not be on either an equal or a personal footing. This limited contact could simply provide opportunities for expressing rather than reducing prejudice (Hogg & Vaughan, 2008). More positively, Pettigrew and Tropp (2006) reviewed over 700 relevant studies and claimed that, while meeting Allport's conditions enhances the prejudice-reducing impact of contact, contact may also reduce prejudice in the absence of these conditions.

11.4.2 SUPERORDINATE GOALS

The concept of **superordinate goals** derives from realistic conflict theory. Remember that the third summer camp study run by Sherif had a final stage in which attempts were made to reduce conflict. After some failed attempts at contact (e.g. eating together just produced 'garbage wars' in which the groups threw food at each other) some 'superordinate' goals were introduced. These are goals which the groups shared but which they could only achieve through cooperation. The reasoning was that, if conflict arises from competition, reduced conflict should follow from cooperation in contexts in which the groups are dependent on each other for achieving their goals. Therefore the staff engineered a series of 'problems', such as the water supply failing or the bus breaking down, which could only be solved by the groups working together. This was successful and at the end of the camp the groups, rather than being on hostile terms, chose to go home together in the same bus (we told you it had a happy ending!)

It helped that the two groups in Sherif's study were not actually very different or well established, thus facilitating their *recategorisation* as one large group rather than two separate groups (Gaertner & Dovidio, 2000). They also succeeded in their cooperative task. Worchel (1979) has shown that failure on such a task may lead one group to blame the other for the failure. Nevertheless this simple idea has had a great deal of influence. It is the root of 'jigsaw classrooms'. These consist of small desegregated groups of children who have to rely on each other to learn material and succeed in class, as each pupil has key elements of information necessary to complete a task. Aronson (2008) claims success in improving self-esteem and performance in minority group children using this technique.

11.4.3 CROSSED CATEGORY MEMBERSHIP

Social identity theory argues that we each have many social identities depending on the groups we belong to. Which of these social identities is salient at any one time will depend on the context. At one moment you may be talking to a lecturer and your identity as a student may be most salient, but if you discover a shared interest in the music of a particular band then the social identity of 'fan' may become more relevant. In conflict situations, this fluency of identity may be decreased and simple 'us–them' distinctions may predominate, leading to ethnocentrism.

KEY RESEARCHER   Richard Crisp

Richard Crisp is a Professor of Psychology in one of the world's leading centres for social psychological research, the Centre for the Study of Group Processes at the University of Kent. His research focuses on how an awareness of diversity can help to improve intergroup relations. Seeing identity as multifaceted, he argues that there is a need to move away from a simple us vs them view of the world while still recognising the core value that group membership can have for people. If societies and cultures concentrate on the many different ways that they can construe themselves and others, whilst minimising the threat of this questioning to the value of their group memberships, then this can lead to a reduction of intergroup bias. This could then balance the need to belong with acceptance of relationships within and across different groups. His most recent work is concerned with extending the contact hypothesis to examine the positive effects of imagined contact.

FIGURE 11.2   Richard Crisp

Richard Crisp has gained several prizes including the Society for the Psychological Study of Social Issues Louise Kidder Early Career Award in 2003. In 2006 he gained the British Psychological Society's Spearman Medal, which is awarded to a psychologist who has made an outstanding contribution to psychological research within 10 years of graduating. This recognition shows the importance of his work and the continuing significance of research on intergroup relations.

This suggests then that making people more aware of their multiple group memberships could play a part in reducing conflict. However, this is only likely to work if the various group memberships are cross-cutting rather than simply overlapping (Deschamps & Doise, 1978). If you and your friends are prejudiced against engineering students but rather like rugby players, then an encounter with the engineering department's rugby team might be less problematic than with a group of non-rugby-playing engineers. Of course, if you are also prejudiced against rugby players this might not be the start of a wonderful evening!

There is considerable evidence that cross-cutting group memberships reduces intergroup conflict (Brewer & Brown, 1998). More recently, Crisp et al. (2001) researched students' prejudice against other students at different universities (such rivalries between universities are sometimes fierce). After asking the students to think of as many ways as possible in which they could describe the other students rather than simply thinking they attended a different university, intergroup bias was reduced. In many contexts, however, one dimension of group difference may outweigh all others in importance. Hewstone et al. (1993) in a study in Bangladesh found that religion (Muslim or Hindu) greatly outweighed nationality (Bangladeshi or Indian) in importance, and thus the effect of cross-cutting categorisations was reduced. Nevertheless, after reviewing some of the evidence, Crisp concludes: 'Our multiple identities may ultimately prove critical in addressing some of the most pressing social issues that we face' (2008: 209).

CHAPTER SUMMARY

11.5

In this chapter we have looked at the effect that group membership can have on our behaviour. It is easy to slip into supporting your group, and often this has positive effects – but not always. Supporting each other is what makes a community strong, and can make life simpler and better for the individual members. The problems arise for people who are either rejected by the group or not in the group. This can create conflict at an individual level and also at a group or even national level. The puzzle for us is to balance the benefits of group cohesion with the obvious downsides of ethnocentrism.

 ## DISCUSSION QUESTIONS

Social psychologists often assume that the same processes occur both in 'big' political and historical events and in small-scale everyday actions. Theories tested in studies of small groups are then applied to larger-scale social processes and conflicts. How appropriate do you think this is?

SUGGESTIONS FOR FURTHER READING

Hogg, M.A., & Vaughan, G.M. (2008). *Social psychology* (5th edn). Harlow: Prentice Hall. With more emphasis on European research than most American textbooks, this provides a good overview of mainstream social psychology and shows how intergroup relations overlaps with other topics in social psychology.

Aronson, E. (2008). *The social animal* (10th edn). New York: Worth. This is a very readable and entertaining account of social psychology, with an emphasis on 'real-world' applications such as Aronson's work on jigsaw classrooms.

Brewer, M.B. (2003). *Intergroup relations* (2nd edn). Buckingham: Open University Press. Written by one of the major figures in the area, this comprehensive but readable review covers most facets of intergroup relations from basic cognitive processes to international relations and war.

Hogg, M.A., & Abrams, D. (2001). *Intergroup relations: essential readings.* Philadelphia: Psychology Press. Provides an easily accessible opportunity to read the original classic papers of writers such as Sherif and Tajfel alongside later authors whose research has built on these foundations.

12 SOCIAL JUDGEMENTS AND BEHAVIOUR

Lead authors **Alex Meredith** and **Monica Whitty**

CHAPTER OUTLINE

INTRODUCTION

12.1
Human beings are very social creatures. We spend most of our lives in the company of other people. The way we behave towards them is affected, among other things, by our attitudes to them and the explanations that we give for their behaviour. In this chapter, we will consider three different facets of social interaction: attributions, attitudes and prosocial behaviour.

In the section on attributions, we will look at the decisions you make when deciding why things have happened. When considering attitudes, we will discuss what an attitude is, the relationship between attitudes and behaviours, and how attitudes can be changed. Finally, we will examine prosocial behaviours and the factors that determine whether people will go to the aid of those in trouble.

? FRAMING QUESTIONS

How do you predict what someone will do in a given situation?

In the case of some particular attitude you have, consider how you acquired that attitude.

Do your attitudes always predict what you'll do, or can you think of a situation where you acted differently than the way you felt? Why was this?

Imagine you are trying to change someone's mind about something: how would you go about it?

If you have helped someone in trouble, is it because you wanted to or because you felt you should do? Did it make any difference as to who they were? Or whether anyone else was around?

What factors might make it either more or less likely that you would help someone in difficulty?

ATTRIBUTIONS

12.2
A friend, Chardonnay, turns up to an important meeting 15 minutes late. You turn to the friend next to you and say, 'That's so typical of Chardonnay, she's always late!' Psychologists would argue that what you are doing is making an **attribution**; that is, attributing a cause to an event (i.e. the reason that Chardonnay is late). This section considers how we come to a decision about whether something that has happened was down to the person themselves or whether it was out of their control (and due to the situation they were in), and how we can go wrong in the process of making that attribution.

> **Attribution**   The process of giving reasons for why things happen.

When we make decisions about why someone has behaved in a certain way, we take into account either their *disposition* (e.g. their individual personality characteristics or traits, such as always being late) or the *situation* (whether something happened in the outside world to bring the situation about). In the above example, the attribution made was dispositional (Chardonnay is *always* late for everything). Had you attributed Chardonnay's behaviour to a traffic jam on the motorway, it would have been situational (the outside world was at fault).

12.2.1 THEORIES AND MODELS OF ATTRIBUTION

Some psychologists have argued that individuals, as part of their everyday lives, seek out causes for others' behaviours. In 1958, Fritz Heider stated that people try to understand others' behaviour in a rational manner as **naive scientists**, rather than through haphazard guesswork. He argued that this outlook may be summarised by three principles: (1) as individuals we look for causes or reasons as to why other people do things; (2) in looking for causes, we attempt to find stable and enduring traits in others and the world around us; and (3) in attributing causality, we either assign it to either an internal (dispositional) cause or an external (situational) cause. Heider's work was instrumental in opening up the area of how we attribute causality to other people's actions.

> **Naive scientist**   The idea that when making attributions we try to understand other people's behaviour in a rational way, seeking to find stable causes, in a naive scientific manner (Heider, 1958).

Two contemporary models that have provided coherent accounts of how we attribute causality in a situation are the correspondent inference theory (Jones & Davis, 1965) and the covariation model (Kelley, 1967).

12.2.2. CORRESPONDENT INFERENCE THEORY (CIT)

The correspondent inference theory argues that we try to infer whether the actions of someone *correspond* to an internal disposition within that person, and we ask ourselves a series of questions to work out the answer:

1   First, was the behaviour *intended* and were the consequences *foreseeable*? If it is apparent that the individual intended the action to occur and that s/he would have known the consequences, we attribute the action to an internal factor (disposition) and think it less likely that an external (situational) factor was involved.

2   Was the action a consequence of the person's *free will*? If it is apparent that the action was taken by the individual without external pressure (say, there wasn't a gun pointed at their head!) and by their own volition, we will attribute it to a dispositional factor.

3   Is the behaviour *socially desirable*? If it is (e.g. if the person waits nicely in a queue for their turn at the checkout rather than trying to push in), it is more likely that it is being influenced by societal norms, and is thus attributable to situational factors.

4   Does the behaviour produce *exclusive* effects? We can also infer intention on the basis of how unique the result of a behaviour is. If a behaviour produces a variety of effects, this tells us very little about the person. However, if a singular or unique effect is produced (e.g. something strange happens as a consequence of the behaviour), it is more likely that this was the actor's intention and it can therefore be put down to dispositional factors.

However, correspondent inference theory has some drawbacks. It has trouble explaining *unintentional* behaviour, given its emphasis on intentional actions. In addition, it argues that we evaluate the numerous possible results any behaviour can have; however, research by Nisbett and Ross (1980) found that most people do not focus on analysing others in so much detail!

12.2.3. COVARIATION MODEL

Kelley (1967) argued that whilst the correspondent inference theory considered internal factors, it did not sufficiently cover events *outside* the immediate situation. He put forward three factors for consideration in a covariation model:

1   *Consensus*: Are there any other people in the situation doing the same thing as well? If there are, it is likely that they are all reacting to something in the environment, and, as such, it is unlikely to be an internal dispositional factor unique to any one individual.

2   *Distinctiveness*: Is the action unique to this situation, or does the person act this way in other situations? If the action is not unique, it is likely to be due to an internal dispositional factor; whereas if it is unique, the action is more likely to be understandable in terms of situational factors.

3   *Consistency of the behaviour*: Has the person performed this before in similar situations? If the action has occurred consistently, it is more likely that the empowering influence is a dispositional one, whereas inconsistency would indicate an external situational factor.

There is evidence to suggest that through the use of **heuristics** we speed up the process of decision making. This has led to Fiske and Taylor (1991) proposing the **cognitive miser** model which argued that, contrary to Heider's view of us as naive scientists, we do not seek out rational answers. Instead, we are cognitive misers who use heuristics to save mental time and effort (see Chapter 6 for an explanation of heuristics).

Heuristic   Rule of thumb that aids us in problem solving.

12.3 BIASES IN ATTRIBUTION

12.3.1 THE FUNDAMENTAL ATTRIBUTION ERROR

From the previous sections, it should be apparent that we do not attribute causality in the clinical way first described by Heider: the process is much more flexible. In this section, we shall consider some of the biases which interfere with the process of attributing causality.

Fundamental attribution errors identified initially by Ross (1977) and Jones (1979) refer to the tendency of people to attribute behaviour to the character (disposition) of individuals.

In a classic study, Jones and Harris (1967) asked participants to judge whether fellow students were for or against the Cuban revolutionary leader, Fidel Castro,

> **Fundamental attribution error**   The tendency to attribute the actions of a person we are observing to their disposition, rather than to situational variables.

after hearing their fellow students read speeches either for or against him. The students had no choice over which speeches they were allocated to read. Despite knowing that their fellow students had no choice over what they read, participants were more inclined to think that the speech fitted the attitude of the reader (dispositional explanation) rather than being 'pot luck' (situational explanation). There have been three reasons proposed to explain why the fundamental attribution error occurs:

1 *Salience*: When we are attending to a situation, we mostly focus on the main agent in the process. This focus on the individual increases their salience in comparison to the situation, so we are more likely to make a dispositional attribution. Research by Krull (1993) has shown that when people are directed or motivated to attend to situational factors, the fundamental attribution error is negated or its effect is lessened.

2 *Differential forgetting*: There is evidence to suggest that both situational and dispositional information can be forgotten with time. This might lead to the fundamental attribution error. Funder (1982) suggests that the direction of the effect depends on the focus of attention.

3 *Cultural factors*: There is strong evidence to suggest that fundamental attribution error is culturally specific, with a higher prevalence in Western countries. Whilst individuality is valued in Western culture (Beauvois & Dubois, 1988), in many non-Western cultures the emphasis is more on interdependence and the community (Morris & Peng, 1994). This change of emphasis can explain why the error is not as fundamental as Ross (1977) originally thought.

12.3.2 ACTOR–OBSERVER EFFECT

Jones and Nisbett (1972) first identified the **actor–observer effect**, which suggests that we are more likely to explain someone else's behaviour by a dispositional effect, whereas we account for our own behaviours through situational factors. So Chardonnay is late because she is always late and that is the sort of thing she does, but when I am late it is because the bus broke down or there was a rip in the fabric of space and time (and hence not my fault at all). This is the basis of many personal disputes, as we blame other people for what happens while at the same time denying all responsibility ourselves. It also seems to be a feature of political life, as when things go wrong politicians blame global events while at the same time saying that everything that goes right is due to their brilliant leadership.

So, why does the actor–observer effect occur? Two factors have been implicated:

1   *Perceptual focus*: In a similar fashion to salience (a fundamental attribution error), an actor is only able to observe the background since s/he cannot see themselves in the situation.

2   *Informational differences*: Jones and Nisbett (1972) have suggested that, as actors in the theatre of life(!), we know how we have acted in a variety of situations and are therefore able to make a more informed assessment as to whether our behaviour is dispositionally or situationally motivated. Observers do not have this information and so are more likely to make a dispositional attribution.

12.3.3 FALSE CONSENSUS EFFECT

Ross et al. (1977) noted the **false consensus effect,** in which people overestimate the probability of people behaving in the same way as themselves. In their study, they asked students if they would walk around with a sign advertising a café. Of those that agreed, 62 per cent thought the other participants would do the same, whilst 67 per cent of those who refused thought their peers would refuse as well. So, when we do something, we think that others are likely to do the same.

12.3.4 SELF-SERVING BIAS

The self-serving bias is a tendency to attribute our successes to our own personal skills and dispositions, but to blame our failings on external situational factors (Miller & Ross, 1975). There are two explanations for the self-serving bias – a cognitive one and a motivational one. The former argues that we expect to succeed, due to the inherent effort that we have made, and therefore it follows that *we* were instrumental in whatever success occurred. The motivational explanation, as proposed by Greenberg et al. (1982), argues that the bias occurs to protect or enhance our self-esteem (so it's not our fault if things go wrong!).

ATTITUDES

12.4

What is your view on the existence of global warming, or the ethics of cloning humans, or the price of blancmange? Psychologists would call your stances on these matters **attitudes**. They are an integral part of our personal and social lives, and as we will see in this section, they simplify our interaction with the world.

Eagly and Chaiken defined an attitude as: '*a psychological tendency that is expressed by evaluating a particular entity with some degree of favor or disfavor*' (1993: 1). An attitude is therefore an evaluation of a target where we decide what we think and feel towards an object. Attitudes may also be ambivalent, since they can contain conflicting elements within them (Thompson et al., 1995): for example, we might think it is a good thing to recycle and save the planet, but might also think that loading your stuff up and carrying it down to the recycle centre is too much effort.

12.4.1 ATTITUDE MEASUREMENT

Having established what an attitude is, the next step is to find a reliable means of measuring one. There are a variety of methods, the two main types being self-report measures and non-verbal measures.

Likert scales

Named after their developer, Rensis Likert, these measure attitudes on a continuum (see Figure 12.1). This type of measure assumes that not all attitudes are held with equal strength, but whether Likert items should be considered as interval-level data or ordinal data is up for debate. Advantages of **Likert scales** are that they are easy to construct, can be completed quickly and easily by participants, and are reliable (although the researcher must be sure that each statement is relevant to the attitude being assessed).

How interested are you in these areas of psychology?					
	1: Very interested	***2:** Somewhat interested*	***3:** Neutral*	***4:** Not very interested*	***5:** Not at all interested*
Biological					
Cognitive					
Social					
Developmental					

FIGURE 12.1 A Likert scale

Semantic differential scales

First developed by Osgood et al. (1957), **semantic differential scales** (SD scales) have two diametrically opposite adjectives such as 'good' and 'bad' and a scale along which the participant indicates which option they prefer and by how much (see Figure 12.2). Typically, there will be a single statement and a variety of adjectival pairs on which the participant marks their choice. Through this mechanism, SD scales are able to measure both the *directionality* of an attitude and the *intensity* with which it is held. As with Likert scales, not all attitudes are of the same strength, so SD scales have the functionality to measure strength as well as direction.

Your view of aliens								
	1	2	3	4	5	6	7	
Do not exist								*Do exist*
Will be peaceful								*Will want to kill us all*
Would be fascinated by us								*Would not be interested in us*
Will love Marmite								*Will hate Marmite*

FIGURE 12.2   A semantic differential scale

Whilst both Likert scales and semantic differential scales are very practical, neither is flawless as a means of accurately assessing attitudes. The first criticism is that people do not always know their own attitudes and feel forced to give an answer. Participants might also opt to present themselves in a socially desirable manner (loves animals and children and wants to save the world).

Given that self-report measures contain biases, researchers have developed other ways of assessing attitudes, such as examining behaviours that link to attitudes or using physiological measures to determine our stance on something.

Non-verbal behaviour as an indication of attitude

In an attempt to get round the problem described above, researchers have looked at what people actually do, as well as what their attitude is. Breckler (1984) measured participants' willingness to approach a live snake, and took this as an indication of their attitude towards snakes. An advantage of this method is that it can be unobtrusive (though not in this example!), but it does have some problems. First, it is not possible to measure all behaviours in such a way (think about measuring fear of crime this way!). Second, there may be ethical problems as in the example above, where people are exposed to stressful situations such as being asked to approach a live snake!

Non-verbal physiological measures

Physiological measures seek to assess our attitudes by measuring physical attributes and trying to correlate this reaction to how we feel. Various measures have been used, including galvanic skin response and heart rate monitor. However, whilst this battery of techniques can measure minute fluctuations in our physiological response, they have some drawbacks.

First, there are a variety of physical reactions that can produce these results including fear, anger and arousal. Second, whilst the results may indicate a strong response, they give no clue as to direction, so that two participants with totally opposite views might have the same response. For example, you might have a strong physiological response to a slice of Marmite on toast being waved in front of you – your heart starts beating faster and faster – but is that because you hate Marmite or you love it?

12.4.2 ATTITUDE FORMATION

Attitudes can be formed as we consciously search out information on something we want to find out about. For example, suppose you had just heard about the health benefits of eating blue Smarties and you decided to look at Wikipedia to find out more. From what you read you come to the conclusion that eating blue Smarties would be a *good* thing. However, you do not have to actively search for information to form an attitude to it. Zajonc (1968) found that **mere exposure** to something will result in more positive feelings (advertisements work on this basis!). In one study, he asked non-Chinese-literate participants to rate whether a word in Chinese script actually translated into a word meaning 'good' or 'bad' in English. The results indicated that the more often a word had been seen by the participant, the more likely that they would rate it as meaning something good. One explanation is that as we become more familiar with an object, we experience less uncertainty towards the object itself. Sulmont-Rosse et al. (2008) provided evidence in support of mere exposure with respect to liking various drinks: thus, the more we see the drinks, the more we like them!

Of course, we also form attitudes less consciously through soaking up what other people think, particularly those we like or admire such as celebrities, family and friends. Another way that we unconsciously acquire our attitudes is through the media in the form of television, newspapers and magazines. We need to ask whether this is a good thing. Is it really the case that the media always tell the truth, the whole truth and nothing but the truth?

Social learning theory has also been utilised to explain attitude formation. Following the work of Bandura (1977), attitudes can be shown to form as people observe the actions of others. As with learning behaviours, children learn from watching what their parents do rather than necessarily what they say. Others have argued that it is important to be self-aware of our own behaviours: for example, Bem (1965) found that we can form attitudes by observing our own behaviour, a concept known as *self-perception theory*. Furthermore, if the behaviour is freely chosen, it is more likely that we will attribute the cause to an internal value or opinion that we hold. In addition, Strack et al. (1988) found that participants could be induced to believe they were experiencing a particular attitude, based on their physiological condition. These researchers divided their participants into two groups: group A were asked to hold a pen in their mouths using their teeth, whilst group B held the pen using their lips (Figure 12.3). The researchers then asked both groups to rate how funny a series of cartoons were, and found that group A rated them funnier. This result they believed was achieved because holding a pen with one's teeth feels more like smiling, whereas holding it using the lips feels more like frowning. Named the *facial feedback hypothesis*, it argues that people feel their own facial expression and conclude what they must be feeling from this sensation.

KEY STUDY   Harrison, K. (2000). Television viewing, fat stereotyping, body shape standards, and eating disorder. *Communication Research, 27* (5), 617–640.

Psychologists have been concerned over the last 30 years or so about women and eating disorders. One concern has been that the media have moulded individuals' attitudes towards the ideal woman's body shape. Research suggests that these attitudes are acquired fairly early on in life. For example, Harrison (2000) surveyed over 300 6- to 9-year-old children and found that television viewing predicted both increased stereotyping of 'fat females' by the male children, and an increased prevalence of eating disorder symptoms in both male and female children.

FIGURE 12.3   Will holding a pen in your mouth make you find even the jokes in this textbook funny? Try it out

12.4.3 ATTITUDES AND BEHAVIOUR

In a famous study, LaPierre (1934) travelled around America with a Chinese couple to see how many times they would be refused service in restaurants. At the time America had just come out of the Great Depression, and there was open hostility towards many minority ethnic groups. However, they were refused service only once out of the 251 restaurants and hotels when they checked in. Several months later, LaPierre sent a questionnaire to the establishments he and the Chinese couple had previously visited which asked specifically if they would serve Chinese customers. Of those that replied, 90 per cent said they would not serve them. This huge discrepancy led LaPierre to conclude that attitudes do not necessarily predict behaviour. However, a number of factors may influence the accuracy of prediction between attitude and behaviour. Fishbein and Ajzen (1975) criticised LaPierre's study because it did not examine specific attitudes. Whilst the restaurant owners replied that they

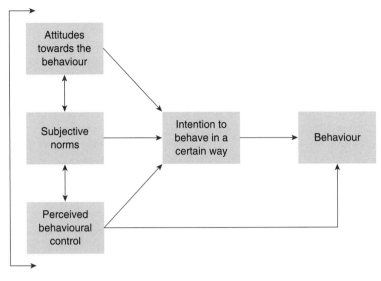

FIGURE 12.4 The theory of planned behaviour (Ajzen, 1991)

would not serve Chinese people as a whole, the study had not asked whether they would serve that *particular* couple (though this seems to be splitting hairs really, as the couple presumably looked like a 'typical' Chinese couple).

12.4.4 THE THEORY OF PLANNED BEHAVIOUR

Ajzen (1991) designed the theory of planned behaviour (TPB) to address how various disparate factors combine to form an intention to act a certain way. As Figure 12.4 illustrates, three factors feed into the intention to act in a certain way. First, there is the person's attitude towards the behaviour and any possible rewards and/or consequences of engaging in that behaviour. Second, there are subjective (or social) norms that exist with respect to the behaviour, and how much the actor is concerned about conforming to those normative beliefs. Finally, there is perceived behavioural control, which refers to the extent to which the person believes they are capable of engaging in the behaviour they are considering. This might relate to whether they can physically do the behaviour, but also whether they have the emotional strength to do it. These three factors combine to form an intention to behave in a certain way, but it is important to remember that this does not necessarily mean the person will actually engage in the behaviour. In this model, the *intention to act* is more important than the *actual behaviour*. There is a direct link between perceived behavioural control and behaviour, because in some situations a person may wish to act but not have the physical and emotional capacity to do so.

The model has received extensive support including research by Huchting et al. (2008) who examined drinking behaviour in college students and found that subjective norms mediated the intention to drink, more so than either attitude towards drink or perceived behavioural control. This suggests that the subjective norm of a binge-drinking culture would mean many individuals end up drinking far more than they might actually want to.

EXERCISE   Start a (friendly) argument!

Try starting a discussion with a friend: it'll give you a good opportunity to think about your own opinions and those of other people, and why they might be different.

When you're next with a good friend, try asking their opinion about something relatively innocuous ... maybe what the weather will be like next week, or what their favourite club/pub is. Whatever your opinion is, try taking the opposing one to theirs and convince them you're right!

Assuming it wouldn't start a fight, try talking about a more contentious issue – maybe religion, trebling the salaries of psychology staff in universities, drug taking or the use of aliens in biomedical research. Give it another go: see what they think, and take an opposing position! As you do, try to be aware of what kind of differences exist in your opinions, what those differences are based on, and finally what type of arguments seem to be more effective in changing their minds.

PROSOCIAL BEHAVIOUR

12.5

Despite the images of social decay and mayhem on the streets that we see on the television every evening, people being nice to other people and helping each other is a daily experience for most of us. Though psychologists seem to prefer to study the mayhem side of life, they do sometimes also look at the many positive ways we interact with each other! Research into prosocial behaviour concentrates on two core areas: (1) **helping behaviour**, where the person intentionally and voluntarily helps someone else but may be expecting to get something in return; and (2) **altruism**, where the behaviour helps others but nothing is expected in return (Batson & Coke, 1981).

> **Prosocial behaviour**   The act of helping out another person, whether as a helping behaviour or as an act of altruism.

12.5.1 EVOLUTION MEETS PROSOCIAL BEHAVIOUR

The *evolutionary approach* argues that we are biologically predisposed to help members of our own family, as this will increase the chances of our own genes surviving. In this regard, the genes that promote prosocial behaviour can be seen as self-selected, and, as such, being helpful is a heritable trait. Stevens et al. (2005) argue that four different types of behaviour can be used to explain evolutionary prosociality:

Kin selection: Genetically related individuals are more likely to help each other, as this will increase the chance of the common genes surviving.

Reciprocity: Help is given on the assumption of being helped at a later time.

Mutualism: Cooperative behaviour will help both individuals.

Sanctioning: Aberrant behaviour is punished to prevent repetition in the future.

Burnstein et al. (1994) found that participants were more likely to help relatives and healthy individuals in a critical situation. This has been replicated by Maner and Gailliot (2007) who found that the factors motivating prosocial behaviour with respect to relatives are different from those factors encouraging such behaviour with strangers. However, this does not account for why we help friends or even strangers who may have no genetic similarity with ourselves, so further explanations must be found. Indeed, social psychologists argue that there is no clear evidence to support prosocial behaviour that can be put down to evolutionary advantages, since no longitudinal research has been completed. Also, it does not explain why people help in some situations and not in others.

12.5.2 THE SOCIAL PSYCHOLOGIST'S EXPLANATION OF PROSOCIAL BEHAVIOUR (OR WHY WE PLAY NICELY)

Social psychology argues that there are a number of theories that can explain prosocial behaviour, including social norms and social learning. Throughout the world, virtually all cultures have social norms that dictate that individuals ought to help someone in need. There are descriptive norms that dictate what is typically done, and injunctive norms that determine what is approved and disapproved of. The activation of social norms is determined by two principles – **reciprocity** and **social responsibility**. Gouldner (1960) identified reciprocity as a factor in social norms, in which we help people that help us. It is a universal common denominator in social transactions and underpins social bonding – the idea that we will help others and expect to be helped in return. In addition, Tesser et al. (1968) found that participants were likely to reciprocate if the helper had made a big and unexpected contribution. The social responsibility norm says that we should help other people, whether they will help us in return or not. Berkowitz (1972) found that this is not entirely true, but rather people are *selective* as to whom they will help. This is related to Lerner and Miller's (1978) **just-world hypothesis** which states that people generally believe that individuals 'get what they deserve'. As such, within this model, if someone seems to be suffering unfairly then we have to help in order to realign this view of the world as a fair place.

> **Just-world hypothesis**   The belief that people have a need to believe that we live in a world where people generally get what they deserve and deserve what they get.

KEY RESEARCHER   Mark Levine

FIGURE 12.5   Mark Levine

Mark Levine is a UK researcher at Lancaster University who is conducting some interesting research on the behaviour of bystanders in emergencies. Mark's work includes both experimental and observational studies. The football shirt study summarised later in this chapter is an example of one of his experiments. He looks at real-life data by analysing CCTV footage. In this analysis he examines how violent incidents play out, including examining the behaviour of the perpetrators, victims and bystanders.

Recent work uses virtual reality environments to study the behaviour of bystanders in violent emergencies. The virtual environment creates the conditions where participants can be exposed to violence in an ethically acceptable manner, and then their behaviour (from eye gaze to autonomic responses to physical proximity) can be studied in real time.

The work on bystander behaviour has also led to studies on social relations in public, for example the way that technologies of control such as CCTV and public drinking legislation are understood, and how they shape our behaviour. Another area of work concerns interactions in the night-time economy such as the relationship between police, private security staff ('bouncers') and the public.

Social learning theories, based on the social learning theory of Bandura (1977), argue that we learn prosocial behaviour from watching other people. This was replicated by Forge and Phemister (1987) who found that children who watch television with examples of prosocial behaviour are more likely to become generous and cooperative themselves. Bryan and Test (1967) found evidence for this, after participants who had seen an experimental confederate giving help were more likely to give help themselves. Similar results were found by Rushton and Campbell (1977) who found that participants were more likely to give blood if an experimental confederate had agreed to do so beforehand (the 'stooge' effect).

12.5.3 BYSTANDER INTERVENTION AND BYSTANDER EFFECTS

A newspaper report of the murder of a young woman in New York in 1964 first brought to psychologists' attention the **bystander effect**. In the media's account, despite the fact that 38 neighbours heard the woman's cries for help, no-one raised the alarm by calling the police until almost 45 minutes had passed after the attack. Psychologists have since shown that the media's account of the story was more fiction than fact (Manning et al., 2007); the story has nonetheless been used to illustrate some psychologists' views about circumstances when we look on and do nothing to help an individual in distress. Latané and Darley (1969) put forward a model for *bystander intervention* which argued that there are five steps involved in making a decision to help or not:

1 *Noticing*: The first step required is that the bystander has actually *noticed* that something has occurred and that it requires more of their attention.

2 *Interpreting*: Once the bystander has noticed that something has happened, s/he must decide whether the situation is one that requires intervention. Of relevance here is the concept of *pluralistic ignorance*, a situation where bystanders use the behaviour of other people as a yardstick for their own actions. The individual bystander assumes that everyone else must have some additional information at their disposal, which explains their lack of action. However, the reality is that everyone is confused and looking for a cue to act.

3 *Taking responsibility*: Having identified that a situation exists that requires attention and that someone does need help, the bystander must decide whether they are responsible for helping. In this situation, **diffusion of responsibility** can mean that someone might not act if they think that someone else will do something, though obviously this effect is negated if they are the only one in the situation. It can also be negated though if the individual sees the required action as part of their expertise (Cramer et al., 1988) or a professional duty (e.g. medical doctors), or if they hold some position of authority in which action is expected as part of their role (Baumeister et al., 1988).

4 *Assessing whether help can be provided*: Having decided to take responsibility, the individual must assess whether they have the required skills to help. Often, however, the most intelligent course of action is to summon help from professionals.

5 *Providing help*: Having moved through all four stages, the individual still has to decide whether they will help or not. At this point, they will weigh up the potential advantages or disadvantages of helping (Fritzsche et al., 2000) and make their decision.

EXERCISE   The bystander model

The bystander model suggests that the greater the numbers of people present, the less likely it is that people will be helpful. Applying this model to the internet, given the large numbers of people present online we might expect that there are very few incidences of helping taking place. From your experience, how true is this? Does helping ever happen online (e.g. in virtual environments such as Second Life or World of Warcraft?) If so, why?

12.5.4 THE BYSTANDER-CALCULUS MODEL

Piliavin et al. (1981) argued that when we see someone in distress, we go through three stages of cognitive and physiological analysis:

1   *Physiological response*: Our initial response is a physiological response, in which the stronger the sense of empathic arousal, the more likely that help will be given (Piliavin et al., 1981). This is also affected by non-social factors such as the clarity and severity of the victim's troubles (Geer & Jarmecky, 1973).

2   *Labelling the arousal*: According to Piliavin et al.'s model, we label the arousal we feel as a particular emotion, and the nature of this dictates our response. This can be either personal distress or empathic concern. In the former, we act to reduce the arousal we feel, whereas with the latter, we act out of genuine sympathy for the victim.

3   *Evaluating the consequences*: Potential helpers then evaluate what action is possible to take, with the lowest potential cost to themselves. As identified by Batson et al. (1978) the primary costs are time and effort, though personal injury is an additional concern.

Psychology does provide some grounds for optimism regarding bystander behaviour: Banyard et al. (2007) identified that the prevention of sexual violence could be enhanced through bystander education techniques. So knowing the above should make you more likely to try to rescue, well, just about anyone in distress.

Of course, the model is not without its doubters (or critical evaluators) and several criticisms have been put forward about the bystander effect. For example, in their reconsiderations of the bystander effect, Levine and Thompson argued that 'it is not simply the presence or absence of others that affects a bystander's intervention, but who the bystander perceives those others to be' (2004: 231). There is some empirical evidence to support this view. For example, Levine et al. (2005) found that an injured stranger wearing an 'ingroup' football shirt was more likely to be helped than an injured stranger wearing a rival football shirt or a neutral shirt.

12.5.5 TO HELP OR NOT TO HELP (THAT IS THE QUESTION)

Locus of control   Refers to what people perceive to be the source of what happens to them. An internal locus of control means that people see it as coming from within themselves – so they are largely in control of what happens to them, or at least in a position to influence it. An external locus of control means that it is perceived as coming from sources outside the person, and so is not something which the individual can influence.

Other factors are also important to consider when predicting helping behaviours. Eisenberg et al. (1999) found that preschool children who exhibited prosocial behaviour were also more likely to engage in prosocial behaviour in the rest of their childhood and early adulthood. Furthermore, Rushton et al. (1984) found that there might be a possible genetic bias as monozygotic twins were more likely to help their twin than dizygotic twins.

In addition, Bierhoff et al. (1991) found that helpers have a higher **internal locus of control** than non-helpers. This meant that they believed they were able to control events around them, whereas those with an **external locus of control** felt that the situation was out of their control (see Chapter 16 for an explanation of locus of control).

However, the association with having an internal locus of control does not mean necessarily that this causes helping behaviour. It means only that there is a relationship between the two variables, i.e. between (1) locus of control and (2) helping behaviour. In psychology we need to be wary of assuming that a relationship between variables is necessarily a causal one. To see why, just consider that an association between the number of ice creams sold and the number of people drowning has been demonstrated; this does not mean that buying an ice cream *causes* people to drown, merely that there is an association between the two. The fact that hot weather leads to increased ice cream sales *and* more people going swimming shows how this association is brought about by a common factor – hot weather!

It has been found that if a person feels they are competent and capable of helping, then they are substantially more likely to do so (Korte, 1971). Pantin and Carver (1982) commented that watching a film on first aid would increase the chances of the participant helping. Jonas et al. (2002) have put forward the *terror management theory* as another factor involved in prosocial behaviour. Their research shows that when people are reminded of their own mortality, they are more likely to have prosocial thoughts. It has also been found that people in a good mood are more likely to help than people in a bad mood.

12.5.6 WHO GIVES HELP? WHO GETS HELP?

As well as there being certain characteristics of the 'giver' that make it more likely that they will help, there are also characteristics of the 'receiver' of that help which will make the help more likely. Research has shown that we are more likely to help someone if we feel they are similar to us (Emswiller et al., 1971). As argued above, help will also be more likely if the receiver is seen as being an 'ingroup' member rather than an 'outgroup' member. For example, Ellis and Fox (2001) found that heterosexuals were more likely to help people they had identified as also being heterosexual, rather than someone who was homosexual or lesbian.

Attractive people are also more likely to be helped. Benson et al. (1976) found that whilst physically attractive people received more help, those seen to have an attractive *personality* were also more likely to get help. Moreover, DePalma et al. (1999) found that someone is more likely to be helped if they are seen as being in a situation that is out of their control. In their research, participants were prepared to help someone with a medical condition, but only if they were not responsible for the onset of the condition.

Research has indicated that females are perceived as kinder and more compassionate than males (Ruble, 1983), but this has also been challenged. Eagly and Crowley (1986), for example, completed a **meta-analysis** investigating whether there was a difference in prosocial helping between genders. They concluded that there was no difference in the amount of helping behaviour, but instead a difference in the type of helping engaged in. Males were reported as being more likely to help females than males (though it is unclear if sexual orientation was taken into account). Males are also more likely to help in dangerous situations, whereas females helped either

Meta-analysis Where a researcher uses statistics to combine results from (typically) a large number of studies about a particular topic.

gender, and in more everyday situations, particularly in ones requiring emotional support (Otten et al., 1988). In addition, Batson et al. (1996) found that having had a similar experience was more like to produce empathy in females than males (do not pass go, but return to Section 12.5.4 on how empathy produces helping behaviour).

12.5.7 THE COST OF NOT HELPING (DON'T BOVVER!)

Piliavin et al. (1981) also identified potential costs in *not helping*: specifically, they suggested there were empathy costs and personal costs in not helping. In this situation, empathy cost refers to the unpleasant arousal felt when seeing someone in trouble, which is then *not* released by activity. A personal cost refers to possible social or personal vilification that might be experienced after the event, since helping is the social norm and going against that incurs costs.

> ### EXERCISE   A more interesting thing to do: help someone!
>
> Try a random act of kindness yourself and see how it makes you feel. *Or*, better still, work your way through Danny Wallace's book *Random acts of kindness: 365 ways to make the world a nicer place* (2004) (naturally making sure you abide by all the laws of the country, health and safety legislation and anything else we need to dodge responsibility for!). And don't be surprised if people view your kind acts suspiciously; after all, there is something strange about people who help for no reason at all, isn't there? Why don't people trust you when you are just trying to help unless they know what you are getting from it? What are you after? Or are you just a bit weird? Hmm. Interesting. See for yourself what reaction you get when you perform a random act of kindness ...

CHAPTER SUMMARY

12.6

As we have highlighted in this chapter, individuals do not always accurately attribute causes to others' or their own behaviours. This is partly because, as Fiske and Taylor argue, most people act as cognitive misers, and make attributions to try to save on mental time and effort. Because of this, errors are often made, such as the fundamental attribution error.

We also learnt that predicting behaviours by attitudes alone can be challenging. The classic study by LaPierre provides a clear illustration of how attitudes towards minority groups did not predict how people behaved towards them. The theory of planned behaviour was put forward as a way to better predict behaviour. This model considers subjective norms, the consequences of engaging in the behaviour, and the extent to which the person believes they are capable of engaging in the behaviour.

Finally, we looked at prosocial behaviour. Several theories have been offered to explain why individuals engage in helping behaviours. Social evolutionary theorists suggest that we are biologically predisposed to at least help members of our own family. Others instead suggest that individuals are helpful simply because they are following social norms. Of course, not everyone helps others in need. But then again, some people (e.g. comedian Danny Wallace) encourage us to break social norms and help anyone and everyone whether they are in need or not.

DISCUSSION QUESTIONS

This section has been all about why people do or do not help others. Bearing in mind what we've just covered in this chapter, can you remember a situation in the recent past where someone needed help? If so, try using the following questions to help you reflect on the situation:

- Did you help them? Or did you decide not to?
- What were the reasons for your choice?
- Can you think of any particular factors in the situation, about the person or about yourself, which made a difference?
- In the future, what situations do you think you might help in?
- What might make a difference when you next encounter someone who needs help?

SUGGESTIONS FOR FURTHER READING

If you are interested in ideas around changing attitudes, why not read Brown, R., Vivian, J., & Hewstone, M. (1999). Changing attitudes through intergroup contact: the effects of group membership salience. *European Journal of Social Psychology, 29* (5–6), 741–764. Also, why not put your feet up and watch the film *An Inconvenient Truth* where Al Gore attempts to change people's attitudes towards 'global warming'. What sorts of persuasive techniques does he seek to employ, and how effective are they?

HOW WE GROW AND CHANGE

Developmental Psychology

The transformation from gurgling and gurning baby to thinking and feeling adult is something that never ceases to amaze. Watch a baby and you can't help but wonder how we change from the unknowing, wriggling infant to being aware of our surroundings and ourselves. Developmental psychology looks at the changes that individuals go though during their lives. It is often thought of as child psychology because much of the research has focused on children, but this view would be misleading because psychologists are actually interested in how we develop 'from the cradle to the grave'. In fact, modern scientific techniques mean that we can track development even before the cradle and so we should really say 'from conception to the grave'. Having said this, the research we cover in this section reflects the traditional preoccupation with children.

Modern developmental psychology is often dated back to William Preyer's book *The mind of the child* which was published in 1882. Like many of the developmental psychologists that followed him, he based his work on observations of his own child. In fact, this use of psychologists' own children is one of the very cute/deeply irritating (delete to taste) aspects of the subject. What distinguished Preyer's work and what set the pattern for developmental psychology was the use of scientific procedures, in particular accurate and thorough recording of behaviour and the identification of patterns of change in that behaviour.

Over the last 130 years psychologists have focused on various areas of development, especially the development of cognition (for example the work of Jean Piaget and more recently the research into autism), emotion (for example the work of Sigmund Freud and later Mary Ainsworth) and behaviour (for example the work of the behaviourist John Watson and later Albert Bandura). In this section we will look at all these areas and see what current research can tell us about how we change from babies to hoodies.

KEY ISSUES

There are two key issues for developmental psychologists. One is the nature–nurture question (see Chapter 13) which explores how much of a behaviour is the product of genetically determined factors (nature) and how much of experience (nurture). We are born with some remarkable behaviours: for example, babies under six months old have a diving reflex, so if they go under water they automatically hold their breath and make swimming-like movements. Also we clearly share some characteristics with our parents, but how much of that is due to being brought up by them and how much to sharing their genetic structure?

The second key issue is about the timing and plasticity of development. Some behaviours develop at specific times in our lives: for example, the diving reflex mentioned above fades by the age of one. The concept of plasticity refers to the amount that a behaviour can change and adapt or how rigid it will be once it has developed. Some psychologists see the changes as developing steadily and progressively, and some describe the changes as going through a series of stages. The interest for all developmental psychologists is in the things that bring about these changes.

EXERCISE   What is a child?

The answer to the question 'What is a child?' is not as obvious as you'd think. Different cultures and different times in history clearly have a range of views about what it means to be a child. For example, have a look here at the painting of a child from the Middle Ages. There is something very strange about it. You will notice that it looks not like a child but like a scaled-down adult. The head is too small and the face too grown-up. Does this mean that the people of this time saw children in this way?

Your task is to make a list of the similarities and differences between children and adults and, more problematically, consider at what age a child takes on the characteristics of an adult.

Example of medieval art showing the adult features of the child
© Arte & Immagini srl/Corbis

THIS SECTION

In this section we have three chapters looking at how children develop. Chapter 13 looks at the early years from before birth up till about four years of age. It looks at some of the innovative methods that psychologists have created to study children and explores the issues identified above. It also looks at how infants make sense of the world, moving from early mental representations of the world to early language development, and finally it examines how the environment can assist in the development of later social interactions. Chapter 14 looks at how children develop through the school years, focusing on language and social reasoning. It goes on to consider how the social world of children changes as they enter school and how this is reflected in the importance of peer relationships, friendships and experiences of bullying. Finally in Chapter 15 we look at atypical development and how we can understand and respond to the unique needs of each individual child.

13 DEVELOPMENT DURING THE EARLY YEARS

Lead authors **Lucy Betts, Lee Farrington-Flint, James Stiller, Rebecca Larkin** and **Gareth Williams**

CHAPTER OUTLINE

INTRODUCTION

13.1

What goes on inside the mind of an infant? Remarkably we can never really know the answer to this despite the fact that we were all infants once ourselves. This chapter introduces you to the topic of developmental psychology during the early years, focusing on the cognitive and social skills developed through early infancy. The chapter explores some of the factors that influence an infant's early cognitive and social development. For the purpose of this chapter we have defined the 'early years' from prenatal through to the age of four. The chapter explores whether we are born with **innate** capabilities or whether the skills we acquire are learnt from interactions with the environment. Additionally, we evaluate some of the methods used to examine development during the early years and consider whether the data generated from these can be interpreted in a way that clearly illustrates innate abilities in infants. We also discuss how infants make sense of the world, from early mental representations of the world to early language development, and also how the environment can assist in the development of social interactions.

?

FRAMING QUESTIONS

How important are the environment and our genetics in development?
What methods can psychologists use to examine development?
What abilities do newborn infants have?
To what extent can young infants recognise familiar faces and objects?
Do infants develop mental representations of objects in their environment?
Can infants recognise familiar voices or melodies?
How important is the environment in children's development of language?
What is the role of child-directed speech?
How important are first relationships in an infant's early emotional development?
What are the advantages of forming strong secure attachments with primary caregivers?
What processes are involved in the development of self-awareness in infants?

INFLUENCES ON INFANT DEVELOPMENT

13.2

One of the most contentious issues within developmental psychology is whether or not our development is driven by nature (i.e. genetics) or nurture (environment). The first part of this chapter explores the evidence for both sides of this argument.

There is growing evidence that our genes, in conjunction with other prenatal influences, shape who we are. For example, exposure to some maternal hormones before birth can influence the development of borderline personality disorders in later life (Evardone et al., 2008). Also, factors such as high maternal stress during pregnancy have been linked to emotional development: infants who are exposed to higher maternal stress are more likely to have lower levels of emotional response at the age of four months (Mohler et al., 2006). Some researchers report that 50 per cent of internalising problems (for example, anxiety) can be accounted for by genetics (Saudino et al., 2008).

Although there is evidence that our genetic composition is important for our development, the studies conducted so far fail to provide evidence that the link between our genetics and our development is a complete match. Therefore, this implicates the importance of other factors for development. According to the nurture side of the debate, the environment is more influential. Returning to prenatal development, environment influences can impact on the developing child. During pregnancy, there are a number of critical periods when certain environmental factors can cause substantial changes to organ development in the unborn infant (Thornton, 2008). The timing of these critical periods differs for each organ. For example, for the nervous system the most sensitive period is three to six weeks post-conception, whereas for the heart it is four to seven weeks. However, outside these times the developing infant is still at risk from environmental influences.

One of the most likely causes of disruption to the developing child during the critical period is **teratogens**. Common examples of potential teratogens are alcohol and nicotine. Consuming alcohol during pregnancy can lead to **foetal alcohol syndrome**. Foetal alcohol syndrome affects 1 to 7 per 1000 births, and symptoms include changes in brain structure, cognitive impairment and behavioural problems that become more pronounced during adolescence (Kodituwakku, 2007; Niccols, 2007). Smoking during pregnancy has been linked to attentional problems, hyperactivity and conduct problems (Button et al., 2007).

> **Teratogens** Substances or environmental influences that affect development of the foetus resulting in physical abnormalities.
>
> **Foetal alcohol syndrome** Foetal abnormalities caused by alcohol consumption during pregnancy.

The transactional model seeks to explain possible links between genes and the environment (Sameroff & Chandler, 1975). According to this approach, a child's development should be regarded as a complex interaction between the child, the child's social context and the child's immediate environment. This makes intuitive sense: while our genetic composition may predispose development, the environment is fundamental to acting as a trigger. Consequently, it seems that it is the combination of these factors that shapes an individual's development (Thornton, 2008).

MAKING SENSE OF THE SOCIAL WORLD: INFANCY AND BEYOND

13.3

In the remainder of this chapter we explore aspects of infant development and consider innate and environmental influences in the development of cognitive, language and social skills. First, however, let's consider how researchers study infant behaviour.

13.3.1 METHODS OF STUDYING INFANT BEHAVIOUR

Early studies into infant visual perception were primarily based upon observations of how infants interact with the visual environment around them. However, these studies did not allow researchers to examine experimentally what properties of a visual stimulus, or what environmental conditions, the infant was responding to. The primary difficulty in conducting such experimental research is that infants do not necessarily understand complex instructions and they cannot provide complex verbal feedback on their thinking or understanding. Similarly, preverbal infants become easily distracted and can be rather unpredictable participants. Nonetheless, psychologists have devised several innovative methods to examine early infant cognition:

1   Preferential looking technique builds on the idea that young infants have an innate predisposition to respond to novel stimuli in their visual environment. So, when presented with two objects, infants would gaze at the object that was of greater interest or was unfamiliar to them. The time spent looking at each stimulus indicates the infant's ability to discriminate between novel and familiar stimuli. If an infant spends longer observing one of the stimuli, this demonstrates an ability to discriminate between the two objects.

2   **Habituation** tasks are a refinement of Fantz's (1963) original preferential looking tasks (see Figure 13.1). They take advantage of an infant's uncanny ability to become bored very quickly. In the initial stages of the habituation paradigm the infant is familiarised with a stimulus until they pay little or no attention to it. The infant can then be presented with another stimulus alongside the habituated one, and the preferential looking task can be reapplied. If the infant focuses their attention on the new stimulus then it can be assumed that the new stimulus has captured their attention.

3   Preferential sucking technique allows for a range of different non-visual stimuli to be tested (such as recognition of familiar sounds or voices). If a novel stimulus attracts the infant's attention then there is a subsequent reduction in the rate of their sucking behaviour.

It is clear that such techniques provide an insight into infants' interactions in their environment and their underlying cognition. However the techniques depend on the experimenters' interpretation, so they may not have measured preferences in the infant. Nonetheless, in the following sections we illustrate the importance of using such methods to examine the underlying cognitive skills in infancy, from facial recognition to early categorisation of objects. All the evidence suggests that although young infants are born with some strong innate predisposition to understand their world, such understanding requires active involvement in their environment and social interactions with others.

13.3.2 FACE PERCEPTION AND IMITATION

A big question regarding infant processing of facial stimuli is whether or not this is an innate behaviour. So, it asks whether infants are predisposed to recognise human faces or particular

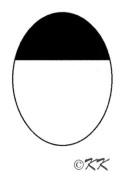

©*KK*

FIGURE 13.1 The jumbled faces task devised by Fantz was used to show that very young children can tell the difference between a face and another interesting pattern

pattern types, or whether visual processing of facial stimuli is the result of learnt expertise. One of the earliest and most influential experimental studies into infant face perception used the preferential looking task. Fantz (1963) demonstrated that two-month-old infants show a preference for patterned stimuli and, in particular, for face-like stimuli over jumbled face-like stimuli or patterned stimuli with facial configurations (see Figure 13.1). However, more recent studies have shown that, straight after birth, infants prefer to look at face-like patterns and images over scrambled faces or non-face-like stimuli (Goren et al., 1975; Johnson & Morton, 1991; Valenza et al., 1996). This ability to differentiate between face and non-face stimuli has led some researchers to suggest that infants are born with an innate inbuilt ability to recognise faces.

An ability to recognise faces is not much use by itself, if the newborn infant cannot understand their significance or learn their significance. Imitation provides one way for infants to make sense of the overwhelming wealth of information provided by the average face. Meltzoff and Moore (1977; 1983) showed that 12- to 21-day-old infants are capable of imitating facial gestures and body movements. Again this could be explained in terms of novelty because newborn infants have an innate preference for things that change. However, imitation of facial gestures, and body movements, suggests that infants are born with an innate ability to respond to the actions of people and that infants possess an innate representation of their own bodies. Nonetheless, such imitative behaviours could be considered innate reflexes or responses rather than specifically guided imitation to human facial expressions.

13.3.3 OBJECT AND CATEGORY PERCEPTION

The human infant is aware of their surroundings and can differentiate between novel and habituated stimuli. However, this does not provide any evidence to suggest that the infant is capable of understanding what characteristics define a particular object or stimuli. Some physical properties of the infant's visual environment appear to be innate. One example is depth perception. This was shown by the 'visual cliff' experiment in which Walk and

Gibson (1961) demonstrated that most infants, moving towards a precipice across a piece of Plexiglass, would stop at the point where the floor beneath them appears to drop off. This suggests that infants have an understanding of depth and perspective.

Recently, Quinn et al. (2006) showed that six-month-old infants can categorise objects. Infants were familiarised with images of cats, and the **event-related potentials** associated with the presentation of the images were recorded. Once the infant was familiarised with the cat stimulus, they were then presented with novel cat images interspersed with dog images. The event-related potentials recorded for the cat and dog stimuli were significantly different, suggesting that we have the relevant neural architecture in place for object categorisation within the first six months of life. This experiment also suggests that the habituation task itself might reflect object categorisation via a preference for novelty in young infants. Further studies suggest that between 14 and 18 months old, infants can start to understand categories and attribute objects to categories (Booth & Waxman, 2002).

> **Event-related potentials**   A characteristic electrophysiological response by the brain to a stimulus, usually recorded using EEG (electroencephalography).

13.3.4 IMPLICATIONS FOR THE DEVELOPMENT OF MENTAL REPRESENTATIONS

Having established that infants are capable of recognising faces and objects from a relatively early age, we can ask questions concerning whether infants develop mental representations of objects. Similarly, questions can be raised concerning the underlying cognitive structures that are developing as infants interact with their social environment.

Piaget's description of the sensorimotor stage of development (between birth and two years) pioneered discoveries in children's thinking in early infancy. During the sensorimotor stage, Piaget argued, infants are essentially limited in their thinking and show a primitive understanding of objects in their environment. They are learning to match up what they experience (their senses) with what they do (their actions or motor activity) – hence this is known as the sensorimotor stage. Further, infants are essentially **egocentric** in their thinking, and before nine months cannot form **mental representations** of the objects in their environment or recognise that when an object is out of view it continues to exist.

> **Egocentric thinking**   When an individual has little regard for the views or interests of others, which may involve individuals memorising objects in relation to themselves.
>
> **Mental representations**   An internal cognitive map of stimuli.

To test these theories Piaget (1952) devised a simple retrieval task to examine the mental representations of six- to nine-month-old infants for everyday objects. During the task, a toy and a cloth were placed in front of the infant and, once the infant was interested in the toy, the toy was either partially or completely hidden under the cloth. The infant's ability to retrieve the object was then observed. At around six to seven months, infants failed to retrieve the object even when it was partially hidden; but by eight to nine months, infants would retrieve the hidden object, suggesting that they had developed a mental representation of the object even when it was out of sight.

In subsequent studies, with nine- to 12-month-old infants, Piaget (1952) used two cloths in front of the infant with a toy hidden under one of the cloths. In this situation, nine-month-olds retrieved the toy on most trials. After several trials of hiding the toy under one of the cloths, the toy was then moved under a different cloth in full view of the infant. However, nine- to 12-month-olds failed to retrieve the toy once it had changed location, with the majority of infants looking under the original cloth. Piaget used these findings as evidence that infants are largely egocentric in their thinking, failing to make a distinction between objects in the world and their own actions.

There are, nonetheless, alternative explanations to Piaget's interpretations of these results. Harris (1973) suggested that Piaget's results indicate the fragility in infants' short-term memory. However, Butterworth (1977) argued that the results were evidence of the infant's inherent difficulty in coding or memorising positions of objects with their location. He suggested that nine- to 12-month-olds were not using **allocentric** forms of coding the location of the object but instead using egocentric forms of coding.

In summary, it is clear that infants between nine and 12 months do develop some form of mental representations of objects they see within their immediate environ-

> **Allocentric**   The skill of memorising the position of an object in relation to other objects.

ment, allowing them to search for objects even when completely out of sight. However, while Piaget's findings have been replicated, the interpretations of these findings have been challenged (for further information on Piaget see Chapter 14). What remains clear is that young infants continue to demonstrate an understanding of the social world and continue to interact with the social world, and because of this interaction they are developing internal mental representations of objects, whether these objects are shapes, toys or human beings.

EARLY LANGUAGE DEVELOPMENT

13.4

Language is arguably what makes humans special, as no other species has mastered communication at such a complex level. How humans develop language skills is therefore a key area of study in developmental psychology, and has been subject to much debate. In this section we consider early language development. It is worth avoiding falling into the traditional assumption that newborn infants lack any language skills. In fact, similar to their perceptual capabilities, even from the early days of life, newborns are inbuilt with facilities to make sense of people's speech as language rather than as general sounds.

13.4.1 DISCRIMINATING BETWEEN SPEECH SOUNDS

Infants show considerable skills in discriminating between sounds even before birth, and complex learning of sound discrimination develops during infancy. There is considerable evidence that an infant's interaction with their environment is fundamental in their learning of language. DeCasper and Fifer (1980) examined infants' ability to discriminate between different voices using infants from birth to three days old and the preferential sucking technique. Infants showed a preference for their mother's voice compared to a stranger's voice. This evidence suggests that young infants are perhaps pretuned to recognise, and respond to, their mother's voice from birth.

KEY STUDY **DeCasper, A.J., Lecanuet, J.P., Busnel, M.C., Granier-Deferre, C., & Maugeais, R. (1994). Fetal reactions to recurrent maternal speech. *Infant Behavior and Development*, 17, 159–164.**

By the seventh month of gestation, the auditory apparatus of the human foetus is fully functioning. However, as the foetus is snugly encased within the womb, speech sounds have to travel through membranes, muscle and fluid. By the time the sound waves finally reach the foetus, the high-frequency sounds have been filtered out and what remains is the rhythm, stress and intonation of speech, otherwise known as the *prosody*.

Starting at the 33rd week of gestation, DeCasper et al. asked pregnant women to repeat a short children's rhyme three times a day over a four-week period. During the testing phase of the study, two rhymes were played to the foetus: the rhyme which had been repeated by the mother, and an unfamiliar control rhyme spoken by a female graduate student. Whilst this was happening the pregnant women wore headphones, to ensure they did not react to the rhymes being played and thus confound the experiment. The heart rates of the foetuses were recorded whilst the rhymes were played to measure their reaction. It was found that the foetuses' heart rates reduced when they heard the familiar rhyme, indicating that they recognised the sequence of speech sounds.

The study by DeCasper et al. is extremely important because it demonstrated that humans are able to recognise familiar speech patterns whilst they are still in the womb. Furthermore, this study showed that this recognition is not limited to the voice of the foetus's mother. The foetus can in fact distinguish between a familiar and unfamiliar story being read by a complete stranger.

Nonetheless, it could be argued that, at two to three days old, these infants had been exposed to language and therefore DeCasper and Fifer's (1980) findings could be the direct results of learning. While this is a reasonable interpretation, there is evidence that young infants are capable of learning even before birth, with studies providing evidence of prenatal speech learning. A study by Lecanuet (1998) revealed that two-day-old infants could demonstrate a preference for melodies that had been repeatedly played during pregnancy compared to unfamiliar melodies. Moon et al. (1993) also illustrated young infants' ability to demonstrate a preference for their own native language (English) over non-native languages (such as Spanish) at two to three days after birth.

However, a key limitation is that researchers can only infer the occurrence of prenatal speech learning: they cannot test this directly. There is one exception (DeCasper et al., 1994), which is described in the key study. Clearly, this evidence suggests that infants are capable of learning about language from an early age. Even within the womb, we are actively learning about the outside environment and developing skills to discriminate between different speech sounds. Therefore, language development begins well before birth.

There is evidence that newborn infants are highly attuned to attend, and respond, to spoken language. Infants can notice elements of speech when it is played forwards but not backwards, suggesting there is something unique to speech over other sounds (Ramus et al., 2000). Also, infants can spot changes in syllables of spoken speech (Bijeljac-Babic et al., 1993) and when prerecorded sounds change from 'ba' to 'da'. These processes are, to some degree, available to other animals as well. For example, tamarin monkeys (Ramus et al., 2000) and macaques (Kuhl & Padden, 1982) can also discriminate between changes in human speech patterns. However, it is from these basic processes that newborn humans begin to sample the world around them and begin to acquire the language of their environment. Picking up where words begin and end, and the main features of the language allows infants to start to piece together the vocabulary of the world around them. Acquisition of language generally needs two things: vocabulary development and, much later, grammar acquisition. In the main, much of what is acquired initially are words to describe things.

Language acquisition therefore clearly involves a complex interaction between the infant and the world around them, especially in the early years of development (see the later section on child-directed speech).

13.4.2 EARLY LANGUAGE PRODUCTION

Language production is an area of rapid progression for an infant, moving in a set of noticeable stages from cooing to short sentences by around two years of age. A newborn has cooing and crying (and more crying) at their disposal initially when it comes to language communication, representing the first noticeable type of language production. One of the main problems with crying is that parents often need to resort to either trial-and-error or context to work out what the crying is about (Thompson et al., 2007).

Crying generally gives way to **babbling** at around seven months of age, which is considered a universal step in typical language development (Harley, 2001). At this stage, whole ranges of consonant and vowel combinations are spoken and these tend to be strung together in repetitive utterances. Some months later, infants tend to only babble those consonant–vowel combinations that occur in the language around them. Hearing infants of deaf parents, where speech is not present in the surroundings, tend to stop babbling at this stage. However, recent research has shown that these babies do continue to babble, but with hand signals instead (Petitto et al., 2004). Generally both babbling and the reduction in consonant–vowel

Babbling A child appears to be experimenting with making the sounds of language, but is not yet producing any recognisable words.

combinations suggest that the process needs a mixture of sampling from the environment and inner processes of development for speech to progress.

At around 12 months, infants start to make single-word utterances. These are not always clear words but are the beginnings of intelligible speech. Often a word is used to represent a range of objects: for example, 'car' may be used for four-wheeled objects like cars and trucks but not for other things in the infant's environment (Boelens et al., 2007). Learning what words go with which objects might have much to do with what interests the infant at the time the word is spoken (Pruden et al., 2006). From only a few words at 12 months, spoken vocabulary and naming tend to expand quite rapidly between 18 months and two years of age, with a large range of words available by the end of this period (Hamilton et al., 2000). Further, around this age infants are starting to put words together to make two-word sentences. Clearly this vocabulary spurt provides an adequate basis for later (and more sophisticated) language development.

13.4.3 IMITATION AND REINFORCEMENT

Early theories of language development suggested that children learn through imitation of adults around them. This theory emphasises the importance of the environment for language learning, and coincides with research demonstrating that children from families with limited education know fewer words than children from less deprived backgrounds (Snow, 1999). However, children's spoken language is often quite different from that of adults, which causes a problem for the theory. The best illustration of this is when young children aged three to four years overgeneralise regular verb endings to irregular verbs (e.g. a child might say 'I falled over' instead of 'I fell over'). Adults do not produce such errors, so how can children have learned to do this through imitation?

Skinner (1957) built on the idea of imitation and suggested that children learn language through reinforcement from adults. In this way, vocabulary, grammar and syntax can be gradually shaped, expanded and improved. Yet Skinner has been criticised for failing to appreciate that adults rarely correct children's grammar, but rather tend to be interested in the content of children's utterances.

13.4.4 CHILD-DIRECTED SPEECH

If you have had any contact with small children in the past, think for a moment about how you spoke to them. You may recall that you spoke more slowly than usual, used simple grammar and **concrete vocabulary**, and exaggerated the pitch and intonation of your speech. This adaptation of speech when talking to small children used to be called **motherese**, but is now more sensibly called **child-directed speech**.

Another notable feature of child-directed speech is repetition of key words and phrases. Research shows that infants prefer to listen to child-directed speech compared to normal speech (Cooper & Aslin, 1990) and this may help explain infants' rapid language development. However, this argument is limited because child-directed speech is not present in all cultures (Pye, 1986), yet nearly all children develop impressive language skills within the first two years of life.

Therefore, whilst child-directed speech is known to facilitate language learning, it is not needed for children to develop a complex understanding of grammar and a wide vocabulary. This brings us back to the argument for an innate predisposition towards learning language, which may set humans apart from other species.

> **Child-directed speech (motherese)** The act of using a sing-song voice, speaking slowly, or using simple language when talking to an infant.

LATER LANGUAGE DEVELOPMENT

13.5

At around 24 months, children are producing two-word sentences, which are still very basic. However, children's development of language beyond this telegraphic phase has been questioned (Smith et al., 2003). This section will consider the development of more complex forms of language, namely the understanding of grammar and later syntactical development.

13.5.1 PIDGINS AND CREOLES

Children are actively constructing their own understanding of language through interactions with the environment. Spoken communication tends to develop between people irrespective of differing language backgrounds. **Pidgin and creole** languages are examples of this and suggest that we may have innate language ability. These types of languages occur where people with different languages are displaced by wider social factors and come together as a community. Aspects of different languages become mixed together and what emerges is a 'good enough' language for daily use. Pidgin languages are typically only oral languages and tend to be uncomplicated in structure (Baptista, 2005).

Later-generation speakers of pidgin languages tend to formalise the language to follow particular grammar rules and include or exclude certain vocabulary; languages where this has occurred tend to be called creoles. Creoles might arise from a pidgin language but they can also appear without it (Kam & Newport, 2005). One possible theory is that children of pidgin speakers tend to turn the language into a more regular structure using innate principles for things like grammar and the structure of languages (Bickerton, 1984). But this self-organising process in communication, where languages appear to emerge from interaction irrespective of original languages, has led some to argue that this is evidence of strong innate drives to the structures found in languages (Pinker, 1995).

> **Pidgin and creole**   A shared language developed when two communities with different languages join together.

13.5.2 SYNTACTIC DEVELOPMENT AND GRAMMATICAL UNDERSTANDING

Around two years of age, infants develop a more sophisticated understanding of language and have already started to make simple one- or two-word sentences and progress through the telegraphic stage of language. Two-word sentences have been the focus of a number of studies; early research suggested that children use a particular set of grammar rules (Brown, 1973), possibly providing evidence of a primitive prototype language. On the other hand, these two-word utterances might simply reflect limitations of the child's cognitive system, with children applying the words that are most available for a given situation to achieve a certain goal (Tomasello, 2000).

The progression of grammar rules actually occurs by three to four years of age, and while vocabulary still develops as children grow older, much of the focus moves to picking up the rules needed to put words in the right order to make sentences. By the time that children reach school they have gone from crying and cooing to babbling, to limited one-word speech, to being able to produce complex sentences.

EARLY SOCIAL DEVELOPMENT IN INFANCY

13.6

In the next part of the chapter we turn our attention to children's social development. The most immediate consideration is the family structure. However, as children grow up socialisation occurs outside the immediate family and they start becoming integrated into more and more social networks including wider family, friends, religious groups or cultural groups. These social networks provide a reference point for the children's knowledge and opportunities for the acquisition of the behaviours and norms that govern social interactions (Lewis, 2005). This section considers the implications of the early interactions for social and emotional development.

13.6.1 THE IMPORTANCE OF EARLY RELATIONSHIPS

As we have seen, infants are tuned into their environment, show a readiness to relate to faces, voices and social beings, and are biologically predisposed to interact with others. The nature of an infant's first relationship is particularly crucial to understand because the mother–infant dyad is important to securing early social relationships (Winnicott, 1964). One way of understanding this early relationship is to look at the concepts of **meshing** and **protoconversations**.

Meshing   How an adult's and an infant's behaviours fit together.

Protoconversations   Early turn-taking behaviour between adults and infants, whereby adults tend to vocalise when the infants are not vocalising.

Observations of protoconversations are important in showing how strikingly the baby's and mother's behaviours are meshed during their early interactions (see Oates, 2005). This form of meshing can occur through both non-verbal behaviour and verbal interactions, such as speech and turn-taking. Turn-taking in conversations is an important aspect of establishing social relationships (Kaye & Fogel, 1980). Over time the type and frequency of infants' face-to-face greetings change from earlier reactive types of interactions (responding solely to interactions) to more proactive types of interactions (such as sustaining or initiating the interaction). Therefore, adults initiate more interactions than infants, especially in the first few months. However, aside from face-to-face actions, turn-taking also occurs through a variety of other non-verbal interactions, such as feeding. Kaye and Brazelton (1971) showed the importance of turn-taking through feeding in terms of jiggling infants on the knee. Remarkably infants show a reduction in feeding behaviour during this jiggling but resume feeding when it stops. In fact synchronizing this behaviour establishes a 'conversation-like' interaction.

We have already seen the importance of imitation for examining infants' representations of facial features earlier in this chapter. However, imitation can also be seen as an important precursor to social development. While previous work has acknowledged the extent to which infants can imitate their mothers' facial features, such as tongue protrusion or widening of the mouth (Meltzoff & Moore, 1977), in reality it is not the infant that is engaging with imitation. Work has shown that it is the mother (or caregiver) that imitates their baby's facial features more frequently as a way of securing a bond and establishing communication with their infant (Pawlby, 1977). Therefore, infants produce behaviours but it is the caregivers that actually use these behaviours to frame interaction sequences accordingly (Pawlby, 1977). This imitation of infants' behaviours decreases in both frequency and duration over the first year of the infant's life as the dyadic (two person) relationship between caregiver and infant becomes more secure (Kaye & Marcus, 1981). In some ways, this ability to frame interactions and imitate infants' behaviours can be seen as methods for scaffolding social interactions (e.g. Bruner, 1975).

13.6.2 IMPORTANCE OF ATTACHMENT AND RELATIONSHIPS

Perhaps the most influential relationship of all is that which the child forms with their primary caregiver during infancy. John Bowlby was one of the first, through his attachment theory, to highlight the importance of the relationship we have with our primary caregiver. Whilst working during the 1930s with boys experiencing adjustment problems, he began to formulate his ideas that disruption to the maternal bond during early childhood is detrimental to later adjustment in the form of psychopathology (Bretherton, 1991).

Bowlby's (1969) deprivation theory states that any interruption to the attachment process will result in problems associated with attachment quality (Thornton, 2008). Four phases of attachment are outlined:

- *Phase 1:* Pre-attachment (birth to two months) in which the infant interacts socially with everyone and does not show a specific preference for a particular caregiver.

- *Phase 2:* Early attachment (two to seven months) in which the infant begins to discriminate between caregivers and develops a strong preference for the primary caregiver. As the strength of the preference for the primary caregiver increases, the child moves to phase 3.

- *Phase 3:* Attachment (seven months to two or three years) where the child exhibits **separation anxiety** if they are not in contact with their primary caregiver. Also the child shows stranger anxiety, which means that they are fearful of people who they do not know. As the child gets older, the attachment figure becomes a resource and this is marked by entry to phase 4.

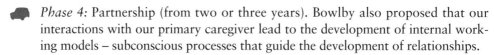 *Phase 4:* Partnership (from two or three years). Bowlby also proposed that our interactions with our primary caregiver lead to the development of internal working models – subconscious processes that guide the development of relationships.

Although Bowlby outlined the importance of attachment, Mary Ainsworth and her colleagues were instrumental in current thinking on attachment through the development of the 'strange situation' studies. Ainsworth et al. (1978) developed the strange situation as a method of assessing children's attachment to their primary caregiver. Specifically, through a series of observations where the primary caregiver and infant (1) interact, (2) are separated and (3) are reunited, it is possible to classify the attachment relationship between the individuals. The central premise is that the infant uses the primary caregiver as a method of exploring the world around them. Through these studies Ainsworth initially developed three attachment classifications: insecure avoidant; securely attached; and ambivalent/resistant. Later a fourth category – disorganised – was added by Main and Solomon (1990). Insecure avoidant is characterised by the child subtly avoiding the primary caregiver. Secure attachment is characterised by the infant using the mother as a secure base to explore the situation and the new environment. Ambivalent/resistant attachment represents a child who clings to the primary caregiver throughout the experience and may show signs of ambivalence. Finally, a disorganised attachment represents those children whose behaviour and interaction patterns do not fit into any of the other categories.

KEY RESEARCHER   Mary Ainsworth

Mary Ainsworth (1913–1999) obtained her PhD in developmental psychology in 1939 and then joined the Canadian army. After the Second World War, Ainsworth held academic positions at various institutions including the Tavistock Clinic in London and the University of Virginia. In 1985 she received an Award for Distinguished Contributions to Child Development; in 1989 she received a Distinguished Scientific Contribution Award from the APA; and in 1998 she received a Gold Medal Award for Life Achievement in the Science of Psychology from the APA.

Her research focused on early social development, including the effects of maternal separation for personality development. Although she is most famous for the strange situation paradigm, she also wrote a number of books and articles exploring aspects of infant development. In particular, she conducted a longitudinal study examining the infant–mother attachment processes in Uganda.

The importance of developing a secure attachment cannot be underestimated. Some researchers argue that a secure attachment is crucial because it helps to protect the child from stress and provides emotional security (Slater, 2007) and promotes positive psychosocial adjustment (Bridges, 2003; Thompson, 2000). Children who develop an insecure attachment or those maltreated by their primary caregiver are more likely to develop emotional disorders (Morton & Browne, 1998). Due to the importance of developing a secure attachment, a number of policy changes have been implemented across the world. In the UK, these include changes to the provision of nursery care, decisions made by the courts in response to custody proceedings, hospital care for children, practices implemented by social services, and the Sure Start initiative (Slater, 2007).

Although many researchers have advocated the importance of secure attachments for children's development, attachment theories are not without their critics. For example, attachment theories have been wrongly used as a tool to pressure mothers to stay at home and to 'blame' mothers for their actions if they return to work and use day care (Slater, 2007). However, there is evidence that children can develop resilience in response to poor attachments (Lewis, 2005). So, despite their poor attachment qualities, these children are still well adjusted. Also, attachment theories are limited in their consideration of the father's role and the role of the wider family (Lewis, 2005). Therefore, traditional attachment theories may fail to fully take into consideration the range of social relationships that infants engage in.

As noted above, some have argued that attachment theory has been used as a tool to criticise those parents who place their children into day care. So, are there implications for children if they attend day care? It is argued that day care is a protective influence for some children and can actively promote the development of a strong parent–child attachment (Ahnert et al., 2006). Day care can be particularly effective when there are low child-to-carer ratios, and the child is cared for in small groups (Ahnert et al., 2006). Another important fact is that day care can be one environment where children interact with their peers, and during this time children acquire a range of social skills.

REASONS TO BE SCEPTICAL   Not all childhoods are the same

Most of the studies on child development are carried out on Western children in wealthy countries. Around the rest of the world, children have very different experiences, and some of them are very hostile. For example, it is estimated that there are 300,000 child soldiers worldwide (UNICEF website) in at least 18 countries. Although the term 'child soldier' commonly brings up a picture of gun-waving teenage boys, the reality is a little different. A number of child soldiers are girls, maybe as many as 40 per cent in some countries, and many of the soldiers are as young as seven or eight. Not all of these children carry weapons, but their roles as support to weapons units puts their lives in danger (Figure 13.2).

(Cont'd)

FIGURE 13.2   Not all childhoods are the same. Thousands of children around the world end up in armies and militias
© Maurizio Gambarini/dpa/Corbis

Some children take up arms to deal with poverty, abuse or discrimination. Some are seeking revenge for violence against themselves or their families. Sometimes they are abducted and forced to join armed groups, and sometimes they become separated from their families and the armies are their only source of food and shelter.

The subsequent recruitment and mobilisation of child soldiers are made possible by the widespread availability of small arms: some 638 million are currently in circulation. Many weapons are so light and portable that a 10-year-old can easily carry, strip and load them.

As well as being influenced by the relationship that infants develop with their primary caregiver from very early on in life, children are influenced by their peers. Specifically, newborn babies are believed to influence the propensity with which other babies cry, with one crying infant triggering crying in others (Hay et al., 1981). This social interaction and preference for similar age mates continues as the infant develops, and by the time that infants are six months old they show preferences for other similar aged infants through reaching out to touch them and also through smiling (Hay et al., 1983). During the first year of life, children's relationships with their peers are characterised by prosocial behaviour, but as infants approach their first birthday they also begin to engage in aggressive behaviour (Hay et al., 2004). From approximately 18 months old, children develop preferences for specific playmates, and by the time a child reaches their third birthday they have developed strong preferences for particular playmates (Hay et al., 2004). Other preferences continue to be established, such as an increasing preference to play with same-gender peers during early childhood (Maccoby, 1988; 1990).

13.6.3 DEVELOPMENT OF SELF-AWARENESS

During the first year of life, infants begin to develop a sense of self-awareness. This involves the development of the subjective self and the objective self. The subjective self is the recognition that the individual is separate from others, whereas the objective self is the recognition that the self is an object with properties (Bee & Boyd, 2005). Self-awareness has been assessed using the rouge test in which an infant is positioned in front of a mirror, a dot is placed on their head and then their reaction is measured (Bertenthal & Fischer, 1978; Lewis & Brooks-Gunn, 1979). If the infant tries to remove the mark then they are showing a sense of self-awareness. As a child's self-awareness increases, they begin to insist on doing things for themselves, show a possessive attitude towards their toys and eventually begin to develop an awareness of their own competencies (Harter, 1982; 1987).

13.6.4 DEVELOPMENT OF GENDER ROLES

Alongside the development of a sense of self, children also begin to develop an awareness of their gender. For a child to apply the gender categorisation to themselves they must move through the processes of gender identity, gender stability and gender consistency. Gender identity involves the infant being able to correctly label other people according to their gender. By the age of two, when shown photographs, children can correctly identify which of the people in the photographs is the same gender as themselves (Ruble & Martin, 1998). Gender stability is the recognition that people remain the same gender throughout their life (Bee & Boyd, 2005). The final stage is gender consistency, which is the notion that people's biological sex remains the same even though their appearance can change. During the development of children's gender roles, children also begin to show an awareness of gender role stereotypes. For example, three- to four-year-olds can apply stereotype knowledge to jobs, with children able to say which job is stereotypically performed by adults of each gender (Ruble & Martin, 1998). Children also show a preference to play with gender-stereotyped toys from about the age of 18 months (O'Brien, 1992), and from the age of three children prefer to interact with same-gender peers (Maccoby, 1988; 1990).

CHAPTER SUMMARY

13.7

In this chapter we have looked at the development of cognitive, language and social skills in relation to development during the early years. We have also evaluated the methods used to examine development, especially in young infants. Hopefully, you should now be able to reflect on the appropriateness of these different methodologies and to question the types of conclusions drawn from studies using these methods.

One of the main questions we have discussed is the validity of researchers' *interpretations* of research evidence concerning infants' early mental and cognitive capabilities. As we have illustrated, though results from experiments may often be replicated, interpretations of these results may vary according to the nature of the study.

Finally, we have illustrated how the interaction between genes and the environment should be seen as a complex relationship. Through this interaction infants can begin to develop a better sense of the social world, through the development of mental representations, language skills and social relationships.

DISCUSSION QUESTIONS

Can we accurately measure perception in infants? What implications does this have for the conclusions drawn from research with regard to innate predispositions?

Can the nature–nurture debate ever be settled with regard to development in the early years?

What evidence can you find in support of the view that young infants develop a relatively early understanding of language?

What methods are used to study cognitive skills in young infants?

To what extent do day care settings encourage the development of attachment in young infants?

How important is attachment in the understanding of infants' early emotional development?

 # SUGGESTIONS FOR FURTHER READING

Bremner, G., & Fogel, A. (2004). *The Blackwell handbook of infant development*. Oxford: Wiley Blackwell. This book provides answers to the key questions that are pertinent to infants' development. The book brings together theory and research across a range of key areas.

Oates, J., & Grayson, A. (2004). *Cognitive and language development in children.* Oxford: Blackwell. This book provides an overview of how children's language and thinking skills develop and also outlines the links between these two topics. Chapters 2 and 4 provide a particularly helpful overview of children's first words and how children develop an understanding of grammar.

Smith, P.K., & Hart, C.H. (2010). *Wiley-Blackwell handbook of childhood social development* (2nd edn). Oxford: Blackwell. This book provides an overview of children's social development from preschool to adolescence. The text also includes details of a range of theories and research pertinent to the area as well as providing details of the historical background to the area.

14

DEVELOPMENT DURING THE SCHOOL YEARS

Lead authors **Lee Farrington-Flint, Lucy Betts, Rebecca Larkin, James Stiller, Mark Torrance** and **Gareth Williams**

CHAPTER OUTLINE

INTRODUCTION

14.1

How do children develop their abilities and become adults? This chapter will consider the role of child development during the school years. We will focus on the development of cognitive, language and social skills. We begin by discussing factors that influence children's development within the school environment and how the environment plays a fundamental role in refining our understanding of how children continue to develop throughout their school years. Following on from Chapter 13, we will discuss theories of cognitive development, including the work of Piaget and Vygotsky, and the implications of these theoretical approaches for children's learning and their schooling. The chapter will then consider children's language development and changes that occur in children's theory of mind and social reasoning, all of which are important for the development of social skills in later years. We will also discuss the skills that children learn whilst they are at school and the processes that underlie the development of language and reading ability. Finally, in this chapter we will consider how the social world of children changes as they enter school and how this is reflected in the importance of peer relationships, friendships and experiences of bullying.

? FRAMING QUESTIONS

How can the theories of (1) Piaget and (2) Vygotsky be applied to education and schooling?

How important are cultural tools in children's development?

What is theory of mind and how does it help us understand the world?

What are the important skills in learning to read?

How important is social adjustment to children's schooling?

What are the functions of peers and friends during the school years?

COGNITIVE DEVELOPMENT

14.2

As outlined in Chapter 13, it is clear that we are born with a range of cognitive abilities. In this chapter, we begin by discussing how children's cognitive abilities develop during the school years. We look at some of the implications for children's development within school context and classroom instruction, with a particular emphasis on the relative importance of **cultural tools** and teaching. It is argued that a child's interaction with their immediate environment is important to enable them to develop and learn new skills. However, to understand children's development in the later years it is important to appreciate the role of social context and to recognise how children develop skills with the assistance of others through scaffolding and peer collaboration.

14.2.1 PIAGET'S STAGE ACCOUNT OF LEARNING AND DEVELOPMENT

Jean Piaget (1896–1980) challenged the way in which psychologists understood how a child's mind develops, and he is arguably the most influential theorist of cognitive development. Piaget considered a child to be like a small scientist, actively discovering the world around them, rather than a passive sponge that absorbs knowledge passed down by adults. Many of Piaget's findings have been challenged by more recent research. However, Piaget's work has been hugely influential in terms of developing our understanding of how children think and, importantly, how children's thought processes differ from those of adults.

> **Cultural tools**   Tools that help us to understand the world more fully by solving problems, measuring the environment, making calculations and storing information (e.g. computers and calculators).

Piaget (1952) proposed a theory of cognitive development that he considered to be universal, regardless of a child's background or culture. This theory is a 'stage theory', because it consists of a set of qualitatively distinct stages through which each child progresses during childhood and adolescence. Piaget also argued that all children must complete the stages in the same order, although some children will progress through them at a faster rate than others.

Piaget's theory centres on children developing **cognitive schemas**. Simply put, these schemas are cognitive structures that represent the world around the child. As children encounter new experiences in the world, their schemas need to be adjusted to take into account this new and revised understanding. Piaget used the term **assimilation** to refer to how children try to fit new information from the world into an existing schema. For example, a child who has never seen a cat before but has plenty of experience of dogs might see a cat for the first time and fit it under the schema of 'dog'. After all, it has four legs, a tail and is furry. However, the child might then notice that this new 'dog' has very pointy ears and whiskers and makes a strange 'miaow' sound. This information no longer fits in with the existing schema for 'dog', so the child is forced to adjust their view of the world and make a new place within this schema for the cat. This process, by which children adjust existing schema to take account of new information, is **accommodation**. In order for a child to be comfortable with and understand the world around them, a balance between the processes of assimilation and accommodation is needed. Piaget used the term **equilibration** to refer to this balance between these two processes.

> **Assimilation**   The incorporation of new experiences into pre-existing cognitive schemas.
>
> **Accommodation**   The modification and expansion of pre-existing cognitive schemas in order to adapt to new experiences.
>
> **Cognitive schemas**   Mental representations and plans used to enact behaviours.
>
> **Equilibration**   This is when a child's set of schemas are balanced and not disturbed by conflict.

TABLE 14.1 An illustration of the four stages of development in Piaget's theory (adapted from Smith et al., 2003)

Stage	Approximate ages	Key characteristics
Sensorimotor	0–2 years	Symbolic thought develops, object permanency (egocentrism)
Preoperational	2–7 years	Egocentrism, animism, centration
Concrete operational	7–12 years	Able to conserve, able to think logically
Formal operational	12 + years	Able to carry out abstract and hypothetical reasoning

Table 14.1 outlines the four main stages highlighted in Piaget's theory. The ages given alongside each stage are only approximations; this is because Piaget was aware that children develop at slightly different rates. Some of the key characteristics of each stage are also included in Table 14.1 and these will be discussed in more detail below.

Piaget's first stage occurs before school age. Between birth and two years, infants gradually develop an awareness of the world around them, accumulating the ability to develop more sophisticated coordinated reflex actions, and this interaction with the environment allows them to develop a better understanding and greater use of language (**symbolic thought**). One of the hallmarks of this stage is the infant's ability to understand that just because they cannot see something it does not necessarily mean that the object no longer exists (**object permanency**). Piaget argued that towards the end of the sensorimotor stage infants are able to understand that out of sight does not have to mean out of mind. For example, an infant who has acquired object permanency will actively search for a toy that has suddenly been removed from view (and probably be very surprised that the object was moved in the first place!).

Object permanency This is the ability to understand that an object still exists even if it is no longer visible.

Symbolic thought The representation of reality through the use of abstract concepts such as words, gestures and numbers.

Animism The attribution of life-like qualities to inanimate objects (for example toys).

By the time the child enters the preoperational stage, they have acquired an awareness of the world around them, and are rapidly developing their language skills. As part of this process, children tend to engage in pretend play, often attributing human characteristics to inanimate objects (**animism**). Children in this stage will also tend to be rather egocentric, which means that they seem preoccupied with their own thoughts and ideas rather than paying attention to other people's. You may have noticed that when young children play together they often seem to be involved in quite different aspects of the game, and pay little attention to what another child says or does.

Centration is also an important characteristic of the preoperational stage, whereby children tend to be able to concentrate on only one aspect of a problem at any one time. The classic tasks Piaget used to assess this were based around the idea of **conservation**. This refers to the understanding that something remains the same even if superficial characteristics are changed (Figure 14.1).

In one famous conservation task, children were presented with two rows of counters. There were equal numbers of counters in each row, and the tester would initially arrange them so the two rows were identically spaced out. The child would be asked whether the number of counters was the same in each row, to which most children would reply 'yes'. The tester would then increase the spaces between the counters in one of the rows so that it looked longer. Again, the child would be asked whether the number of counters was the same in the two rows, to which children in the preoperational stage tend to reply 'no'. Piaget argued this error occurs because the children are only able to focus on one aspect of the problem, in this case the difference in length between the two rows.

In the concrete operational stage, children are able to carry out conservation tasks successfully. Children are also able to carry out problem solving tasks in a logical manner. There are limits to this logic, however, and they struggle with abstract ideas such as algebra. Finally, in the formal operational stage, children are able to carry out hypothetical and abstract reasoning, and this continues to develop later into adulthood (in line with the transition into secondary school and beyond). With this type of thinking they approach a problem in a methodical way, exploring all the possibilities in the way that we like to think that science is done.

> **Centration**   The focusing of attention on one aspect of a situation while excluding the rest of the scenario.
>
> **Conservation**   The understanding that certain properties of objects remain the same under transformation. These properties include quantity, weight and volume.

14.2.2 CHALLENGES TO PIAGET'S WORK

Piaget's theory has been challenged on several points. Perhaps the most general criticism is that he overlooked the importance of social influences on children's development. He concentrated on the ways that individual children solve problems and make sense of the world by themselves. However, it should be noted that while Piaget emphasised that children learn by discovery, he did not argue that this should occur in isolation.

Researchers such as Margaret Donaldson have also argued that Piaget's tasks were often too difficult for children to understand, leading to an underestimation of young children's cognitive abilities. For example, think back to Piaget's conservation task with the rows of counters. Children were asked the same question twice (i.e. 'Are the number of counters the same in the two rows?'). In a classroom situation, teachers only tend to ask the same question twice if the first answer was wrong. Therefore, many children may change their initial answer for this reason, and not because they do not understand how to conserve number. Accepting Piaget's theory also relies on us being happy to think of development occurring in discrete, qualitatively distinct stages. Is this what really happens in the context of everyday learning?

Despite the many criticisms of Piaget's work, researchers (referred to as neo-Piagetians) have continued to develop his ideas over the past 40 years. Like Piaget, these researchers argue that children develop their own knowledge through exploration and discovery.

FIGURE 14.1   Six year old Sonia studies her choices carefully, while taking her simulated Piaget Conservation Tests. The psychology exercise will check her development of conservation skills using equal amounts of liquids in different glasses
© Laura Dwight/Corbis

Neo-Piagetians also agree that children progress through a series of discrete stages. Their work has shown us more about the ways that children process information and make decisions (see Morra et al., 2007).

REASONS TO BE SCEPTICAL   Piaget's stages of development

Piaget suggested that his four stages of development were universal and characterise key changes in children's thinking and reasoning throughout development. However, how reliable are these four distinct stages? Consider how valid these stages are in the light of the following:

- changes in cultural norms and values
- children with distinct learning difficulties
- children without access to formal schooling
- delay in language development.

Clearly, there are environmental factors that may not allow children to meet these distinct stages in line with other children, which would lead us to question the validity of using these developmental milestones as fixed.

14.2.3 VYGOTSKY: LINKING SOCIAL AND COGNITIVE DEVELOPMENT

Unlike Piaget, Lev Vygotsky (1896–1934) did not produce a detailed model of how children's internal mental representations or cognitive skills develop. Instead, Vygotsky emphasised the broad link between cognitive and social development. Whilst Paiget considered the child to be a discoverer of the world around them, Vygotsky argued that children learn most from interaction with other children and adults.

Vygotsky used the term *cultural tools* to refer to the tools with which children can develop the appropriate psychological skills, and the values passed on to children by older generations. These tools may provide one path for children's intellectual adaptation through computers or teaching methods. Language can be considered the most important cultural tool, and Vygotsky believed that use of language underpinned the development of reflective thought. Children's development of language begins with the social environment (social speech – talking to others) and then over time this becomes internalised (private speech – talking to yourself) to guide and develop thought.

Vygotsky's (1978) emphasis on social interactions to guide children's learning and cognitive development is clearly demonstrated in the following quotation:

> Every function in the child's cultural development appears twice: first, on the social level, and later, on the individual level; first, between people (interpsychological) and then inside the child (intrapsychological). This applies equally to voluntary attention, to logical memory, and to the formation of concepts. All the higher functions originate as actual relationships between individuals. (1978: 57)

However, we can still ask how the environment provides children with appropriate skills for development. Vygotsky and his **social constructivist** account do not deal with fixed stages of development but describe 'leading activities' typical of certain age periods around which intellectual development is organised. It is through such leading activities that children interact with their environment and develop appropriate skills in learning and thinking. The emphasis is clearly on guiding children's development across a range of different activities and this, according to Vygotsky, governs children's intellectual development and rate of learning.

As a way of explaining the importance of guiding children's learning, Vygotsky developed the idea of the **zone of proximal development,** based on his argument that children can only achieve a limited amount on their own. With assistance from adults or more developed peers, children can achieve considerably more. **Scaffolding** refers to how a child can be helped to achieve their goal with structured support from an adult or an older child. As the child becomes more competent at the task, the support (or scaffold) is gradually removed. Having a dynamic, flexible scaffold – or framework – therefore assists the child in mastering new skills or

Scaffolding   This occurs when adults guide the learning of a child by simplifying the structure of the child's learning environment.

Social constructivism   A theoretical approach that emphasises the role of culture and context in children's understanding and development.

Zone of proximal development (ZPD)   This is the gap between what a child can do by themselves and what they can achieve under adult guidance or collaboration.

obtaining new information. Ultimately this can be seen as a tool to aid development. The idea of scaffolding was later developed to refer to other leading activities such as guided participation, which involves the use of adult or peer collaboration to guide children to the next level of understanding through leading activities (Rogoff, 1990).

LATER LANGUAGE DEVELOPMENT

14.3

As suggested in Chapter 13, the process of language development is rather complex. Although infants are born with some ability to recognise familiar sounds or their mother's voice from an early age, this process does not end in infancy. In fact, language skills are still developing when children enter the later years, especially during school. The development of later language skills will be examined in this section, with a particular focus on syntactic development and understanding of grammar.

Many early theories of language development emphasise imitation or learning with reinforcement as processes that drive language learning in early years. Yet there are a number of problems with this as an explanation. The main one is that languages are complex and dynamic, and users of languages tend to be very creative in how they communicate. Few utterances are ever the same, and so it is unlikely that someone could learn a language only from imitating others. We are predisposed to explore and use language from an early age and this goes beyond what would be expected from simple learning and reinforcement from others.

14.3.1 LANGUAGE ACQUISITION DEVICE (LAD)

In the 1960s Noam Chomsky developed an influential theory to explain how children are able to develop language skills so quickly and to such a high degree of complexity. They argued that all children are born with an innate **language acquisition device (LAD)**, and that there is an area (or a module) in the brain that is preprogrammed to learn language. When a child is exposed to language in their environment, their LAD will gradually be switched to the relevant settings for their native tongue. Chomsky referred to this as setting the parameters of the LAD. Therefore, whilst all children are born with the capacity to adapt to any language, their environment will quickly determine which language(s) they actually develop. Lenneberg (1967) added to this theory by suggesting that there is a critical period for language learning which occurs before children reach puberty. Learning language outside this critical period is thought to be very

Language acquisition device (LAD) A system proposed by Chomsky that young infants have. It helps them navigate the grammar of language, which in turn helps language development.

difficult and may explain why older children and adults have difficulties in learning other languages.

14.3.2 GRAMMATICAL AWARENESS

How do children develop their awareness of grammar? Some ideas have come from the mistakes that young children make while learning to apply grammatical rules. This applies especially to the overgeneralising of rules which have regular grammatical forms to those which are less regular. Evidence for the LAD was largely based on the finding that children produce over-regularisation errors that they could not have learned from imitation. Therefore, this aspect of spoken language would seem to have come from inside the child, rather than from the external environment. However, these types of errors are actually very rarely produced by children (Thornton, 2008). Therefore, they provide limited support for Chomsky's universal theory that children's grammar is being driven by an innate language module.

Let's consider some examples. When you talk about things that happened in the past, you might say that you have *closed* doors or *cleaned* cars but you won't have *teached* history or *eated* an apple. For word plurals, you can have *cats*, *dogs* and *lions* but only *sheep*. To take the example of past tense, there are two routes to apply past tenses in grammar (Pinker & Prince, 1988). One route is for common grammar forms, and in the case of past tense we follow the rule: apply 'ed' *to the end of the word*. A second route stores information about irregular past tenses: that is, when the word needs to be modified in other ways (for example, *eat* becomes *eaten* and *teach* becomes *taught*). When the tense of a word needs to be applied, the route with the irregular forms is looked up; if there is no irregular form for the word, then 'ed' is added to the end of the word. Over time more irregular past tenses are stored, and so these will be applied in place of simply adding 'ed' to the end of the word. A similar process would take place for applying plurals to words.

In summary, we may have a general preset guide that is sensitive to the idea that rules are needed to take individual words and use them for communication. Then a child's interaction with the world around them and the feedback that they get help them to navigate the subtleties of the language in their environment.

THEORY OF MIND (TOM) AND SOCIAL REASONING

14.4

If you are going to interact with other people effectively, you need to understand that they are likely to have different thoughts, beliefs and views of the world to yourself. This understanding will be based on the possession on your part of what is known as a **theory of mind** (or ToM) (Premack & Woodruff, 1978). The ability to attribute a theory of mind to another person seems to be a very easy thing to do for most adults, but just a brief thought about what we are doing to achieve this shows that it is a task that requires a lot of skill.

Consider here an important paper by Heider and Simmel (1944) on attributing beliefs and emotional states to abstract moving objects. In one study from Heider and Simmel's paper, participants viewed a series of triangles and circles moving around a screen; on occasion the shapes moved in and out of a non-moving square, bumping into each other along the way. The participants were then required to describe what they observed. A large proportion of the participants used anthropomorphic terms describing the shapes as animate beings with individual beliefs, desires and personalities moving in and out of a stationary house (the square). However, studies of child development suggest that the ability to take the viewpoint of others is not so straightforward, and studies have shown that young children below the age of four often have problems taking the viewpoint of other individuals (for example Piaget's three-mountain task) and often fail at solving simple false belief tasks.

14.4.1 STUDYING FALSE BELIEF IN CHILDREN'S REASONING

The false belief task described below is based upon the assumption that in order to understand if someone has been deceived (or possesses a **false belief** about a situation) an individual needs to understand that others have their own individual viewpoint.

One widely recognised test of theory of mind is the Sally–Anne task (Baron-Cohen et al., 1985). This examines false beliefs by using two dolls, Sally and Anne. Sally has a basket and Anne has a box. Sally also has a marble, and places this in her basket before disappearing out of sight. Anne quickly moves the marble from the basket into her box.

The child is then asked, 'When Sally returns, where will she look for her marble?' Baron-Cohen et al. found that three-year-old children tend to say with confidence that Sally will look in the box. This is because the child knows the marble is in the box, and is unable to appreciate that Sally has a different view of the world (a false belief). In contrast, four-year-old children are usually able to understand that Sally thinks the marble is still in her basket, thus demonstrating a theory of mind.

False belief   This is when an individual incorrectly believes a statement or scenario to be true when it is not. This is the basis of the false belief tasks used in the theory of mind experiments.

Theory of mind   The ability to attribute mental states such as beliefs, intentions and desires to yourself and others, and to understand that other people have beliefs, desires and intentions that are different from your own.

However, these techniques of assessing theory of mind have recently come under some criticism, as they are subject to the 'curse of knowledge'. This refers to having too much information and then focusing on the wrong bit. The curse of knowledge suggests that a child (or even an adult) can fail a false belief task as the additional information they are provided with in the scene they observe and personal experience can influence their decision, resulting in a wrong conclusion (Birch and Bloom, 2007).

Even when these false belief tasks are more realistic and relevant to the participant, the child may still fail. For example, Perner et al. (1987) developed the Smarties task, where a child is shown a Smarties tube and asked what is inside. The child (normally) responds with 'Smarties' or 'sweets'. The experimenter then shows the child, to their surprise, that the tube is actually full of not very tasty pencils. The child is then asked what their friend, not present during the experiment, will think is in the tube. Again children below the age of four tend to falsely rely on their current world-state knowledge and suggest that their classmate will think there are pencils in the Smarties tube, rather than the correct belief-state assumption that their friend will make the same conclusions that they originally made, i.e. there are sweets in the tube.

There is evidence that children may fail these theory of mind tasks before the age of four years. False belief tasks require considerable mentalising on the part of the child. It has been suggested that the ability to perform tasks that require the mental rotation of different people's viewpoints are strongly associated with a child's verbal ability (Hughes et al., 2005) and the child's general language ability (Ruffman et al., 2003). This strong association with language could suggest that by improving the quality of social interaction and communication a child can better develop their understanding of others' belief states (see the key study).

14.4.2 RELEVANCE OF THEORY OF MIND TO SCHOOLING AND EDUCATION

A well-developed theory of mind is essential for children to survive the daily politics of school life, and to engage emotionally with fiction and drama, as well as to comprehend the complex distinctions between fiction and reality. Some researchers have suggested that theory of mind is in fact a domain-specific function with a specific neural architecture that is used for solving social problems and examining the beliefs and desires of others. Deficits in this theory of mind module (TOMM) have been suggested as being one of the key symptoms of autism (Baron-Cohen, 1995). It is considered that theory of mind development is crucial in being able to work with others and to engage in peer relationships within and around the educational setting.

KEY STUDY Lohmann, H., Carpenter, M. & Call, J. (2005). Guessing versus choosing – and seeing versus believing – in false belief tasks. *British Journal of Developmental Psychology, 23*: 451–469.

Between three and a half and four years old, children's performance on the traditional false belief task (Baron Cohen et al., 1985; Wimmer & Perner, 1983) has been shown to result in a 50:50 chance of getting the correct answer.

In the traditional false belief task, a main protagonist places an object in a box and then leaves the room; a second protagonist enters and, unseen by the main protagonist, moves the item to a new location. When the main protagonist returns they are unaware a switch has occurred. Lohmann et al. (2005) decided to investigate whether or not children were just guessing or whether they were certain in their

(Cont'd)

beliefs, and whether the children were relying solely on the visual cues present in the traditional task. So, in addition to this false belief scenario, Lohmann et al. introduced three other conditions; a first condition where the main protagonist knew the location of the item; a second condition where the main protagonist is lied to about the position of the item (a verbal version of the false belief task); and a third scenario where the main protagonist would have to guess the location of the object.

In the condition where the main protagonist knew the item's location – by witnessing the switch, by being told about the switch, or by knowing that the object was not moved – the children consistently performed better in the 'no switch' scenario, which entails low processing demands compared with the verbal and visual equivalents. In the guess condition, the main protagonist is not present when the second protagonist hides the object in a box. The scenario is then obscured, providing no indication to the child or main protagonist as to the object's location. The children performed at chance on this condition.

Over half the children in the sample failed the false belief task, replicating the findings of Wellman et al. (2001). However, in terms of uncertainty, the children showed less uncertainty in the false belief task (regardless of whether it was the verbal lie condition or the traditional visual scenario) than in the guessing task, and these levels of certainty did not significantly vary between the children that passed and failed the tasks. This suggests that the children in this age range are not simply guessing answers to the false belief task but do have a certain belief about the outcome of the task.

Lohmann et al. (2005) next examined the individual differences in children's performance and showed that children that had higher vocabulary and grammar scores were more likely to pass the traditional false belief task and the lie condition. In conclusion, the children are not guessing but relying on their own knowledge and performance, and this is largely governed by the child's linguistic abilities.

SCHOOL-LED DEVELOPMENT AND INSTRUCTION

14.5

As we have already seen, the social environment plays a key role in the context of children's learning – especially in the provision of appropriate opportunities for children to learn. Vygotsky emphasised the role of scaffolding and collaborative learning and how these processes are guided by a more skilled individual who scaffolds the child's progress (Wood et al., 1976). As the child develops on certain tasks, the level of scaffolding or support should change to allow autonomy over their own learning. As a result there is a strong emphasis on the use of cultural tools and receiving tuition to help develop skills across schooling, especially with regard to children's language and literacy development. This section considers children's reading development and how instruction plays a fundamental role in developing literacy skills.

14.5.1 DEVELOPMENT OF READING SKILLS

Learning to read is a fairly complex task which involves the combination of a variety of cognitive skills including the development of spoken language. Although the link between early language skills and reading seems fairly obvious, in some ways children do need to show some competency in their own native language before acquiring skills in reading; however, reading itself is not an automatic process but instead requires formal instruction. In fact reading is a linguistic skill that is learned only after children have acquired considerable proficiency in using oral language.

It is clear that many children develop linguistic awareness through everyday communicative activities, but learning to read is not solely determined through the development of such language skills. In fact, reading is an artificial activity that requires explicit teaching.

14.5.2 IMPORTANCE OF PHONOLOGICAL AWARENESS

The most important set of linguistic abilities that a child requires in order to read is knowledge of sounds – often referred to as 'phonological awareness'. Phonological awareness is defined as the ability to perceive and manipulate the sounds of spoken words. Three important levels of phonological awareness have been distinguished within the reading literature: syllables, **rimes** and **phonemes** (Goswami & Bryant, 1990). Phonological awareness is unique for learning to read an alphabetic language. The importance of different levels of phonological awareness through syllables, rimes and phonemes, and the link between these levels of phonological awareness and reading development, are now fairly well established (Goswami & Bryant, 1990).

> **Phonemes** The smallest unit of sound that is able to carry some meaning in language.
>
> **Rime** The vowel sound of a word followed by the subsequent consonants: for example, the rime of 'ham' is 'am'. When two words share the same rime unit, they can be said to rhyme.

The awareness of syllables, onsets and rimes appears to emerge around three to four years of age, before the child enters formal schooling. The awareness of phonemes, by contrast, appears to emerge around the age of five to six years when children in the UK are taught to read formally (see Carroll et al., 2003). Primarily the reason for phoneme awareness developing at a later age is that phonemic judgements are often difficult for young children to grasp without any prior reading experience. This often occurs as they begin to learn about alphabet, combining written letters with spoken sounds. The question therefore remains as to which aspect of phonological awareness contributes the greatest to developing proficiency in learning to read.

There is evidence for rhyme awareness and links to later reading development. It has been shown that children as young as three years can solve rhyme oddity tasks, that is, identifying the odd word out from a selection (e.g. *cat*, *hat* and *pin*: Bradley & Bryant, 1983), and this ability is linked to the progress they make in learning to read. There is also strong support for the relationship between an early sensitivity to rhyme (nursery rhymes) and later reading development (see Bradley & Bryant, 1983). The question we need to ask is how this early awareness of rhyme contributes to the development of early word reading. Goswami's (1986; 1988) early work explicitly tested the relationship between early rhyme awareness and children's alphabetic literacy through the use of orthographic analogies. Her work has shown that many young children (even before learning to read) can use existing knowledge of words from memory (e.g. *look*) to aid their attempt at identifying other unknown printed words that share similar rime units (e.g. *took*, *cook*). This use of analogies has since been shown to be extremely useful in teaching words, even to prereaders and those in the first year of receiving formal instruction.

Although rhyme is important, there is strong evidence to show that a child's understanding of phonemes (the smallest phonological unit) is also an important aspect of early reading development (Hulme et al., 2002). Studies have found that phoneme skills are strong predictors of children's reading success even two to three years later (Duncan et al., 1997). In fact, several of these studies directly compared the contribution of rhyme and phoneme skills to children's later reading within the same study and found that phoneme skills were the best predictor after the contribution of rhyme skills was controlled (Hulme et al., 2002). Therefore, despite some studies finding that when rhyme and phoneme skills are measured in the same way, such as using similar tasks, both contribute well to reading. However, there does seem to be a greater emphasis on phoneme awareness as a predictor of early word reading in children.

14.5.3 READING INSTRUCTION

Given the importance of these phonological skills, how should they be taught in schools? One answer that is fashionable at the moment is to promote reading skills in young children through phonics teaching. There is a distinction to be made here between two approaches, namely (1) synthetic phonics and (2) analytic phonics. They emphasise different phonological units as a way of promoting reading discovery. However, in analytic phonics, the predominant method in the UK, letter sounds are taught after reading has already begun; children begin using a whole word approach to identify text, usually initially learning to read words by sight, often in the context of meaningful text. There is a strong focus on the recognition and identification of spelling patterns. For instance, analytic phonics emphasises the importance of onset-rime units, especially how the rimes of words can be used to help children read and spell by analogy.

Synthetic phonics, by comparison, is a much more accelerated form of phonics that focuses primarily on phoneme skills and letter-sound knowledge. After the first few of these have been taught, children are then taught series of different phonemes (the smallest units of sound) and their related **graphemes** (the written symbols for the phoneme) and they are shown how these sounds can be blended together to build up words. But which approach is more efficient in accelerating children's early reading skills? There is evidence that receiving synthetic phonics training leads to better reading, spelling and phonemic awareness than an analytic phonics approach (Johnston & Watson, 2004)

Researchers have argued that synthetic phonics has a major and long-lasting effect on children's reading and spelling attainment and even accelerates the reading and spelling skills in children who have English as a second language (Stuart, 1999). Indeed, explicit phoneme-based training seems to be a good intervention for young children at potential risk of developing reading difficulties, such as dyslexia (Hatcher et al., 2004). Nonetheless, irrespective of our approach to reading instruction, the conclusion is that a focus on teaching children phonological skills generally is crucial to supporting their later reading development. However, when evaluating different methods for teaching reading skills, it is important to be aware of how reading skills may develop in different ways across different languages (see Goswami et al., 2003).

KEY RESEARCHER   Usha Goswami

FIGURE 14.2   Usha Goswami

Usha Goswami is Professor of Education at the University of Cambridge and a Fellow of St John's College, Cambridge. In 2005 she became Director of the new Centre for Neuroscience in Education at the faculty. She received her DPhil from Oxford University in 1987. Her research topic was reading and spelling by analogy. Her current research examines relations between phonology and reading, with special reference to rhyme and analogy in reading acquisition, and rhyme processing in dyslexic and deaf children's reading.

A major focus of the research is cross-linguistic and current projects include: cross-language studies of the impact of deficits in auditory temporal processing on reading development and developmental dyslexia; neuro-imaging studies of the neural networks underpinning reading in good and poor deaf adult readers; and precursors of reading development in deaf children with cochlear implants.

Usha Goswami has made a significant contribution to our knowledge regarding the role of phonological representations and auditory processing in children with dyslexia. She remains one of the most prominent UK figures in developmental psychology with regard to her work in children's reading development.

We have examined how children learn to use language and to read. There are a number of other skills that children develop at the same time, such as writing and understanding mathematics. Psychologists give as much importance to these skills as they do to language, but we decided in this text to concentrate on language.

CHANGING DYNAMICS IN A SOCIAL WORLD

14.6

Having considered the development of cognitive skills in the school years, the next stage is to consider some of the social issues that many children face as they progress through the school years. In this section we will consider the impact that different social situations may have on a child's later development, with specific emphasis on their school adjustment, the importance of peers and friends and the role of bullying within the school context.

14.6.1 SCHOOL ADJUSTMENT AND SOCIAL DEVELOPMENT

As children enter school they are exposed to both changes in the physical and social environment and changes in the demands placed upon them. During this time, children must negotiate the complexity of new interpersonal relationships and learn how to behave in an appropriate and conventionally accepted manner (Wentzel, 1999). Therefore, the relationships that children develop with their peers and teachers are particularly important. Also, by developing positive relationships with teachers and peers, children are likely to benefit from the facilitative nature of these relationships during the transition to school (Johnson et al., 2000).

The early years of school are particularly important for fostering a sense of school adjustment, but 13–35 per cent of children experience problems adjusting to school (Hughes et al., 1979). The reason why children's initial school adjustment is so important is that the early years of school shape children's trajectories throughout their school career. Further, it is thought that early adjustment problems can lead to continued poor adjustment throughout children's school careers and also poorer academic performance. The reason for this, according to the cumulative deficit hypothesis, is that adjustment problems are perpetuated from one year to the next and cause the children to become more disadvantaged (Ackerman et al., 2003). Alternative accounts, such as the developmental transaction systems perspective, suggest that children's school adjustment is influenced by the interaction between themselves and the hassles and uplifts in the environment (Santa Lucia et al., 2000). Finally, children's attributions towards their scholastic abilities may also influence their feelings towards, and behaviour in, school and ultimately bear on their adjustment. Therefore, adjustment problems are not transient or trivial but are influential for later performance and adjustment (Dunn, 1988).

14.6.2 IMPORTANCE OF PEERS AND FRIENDS

One of the important aspects in children's social development concerns their relationship to peers and friends in the school environment. Children form two distinct types of relationships with their peers during the school years: companionship and intimate relationships (Buhrmester & Furman, 1987). Companionship represents the extent to which children are sociable with their peers and the extent to which they spend time sharing in common activities with others. Recently, companionship has been regarded as the extent to which children are accepted by their peers. Peer acceptance is an indicator of how an individual child is regarded in terms of whether they are liked or disliked by a group of other children (Ladd et al., 1999). Intimate relationships, on the other hand, are regarded as much more exclusive and specific. Friendships are an example of an intimate relationship because they constitute a positive dyadic relationship which is characterised by an emotional connection between individuals (Ladd et al., 1999). Although both boys and girls develop relationships characterised by intimacy and companionship, there are some differences. Girls tend to have a smaller group of close peers compared to boys, as well as having greater intimacy, companionship and prosocial support with their same-gender peers than boys (Hussong, 2000).

Research suggests that it is important for children to have friends whilst they are at school. Friendships facilitate children's adjustment to school because they provide academic and scholastic support. Also, children with a higher number of friends perform better academically than children with a lower number of friends. The reason why children's peers are so important for their performance at school is that peers can provide support networks and foster emotional and cognitive development (Hay et al., 2004). Further, the importance of these support networks does not stop when children leave school because children who experience difficulties in establishing and maintaining peer relationships are more likely to experience maladjustment in later life. Also, having friends during adolescence has been linked to higher levels of self-esteem and fewer mental problems during adulthood (Bagwell et al., 1998).

14.6.3 BULLYING AND SOCIALISATION

Recent figures suggest that almost half of all children report that they have experienced bullying at school, whilst teachers report that between 40 and 70 per cent of pupils experience bullying (Bradshaw et al., 2007). 'Bullying' may cover a range of behaviour. Typically it involves physical, verbal or relational aggression that is repeated and that involves a power difference between individuals. Children report that bullying occurs within the classroom, cafeteria, hallway and playground, with 70 per cent of children asked by Bradshaw and colleagues (2007) reporting that they had witnessed an instance of bullying within the last month whilst at school. Bullying is widespread and may adversely affect children's performance at school. Typically, those children who experience bullying tend to have lower academic performance and decreased self-efficacy, which can ultimately influence an individual's later socioeconomic status (Schwartz et al., 2005).

14.6.4 MORAL DEVELOPMENT

Although developing a sense of morals is a complex process, children appear to be able to have an understanding of morality by the age of five (Helwig & Turiel, 2002). Similar to Piaget's stage theory, Kohlberg (1976) proposed a six-stage theory of moral development. Moral development was assessed through responses to a series of short stories. One of these was about Heinz, whose wife was near to death. A life-saving drug was available; however, the drug was very expensive and Heinz could not afford it. Children were asked whether or not Heinz should steal the drug to save his wife.

Based on a series of studies, Kohlberg concluded that we progress through three levels of moral development, each of which has two stages. Stages 1 and 2 represent the pre-conventional level of moral reasoning. In the first stage, obedience to authority represents the right thing to do in a given situation whereas disobedience is the wrong thing. In the second stage, right is regarded as doing what is in the individual's own interest and, as such, has been termed naive hedonism (Bee & Boyd, 2005). The conventional level (based on agreed rules) contains the third stage of right, in which people judge behaviour by what an individual is expected to do based on their current social role ('I was following orders'). Conversely, in the fourth stage, right is regarded as an action that supports the community and prevents the breakdown of society, so the societal norms are becoming more important in moral reasoning.

The fifth and sixth stages represent post-conventional reasoning (beyond socially agreed rules) where right is considered with regard to universal ethical principles and human rights. People using this level to make judgements will be looking beyond their own advantage, the advantage of their family and even their community when they make their judgements. If you think about the use by the USA of torture to obtain information from prisoners, then at a conventional level you might judge it to be acceptable because it might benefit the USA in their military campaigns; but at the post-conventional level you may judge it to be wrong because it infringes the human rights of the people being interrogated, regardless of who they are and what they have done. Later Kohlberg and Power (1981) argued that there was a seventh, more advanced stage of moral development. Kohlberg's approach remains very controversial, not least because it seems to be culturally biased and to present people in the USA as more moral than people in most other countries. However, recent research does suggest that the stage descriptions are a useful way of looking at moral development (Boom et al., 2007).

EXERCISE   Moral development: how moral are we as adults?

Read the passage below, an adaptation of Kohlberg's passage, and then consider the five questions that follow. There are no right or wrong answers, but your attempt at answering the questions should provide a nice illustration with regard to some of the difficulties that many children face in developing moral understanding.

A woman is very ill, and the only drug that the doctors thought might save her costs around £2000. The drug was expensive to make, but the chemist was charging ten times what the drug cost him to make – he paid £200 for the drug and charged £2000 for a small dose to each customer. The sick womans husband Heinz went to everyone he knew to borrow the money, but he could only get together £1000. There was no way he could raise the money to save his wife. So Heinz became desperate and considered breaking into the chemists store to steal the drug for his wife.

1 Should Heinz steal the drug? Why or why not?

2 It is against the law for Heinz to steal. Does that make it morally wrong? Why or why not?

3 Should people do everything they can to avoid breaking the law?

4 How does this relate to Heinz's case?

5 Is there anything else that Heinz can do that is morally right?

Children typically give moral reasons for actions that suggest that they have an understanding of moral behaviour equivalent to stage 1 in Kohlberg's model, with later stages becoming evident as children develop (Helwig & Turiel, 2002). However, there is debate over this notion of development, since some evidence suggests that individuals may on occasion regress to earlier stages (Gibbs et al., 2007). An adult example would be the expenses crisis in the UK Parliament in 2009. The Members of Parliament are used to making decisions based on the highest moral values, and some of them chose to go against their colleagues and the government to vote against the war on Iraq (stage 6). However, some of these same people used the much lower-level defence of 'it was in the rules' (stage 3) when they came to filling out their expenses and claiming for their moats to be cleaned or houses for their parents to live in.

In addition, some researchers argue that the methods used to assess children's morals are very different from children's day-to-day experiences. More recently, researchers have used prosocial reasoning tasks (Eisenberg, 1986; 1992) and distributive justice tasks (Damon, 1977; 1980) to overcome the problems of asking the children to choose between two negative acts as in the case of the original Heinz story. The distributive justice task is an experimental task that allows researchers to examine children's understanding of social norms. It measures children's knowledge of a range of different social norms while at the same time maximising rewards for themselves. This task has more recently been used to capture children's moral understanding.

CHAPTER SUMMARY

14.7

In this chapter we have looked at the concept of children's development during the school years, with a particular focus on cognitive, language and social skills. Specifically, we have examined what factors influence children's development as they enter school. We have discussed cognitive development during the school years and considered the implications of Piaget's and Vygotsky's theories for understanding children's learning. Additionally, the chapter has focused on how children develop language, theory of mind and social reasoning during the school years, all of which are important skills for later development and social interactions. We have also discussed aspects of children's development within the context of school including the importance of cultural tools and classroom-led instruction, with a particular focus on early reading development and mathematical understanding. Finally, the chapter reviewed the changing dynamics of children's social world as they enter school by discussing school adjustment, socialisation and friendships and the development of moral understanding. All of these topics emphasise the relative importance of the social context in explaining and understanding children's development in the school years and reinforce the argument that development can only occur through a child's interaction with their social environment.

 ## DISCUSSION QUESTIONS

How can the theories of cognitive development be applied to children's learning in school?

What are the key similarities and differences between Piaget's and Vygotsky's theories of development?

Can children function in a social world without a well-developed theory of mind?

How important are cultural tools in children's educational development?

What are the best ways to teach a child to read?

How do children develop a sense of moral understanding during the school years?

How important are peer relationships to children's social development?

 ## SUGGESTIONS FOR FURTHER READING

Crain, W.C. (2000). *Theories of development: concepts and applications*. Engelwood Cliffs, NY: Prentice Hall. A good text that covers a range of different theories and perspectives predominant in developmental psychology and introduces students to varying perspectives in understanding child psychology.

Smith, P., Cowie, H., & Blades, M. (2003). *Understanding children's development* (4th edn). Oxford: Blackwell. An introductory text that covers a range of approaches, including different social, emotional and cognitive aspects of children's development, in an easily accessible format.

Pinker, S. (1995). *The language instinct: the new science of language and mind.* London: Penguin. This text is primarily aimed at addressing the development of language from an innate perspective, and allows students to understand the arguments in favour of nativist approaches to explaining early language development.

Goswami, U., & Bryant, P. (1990). *Phonological skills and learning to read.* Hove: Erlbaum. A good text that clearly outlines the way in which children learn to read, with supporting evidence and clear psychological models of reading acquisition.

Smith, P.K., & Hart, C.H. (2010). *Wiley-Blackwell handbook of childhood social development* (2nd edn). Oxford: Blackwell. A very detailed text that examines children's early social development across a range of different perspectives. This will provide a solid foundation for examining recent studies in social development.

15 ATYPICAL CHILD DEVELOPMENT

Lead authors Gayle Dillon, Susannah Lamb and Andrew Grayson

CHAPTER OUTLINE

INTRODUCTION

15.1 Every child is unique, possessing their own collection of abilities and talents which develop at their own pace. Nonetheless, many children follow more or less predictable patterns of growth, and common features may be observed in the ways that cognitions, feelings and behaviours develop. This means we can build up a pattern of how many children develop (typical development) while being aware that not everyone follows this pattern (atypical development). Psychologists need to understand how typical development comes about and also what the implications of this are when dealing with children who develop atypically. The study of atypical development is essential for aiding our understanding of the diversity of paths that children can develop along and also for understanding their individual needs.

FRAMING QUESTIONS

What is typical development?
What is atypical development?
How do factors (1) within the child and (2) external to the child contribute to atypical development?
Are explanations of 'within' and 'external' factors of atypical development mutually exclusive?

WHAT IS ATYPICAL DEVELOPMENT?

15.2 Previous chapters have mainly been concerned with typical patterns of child development. However, not all children follow a typical developmental trajectory. Understanding why some children develop problems or difficulties that require specialist support or intervention is a key concern of developmental psychologists. Before we can begin to explore what is meant by the term 'atypical development', it is important to be clear about what typical development entails. Children who are classed as typically developing are those who follow a predictable developmental trajectory of physical and psychological development, achieving various milestones along the way. Such milestones relate to cognition (such as thinking, reasoning, problem solving, understanding), language, motor coordination (crawling, walking, jumping, hopping, throwing, catching), social interaction (for example, initiating peer contact, group play) and adaptive development (dressing, eating, washing).

However, this developmental process may be disrupted by biological or environmental factors, or by an interaction between the two, which can result in a child developing in ways which do not follow an expected trajectory. The term 'atypical child development' is, therefore, used to describe children whose differences in development appear to be inconsistent with typical child development.

Many cultural, societal, ethnic and personal values affect our classifications of typical and atypical development. For example, typical sleep patterns of young infants can vary dramatically across cultures. In their discussion about this kind of cross-cultural variation in development, Super and Harkness (1977) make a comparison between mothers in the USA and mothers of infants in rural western Kenya. Because of the different family practices framed by these different cultures, babies in the USA demonstrate much longer periods of sustained sleep compared with rural Kenyan babies. As well as recognising the role of culture in our description of what is typical and not typical, we need to acknowledge variation in development which can be attributed to individual differences. Just because one seven-year-old child demonstrates a particular ability and their friend of the same age does not, this is not necessarily an indication that either child's development is atypical. In any analysis of child development there is an acknowledgement that there can be a great deal of variation in the rates at which children 'typically' acquire certain skills.

The aim of this chapter is to discuss atypical child development from two key perspectives: explanations of atypical development that occurs as a result of factors described as arising from *within* the child, and explanations of atypical development that occurs as a result of factors that are *external* to the child. Within these two perspectives, issues such as the impact of damage to the brain, genetics, and the impact of societal expectations and labelling will be covered.

INFLUENCES ON ATYPICAL DEVELOPMENT WITHIN THE CHILD

15.3

This section aims to highlight the role of several factors which psychologists might describe as being 'internal' to the child which might contribute to atypical development. In particular, it focuses on four explanations. These include abnormalities or damage to a child's brain; genetic factors; the concept of a developmental or maturational lag; and the notion of a critical or sensitive period of development.

15.3.1 ABNORMALITIES, DYSFUNCTION OR DAMAGE TO THE BRAIN

Our brains begin to develop around three weeks after conception, and at around seven months after conception the basic structure of the brain is complete (Nowakowski & Hayes, 2002). In the months following birth, the brain grows rapidly to end up forming a highly specialised mature brain with different psychological functions localised to particular regions, such as the ability to make and carry out plans. Of particular interest to developmental psychologists is what impact abnormalities or damage to the brain have on child development.

Numerous studies have investigated the impact of brain damage on development, in particular with respect to the timing of the damage relative to developmental stage. For example, Stiles et al. (2005) report that young children often recover skills after brain injury better than older children and adults. This is thought to be because certain functions are more easily reorganised in the young brain which may have greater **plasticity** (flexibility of organisation) than older brains. Take, for example, a child who has been involved in a collision with a car in which some degree of brain damage occurred. If this damage leads to impaired language skills (because the left hemisphere of the brain took most of the impact from the collision) it would not be unusual for a young child's brain to be able to compensate for the damage and for full language skills to be restored several months later. This is because, in young children, the job of the damaged neural structures can be taken on by other structures which have not yet become specialised to other areas.

However, brain damage does not just occur through traumatic injury. During development, the process of brain organisation can be interrupted or changed through other causal mechanisms, which are hypothesised to be the cause of several types of atypical development such as **autism** or **attention deficit hyperactivity disorder** (ADHD). In the case of autism, Baird et al. (2003) argue that a variety of causes can underlie the atypical or disrupted development of the central nervous system that results in brain structures, such as the cerebellum, working differently in children and adults with autism (Allen & Courchesne, 2003).

> **Attention deficit hyperactivity disorder**   A behaviour disorder, usually first diagnosed in childhood, that is characterised by inattention, impulsivity and, in some cases, hyperactivity.
>
> **Autism**   A form of pervasive developmental disorder. It can range from high functioning to severe in nature. Diagnosis is usually made according to difficulties found in aspects of communication, social skills and the use of imagination.
>
> **Plasticity**   The ability of the brain to adapt to deficits or injury.

Similarly, in the case of ADHD, one of the leading biological explanations suggests that hyperactivity is caused by brain abnormalities in three areas of the brain: the frontal lobes, the basal ganglia and the cerebellum (Casey, 2001). Interestingly, this explanation has recently been challenged in light of further research that suggests that ADHD is actually predominantly a genetic disorder (Campbell, 2000; Nadder et al., 2001). For example, twin studies show that identical twins are often both diagnosed with ADHD, whereas in fraternal twins (non-identical twins), this is uncommon (Pennington et al., 2005; Plomin, 1990). The exact primary cause of ADHD remains unclear, although many researchers would agree that it is the result of an interplay between genetics, brain abnormalities and the environment (Gelfand et al., 1997).

KEY RESEARCHER   Simon Baron-Cohen

Simon Baron-Cohen is director of the Autism Research Centre (ARC) in Cambridge. He is also Professor of Developmental Psychopathology at the University of Cambridge. Baron-Cohen's first degree was in Human Sciences from New College, Oxford, followed by a PhD in Psychology from University College London, and an MPhil in Clinical Psychology from the Institute of Psychiatry.

(Cont'd)

Baron-Cohen's main research interests lie in seeking to identify the basic mental processes that are specific in autistic spectrum conditions. One of his key contributions to this area of research was the suggestion that children with autism find it difficult to read and understand other people's minds, which he termed 'mindblindness'. Whereas typically developing individuals are suggested to be able to effortlessly read others' minds in everyday life, Baron-Cohen argues that individuals with autism find it difficult to understand another person's thoughts, desires and intentions. This in turn, he suggests, impacts on an individual's ability to communicate and interact in the social world.

Baron-Cohen's current research focuses on testing the 'extreme male brain' theory of autism. This theory is based on the idea that babies who are exposed to high levels of male hormones in the womb (and thus who are more likely to develop what Baron-Cohen describes as an 'extreme male brain') are more likely to develop traits that are typical of autism.

FIGURE 15.1   Simon Baron-Cohen

15.3.2 GENETIC FACTORS

The field of genetics looks at the way that traits and characteristics are passed down from one generation to another through a person's genes. The first stage of development begins at conception when each of us receives a unique combination of genes from our parents. At conception, 23 **chromosomes** from a father's sperm cell unite with 23 chromosomes from a mother's egg cell to form a new life. Contained within these chromosomes are our genes which are the basic units of heredity, which in turn are composed of a chemical called **deoxyribonucleic acid** (our **DNA**) (Kail, 2007).

In typical development, the newly fertilised egg proceeds through a process of rapid cell division and eventually, after around nine months of gestation, a baby is born. However, not all successful conceptions result in the birth of a child, with two out of every three being spontaneously aborted in the early months of pregnancy. In the majority of these cases the embryo has genetic or chromosomal abnormalities (Rosenblith,

Chromosome   A thread-like strand of DNA that carries the genes.

DNA   Deoxyribonucleic acid, a chemical found primarily in the nucleus of cells. DNA carries the instructions or blueprint for making all the structures and materials that the body needs to function.

1992) and the body's expulsion of the embryo is considered to be an example of natural selection. The more severe the abnormality, the less likely it is that the baby would survive to term or survive the trauma of birth.

Thousands of genetic disorders have been recognised so far. However, there are only a small number of these disorders for which we know what the contributing genes are and the ways in which these are thought to contribute. We do know, however, that the genetic contribution to a disorder can occur in one of several ways. The first is through single-gene effects where an abnormality is due to the action of a recessive gene which both parents carry and which is passed on to the foetus at conception. **Phenylketonuria** (PKU) is an example of a recessive gene disorder which affects the metabolic system. The second is through dominant gene conditions. These are rarer than recessive single-gene conditions and can be passed down from one parent only (giving the child a 50 per cent chance of inheriting the condition). The condition will usually manifest in all carriers and so is relatively easy to identify. **Huntingdon's disease**, which affects the central nervous system to produce progressive dementia and involuntary movements, is an example of a dominant gene condition (Simpson & Harding, 1993).

Chromosomal disorders arise due to abnormalities in one or more pairs of chromosomes which are present in every cell of the body. The most frequently used example of a chromosome disorder is **Down syndrome** in which there is typically an extra chromosome 21 (so instead of having two copies of chromosome 21, individuals with Down syndrome have three). Down syndrome, which occurs in approximately 1 in 1000 individuals, is thought to be caused by one-off faults in either the egg or the sperm cells. Children born with the syndrome have characteristic facial features and may have some degree of learning difficulty (Figure 15.2).

> **Down syndrome** A congenital disorder, caused by the presence of an extra 21st chromosome, in which the affected person has mild to moderate learning difficulties and distinctive facial profile. Also called trisomy 21.
>
> **Huntington's disease** A dominant genetic disorder in which a protein is produced abnormally, leading to the breakdown in the parts of the brain that control movement.
>
> **Phenylketonuria** An inherited, metabolic disorder that can result in learning difficulties and other neurological problems. People with this disease have difficulty breaking down and using the amino acid phenylalanine. PKU can be managed by a diet restricted in foods that contain this amino acid.

15.3.3 DEVELOPMENTAL OR MATURATION LAG

Another key issue in the study of atypical development is the concept known as the developmental or **maturation lag**, which refers to delayed maturity in one or more areas of development. This explanation again mainly attributes the cause of atypical development to factors within the child. For example, children diagnosed with learning difficulties have been described as being characterised by a maturation lag which reflects delayed progress in certain aspects of neurological development. Since their rate of development is significantly slower than that of typically developing children, children with learning difficulties more

FIGURE 15.2   Young man with Down syndrome
© Mika/Corbis

frequently function at an immature stage for their age and consequently fail to attain the same final level of competence. This concept of immaturity suggests that the child continues to develop in the area of difficulty and may eventually reach a more typical level of competence in certain tasks. One of the main areas of research that has utilised the idea of the developmental lag is reading development, where researchers have investigated at what point parents and educators should be concerned about delays in a child's reading ability (Satz et al., 1978).

15.3.4 CRITICAL OR SENSITIVE PERIODS

A critical or sensitive period is a time during the lifespan in which an organism may be affected by a specific experience or event, more so than at any other time in development (Colombo, 1982). According to the critical period hypothesis, a child is more susceptible to environmental stimulation during a critical period than at other times during the lifespan. If specific experiences occur during this period, then development will continue on its typical course. If these specific experiences do not occur, there may be a significant disruption or difficulty in subsequent development.

The concept of a critical period is drawn predominantly from the work of ethologist Konrad Lorenz (1981), who noted that the young of some species, for example hens and ducks, learn to follow their mother around soon after birth. Lorenz found that while the following behaviour was driven by instinct (also known as a canalised process) there is some flexibility in learning what or whom to follow. Typically, young birds were found to learn the characteristics of a moving object during a period soon after hatching, which the birds then followed. This process of knowing which object to follow is known as *imprinting* and usually occurs in relation to the mother, since she is the main figure the offspring encounters during the critical or sensitive period after birth. Imprinting in which the young learn the characteristics of the parent is known as filial imprinting. However, Lorenz also found that imprinting to other objects can occur and he successfully imprinted ducklings on himself so that they then followed him.

Following on from this work on imprinting, Lorenz introduced the term **critical period** to describe the restricted period in which he believed imprinting took place. The critical period is defined by a window of opportunity which begins and ends abruptly and is a period beyond which a phenomenon will not appear. This is contrasted with the notion of a **sensitive period** which is believed to begin and end more gradually than a critical period. The sensitive period refers to a time in which the organism is in a stage of maximum sensitivity rather than a strict window of opportunity.

Critical period   A limited period, usually early in life, in which a child is required to be exposed to a particular skill or experience in order for it to be learned.

Sensitive period   A period of development, usually early in life, during which the individual is most sensitive to certain types of experience or learning. Refers to a period that is more extended than a critical period.

ASIDE

Konrad Lorenz, along with Niko Tinbergen and Karl von Frisch, was awarded the 1973 Nobel Prize in Physiology or Medicine for 'discoveries concerning organisation and elicitation of individual and social behaviour patterns'. A remarkable story concerns the different routes that these scientists took during their collaboration. Lorenz and Tinbergen met before the Second World War (1939–1945) but found themselves on different sides when the hostilities began. Tinbergen was Dutch and spent much of the war as a hostage in a prison camp. Lorenz, on the other hand, was conscripted into the German army and later spent some time in a Russian prison camp. Before his time in captivity Lorenz had associated with the German Nazi Party and wrote a scientific justification for what we now call ethnic cleansing. Tinbergen clearly did not share these views, and it is testament to his humanity that he could look past this after the war and renew his collaborative work with Lorenz.

The idea of critical and sensitive periods has been shown to be valuable in studies of many aspects of development including language acquisition and the development of attachment behaviours (Schaffer, 2000). In 1967, Eric Lenneberg first proposed the notion of a critical period for language acquisition. He suggested that the period between infancy and puberty (the beginning of adolescence) was a critical period for language acquisition. This period was thought to end at puberty because of important maturational changes in the brain that occur at this time. Evidence to support the notion of a critical period in language development comes from studies of children brought up in deprived circumstances.

KEY STUDY Curtiss, S. (ed.) (1977). *Genie: psycholinguistic study of a modern-day 'Wild Child'*. New York: Academic.

Genie was a girl discovered in 1970s America at the age of 13 after having been kept in virtual isolation for the majority of her life. After being told that Genie had possible learning difficulties at the age of two, her father kept her locked in her bedroom. She was tied to a potty chair for the majority of the day, and at night she was placed in a cot covered with a metal cover to keep her inside. Her mother and brother were forbidden to talk to her and she was growled at like a dog if she made a noise in order to keep her quiet.

Eventually, Genie's mother ran away, taking Genie to a welfare office in California. Genie's parents were initially charged with child abuse after welfare officers became concerned by Genie's poor development relative to her age. When she was discovered at around the age of 13, she had some understanding of language but did not speak. After a year of intensive training and instruction, she had a vocabulary of about 200 words and was speaking in two-word sentences. She walked awkwardly, had very little language and only ate baby food. After spending around a year in hospital, Genie went to live with one of her therapists. She was placed on an intensive programme of language and social development in the hope that those looking after her could establish whether there was a critical age for language acquisition.

Although Genie made good progress in terms of her language development, she never became a proficient user of language and grammar. She also demonstrated some difficulties in forming attachments. After four years of living with her therapist, the funding that had been allocated to look after her was cut and she was returned to hospital, and eventually her biological mother. Despite having made much progress, Genie still displayed some difficult behaviour such as tantrums, and her mother found her difficult to cope with. Genie was subsequently placed in a series of foster homes where she was sometimes treated very badly, and she regressed dramatically.

What Genie's case shows us is that extreme deprivation and neglect have serious and long-lasting effects on both emotional and cognitive development. Whilst the effects of such deprivation can be tempered by good support systems in later years, it appears to be very difficult to encourage development along a more typical developmental trajectory where severe deprivation has been prolonged and sustained.

Illustrative examples of the concept of a critical or sensitive period can also be found in the domain of social development. One particularly interesting example is the formation of the infant–parent attachment relationship. **Attachment** is defined as the strong emotional ties between an infant and a caregiver and is thought to develop over the first year of the child's life, in particular during the second six months of the first year (see also Chapter 13).

John Bowlby, a twentieth-century English psychiatrist, formulated and presented a comprehensive theory of attachment. Bowlby was the first to propose that there is a strong biological basis for the development of attachment behaviours, and accordingly the infant–parent attachment relationship was suggested to develop because it is important to the survival of the infant. It also provides a secure base from which the infant can feel safe exploring their environment.

> **Attachment behaviour** Any behaviour that helps to form or establish an emotional bond between two individuals. Strong attachment bonds are usually formed between an infant and his or her caregiver.

Bowlby (1944; 1969) suggested that there was a sensitive period for the formation of the attachment relationship by which he meant that attachment would only happen within a constrained time frame. Bowlby's hypothesis was based in part on the findings from his work with juvenile thieves, the majority of whom he established had experienced early and prolonged separation from their mothers. Bowlby concluded from this that there is a significant relationship between maternal deprivation in infancy and subsequent emotional maladjustment.

However, it is now recognised that even if an infant does not have access to a secure and loving relationship with a particular caregiver early in life, but does so later in life, it is still possible for an affectionate bond to be established. As a group, however, children who develop a bond later in life appear to be at an increased risk for insecure or maladaptive attachment relationships with their adopted parents (DeKlyen & Speltz, 2001).

OUTSIDE INFLUENCES ON ATYPICAL DEVELOPMENT

15.4

Previous sections of this chapter have illustrated psychology's contribution to understanding how and why development might not proceed as expected. These explanations have focused on factors which are considered to be 'internal' to the child, and generally arise from attempts to identify specific genetic, biological and cognitive differences which can be related to a developmental trajectory which is considered atypical. This range of behaviours, as we have seen, may include aspects of social behaviour, communication and learning. Sometimes we observe unusual patterns of behaviours which we do not expect to see (for example, in autism). In other cases, we observe behaviours that are more typical but occur later than we would expect (as we see in children with some learning difficulties). By understanding the internal causes of atypical development, we gain insight into the educational and social support that children might need, and at the same time we increase our theoretical understanding of typical development.

There are, however, other considerations when we are thinking about atypical development. Some of these considerations require a shift in the way we think about our expectations of the developmental trajectory: and we will return to these towards the end of the chapter. First, however, we will consider some aspects of psychological understanding that illustrate the significant contribution of factors which are external to the child, but which may play a part in the development of atypical behaviour. To do this we will first identify some environmental factors which have been demonstrated to relate quite clearly to children's development – particularly with respect to school performance and social and emotional development. The remainder of the discussion will then focus on a range of psychological constructs that contribute to our understanding of the causal effects (on typical and atypical development) of aspects of the child's environment.

15.4.1 'OUTSIDE-THE-CHILD' FACTORS

There are a range of factors 'external' to children which are thought to have an effect on children's behaviour and which may indeed be thought to play some causal role in atypical development. The research we refer to here has attempted to describe the disadvantageous effects of different environments in which children might be brought up. For example, there has been much research into the effects of poverty on children's development. Duncan et al. (1994) demonstrated that poor children usually do less well in school and score lower on standard IQ tests. Another aspect of the child's environment which has been of interest to researchers is that of family background – particularly with respect to the potential effects of divorce or separation. We use the word 'potential' here to highlight the fact that although there is evidence which has demonstrated the significant distress and consequent effect on children's behaviour when parents separate, this is not the only outcome for children of split families. Where the separation is managed carefully and the child's perspective is taken into account, the children might actually be at lower risk for the range of social, behavioural and academic problems which are sometimes associated with family discord (Hetherington & Stanley-Hagan, 1999).

15.4.2 EXPECTATION AND THE SELF-FULFILLING PROPHECY

In 1968, a study was undertaken by Rosenthal and Jacobson which has important implications for our understanding of children's development. These researchers demonstrated that, within a school situation, teachers' beliefs about children's abilities can affect how much children learn. More specifically, teachers in this study were told that some of the children in their classes had been identified through tests to be very likely to make great progress in the coming year. In actual fact, the children identified in this way had simply been selected at random from the school population.

What seemed to happen over a period of time was that those children who were expected by the teachers to do well actually *did* do better than those children for whom their teachers' expectations were lower, despite the real similarities of the groups. That is, the *expectations* of the teachers seemed to be exerting a causal effect on the children's learning. Notwithstanding various methodological critiques of the study (Snow, 1969; Thorndike, 1968) this stands as an example of what has been termed a **self-fulfilling prophecy** (Merton, 1957). This refers to the suggestion that people tend to act in the way that others expect of them, or indeed in ways that they have come to expect of themselves.

The fact that our own and others' expectations may influence behaviour is therefore a potentially significant factor for our understanding of the influences on development which lie outside the child. Rosenthal and Jacobson were specifically interested in the effect of teachers' expectations on children's performance on school tasks. However, given the many other studies which have investigated the impact of the self-fulfilling prophecy, it would seem reasonable to apply the same logic to other aspects of children's behaviour across other contexts. For example, if teachers' expectations can be demonstrated to affect children's learning, then maybe there are examples of adult expectations about other aspects of development (for example social behaviour or communication) which also have an effect on children's behaviour.

> **Self-fulfilling prophecy**   A prediction that directly or indirectly causes itself to become true.

One question we can ask here, for example, concerns what happens when a parent learns that their newborn baby has a severe disability. Not surprisingly, a range of emotional reactions comes with hearing this news, with feelings of anxiety and shock very often followed by elements of denial or disbelief. Of course this very difficult situation is at times further exacerbated by the mothers having more limited contact with their babies in the period after birth than would normally be the case. Ludman et al. (1992) found that infants who underwent major surgery during their early days, and thus who were separated from their parents for lengthy periods, demonstrated an increased incidence of behaviour problems at age three, with higher rates of difficulties in the mother–child relationship compared with controls. The question here is whether these factors (maternal anxiety and the effects of early separation) alter the mother–child relationship in a way that will have consequences for the child in the long term. The jury is still out on this case (see Leifer et al., 1972), but this is a good example of the potential 'external' influences on atypical behaviour.

Here then a range of evidence indicates that it is important to consider people's expectations when reflecting on possible 'outside' influences on behaviour. With respect to understanding atypical development, there would appear to be a continuum on which we might judge the significance of this effect. At one end of this continuum, it might be the case that expectations of others serve to increase aspects of the atypical behaviour; at the other, there may be examples of expectations actually *causing* atypical development. For example, one of the key factors in adolescent drug abuse is known to be the availability of drugs and people to tempt such use (Herbert, 2008). Key characteristics of those using drugs are commonly cited as low self-esteem, a poor sense of psychological wellbeing and low academic aspirations (Herbert, 2008). As previous research has demonstrated the links between societal expectations, the self-fulfilling prophecy and self-esteem (Krishna, 1971), it is clear that there may be a causal link between expectation and atypical behaviour.

15.4.3 LABELLING

At this point it is important to refer to the process of 'labelling'. This creates a real tension within groups of people who are associated with children demonstrating atypical develop-ment, for example, parents, educationalists and clinicians. By labelling, we refer to the business of identifying a particular pattern of atypical behaviours and consequently attaching a label of diagnosis to the child demonstrating those behaviours. Many parents feel that having a label to describe their child's behaviours (for example, dyslexia or autism) is an important step in ensuring that their child receives appropriate educational, social and financial support. It can also provide the child with a useful understanding about why they find some aspects of their work more difficult than their peers.

On the other hand, as we have just seen, a label might make other people expect a certain pattern of behaviour which may indeed lead to an increase in this behaviour. A good example here is to consider the potential effects of the label of dyslexia on a school-aged child. It could be that being labelled dyslexic not only gives the child an 'excuse' for not doing well at school, but also means that the teacher may assume that the child is not going to succeed at the same level as their peers.

REASONS TO BE SCEPTICAL   Over-interpretation of evidence and understanding research agendas

In some areas of enquiry, researchers and consumers of research findings can be guilty of over-interpreting evidence and making claims that are not fully supported by evidence. One clear example of over-interpretation of empirical findings is in the autism research literature, where it is sometimes claimed that people with autism *lack* a theory of mind (the understanding of another person's thoughts and feelings). What actually appears to be the case is that people with autism may experience some challenges when it comes to engaging with the thoughts and feelings of others. This is quite different from 'lacking' a theory of mind.

It is also important to consider the importance of certain areas of research, relative to the amount that is published about them. For example, if we refer back to the issue of theory of mind in autism, a brief literature search using the term 'theory of mind' will result in the return of a large number of published papers in the area. Whilst this is an important area of research, a similar search for example investigating 'sensory issues in autism' results in the return of considerably fewer published articles. This does not mean that understanding sensory issues in autism is any less important than understanding theory of mind, although it might appear so based on the number of articles published in each area. The number of articles published in an area may have more to do with trends of thought and sources of funding than with the relative importance or otherwise of that area.

15.4.4 PROVIDING APPROPRIATE OPPORTUNITIES

So far, we have considered effects on development which have come about by, or are exacerbated by, the expectations and behaviours of others. At this point, we ought to acknowledge another – less direct but possibly more potent – way in which other people's expectations may exert an effect on development, and which is particularly pertinent when considering children who demonstrate patterns of atypical development. Patterns of behaviour which we find challenging, either because they are very different from what we expect, or because we do not understand them, may lead us to make false assumptions about the abilities of the children demonstrating these behaviours. These assumptions may result in us failing to provide opportunities for children to develop in more typical ways – just because we believe that they cannot benefit from these opportunities.

For example, children with autism may live in a very unusual sensory world in which sights and sounds can be confusing, distracting, uncomfortable and even painful (Williams, 1996). A noisy, visually stimulating classroom might make it extremely difficult for a child with autism to participate with others, or to understand the words that are spoken to them which may not be 'sifted out' from the mass of information that is bombarding their senses. That child might employ behavioural strategies that are designed to help them cope with the situation, such as stereotypical hand flapping, or even behaviours that result in them being removed from the classroom. An outsider, looking in on that child's behaviour, might conclude wrongly that the child does not want to participate with others and that the child does not have a good understanding of spoken language. However it can often be the case that if the sensory context can be adjusted to better suit the child, the opportunities for that child increase dramatically (Gillingham, 2004).

15.4.5 PROVIDING APPROPRIATE LEARNING CONTEXTS

To examine a further way in which adults' expectations may come to influence development, we need to consider the ideas of the Soviet psychologist Lev Vygotsky (1896–1934), whose work is also discussed in Chapter 14. Vygotsky's theoretical account of development was concerned with the relationship between language and communication and intellectual development. Vygotsky argued that higher-level cognitive processes are realised during interactions with others. When taking part in social interactions children are observing, experimenting with and practising a range of behaviours which gradually become internalised and employed on an intra-individual level.

A central concept in Vygotsky's (1978) theory is the **zone of proximal development** (ZPD). The ZPD is located between what a child can achieve on his or her own and what that same child can achieve with the help of either an adult or a more capable peer (see Figure 15.3). For learning to be most effective, teaching needs to be sensitive to the child's zone. Directing efforts below the level of the zone will result in no learning, because this is what the child can do already. Interactions directed above the zone will also result in little learning, as this will be at a level too difficult for the child to understand. Guiding the child within the ZPD, however, is likely to lead to the child learning.

Pioneering work by Wood et al. (1976) began to explore the characteristics of these 'successful' interactions. These researchers coined the term **scaffolding** to describe the nature of the activities that the adult employs in these interactions (Figure 15.3). The studies of Wood and colleagues were restricted to experimental situations where the teaching techniques of mothers were observed while they supported their children in learning how to assemble a construction toy. In an attempt to look more widely at this phenomenon, Barbara Rogoff (1990) drew on wider cross-cultural observations of

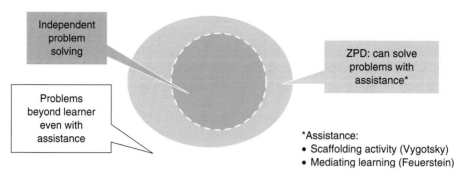

FIGURE 15.3 The zone of proximal development

Zone of proximal development The zone or distance between what a learner can achieve alone and what he/she can achieve with assistance.

Scaffolding A teaching strategy in which instruction begins at a level encouraging students' success and provides sufficient support to move students to a higher level of understanding.

interactions between children and their carers, and used the term *guided participation* to describe a range of behaviours which not only characterise deliberate attempts to teach but also can be observed in playful interactions and in everyday activities shared by adults and children.

You may now be wondering why we are spending time here considering a theoretical approach which was primarily developed through observations of interactions between typically developing children and their parents or peers. However, what we would like to suggest is that, within the framework of teacher expectations being proposed above, Vygotsky's thoughts about development generally, and about the ZPD specifically, may also have an important part to play in our understanding of atypical development. As has been established, learning through collaboration with others is most likely to occur when your partner (either an adult or a more capable peer) is able to provide a level of interaction that is within your ZPD. If a child's abilities are not clearly understood, it is likely that the level of interaction that is available to the child may not be appropriate for effective learning to take place.

A number of studies have explored aspects of teaching and learning for children demonstrating atypical developmental trajectories (see, for example, Cains, 2000; Hobsbaum et al., 1996; Lamb et al., 1998). Several of these studies draw attention to the fact that for many of these children, learning interactions have not been appropriately directed. When careful consideration is given to the nature of the interactions among children and between children and adults, significant changes in children's learning have been observed. This is also the case for children who have had a history of failure in school learning. For example, Ann Brown and her colleagues provide compelling evidence to demonstrate that children who have real difficulties with reading comprehension can make significant gains in reading achievement through a series of structured group reading events

(Brown & Campione, 1990). This approach, which is known as 'reciprocal teaching', is informed quite explicitly by Vygotskian thinking about interaction and collaboration. In the reading groups, the teacher models appropriate reading behaviours and scaffolds the children in the use of a range of comprehension skills, for example, questioning, clarifying, summarising and predicting. Through guided practice in applying these strategies, these comprehension-enhancing skills start to become an automatic part of the child's own reading process.

Researchers using integrated play groups (IPGs), whereby children with autism are introduced to groups with typically developing children as a means of promoting play, have also used Vygotskian principles to good effect. Such groups have been found to result in increases in social play and less isolated play by the children with autism (Bass & Mulick, 2007; Wolfberg & Schuler, 1993). What is important to recognise in these studies is that the children involved demonstrate 'atypical' development, and for many of them it had been assumed that progress in a range of different areas was unlikely. However, by providing an appropriate learning environment which is designed to take into account the specific nature of these children's abilities, progress in learning can be made.

15.4.6 MODELS OF DISABILITY

In the discussion that has been presented in this latter half of the chapter, we have suggested that it is necessary to look beyond the 'inside' of the individual child when considering the causes and developmental trajectory of children who are described as demonstrating atypical development. Specifically we have drawn attention to the potential effect that the behaviours, knowledge and decisions of other people (in particular other adults) can have on a child's development.

We can take this argument one step further by considering the wider consequences and implications of some of the ideas presented here. One way of thinking about these issues is to refer to the distinction made between two different models of disability – the 'medical' model and the 'social' model. The medical model describes difficulties associated with atypical development as arising from within the individual, who needs to be supported by society or 'made better'. This is the model within which much of the research discussed in the first half of this chapter is framed. An important feature of the medical model is the need for diagnosis and labelling of the child. In contrast, the social model regards the problem as lying not within the individual, but within the attitudes, behaviours and assumptions of society that frame the transactions of each individual with that society. Within this framework, disability is the product of a society which builds barriers that prevent someone from being able to be fully included in that society. These barriers may be organisational, physical or social and are found to exist in many settings. From this point of view, for a disabled individual to play a full role in society, it is not the person that needs to change, but society itself.

We raise this issue here to encourage you to think about the wider issues associated with an understanding of atypical development. Knowledge about the range of different courses that development may take as a consequence of a range of different genetic, biological and cognitive characteristics is important for a variety of reasons. Also important is an understanding of how society views these developmental differences and the potential effects of our assumptions about these differences.

CHAPTER SUMMARY

15.5

This chapter has outlined some of the factors which we know contribute to development that can be described as following an atypical trajectory. We identified two key perspectives and considered the factors within two corresponding groups: those arising from *within* the child (such as brain damage, genetics and the importance of critical or sensitive periods of development); and those *external* to the child (such as societal expectation and the self-fulfilling prophecy, labelling and the provision of appropriate opportunities and learning contexts).

This discussion of 'within' and 'external' factors deliberately raises the issue of the interplay between these two perspectives. It is increasingly recognised that the way we think about atypical development needs to take account of these two perspectives and consider the implications for how we help children developing atypically. At the beginning and end of this chapter we discussed the question of how society views developmental differences and the role that individual differences play in determining whether development is considered to be atypical. As educators, parents and policy makers, when discussing atypical development and determining the nature of any subsequent help that is provided, we need to give consideration to the nature of societal expectation and the model of disability that we ascribe to.

Historically, those factors considered to be within the child received more attention and were ascribed greater importance than factors external to the child. Current thinking, however, is that we need to be engaging with a more rounded description of atypical development that takes into account the full range of factors that are considered to contribute. This shift is important not only for our understanding of atypical development, but also for the way in which we, as society, provide appropriate support and opportunities.

 ## DISCUSSION QUESTIONS

William James is quoted as saying 'to study the abnormal is the best way of understanding the normal'. What does the study of atypical child development tell us about typical development? How much can we learn if we follow this principle? Should we follow this principle?

According to the Austrian psychologist Alfred Adler, 'the only normal people are the ones you don't know very well'. How would you apply this quotation to the arguments in this chapter? Consider your own definition of 'typical' and 'atypical'.

SUGGESTIONS FOR FURTHER READING

Bornstein, M. (1989). Sensitive periods in development: structural characteristics and causal interpretations. *Psychological Bulletin*, *105*, 179–197. A key journal article outlining the nature and definitions of sensitive periods.

Empson, J.M., & Nabuzoka, D. (2004). *Atypical child development in context*. Hampshire: Palgrave Macmillan. This book discusses definitions of both typical and atypical development, examining a variety of topics such as emotional and behavioural difficulties and learning difficulties. It also explores possible explanations of the causes of atypical development in light of current research.

Herbert, M. (2008). *Typical and atypical development: from conception to adolescence*. Malden, MA: Blackwell. This text describes the development a child undergoes whilst in the womb right through to adolescence. It is split into two: the first half of the book is dedicated to describing typical development; the second half provides an outline of atypical development, examining areas such as genetic disorders and emotional and behavioural difficulties.

Plomin, R., DeFries, J.C., McClearn, G.E., & McGuffin, P. (2005). *Behavioral genetics* (5th edn). New York: Worth. This is another key text that introduces findings from genetic studies of cognitive and developmental abilities, with a focus on the interplay between nature and nurture.

Smith, P.K., Cowie, H., & Blades, M. (2003). *Understanding children's development* (4th edn). Malden, MA: Blackwell. This is a core text which is comprehensive and provides a good introduction to the general area of child development.

HOW WE KNOW AND MEASURE OUR INDIVIDUALITY

The Psychology of Individual Differences

Half of the people you know are below average.

Steven Wright

In our modern world, we categorise people on a whole range of abilities. 'He's very bright, you know', says the competitive (i.e. every) parent, as if it mattered, or as if they had actually tested their child and compared them to other children. In everyday conversation, we are always making comparisons between our expectations of individuals and how they actually behave. These differences between individuals have been one of the key concerns of psychology for over 100 years.

THE HISTORY OF INDIVIDUAL DIFFERENCES

The study of individual differences can be traced back to the work of Francis Galton who invented and defined the field. In 1884, Galton created a mental testing laboratory – an anthropometric lab for testing data about people, such as visual acuity, strength of grip, colour vision, hearing acuity and hand preference. He hoped to use these measures to estimate people's hereditary intelligence. This is a key feature of much subsequent research, and the genetic explanation of individual differences has dominated the field.

Galton was the cousin of Charles Darwin and was greatly impressed by Darwin's ideas on individual variability and selection. Before Galton, psychology had been looking for general principles of experience. By contrast, Galton's anthropometric laboratory looked for individual differences and tried to place them within a theory of evolution. Although we would not recognise Galton's tests as measures of mental abilities today, they do mark the beginning of mental testing.

Galton was remarkably inventive and he is credited with developing a range of techniques and concepts that define the field even today (see Fancher, 1996):

- *Self-report questionnaires*: In 1873, Galton wrote to all the Fellows of the Royal Society (eminent scientists) with a lengthy questionnaire to discover the common features of people who are successful in science.

- *Nature and nurture*: He invented this term to describe the difference between environmental and inherited influences.

- *Twin studies*: He devised the first of these, as well as carrying out the first comparisons of natural and adopted children with their parents.

- *Scatterplots*: Galton wanted to find ways to present his data on family resemblances and he devised the scatterplot.

- *Statistics*: Galton developed regression lines and the correlation coefficient.

The above is a phenomenal list but it is only a selection of his output – and you can add word association to it. Galton devised a word association technique; his paper on this was

Galton's anthropometric laboratory that was set up at the International Health Exhibition in London in 1885
© Science Museum/Science & Society Picture Library

read by Sigmund Freud and contributed to the development of one of the major techniques of psychoanalysis. And if you're still not impressed, then he also invented the weather map, and hence weather forecasting.

KEY ISSUES

One of the key issues in the field of individual differences concerns the usefulness of measuring and categorising people. The measured differences between us are usually very small but are used to rank people and to distinguish one person from another. This is fine, but another view of people could highlight how much we have in common. People are able to communicate, they are sociable, they have warm attachments to other people that endure over time, and they perceive and make sense of the world around them in very similar ways. However, at this point in our history we seem more bothered about what distinguishes one person from another than about what unites us. Hence the rise in importance of individual differences in psychology.

Another key issue for individual differences is the discussion over nature and nurture. This was first framed by Galton but has burned brightly ever since, as we try and explain why one group of people is better or worse than another group at a particular skill. The importance of this discussion is that the answer you come to guides you to certain solutions to social problems.

THIS SECTION

In this section we have three chapters looking at the core areas of individual differences. Chapter 16 explores what psychologists have to say about personality: what is it? Is there such a thing as a normal or abnormal personality? How is personality measured? In Chapter 17 we look at differences in cognitive performance, and the most prominent concept here is intelligence. Is intelligence just the ability to learn, or is it problem solving ability? Do we become 'more' intelligent as we grow older? Finally, in Chapter 18, we look at the self and ask who am I? How do I know who I am?

16 PERSONALITY

Lead authors **Glenn Williams, Jamie Murphy** and **James Houston**

INTRODUCTION

16.1

When we are asked what we admire in another person, we might comment that they have a 'nice personality' or a 'strong personality'. But what exactly do we mean by these comments, and what is this thing called personality? We think about a person's personality in the way that we think about their appearance: it has a number of features that are similar to a few other people, a number of features that are similar to a lot of other people, and a number of features that seem to be unique. In this chapter we will look at how psychologists have defined and researched personality and then consider how these theories can be applied to real-life situations.

? FRAMING QUESTIONS

What is this thing called 'personality'? What is it made up of?

What type of personality would you say that you have? Think about what might have influenced you to have this personality type. To what extent does your personality result from your genes and to what extent from the way you have been brought up?

Do you think your personality stays the same as you get older? Do you think that your personality changes in different situations? Do you have the same sort of personality with your friends as you do with your family?

What do think constitutes an 'abnormal' personality? How might it be different to a so-called 'normal' personality? How might 'normal' personalities develop into 'abnormal' ones?

WHAT IS PERSONALITY?

16.2

This question of what personality involves is a difficult one to answer because 'personality' means different things to different psychologists. There are a number of approaches to personality, known by such labels as psychodynamic, humanistic, feminist and existential. Here we will focus on one of the most popular theoretical perspectives, namely the study of personality traits. We will show the relevance of examining personality traits in a variety of real-life situations, especially in relation to people's experiences of health and illness and also when applied to education and the workplace. In doing so, we have departed from traditional textbook practice: we have concentrated less on the development of the subject through history and more on its relevance to applied settings.

The following two definitions should provide an insight into how much psychologists vary in their understanding of what it means to have a certain type of personality. One definition of personality emphasises *differentiation* between people. It states that personality is:

those internal stable factors that make people systematically and predictably different from one another. (Furnham & Heaven, 1999: 1)

Another definition instead emphasises *similarities*; it focuses on the common features between people. It says that personality is:

a stable set of tendencies and characteristics that determine those commonalities and differences in people's psychological behaviour. (Maddi, 1989: 8)

Although there is some variation in how personality is defined, there does seem to be some common ground between psychologists. Furnham and Heaven (1999) argue that psychologists' conceptions of personality tend to include the following:

- individual differences, with a stress on the uniqueness of individuals but also the importance of being able to categorise, classify or describe this uniqueness along dimensions of personality
- a combined system of cognitions, emotions and behaviours
- stable, and sometimes predictable, behaviour
- general dispositions, which are linked to specific needs or drives.

Clearly, therefore, there are a number of things that need to be considered when examining personality. Each of us has our own personality, and this is evident in everyday life, in what we think about certain aspects of life, how we act around other people, what choices we make, and how we work. There can be a bewildering array of reasons to explain why we think, feel and act the way we do. For example, if you are reading this chapter, it may be that you are an extremely conscientious student who has decided that you would like to know more about personality for a course that you will be pursuing in the future; or you may be someone who has a piece of work to hand in tomorrow morning and has only just decided to make a start!

Many personality psychologists (or 'personologists' as they are sometimes called) agree that we are all very different. However, they have also argued that personality involves a prevailing behaviour pattern within each of us that appears to remain stable across time as well as circumstances. This approach is typified by the trait perspective on personality.

TRAIT APPROACHES TO PERSONALITY

16.3
In Chapter 2 you were introduced to the nomographic or **nomothetic** approach to psychology, which involves looking at a range of separate concepts and evaluating the degree to which a person matches what is 'normal' for that person's age group and sex. Personality researchers who use the

nomographic approach usually focus on two main units of analysis: personality **traits** and personality **types**. Personality types are typified by analysis of categories and the extent to which an individual can be described according to one personality category versus another. For example, the Myers–Briggs Type Inventory (MBTI) seeks to classify personalities by types. Thus, people are classified as either sensates or intuitives (they are one or the other). *Sensates* focus on the physical world and are down to earth, making decisions on the evidence of their senses; whilst *intuitives* are more likely to focus on the mental or spiritual world, rely on hunches or gut feelings, and be more interested in 'what can be'.

Conversely, trait approaches have involved viewing personality along a continuum or a series of personality dimensions.

> **Nomothetic and idiographic**
> Nomothetic approaches look for laws of behaviour and collect measures that can be observed and verified and quantified. They are concerned with averages and norms. By contrast, idiographic approaches look for unique and individual experiences.

Over the past 30 years, several models of the **trait** structure of human personality have been particularly prominent. They are the sixteen-factor model (Cattell et al., 1970), the five-factor model (Costa & McCrae, 1992; Norman, 1963) and the three-factor model (Eysenck & Eysenck, 1991). These different types of trait model have been labelled 'factor' models as the authors have all used the statistical technique of **factor analysis** to find the underlying structure to people's major personality traits. Here we will look at the main personality factors in the three-factor and the five-factor models.

16.3.1 EXTRAVERSION AND NEUROTICISM

Two personality traits that are common to both the three-factor and five-factor models of personality are **extraversion** and **neuroticism**. A typical extravert has been defined as someone who enjoys being with other people and 'craves excitement … acts on the spur of the moment, and is generally an impulsive individual' (Eysenck & Eysenck, 1991: 4). An **introvert**, on the other hand, is described as someone who is 'introspective, fond of books rather than people … [and who] tends to plan ahead … [and] does not like excitement' (1991: 4).

> **Trait**   An enduring pattern of perceiving and behaving in the world that is relatively consistent and predictable.
>
> **Factor analysis**   A method of statistical analysis which examines intercorrelations between data in order to identify major clusters of groupings which might be related to a single common factor.

Neuroticism is characterised by persons who are prone to anxiety and depression, and who are often tense and susceptible to mood swings. Both extraversion and neuroticism are core components of the three-factor and five-factor models, which we will visit in turn.

KEY RESEARCHER   Hans Eysenck (1916–1997)

FIGURE 16.1   Hans Eysenck

Hans Jurgen Eysenck was one of the most colourful characters in psychology and his work often attracted a great deal of emotive debate. He has frequently been at the centre of controversies including those concerning racial differences in intelligence (he argued there were substantial differences and these were due to genetic factors); claims made about the link between smoking and cancer (he argued that the links between the two were tenuous, to say the least); and his vocal criticisms of the efficacy of psychoanalysis, particularly Freudian psychotherapy.

Eysenck was an advocate of behavioural therapy for psychological problems and supported the notion that personality and intelligence were largely influenced by genetic and other physiological factors. He was also intrigued by the notion that personality dimensions could be influenced by astrological factors, and he even wrote a book entitled *Know your own psi-Q* which delved into this area.

Eysenck communicated complex psychological ideas to a general audience in books like *Uses and abuses of psychology* and *Sense and nonsense in psychology*. He was very keen to make sure that psychology could be approached in a scientific way and this commitment could be traced back to his unfulfilled desire to study physics at university.

However, Eysenck had an enduring and wide-ranging impact on psychology, particularly in the areas of personality, individual differences and intelligence. Eysenck published over 600 journal articles or book chapters and over 60 authored or edited books. His widow, Sybil Eysenck, is another prolific psychologist, who is an editor of the journal *Personality and Individual Differences*, and his son is Michael Eysenck, an eminent cognitive psychologist.

16.3.2 THE THREE-FACTOR MODEL

Eysenck (1967) developed the **three-factor model** of personality from Galen's (129–199 AD) concept of the four 'humours', which was later expanded upon by Immanuel Kant (1907/1978). According to Galen, the four **humours** (or **temperaments**) were typified by melancholic, choleric, phlegmatic and sanguine characteristics. The first two temperaments predominantly involved volatile, strong emotions, whereas the latter temperaments depicted relatively less emotional, and more stable, types of personality. Melancholic persons would tend to have *anxiety-prone* personalities. Kant saw the melancholic person as being different from the sanguine predisposition in that:

> Everywhere he [the melancholic] finds cause for concern and he directs his attention first of all to difficulties, while the sanguine person relies on the hope of success. (1907/1978: 199)

According to Eysenck's theory, the melancholic would be the equivalent to the unstable introvert. Introverts would be usually less impulsive, sociable and sensation seeking than extraverts would. Unstable introverts would not tend to seek social support in times of stress and would often be self-critical.

In contrast to the melancholic person, the choleric would tend to possess an *anger-prone* personality. Kant defined the 'choleric' individual as 'hot tempered, and … quickly ablaze like a straw fire' (1907/1978: 199). The choleric would tend to direct their frustrations and aggression outwardly at other people or other objects, whereas the melancholic would tend to direct negative emotions inwardly, which would usually manifest itself in anxiety or depression. According to Eysenck's personality theory, the choleric individual would be similar to the unstable extravert. Both unstable extraverts and unstable introverts are depicted in Figure 16.2.

The inner circles in the diagram have incorporated Galen's model of the temperaments, and the outer circle shows the characteristics of extraversion and introversion and how they interrelate. Eysenck (1967) used data to suggest that differences between extraverts and introverts could be explained biologically by the low levels of arousal in the extravert's

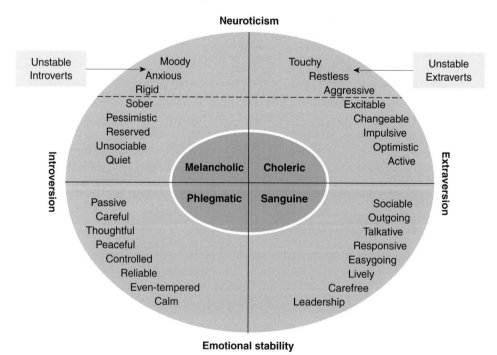

FIGURE 16.2 The Eysenck personality circle
Adapted from Eysenck & Eysenck, 1991.

ascending reticular activating system (ARAS) in the brain, whereas the introvert would have continuous overarousal in the same area. Extraverts are 'stimulus hungry' because they seek out stimulation in the ARAS, whereas introverts are 'stimulus averse' because they try to avoid too much stimulation to the ARAS (Eysenck & Eysenck, 1985). This is one reason why extraverts might prefer sociable situations as they physiologically thrive on being around the stimulation provided by others, whilst introverts would often tend to avoid such less controllable and overstimulating environments.

Another biological basis for personality in the three-factor model is neuroticism's link to the **autonomic nervous system** (ANS), in which a person's tendency to get into a 'fight-or-flight' response when under stress is associated with higher levels of neuroticism (Eysenck & Eysenck, 1985).

> **Autonomic nervous system**
> A network of nerve fibres running from the brain stem and spinal cord, which can activate the body for action, or set it into a quiescent state.

The third component to personality according to Eysenck is **psychoticism**. This is very much separate from the other two personality factors. High levels of psychoticism are characterised by individuals who are emotionally cold, antisocial in behaviour, impersonal and unable to empathise with other people's feelings and thoughts. In terms of support for the three-factor model, various studies have confirmed its essential structure and validity. Overall, the three-factor model has been replicated widely in a wide range of clinical and other applied settings (Eysenck & Eysenck, 1991; Kline, 1993).

16.3.3 THE FIVE-FACTOR MODEL

Arguably the most popular contemporary model of personality trait structure is the **five-factor model** (Digman, 1990; McCrae & Costa, 1997). This model has also been termed the Big 5 (Deary, 1996) or the Norman 5 (Norman, 1963) and was developed in a non-theoretical way by using lists of adjectives (e.g. quiet, assertive, sociable, proud) and grouping similar concepts together (e.g. loud, talkative, chatty, assertive, domineering), producing five main dimensions or factors. Paul Costa and Robert McCrae's (1992) five-factor model has been called the OCEAN model, after the initial letters of openness to experience, conscientiousness, extraversion, agreeableness and neuroticism.

REASONS TO BE SCEPTICAL   How many personality traits do we *really* have?

There is plenty of evidence to suggest that there is no clear-cut set of personality traits that are common to all of us. Personality researchers have come up with different labels for personality traits that use the same measuring instrument, whereas others have argued long and hard over the organisation of people's personalities. In the past, sensation seeking used to be part of Eysenck's notion of extraversion, but now it is more commonly seen as a part of psychoticism.

(Cont'd)

> With the five-factor model, there has also been some inconsistency in the characterisation of each factor. For-example, one study itemises impulsivity as part of extraversion, whereas another study shows it as a vital part of neuroticism.
>
> Why do you think there is so much variation with how the personality traits are labelled and organised?

We have already introduced you to the traits of extraversion and neuroticism. The other three personality traits involve the following main characteristics:

- Someone who has high levels of **openness to experience** appears to have very creative tendencies. Openness, in short, involves having a thirst for knowledge and an active imagination. High scores on openness might also indicate the drive to pursue an unconventional lifestyle.

- **Conscientiousness** is indicated by high degrees of being diligent, hardworking, reliable and thorough. Conscientious individuals have a need to accomplish things and have the attributes that are required to do this, for example efficiency and steadiness, as well as being organised, systematic and practical (Goldberg, 1992).

- **Agreeableness** entails the ability to generally 'get on' with others by being altruistic, trustworthy, compliant to people's requests for help and generally tender-minded. It is possibly the polar opposite of Eysenck's (1991) concept of psychoticism.

The OCEAN model has been subjected to a wide-ranging test of its validity and cross-cultural applicability (Costa & McCrae, 1992; McCrae & Costa, 1997). It has also been subjected to some criticism. Whilst the three-factor model has strong biological underpinnings, there is not much research into the biological processes underlying all five personality factors. The five-factor model was mainly developed from how people talk about personality characteristics. It may, therefore, be a function of the language that people use about it, rather than of the mechanisms involved in each personality trait (Block, 1995; 2001). Despite the reservations that some psychologists have had about the five-factor model, it is one that has endured and remains extremely popular as the basis for personality measurement in the workplace, in education and in health.

KEY STUDY   Costa, P.T. Jr, & McCrae, R.R. (1976). Age differences in personality structure: a cluster analytic approach. *Journal of Gerontology, 31*(5), 564–570.

This study might seem an unlikely piece of research to choose as a key study, but it was one of the first studies that Costa and McCrae published together and demonstrated that they were already beginning to think of personality traits beyond the three-factor and sixteen-factor models.

In this seminal study, Costa and McCrae used a questionnaire commonly used to measure 16 personality factors. They took a sample of 969 adult male volunteers and separated their participants into three major age groups (25–34 years, 35–54 years, 55 years or over). They were able to find age group differences in relation to a new personality trait at the time, namely openness to experience. Costa and McCrae had not found any age differences on the traits of anxiety–adjustment (similar to the modern-day concept of neuroticism) and introversion–extraversion. Openness to experience, on the other hand, appeared to have three main dimensions: openness to (1) feelings, (2) ideas and (3) feelings and ideas combined. Costa and McCrae found that the youngest group of participants were more open to feelings, whereas those in the group aged 35–54 were more open to ideas. The oldest age group were found to be more open to feelings and ideas.

This study was a landmark move away from viewing personality as being mainly constituted of core neuroticism and extraversion traits, and began to show the possibilities for the existence and utility of alternative traits such as openness to experience. From then on, Costa and McCrae began work on developing ways of understanding and measuring personality traits using the NEO (neuroticism, extraversion and openness to experience) questionnaire, and this eventually led to the emergence of the NEO-Personality Inventory (NEO-PI; McCrae & Costa, 1983). This breakthrough work has spawned a great deal of research work. As a result, the five-factor model of personality traits remains one of the most popular in the world today.

Overall, the trait approach in general is not without its critics. We will see in the following section how this perspective may be limited in predicting and explaining human behaviour.

REASONS TO BE SCEPTICAL   How consistent are personality traits?

Research tends to support the argument that our personality traits are not that strong in predicting how we will behave in any given situation. How useful is the trait approach in predicting how we think, feel and act? Think about the following as a way of testing this: in which ways have your personality characteristics changed or stayed the same over the years? If you saw some of your classmates at a reunion 10 years later, do you think they would recognise you and your core personality? Do you think you act the same way at all social events? What conclusions do you reach on how consistent people generally are?

THE SITUATIONALIST CRITIQUE OF TRAIT PSYCHOLOGY

16.4

In the previous section, we have looked at the potential for identifying people's personality traits and the use of traits as a common 'language' with which to understand variation and similarities in personality. However, some issues remain unresolved, particularly with the role of the situation in determining how people will act in given environments (Figure 16.3). Trait psychology, with the regular use of characteristic adjectives of how human beings *generally* are, may be ill-equipped to account for 'the kind of person who is affable with peers, deferent to superiors, and nasty to individuals of lower rank' (Block, 1995: 196). The problems that lie within the trait approach are mainly to do with being consistent with one's thoughts, emotions and actions across a wide range of situations and contexts. With trait psychology, there is an assumption that we have an inner core to our personalities that will remain stable over time and will continually affect how we act, think and feel.

Sarah Hampson has argued that the trait approach finds it difficult to explain why people act in ways that do not conform to their so-called traits. For example, Hampson (1999) questions how we can explain an introverted person who is shy in small-group situations but also an effective public speaker in front of large groups. If someone is highly introverted, they may find it more comfortable to spend time by themselves rather than with others; but how come they might also be a good public speaker? In essence, we need to understand the dynamics of each situation and the behaviour required of it, and authors such as Walter Mischel have argued that these dynamics are too often neglected by personality psychologists.

FIGURE 16.3 Nobody likes to think of themselves as a cheat. But given the opportunity what is most likely to affect your behaviour? Your personality or the situation you are in?
© Michael Haegele/Corbis

16.4.1 MISCHEL'S CRITICISMS OF TRAIT PSYCHOLOGY

Mischel (1968) has argued that humans are consistently inconsistent. By looking at a wide range of studies into how personality traits are related to units of behaviour, Mischel was only able to find an average correlation of 0.30. He found that correlations between two single behaviours in two separate situations were rarely higher than 0.30, which seemed to suggest that humans are often very changeable in terms of adapting and trying various ways of coping with situations. This 'magic' number of 0.30 was labelled by Mischel the **personality coefficient**. Personality then accounted for only around 10 per cent of variation in people's behaviours: this was calculated by multiplying the coefficient by itself (0.30 x 0.30) and then multiplying by 100 to show the percentage of variation accounted for by personality. Mischel concluded that personality traits had minimal input into how we behaved and that behaviour was largely a function of the situations within which we are placed.

16.4.2 RESPONDING TO THE SITUATIONALIST CRITIQUE

Mischel's criticisms of the utility of personality traits seem quite damning. Should we reject using traits as a universal language of portraying the very essence of people's personalities? However, there are ways in which Mischel's assumptions can be questioned. Most importantly, just because personality may only account for, on average, 10 per cent of a given behaviour, it does not follow that the remaining 90 per cent is necessarily due to situational constraints. Furthermore, though traits may be relatively poor predictors of behaviour in a laboratory setting, they may be robust indicators of how people will act over wide-ranging situations and within a given time (McAdams & Pals, 2006). There are a wide range of influences to our behaviour beyond needing to seek pleasure and avoid pain. If behaviours were solely a function of situations, then we would be assuming that the individual is like a 'blank slate' upon which a stimulus would produce a predictable response. There is evidence to show that we are not like blank slates and that we bring to bear a great deal of innate responses that transcend a knee-jerk reaction, with many human behaviours thought to be determined through human nature rather than nurture (Pinker, 2002).

A more advanced method of understanding the role of personality traits and when they become prominent in specific situations has been put forward by Buss (1989). Buss found that situational influences only seemed to have a major role when what is required of us is only for a brief duration and there is little choice over what we can do. We are more likely to comply with the norms of what might be expected of us in situations that are public, formal and novel. For instance, at a graduation ceremony it would be very unlikely (and shocking!) if a student who is graduating were to walk onto the stage where the vice-chancellor is handing out degrees and suddenly start body popping!

Our traits are more likely to show themselves as influences when we are in situations that are likely to last over a long time, there are choices over what we can do, and the social environment is relatively informal and private. If we use a similar example of enjoying one's graduation at a ball, body popping or any other way of expressing one's individuality would be perfectly acceptable and even encouraged by everyone dancing at the same time.

Overall, it seems that the most appropriate way forward for personality psychology is to adopt a method of seeing how personality traits interact with various situations while not assuming that traits are going to drive us to act in an automatic and unthinking way. The environment that surrounds us may shape our personalities and the goals that we aspire to achieve, but we are active participants in attempting to reshape our environment. In the following sections, we will look at how personality interacts with a range of environments from health care to the workplace to education.

REAL-WORLD APPLICATIONS OF PERSONALITY THEORIES NO. 1: CAN YOUR PERSONALITY MAKE YOU ILL?

16.5

Knowledge of personality can help us to understand how our personalities can have a damaging or protective role when it comes to our health, especially our susceptibility to physical or psychological ill-health. Two main perspectives have been used to explain the possible influences that personality can have on health: (1) the **specificity approach** and (2) the **generality approach**. With the specificity approach, personality is seen as being a direct, causal factor in disease. In other words, our personalities can have a major role in making us prone to experiencing particular illnesses, like peptic ulcers, hypertension and some types of eczema (Alexander, 1950).

The generality approach, on the other hand, does not view personality as being one of the main causes of disease. Instead, personality has an indirect role by influencing our emotions and behaviours that will, in turn, have some form of impact on our health. For example, if we look at the concept of **locus of control** there is evidence to suggest that people who have an internal locus of control are more likely to adopt health-enhancing behaviours, like taking up exercise or having a healthier diet, when compared to people with an external locus of control (Strickland, 1989).

Locus of control   Refers to what people perceive to be the source of what happens to them. An internal locus of control means that people see it as coming from within themselves – so they are largely in control of what happens to them, or at least in a position to influence it. An external locus of control means that it is perceived as coming from sources outside the person, and so is not something which the individual can influence.

It has also been found that, with an internal locus of control, there is more of a tendency to take interest in messages relating to health/illness, and there will be active efforts by 'internals' to control factors that could affect their health. There is evidence that people with high levels of conscientiousness live longer than people who have low levels of conscientiousness (Bogg & Roberts, 2004). This might be because those people with high levels of conscientiousness are much more likely to be careful in following specialist and general medical advice when compared with people low in conscientiousness. In the rest of this section, we will consider personality as an indirect influence on ill-health. To do this we will focus on the notion of a type A personality.

16.5.1 TYPE A PERSONALITY

This personality type has been linked to an individual's proneness to having coronary heart disease (CHD). CHD can include a wide range of heart problems, including angina pectoris and myocardial infarction (commonly known as a 'heart attack').

It was almost a century ago that William Osler (1910) made the link between CHD and personality. Although he had not identified and labelled a set of coronary-prone behaviours as part of a type A personality (that came much later in 1974: see Rosenman and Friedman, 1977), his portrayal of the coronary-prone personality resonates with the main features of being a type A. Osler wrote that the coronary-prone person was:

> The robust, the vigorous in mind and body, the keen and ambitious man, the indicator of whose engine was always at full speed ahead. (1910: 839)

What we were later to find out was that it wasn't the hurrying-type behaviour that was the most problematic when it came to posing a risk of CHD. Early ways of understanding type A personality posited a person's 'hurry sickness' as a vital component, but in the 1980s research began to show that being anger-prone was the killer (see Booth-Kewley & Friedman, 1987; Williams et al., 2000).

In the mid 1970s, Meyer Friedman and Ray Rosenman reported on the Western Collaborative Group Study, which involved repeatedly testing 3000 men for eight years. Although there was accumulating medical evidence for smoking, obesity and lack of exercise as risk factors for CHD at the time, Friedman and Rosenman also discovered that a person's risk of getting CHD was affected by that person's behaviour patterns. These behaviours were labelled the **type A behaviour pattern** and this is commonly termed the **type A personality**. The common features of being a type A can be found in Table 16.1.

TABLE 16.1 Common type A behaviours

Very competitive
'Hurry sickness':

- Restless and alert
- Always moving, walking and eating rapidly
- Speaking rapidly and interrupting others whilst they are talking
- Often trying to do more than one thing at a time

Feeling guilty when attempting to relax or doing something not related to work
Compulsive tendencies
Having a strong need for advancement in one's career
Having aggressive and hostile feelings towards other people
Depressive/neurotic tendencies
Low on introspection (i.e. doesn't spend much time to stop-and-think before acting)

Friedman and Rosenman were not the only researchers to find this trend, as another large-scale study among residents of the town of Framingham in the United States showed similar patterns (Haynes & Feinleib, 1980). There was also a growing body of evidence to show that people with a type A personality were often very competitive and career oriented and tended to harbour hostile attitudes towards others. They would get impatient with people who were not meeting a type A's exacting standards of behaviour. As mentioned earlier, the 'hurry sickness' that Osler (1910) identified was also found to be characteristic of having a type A personality. A really extreme example of the hostility that someone with a type A personality could harbour can be seen in Figure 16.4.

Patient:	Doctor, you must help me. I'm under a lot of stress. I keep losing my temper with people.
Doctor:	Tell me about your problem.
Patient:	I JUST DID, DIDN'T I? YOU USELESS TWAZZOCK!!!

FIGURE 16.4 *Type A personality*

16.5.2 PERSONALITY AND GOOD HEALTH

Personality has been used to account for differences in health and overall wellbeing. Aaron Antonovsky (1987) used the term **salutogenesis** to represent the science of studying wellbeing, after the Latin and French for good health (*salus* and *salut* respectively) and *genesis* – the Greek term to denote a beginning. Health could encompass many things relating to someone's quality of life, and Antonovsky identified a phenomenon that could help in preserving quality of life, namely the **sense of coherence** (SOC). With SOC, a person sees the world as comprehensible, manageable and meaningful. Rather than seeing as threatening (as in the case of the person who feels the need to restrain their emotions) or as unjust (as in the case of the anger-prone type A individual), the person with high levels of SOC sees some elements of their worlds as controllable. There is evidence from a sample of patients with schizophrenia living in a community setting that people with high SOC can have reduced psychopathology and greater social support networks than those low in SOC (Bengtsson-Tops & Hansson, 2001). SOC also interacts with employees' experiences of demanding work environments, protecting them from stress (Söderfeldt et al., 2000).

Although there has been a great deal of research into how personality may make us prone to certain diseases, there is also a flourishing body of evidence to indicate that specific types of personality can help in bringing about good health. A review by Booth-Kewley and Vickers (1994) has shown that the OCEAN five-factor model can indicate associations between personality type and health. Extraversion and conscientiousness have been related to adopting healthier lifestyles, and conscientiousness has been especially linked to living a longer life. On the other hand, agreeableness and conscientiousness have been inversely (i.e. negatively) correlated with taking more chances when driving and thus posing more of a risk of being involved in traffic accidents. Openness to experience has also been linked to hazardous health-related behaviours, like using illegal drugs. Overall, not only can your personality make you more likely to be ill but it can also help to make you less likely to suffer from some illnesses as well.

REAL-WORLD APPLICATIONS OF PERSONALITY THEORIES NO. 2: CAN KNOWLEDGE OF YOUR PERSONALITY HELP YOU TO BECOME A MORE EFFECTIVE WORKER?

16.6 It may not be obvious to you, but knowledge of your personality is something that is highly sought after by many employers. Companies spend vast sums of money trying to identify what personality type constitutes the most effective worker and whether or not you or I fit the bill.

'So,' you may ask, 'how does all this information about extraversion, introversion and neuroticism inform employers as to how suitable I am as an employee and whether or not I'm going to line their deep pockets with cash?' Well these bigwigs turn to occupational and personality psychologists (who are well versed and informed about the trait approaches to personality) to assist them in making the best possible hiring decisions. Among the many high-profile tasks for occupational psychologists have been the appointments of the heads of UK banks. To begin with, these psychologists complete a **job analysis**, that is, they conduct a thorough analysis of the requirements and demands of the job in question. They might start this analysis by interviewing the employees and managerial staff of a company to gain some understanding of their personal experiences and how they perceive their own role within the company as well as the roles of others. The psychologists might also devote time to observing the workers and assess the skills that are required and utilised to achieve maximum performance and success. An assessment of the working environment may also be carried out to identify the physical and social context and demands within which the work must be performed.

Having completed this job analysis, the psychologists, using their extensive knowledge of personality, develop hypotheses to test associations between certain personality traits and abilities and job-related tasks. Different jobs present different demands, and it is unsurprising that occupational and personality psychologists invest their time assessing which personality traits are most suitable for the successful execution and completion of specific jobs and job-related tasks.

Take the extraversion–introversion trait that we dealt with earlier in the chapter. Research has shown that extraverts tend to outperform introverts on certain tasks. It has been established in particular that extraverts are more competent in executing tasks that require divided attention amidst distraction and interference (Eysenck, 1982; Furnham & Allass, 1999). Extraverts, unsurprisingly given their social nature, also display superior performance in processing verbal information compared to that displayed by introverted individuals (Dewaele & Furnham, 1999; LePine & Van Dyne, 2001).

Conversely, introverted individuals outperform extraverts on tasks that require vigilance and focused attention and on particular kinds of problem solving (Amelang & Ullwer, 1991). It has been noted that extraverts generally have a preference for response speed, which has been shown to have a detrimental effect on response accuracy; this is less commonly identified in introverted individuals (Eysenck, 1967; Koelega, 1992). Brebner and Cooper (1985) differentiate between extraverts and introverts, stating that 'extraverts are geared to respond' while 'introverts are geared to inspect'. You might ask yourself therefore on the basis of this information, 'Can I think of particular job-related tasks that might suit extraverts and others that might suit introverts?'

This is exactly what personality and occupational psychologists strive to achieve. For example, the above information on task performance applied to a job-related task indicated that individuals employed as train drivers who were also characterised as extraverts were better equipped to respond to and detect railway signal stimuli (Singh, 1989). Matthews et al. (1989) showed that extraverted post office workers, when assessed on a speeded mail-coding task, were more efficient than introverted employees.

Studies assessing differences in task performance are not confined to those between extraverts and introverts; they are also conducted on the various other traits elaborated upon earlier in the chapter. Knowledge and evidence of these trait differences in performance is applied to occupational contexts to establish who out there is fit and suitable for employment. Thousands of personality tests have been published (Spies & Plake, 2005) and many companies use these tests to assist businesses in the selection of their workforce. Knowledge of your personality therefore may not help you to become a more effective worker, but you can be pretty certain that behind-the-scenes knowledge of your personality is a highly valued commodity to many others. For a more detailed and comprehensive account of personality and job-related performance, read Larsen and Buss (2008) or Matthews et al. (2003).

REAL-WORLD APPLICATIONS OF PERSONALITY THEORIES NO. 3: CAN KNOWING ABOUT A STUDENT'S PERSONALITY BRING ABOUT A BETTER EDUCATIONAL ENVIRONMENT?

16.7 Personality has been linked in many ways to education: for example, psychologists have examined how anxiety can influence performance in exams, and alternatively, how people who are high in motivation and persistence can achieve academic success (for example, Underwood et al., 2007a). A great deal of the research in this area examines positive personality traits in relation to success in education. Having said this, however, a number of personality traits have been linked to negative behaviour in the educational arena, for example, with regard to the nature of bullying in schools. Here we will first examine research that has linked personality to academic achievement, and second will examine evidence relating personality to the different roles that children play in school with specific regard to bullying.

16.7.1 EDUCATIONAL ACHIEVEMENT AND PERSONALITY

If we were to ask what makes a student successful in school or at university, the first thing that would pop into a lot of minds is the word 'intelligence'. Whilst this is of course a strong predictor of educational success, some psychologists have suggested that there are many characteristics which influence an individual's educational achievement. For example, Neisser et al. (1996) suggest that personality characteristics, such as willingness to study, persistence and interest in school are important in terms of academic achievement. In fact, as far back as Cattell (1965), differences in personality and motivation were seen to be just as important in predicting academic achievement as differences in intelligence for college students.

A lot of the early work in this area suggested that before the age of around 11 or 12 years, extraverted children were superior to other students at school (e.g. Eysenck & Cookson, 1969). In many ways, from what we know about those who are high in extraversion, this would make sense. For example, extraverted people have lots of energy and they are extremely active and outgoing. Some research however has also suggested that extraverts have a tendency to socialise a lot during school or in college as opposed to doing work, and therefore have difficulty concentrating, as they are busy seeking other, more social ways of using their energies (Eysenck, 1982).

Two other personality traits (from the five-factor model) that have been investigated in relation to educational achievement are agreeableness and conscientiousness. There are obvious implications for high educational achievement for people who possess conscientiousness, given that they are typically hardworking and thorough.

Possibly a slightly less obvious positive personality trait in relation to educational success is agreeableness. Some research has however found that agreeableness can have an effect on educational success. For example, Stevens and Slavin (1995) suggested that when students are learning in a cooperative environment there can be significant effects on achievement. Agreeable people are more likely to cope better with others in a school or university setting, and therefore what might be more significant in terms of the relationship between agreeableness and education is the way we conduct ourselves within the educational environment, and with this, the relationships that we develop with others. For some, however, these relationships, particularly in this setting, are sometimes very negative. This has obvious implications for an individual's chance of achieving academic success. One negative behaviour in the school environment that has been linked to personality is bullying and we will look at this in more depth in relation to personality.

16.7.2 BULLYING IN SCHOOL AND CHILDREN'S PERSONALITY

Although there has not been a great deal of research with regard to the personalities involved in **bullying**, research has concentrated on the Eysenck and Eysenck (1975) factors of psychoticism, neuroticism and extraversion. According to Eysenck and Eysenck, individuals scoring high on psychoticism are typically identified as solitary, impulsive individuals who are hostile towards others, lack cooperation, are low in social sensitivity and lack feelings of anxiety and inferiority. Individuals who score highly on neuroticism are fearful, low in self-esteem, lacking in autonomy, obsessive and prone to guilt, and those scoring high on extraversion are characterised as outgoing, talkative and high on positive affect. We might therefore expect victims to score highly on neuroticism, but some research has suggested that this is not the case. Slee and Rigby (1993), for example, concluded that the major factor differentiating victims from bullies is introversion, not neuroticism. Introverts are described by Eysenck and Eysenck (1975) as preferring their own company to that of others, as well as being relatively quiet individuals who rarely show signs of aggression. Additionally Slee and Rigby (1993) found bullies scored significantly higher on psychoticism than victims. In contrast to this, Connolly and O'Moore (2003) found bullies to score significantly higher than victims on psychoticism, extraversion and neuroticism, indicating that neuroticism is more likely to be part of the personality of a bully as opposed to a victim. Psychoticism therefore seems to be most closely associated with bullies, whereas research is more unclear in relation to extraversion and neuroticism.

Research therefore suggests that an individual's personality may have a significant effect on whether or not they become involved in bullying in school, and which role they will play within the bullying arena, as either a 'bully', a 'bully/victim', a 'victim' or indeed none of these. Personality research in relation to the nature of bullying in schools has many implications for the safety of children: for example, it could lead to early identification and therefore early intervention, which would serve to reduce bullying in schools.

CHAPTER SUMMARY

16.8 This chapter has introduced you to some leading theories in personality research, as well as how these theories have been applied. We first examined personality in terms of the trait approach, outlining the three- and five-factor models (Costa & McCrae, 1992; Eysenck & Eysenck, 1991) and some commonalities between these models with regard to extraversion and neuroticism. However, the trait approach has been criticised in some circles for being too general, and for *not* being equipped to discriminate how we behave across the wide range of situations and contexts that we find ourselves in throughout our lives. Additionally, it is not clear why we sometimes act in ways that are different to what trait approaches would describe as our dominant traits. This led us to a critique of the trait approach to personality, with arguments by Walter Mischel (1968) who suggested that humans are consistently inconsistent.

Finally, we have outlined a number of ways in which psychologists have used personality theories in a real-world setting, for example, with regard to our physical and mental health, as well as (importantly for you, perhaps) an examination of personality in terms of educational and occupational success.

DISCUSSION QUESTIONS

From the evidence provided in this chapter, it is clear that our personalities (and the situations that we find ourselves in) can have an impact on how we behave in the long term. With this in mind, think about the following questions in relation to personality, education and the workplace:

- Do you think that someone who has been bullied at school will be bullied in the workplace when they are older?

- Will someone continue to be a bully in the workplace if they have been a bully at school?

- Are there other things that might influence whether someone will carry the role that they had in school into the workplace, apart from their personality?

Furthermore:

- What type of studies could we use to get the types of information specified above?

- What are the limitations/benefits of these types of studies? For example, if **longitudinal studies** are used, would there be issues in relation to 'tracking' people over time? Or if we use studies that only assess people on one occasion, how accurate do you think adults' retrospective accounts of what happened to them in school can be?

SUGGESTIONS FOR FURTHER READING

If you are interested in reading further in relation to some of the leading figures within the personality arena, as well as the theories that we have not examined in this chapter, there are a number of very good introductory texts.

For a good outline and critique of the main personality theories, you could look at

Maltby, J., Day, L., & Macaskill, A. (2006). *Personality, individual differences and intelligence*. Harlow: Pearson.

There are also comprehensive textbooks in the field of personality, such as:

Pervin, L.A., Cervone, D., & John, O.P. (2004). *Personality: theory and research* (9th edn). Chichester: Wiley.

Carver, C.S., & Scheier, M.F. (2007). *Perspectives on personality*. Boston: Allyn & Bacon.

Hergenhahn, B.R., & Olson, M.H. (2002). *An introduction to theories of personality* (international edn). Englewood Cliffs, NJ: Prentice Hall.

Schultz, S.E., & Schultz, D. (2004). *Theories of personality*. Belmont, CA: Wadsworth.

In addition, if you would like to find out more about how personality traits are measured, and for samples of scales, visit http://ipip.ori.org/ipip/

17 INTELLIGENCE: MEASURING THE MIND

Lead author **Eva Sundin**

CHAPTER OUTLINE

INTRODUCTION

17.1

This chapter will show how our thoughts about intelligence have changed from the end of the nineteenth century until today. We will start by examining two early and fundamentally different approaches to the concept of intelligence. The chapter will lay out how these intelligence theories were developed in an attempt to understand what is meant by intelligence, and also to provide a basis for measuring differences among children and adults. You will see how the first intelligence test was developed from some of these theoretical assumptions. You will also see that important themes introduced by these pioneers continue to be debated by later intelligence researchers.

The chapter will then introduce you to some of the theoretical positions that represent 'the psychometric approach' to intelligence, which uses factor analysis and other statistical techniques to understand intelligence. We will see how these theorists debate whether human intelligence is best understood as one general factor or as multiple dimensions of intellectual abilities.

The chapter will also familiarise you with current trends within intelligence research. One group of theorists combines the assumption that intelligence is one general factor with the notion that it consists of several dimensions of abilities into a hierarchical model. You will see that a second group of theorists opposes the idea that there is one, general intelligence altogether; at the same time they have different views on the abilities that constitute intelligence. Finally, the chapter will review group differences in intelligence.

FRAMING QUESTIONS

What is intelligence? Is there such a thing as general intelligence, or are there instead many different kinds of intelligence?

Can we measure intelligence? If so, how?

What accounts for differences in intelligence? What is the role of (1) hereditary and (2) environmental factors?

What differences in intelligence exist, or appear to exist, between groups (for example, between sexes or between races)? What are we to make of claims about such differences? Is there such a thing as a culturally unbiased intelligence test?

Can we say anything sensible about differences in average IQ scores of people from different 'races'?

DIFFERENT VIEWS ON INTELLIGENCE

17.2

In research into intelligence, a number of questions recur. Just what does it mean to be intelligent? Is intelligence the ability to learn? Or how quickly we understand new information? Or is it the ability to learn from experience, to apply knowledge to solve problems and formulate new solutions to adapt in a new context? Is intelligence a single, general ability or is it many? Do we inherit intelligence from our parents or is intelligence developed as we go through life? Although researchers and scholars have struggled with these questions since the end of the nineteenth century, there is still no universal agreement on what the term 'intelligence' means.

EXERCISE   Intelligence-related words, part 1: name that dunce

Intelligence is a very important concept for us. You can see this by thinking about the number of words you use to describe intelligence. (The point here is that the more important something is to use, the more words we have for it.)

Make two lists: one of words that describe intelligence in a positive way (e.g. 'brainy') and one that describes it in a negative way (e.g. 'moron'). Make each list as long as you can. It may help to involve members of your household as you do so.

You will probably find that you list more negative words than positive ones. Many of these words we use on an everyday basis. Retain these lists: we'll come back to them later in the chapter.

Social psychologists have shown that the way we understand the world guides our perceptions of present and past events, as well as our predictions about the future (Fiske & Taylor, 1991). For example, people's views of intelligence have implications for their motivation and achievement. North American psychologist Carol Dweck (2002) has shown that people's understanding of their own intelligence influences their enthusiasm to learn. Her research says that those who believe intelligence to be a fixed, inborn entity are more likely to feel helpless if they fail. In contrast, those who believe that intelligence can expand and develop are more likely to try again, even if their first attempt was a failure.

In similar ways, scientists are guided by their theoretical ideas about the nature of intelligence. Just as in the story about seven blind men who encountered an elephant: each of the men touched different parts of the animal and each of them developed different ideas of what an elephant is. The intelligence researcher Robert Sternberg warned that 'until scholars are able to discuss their implicit theories and thus their assumptions, they are likely to talk past rather than to each other in discussing their explicit theories and their data' (2004: 13).

ASIDE   Definitions of intelligence – past and present

Here are a number of quotations showing different ways in which psychologists have characterised intelligence. As you read through them, try to identify similarities and differences between them.

It seems to us that there is a fundamental faculty in intelligence, any alteration or lack of which is of the utmost importance for practical life. This is judgement, otherwise known as common sense, practical sense, initiative, the ability to adapt oneself to circumstance. To judge well, to comprehend well, to reason well, these are the essential ingredients of intelligence. (Binet & Simon, 1905: 196–197)

Intelligence is what is measured by intelligence tests. (Boring, 1923: 36)

We shall use the term 'intelligence' to mean the ability of an organism to solve new problems. (Bingham, 1937: 36)

[Intelligence is] a quality that is intellectual and not emotional or moral: in measuring it we try to rule out the effects of the child's zeal, interest, industry, and the like ... [It] denotes a general capacity, a capacity that enters into everything the child says or does or thinks; any want of 'intelligence' will therefore be revealed to some degree in almost all that he attempts. (Burt, 1957: 64–65)

A global concept that involves an individual's ability to act purposefully, think rationally, and deal effectively with the environment. (Wechsler, 1958: 7)

Intelligence is assimilation to the extent that it incorporates all the given data of experience within its framework ... There can be no doubt either, that mental life is also accommodation to the environment. Assimilation can never be pure because by incorporating new elements into its earlier schemata the intelligence constantly modifies the latter in order to adjust them to new elements. (Piaget, 1963: 6–7)

Intelligence is the ability to solve problems, or to create products, that are valued within one or more cultural settings. (Gardner, 1993a: x)

In a sense we have two brains, two minds – and two different kinds of intelligence: rational and emotional. How we do in life is determined by both – it is not just IQ, but *emotional* intelligence that matters ... the abilities called here emotional intelligence, [which] include self-control, zeal and persistence, and the ability to motivate oneself. (Goleman, 1996: 28, xii)

Individuals differ from one another in their ability to understand complex ideas, to adapt effectively to the environment, to learn from experience, to engage in various forms of reasoning, to overcome obstacles by taking thought. (Neisser et al., 1996: 77)

The important point is not whether what we measure can appropriately be labelled 'intelligence', but whether we have discovered something worth measuring. (Miles, 1957: 159)

EARLY CONCEPTS OF INTELLIGENCE

17.3

Although people may have speculated about the nature of intelligence for centuries, it was not until the end of the nineteenth century that a systematic investigation of individual differences in intelligence was carried out, and that is where we will start our exploration of intelligence theories.

17.3.1 PIONEERS IN PSYCHOMETRIC THEORY OF INTELLIGENCE

One of the first to study individual differences in intelligence was a British psychologist, Sir Francis Galton (1822–1911). Galton believed that complex intellectual abilities were built on less complex abilities like capacity for labour (or energy), sensitivity to stimuli (for example, touch, visual and auditory) and reaction time. Highly intelligent people supposedly had more capacity for labour and better abilities to process sensory information than less intelligent people. Galton also believed that we inherit intelligence from our parents. In his book *Hereditary genius* (1869) he examined the family background of a group of 'eminent men' – judges, statesmen, commanders, scientists, poets, musicians, painters, divines, oarsmen and wrestlers. He found that an unexpectedly large proportion of these men had distinguished relatives. Based on this observation he concluded that genius is passed down from generation to generation. Galton believed this link was genetic. However, there is of course an alternative plausible explanation, namely that children from the homes of distinguished people had better education and better employment opportunities and hence more chance to develop their own skills. The link between heredity and intelligence, Galton hypothesised however, was to be found in sensory discrimination, the reason for this being that genetic inheritance influences the system that processes sensory information – the nervous system.

Galton is considered a pioneer in the experimental study of intelligence. He is known for his pioneering work on measuring intelligence quantitatively, and for his attempts to examine the relationship between intelligence and sensory discrimination and reaction time, and he actually invented the statistical analysis of correlations while mapping out the relationship between these variables. Galton himself concluded that his use of sensory tasks was a failure: he expected to find strong correlations between intellectual abilities and sensory discrimination and reaction time, but the correlations he obtained were in the moderate range. He concluded that his studies failed to support an association between psycho-physiological processes and intelligence. Although Galton discarded his theoretical assumptions, his contributions inspired other, more recent researchers. It is noteworthy that the correlations that Galton reported were of the same magnitude as those observed by contemporary intelligence researchers. In contrast to Galton, these researchers interpret the correlations as indicators of a substantial association: reaction time is closely connected with intelligence (Hunt, 2005).

During the same period, a French physician Alfred Binet (1857–1911) developed an interest in the study of human intelligence. As we will see, Binet, unlike Galton, viewed practical knowledge, reasoning, vocabulary and problem solving as better indicators of intellectual ability than sensory discrimination.

Binet developed a scale that is known to us as the first intelligence test. The background of this initiative was that the French government had enacted a law that all children should be provided with public education. This implied that children who had learning difficulties should be given appropriate opportunities for education. In consequence, how children who were in need of special education were identified became an issue. The government asked Binet to develop an instrument that could be used to detect children with lesser intellectual resources so that they would be given an adequate education.

Binet accepted the task. Together with Theodore Simon, he developed a scale to determine whether a child ought to receive special education or conventional classroom instruction. In other words, the Binet–Simon scale was primarily developed as a rough guide for identifying children with learning difficulties, not as a device for rank ordering intelligence in children with normal cognitive functioning.

The Binet–Simon scale has become known as the first intelligence test. One reason for this may be that the Binet–Simon scale was developed in a format commonly used in more recent intelligence tests. Thus, the scale consisted of a battery of subtests, for example word problems, paper cutting tasks and block comparison.

Second, when the scale was developed, large numbers of performance and paper/pencil tests were taken by different groups of children, and these children were also interviewed. The next step was to compare children's test scores with their school grades. Tests that did not differentiate between children similarly to the interviewers' ratings, or that failed to rank order children similarly to their school grades, were removed.

During the development of the scale, Binet and Simon also became aware of the need to consider the possible influence of interviewer bias. They paid attention to key principles in psychometric theory, especially various forms of validity. Specifically, they attended to questions of: internal validity (that is, whether the test is a coherent measure of the trait it purports to measure); external validity (that is, whether the test scores agree with 'real-world performance'); and inter-rater **reliability** (that is, whether different raters who rate the same data agree with one another).

Not only was the Binet–Simon scale developed to meet the basic psychometric standards of validity and reliability, it was also standardised. Standardisation is the process of testing a pilot group who are similar to the people taking the test to see the scores that are attained. When using a standardised test, each child can compare their score with the standardisation group's score. The first version of the scale was introduced in 1905. Subsequently, Binet and Simon undertook several standardisations of the scale, using different samples of children from different age groups, representing children with different levels of cognitive functioning.

> **Reliability** The reliability of a psychological measuring device (such as a test or a scale) is the extent to which it gives consistent measurements. The greater the consistency of measurement, the greater the tool's reliability.

A third important aspect was that Binet and Simon revised the scale several times. Based on the theoretical assumption that intelligence increases with age, the tests were arranged in accordance with performances by the average child in different age groups. The scale could then be used to establish a child's *mental age*, as opposed to his or her chronological age.

Finally, when the Binet–Simon scale had been translated and revised for usage in the United States, it quickly became the standard of intelligence testing. As we will see, intelligence testing was soon used throughout the US in a variety of ways, including for the screening and placement of recruits during the First World War (1914–1919), school placements, admissions to university studies, and identifying children in need of learning difficulty services.

To adapt the Binet–Simon scale for use in the US, Lewis Terman (1877–1956), who was Professor of psychology at Stanford University, revised some of the tests in that scale and added a large number of new ones. The revision resulted in the Stanford–Binet scale, which consisted of 90 items, and aimed to measure cognitive abilities of children and adults with inferior, normal or superior intelligence. The Stanford–Binet scale assesses four types of cognitive abilities: verbal reasoning, quantitative reasoning, abstract/visual reasoning and short-term memory.

When the US entered the First World War in 1918, many were convinced that an intelligence test was needed to help determine the US army's placements of recruits. To find a way of testing the large numbers of recruits within a reasonable time frame, a simplified adaptation of the Stanford–Binet scale was developed in two versions: a verbal version (the Army Alpha) and a non-verbal version (the Army Beta) for illiterate and non-English-speaking recruits. By the end of the war, the tests had been taken by more than 2 million men (McGuire, 1994). After the war, a new version of the military tests, the Scholastic Aptitude Test (SAT), was introduced. The SAT was soon used by colleges and universities throughout the US as part of their admission criteria.

The widespread usage of intelligence testing in the US provided researchers with large amounts of empirical data to examine differences in intelligence between individuals and groups. A research result that immediately raised controversy was the finding that the average score for populations with African heritage was below the average score for populations with European heritage, and we will come back to that finding later in the chapter. Many of the early **intelligence quotient** (IQ) test pioneers including Galton and Terman (as well as Spearman and Pearson, who devised the correlation tests you use with your data) shared a common belief in eugenics (a subject we discuss below). It was this belief that gives intelligence its controversial edge – an edge that has stayed with it until the present day.

> **Intelligence quotient (IQ)**   A numerical figure, believed by some to indicate the level of a person's intelligence, and by others to indicate how well that person performs on intelligence tests.

17.3.2 EUGENICS

A number of scientists (including Galton and Terman) believed that much of human behaviour is under genetic control and has developed through the forces of natural selection. These scientists noticed that better health care and social conditions at the end of the nineteenth century meant that not so many people were dying at a young age and they feared that the effect of natural selection was being blunted. In other words, if the weak survived then they would pass on their weak genes to the next generation. They proposed that instead of allowing the environment to (in effect) selectively breed the better members of the species, this selection needed to be organised by society. Galton coined the term **eugenics** to describe his project of improving the race through selective breeding.

> **Eugenics** The political idea that the human race could be improved by eliminating 'undesirables' from the breeding stock, so that they cannot pass on their supposedly inferior genes. Some eugenicists advocate compulsory sterilisation, while others seem to prefer mass murder or genocide.

This selective breeding of a superior class of people could then be used to improve society and remove people who, for example, would not put the top back on a tube of toothpaste once they had used it. This is, in fact, no laughing matter: the approach had some powerful supporters who put forward views that make our hair stand on end today. For example:

> There exists a sentiment for the most part quite unreasonable against the gradual extinction of an inferior race. (Francis Galton, 1883, cited in Rose et al., 1984: 30)

> If we would preserve our state for a class of people worthy to possess it, we must prevent, as far as possible, the propagation of mental degenerates. (Lewis Terman, 1921, cited in Kamin, 1977)

The big words disguise the sentiments of the quote. To paraphrase Terman, he is saying we must stop poor and uneducated people from having children. All this would seem unpleasant but unimportant, were it not for the fact that over half of the states in the US brought in sterilisation laws for the 'feeble minded' and carried out tens of thousands of operations (Kamin, 1977). On top of that, Terman provided scientific evidence to US politicians that influenced them to bring in immigration quotas based on race (Gould, 1981).

17.3.3 INTELLIGENCE TESTING AND RACE

Perhaps the most controversial use for IQ data has been to look at average differences in scores for people from different groups, for example race. If you give the same IQ test to various groups of people then they will achieve different average scores. The BBC occasionally runs a programme called 'Test The Nation' where groups of people take IQ tests. In this show they compare average scores of, for example, a group of plumbers with a group of undertakers. This is all good fun and doesn't have any real consequences.

However, if you do the same exercise with different ethnic groups then the results become more controversial and more important. Say, for example, we find that one group of people called the Tralfamagorians (made-up nation) all do very badly on our IQ test: what should we do about it? If we believe that differences in IQ scores are mainly due to genetic effects (the hereditarian position) then we would think that there is nothing we can do for the Tralfamagorians and we just make sure they only do menial jobs. On the other hand if we believe that IQ scores are mainly influenced by our education and our environment (the environmentalist position) then we offer extra support and better education programmes. You can see, then, why the issue of the inheritance of differences in intelligence is a hot topic and one that has generated a lot of controversy over the years.

The debate over racial differences in intelligence is one of the major scientific and political disputes of the past century and the issue is still not resolved. We return to this in Section 17.5.2.

17.3.4 FACTOR ANALYSIS AND THE STRUCTURE OF INTELLIGENCE

Until the early 1900s, the approaches to intelligence had been pragmatic: tests of intellectual abilities were developed for particular needs. At that time, the British psychologist Charles

Spearman (1863–1945) reported an observation that has impacted on later theories of intelligence. When he examined the data on many different cognitive abilities, using several different instruments, he found that all correlations between these tests were positive. Thus, if an individual obtains high scores on a test of verbal reasoning, s/he could be expected to obtain high scores on a second test, such as mathematical abilities. In the same way, individuals who had low scores on one test of cognitive abilities could be expected to score low on the other tests as well. Spearman labelled the trend that cognitive tests tended to correlate positively with each other as positive manifold. He argued that this overlap, or intercorrelation, indicated that these tests measure a general component of intelligence, in addition to measuring specific intellectual abilities.

To be able to examine the nature of the relationships between scores from several different tests, Spearman developed a mathematical method which in a refined version is known to us as **factor analysis**. As you will remember from the previous chapter, factor analysis is used for reducing a mass of information to a simple description. In this case, factor analysis involves exploring the underlying structure of many intelligence test scores. Spearman used factor analysis as a tool to examine whether intelligence had one big underlying factor or a range of many factors. He showed that one major factor was regularly being extracted in his analyses.

General factor(g) The theoretical general factor of intelligence that some scientists believe underpins all cognitive activity.

Factor analysis A method of statistical analysis which examines intercorrelations between data in order to identify major clusters of groupings, which might be related to a single common factor.

From this observation, Spearman formulated his assumption that a general intellectual ability, or *g*, underlies all human cognitive performance and could account for individual differences in scores on mental tests. Spearman believed that *g* should be considered as intelligence and he called the approach 'the two-factor theory of intelligence'. This approach indicates that the **general factor**, *g*, represents what all of the mental tests had in common. The second factor was identified as the **specific factor**, or *s*. The specific factor related to the unique ability that was measured by each test. The hierarchical model of intelligence is shown in Figure 17.1.

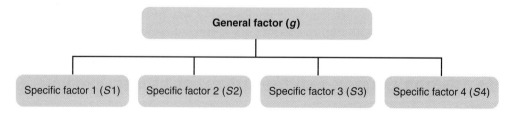

FIGURE 17.1 The hierarchical model of intelligence

Spearman did not seek to specify how many specific cognitive abilities exist: he was more interested in the general (*g*) factor. It is useful at this point to consider the relationship between Spearman's approach and that of Galton and Binet. Like Galton, Spearman assumed that individual differences in intellectual abilities are mainly hereditary. Spearman also agreed with Galton that sensory discrimination is positively correlated with intellectual ability. Not surprisingly, Spearman found it difficult to see benefits in Binet's intelligence scale. Binet was equally sceptical over Spearman's approach. Especially, Binet argued that it is not meaningful to measure someone's intelligence with a single score because two different individuals could obtain the same score although they had very different types of abilities.

Binet's criticism, and the fact that the research by Galton and others had failed to support the assumption that intelligence and acuity of perception are correlated, did not discourage Spearman. Instead he suggested that the disappointing findings in previous research had resulted from not having taken account of uncertainties in the measurement. Spearman (1904) created a formula, *correction for attenuation*, which has been used since then to calculate the correlation between two variables as if they had been measured perfectly, without any measurement error. When he calculated the analysis using the new formula, the results of his study were in support of Galton's hypothesis.

Since Spearman presented his theory, other researchers have either expanded on his concept of *g* or challenged his approach. Many theorists, for example, have argued that people can be intelligent in many different ways. One of the first to do so was Louis Leon Thurstone, a US psychologist. His analysis suggested that, rather than there being one general factor, there is a small set of independent factors (mental abilities) of equal importance. His analysis suggested that there were seven unrelated components:

1 verbal comprehension (understanding of written words)

2 word fluency (speed of generating words)

3 arithmetic ability (solving mathematical problems)

4 memory (remembering lists of words and numbers)

5 perceptual speed (speed of recognising forms and symbols)

6 inductive reasoning (finding rules for solving problems)

7 spatial visualisation (imagining rotations of objects or pictures).

From this finding, Thurstone concluded that human intellectual ability should be presented as a cognitive ability profile rather than as a single IQ score.

17.3.5 SUMMARY: THE SEARCH FOR INTELLIGENCE

The ideas presented by Galton and Binet may appear to contradict one another. It has been suggested, however, that in fact they represent two different aspects of intelligence. Despite this, since Binet's days, one of the most persistent disputes in the field of intelligence has circled around the question: is human intelligence best understood as one general factor (*g*) or as multiple dimensions of intellectual abilities? Although this might seem like a dry theoretical issue, it has an important implication. If you are proposing that the differences between people in their intelligence are largely due to heredity then there must be something that you can call intelligence and something you can inherit. Some people might argue that if there are many intelligences then the hereditary argument collapses.

In the next section, we will see that this debate among theorists and researchers continues to flourish.

17.4 CURRENT CONCEPTS OF INTELLIGENCE

17.4.1 THE ONE-FACTOR MODEL OF INTELLIGENCE REVISITED

Most researchers acknowledge that intelligence involves several specific cognitive abilities; however, some emphasise the central importance of Spearman's *g*. Others suggest that neither Spearman's nor Thurstone's model gives a good account of intelligence because they emphasise different aspects of human intelligence rather than representing two complete models. These theorists have developed their own models by combining Spearman's and Thurstone's models in different ways. We will begin by examining the one-factor approach, and then the hierarchical approach to intelligence will be scrutinised.

Why is it important for some to defend a position where only the general factor is of importance? And how is Thurstone's notion of **specific factors** treated in the one-factor approach? Theorists who support the one-factor model maintain that *g* is a biological, hereditary component of intelligence that explains a large proportion of the variance in many measures of intelligence. These theorists have formulated a number of arguments, derived from psychometric research:

1   In his research, Hans Eysenck (1916–1997) showed that measures of reaction time were strongly related to total score on a *IQ test*, which supported the assumption that 'speed of information processing is the essential basis of *g*' (Jensen, 1993: 54).

2   The *g* factor is strongly related to all tests of cognitive abilities (Jensen, 1998). Jensen argued that the *g* factor, or the total score on a test battery, gives more information about individual differences in intelligence than the specific factors, or the subscale scores.

3   *g* gives a better explanation of test performance on many cognitive ability tests than the specific factors do (Gottfredson, 1998).

4   *g* is a good predictor of educational achievement and work performance (Gottfredson, 1998).

In summary, the one-factor approach argues that it is necessary and sufficient to study one general underlying factor – and essential if you want to maintain the hereditarian position on intelligence. Jensen, Eysenck and Gottfredson have all been strong supporters of that position.

17.4.2 THE HIERARCHICAL MODELS OF INTELLIGENCE REVISITED

Other theorists have attempted to combine Spearman's and Thurstone's approaches into a **hierarchical** approach. A hierarchical theory implies one or more higher-order factors and one or more lower levels with several factors. One of the first to develop a hierarchical theory was the British psychologist Philip Vernon (1905–1987). Vernon assumed that intelligence comprises abilities at four different levels of generality, where two new levels were inserted between Spearman's *g* and Thurstone's specific factors.

A British psychologist, Raymond Cattell (1905–1998), designated a model with two levels. On the highest level, there were two types of general intelligence: **fluid intelligence** (*gf*) and **crystallised intelligence** (*gc*). The general cognitive abilities are based on a large number of subordinate factors: *gf* includes reasoning and the cognitive ability to draw inferences; *gc* comprises the knowledge and skills that people gain throughout their lives.

A North American psychologist, John Carroll (1916–2003), created a model with three levels or *strata*. In the first stratum, specific or 'narrow' abilities are included; in the second stratum, we find complex or 'broad' abilities; and, finally, the third stratum comprises a single general ability.

There is a common basis to the models by Vernon, Cattell and Carroll: all of them are developed within the **psychometric approach** to intelligence. That is, they endorse the presumption that intelligence is a measurable phenomenon.

> **Psychometric tests**   Instruments which have been developed for measuring mental characteristics. Psychological tests have been developed to measure a wide range of things, including creativity, job attitudes and skills, brain damage and, of course, 'intelligence'.

Other intelligence theorists are more critical of the psychometric approach and acknowledge that intelligence test scores are stable predictors of educational achievement. However, they believe that the attempt to 'base a concept of intelligence on test scores alone is to ignore many important aspects of mental ability' (Neisser et al., 1996: 78–79). Some of the aspects of mental ability that are ignored by the psychometric theory are emphasised in the approaches discussed below.

17.4.3 MULTIPLE INTELLIGENCES

A number of theorists have questioned the theoretical assumption that there is only one type of intelligence, which is measurable with intelligence tests. Instead, 'there are many different "intelligences" (systems of abilities), only a few of which can be captured by standard psychometric tests' (Neisser et al., 1996: 78). Thus, in addition to the cognitive abilities that we normally think of as intelligence, according to this school of thought there are several other types of intelligence. This theoretical approach is labelled cognitive-contextual: the focus is on the individual's abilities to adapt in different environmental contexts.

One influential theory about '**multiple intelligences**' was developed by an American psychologist, Howard Gardner. Gardner is critical of contemporary intelligence theorists' reliance on mental testing to assess intelligence while other ways of assessing cognitive abilities are devalued. If IQ tests are indispensable tools to assess intellectual abilities, how did people manage before the IQ test was invented? 'Were we incapable of making judgments about intellect before Alfred Binet and Francis Galton cobbled together the first set of psychometric items a century ago?' (Gardner, 1998: 18). Gardner pointed out that an abundant body of research has shown that the conventional method of intelligence assessment (that is, multiple choice tests) provides information about abilities in only one or two domains; that is, multiple choice tests may measure linguistic intelligence and logical-mathematical intelligence, but not the kinds of intelligence found in other domains.

Gardner defined intelligence as the capacity to solve problems and to create products that are valued in society (Gardner & Hatch, 1989). He developed the theory of multiple intelligences based on research findings which suggested that humans have a number of different intelligences that operate from different areas of the brain and thus the notion of a single intelligence is faulty. He also stated that different individuals have different combinations of the many intelligences.

Gardner initially defined seven different intelligences; however, he suggested that there may be additional ones.

1   **Linguistic intelligence** is the capacity to use spoken and written words and languages.

2   **Logical-mathematical intelligence** is the capacity for logic reasoning and dealing with numbers.

3   **Musical intelligence** has to do with hearing and performing sounds, rhythm and music.

4   **Spatial intelligence** is the ability to perceive spatial information.

5   **Bodily-kinaesthetic intelligence** is the ability to use one's body in various movements and activities.

6   **Interpersonal intelligence** is the ability to understand others and interact based on that understanding.

7   **Intrapersonal intelligence** is the capacity to understand one's own behaviours, thoughts and emotions.

17.4.4 THE ROONEY CONUNDRUM

There is a common misconception about Wayne Rooney, the English footballer (Figure 17.2), that he is not very intelligent. However, a brief look at Gardner's intelligences show that Rooney is an exceptional performer on at least three of the dimensions. His spatial awareness allows him to create and respond to cognitive maps, and this allows him to pass

FIGURE 17.2 Wayne Rooney: an intelligent footballer
© Ben Radford/Corbis

to team mates and understand where to be at the best time to score a goal. His body control is clearly excellent, but so is his ability to read the behaviour of others. This allows him to anticipate and predict what other players will do, where they will be, and how they will respond. It also allows him to disguise his own intentions and bluff opponents. He is clearly exceptionally intelligent. So why is he not always given credit for this? Maybe that is more to do with issues of class (Rooney coming from working-class origins) and prejudice than clear thinking about intelligence.

17.4.5 SUCCESSFUL INTELLIGENCE

Building on Gardner's theory of multiple intelligences and cognitive psychology, American psychologist Robert Sternberg distinguished between different aspects of intelligence. Similar to Gardner, Sternberg saw conventional notions of intelligence as being too narrow. But he did not agree that the alternative theory of intelligence should encompass abilities such as musical and bodily-kinaesthetic ones. This was because, following his definition of intelligence as the individual's 'adaptation to, shaping of, and selection of real-world environments' (Sternberg, 1984: 271), these abilities do not match the criteria for intelligences. Instead they should be thought of as talents.

Sternberg's triarchic (i.e. three-part) theory specifies three different aspects of intelligence: *analytic*, *creative* and *practical*. When someone has the ability to balance and use the three aspects of intelligence effectively, s/he has a **successful intelligence**.

The individual uses **analytical intelligence** when accomplishing tasks and overcoming obstacles to solve problems that s/he is familiar with. For example, when you think about how to get home from a night out, you might first consider the different modes of transport available – which are running, at what times and cost, how safe they are etc. – in your analysis of how best to get home that night.

When the task is to function well in one's sociocultural environment, **practical intelligence** is applied. The individual's thinking draws from previous, often tacit, experiences when adapting to a certain environment, reshaping that environment, or selecting a new environment. So, you have previously fixed your Playstation when it broke from overuse. You can use that experience to help you fix your Wii.

When people find themselves in a relatively new context, or are facing a new kind of problem, they are using **creative intelligence**. What would you do if an axe-wielding maniac suddenly appeared from nowhere and started running towards you screaming loudly? You would have to rely on your creative intelligence to come up with a way of dealing with this situation (which you probably haven't come across before).

EXERCISE   Intelligence-related words, part 2: intuitive models of intelligence

Go back to the list of intelligence-related words we suggested you wrote in the exercise at the beginning of the chapter. Look at these words and think about when either you have used them yourself or someone has used them at you. What was happening to provoke the use of these words? For example, I forgot my phone the other day and immediately thought to myself, 'What a fool.' So, forgetting my phone made me think I had been stupid.

Make a long list and then look at what is behind each of these acts. That way you will get an idea of the things you think are intelligent and unintelligent. You might like to go one step further and look at an IQ test to see how many of the items you came up with are covered by the test. You will be surprised how few are there.

17.4.6 SUMMARY: INTELLIGENCE, ONE OR MANY?

Compared to the conventional view on intelligence, Gardner's and Sternberg's theories represent a completely different perspective. Both have questioned whether conventional tests really assess all abilities necessary to succeed in life and in school.

Gardner's theory of multiple intelligences has been well received, especially perhaps among practitioners. One example of how his work has been used is a report by Hoerr (2000) which seeks to show how Gardner's theory can be used in schools. Hoerr's idea is that the teacher who uses a teaching model based on Gardner's theory will recognise that not all people learn in the same way, nor do they prefer the same way of demonstrating their understanding. In Gardner's words there 'is no reason why everyone has to learn … in the same way' (1993b: 21).

17.5 GROUP DIFFERENCES IN INTELLIGENCE

17.5.1 GENDER DIFFERENCES

Most intelligence theorists agree that there is no difference in overall average intelligence scores between genders (Neisser et al., 1996). Over the years, this non-difference has been confirmed in many studies, yet there are some who claim that there are gender differences, with males having a higher average score than females. A strong advocate of this notion is Richard Lynn, a controversial UK psychologist.

Others have pointed out that research on gender differences in brain size has reported inconsistent findings (Witelson et al., 2006). Others again have suggested that the size of the brain is not that important. Instead, what matters is that the female brain has other advantages, such as a greater density of neurons, which results in more efficient processing (Jensen & Johnson, 1994).

North American psychologist Richard Haier and his co-workers are using brain imaging to study intelligence in men and women (Haier et al., 2004). They have concluded that there is no difference in general intelligence between men and women; and that men and women can achieve similar results on an intelligence test using different brain regions.

Although the difference between men and women in overall intelligence scores is either very small or non-existent, there are gender differences in specific abilities. Thus, many studies have reported that females perform better on some tasks and males perform better on others. Such findings seem to suggest that women tend to have different cognitive abilities than men. For example, women outperform men on tests of verbal abilities, such as reading, and certain memory tasks (Halpern et al., 2007). Men, on the other hand, perform better than women on mathematical reasoning and mechanical tests (Neisser et al., 1996).

How can we understand the gender differences in cognitive abilities? Researchers who have chosen to study intelligence from a biological psychology perspective provide answers from studies of brain activities and structures. At the other extreme, we find researchers who emphasise the importance of the external cultural context for understanding intelligence. In between, there are those who believe that it is difficult for any single theoretical approach to explain the difference. Halpern and colleagues (2007) proposed a psychobiosocial model, which emphasises the complicated interaction of biological, psychological and psychosocial/environmental factors. A similar thought was presented by

Race Commonly used to refer to groups of people such as white people or black people. It implies a genetic component to the differences between these groups, but research shows that the term 'race' has no biological validity and is best described as a political construct.

Racism The use of the pervasive power imbalance between races to oppress dominated peoples by devaluing their experience, behaviour and aspirations.

Neisser and co-workers: 'It is clear that any adequate model of sex differences in cognition will have to take both biological and psychological variables (and their interactions) into account' (1996: 92).

17.5.2 RACE AND INTELLIGENCE

Race has been an issue in psychology for over 100 years. As we saw above, there has been a view that it is possible to measure differences between races to show the superiority of one race over another at certain tasks. A battleground for these arguments has been intelligence. This section is designed to give you a flavour of this controversy and show why the scientific argument matters.

Earlier in the chapter we described the mass testing of US soldiers at the beginning of the twentieth century and the observations that were made about differences in the average scores of people of different nationalities and races. Of course there are a number of possible explanations for these differences. Have a quick look at three of the questions from the written test and consider who would be more likely to know the answers:

> Washington is to Adams as first is to:
>
> Crisco is a: patent medicine, disinfectant, toothpaste, food product.
>
> Christy Mathewson is famous as a: writer, artist, baseball player, comedian.

The psychologist who ran the tests, Yerkes, asserted that the tests measured 'native intellectual ability' (cited in Gould, 1981: 349), yet it is clear that in fact you need a good level of general and cultural knowledge to get the answers right.

There were also a number of problems in the administration of the tests. In particular, many who were illiterate in English were still allocated to the Alpha test (which required reading and writing) and so scored zero or near to zero. This created a systematic bias in the test since recent immigrants who had a poor grasp of English, and black men who had been given little, if any, formal education were unable to score on the Alpha test. Another problem arising from the way the tests were administered was that even the Beta test (using pictures) required the use of a pencil and the writing of numbers, and many men had never held a pencil in their lives.

In his critical review of the tests, Gould (1981) reported that three 'facts' were created from the testing data:

1   The average mental age of white Americans was about 13. (Unfortunately, this had been defined as the intellectual level of a moron, so the tests appeared to indicate that the average American was a moron.) (Note: I advise readers to hold their ethnocentrism in check at this point!)

2 European immigrants could be graded by their country of origin.

3 The average score of black men was lower than the average score of white men.

These three 'facts' can be adequately explained by the administration difficulties of the testing and the level of literacy of the groups of people taking the tests. In fact, a reanalysis of the data showed that performance depended on the length of time a person had lived in America, suggesting that culture and language played a large part in test performance. However, a much more sinister explanation was given for the results. It was argued that white people were superior to black people, and that Americans were superior to many European peoples.

Political beliefs triumphed over scientific analysis and the eugenic explanation took hold. One of the consequences of this was the passing of the Immigration Restriction Act in 1924 by the American Congress, which selectively stopped certain national groups from emigrating to the USA. The scientists who supported the eugenics argument lobbied the politicians and, according to Gould, 'won one of the greatest victories of scientific racism in American history' (1981: 352). Please note, this is obviously *not* a good thing!

17.5.3 INTELLIGENCE TESTING AND RACE

The idea of there being racial differences has simmered for the last 100 years. It is common even today to suggest that there are measurable differences between groups on all manner of abilities including musicality, personality (e.g. 'the Latin temperament'), sexuality and intelligence, but there are a number of scientific and political objections to this view. In the first place, we can only investigate racial differences if we can first define what race is and then carry out appropriate studies. As Jones (1991) points out, there are a number of problems including:

- It is difficult to define race.

- The history of social movement has meant that many people have ancestors from many parts of the world.

- Within-race variability is much greater than between-race variability, or in other words you cannot use someone's race to predict how intelligent they are likely to be as there is a wide range of abilities in all groups.

- When comparative research is carried out, it has so far been impossible to obtain comparable samples of people from different races.

The idea that there are biologically different races of people is controversial to say the least. For example, how do we define 'race'? By country of birth? Or parents' birth? Any definitions of race come down to social criteria and not biological ones, and the differences are most likely to be due to social differences, such as income and opportunity.

As mentioned above, early IQ tests were used to suggest differences between different racial groups. This is an argument that has rumbled on for over 100 years without ever

Heritability The proportion of variance in the phenotype that can be attributed to genetic variance. It is a widely misunderstood concept and is commonly misused in debates about nature and nurture. It is a measure that may vary with the range of genetic backgrounds and range of environments studied. It is therefore a mistake to argue that a high figure for heritability in a particular population in a particular environment means that the characteristic is genetically determined.

resolving itself. There are many problems with attempting any exploration of racial differences, especially where the issue of intelligence is concerned. Controversy typically arises from the fact that differences between one group and another have often been assumed to represent differences in ability rather than differences in performance. In truth, the only evidence we have are performance scores, and we have to explain why groups perform differently. This could be due to a range of cultural, educational and motivational factors, and these explanations are much more plausible than any genetic explanations for the reasons described by Jones.

There is also the matter of how the genetic effect is calculated, and the statistic that is commonly cited is **heritability**. This statistic estimates how much the variation within any given population is due to genetic factors. It does not, however, tell us about why two populations will differ and so contributes nothing to our understanding of this issue (see Rose et al., 1984). It also fails to tell us anything about how much genetics affects the characteristics of an individual.

Problems like these make assertions about racial differences very difficult, and in fact a leading psychometrician suggests that:

> The only advantage in setting out the different scores on IQ tests of racial groups is to give ammunition to those who wish to decry them. It adds nothing to theoretical understanding or to the social or educational practice. (Kline, 1991: 96)

KEY STUDY Sternberg, R.J., Grigorenko, E.L., Ngrosho, D., Tantufuye, E., Mbise, A., Nokes, C., Jukes, M., & Bundy, D.A. (2002). Assessing intellectual potential in rural Tanzanian school children. *Intelligence, 30*, 141–162.

Some controversial researchers (Lynn & Vanhanen, 2002; Rushton & Jensen, 2005) have suggested that some populations with African heritage perform at lower mean levels on conventional IQ tests compared to populations with for example European heritage.

This interpretation of the test results has been questioned by many other researchers, who have claimed that the IQ test measures intellectual abilities that are less relevant for black Africans who live in non-Westernised environmental contexts. In addition, these people may have no prior experience with the procedures of taking an IQ test.

To examine this claim, Sternberg and colleagues (2002) used an alternative to conventional testing to examine the performance of 358 children who were 11 through 13 years of age from 10 schools in rural Tanzania. The alternative procedure used dynamic testing, which is based on Vygotsky's idea of the zone of proximal development (you will find more details about Vygotsky's theory in Chapter 14). Dynamic testing differs from conventional testing in three important ways: (1) it emphasises the psychological processes that are involved in learning and change rather than measuring pre-existing abilities; (2) the test taker receives feedback from the test administrator; and (3) the relationship between the test taker and the test administrator is an active two-way interaction characterised by teaching and support.

The performance of the children in the experimental group was compared to the performance of a sample of 100 children who took the test administered using conventional procedures. A set of three tasks was administered to the children in the experimental group using the alternative procedures, and the same set of tasks was then administered to the control group, this time using conventional procedures. Each test given to the experimental group comprised (1) pre-test; (2) feedback and the teaching of skills and strategies that contributed to improve the test results; and (3) post-test. Children in the control group received only the pre-test and the post-test. The results showed that children in the experimental group improved significantly more from pre-test to post-test compared to the children in the control group who did not receive feedback. Sternberg et al. concluded that the children in the experimental group had intellectual abilities not measured by conventional IQ tests.

CHAPTER SUMMARY

17.6 In this chapter we have looked at different theories of intelligence. Specifically, we have examined how the theoretical assumptions about the mechanisms underlying intelligence determine our view of intelligence and how intelligence can be measured.

To understand where the current IQ test had its beginning, we have discussed the early attempts by Galton and Binet. We explored how the psychometric approach, which assumes that intelligence is a measurable factor, continued to be developed by Spearman, who believed that intelligence is one single factor, and Thurstone, who argued that intelligence is many different intellectual abilities.

We also looked at more recent intelligence theories that acknowledge that intelligence comprises a number of different abilities. We saw that one strand of thought, represented by theorists such as Carroll, Cattell and Vernon, emphasises that the psychometric approach can be developed further through combining the models of Spearman and Thurstone. We examined the theories of Gardner and Sternberg, both of which argue that the psychometric approach leaves out much of what intelligence is.

Finally, we examined gender, racial and cultural differences in intelligence, and found that this work is a minefield of controversy as scientists seek to further their beliefs about people through their work. We also found that both researchers who claim that intelligence is in the genes, and those who argue that the environment plays an important role in intelligence, often have a general understanding that both genes and the environment are important for intelligence. The chapter emphasised that psychologists generally acknowledge that there is an ongoing interaction between the genes and the environment, and this interaction shapes our intellectual abilities.

DISCUSSION QUESTIONS

1   We have seen that there has long been a debate over whether there is one general kind of intelligence or several different kinds. Where do you stand on this question? What reasons can you give in support of your views?

2   There has also been lengthy debate over the role of (a) nature and (b) nurture in accounting for differences in intelligence. Which do you think is most important? What reasons can you give in support of your views?

3   What do you think IQ tests actually measure?

4   Consider the differences between the major theories of intelligence outlined above. What are the implications for: (a) intelligence testing; (b) learning; (c) schooling?

SUGGESTIONS FOR FURTHER READING

You may wish to read about the development of intelligence, IQ testing or recent views on intelligence. The latter include the concept of 'emotional intelligence' put forward by Daniel Goleman. A good and interesting starting point for any student interested in intelligence is Mackintosh, N.J. (1998). *IQ and human intelligence.* Oxford: Oxford University Press.

On the history of intelligence, see Deary, I.J. (2000). *Looking down on human intelligence: from psychometrics to the brain.* Oxford: Oxford University Press; Richardson, K. (1991). *Understanding intelligence.* Milton Keynes: Open University Press; Sternberg, R.J. (ed.) (2000). *Handbook of intelligence.* Cambridge: Cambridge University Press.

For information about IQ tests, see Gould, S.J. (1996). *The mismeasure of man.* New York: Norton; Mackintosh, N.J. (1998). *IQ and human intelligence.* Oxford: Oxford University Press.

For recent views on intelligence, see Khalfa, J. (ed.) (1994). *What is intelligence?* Cambridge: Cambridge University Press; Sternberg, R.J., & Grigorenko, E. (2007). *Teaching for successful intelligence: to increase student learning and achievement* (2nd edn). Thousand Oaks, CA: Corwin. If you are interested in an alternative view on intelligence, you may wish to look up literature on emotional intelligence, starting with a pop psychology book: Goleman, D. (1996). *Emotional intelligence.* London: Bloomsbury.

18 SELF

Lead authors **Jill Arnold** and **Brendan Gough**

INTRODUCTION

18.1

Who am I and how do I know who I am? When challenged to say who we are we commonly reply with our name and a list of categories of things we do and places we go. Awareness of ourselves as individuals, the notion of a 'self', is something that most people believe differentiates us from other animals. Over the years, psychologists have proposed numerous explanations of what the self is and numerous techniques to investigate and describe the self. This chapter introduces some of the most important discussions and methods.

?

FRAMING QUESTIONS

Can you be whoever you want to be?
Are you really what you wear?
Does what you own change who you are?
What does it mean to 'perform' your 'gendered self'?
How can we know ourselves when we change so much?

EXERCISE   Who am I? Part 1

Write down as many responses as you can (up to 20) as quickly as possible to the question, 'Who am I?' Keep these responses for analysis later on in the chapter.

18.2 THE QUESTION OF SELF

'Who are YOU', said the Caterpillar.

Alice replied rather shyly, 'I hardly know sir, just at present – at least I know who I WAS when I got up this morning, but I think I must have changed several times since then'.

'What do you mean by that?,' said the Caterpillar sternly. 'Explain yourself!'
'I can't explain MYSELF, I'm afraid sir,' said Alice, 'because I'm not myself you see.'
(Carroll, 1865: ch. 5)

Psychologists trying to explain 'self' can fully appreciate the dilemma faced by Alice: 'Somehow psychological theory of the self must encompass both the stability and uniqueness; the variability and multiplicity' (Harré & Van Langenhove, 1999: 60). It seems so obvious that we are individual selves ('myself' or 'my self'), that we each have a *sense* of the self or know about it, can refer to ourselves and what we are like. It is also often taken for granted that we have many roles or **identities** that are recognisable by others. Even mere passers-by (like Alice's caterpillar!) may assume they know what kind of person we are. If we are in doubt, or we are challenged about who or what we are, we can usually refer to our name, where we live, or our school, and perhaps offer ID, such as a driver's licence, to provide evidence for our claims. That we have an individual character – influenced by our families and biology, and shaped by events and experiences – that can be readily categorised is familiar 'folk psychology'.

There are a number of questions for psychologists to consider concerning identity. On the one hand, we each seem unique; on the other hand, in many ways we resemble other people. Each person may remain the same individual bodily, yet also change a good deal across the lifespan or even from one situation to another: that is, the roles we adopt may change. However, a key issue faced by psychology and which continues to be a challenge (as the quote above suggests) concerns the complexity of self and identity: yes, people are unique and always the same *bodily* person, i.e. an *individual,* but at the same time they will appear to be quite a lot like some others (judging from the way they dress or talk or eat food, or do certain jobs). Moreover, although we *are* just one person, at times we will play very different roles; for example, when we are at home we may not swear or drink, but being out with mates reveals a different side to us. So how do we understand and research these tensions concerning identity? This chapter will provide a tour of key psychological concepts which have been developed to address the complexities of being a person. These concepts arise from diverse theories and often deploy distinctive methods for understanding selfhood, as we shall see.

> **Identity** Awareness of shared distinctive characteristics by members of a group. Identity may be considered in a number of ways, e.g. in cultural terms as ethnic identity, or in terms of sexual orientation.

SELF AND PERSONALITY

18.3 Who in the world am I? Ah, that's the great puzzle. (Carroll, 1865: ch. 2)

EXERCISE Who am I? Part 2

Reflect on your responses to our opening 'Who am I?' exercise. Consider how many of your responses relate to personality traits (extraverted, intelligent, humorous etc.). Then think how many relate to social categories, roles and group memberships (as, for example, son, daughter, partner, student, Scottish, woman, man). Would you say those responses produced first are more important to your sense of self? How difficult do you find it to provide a satisfactory answer?

Mainstream psychology approached the 'puzzle' of self largely through the concept of **personality** and the idea that each individual possesses a recognisable character or set of attributes which are relatively fixed throughout life. In fact, though, the notion of personality is a very Western construct reflecting the individualist ethos of nations like the USA and UK (Rose, 1989): in other nations such as Japan, India and Brazil (which are more *collectivist*), group memberships, social roles and obligations are emphasised rather than individual traits, preferences and achievements. Western psychology therefore reflects the common-sense thinking of its surrounding culture.

However, psychology moves away from common sense when it comes to the idea that self and individuality can be categorised and measured. Traditional personality theories and psychometric approaches use tests, scales and questionnaires so that individuals can be classified as, say, 'extroverted', 'achievement oriented' or 'nurturing' (see Chapter 16 for an account of this approach to personality and Chapter 17 for psychometrics). These approaches rest on the belief that we have personality structures with qualities, traits, characteristics and preferences and that we know enough about the social and cultural practices of people to ask them the questions that will elicit responses that provide standardised scores.

> **Personality**   The characteristic patterns of thoughts, feelings and behaviours that make a person unique.
>
> **Psychometric approach**   Any attempt to assess and express numerically the mental characteristics of behaviour in individuals, usually through specific tests for personality or intelligence or some kind of attitude measurement.

> **Humanistic psychology**   The humanistic approach explains the subjective experience of individuals in terms of the way they interpret past events. Humanistic psychology partly arose in reaction to the mechanical (stimulus/response) models of behaviourism. Borrowing ideas from psychoanalysis, it sought to affirm the dignity and worth of all people.
>
> **Phenomenology**   Based on the idea that the ordinary world of lived experience is taken for granted and often unnoticed, phenomenology attempts to discover how people know and understand objects (and other people) from the way they perceive and construct ideas about the social world around them.

18.3.1 THE SUBJECTIVE EXPERIENCE OF 'BEING ME'

The concept of personality (and its measurement) has been criticised however for failing to recognise the complex, dynamic and socially embedded nature of subjective experience. Personality scales in psychometric tests offer only a limited range of mutually exclusive options (for example, yes/no, agree/disagree) and therefore do not allow individuals to elaborate on their responses. In contrast, psychologists who use qualitative research methods encourage individuals to talk about themselves and their experiences in their own terms. **Humanistic** and **phenomenological** psychologists, for example, are interested in finding out about how people's **self-concept** is influenced by life events, typically involving a transition (e.g. falling ill, divorce, changing jobs) (see Stevens, 1996). All manner of experiences have been studied through compiling and analysing individuals' accounts, from being a victim of crime to enjoying 'peak' or 'flow' experiences, though the focus is often on 'lived experience', i.e. those set in the context of their lifeworld.

An assumption in such research is that individuals 'know' their own lives and can provide descriptions of their experiences. It is the job of the researcher to capture and identify the psychological aspects of these experiences. Another characteristic of this approach is that individuals' experiences are treated as unique (at least to some extent) and so everyone has a distinctive 'self', and whatever the experience being studied, the overarching aim of the analysis is to reveal some of a person's authentic sense of self. In the UK, the methodology known as **interpretive phenomenological analysis** (shortened to IPA: see Smith, 2004) is a popular qualitative approach for understanding individual experiences using in-depth, semi-structured interviews and systematic analysis of transcripts. IPA is notably used to investigate how individuals deal with life experiences. See the key study for a summary of one such analysis.

Self-concept or **self-identity** Self-knowledge and memory allow people to develop a life story and to understand how others perceive them. The self-concept is the product, therefore, of self-assessments – some relatively permanent, such as personality attributes and knowledge of skills and abilities, others less so, such as occupation, interests and physical status.

Interpretive phenomenological analysis (IPA) An experiential qualitative approach to research in psychology and the social sciences. It was developed by Jonathan Smith and it offers insights into how a person makes sense of a particular experiential phenomenon – the 'insider's perspective'.

KEY STUDY Smith, J.A., & Osborn, M. (2007). Pain as an assault on the self: an interpretive phenomenological analysis. *Psychology and Health*, *22*, 517–534.

Smith and Osborn's paper presents an in-depth study, illustrating how chronic, benign, low back pain may have a serious debilitating impact on the sufferer's sense of self. Six patients were interviewed and transcripts were subjected to interpretive phenomenological analysis. The analysis pointed to the powerful ways in which chronic pain has a negative impact on patients' self and identity, and some participants describe how the ensuing derogatory self-image seemed to lead to their directing negative emotions towards other people.

The analysis gives a detailed account of these processes at work, which are then considered in relation to the literature, including studies of illness and identity, shame and acceptance.

18.3.2 PERSONAL CONSTRUCT THEORY

Not all humanistic-phenomenological approaches rely on interview-based accounts. A notable exception is the *repertory grid* (RG) devised by George Kelly (1955), the pioneer of *personal construct theory*. PCT maintains that the self is defined by perceptions, or constructs, concerning our personal world. Further, each person's construct system is regarded as relatively distinctive, i.e. individuals will see things in different ways, using particular constructs which help make sense of the world around them. For example, the construct religious–secular (constructs are 'bipolar', i.e. two-sided) may be a core construct which some individuals use to differentiate people and events in their world, whereas other individuals perceive the world in terms of liberal–conservative, or weak–strong, and so on.

So, an individual will use one or a few core constructs to help understand, simplify and predict relevant people and experiences. They will also have other, less important or peripheral, constructs which they use only occasionally or only in relation to specific events. So, even if two people share the same core constructs, the content and range of their construct system will likely differ, and in any case the way they define and apply their core constructs may well differ.

In short, Kelly stressed the uniqueness of personal construct systems as a consequence of a person's life history. His theory also emphasises *personal agency*: people actively interpret their environment and try to anticipate future events, much like psychologists in fact! Kelly's RG method is a relatively straightforward tool for generating insights into an individual's current construct system.

In brief it works like this. First, you select a topic that is important, for example your life at university. Second, you select around 12 elements in that life which are most likely people you know at the university like lecturers, housemates, work colleagues, friends etc. Third, you select three of these elements and identify how one of the elements is different to the other two. So let us say you choose the three elements of 'lecturer', 'housemate' and 'friend' and you differentiate between them on the basis of how much fun they are. You might consider your friends and housemates to be 'fun', and lecturers 'not fun'. In this case, 'fun–not fun' is the construct you are using to analyse the elements. You repeat this process with a number of different sets of three elements, having thought up a number of ways in which they differ (i.e. more constructs). Finally you draw a grid of your construct and elements and rate each combination of element and construct on a seven-point scale. It takes a while to do but it allows you to identify your own unique way of analysing the world.

The repertory grid can be a useful tool to help illuminate how a person is currently thinking about themselves in relation to others within a particular context (university, work, home etc.). It provides a snapshot rather than a portrait of the whole person, so it would be interesting to contrast grids over time and place to help gauge levels of change, continuity and consistency of personal constructs.

Humanistic and phenomenological approaches have been criticised for neglecting the wider social and cultural contexts which influence and constrain individual experiences and identities. According to their critics, these approaches are preoccupied with the private and personal, and miss out the public and social. This is not to say that interpersonal relationships and environmental factors are not recognised by humanistic and phenomenological approaches or that social influences are not reported by research participants; rather, the emphasis tends to be on personal experiences and perceptions. In this way, humanistic-phenomenological approaches share a psychological emphasis with the psychometric focus on personality, despite underlying methodological and theoretical differences. At the other end of the psychological spectrum, *social* psychologists have been concerned with studying those group and social identities to which individuals are drawn, and it is to these approaches which we now turn.

GROUP MEMBERSHIP AND SOCIAL IDENTITY

18.4

One of the most important concepts in social psychology is the idea of the social or cultural group. A great deal of attention has been paid to investigations into the effects of intragroup (within-group) and inter-group (between-group) dynamics (see Chapters 10 and 11 respectively). According to Henri Tajfel's (1981) **social identity theory,** identifying (or indeed refusing to identify) as a member of a group, and whether membership is chosen (for example Manchester City Football Club fan) or designated (for example by sex, age, nationality, ethnicity), can affect how we see and feel about ourselves. This theory suggests that personal identity is linked to **social identity** and that group memberships are important to our sense of self and help define who we are. Further, Tajfel suggests that self-esteem may be boosted if our 'ingroups' are positively evaluated. For example, if our national identity is enhanced by, say, sporting success in international competitions (for example, our team wins the World Cup), then it follows that we will feel good about ourselves. In fact, Tajfel maintains that we are motivated to perceive our 'ingroups' in positive ways, as this will lead to positive feelings about self. Conversely, we will also be motivated to perceive other 'outgroups' in negative ways to help ensure that our ingroups are viewed positively, relatively speaking. The theory has been influential as a way of explaining intergroup prejudice and conflict:

> According to social identity theory, the distinctive characteristics of group behaviour arise from the psychological processes of categorisation and self-enhancement. These psychological characteristics include depersonalisation, ethnocentrism, and relative uniformity of action and attitude among group members. (Abrams, 1992: 57)

There are many other aspects of social identity theory (SIT) (see Chapters 10 and 11 for further discussion) that help us to appreciate how our self-image or identity is bound up with our identification with others in our group.

SIT has, however, been criticised on several grounds. For example, there is the problem of what counts as a group. Being male or female (or any other biological category such as being, old, diabetic etc.) is not the same as a social group such as following a football team

Social identity theory Tajfel and Turner's (1979) social identity theory examines intergroup and ingroup discrimination based on the idea that a person has several selves that function at different levels of social circles, e.g. personal, family, community, national.

or a religious system, though all such categories carry social meaning according to the culture as to what a man or woman 'should' be like, or expectations about the behaviour of a patient, a pensioner or a student. Also, people may feel ambivalent about the groups they are associated with and have a complex, shifting perspective on group membership which may not entail hostility toward other groups. For example, someone may identify as a Catholic but disagree with edicts on contraception and women priests, while being sympathetic to aspects of Buddhist teachings. SIT therefore presents individuals as rather mechanistically 'contained' within a group and responding to group values and norms in predictable ways, almost as if we are cognitively wired to maximise intergroup differences in self-serving ways (see Billig, 1985; Radley, 1995).

18.4.1 SOCIAL ROLES, THE PRESENTATION OF SELF AND THE DRAMATURGICAL ANALOGY

In contrast to psychological approaches which focus on individuals' identification with the group, social psychologists are also interested in how the self is manifested in a wide range of social *situations*. One formerly popular perspective, especially in the USA, was **role theory** (e.g. see Dahrendorf, 1973), where individuals are characterised by their different roles in different situations (e.g. work, home). Unlike the humanistic-phenomenological emphasis on a singular private self, role theories consider multiple *personas* across different social contexts. So, for example, we would expect a person's behaviour as a mother to be different from her behaviour as a work colleague or an athlete etc. Each social role carries different expectations: for example, motherhood is normatively associated with being responsible and nurturing, while a work colleague will be expected to be hardworking and task oriented. In addition, some social roles will be more important than others, so being a parent might be central for some people, while being a professional might be key for others.

Trying to fulfil many (competing) demands of roles may result in **role conflict**. For example, trying to achieve good grades as a student while also being a paid worker to finance one's studies may create difficulties. Historically, some theorists (e.g. Parsons, 1954) assumed that social roles were adopted in a mechanical, conformist fashion, suggesting that individuals were fixed in place by social constraints. However, there may be an element of choice in deciding which roles are core, and some theorists have therefore emphasised personal agency over social constraints.

> **Role theory** A perspective in social psychology that considers how we manage everyday activity (rights, duties, expectations and norms of behaviour) by fulfilment of socially defined social roles (e.g. mother, manager, teacher).

Traditional role theory considered the *actual* roles we play in everyday life (such as student, sister, customer) and their constraints (such as sex, social class) and the expectations people have about them. A contrasting theoretical approach to social self is based on what Erving Goffman (1959) called the **dramaturgical analogy**. This approach looks at social life as if individuals were *performing* their everyday roles in ways thought acceptable or sometimes strategically, to secure certain social outcomes. For example, a child may *present* as ill in order to receive sympathy from a parent and miss school, or an adolescent boy may present himself (his *self*) as 'cool' when interacting with a girl he likes in front of his male friends, and so on. Goffman invites us to think of self, therefore, as negotiated in the process of social interaction – a set of 'performances' which evolve in the presence of others and which shift across time and place. In order to be convincing in our various roles, avoiding embarrassment or conflict in the presentation of self, emphasis is placed on preparation for the performance of self (usually away from the public gaze, for example the business of getting dressed in the morning) and the need to choose the necessary 'props'. This perspective, according to which the self is multiple and performed, has been developed in different ways by **ethnomethodologists** (e.g. Garfinkel, 1967) and more recently by social psychologists interested in discourse practices (e.g. Edwards & Potter, 1992; Potter & Wetherell, 1987) and the socially constructed self (see later sections) and even the presentation of self in virtual spaces (Miller & Arnold, 2001).

Dramaturgical analogy Erving Goffman proposed a theatrical metaphor as a way of understanding self in everyday life and seeing social interactions as though they were dramatic performances, considering the costumes, the props etc. which go towards making up the 'scenes' played out by people.

Ethnomethodology Not a formal research method, but an approach to empirical study that aims to discover the things that people *do* in particular situations and how they create the patterns and orderliness of social life to gain a sense of social structure.

EXERCISE Social roles

Reference to Goffman here acknowledges his important ideas about how we manage the 'multiplicity of social identities or selves'. As you read the rest of the chapter, we invite you to consider the following questions and see how many different ways you could answer them:

- We may play different roles, but does this mean we have no 'true' self?
- How would other people describe you (e.g. parent, friend, colleague)? Do these descriptions differ and, if so, are you all of these selves? Are any of them how you see yourself? How do you 'manage' discrepancies?
- Are you ever aware of trying to fulfil too many or conflicting roles? How do you feel when this happens, and why?
- What happens when people challenge 'you', i.e. when they are not convinced about your identity, authenticity or role? They may say things like 'You look too young', 'You're just a girl' or 'Who do you think you are?'
- Can we be ourselves without an audience? How much do we rely on others to help us be ourselves?
- How much could you be yourself without the appropriate 'props' and costume? What do *you* rely on to be you?

18.5 EXPLAINING IDENTITY

18.5.1 DISCOURSE AND IDENTITY

Role theories and SIT examine social identities by designing experiments involving group judgements or by observations of the way people manage the performance of identity in social interactions. Another way of studying self and identity is to examine how people actually talk about themselves (and others) in practice. Social psychologists interested in discourse and social interaction have looked at the construction and negotiation of self and identity in different social contexts (see Burman & Parker, 1993; Potter & Wetherell, 1987).

In this body of work, *self* is regarded as a *construct* which is presented and negotiated during interactions with others. As such, self is not a 'thing' we can feel or touch but an ongoing project which evolves and changes within diverse social contexts. Here the focus is on how self-presentations are informed by culturally important discourses, or representations. For example, the notion of 'personality' is a popular way of conceiving self in Western cultures and is constantly deployed in mass market magazines, pop psychology texts and everyday talk. It is inevitable that in such contexts people will describe themselves and others as having a particular type of personality or character. But we also use other language to describe self and identity, including concepts of 'true' selves, social roles, performance and group identification – highlighting that psychological theories are linked to common understandings.

KEY RESEARCHER   Margaret Wetherell

FIGURE 18.1   Margaret Wetherell

In 1987, Margie Wetherell and Jonathan Potter wrote a ground-breaking book *Discourse and social psychology: beyond attitudes and behaviour.* It set out the principles of a psychological approach that challenged traditional ways of understanding social interactions and showed how discursive psychology, discourse analysis and the wider implications of patterns in people's talk was at the centre of the study of self and identity. These ideas have developed since then with increasingly diverse research (using ethnographic and other qualitative methods in social psychology) as part of postmodern, critical, social constructionist or feminist approaches to natural language use. Margie Wetherell has played a key role in developing this research and our understanding of psychological states and subjectivity (including emotion and memory) but also ideology and collective sense-making and the exploration of constructive and constructed language.

Such developments have also contributed to our understanding of self in relation to such issues as: racist discourse; health care decision making; gender identities (in particular studies of men's identities), ethnic diversity, citizen participation and democratic decisions.

Discourse analysis of talk about race, gender or disability can be valuable in highlighting contemporary forms of group membership prejudice and ways of 'doing' identity. For example, research suggests that the use of disclaimers (Hewitt & Stokes, 1975) is common in the process of potentially controversial claims about groups. In the context of race, the classic formulation runs 'I'm not racist but ...'; in other words, a prefacing statement is used before uttering one which could be heard as prejudiced to manage possible accusations of racism (see Billig, 1988). Such talk is also a way of doing what social psychologists call 'identity work', i.e. implicitly presenting one's own group as superior. Research by Gough (e.g. 1998; 2002) has examined heterosexual men's talk about women and gay men and highlighted similar disclaimers (e.g. 'I've always tolerated it but ...'). Gough argues that such patterns of talk are designed to inoculate the speaker against criticism while at the same time presenting self and (heterosexual) men in general as 'masculine'. In this way identity is relational – meaning that we describe ourselves implicitly or explicitly in relation to (or against) particular others.

Discourse analysts have also shown that talk about our selves is oriented to issues of 'stake' and 'accountability'. In other words, speakers are often concerned about attributing personal interest (stake) about an issue to self and others as well as attending to matters of blame and responsibility. For example, a house meeting arranged to discuss domestic chores might involve all sorts of claims from different parties about who is (un-)interested in cleaning and who is (ir-)responsible in matters of tidiness. Throughout this discussion, identities are being constructed, defended, negotiated, challenged and disavowed. For example, Sally's claim about being tidy might be disputed, while Dan's promise to clean the bathroom might be treated with disdain. *Identity work* gets done in mundane situations like these all the time in interactions with partners, colleagues, peers, children and parents. People are highly skilled and creative when discussing, arguing, joking, complaining and praising, all the while negotiating subject positions for themselves and others.

It is clear, however, that some subject positions are more difficult to successfully claim than others because of *prevailing normative assumptions*. For example, for a man to claim an interest in cosmetics risks censure because of stereotypical notions of masculinity, while for a woman to profess an interest in weightlifting also courts controversy. Research by Wetherell and Edley (1999), based on group discussions with men, highlighted how many men are concerned to avoid claiming stereotypical 'macho' identities for themselves while instead positioning themselves as 'ordinary' or 'rebellious'.

Hegemony   A situation where the interests of the powerful can marginalise and counter the claims of other groups. Hegemonic masculinity is therefore one that subordinates women's activities and other (usually more effeminate) ways of being masculine. Wetherell and Edley (1999) provide a critical analysis of the concept of hegemonic masculinity. You could also consider how discourse around other aspects of gender perpetuates hegemony.

18.5.2 PERSONAL HISTORIES

Discourse analysts have produced rich, sophisticated accounts of identity work in a wide range of social contexts. However, the emphasis on social interaction perhaps glosses over issues of personal history and presence that shape interpersonal relations. For this reason, other researchers have turned to psychoanalytic concepts to help situate questions of identity within *personal* as well as social contexts, and it is this aspect we now consider.

In order to unravel the influence of life (his)stories on current self-presentations, some theorists have recently returned to narrative and psychoanalytic traditions in psychology. Notwithstanding the influences and constraints which shape self-presentation within different social interactions, writers such as Wendy Hollway (e.g. Hollway & Jefferson, 2000) and Stephen Frosh (e.g. Frosh et al., 2001) point to the role of early experiences, especially within family contexts, on the performance of identities in the present. Of course, researchers cannot access an individual's early experiences directly and so make use of the life stories people provide during research interviews. Such interviews involve minimal intervention from the researcher in order to encourage the participant to provide as much detail as possible, in their own terms, on topics which they introduce as significant.

Evidence suggests that two people who share similar backgrounds (even those from the same family) may offer very different accounts of their upbringing and place emphasis on particular features over others. For example, the absence of a drunken father could be construed as a positive or negative factor depending on the perspective of the individual, and the perspective adopted could in turn help shape gender identities and attitudes to parenting. According to Hollway and Jefferson (2000), everyone experiences anxieties based on early life events which are difficult to tolerate and so lead to *unconscious defence mechanisms*. So, an individual might deny difficult encounters with the mother from the past and instead idealise her so that tensions and difficulties are pushed away (and into the unconscious).

These repressed tensions may well resurface, however, during times of stress or during situations which invoke maternal relations (e.g. becoming a parent) resulting in the breakdown of defences and a need to confront and resolve conflicts head on. Adam Phillips (1993; Phillips & Taylor, 2009) has provided accounts of how infants come to realise that they have separate selves and how they creatively (but often slowly) *invent* an identity with repercussions that last throughout life. Psychoanalytically informed research can yield rich, emotion-laden data relating to a person's biography and central values.

18.5.3 EMBODIED SELVES: MATERIAL AND VIRTUAL WORLDS

Until relatively recently, psychologists have given little emphasis to *the embodied self*. That is, they have tended to concentrate on cognition rather than on the psychological significance of people's bodies. Recently, however, the embodied self has emerged as a major theme in psychology. It is clear that, for example, judging ourselves (or being judged) as fat, attractive, tall, cool, bald etc. will have implications for our self-image. Our feelings about self will certainly change if we experience a bodily trauma, such as an injury, an illness or a disability, and many people spend time and effort on body care as self-enhancing – whether

FIGURE 18.2 Are adverts for 'manscara' changing the way men think about their bodies?
© Ron Chapple Stock/Corbis

by applying cosmetics, bodybuilding, dieting, purchasing fashionable clothes, hair styling and so on. The use of beauty and health products is no longer the preserve of younger, female-dominated groups since older people ('middle youth') and, increasingly, men are investing in their appearance (men are now being targeted with cosmetic products such as 'manscara' and 'guyliner': Figure 18.2).

Some social psychologists regard the body as a key *site* for self-identity and personal development in the twenty-first century. Body 'projects' such as exercising, hair transplants, tattoos, sunbathing etc. can be regarded as attempts to define who we are and to differentiate ourselves from others. So our bodily practices are clearly a way of being part of the culture we live in and are performed according to prevailing norms, particularly around gender, age and social class: few men in the1950s bought even deodorant, and some women now consider facelifts as normal. Of course, body image also changes according to age and life stage (for example, teenage), bodily changes (for example, pregnancy) and life events (for example, accidents). Social class is also associated, for example, with fashion preferences for 'chav', 'preppy' or designer clothes, though everyone attempts (and possibly fails: see Woodward, 2007) to represent 'who we are' through clothes and the *way* they are worn. Further, such projects can be interpreted as a means of testing and *changing* our self-presentations so that we may feel more confident, attractive, successful etc. The internet has become a site for self-presentation, to which numerous popular social networking sites such as Facebook and Bebo attest.

Our embodied identities are of course always social. However, they are also bound up with possessions and sundry desired items that are part of our cultural worlds. Humans are 'natural-born cyborgs' (Haraway, 1991) and our goods and possessions have been acknowledged as part of our self-identity since William James's *Principles of psychology* (1890). Some concerns (for example, that our interactions with machines change us) are well founded (Clark, 2003; Ong, 1982), but these ideas are countered by psychologists who argue that our relationship with even rapidly changing technology helps us to understand the psychology of self and identity (Gergen, 1996; 2000). Perhaps one of the most *valued* possessions today for its ability to enable us to be ourselves is the mobile phone; indeed it is regarded by many as an *extension of self* because of the personally relevant information (numbers, images, texts, voicemails, songs etc.) it contains. Similarly, laptops and other portable devices, e.g. MP3 players, will be treasured by many. When such items are lost or stolen it can feel as if the self has been violated and a period of disorientation may ensue before the self can be rebuilt and re-established (Breakwell, 1986; Dittmar, 1992).

EXERCISE   What makes you a material girl or boy?

FIGURE 18.3   Madonna
© Ronald Wittek /Corbis

You can define your material self by where you get your clothes and belongings (Figure 18.3). Check out the objects you have on you or are carrying and what you are wearing. Which of them is: old, new, borrowed, of sentimental value, essential to your identity? We may be what we wear, but in what way are objects necessary for being ourselves? Are they personal expression or what others expect? What items would make you less 'you'? What are the items without which you would not be able to function as yourself?

To test this, think about the times you have lost, broken or changed bits of your material world – and this might include your embodied self: your hair, your ability to run fast, your eyesight without glasses etc. Do you have objects in your room that symbolise where you are from or your interests (team T-shirt, posters, concert tickets etc.)? What do the mementos you have in your room – postcards, that old swimming trophy, or photos of yourself when younger etc. – do for you now?

Everyday and conventional items (that we keep in our homes, personal spaces, bedrooms or garden sheds) can resonate with personal significance, such as treasured family photographs, coveted coffee mugs, DVDs, old records, posters, letters, a skateboard, and even pieces of furniture (and see Gosling, 2008, on snooping in personal spaces). The contemporary trends for home (and self) makeovers highlight just how much we are inclined to invest in our living spaces, which seem to provide another opportunity for self-expression. Indeed, it is difficult to think of areas which have yet to be colonised by taste makers and television producers as outlets for identity statements and practices.

Sometimes these are not individual or personal choices but the requirements of social or cultural circumstances, for example, wearing gender- , age- or work-appropriate clothes at school or a family wedding. Our choices and opportunities will of course be restricted (by time, money etc.), but we do seem to live in a world where self and identity can be (re)made in all manner of contexts.

That many items we value are tools for communication and connection to others, in both virtual and 'real' space, emphasise the importance of our *relational selves* (Gergen, 1994; 2009; Gilligan, 1982) and our ability to exploit technology. Playing out roles as online presences offers people opportunities to express aspects of 'self' in ways that are different from or even impossible in 'real life' (Miller & Arnold, 2000). That said, people having a presence on Facebook, web pages or blogs draw on the same self-management skills (such as decisions about what to reveal about themselves) as they did when there were only phones or pen and paper (Miller & Arnold, 2001; 2003; 2009).

EXERCISE What would *your* avatar be like?

FIGURE 18.4 An avatar

Before you answer the question above, consider if you already have representations of your *self* in cyberspace (for example, your photos on Facebook or the name or 'character' you adopt when you play computer games). Think about how far you *identify* with the 'Facebook you', or what you choose to reveal about yourself with the photo of your friends on a night out, your status, links to 'friends', your interests, links to your favourite YouTube clip, and so on. Does your virtual self represent or contradict aspects of your personality? Many people have an online 'presence', but how far does the cyborg activity of texting and tweeting also demand identity creation and maintenance?

If you now return to thinking about your avatar – would it be an alternative you or would it represent some facet of you? In Second Life you can create and customise your own digital persona in 3D' and shop for 'unique clothing, hair and fashion accessories' (Second Life web page). It is fun to do – and there are many people who take advantage of the possibilities afforded in these new social/cultural spaces, when bodies are not restricted as in First Life. For example, some people who have particular disabilities find it offers new experiences and choices, and they gain confidence and skills that transfer to life this side of the screen.

You can read more about the issues raised when people create an avatar (for example, Meadows, 2008) and there is increasing cyberpsychology research into self and identity and computer-mediated communications and interactions of every kind: social networks, blogs, online dating and relationships (Ellison et al., 2006; Whitty, 2008) and many more.

18.5.4 SOCIAL CONSTRUCTIONISM

In 1973, Kenneth Gergen wrote a paper called 'Social psychology as history', a milestone for the psychology of self and identity and for the development of key concepts in **social constructionism**, which is the last, but not least, of our approaches to understanding self. Gergen argued that there were *alternative* ways of understanding and doing social psychology (to be critical, interpretive and culturally specific). This theoretical and postmodern approach to understanding the dynamic *process* of maintaining a sense of self is one that recognises how our experiences are incorporated into our life story and how we actively manage the struggles and conflicts, as well as the positive experiences (Gergen & Gergen, 2003).

The social constructionist approach also suggests an alternative to the traditional approach to personality: it views the self as a *product* of social encounters and relationships, rather than the source of personality (Gergen, 1994; Gergen & Gergen, 1988). Further, it suggests that people's *understanding* of self comes from communications and interactions with others (Burr, 2003) together with life story memory (Neisser & Fivush, 1994; Neisser & Joplin, 1997) and our cultural narratives (Polkinghorne, 1996).

> **Social constructionism**   An approach to psychology which focuses on *meaning* and *power*; it aims to account for the ways in which phenomena are socially constructed.
>
> **Gendered identity**   The way that people *perform* their biological sex. Just how or in what way gender is demonstrated will vary depending on social or cultural understanding, circumstances, expectations or requirements.

Social constructionists have generated interest in the idea of diversity of experience rather than difference, and the importance of cultural, geographical and historical contexts in which interactions take place. So they study how people view themselves from multiple perspectives and in particular contexts such as at work, at school, at the doctors etc. Some theorists think that the idea of a socially constructed self neglects bodily identity (Cromby, 2005), but feminist and critical psychologists have developed social constructionist approaches to understand for example **gendered identity** and sexuality, whereby the bodily identity (as male or female) is constructed, managed and performed according to prevailing cultural notions of gender (Burman, 1998; Kitzinger & Wilkinson, 1996). One of the original 'puzzles of self' was the way we assume a 'consistent self' despite a changing body (perhaps not as dramatically as Alice experienced, but nevertheless as real), but social constructionist concepts explain how the sense of self results from active *processes* – constructing an 'on-going sense of self as we age and change roles etc.' (Markus & Wurf, 1987).

As mentioned above, in order to be ourselves in whatever context – as man or woman, worker or student – we use the objects we carry in our bags and indeed the bag itself, clothes and bodily adornment or arrangements to convey or communicate *something* (deliberately or inadvertently) about ourselves. We display our status or social class (e.g. police uniform or business suit), interests (badges, sports T-shirts), gender (style of clothes, jewellery, haircut), individuality and character (personal items) and we present ourselves as a certain *kind* of person (lifeguard, shopper) (see Csikszentmihalyi & Rochberg-Halton, 1981; Finkelstein, 1991). Social constructionism proposes that our ideas about ourselves are both individual and social, with the narratives we create about ourselves (our life stories) used as a reference point for how we portray our *future* selves, i.e. what we might think or do in situations in the future (Crossley, 2000; Csikszentmihalyi, 1993; Polkinghorne, 2000). The culture in which we belong is, therefore, not 'out there' to influence; it is not a 'container' to control us (Radley, 1991) but is there to provide us with stories, discourses from which we come to understand what to expect in our interactions with others.

Social constructionism has enabled psychologists to develop ideas about self and how it relates to identity (social and performed) and personhood (political and ideological). It has also enabled them to develop the methodologies that allow rigorous exploration of subjective experience as well as what happens as we engage in social or cultural discourse and interactions in real and cyborgian places.

CHAPTER SUMMARY

18.6 In this chapter we have tried to address poor Alice's dilemma in answering the question – who are you? The earliest psychologists thought that it was a fundamental matter for psychology to investigate and devise theories that answered questions in their own terms and not those of the philosophers or playwrights (though Shakespeare did a good job). We have considered the main ways that, over the last 50 years or so, approaches have been successful, but which have in turn raised further issues: of methodology, ontology and levels of explanation. We have shown that recent studies have moved away from the traditional understanding of self as a fixed 'thing' that is 'real' or 'true', towards self as being produced through interactions that take place in specific cultural, political, social, temporal, geographic and increasingly virtual contexts or spaces. We see that psychological research can be interdisciplinary and provide useful understandings for people in our increasingly technological world.

DISCUSSION QUESTIONS

What do critical social psychologists think are the best ways to study 'self'?

Why might it be important to ask questions that are not based on determinist assumptions of biology?

How come it matters how and who does the research?

In what ways could critical research on self have beneficial applications for people?

SUGGESTIONS FOR FURTHER READING

Adopt a critical approach to psychology. First, check out how the concept of 'self' is central to everyday life situations and understanding people in social interactions. Discover for yourself, from suggested reading and from chapter discussions and examples, what the various theories and approaches offer for education, health, occupation, gender relations etc.

Discover how critical social psychology throws new light on many aspects of self-in-action discussed in this chapter. A wide range of references – journals and other source materials – will help, but you can also develop ideas through engaging in discussion of matters and questions we have raised, amongst your friends, on Facebook or as blogs. Try the following:

Gough, B., & McFadden, M. (2001). *Critical social psychology*. Basingstoke: Palgrave.

Parker, I. (1989). *The crisis in modern social psychology, and how to end it*. London: Routledge.

Parker, I. (2007). *Revolution in psychology: alienation to emancipation*. London: Pluto.

Sherif, M. (1977). Crisis in social psychology: some remarks towards breaking through the crisis. *Personality and Social Psychology Bulletin, 3*(3), 368–382.

Walkerdine, V. (2002). *Challenging subjects: critical psychology for a new millennium*. Basingstoke: Palgrave.

If you pay attention to how psychology is generally reported in the media (full of so-called 'personality tests' and 'bad science') you will know that sharing psychological understanding of 'who we are' is a difficult task. Consider how (as critical approaches suggest) psychology could be 'given away' to empower people and:

- move from the notion of an *essential* self (discoverable and measurable) to an active, discursive and performed self

- recognise the importance of culture – politics, geography, ideology, gender representations, media narratives etc.

- understand the importance of symbolism, the unconscious self and the dynamics of social relations

- challenge what counts as legitimate psychology and what difference it makes who owns psychology

- ask questions that are meaningful to people in everyday situations.

GLOSSARY

5-alpha reductase syndrome   Individuals who are genetically male but appear to be female at birth. During puberty, male genitalia then develop and the majority of such individuals develop a male gender identity.

Absolute refractory period   In a neurone, the period of time following an action potential during which another action potential cannot be generated.

Accentuation principle   Categorisation theory suggests that differences between members within the same category are underestimated and differences between members of different categories are accentuated.

Accommodation   The modification and expansion of pre-existing cognitive schemata in order to adapt to new experiences.

Acetylcholine (ACh)   Neurotransmitter abundant in the nervous system that acts as a fast excitatory neurotransmitter at the neuromuscular junction, although it can have inhibitory effects elsewhere.

Acetylcholineresterase (AChE)   Enzyme that inactivates acetylcholine.

Action potential   Mechanism of signalling information from one end of a neurone to the other achieved by the transitory change in membrane potential travelling down the neurone.

Activational hormones   Hormones that circulate in the bloodstream and can affect behaviour or physical characteristics when they bind to a receptor site.

Actor–observer effect   An extension of the fundamental attribution error. Whilst attributing the actions of targets to their disposition, we are more likely to explain our own behaviour as influenced by the situation.

Affordances   The notion that the function of objects can be directly perceived, with no prior experience being necessary.

Agonist   Drug that enhances effects of a neurotransmitter on the post-synaptic neurone.

Agreeableness   This personality trait mainly involves being motivated to help, serve and please others. A person with high levels of the agreeableness trait will often comply with requests for help and sometimes do things without worrying about their own interests. Agreeableness is a part of the five-factor model of personality.

Allocentric   The skill of memorising the position of an object in relation to other objects.

All-or-none law   The result of the threshold of excitation. An action potential is either triggered or not and so is always of the same strength.

Altruism   The act of helping someone, but without any expectation of getting something in return.

Amygdala   A structure of the limbic system located in the medial temporal lobe involved in emotional processes.

Analytical intelligence   The ability to evaluate ideas, solve problems and make decisions through analysing, evaluating and making inferences.

Androgen   A class of male sex hormones responsible for the maintenance and development of male characteristics.

Androgen insensitivity syndrome   A male with this condition is insensitive to the masculinising effects of androgens in the womb. Such individuals appear to be female, although they possess testes.

Animism   The attribution of life-like qualities to inanimate objects (for example, toys like Edmund Elephant).

Antagonist   Drug that inhibits the effects of a neurotransmitter on the post-synaptic neurone.

Anterograde axoplasmic transport   Forward conveyance of material such as neurotransmitter vesicles, along the axon of a neurone (from soma towards synaptic button).

Anthropocentrism or **anthrocentrism**   The belief that people (*anthro*) are the most important thing in the universe rather than the worthless pile of brown stuff that we really are!

Ascending auditory pathway   The pathway that runs from the ear to the brain.

Ascending reticular activating system (ARAS)   Sometimes known as the reticular activating system, this is a part of the brain that affects, among other things, an individual's level of wakefulness and attentiveness. Hans Eysenck claimed that this part of the brain is what differentiates extraverts and introverts; extraverts seek out stimulation to the ARAS (i.e. being 'stimulus hungry') whereas introverts avoid stimulation in the ARAS if they can help it (i.e. being 'stimulus aversive').

Assimilation   The incorporation of new experiences into pre-existing cognitive schemas.

Astrocytes   Glial cells shaped like stars that perform various functions for neurones within the CNS including physical support, producing the blood–brain barrier, isolation of synapses, providing nutrition and keeping the extracellular environment clean.

Attachment behaviour   Any behaviour that helps to form or establish an emotional bond between two individuals. Strong attachment bonds are usually formed between an infant and his or her caregiver.

Attention   Concentration of cognitive resources on some aspect or aspects of an environment whilst ignoring others.

Attention deficit hyperactivity disorder   A behaviour disorder, usually first diagnosed in childhood, that is characterised by inattention, impulsivity and, in some cases, hyperactivity.

Attenuate   The reduction of a signal or information.

Attitudes   The thoughts and opinions you have about any number of objects in the world.

Attribution   The act of making a decision as to why someone has acted in a particular way.

Auditory canal   The 'tube' running between the pinna and the tympanic membrane.

Authoritarianism   The theory that a person with this type of personality will be hostile to minority groups and has a predisposition to show prejudice.

Autism   A form of pervasive developmental disorder. It can range from high functioning to severe in nature. Diagnosis is usually made according to difficulties found in aspects of communication, social skills and the use of imagination.

Autonomic nervous system (ANS)   This is part of the nervous system that stimulates activity to the heart and muscles and is especially important to get the person to defend (i.e. the 'fight-or-flight' response) against any perceived threats. The ANS has been associated with the personality trait of neuroticism, with persons who have high levels of this trait being poor in controlling the ANS.

Autoreceptor   Pre-synaptic receptor that detects and signals levels of neurotransmitter in the synaptic cleft and so regulates release.

Axon   The long slender projection from cell body to axonal branches or synaptic buttons. Its main purpose is to convey action potentials.

Axon hillock   Region of the axon that is adjacent to the soma (also known as the initial segment). It is here that post-synaptic potentials typically accumulate and determine whether an action potential is triggered or not.

Axonal branches   The division of the axon of the neurone into two or more sections. Occurs in certain types of neurones and only at the synaptic end.

Axoplasm   The fluid inside the axon.

Babbling   A child appears to be experimenting with making the sounds of language, but is not yet producing any recognisable words. Also, what boys do when they are trying to ask someone out on a date.

Basal ganglia   A group of forebrain structures that integrates voluntary movement and consists of the caudate nucleus, globus pallidus and putamen.

Base rate fallacy   Ignoring the base rate of an event occurring when computing a probability.

Basilar membrane   A flexible membrane in the cochlea that moves in response to sound.

Bayes theorem   A method of computing the probability of a hypothesis being true given some factual evidence related to the hypothesis.

Bipolar cells   A type of neurone which is specialised for dealing with sensory information.

Bipolar neurone   A type of neurone (usually a sensory neurone) named for its structure, having two processes arising from the cell body.

Blind spot   The point on the retina where there are no photoreceptor cells.

Blood–brain barrier   Protective barrier between the brain and blood vessels, providing a mechanism by which certain substances are prevented from entering the brain.

Bodily-kinaesthetic intelligence   The ability to use one's body in various movements and activities.

Bottom-up processing   A cognitive process that starts with simple (low-level) processes and builds up to the more complex higher levels. It doesn't depend on prior knowledge.

Brain stem   The part of the brain that regulates vital reflexes such as heart rate and respiration; it consists of the midbrain, the pons and the medulla. It is activity or the lack of it in this region that is used by medics to establish if a patient is 'brain dead'.

Bullying   This is a process involving exercise of power and control over a more vulnerable person. Bullying may take a verbal form (e.g. insults, threats, and use of language to make the victim feel fearful). It might also be physical in nature such as when a group of bullies surrounds the victim (i.e. 'mobbing') in order to intimidate them.

Bystander effect   Lack of action in a given situation, based on the presence of other people. The higher the number of participants, the lower the probability that anyone will act.

Cardinality   The principle that a set of items has a cardinal value (a quantity), and this quantity is equal in value to another set of items with the same quantity. For example, although three horses might look visually different to three ducks, the principle of cardinality suggests that there are the same number, i.e. three.

Cartesian dualism   The idea that we are made up of two parts, a mind and a body. The body is like all other material objects and can be examined using the material sciences, whereas the mind is not physical and cannot be measured.

Catharsis   Release of pent-up energy (usually frustration or aggression) by acting out the emotions stored up within the individual.

Cell theory   Schwann's (1839) theory that all bodily tissues are composed of individual discrete cells.

Centration   The focusing of attention on one aspect of a situation while excluding the rest of the scenario.

Cerebellum   The lower part of the brain responsible for balance and coordination.

Cerebral cortex   The layer of neural tissue which covers the cerebral hemispheres and is involved in higher-order cognitive processes.

Cerebral hemispheres   The right and left halves of the most anterior part of the brain. They play a primary role in most of our mental abilities, such as language, attention and perception.

Cerebrospinal fluid   The clear fluid that protects the central nervous system and fills the ventricular system, the subarachnoid space and the central canal.

c-fibres   Neurones that are found in the somatic sensory system and are unique because, unlike most other nerves in the nervous system, they are unmyelinated. They have a role in the transmission of pain.

Chemical synapses   Synapses that depend upon chemicals (transmitter substances), released by the pre-synaptic cell and recognised by the post-synaptic cell, for communication.

Chemically gated ion channels   Ion channels whose state (open or closed) is determined by the docking of an appropriate chemical onto a nearby receptor.

Child-directed speech (motherese)   The act of using a sing-song voice, speaking slowly, or using simple language when talking to an infant.

Chloride (Cl-)   Negatively charged ion that plays a role in producing and maintaining membrane potentials.

Chromosome   A thread-like strand of DNA that carries the genes.

Chunk decomposition   The process of breaking down something that was initially perceived as a whole into its constituent parts – such as X being seen as two individual lines rather than as a letter of the alphabet.

Cisternae   Found in some synaptic buttons, cisternae repackage transmitter substances into vesicles.

Cochlea   The spiral-shaped structure in the inner ear which generates electrical impulses in response to sound.

Cochlear duct   A fluid-filled chamber in the cochlea.

Cognitive dissonance   The argument that if our own attitudes, thoughts or actions disagree with each other, a state of dissonance is created. This acts as a motivation to change one or more of these internal elements (Festinger, 1957).

Cognitive miser   In contrast to Heider's naive scientist perspective, the idea that we try to conserve mental energy and take shortcuts when making attributions (Fiske & Taylor, 1991).

Cognitive schemata   Mental representations and plans used to enact behaviours.

Competitive binding   The situation where drugs and neurotransmitters are in competition for the same receptor sites.

Concrete vocabulary   A precursor to abstract vocabulary, whereby children name objects at a subordinate level, e.g. chair and table, as opposed to an abstract superordinate level, e.g. furniture.

Cones   The photoreceptor cells in the eye responsible for colour vision and visual acuity.

Conflict resolution   When more than one rule (or production) is able to be used at any one time in a production system, it is said to be in conflict. Conflict resolution is the strategy used to resolve this conflict.

Congenital adrenal hyperplasia   A female with this condition is exposed to an excess of androgens, produced by the adrenal glands, during prenatal development. As a consequence, a number of physical and personality characteristics are shifted in a male-typical direction.

Conscientiousness   This personality trait is often demonstrated by an individual in a work or study setting, in which the individual is industrious and has an eye for detail in the work that is being done. People with high levels of conscientiousness are very practical and like to finish a project once they have started it. Conscientiousness is a part of the five-factor model of personality.

Consciousness   Often used in everyday speech to describe being awake or aware in contrast to being asleep or in a coma. In psychology, the term has a more precise meaning concerning the way in which humans are mentally aware so that they distinguish clearly between themselves and all other things and events.

Conservation   The understanding that certain properties of objects remain the same under transformation. These properties include quantity, weight and volume.

Consolidation theory   The idea that memories are fragile and require time to consolidate before they can be stored in long-term memory.

Constraint relaxation   The process of relaxing constraints that were unnecessarily imposed on a problem – such as believing coins could not be stacked on top of each other in the eight-coin problem.

Constructivist   An approach which assumes that our perceptual experiences are constructed based on a combination of sensory input and what we know about the world.

Contact hypothesis   The theory that bringing members of two different groups together within a cooperative, equal and supportive environment can reduce conflict between those two groups.

Context-dependent memory   Where memory for an item improves when the original context in which it was presented is reinstated at test.

Cornea   The transparent protective layer on the surface of the eye.

Corpus callosum   The largest commissure in the brain that connects the two cerebral hemispheres.

Cranial nerves   Part of the peripheral nervous system composed of a set of 12 pairs of nerves or pathways which transmit sensory and motor information to and from the brain.

Creative intelligence   The ability to draw upon previous experience in order to come up with new solutions to both old and new problems.

Critical period   A limited period, usually early in life, in which a child is required to be exposed to a particular skill or experience in order for it to be learned. Alternatively, the time during pregnancy when exposure to certain substances has lasting consequences on development.

Crossed category membership   The theory that encourages people to view others' membership in lots of different categories to reduce intergroup bias (this can include race, age, ethnicity, gender, university enrolment and economic status, to name just a few).

Cryptarithmetic   A problem where an arithmetic sum is given using letters rather than numbers, with the goal of identifying which number from 0 to 9 corresponds to each of the letters.

Crystallised intelligence (*gc*)   The ability to think and reason about abstract ideas, and to use knowledge and skills to solve problems.

Cued recall   Where specific prompts or cues are used to direct recall (e.g. paired-associate learning).

Cultural tools   Tools that help us to understand the world more fully by solving problems, measuring the environment, making calculations and storing information (e.g. computers and calculators).

Cytoplasm   Gel-like fluid, rich in salts, that is contained within the cell and surrounds organelles.

Decay   An explanation of forgetting that suggests memories fade or deteriorate over time.

Declarative knowledge   Factual information such as that Paris is the capital of France.

Deductive reasoning   A type of reasoning that uses a rule or a set of premises applied to specific instances to produce a conclusion.

Deindividuation   A process whereby the presence of others leads an individual to lose their sense of personal identity and to feel anonymous, becoming less socially responsible and guided by moral principles.

Dendrites   The branching processes that emanate from the soma and receive inputs from other cells.

Dendritic arborisation   The number and organisation of dendrites.

Deoxyribonucleic acid (DNA)   Nucleic acid found in cells that contains the genetic instructions vital for development and functioning of organisms.

Desired state   The ultimate state, i.e. when the problem is solved.

Determinism   The idea that every event including human thought and behaviour is causally determined by an unbroken chain of prior events. According to this idea there are no mysterious miracles and no random events.

Diencephalon   The division of the forebrain that contains the thalamus and hypothalamus.

Diffusion   Natural movement of molecules in solution from areas of high to low concentration.

Diffusion of responsibility   The phenomenon of individuals taking less responsibility for events when there are other people present because they feel less personally responsible for what is happening.

Dihydrotestosterone   An androgen converted from testosterone by the actions of the enzyme 5-alpha reductase.

Discrimination   The consideration or treatment of others (typically negative) based on general factors (e.g. their race, religion or some other grouping), rather than on individual merit.

Displacement   Swapping negative feelings or aggression from one group or individual to another target.

Dogmatism   A rigid, inflexible approach which can cause prejudice through intolerance.

Double dissociation   A term used in brain sciences to indicate that two cognitive processes are distinct, such that damage to a particular brain region affects one of those processes but not the other. For example, damage to Broca's area of the brain means a patient cannot speak but can still understand speech, whereas damage to Wernicke's area means a patient cannot understand speech but can still speak.

Down syndrome   A congenital disorder, caused by the presence of an extra 21st chromosome, in which the affected person has mild to moderate learning difficulties and distinctive facial profile. Also called trisomy 21.

Dramaturgical analogy   Erving Goffman proposed a theatrical metaphor as a way of understanding self in everyday life and seeing social interactions as though they were dramatic performances, considering the costumes, the props etc. which go towards making up the 'scenes' played out by people.

Drugs   Substances that produce observable changes to physiological processes and/or behaviour at relatively low doses.

Dynamic equilibrium   When two opposing processes operate at equivalent rates.

DZ and MZ twins   Fraternal or dizygotic (DZ) twins occur when two different eggs are fertilised by two different sperm. Identical or monozygotic (MZ) twins occur when a single fertilised egg divides into two identical copies.

Egocentric thinking   When an individual has little regard for the views or interests of others, which may involve individuals memorising objects in relation to themselves.

Elaboration likelihood model   Examines how attitudes are formed and changed by focusing on two routes to persuasion: the 'central route' and the 'peripheral route'.

Electrical synapses   Synapses that depend upon electrical charge accumulated in the pre-synaptic cell passing to the post-synaptic cell for communication.

Electrostatic pressure   The force created because particles of opposite polarity (+ and −) are attracted towards each other and those of the same polarity are repelled.

Emotional intelligence   An ability to identify, assess and manage the emotions of yourself, other individuals and groups.

Encoding   The stage of memory involving interpreting and transforming incoming information in order to 'lay down' memories.

Encoding specificity principle   This principle states that specific encoding operations performed at presentation determine what is stored, and therefore determine what retrieval cues are effective at test.

Endocrine system   A series of small organs responsible for producing hormones that regulate a variety of processes including growth and development, metabolism and puberty.

Endogenous   Substances naturally found within the body (e.g. neurotransmitters).

Entitativity   Refers to how coherent and connected a group is, that is, how much the people in the group can be seen as being a part of the group rather than being a collection of individuals.

Enzymatic degradation   Process by which certain neurotransmitters are broken down by enzymes.

Enzymes   Typically proteins that are catalysts important for biological reactions.

Equilibration   This is when a child's set of schemas are balanced and not disturbed by conflict.

Equilibrium potential   Each type of ion has its own equilibrium potential, which is the voltage at which the net effect of the passage of a given ion in and out of the cell is zero.

Ethnocentrism   A stance in which an individual believes that their own race or ethnic group (or aspects of it, e.g. its culture) is superior to other groups.

Ethnomethodology   Not a formal research method, but an approach to empirical study that aims to discover the things that people *do* in particular situations and how they create the patterns and orderliness of social life to gain a sense of social structure.

Eugenics   The political idea that the human race could be improved by eliminating 'undesirables' from the breeding stock, so that they cannot pass on their supposedly inferior genes. Some eugenicists advocate compulsory sterilisation, while others seem to prefer mass murder or genocide.

Eustachian tube   A structure in the middle ear which helps regulate air pressure.

Event-related potentials   A characteristic electrophysiological response by the brain to a stimulus, usually recorded using EEG (electroencephalography).

Excitatory post-synaptic potentials (EPSPs)   Graded post-synaptic potentials that increase the likelihood that the post-synaptic cell will produce an action potential.

Exocytosis   Process by which substances are released from a cell.

Exogenous   Substances originating outside the body (e.g. drugs).

Explanatory pluralism   Holds that different levels of description, like the psychological and the neurophysiological, can coevolve, and mutually influence each other, without the higher-level theory being replaced by, or reduced to, the lower-level one.

Explicit memory test   Where the participant is told at test that the task involves memory for material presented earlier.

External locus of control   People with an external locus of control will usually see their lives as mainly subject to influence and control by other people (e.g. destiny affected by someone's family members, friends, boss etc.).

Extraversion   The main feature of extraversion is having a focus on other people and their interests. A typical characteristic of having high levels of extraversion is someone who seeks out social situations, like parties, and enjoys being in this type of environment. Extraversion is a personality trait that is common to all major personality factor models and is best understood as having two extremes of people, with high extraversion levels being called 'extraverts' and those with low extraversion levels being seen as 'introverts'.

Factor analysis   This is a statistical method that is used to reduce complex information into more manageable units. The technique entails analysing personality by examining how certain behaviours, motivations and feelings are correlated with each other. Strong relationships between some of these measurements might indicate an underlying personality factor. This technique has been used to aid the development of many of the major personality factor models, like the three-factor, five-factor, and sixteen-factor models.

False belief   This is when an individual incorrectly believes a statement or scenario to be true when it is not. This is the basis of the false belief tasks used in the theory of mind experiments.

False consensus effect   The effect seen when people overestimate the probability of other people thinking, feeling or acting the same way as they do.

Filter   In the context of attentional processing, a filter serves the purpose of allowing some sensations of stimuli through to be processed whilst screening out others. This is based on the theoretical approach that we can only cope with a limited amount of information and so select which stimuli to process.

Five-factor model   This model of personality traits is sometimes called the Big 5 or the OCEAN model (after the initials for each of the five major traits: openness to experience, conscientiousness, extraversion, agreeableness and neuroticism). It is commonly used to assess personality in a range of settings, including the workplace. The model is highly popular in personality psychology and has been developed and promoted by Robert McCrae and Paul Costa Jr, both working at the National Institute of Aging, National Institutes of Health in the United States of America.

Fluid intelligence (*gf*)   The ability to learn from previous experiences.

Foetal alcohol syndrome   Foetal abnormalities caused by alcohol consumption during pregnancy.

Folk psychology   Ways of thinking about the mind that are implicit in how we make everyday attributions of mental states to ourselves and others.

Forebrain   Most anterior division of the brain, containing the telencephalon and diencephalon.

Forgetting function   The mathematical equation that determines the precise rate of forgetting as a function of time.

Fovea   The part of the eye located in the centre of the macula which is responsible for high visual acuity.

Fraternal birth order effect   The increased rates of homosexuality observed in males with a large number of older brothers.

Free recall   Where the prompt for recall is quite general (e.g. 'remember as many words as you can from the first list').

Frustration-aggression hypothesis   The theory that frustration leads to aggression; this can be used to explain prejudice.

Functional fixedness   When one becomes fixated on the function of an object rather than considering other uses that the object could be applied to.

Functionalism   In the philosophy of mind, functionalism refers to the idea that mental states can be defined by their causes and effects.

Fundamental attribution error   The tendency to attribute the actions of a person we are observing to their disposition, rather than to situational variables.

G protein   Guanine nucleotide-binding proteins are coupled to metabotropic chemical receptors and are involved in cascade effects that result in the opening of ion channels.

Gendered identity   A person's gendered identity is the way that people *perform* their biological sex. Just how or in what way gender is demonstrated will vary depending on social or cultural understanding, circumstances, expectations or requirements.

Gene   A discrete portion (sequence) of DNA (deoxyribonucleic acid). DNA is the building block of our chromosomes. In *Homo sapiens* there are 23 pairs of chromosomes contained in the nucleus of each cell. For each pair, one of the chromosomes is inherited from the mother and one from the father. We have around 20,000 to 25,000 genes.

General factor (g)   The theoretical general factor of intelligence that some scientists believe underpins all cognitive activity.

General problem solver (GPS)   A computer program created in 1957 by Herbert Simon and Allen Newell to build a universal problem solving machine.

Generality approach   Researchers studying the link between personality and health may use the generality approach by analysing specific health-related behaviours that are influenced by personality. In essence, this approach assumes that health is affected by an indirect route from a personality trait or type contributing to a behaviour that is likely to impact upon health (e.g. smoking, alcohol use, taking fewer risks when driving etc.).

Generate-recognise theory   The theory that people use an initial prompt to generate a series of cues during recall until one of them matches an item shown at presentation and is recognised.

Genetic predisposition   Any behaviour or physical characteristic that is present within an individual's genetic code. These characteristics may not always be activated, but there is a potential for them to be developed.

Genotype   Genes that make up the genetic code for an individual are described as the genotype. In humans the genotype comprises approximately 25,000 genes. Genes mostly come in pairs. Each member of a pair of genes is referred to as an allele.

Genus   A class, group or category that possesses common attributes. Our own species exists in the genus *Homo* alongside other species (all of which are now extinct).

Gestalt psychology   A school of psychology that began in Germany in the first half of the twentieth century. It proposed that an experience or behaviour can only be understood as a whole, not by understanding the individual constituent parts.

Glial cells   Non-neuronal cells performing a number of supporting roles in the nervous system.

Goal state   A desired state for a subgoal of the problem solving process.

Graphemes   The graphical representation of a sound in written form.

Groupthink   A style of thinking shown by group members who try to minimise conflict and reach a consensus without critically testing and evaluating ideas.

Habituation   A method of measuring infant attention, by habituating an infant to a particular stimulus until they become uninterested in the stimulus.

Hegemony   A situation where the interests of the powerful can marginalise and counter the claims of other groups. Hegemonic masculinity is therefore one that subordinates women's activities and other (usually more effeminate) ways of being masculine.

Helping behaviour   The act of helping someone, but with the hope or expectation of getting something in return.

Heritability   The proportion of variance in the phenotype that can be attributed to genetic variance. It is a widely misunderstood concept and is commonly misused in debates about nature and nurture. It is a measure that may vary with the range of genetic backgrounds and range of environments studied. It is therefore a mistake to argue that a high figure for heritability in a particular population in a particular environment means that the characteristic is genetically determined.

Hermaphrodite   A term derived from Hermaphroditus, a Greek deity believed to possess both male and female attributes. Such individuals possess both testicular and ovarian tissue.

Heuristic   A mental shortcut (or rule of thumb) that represents a 'best guess', allowing people to make solution attempts or make decisions quickly and efficiently (though not always correctly).

Heuristic systematic model   Explains that, when making decisions, individuals either use heuristics and shortcuts or systematically process the merits and problems with a given argument.

Hierarchical models of intelligence   These models imply one or more general, higher-order factor(s) of intelligences and one or more lower levels with several specific intelligence factors.

Hindbrain   Most posterior division of the brain, containing the metencephalon and myelencephalon.

Hippocampus   Structure of the limbic system located in the medial temporal lobe that plays an important role in memory.

Hormones   From the Greek *horman,* 'to excite' or 'impetus'. Hormones are chemical messengers, released by the endocrine system, that are carried to other areas of the body through the bloodstream. Once they have reached a specific area of the body, they bind to certain receptor sites within tissues or organs and induce physiological change. Hormones have powerful effects on physiology and behaviour.

Humanistic psychology   The humanistic approach explains the subjective experience of individuals in terms of the way they interpret past events. Humanistic psychology partly arose in reaction to the mechanical (stimulus/response) models of behaviourism. Borrowing ideas from psychoanalysis, it sought to affirm the dignity and worth of all people.

Humours   Refers to the physical elements that ancient Greek and Roman doctors thought were flowing through a person's body. According to the Roman physician Galen, four main humours characterised a person's temperament, which were related to being sanguine, choleric, phlegmatic and melancholic. A person would tend to have a larger proportion of one or other of the humours and this would dictate how the person consistently reacted in a variety of situations.

Huntington's disease   A dominant genetic disorder in which a protein is produced abnormally, leading to the breakdown in the parts of the brain that control movement.

Hypothalamus   A part of the brain which controls the actions of the pituitary gland and as such controls hormone production in the human body. It is also involved in a variety of physiological processes such as hunger, thirst, circadian rhythms and sexual behaviour.

Hysteria   A condition in which physical symptoms appear in the absence of any obvious physical cause.

Identity   Awareness of shared distinctive characteristics by members of a group. Identity may be considered in a number of ways, e.g. in cultural terms as ethnic identity, or in terms of sexual orientation.

Idiographic or idiothetic approach   This perspective focuses on the uniqueness or idiosyncrasies of the person. It does not require trying to get a common language of personality traits or types to compare between people. Instead, it allows people to tell their stories of how they develop over time and attempts to understand their perceptions of why they say and do things. It recognises that a person evolves over time and that changing moods and perceptions can influence what that person may do in any given situation.

Illusion   An error in perception.

Impasse   When one becomes stuck during problem solving and cannot see a solution.

Implicit memory test   Where participants perform an activity at test that is apparently unrelated to the material that was originally presented.

Incidental learning   Where participants are not told at presentation that their memory for the material will later be tested.

Inductive reasoning   A type of reasoning that starts from specific instances or facts to produce general rules or theories.

Inferior colliculi   Nuclei of the tectum in the midbrain that receives auditory information.

Ingroup   A group of which an individual believes they are a member.

Inhibitory post-synaptic potentials (IPSPs)   Graded post-synaptic potentials that decrease the likelihood that the post-synaptic cell will produce an action potential.

Innate   Being present at birth (usually refers to a characteristic or behaviour that is deemed hereditary).

Inner ear   The part of the ear which consists of the cochlea and the semicircular canals.

Inner hair cells   The sensory receptors in the ear which are responsible for sending electrical signals to the brain.

Insight   This is when we reach a dead end in problem solving, until suddenly – 'aha!' – we suddenly realise the solution. A rare phenomenon.

Intelligence quotient (IQ)   A numerical figure, believed by some to indicate the level of a person's intelligence, and by others to indicate how well that person performs on intelligence tests.

Intentional learning   Where participants are told at presentation that their memory for the material will later be tested.

Interference   An explanation of forgetting in which other learning (old or new) can disrupt or prevent retrieval.

Internal locus of control   People with an internal locus of control see themselves as 'masters of their own destiny'. Locus of control relates to how individuals perceive the causes of events that occur to them. Internal locus of control is a personality type that categorises a person as seeing events that occur around them as being dependent on what they say or do. Someone with an internal locus of control is also said to have 'self-determination' or 'personal control' or 'self-agency', which all refer to people seeing themselves as being integral to what happens to their lives.

Interneurone   A neurone connecting two other neurones. Typically for local connections confined to a specific region of the brain.

Interpersonal intelligence   The ability to understand other people's thoughts, beliefs and intentions, and respond appropriately.

Interpretive phenomenological analysis (IPA)   An experiential qualitative approach to research in psychology and the social sciences. It was developed by Jonathan Smith and it offers insights into how a person makes sense of a particular experiential phenomenon – the 'insider's perspective'.

Intersex   An individual who has undergone atypical sexual differentiation, and has external genitalia that appear to be between those of a typical female and a typical male.

Intrapersonal intelligence   The ability to understand oneself and be aware of one's thoughts, beliefs and intentions, and use this understanding to guide one's behaviour.

Introversion   This is the polar opposite of extraversion and lies at the other end of a continuum of how outwardly focused someone is. Introversion relates to a person being primarily focused on their own needs and drives. The concept is common to most theories relating to personality traits; it has been used in understanding and measuring personality types, as in the analytic psychology developed by Carl Jung and in assessing types through the use of the Myers–Briggs Type Indicator.

Ion channels   Pores (formed by proteins) found in cell membranes that allow or restrict the passage of ions in and out of the cell.

Ionotropic receptors   Chemical receptors that when activated act directly to open ion channels.

Ions   Positively and negatively charged atoms that are vital to maintaining the membrane potential of cells.

Iris   The coloured part of the eye which controls the amount of light that enters the pupil.

Job analysis   This is a process that entails unpacking the main tasks, roles and responsibilities that are undertaken by a person holding a specific job. Job analysis involves a lot of fact finding about the job role but also the characteristics of the person who would be ideally suited to hold that role. Methods of job analysis include collecting data through interviews of current post-holders and observation of their behaviour.

Just-world hypothesis   The belief that people have a need to believe that we live in a world where people generally get what they deserve and deserve what they get.

Klinefelter's syndrome   A male who receives an additional X chromosome during conception (XYY sex chromosomes). Such individuals tend to have a more feminised appearance.

Language acquisition device   A system proposed by Chomsky that young infants have. It helps them navigate the grammar of language, which in turn helps language development.

Lateral geniculate nucleus   An area of the thalamus that processes visual information.

Lens The part of the eye that focuses incoming light onto the retina.

Levels of processing theory The theory that deep, semantic processing leads to better retention than shallow, perceptual processing.

Ligand Any substance (e.g. neurotransmitter or drug) with the capacity to bind to a receptor.

Likert scale Developed by Rensis Likert (1932). A scale for measuring attitudes, typically using a score from 1 to 5 across a range of attitudes such as 'agree strongly' to 'disagree strongly'.

Limbic system A group of interconnected forebrain structures that plays a role in memory and emotion.

Linguistic intelligence The capacity to use spoken and written words and languages.

Lipids Substances that are fat soluble.

Locus of control Refers to what people perceive to be the source of what happens to them. An internal locus of control means that people see it as coming from within themselves – so they are largely in control of what happens to them, or at least in a position to influence it. An external locus of control means that it is perceived as coming from sources outside the person, and so is not something which the individual can influence.

Logical-mathematical intelligence The capacity for logic reasoning and dealing with numbers.

Longitudinal studies This is research that observes the same participants over a period of time. These observations can be over weeks, months or years, or perhaps even over someone's lifetime. These studies are important in areas such as developmental psychology, where researchers are interested in how people develop over a given period. The central feature of longitudinal research is that it tracks the same people. In personality psychology, this can be an important tool to see how people's personalities develop over time and in relation to positive and negative events.

Long-term memory Memory for material that has left consciousness and has to be brought back into mind. This term also describe experiments with a long delay between presentation and test (presumed to measure long-term memory).

Long-term recency Enhanced memory for the most recent of a sequence of items or events that are spread over a long period (e.g. for the last few films seen at the cinema).

Long-term store a key component of the modal model of memory. Items held in the short-term store for an extended period are more likely to pass into the long-term store.

Macula The area of the eye that falls in the centre of the retina.

Material and **immaterial** If something is material it is made up of the atoms and molecules that are building blocks of our world, whereas if it is immaterial it is not made up of these things. We cannot measure or see immaterial things such as 'mind', which challenges their existence. The existence of immaterial things is a matter of belief rather than evidence.

Maturation lag   Slower than expected rate of development for a child.

Means–ends analysis   Setting a goal and then breaking it down to produce subgoals which need to be achieved – thus creating a 'means to an end'.

Medulla oblongata   Most caudal part of the brain stem that regulates breathing and heart rate.

Membrane potential   The voltage difference across the cell membrane, i.e. the differences in voltage between the interior and the exterior of the cell.

Meninges   The three protective membranes (dura mater, arachnoid and pia mater) that surround the brain and spinal cord.

Mental representations   An internal cognitive map of stimuli.

Mental states   In the philosophy of mind, a mental state is unique to thinking and feeling beings, and forms part of our cognitive processes. These processes include our beliefs and attitudes as well as our perceptions and sensations, such as the taste of wine or the pain of a headache.

Mere exposure   The finding that mere exposure to an item will increase positive feelings towards it (Zajonc, 1968).

Mesencephalon   Another name for midbrain.

Meshing   How an adult's and an infant's behaviours fit together.

Meta-analysis   Where a researcher uses statistics to combine results from (typically) a large number of studies about a particular topic.

Metabotropic receptors   A form of G protein coupled chemical receptor that when activated indirectly (via activation of a G protein) opens ion channels.

Microglia   Small glial cells that constitute the major immune system of the CNS, 'swallowing' infectious agents (phagocytosis) and producing inflammatory responses.

Micrometre (μm)   Unit of measurement equal to 10^{-6} m.

Midbrain   The middle division of the brain that includes the tectum and the tegmentum.

Middle ear   The part of the ear that contains the ossicles and the Eustachian tube.

Millivolts (mV)   Unit of measurement equal to one-thousandth (10^{-3}) of a volt.

Minimal intergroup paradigm   An experimental technique used to form groups on an *ad hoc* basis to study social categorisation.

Mitochondria   Organelles found within the neurone. They are important for producing chemical energy in the form of adenosine triphosphate, but also play a vital role in a number of other cellular processes.

Mnemonics   Strategies for helping people to remember information, usually involving cues such as rhyme or imagery.

Modal model   The model of short-term memory exemplified by Atkinson and Shiffrin (1968), which includes a limited capacity short-term store and an unlimited capacity long-term store.

Motherese   More recently termed 'child-directed speech'. The act of using a sing-song voice, speaking slowly, or using simple language when talking to an infant.

Motivated tactician   As a midpoint between the naive scientist and the cognitive miser, the argument that we can use either of those strategies as the situation requires (Kruglanski, 1996).

Motivation   Most commonly, this is defined as the mechanism or process that drives someone to act. However, the main motivations of a person might not be that readily apparent and visible and may need a great deal of study and observation. There are many variables within this complicated process such as being driven to act by what we expect to achieve from our actions (e.g. getting a good grade after putting in many hours of revision) or being driven by habitual ways of acting (e.g. feeling stressed being equated with the need to get drunk).

Motor neurone   Type of neurone with its soma located in the CNS. Responsible for sending outgoing motor information along axons to sites outside the CNS (e.g. to muscles).

Multiple intelligences   The theory of multiple intelligences, proposed by Howard Gardner, holds that there are many kinds of human intelligence in addition to the intelligence that is measured with conventional IQ tests.

Multipolar neurone   The most common type of neurone in the CNS. Typically posesses a long axon and many dendrites.

Musical intelligence   Abilities that involve hearing and performing sounds, rhythm and music.

Myelin   Fatty insulating sheath deposited by glial cells that surrounds the axons of some neurones and nerve cells.

Naive scientist   The idea that when making attributions we try to understand other people's behaviour in a rational way, seeking to find stable causes, in a naive scientific manner (Heider, 1958).

Neurites   Collective term for axons and dendrites (i.e. any projection from the soma).

Neurone doctrine   The widely accepted theory, originally espoused by Cajal, that nerve cells are discrete units and are separate from one another.

Neurone membrane   The 'skin' that bounds the neurone and which is composed of the phospholipid bilayer.

Neurones   Specialised cells found in the CNS that are responsible for communication of information.

Neuroticism   A personality trait characterised by feelings of anxiety, tension, anger and/or depression.

Neurotransmitters   Chemical substances released from neurone terminals into the synaptic cleft that can affect the activation of another adjacent neurone.

Nodes of Ranvier Small gaps in the myelination of axons that are necessary for saltatory conduction of action potentials.

Nomothetic and **idiographic** measures Nomothetic approaches look for laws of behaviour and collect measures that can be observed and verified and quantified. They are concerned with averages and norms. By contrast, idiographic approaches look for unique and individual experiences.

Nucleus Organelle found within the soma of a cell that contains the genetic information necessary for cell form and function.

Object permanency This is the ability to understand that an object still exists even if it is no longer visible.

Old–new recognition A memory test in which one item is presented at a time and a participant indicates if it is a 'new' (unrecognised) or an 'old' (recognised) item.

Oligodendrocytes Glial cells responsible for myelination of neurone axons within the CNS.

Openness to experience One of the personality factors in the five-factor model. This factor refers to people who have high levels of creative tendencies, a thirst for knowledge, and an active imagination. A high score on this factor may also indicate the drive to pursue an unconventional lifestyle.

Optic flow The apparent motion of objects in the visual scene caused by an observer moving through the scene.

Optic nerve An array of axons that carry information from the eye to the brain.

Organ of Corti The sensory organ for hearing located in the cochlea.

Organelles Little 'organs' found within cells such as the nucleus, Golgi apparatus and endoplasmic reticulum. Organelles are membrane bound and perform specialised roles within the cell.

Organisational hormones Hormones that a foetus is exposed to in the womb. Such hormones affect the structure of the developing foetal brain and their effects are set in place for life.

Ossicles The three small bones in the middle ear (stapes, hammer, anvil).

Outer ear The external portion of the ear, consisting of the pinna, the auditory canal and the tympanic membrane.

Outer hair cells The sensory receptors in the ear which are responsible for injecting energy into the movement of the basilar membrane.

Outgroup A group of which an individual believes they are not a member.

Over-regulation errors Children might overuse a rule that they have learnt in a particular context when it seems appropriate in a new context. In language, this might work for some invented words such as 'wug' and 'wugs' but not for irregular plurals such as 'sheep'.

Paraplegia   Paralysis characterised by failure to move and/or feel the lower part of the body due to damage in the thoracic, lumbar or sacral segments of the spinal cord.

Parasympathetic division   Part of the autonomic nervous system that is mainly involved in restoring and preserving levels of energy in the body.

Parsimony   The idea that 'less is better' and, in particular, that a complicated explanation is not needed when a simple one is sufficient.

Pavlov's log   Conditioned reflex action causing bowels to relax as soon as you see the toilet door.

Perception   The process of making sense of the world around us.

Perceptual constancies   The way that perception of an object remains unchanged despite changes in lighting or viewing angle.

Perceptual processing   Processing of material to extract superficial sensory characteristics such as shape or colour.

Perseveration errors   When a participant repeats items in a recall task.

Personality   The characteristic patterns of thoughts, feelings and behaviours that make a person unique.

Personality coefficient   Contrary to the belief that an individual's personality is consistent over time, Mischel suggested that humans are consistently inconsistent. By examining a range of studies into how personality traits are related to units of behaviour, Mischel found an average correlation coefficient of 0.30 (which represents a weak correlation at best) with regard to correlations between two single behaviours in two separate situations.

Phagocytes   Cells which are able to 'swallow' and break down unwanted materials such as pathogens and cell debris.

Phenomenology   Based on the idea that the ordinary world of lived experience is taken for granted and often unnoticed, phenomenology attempts to discover how people know and understand objects (and other people) from the way they perceive and construct ideas about the social world around them.

Phenotype   The characteristics of an organism resulting from the interaction between its genetic makeup and the environment. These characteristics can be biological or behavioural.

Phenylketonuria   An inherited, metabolic disorder that can result in learning difficulties and other neurological problems. People with this disease have difficulty breaking down and using the amino acid phenylalanine. PKU can be managed by a diet restricted in foods that contain this amino acid.

Phonemes   The smallest unit of sound that is able to carry some meaning in language.

Photoreceptor cells   The sensory receptors in the eye which are responsible for converting light energy into electrical signals.

Pidgin and creole   A shared language developed when two communities with different languages join together.

Pinna   The visible part of the ear, on the outside of our heads.

Pinocytosis   The reverse process to exocytosis. The cell 'pinches up' transmitter into vesicles and takes it back into the cell.

Pituitary gland   Endocrine gland, also called hypophysis, that is ventral to the hypothalamus.

Plasticity   The ability of the brain to adapt to deficits or injury.

Pons   Metencephalic structure, ventral in the brain stem, that relays sensory information to the cerebellum and thalamus.

Positive manifold   Charles Spearman's discovery that an individual's performance on any two tests of cognitive abilities is positively correlated.

Post-synaptic events   Events that occur in the post-synaptic cell ('after' the synaptic cleft).

Post-synaptic membrane   Synaptic element associated with the post-synaptic neurone. It is here that neurotransmitters bind to post-synaptic receptors.

Post-synaptic neurone   Neurone that is 'after' the synaptic cleft (that is, the receiving neurone).

Post-synaptic potentials   Graded changes in membrane voltage in the post-synaptic cell (caused by input into that cell) that affects the likelihood that the post-synaptic cell will produce an action potential.

Potassium (K^+)   Positively charged ion that plays a role in producing and maintaining membrane potentials.

Practical intelligence   The ability to solve problems in everyday life. This ability draws upon 'tacit knowledge' which is gained through experience and practice, and is difficult to explain with words.

Precursor   In biochemistry, a substance from which more complex compounds are made.

Prejudice   An unreasonable or unfair dislike of something, or more usually someone – typically because they belong to a specific race, religion, or group.

Presentation   The phase of a memory experiment in which the experimenter presents the to-be-remembered material to participants.

Pre-synaptic events   Events that occur in the pre-synaptic neurone ('before' the synaptic cleft).

Pre-synaptic membrane   Synaptic element associated with the pre-synaptic neurone. It is from here that neurotransmitters are released.

Pre-synaptic neurone   Neurone that is 'before' the synaptic cleft (that is, the transmitting neurone).

Primacy effect   Good recall of the first few items of a set of stimuli (e.g. word list).

Primary auditory cortex   The first cortical structure responsible for processing sound.

Primary dimensions of intellectual abilities   Louis Leon Thurstone found that human intelligence comprises a number of independent cognitive abilities, all of which are of equal importance. Thurstone suggested that there are seven primary dimensions of intellectual abilities.

Primary memory   James's (1890) term for the immediate contents of consciousness and a precursor to the more modern idea of a short-term store.

Probabilistic reasoning   How we reason under varying degrees of uncertainty.

Procedural knowledge   Knowledge that we have that is difficult to put into words, such as how to ride a bicycle.

Production system   A system that uses facts and rules about those facts to govern its behaviour. The term arises because rules are also known as productions.

Progestin-induced pseudohermaphroditism   A similar condition to congenital adrenal hyperplasia, whereby a foetus is exposed to an excess of androgen-like substances (progestin) in the womb.

Prosencephalon   Another name for forebrain.

Prosocial behaviour   The act of helping out another person, whether as a helping behaviour or as an act of altruism.

Protoconversations   Early turn-taking behaviour between adults and infants, whereby adults tend to vocalise when the infants are not vocalising.

Pseudohermaphrodites   These individuals have gonads that are consistent with their sex chromosomes (ovaries in females and testes in males) but have ambiguous internal and external genitalia.

Psychometric approach   Any attempt to assess and express numerically the mental characteristics of behaviour in individuals, usually through specific tests for personality or intelligence or some kind of attitude measurement.

Psychometric tests   Instruments which have been developed for measuring mental characteristics. Psychological tests have been developed to measure a wide range of things, including creativity, job attitudes and skills, brain damage and, of course, 'intelligence'.

Psychoticism   Hans Eysenck suggested a three-factor model of personality in which psychoticism represented individuals who are reckless, unable to empathise with others' situations and likely to commit antisocial acts. Psychoticism has also been termed 'tough-mindedness' (as opposed to 'tender-mindedness') and this is due to people with high psychoticism levels being likely to be ruthless in their dealings with others. Originally, Eysenck believed that high levels of psychoticism could predict an individual's vulnerability to experiencing psychotic symptoms, including schizophrenia.

Puberty The physiological process resulting in sexual maturity. This process is marked in males by the onset of sperm production and a liking for metal music (spermarche) while in females it triggers the onset of the menstrual cycle (menarche).

Pupil The opening in the iris through which light enters the eye.

Qualitative data Describe meaning and experience rather than providing numerical values for behaviour such as frequency counts.

Quantitative data Focus on numbers and frequencies rather than on meaning or experience.

Race Commonly used to refer to groups of people such as white people or black people. It implies a genetic component to the differences between these groups, but research shows that the term 'race' has no biological validity and is best described as a political construct.

Racism A negative attitude towards a group on the basis of their race.

Rape acceptance myths A person's, society's or culture's endorsement or subscription to rape myths. Rape myths are prejudicial, stereotyped or false beliefs about rape, rape victims and rapists which serve to justify and legitimise sexual aggression towards women and shift the blame onto rape victims.

Realistic conflict theory The theory that competition for resources between groups causes conflict.

Recall Where participants are prompted to remember the material that was originally presented.

Recency effect Good recall of the last few items of a set of stimuli (e.g. the last few items on a word list).

Receptors Proteins embedded in cell membranes that respond to ligands (specific chemical substances, e.g. neurotransmitters).

Recessive gene A gene which must be present on both chromosomes in a pair to show outward signs of a certain characteristic.

Reciprocity Helping someone else, on the basis that they will voluntarily help you at some undefined point in the future.

Recognition Where the original material is re-presented and participants indicate whether they remember it or not.

Recognition failure Recognition failure of recallable words occurs when participants recall items that they fail to recognise (a phenomenon impossible in generate-recognise theory).

Reductionism The idea that a complex system is nothing more than the sum of its parts, and that a description of a system can be reduced to descriptions of the individual components.

Reissner's membrane A membrane in the cochlea.

Relative deprivation   An individual's perception that they are getting less than they deserve compared to other people or groups.

Reliability   The reliability of a psychological measuring device (such as a test or a scale) is the extent to which it gives consistent measurements. The greater the consistency of measurement, the greater the tool's reliability.

Retention interval   The gap in time between presentation and test in a memory experiment.

Reticular formation   Network of neurones in the brain stem that regulates arousal and consciousness.

Reticular theory   The theory espoused by Golgi that nerve cells are continuous (actually join) to each other.

Retina   The sensory organ for sight that lines the back of the eye.

Retinal ganglion cells   Cells in the eye which receive information from the rods and cones.

Retrieval   The stage of memory where information is brought back into mind to be used or reported.

Retrieval cue   Any stimulus that helps us recall information, for example a picture, an odour or a sound.

Retrograde axoplasmic transport   Backwards conveyance of material along the axon of a neurone (i.e. from synaptic button towards the soma).

Reuptake   Process by which certain neurotransmitters are taken back into the releasing cell.

Rhombencephalon   Another name for hindbrain.

Ribonucleic acid (RNA)   Nucleic acid that has a number of roles including protein synthesis and gene regulation.

Rime   The vowel sound of a word followed by the subsequent consonants: for example, the rime of 'ham' is 'am'. When two words share the same rime unit, they can be said to rhyme.

Risky shift   When individual group members all favour a relatively risky course of action prior to group discussion, the decision made after group discussion is more risky than the average of individual positions would have predicted.

Rods   The photoreceptor cells in the eye which are extremely sensitive to movement and are responsible for our peripheral vision.

Role conflict   When an individual has two or more different and incompatible roles at the same time, resulting in anxiety and/or stress.

Role theory   A perspective in social psychology that considers how we manage everyday activity (rights, duties, expectations and norms of behaviour) by fulfilment of socially defined social roles (e.g. mother, manager, teacher).

Salutogenesis   This concept focuses on the science of 'good health' and the factors that influence a person's physical and mental wellbeing.

Scaffolding   A teaching strategy in which instruction begins at a level encouraging students' success and provides sufficient support to move students to a higher level of understanding.

Scapegoat   An individual or group who become the target of negative attitudes and/or behaviours, caused by a different group, individual or circumstances.

Schema   A mental representation of some aspect of the world built from experience and into which new experiences are fitted.

Schizophrenia   Schizophrenia is not a single condition but is best described as a syndrome. The typical symptoms include difficulties in organising behaviour (including speech) as well as detachment from reality which may involve delusion and/or hallucinations. Schizophrenia is often misrepresented in the popular media as a case of split or multiple personalities.

Schwann cells   Glial cells responsible for myelination of nerve axons within the PNS.

Scientific revolution   In the sixteenth and seventeenth centuries there was a period of rapid change in the intellectual endeavour of making sense of the world that people lived in. Medieval philosophy was replaced by scientific principles of observation, measurement and experimentation. These developments are linked with Bacon (1561–1626), Galileo (1564–1642), Descartes (1596–1650) and Newton (1642–1727).

Search space   The states that can be visited when trying to solve a problem.

Second messenger   Substance released as part of a series of cascading effects in metabotropic receptors that result in the opening of ion channels.

Self-categorisation theory   The notion that as an individual categorises themselves as a group member, they take on the group identity and the characteristics of a typical group member.

Self-concept or self-identity   Self-knowledge and memory allow people to develop a life story and to understand how others perceive them. The self-concept is the product, therefore, of self-assessments – some relatively permanent such as personality attributes and knowledge of skills and abilities, others less so such as occupation, interests and physical status.

Self-fulfilling prophecy   When an individual's expectations or false beliefs of another influence their interactions and cause that individual to behave in ways which appear to confirm the false beliefs.

Semantic differential scales   Developed by Osgood et al. (1957), a set of diametrically opposite adjectives upon which the participant marks a score.

Semantic processing   Processing of material that extracts meaning from it (e.g. deciding whether it completes a sentence).

Sensation   The stimulation of our sensory systems which cause the nervous system to send electrical impulses to the brain.

Sense of coherence   If a person has high levels of sense of coherence, this has been associated with having good mental health. With sense of coherence, a person's world is seen as controllable (i.e. she or he can influence what happens to them), sensible (i.e. the events that occur can be explained and understood) and meaningful (i.e. that person has a sense of purpose).

Sensitive period   A period of development, usually early in life, during which the individual is most sensitive to certain types of experience or learning. Refers to a period that is more extended than a critical period.

Sensory neurone   Type of neurone that has its cell body located in peripheral ganglia and receives sensory information from organs via (typically) long dendrites. In turn, this information is transmitted along axons to sites within the CNS.

Separation anxiety   The resulting fear or apprehension of a child after the removal of a parent or other significant figure.

Serial position curve   A plot of the percentage of correct responses as a function of order of presentation (e.g. the position of a word in a list).

Sexism   A negative attitude towards a group on the basis of their sex/gender.

Short-term memory   Memory for the immediate contents of consciousness (e.g. maintained by rehearsal or some other process that can act only in the short term). Also describes experiments that have an immediate test or only a brief interval between presentation and test (presumed to measure short-term memory).

Short-term store   A key component of the modal model of short-term memory. Items enter the short-term store as a consequence of attention to environmental stimuli.

Situationalism or **situationalist critique**   Refers to the viewpoint proposed by Walter Mischel and others that our behaviour is primarily determined by factors beyond our personalities. The overall emphasis of this approach is to demonstrate that personality traits or types are not the dominant factor influencing our actions; it is how we interpret situations, and our roles within the situations, that matter.

Snowball effect   Refers to the processes by which the opinions of the majority shift in order to agree with the position of the minority, which is then, strictly speaking, no longer a minority.

Social categorisation   The way in which we categorise people into social groups across society.

Social change   In social identity theory, the rejection of current relations between groups and the collective group effort to bring about a change in those relations.

Social comparison   The comparison of our own attitudes, beliefs and behaviours with other people's in order to establish if they are acceptable.

Social constructionism   An approach to psychology which focuses on meaning and power; it aims to account for the ways in which phenomena are socially constructed.

Social constructivism   A theoretical approach that emphasises the role of culture and context in children's understanding and development.

Social facilitation   Refers to the effect that the presence of one or more people can have to boost our performance.

Social grooming or **allogrooming**   A behaviour seen in many social species including our own. It involves an individual or individuals assisting others to keep clean and in good maintenance. In addition to the obvious health benefits, the behaviour has also taken on a significant social function.

Social hierarchies   Classic research describes a pecking order which determines the dominant and subordinate positions of individuals. This is a pyramid-like form of organisation that has at its head the most dominant individual, while others will be at various levels of dominance or influence.

Social identity   An individual's membership of a social group and their acceptance of the group's attitudes, beliefs and behaviours.

Social identity theory   The explanation of how group membership can influence behaviour. The theory suggests that as a member of a group it is our social self and not our personal self which guides our beliefs and attitudes and therefore our behaviours.

Social inhibition   Refers to how the presence of one or more people can have a detrimental effect on our performance.

Social loafing   The reduction in individual effort that can occur in tasks when only group performance is measured (not each person individually).

Social mobility   In social identity theory, when an individual moves from one group into another group with perceived higher status.

Social responsibility   A social norm that says we should help those in trouble, particularly those who seem to be suffering unfairly.

Sodium (NA+)   a positively charged ion that plays a role in producing and maintaining membrane potentials.

Soma   Cell body; contains the cell nucleus.

Somatic nervous system   The division of the peripheral nervous system that interrelates with the external world.

Somatotopical organisation   The arrangement of brain structures whereby regions of brain represent particular parts of the body. For example, when the hand area in the primary motor cortex is activated, the hand moves.

Sound waves   Fluctuations in air pressure that result from physical vibrations in the environment.

Spatial intelligence   Ability to perceive spatial information.

Species   A group that exists within a genus. Members of a species in the same or in different populations are able to interbreed under natural conditions to produce viable offspring. Species are defined by reproductive isolation. There is one hominid species to which we all belong called *Homo sapiens*.

Specific factors (s)   Spearman's intelligence theory suggested that each individual intelligence test measures a unique or specific factor *s* of intelligence, in addition to the general factor g which all of the intelligence tests have in common.

Specificity approach   This is a way of seeing personality as influencing a person's tendency to experience disease or illness. Through this approach, personality is seen as directly contributing to the cause of a person's illness. For example, someone's personality can directly affect their physiology and make them experience a psychosomatic illness, like having peptic ulcers or some kinds of skin disorders.

Spinal cord   Part of the central nervous system located within the vertebral column.

Spinal nerve   A bundle of axons that transmits information to and from the spinal cord.

SRY gene   The 'sex determining region, Y chromosome' (Haqq et al., 1994). This is part of a group of genes referred to as testes determining factor (TDF).

Stereocilia   The stiff rods (or hairs) that protrude from the inner and outer hair cells in the ear.

Stereotype   An oversimplified, generalised impression of someone or something.

Stereotype threat   The concern of an individual that they will be judged on the stereotypes of the social group to which they belong, and the concern that they will confirm this belief through their own actions (like the self-fulfilling prophecy).

Storage   The stage of memory between encoding and retrieval. Factors such as the length of the retention interval and exposure to interfering material may influence memory during this stage.

Subarachnoid space   Space between the arachnoid layer and the pia mater that is filled with cerebrospinal fluid.

Successful intelligence   In Robert Sternberg's theory, intelligence is the individual's ability to select, shape and adapt to the environment. Someone with a high level of intelligence is successful in interacting with many different environments.

Superior colliculi   Nuclei of the tectum in the midbrain that receive visual information.

Superordinate goal   A goal desired by two or more groups which cannot be achieved by one group on its own, therefore necessitating cooperation between groups.

Syllogism   A form of deductive reasoning consisting of a major premise, a minor premise, and a conclusion. For example, all Liverpool players are divers; Steven Gerrard is a Liverpool player; therefore Steven Gerrard is a diver.

Symbolic thought   The representation of reality through the use of abstract concepts such as words, gestures and numbers.

Sympathetic division   Part of the autonomic nervous system that is mainly involved in spending levels of energy in the body.

Synapse   Junction between cells across which information is transmitted in electrical or chemical form. Comprises a pre-synaptic and a post-synaptic membrane that are separated by the synaptic cleft.

Synaptic buttons   Terminal points of axonal branches from which neurotransmitter is released and which form the pre-synaptic element of a synapse.

Synaptic cleft   Small (20 nanometre) gap that separates the pre- and post-synaptic membranes of a synapse.

Tectorial membrane   A membrane in the cochlea.

Tectum   Dorsal division of the midbrain that consists of the superior and inferior colliculi and receives visual and auditory information.

Tegmentum   Ventral division of the midbrain that consists of the substantia nigra, red nucleus and part of the reticular formation.

Temperaments   In ancient times, a person's temperament was associated with the type of fluid (or 'humour') that was mainly flowing throughout that person's body. Nowadays, some-one's temperament is mainly connected to how a person generally thinks, feels and acts; it is often associated with whether someone is prone to anxiety, anger or a range of other emotions.

Teratogens   Substances or environmental influences that affect development of the foetus resulting in physical abnormalities.

Test   The phase of the task in which the experimenter attempts to measure memory for the material that was presented.

Testosterone   The primary type of androgen, involved in the development of male characteristics and sexual functioning.

Tetraplegia   Paralysis characterised by inability to move and/or feel the lower part and most of the upper part of the body due to damage in the cervical segments of the spinal cord.

Thalamus   Diencephalic structure that relays sensory and motor information to the cerebral cortex.

Theory of mind   The ability to attribute mental states such as beliefs, intentions and desires to yourself and others, and to understand that other people have beliefs, desires and intentions that are different from your own.

Three-factor model   Also known as the PEN model after the initial letters of the three major personality traits that Hans Eysenck claimed were the core parts of people's personalities: psy-choticism, extraversion and neuroticism.

Tonotopic   The spatial ordering (in the ear or brain) of the response to sound frequency, with low frequencies at one location and high frequencies at another.

Top-down processing   A way of explaining a cognitive process in which higher-level processes, such as prior knowledge, influence the processing of lower-level input.

Tower of Hanoi   The Tower of Hanoi is a problem solving puzzle consisting of three rods. On one of the rods are placed a number of disks of various sizes (placed in order of size from large to small). The aim is to move all disks onto another rod in the correct order of size. The constraints are that only one disk can be removed at a time and may not be placed on top of a smaller disk. The aim is to use the smallest possible number of moves to achieve the goal.

Traits   Traits are linked to stable aspects of our personalities. They are usually 'higher-order' parts of our personality that are measured along a continuum and attempt to comprehensively cover the variation in how we think, feel and act.

Transfer-appropriate processing   The idea that similar processing at encoding and retrieval enhances memory.

Transporter molecules   Proteins integral to the cell membrane that are involved in the movement of substances (e.g. neurotransmitters) in and out of the cell.

Trial-and-error   Attempting to solve a problem by not applying any thought to it.

Turner's syndrome   A female with this condition inherits only a single X chromosome (XO sex chromosomes). Such females do not menstruate, are unable to become pregnant, do not develop breasts during puberty and are generally short in stature, but they do not differ from typical females in terms of their behaviour and interests.

Two-alternative forced-choice test   Recognition memory test in which the 'new' and 'old' items are presented simultaneously and the recognised option has to be selected.

Tympanic canal   A fluid-filled cavity in the cochlea.

Tympanic membrane   Also known as the ear drum. A thin membrane that vibrates in response to sound.

Type A behaviour pattern or **type A personality**   This type of personality is normally linked to being at an increased risk of coronary heart disease. Two cardiologists, Friedman and Rosenman, found that the type A personality consisted of a range of typical behaviour patterns ranging from irritability to competitiveness to restlessness. This type of personality is contrasted with people who have type B personality, which mainly involves a set of reactions such as being calm and relaxed and not overly competitive.

Types   Personality types are often categorisations that allow researchers to identify someone's most dominant way of thinking, feeling and acting. Whereas personality traits are assessed on many points on a continuum (i.e. ranging from high to moderate to low levels) on a given personality factor, personality types are often assessed by classifying into one category or another. For instance, if type psychology was being used and a person measured just over the average on an extraversion scale, that person would be labelled as an extravert.

Ultimate attribution error   The tendency to differentially explain similar actions by individuals of different social groups. With a member of an ingroup, if there is good behaviour or achievements this is explained internally (within the individual such as kindness), whereas if there is bad behaviour or failures this is explained externally (societal or environmental factors such as luck). The opposite applies to explanations of the behaviours of a member of another group (an 'outgroup').

Unipolar neurone Type of neurone (usually a sensory or autonomic nervous system neurone), named for its structure, having a single process arising from the cell body.

Ventricle Any of the four cavities in the brain filled with cerebrospinal fluid.

Vesicles Membrane-bound packets of neurotransmitter found within the synaptic button.

Vestibular canal A fluid-filled cavity in the cochlea.

Volition The act of deciding to do something. It is also referred to as 'will'.

Withdrawal symptoms Physiological, behavioural and/or psychological symptoms following the withdrawal of certain drugs.

Word pair Stimulus used in a paired-associate learning cued recall task, in which participants are presented with pairs of words to learn. At test they are presented with one member of the pair as a cue to retrieve the other.

Working memory model A model proposed by Baddeley and Hitch (1974) to account for many of the shortcomings of the modal model of short-term memory.

XXX syndrome A female with this condition inherits an additional X chromosome (XXX sex chromosomes). XXX females do not have any distinguishing features and they are virtually impossible to tell apart from typical XX females.

XYY syndrome A male with this condition inherits an additional Y chromosome (XYY sex chromosomes). Such individuals are virtually indistinguishable from typical males, though XYY males tend to be slightly taller in stature and have larger canine teeth.

Zone of proximal development (ZPD) The zone or distance between what a learner can achieve alone and what he/she can achieve with assistance.

REFERENCES

Abrams, D. (1992). Processes of social identification. In G.M. Breakwell (Ed.), *Social psychology of identity and the self-concept* (pp. 57–99). London: Surrey University Press.

Ackerman, B.P., Brown, E., & Izard, C.E. (2003). Continuity and change in levels of externalizing behavior in school children from economically disadvantaged families. *Child Development, 74,* 694–709.

Adams, D. (1979). *The hitch hiker's guide to the galaxy.* London: Pan Macmillan.

Adorno, T.W., Brunswik, E.F., Levinson, D.J., & Sanford, R.N. (1950). *The authoritarian personality.* New York: Harper.

Ahnert, L., Pinquart, M., & Lamb, M.E. (2006). Security of children's relationships with nonparental care providers: a meta-analysis. *Child Development, 74,* 664–679.

Ainsworth, M.D.S., Blehar, M.C., Waters, E., & Wall, S. (1978). *Patterns of attachment: a psychological study of the strange situation.* Hillsdale, NJ: Erlbaum.

Ajzen, I. (1991). Theory of planned behaviour. *Organisational Behavior and Human Decision Processes, 50,* 179–211.

Alexander, F. (1950). *Psychosomatic medicine.* New York: Norton.

Allen, G., & Courchesne, E. (2003). Differential effects of developmental cerebellar abnormality on cognitive and motor functions in the cerebellum: an fMRI study of autism. *American Journal of Psychiatry, 160,* 262–273.

Allen, L.S., & Gorski, R.A. (1990). Sex difference in the bed nucleus of the stria terminalis of the human brain. *The Journal of Comparative Neurology, 302,* 697–706.

Allen, L.S., & Gorski, R.A. (1992). Sexual orientation and the size of the anterior commissure in the human brain. *Proceedings of the National Academy of Sciences USA, 89,* 7191–7202.

Allen, L.S., Hines, M., Shryne, J.E., & Gorski, R.A. (1989). Two sexually dimorphic cell groups in the human brain. *Journal of Neuroscience, 9,* 497–506.

Allport, A. (1993). Attention and control: have we been asking the wrong questions? A critical review of twenty-five years. In D.E. Meyer and S. Kornblum (Eds), *Attention and performance XIV* (pp. 183–218). Cambridge, MA: MIT Press.

Allport, F.H. (1920). The influence of the group upon association and thought. *Journal of Experimental Psychology, 3,* 159–182.

Allport, G.W. (1954). *The nature of prejudice.* Cambridge, MA: Addison-Wesley.

Almers, W. (1990). Exocytosis. *Annual Review of Physiology, 52,* 607–624.

Altemeyer, B. (1998). The other 'authoritarian personality'. In M.P. Zanna (Ed.), *Advances in experimental social psychology* (pp. 47–92). San Diego: Academic.

Amelang, M., & Ullwer, U. (1991). Correlations between psychometric measures and psychophysiological as well as experimental variables in studies on extraversion and neuroticism. In J. Strelau & A. Angleitner (Eds), *Explorations in temperament*. New York: Plenum.

Amir, Y. (1969). Contact hypothesis in ethnic relations. *Psychological Bulletin, 71*, 319–342.

Anderson, J.R. (1993). *Rules of the mind*. Hove: Erlbaum.

Anderson, J.R. (2000). *Cognitive psychology and its implications* (5th edn). New York: Worth.

Anderson, J.R., & Reder, L.M. (1979). An elaborative processing explanation of depth of processing. In L.S. Cermak & F.I.M. Craik (Eds), *Levels of processing in human memory* (pp. 385–403). Hillsdale, NJ: Erlbaum.

Anderson, J.R., & Schooler, L.J. (2000). The adaptive nature of memory. In E. Tulving & F.I.M. Craik (Eds), *Handbook of memory* (pp. 557–570). New York: Oxford University Press.

Anderson, R.C., & Pichert, J.W. (1978). Recall of previously unrecallable information following a shift in perspective. *Journal of Verbal Learning and Verbal Behavior, 17*, 1–12.

Anderson, S., Dallal, G., & Must, A. (2003). Relative weight and race influence average age at menarche: results from two nationally representative surveys of U.S. girls studied 25 years apart. *Pediatrics, 111*, 844–850.

Antonovsky, A. (1987). *Unraveling the mystery of health: how people manage stress and stay well*. San Francisco: Jossey-Bass.

Archer, J. (2004). Sex differences in aggression in real-world settings: a meta-analytic review. *General Review of Psychology, 8*, 291–322.

Arnow, B.A., Desmond, J.E., Banner, L.L., Glover, G.H., Solomon, A., Polan, M.L., Lue, T.F., & Atlas, S.W. (2002). Brain activation and sexual arousal in healthy, heterosexual males. *Brain, 125*, 1014–1023.

Aronson, E. (2008). *The social animal* (10th edn). New York: Worth.

Atkinson, R.C., & Shiffrin, R.M. (1968). Human memory: a proposed system and its control processes. In K.W. Spence & J.T. Spence (Eds), *The psychology of learning and motivation: advances in research and theory*, vol. 2 (pp. 742–775). New York: Academic.

Awh, E., & Pashler, H. (2000). Evidence for split attentional foci. *Journal of Experimental Psychology: Human Perception and Performance, 26*, 834–846.

Baddeley, A.D. (1978). The trouble with levels: a reexamination of Craik and Lockhart's framework for memory research. *Psychological Review, 85*, 139–152.

Baddeley, A.D., & Hitch, G.J. (1974). Working memory. In G.H. Bower (Ed.), *The psychology of learning and motivation: advances in research and theory*, vol. 8. (pp. 742–775). New York: Academic.

Baddeley, A.D., & Hitch, G.J. (1977). Recency reexamined. In S. Dornic (Ed.), *Attention and performance VI* (pp. 647–667). Hillsdale, NJ: Erlbaum.

Bagwell, C.L., Newcomb, A.F., & Bukowski, W.M. (1998). Preadolescent friendship and peer rejection as predictors of adult adjustment. *Child Development, 69*, 140–153.

Bailey, D.H., and Geary, D.C. (2009). Hominid brain evolution. *Human Nature, 20*(1), 67–79.

Bailey, J.M., & Pillard, R.C. (1991). A genetic study of male sexual orientation. *Archives of General Psychiatry, 48,* 1089–1095.

Bailey, J.M., Dunne, M.P., & Martin, N.G. (2000). Genetic and environmental influences on sexual orientation and its correlates in an Australian twin sample. *Journal of Personality and Social Psychology, 78,* 524–536.

Baird, G., Cass, H., & Slonims, V. (2003). Diagnosis of autism. *British Medical Journal, 327,* 488–493.

Ballard, P.B. (1913). Oblivescence and reminiscence. *British Journal of Psychology Monograph Supplements, 1,* 1–82.

Bandura, A. (1977). *Social learning theory.* Englewood Cliffs, NJ: Prentice Hall.

Banyard, V.L., Moynihan, M.M., & Plante, E.G. (2007). Sexual violence prevention through bystander education: an experimental evaluation. *Journal of Community Psychology, 35*(4), 463–481.

Baptista, M. (2005). New directions in pidgin and creole studies. *Annual Review of Anthropology, 34,* 33–42.

Baron, R.S. (1986). Distraction-conflict theory: progress and problems. In L. Berkowitz (Ed.), *Advances in experimental social psychology,* vol. 19 (pp. 1–40). New York: Academic.

Baron-Cohen, S. (1995). *Mindblindness.* Cambridge, MA: MIT Press.

Baron-Cohen, S., Leslie, A.M., & Frith, U. (1985). Does the autistic child have a 'theory of mind'? *Cognition, 21,* 37–46.

Bartlett, F.C. (1932). *Remembering: a study in experimental and social psychology.* Cambridge: Cambridge University Press.

Bass, J.D., & Mulick, J.A. (2007). Social play skill enhancement of children with autism using peers and siblings as therapists. *Psychology in the Schools, 44*(7), 727–735.

Batson, C.D., & Coke, J.S. (1981). Empathy: a source of altruistic motivation for helping? In J.P. Rushton & R.M. Sorrentino (Eds), *Altruism and helping behavior: social, personality, and developmental perspectives.* Hillsdale, NJ: Erlbaum.

Batson, C.D., Cochran, P.J., Biederman, M.F., Blosser, J.L., Ryan, M.J., & Vogt, B. (1978). Failure to help when in a hurry: callousness or conflict? *Personality and Social Psychology Bulletin, 4,* 97–101.

Batson, C.D., Sympson, S.C., Hindman, J.L., & Decruz, P. (1996). 'I've been there, too': effect on empathy of prior experience with a need. *Personality and Social Psychology Bulletin, 22*(5), 474–482.

Baumeister, R.F., Chesner, S.P., Senders, P.S., & Tice, D.M. (1988). Who's in charge here? Group leaders to lend help in emergencies. *Personality and Social Psychology Bulletin, 14,* 17–22.

Beauvois, J.-L., & Dubois, N. (1988). The norm of internality in the explanation of psychological events. *European Journal of Social Psychology, 18*(4), 299–316.

Bee, H., & Boyd, D. (2005). *The developing child* (10th edn). Boston: Pearson.

Bellezza, F.S., & Bower, G.H. (1981). Person stereotypes and memory for people. *Journal of Personality and Social Psychology, 41*(5), 856–865.

Bem, D.J. (1965). An experimental analysis of self-persuasion. *Journal of Experimental Social Psychology, 1,* 199–218.

Bem, S. (2001). The explanatory autonomy of psychology: why a mind is not a brain. *Theory and Psychology*, *11*(6), 785–795.

Bengtsson-Tops, A., & Hansson, L. (2001). The validity of Antonovsky's sense of coherence measure in a sample of schizophrenic patients living in the community. *Journal of Advanced Nursing*, *33*(4), 432–438.

Benson, P.L., Karabenick, S.A., & Lerner, R.M. (1976). Pretty pleases: the effects of physical attractiveness, race, and sex on receiving help. *Journal of Experimental Social Psychology*, *12*, 409–415.

Bergman, E., & Roediger, H.L. (1999). Can Bartlett's repeated reproduction experiments be replicated? *Memory & Cognition*, *27*, 937–947.

Berkowitz, L. (1972). Social norms, feelings, and other factors affecting helping and altruism. In L. Berkowitz (Ed.), *Advances in experimental social psychology*, vol. 6 (pp. 63–108). New York: Academic.

Berkowitz, L. (1993). *Aggression: its causes, consequences, and control*. New York: McGraw-Hill.

Bertenthal, B., & Fischer, K. (1978). Development of self-recognition in the infant. *Developmental Psychology*, *14*, 44–50.

Bickerton, D. (1984). The language bioprogram hypothesis. *Behavioral and Brain Sciences*, *7*(2), 173–221.

Bierhoff, H.W., Klein, R., & Kramp, P. (1991). Evidence for the altruistic personality from data on accident research. *Journal of Personality*, *59*(2), 263–280.

Bijeljac-Babic, R., Bertoncini, J., & Mehler, J. (1993). How do 4-day-old infants categorize multisyllabic utterances? *Developmental Psychology*, *29*, 711–721.

Billig, M. (1978). *Fascists: a social psychological view of the National Front*. London: Academic.

Billig, M. (1985). Prejudice, a categorization and particularization: from a perceptual to a rhetorical approach. *European Journal of Social Psychology*, *15*(1), 79–103.

Billig, M. (1988). The notion of prejudice: some rhetorical and ideological aspects. *Text*, *8*, 91–110.

Billig, M. (2001). Humour and hatred: the racist jokes of the Ku Klux Klan. *Discourse and Society*, *12*(3), 267–289.

Billig, M., & Tajfel, H. (1973). Social categorization and similarity in intergroup behaviour. *European Journal of Social Psychology*, *3*, 27–52.

Binet, A., & Simon, T. (1905). Méthodes nouvelles pour le diagnostic du niveau intellectuel des anormaux. *L'Anne Psychologique*, *11*, 191–244.

Bingham, W.V. (1937). *Aptitudes and aptitude testing*. New York: Harper.

Birch, S.A.J., & Bloom, P. (2007). The curse of knowledge in reasoning about false beliefs. *Psychological Science*, *18*, 382–386.

Bjork, R.A., & Whitten, W.B. (1974). Recency-sensitive retrieval processes in long-term free recall. *Cognitive Psychology*, *6*, 173–189.

Blackless, M., Charuvastra, A., Derryck, A., Fausto-Sterling, A., Lauzanne, K., & Lee, E. (2000). How sexually dimorphic are we? Review and synthesis. *American Journal of Human Biology*, *12*, 151–166.

Blackmore, S. (1993). *Dying to live: science and the near death experience*. London: Grafton.

Blackmore, S. (1999). *The meme machine*. Oxford: Oxford University Press.

Blackmore, S. (2003). *Consciousness: an introduction*. London: Hodder & Stoughton.

Blackmore, S. (2005). *Conversations on consciousness*. Oxford: Oxford University Press.

Blackmore, S. (2009). *Ten Zen questions*. Oxford: OneWorld.

Blake, R.R., & Mouton, J.S. (1961). Reactions to intergroup competition under win–lose conditions. *Management Science, 7*(4), 420–435.

Blanchard, R. (1997). Birth order and sibling sex ratio in homosexual versus heterosexual males and females. *Annual Review of Sex Research, 8*, 27–67.

Blanchard, R. and Bogaert, A.F. (1996) Homosexuality in men and number of older brothers. *American Journal of Psychiatry, 153*, 27–31.

Blascovich, J., Mendes, W.B., Hunter, S.B., & Salomon, K. (1999). 'Social facilitation' as challenge and threat. *Journal of Personality and Social Psychology, 77*, 68–77.

Block, J. (1995). A contrarian view of the five-factor approach to personality description. *Psychological Bulletin, 117*, 187–215.

Block, J. (2001). Millennial contrarianism: the five-factor approach to personality description 5 years later. *Journal of Research in Personality, 35*, 98–107.

Boelens, H., Hofman, B., Tamaddoni, T., & Eenink, K. (2007). Specific effect of modeling on young children's word productions. *Psychological Record, 57*, 145–166.

Bogaert, A.F. (2006). Biological versus nonbiological older brothers' and men's sexual orientation. *Proceedings of the National Academy of Sciences USA, 103*, 10771–10774.

Bogaert, A.F., & Hershberger, S. (1999). The relation between sexual orientation and penile size. *Archives of Sexual Behavior, 28*, 213–221.

Bogg, T., & Roberts, B.W. (2004). Conscientiousness and health behaviors: a meta-analysis of the leading behavioural contributors to mortality. *Psychological Bulletin, 130*, 887–919.

Bolton, T. (1902). A biological view of perception. *Psychological Review, 9*, 537–548.

Boom, J., Wouter, H., & Keller, M. (2007). A cross-cultural validation of stage development: a Rasch re-analysis of longitudinal socio-moral reasoning data. *Cognitive Development, 22*, 213–229.

Boon, J.C., & Davis, G.M. (1987). Rumours greatly exaggerated: Allport and Postman's apocryphal study. *Canadian Journal of Behavioural Science, 19*(4), 430–440.

Booth, A.E., & Waxman, S. (2002). Word learning is 'smart' evidence that conceptual information affects preschoolers' extension of novel words. *Cognition, 84*, B11–B22.

Booth-Kewley, S., & Friedman, H. (1987). Psychological predictors of heart disease: a quantitative review. *Psychological Bulletin, 101*(3), 343–362.

Booth-Kewley, S., & Vickers, R.R. (1994). Associations between major domains of personality and health behaviour. *Journal of Personality, 62*(3), 281–298.

Boring, E.G. (1923). Intelligence as the tests test it. *New Republic, 35*, 35–37.

Bowlby, J. (1944). Forty-four juvenile thieves: their characters and their home life. *International Journal of Psycho-Analysis, 25*, 19–52, 107–127.

Bowlby, J. (1969). *Attachment and loss. Vol. 1: Attachment*. New York: Basic.

Bradley, L., & Bryant, P. (1983). Categorising sounds and learning to read – a causal connection. *Nature, 301*, 419–521.

Bradshaw, C.P., Sawyer, A.L., & O'Brennan, L.M. (2007). Bullying and peer victimization at school: perceptual differences between students and school staff. *School Psychology Review*, 36, 361–382.

Bray, R.M., & Noble, A.M. (1978). Authoritarianism and decisions of mock juries: evidence of jury bias and group polarization. *Journal of Personality and Social Psychology*, 36, 1424–1430.

Breakwell, G.M. (1986). *Coping with threatened identities*. London: Methuen .

Brebner, J., & Cooper, C. (1985). A proposed unified model of extraversion. In J.T. Spence & C.E. Izard (Eds), *Motivation, emotion and personality*. Amsterdam: North-Holland.

Breckler, S.J. (1984). Empirical validation of affect, behavior, and cognition as distinct components of attitude. *Journal of Personality and Social Psychology*, 47, 1191–1205.

Bretherton, I. (1991). The roots and growing points of attachment theory. In C.M. Parkes, J. Stevenson-Hinde, & P. Marris (Eds), *Attachment across the life cycle* (pp. 9–32). London: Routledge.

Brewer, M.B. (1999). The psychology of prejudice: ingroup love or outgroup hate? *Journal of Social Issues*, 55(3), 429–444.

Brewer, M.B., & Brown, R.J. (1998). Intergroup relations. In D.T. Gilbert, S.T. Fiske, & G. Lindzey (Eds), *The handbook of social psychology* (pp. 554–594). New York: McGraw-Hill.

Bridges, L.J. (2003). Trust, attachment, and relatedness. In M.H. Bornstein, L. Davidson, C.L.M. Keyes, & K.A. Moore (Eds), *Well-being: positive development across the life course*. Mahwah, NJ: Erlbaum.

Broadbent, D.E. (1958). *Perception and communication*. London: Pergamon.

Broks, P. (2004). *Into the silent lands: travels in neuropsychology*. London: Atlantic.

Brown, A.L., & Campione, J.C. (1990). Communities of learning and thinking, or a context by any other name. In D. Kuhn (Ed.), *Developmental perspectives on teaching and learning thinking skills*, vol. 21 (pp. 108–126). Basel: Karger.

Brown, G.D.A., Neath, I., & Chater, N. (2007). A temporal ratio model of memory. *Psychological Review*, 114, 539–576.

Brown, R. (1965). *Social psychology*. New York: Macmillan.

Brown, R. (1973). Development of the first language in the human species. *American Psychologist*, 28(2), 97–106.

Brown, R. (1995). *Prejudice: its social psychology*. Oxford: Blackwell.

Bruner, J.S. (1975). From communication to language: a psychological perspective. *Cognition*, 3, 255–287.

Bryan, J.H., & Test, M.A. (1967). Models and helping: naturalistic studies in aiding behavior. *Journal of Personality and Social Psychology*, 6, 400–407.

Bryden, M.P., & MacRae, L. (1989). Dichotic laterality effects obtained with emotional words. *Neuropsychiatry, Neuropsychology, and Behavioral Neurology*, 1(3), 171–176.

Buhrmester, D., & Furman, W. (1987). The development of companionship and intimacy. *Child Development*, 58, 1101–1113.

Burman, E. (Ed.) (1998). *Deconstructing feminist psychology*. London: Sage.

Burman, E., & Parker, I. (Eds) (1993). *Discourse analytic research: repertoires and readings of texts in action*. London: Routledge.

Burnstein, E., & Vinokur, A. (1977). Persuasive argumentation and social comparison as determinants of attitude polarization. *Journal of Experimental Social Psychology*, *13*, 315–332.

Burnstein, E., Crandall, C., & Kitayama, S. (1994). Some neo-Darwinian decision rules for altruism: weighing cues for inclusive fitness as a function of the biological importance of the decision. *Journal of Personality and Social Psychology*, *67*, 773–789.

Burr, V. (2003). *Social constructionism* (2nd edn). London: Psychology.

Burt, C.L. (1957). *The causes and treatments of backwardness*. London: University of London Press.

Burt, M.R. (1980). Cultural myths and supports for rape. *Journal of Personality and Social Psychology*, *38*(2), 217–230.

Burwood, S., Gilbert, G., & Lennon, K. (1999). *Philosophy of mind*. London: UCL Press.

Buss, A.H. (1989). Personality as traits. *American Psychologist*, *44*, 1378–1388.

Butterworth, G.E. (1977). Object disappearance and error in Piaget's stage IV task. *Journal of Experimental Child Psychology*, *23*, 301–401.

Button, T.M.M., Maughan, B., & McGuffin, P. (2007). The relationship of maternal smoking to psychological problems in the offspring. *Early Human Development*, *83*, 727–732.

Byne, W., Lasco, M.S., Kemether, E., Shinwari, A., Edgar, M.A., Morgello, S., Jones, L.B., & Tobet, S. (2000). The interstitial nuclei of the human anterior hypothalamus: an investigation of sexual variation in volume and cell size, number and density. *Brain Research*, *856*, 254–258.

Cains, R.A. (2000). Children diagnosed ADHD: factors to guide intervention. *Educational Psychology in Practice*, *16*(2), 159–180.

Callaway, M., & Esser, J. (1984). Groupthink: effects of cohesiveness and problem-solving procedures on group decision making. *Social Behavior and Personality*, *12*, 157–164.

Calvin, W.H. (2002). *A brain for all seasons: human evolution and abrupt climate change*. Chicago: University of Chicago Press.

Campbell, S.B. (2000). Developmental perspectives on attention deficit disorder. In A. Sameroff, M. Lewis, & S. Miller (Eds), *Handbook of child psychopathology* (2nd edn). New York: Plenum.

Cantor, J.M., Blanchard, R., Paterson, A.D., & Bogaert, A.F. (2002). How many gay men owe their sexual orientation to fraternal birth order? *Archives of Sexual Behavior*, *31*, 63–71.

Carroll, J., Snowling, M., Hulme, C., & Stevenson, J. (2003). The development of phonological awareness in pre-school children. *Developmental Psychology*, *39*, 913–923.

Carroll, L. (1865). *Alice's adventures in Wonderland*. Harmondsworth: Penguin, 2003.

Casey, B.J. (2001). Disruption of inhibitory control in developmental disorders: a mechanistic model of implicated frontostriatal circuitry. In J. McClelland & R. Sieglar (Eds), *Mechanisms of cognitive development* (pp. 327–349). Mahwah, NJ: Erlbaum.

Castiello, U., & Umiltà, C. (1992). Splitting focal attention. *Journal of Experimental Psychology: Human Perception and Performance*, *18*, 837–848.

Castro, A., Díaz, F., & van Boxtel, G.J.M. (2007). How does a short history of spinal cord injury affect movement-related brain potentials? *European Journal of Neuroscience*, *25*, 2927–2934.

Cattell, R.B. (1965). *The scientific analysis of personality.* Harmondsworth: Penguin.

Cattell, R.B., Eber, H.W., & Tatsuoka, M.M. (1970). *The 16-factor personality questionnaire.* Champaign, IL: IPAT.

Cepeda, N.J., Pashler, H., Vul, E., Wixted, J.T., & Rohrer, D. (2006). Distributed practice in verbal recall tasks: a review and quantitative synthesis. *Psychological Bulletin, 132,* 354–380.

Chalmers, D. (1996). *The conscious mind.* New York: Oxford University Press.

Chávez-Bueno, S., & McCracken, G. (2005). Bacterial meningitis in children. *Pediatric Clinics of North America, 52,* 795–810.

Chemers, M. (2002). Leadership effectiveness: an integrative review. In M. Hogg & R. Tinsdale (Eds), *Blackwell handbook of social psychology: group process.* London: Blackwell.

Cherry, E.C. (1953). Some experiments on the recognition of speech, with one and with two ears. *Journal of the Acoustical Society of America, 25,* 975–979.

Clark, A.J. (2003). *Natural-born cyborgs: minds, technologies and the future of human intelligence.* Oxford: Oxford University Press.

Clarke, S., Bellmann Thiran, A., Maeder, P., Adriani, M., Vernet, O., Regli, L., Cuisenaire, O., & Thiran, J.P. (2002). What and where in human audition: selective deficits following focal hemispheric lesions. *Experimental Brain Research, 147,* 815.

Colapinto, J. (2000). *As nature made him: the boy who was raised as a girl.* New York: HarperCollins.

Colombo, J. (1982). The critical period concept: research, methodology, and theoretical issues. *Psychological Bulletin, 91*(2), 260–275.

Comer, D.R. (1995). A model of social loafing in real work groups. *Human Relations, 48,* 647–667.

Connolly, I., & O'Moore, M. (2003). Personality and family relations of children who bully. *Personality and Individual Differences, 34,* 1–8.

Cook, S.W. (1978). Interpersonal and attitudinal outcomes in cooperating interracial groups: a context effect. *Journal of Personality and Social Psychology, 49,* 1231–1245.

Cooper, R.P., & Aslin, R.N. (1990). Preference for infant-directed speech in the first month after birth. *Child Development, 61,* 1584–1595.

Costa, P.T. Jr, & McCrae, R.R. (1976). Age differences in personality structure: a cluster analytic approach. *Journal of Gerontology, 31*(5), 564–570.

Costa, P.T., & McCrae, R.R. (1992). *NEO PI-R professional manual.* Odessa, FL: Psychological Assessment Resources.

Cottrell, N.B., Wack, D.L., Sekerak, G.J., & Rittle, R.M. (1968). Social facilitation of dominant responses by the presence of an audience and the mere presence of others. *Journal of Personality and Social Psychology, 9,* 245–250.

Craik, F.I.M., & Lockhart, R.S. (1972). Levels of processing: a framework for memory research. *Journal of Verbal Learning and Verbal Behaviour, 11,* 671–684.

Cramer, R.E., McMaster, M.R., Bartell, P.A., & Dragna, M. (1988). Subject competence and minimization of the bystander effect. *Journal of Applied Social Psychology, 18,* 1133–1148.

Creswell, J.W., & Plano Clark, V.L. (2007). *Mixed methods research.* London: Sage.

Crick, F.H. (1994). *The astonishing hypothesis: the scientific search for the soul.* New York: Scribner.

Crisp, R.J. (2008). Recognising complexity in intergroup relations. *The Psychologist*, *21*(3), 206–209.

Crisp, R.J., & Turner, R.T. (2007). *Essential social psychology*. London: Sage.

Crisp, R.J., Hewstone, M., & Rubin, M. (2001). Does multiple categorization reduce intergroup bias? *Personality and Social Psychology Bulletin*, *27*, 76–89.

Cromby, J. (2005). Theorising embodied subjectivity. *International Journal of Critical Psychology*, *15*, 133–150.

Crossley, M. (2000). *Introducing narrative psychology: self, trauma and the construction of meaning*. Buckingham: Open University Press.

Crowder, R.G. (1993). Systems and principles in memory theory: another critique of pure memory. In A. Collins, M.A. Conway, S.E. Gathercole, & P.E. Morris (Eds), *Theories of memory* (pp. 139–161). Hillsdale, NJ: Erlbaum.

Csikszentmihalyi, M. (1993). *The evolving self: a psychology for the new millennium*. New York: HarperCollins.

Csikszentmihalyi, M., & Rochberg-Halton, E. (1981). *The meaning of things: domestic symbols and the self*. Cambridge: Cambridge University Press.

Curt, B. (1994). *Textuality and tectonics: troubling social and psychological science*. Buckingham: Open University Press.

Curtiss, S. (Ed.) (1977). *Genie: psycholinguistic study of a modern-day 'wild child'*. New York: Academic.

Cushing, J.T. (1998). *Philosophical concepts in physics: the historical relation between philosophy and scientific theories*. Cambridge: Cambridge University Press.

Dahrendorf, R. (1973). *Homo sociologicus*. London: Routledge Kegan Paul.

Damasio, H., Grabowski, T., Frank, R., Galaburda, A.M., & Damasio, A.R. (1994). The return of Phineas Gage: clues about the brain from the skull of a famous patient. *Science*, *264*(5162), 1102–1105.

Damon, W. (1977). Measurement and social development. *Counseling Psychologist*, *6*, 13–15.

Damon, W. (1980). Patterns of change in children's prosocial reasoning: a two year longitudinal study. *Child Development*, *51*, 1010–1017.

Danziger, K. (1990). *Constructing the subject: historical origins of psychological research*. Cambridge: Cambridge University Press.

Darwin, C. (1871). *The descent of man, and selection in relation to sex*. London: John Murray.

Davies, M.N.O., & Green, P.R. (1990). Optic flow-field variables trigger landing in hawk but not in pigeons. *Naturwissenschaften*, *77*, 142–144.

Davies, M.N.O., & Green, P.R. (1994). *Perception and motor control in birds: an ecological approach*. Berlin: Springer.

Deary, I. (1996). A (latent) Big Five personality model in 1915. *Journal of Personality and Social Psychology*, *6*, 299–311.

DeCasper, A.J., & Fifer, W.P. (1980). Of human bonding: newborns prefer their mothers' voices. *Science*, *208*, 1174–1176.

DeCasper, A.J., Lecanuet, J.P., Busnel, M.C., Granier-Deferre, C., & Maugeais, R. (1994). Fetal reactions to recurrent maternal speech. *Infant Behavioral and Development*, *17*, 159–164.

DeKlyen, M., & Speltz, M.L. (2001). Attachment and conduct disorder. In J. Hill & B. Maughan (Eds), *Conduct disorders in childhood and adolescence* (pp. 320–345). Cambridge: Cambridge University Press.

DePalma, M.T., Madey, S.F., Tillman, T.C., & Wheeler, J. (1999). Perceived patient responsibility and belief in a just world affect helping. *Basic and Applied Social Psychology*, 21, 131–137.

Deschamps, J.C., & Doise, W. (1978). Crossed category memberships in intergroup relations. In H. Tajfel (Ed.), *Differentiation between social groups*. Cambridge: Cambridge University Press.

Deutsch, J.A., & Deutsch, D. (1963). Attention: some theoretical considerations. *Psychological Review*, 70, 80–90.

Dewaele, J.M., & Furnham, A. (1999). Extraversion: the unloved variable in applied linguistic research. *Language Learning*, 49, 509–544.

Diamond, M. (1997). Sexual identity and sexual orientation in children with traumatised or ambiguous genitalia. *Journal of Sex Research*, 34, 199–211.

Diamond, M., & Sigmundson, H.K. (1997). Sex reassignment at birth: long-term review and clinical implications. *Archives of Pediatric and Adolescent Medicine*, 151, 298–304.

Dickstein, L.S. (1978). The effect of figure on syllogistic reasoning. *Memory and Cognition*, 6, 76–83.

Diener, E. (1977). Deindividuation: causes and consequences. *Social Behavior and Personality*, 5, 497–507.

Diener, E. (1980). Deindividuation: the absence of self-awareness and self-regulation in group members. In P.B. Paulus (Ed.), *Psychology of group influence* (pp. 209–242). Hillsdale, NJ: Erlbaum.

Digman, J.M. (1990). Personality structure: emergence of the five-factor model. *Annual Review of Psychology*, 41, 417–440.

Dion, K.L. (2003). Prejudice, racism, and discrimination. In T. Millon & J. Lerner (Eds), *Handbook of psychology. Vol. 5: Personality and social psychology* (pp. 507–536). Hoboken, NJ: Wiley.

Dittman, M. (2002). Study ranks the top 20th century psychologists. *Monitor on Psychology*, 33, 28–29.

Dittmar, H. (1992). *The social psychology of material possessions: to have is to be*. Hemel Hempstead: Harvester Wheatsheaf.

Dollard, J., Doob, L.W., Miller, N.E., Mowrer, O.H., & Sears, R.R. (1939). *Frustration and aggression*. New Haven, CT: Yale University Press.

Doty, R.M., Peterson, B.E., & Winter, D.G. (1991). Threat and authoritarianism in the United States. *Journal of Personality and Social Psychology*, 61, 629–640.

Duckitt, J. (1992). Psychology and prejudice: a historical analysis and integrative framework. *American Psychologist*, 47(10), 1182–1193.

Dunbar, R.I.M. (1996). *Grooming, gossip and the evolution of language*. Cambridge, MA: Harvard University Press.

Dunbar, R.I.M. (1998). The social brain hypothesis. *Evolutionary Anthropology*, 6, 178–190.

Duncan, G.J., Brooks-Gunn, J., & Klebanov, P.K. (1994). Economic deprivation and early childhood development. *Child Development*, 65, 296–318.

Duncan, L.G., Seymour, P.H.K., & Hill, S. (1997). How important are rhyme and analogy in beginning reading? *Cognition, 63,* 171–208.

Dunn, J. (1988). Normative life events as risk factors in childhood. In M. Rutter (Ed.), *Studies of psychosocial risk: the power of longitudinal data.* Cambridge: Cambridge University Press.

Dweck, C.S. (2002). Beliefs that make smart people dumb. In R. Sternberg (Ed.), *Why smart people can be so stupid.* New Haven, CT: Yale University Press.

Dyson, B.J., & Ishfaq, F. (2008). Auditory memory can be object-based. *Psychonomic Bulletin and Review, 15,* 409–412.

Eagly, A.H. (1995). The science and politics of comparing women and men. *American Psychologist, 50,* 145–158.

Eagly, A.H., & Chaiken, S. (1993). *The psychology of attitudes.* Fort Worth, TX: Harcourt Brace Jovanovich.

Eagly, A.H., & Crowley, M. (1986). Gender and helping behavior: a meta-analytic review of the social psychological literature. *Psychological Bulletin, 117,* 125–145.

Edelman, G.M. (2006). *Second nature: brain science and human knowledge.* London: Yale University Press.

Edwards, D., & Potter, J. (1992). *Discursive psychology.* London: Sage.

Eisenberg, N. (1986). *Altruistic emotion, cognition and behaviour.* Hillsdale, NJ: Erlbaum.

Eisenberg, N. (1992). *The caring child.* Cambridge, MA: Harvard University Press.

Eisenberg, N., Guthrie, I.K., Murphy, B.C., Shepard, S.A., Cumberland, A., & Carlo, G. (1999). Consistency and development of prosocial dispositions: a longitudinal study. *Child Development, 70,* 1360–1372.

Ellis, J., & Fox, P. (2001). The effect of self-identified sexual orientation on helping behavior in a British sample: are lesbians and gay men treated differently? *Journal of Applied Social Psychology, 31,* 1238–1247.

Ellis, L., & Ames, M.A. (1987). Neurohormonal functioning and sexual orientation: a theory of homosexuality–heterosexuality. *Psychological Bulletin, 101,* 233–258.

Ellison, N., Heino, R., & Gibs, J. (2006). Managing impressions online: self-presentation processes in the online dating environment. *Journal of Computer-Mediated Communication, 11*(2), article 2.

Emswiller, T., Deaux, K., & Willits, J.E. (1971). Similarity, sex, and requests for small favors. *Journal of Applied Social Psychology, 1,* 284–291.

Eriksen, B.A., & Eriksen, C.W. (1974). Effects of noise-letters on identification of a target letter in a nonsearch task. *Perception & Psychophysics, 16,* 143–149.

Eriksen, C.W., & Yeh, Y. (1985). Allocation of attention in the visual field. *Journal of Experimental Psychology: Human Perception and Performance, 11,* 583–597.

Evans, J. St B. T., Barston, J.L., & Pollard, P. (1983). On the conflict between logic and belief in syllogistic reasoning. *Memory and Cognition, 11,* 295–306.

Evans, J. St B. T., Newstead, S.E., & Byrne, R.M.J. (1993). *Human reasoning: the psychology of deduction.* Hove: Erlbaum.

Evardone, M., Alexander, G.M., & Morey, L.C. (2008). Hormones and borderline personality features. *Personality and Individual Differences, 44,* 278–287.

Eysenck, H.J. (1967). *The biological basis of personality*. Springfield, IL: Thomas.

Eysenck, H.J. (1991). Dimensions of personality: 16, 5 or 3? Criteria for a taxonomic paradigm. *Personality and Individual Differences, 12*, 773–790.

Eysenck, H.J. (2004). *The decline and fall of the Freudian empire*. Edison, NJ: Transaction.

Eysenck, H.J., & Cookson, D. (1969). Personality in primary school children: ability and achievement. *British Journal of Educational Psychology, 39*, 109–122.

Eysenck, H.J., & Eysenck, M.W. (1985). *Personality and individual differences*. New York: Plenum.

Eysenck, H.J., & Eysenck, S.G. (1975). *Manual of the Eysenck Personality Questionnaire*. London: Hodder & Stoughton.

Eysenck, H.J., & Eysenck, S.G. (1991). *Manual of the Eysenck Personality Scales (EPS Adult). Comprising the EPQ–Revised (EPQ–R), EPQ–R Short Scale, Impulsiveness (IVE) Questionnaire*. London: Hodder & Stoughton.

Eysenck, M.W. (1979). Depth, elaboration, and distinctiveness. In L.S. Cermack & F.I.M. Craik (Eds), *Levels of processing in human memory* (pp. 89–118). Hillsdale, NJ: Erlbaum.

Eysenck, M.W. (1982). *Attention and arousal: cognition and performance*. New York: Springer.

Eysenck, M.W., & Keane, M.T. (2005). *Cognitive psychology: a student's handbook* (5th edn). Hove: Psychology.

Fancher, R.E. (1996). *Pioneers of psychology* (3rd edn). New York: Norton.

Fantz, R. (1963). Pattern vision in newborn infants. *Science, 140*, 296–297.

Fausto-Sterling, A. (2000). *Sexing the body: gender politics and the construction of sexuality*. New York: Basic.

Ferguson, C.K., & Kelley, H.H. (1964). Significant factors in overevaluation of own group's products. *Journal of Abnormal and Social Psychology, 69*, 223–228.

Festinger, L. (1957). *A theory of cognitive dissonance*. Stanford, CA: Stanford University Press.

Festinger, L., Pepitone, A., & Newcomb, T. (1952). Some consequences of de-individuation in a group. *Journal of Abnormal and Social Psychology, 47*, 382–389.

Finkelstein, J. (1991). *The fashioned self*. Cambridge: Polity.

Fischer, E. (1894). Einfluss der Configuration auf die Wirkung der Enzyme. *Berichte der deutschen chemischen Gesellschaft, 27*(3), 2985–2993.

Fishbein, M., & Ajzen, I. (1975). *Belief, attitude, intention and behavior: an introduction to theory and research*. Reading, MA: Addison-Wesley.

Fisher, H. (1999). *The first sex: the natural talents of women and how they will change the world*. New York: Random House.

Fiske, S.T. (1998). Stereotyping, prejudice, and discrimination. In D.T. Gilbert, S.T. Fiske, & G. Lindzey (Eds), *Handbook of social psychology* (pp. 357–411). New York: McGraw-Hill.

Fiske, S.T., & Taylor, S.E. (1991). *Social cognition* (2nd edn). New York: McGraw-Hill.

Ford, T.E., Boxer, C.F., Armstrong, J., & Edel, J.R. (2008). More than 'just a joke': the prejudice-releasing function of sexist humor. *Personality and Social Psychology Bulletin, 34*(2), 159–170.

Forge, K.L., & Phemister, S. (1987). The effect of prosocial cartoons on preschool children. *Child Development Journal, 17*, 83–88.

Freedman, J.L., Klevansky, S., & Ehrlich, P.R. (1971). The effect of crowding on human task performance. *Journal of Applied Social Psychology, 1,* 7–25.

Frith, C. (2007). *Making up the mind: how the brain creates our mental world.* Oxford: Blackwell.

Fritzsche, B.A., Finkelstein, M.A., & Penner, L.A. (2000). To help or not to help: capturing individuals' decision policies. *Social Behavior and Personality, 28,* 561–578.

Frohlich, N., & Oppenheimer, J. (1970). I get by with a little help from my friends. *World Politics, 23,* 104–120.

Frosh, S., Phoenix, A., & Pattman, R. (2001). *Young masculinities: understanding boys in contemporary society.* London: Palgrave Macmillan.

Funder, D.C. (1982). On the accuracy of dispositional versus situational attributions. *Social Cognition, 1*(3), 205–222.

Furnham, A., & Allass, K. (1999). The influence of musical distraction of varying complexity on the cognitive performance of extraverts and introverts. *European Journal of Personality, 13,* 27–38.

Furnham, A., & Heaven, P. (1999). *Personality and social behaviour.* London: Arnold.

Furshpan, E.J., & Potter, D.D. (1959). Transmission at the giant motor synapse of the crayfish. *Journal of Physiology, 145,* 289–325.

Gaertner, S.L., & Dovidio, J.F. (2000). Reducing intergroup bias: the benefits of recategorization. *Journal of Personality and Social Psychology, 57,* 239–249.

Gardner, H. (1993a). *Frames of mind: theory of multiple intelligences.* London: Fontana.

Gardner, H. (1993b). Educating for understanding. *The American School Board Journal, 180,* 20–24.

Gardner, H. (1998). A multiplicity of intelligences. *Scientific American Presents: Exploring Intelligence, 9,* 18–23.

Gardner, H., & Hatch, T. (1989). Multiple intelligences go to school: educational implications of the theory of multiple intelligences. *Educational Researcher, 18,* 4–9.

Garfinkel, H. (1967). *Studies in ethnomethodology.* Englewood Cliffs, NJ: Prentice Hall.

Gauld, A., & Stephenson, G.M. (1967). Some experiments related to Bartlett's theory of remembering. *British Journal of Psychology, 58,* 39–49.

Gay, P. (Ed.) (1989). *The Freud reader.* New York: Norton.

Geer, J.H., & Jarmecky, L. (1973). Effect of being responsible for reducing another's pain on subjects' response and arousal. *Journal of Personality and Social Psychology, 26*(2), 232–237.

Geiselman, R.E., Fisher, R.P., MacKinnon, D.P., & Holland, H.L. (1986). Enhancement of eyewitness memory with the cognitive interview. *American Journal of Psychology, 99,* 385–401.

Gelfand, D.M., Jensen, W.R., & Drew, C.J. (1997). *Understanding child behaviour disorders* (3rd edn). Fort Worth, TX: Harcourt Brace.

Gelman, A. & Hill, J. (2007). *Data analysis using regression and multilevel/hierarchical models.* Cambridge: Cambridge University Press.

Gergen, K. (1973). Social psychology as history. *Journal of Personality and Social Psychology, 26,* 309–320.

Gergen, K. (1994). *Realities and relationships: soundings in social construction*. Cambridge, MA: Harvard University Press.

Gergen, K. (1996). Technology and the self: from the essential to the sublime. In D. Grodin & T.R. Lindlof (Eds), *Constructing the self in a mediated world*. London: Sage.

Gergen, K. (2000). The self in the age of information. *The Washington Quarterly, 23*(1), 201–214.

Gergen, K. (2009). *Relational being*. New York: Oxford University Press.

Gergen, K., & Gergen, M. (1988). Narratives and the self as relationship. *Advances in Experimental Social Psychology, 21*, 17–56.

Gergen, M., & Gergen, K. (Eds) (2003). *Social construction: a reader*. London: Sage.

Gerl, E.J., & Morris, M.R. (2008). The causes and consequences of color vision. *Evolution: Education and Outreach, 1*(4), 476–486.

Gibbons, A. (1991). The brain as a 'sexual organ'. *Science, 253*, 957–959.

Gibbs, J.C., Basinger, K.S., Grime, R.L., & Snarey, J.R. (2007). Moral judgement development across cultures: revisiting Kohlberg's universality claims. *Developmental Review, 27*, 443–500.

Gibson, J.J. (1950). *The perceptions of the visual world*. Boston: Houghton Mifflin.

Gibson, J.J. (1966). *The senses considered as perceptual systems*. Boston: Houghton Mifflin.

Gilligan, C. (1982). *The relational self*. Boston: Harvard University Press.

Gillingham, G. (2004). *Autism: handle with care!* Edmonton, Alberta: Tacit.

Gladue, B.A. (1991). Aggressive behavioral characteristics, hormones, and sexual orientation in men and women. *Aggressive Behavior, 17*, 313–326.

Gladue, B.A., & Bailey, J.M. (1995). Aggressiveness, competitiveness and human sexual orientation. *Psychoneuroendocrinology, 20*, 475–485.

Glenberg, A.M., & Swanson, N.G. (1986). A temporal distinctiveness theory of recency and modality effects. *Journal of Experimental Psychology: Learning, Memory and Cognition, 12*, 3–15.

Godden, D.R., & Baddeley, A.D. (1975). Context-dependent memory in two natural environments: on land and underwater. *British Journal of Psychology, 66*, 325–331.

Goffman, E. (1959). *The presentation of self in everyday life*. New York: Doubleday Anchor.

Goldberg, L.R. (1992). The development of markers of the Big-Five factor structure. *Psychological Assessment, 4*, 2642.

Goleman, D. (1996). *Emotional intelligence*. London: Bloomsbury.

Goodale, M.A., & Milner, A.D. (1992). Separate visual pathways for perception and action. *Trends in Neurosciences, 15*, 20–24.

Goren, C.C., Sarty, M., & Wu, P.Y.K. (1975). Visual following and pattern discrimination of face-like stimuli by newborn infants. *Pediatrics, 56*, 544–549.

Gosling, S. (2008). *Snoop: what your stuff says about you*. New York: Basic.

Goswami, U. (1986). Children's use of analogy in learning to read: a developmental study. *Journal of Experimental Child Psychology, 42*, 73–83.

Goswami, U. (1988). Orthographic analogies and reading development. *Quarterly Journal of Experimental Psychology: Human Experimental Psychology, 40a*, 239–268.

Goswami, U., & Bryant, P. (1990). *Phonological skills and learning to read*. Hove: Erlbaum.

Goswami, U., Ziegler, J., Dalton, L., & Schneider, W. (2003). Nonword reading across orthographies: how flexible is the choice of reading units? *Applied Psycholinguistics, 24*, 235–247.

Gottfredson, L.S. (1998). The general intelligence factor. *Scientific American Presents: Exploring Intelligence, 9*, 24–29.

Gough, B. (1998). Men and the discursive reproduction of sexism: repertoires of difference and equality. *Feminism & Psychology, 8*(1), 25–49.

Gough, B. (2002). 'I've always tolerated it but …': heterosexual masculinity and the discursive reproduction of homophobia. In A. Coyle & C. Kitzinger (Eds), *Lesbian and gay psychology*. Oxford: BPS /Blackwell.

Gould, S.J. (1981). *The mismeasure of man*. Harmondsworth: Penguin.

Gouldner, A.W. (1960). The norm of reciprocity: a preliminary statement. *American Sociological Review, 25*, 161–178.

Gravholt, C., Juul, S., Naeraa, R., & Hansen, J. (1998). Morbidity in Turner syndrome. *Journal of Clinical Epidemiology, 51*, 147–158.

Gray, J.A., & Wedderburn, A.A.I. (1960). Group strategies with simultaneous stimuli. *Quarterly Journal of Experimental Psychology, 12*, 180–184.

Green, D.P., Glaser, J., & Rich, A. (1998). From lynching to gay bashing: the elusive connection between economic conditions and hate crime. *Journal of Personality and Social Psychology, 75*(1), 82–92.

Greenberg, J., Pyszczynski, T., & Solomon, S. (1982). The self-serving attributional bias: beyond self-presentation. *Journal of Experimental Social Psychology, 18*, 56–67.

Gregory, R.L. (1963). Distortion of visual space as inappropriate constancy scaling. *Nature, 199*, 678–691.

Gregory, R.L. (1970). *The intelligent eye*. London: Weidenfeld & Nicolson.

Gregory, R.L. (1997). *Eye and brain: the psychology of seeing* (5th edn). Oxford: Oxford University Press.

Grieve, P., & Hogg, M.A. (1999). Subjective uncertainty and intergroup discrimination in the minimal group situation. *Personality and Social Psychology Bulletin, 25*, 926–940.

Griffiths, M.D., Davies, M.N.O., & Chappell, D. (2003). Breaking the stereotype: the case of online gaming. *Cyberpsychology and Behavior, 6*: 81–91.

Gruber, H.E. (1995). Insight and affect in the history of science. In R.J. Sternberg & J.E. Davidson (Eds), *The nature of insight* (pp. 397–431). Cambridge, MA: MIT Press.

Gupta, D. (2001). *Path to collective madness: a study in social order and political pathology*. Westport, CT: Greenwood.

Guzzo, R.A., & Dickson, M.W. (1996). Teams in organizations: recent research on performance and effectiveness. *Annual Review of Psychology, 47*, 307–338.

Hackney, C. (2002). From cochlea to cortex. In D. Roberts (Ed.), *Signals and perception: the fundamentals of human sensation*. London: Palgrave Macmillan.

Haggbloom, S.J., Warnick, R., Warnick, J.E., Jones, V.K., Yarbrough, G.L., Russell, T.M., et al. (2002). The 100 most eminent psychologists of the 20th century. *Review of General Psychology, 6*, 139–152.

Haier, R.J., Jung, R.E., Yeo, R.A., Head, K., & Alkire, M.T. (2004). Structural brain variation and general intelligence, *NeuroImage, 23*, 425–433.

Hall, J.A.Y., & Kimura, D. (1995). Performance by homosexual males and females on sexually dimorphic motor tasks. *Archives of Sexual Behavior*, 24, 395–407.

Halpern, D.F., Benbow, C.P., Geary, D.C., Gur, R.C., Shibley Hyde, J., & Gernsbacher, M.A. (2007). The science of sex differences in science and mathematics. *Psychological Science in the Public Interest*, 8, 1–51.

Hamer, D.H., Hu, S., Magnuson, V.L., Hu, N., & Pattatucci, A.M.L. (1993). A linkage between DNA markers on the X chromosome and male sexual orientation. *Science*, 261, 321–327.

Hamilton, A., Plunkett, K., & Schafer, G. (2000). Infant vocabulary development assessed with a British communicative development inventory. *Journal of Child Language*, 27, 689–705.

Hamilton, D.L., & Crump, S.A. (2004). Stereotypes. In C. Spielberger (Ed.), *Encyclopedia of applied psychology* (pp. 479–484). New York: Elsevier.

Hampson, S. (1999). State of the art: personality. *The Psychologist*, 12(6), 284–288.

Haqq, C.M., King, C.-Y., Ukiyama, E., Falsafi, S., Haqq, T.N., Donahoe, P.K., & Weiss, M.A. (1994). Molecular basis of mammalian sexual determination: activation of Müllerian inhibiting substance gene expression by SRY. *Science*, 266, 1494–1500.

Haraway, D. (1991). *Simians, cyborgs, and women: the reinvention of nature*. London: Free Association.

Harley, T. (2001). *The psychology of language: from data to theory* (2nd edn). Hove: Psychology.

Harré, R. (1998). *The singular self: an introduction to the psychology of personhood*. London: Sage.

Harré, R. (2006). *Key thinkers in psychology*. London: Sage.

Harré, R., & Van Langenhove, L. (Eds) (1999). *Positioning theory*. Oxford: Blackwell.

Harris, P.L. (1973). Perseverative errors in search by young children. *Child Development*, 44, 28–33.

Harrison, K. (2000). Television viewing, fat stereotyping, body shape standards, and eating disorder. *Communication Research*, 27(5), 617–640.

Harter, S. (1982). The perceived competence scale for children. *Child Development*, 53, 87–97.

Harter, S. (1987). The determinants and mediational role of global self-worth in children. In N. Eisenberg (Ed.), *Contemporary topics in developmental psychology* (pp. 219–242). New York: Wiley-Interscience.

Hatcher, P.J., Hulme, C., & Snowling, M.J. (2004). Explicit phoneme training combined with phonic reading instructions helps young children at risk of reading failure. *Journal of Child Psychology & Psychiatry*, 45, 338–358.

Hay, D.F., Nash, A., & Pedersen, J. (1981). Response of six-month-olds to the distress of their peers. *Child Development*, 52, 1071–1075.

Hay, D.F., Nash, A., & Pedersen, J. (1983). Interaction between six-month-old peers. *Child Development*, 54, 577–562.

Hay, D.F., Payne, A., & Chadwick, A. (2004). Peer relations in childhood. *Journal of Child Psychology and Psychiatry*, 45, 84–108.

Haynes, S.G., & Feinleib, M. (1980). Women, work and coronary heart disease: prospective findings from the Framingham Heart Study. *American Journal of Public Health*, 79, 133–141.

Heider, F. (1958). *The psychology of interpersonal relations*. New York: Wiley.

Heider, F., & Simmel, M. (1944). An experimental study of apparent behavior. *The American Journal of Psychology*, 57, 243–259.

Helwig, C.C., & Turiel, E. (2002). Children's social and moral reasoning. In P.K. Smith & C.H. Hart (Eds), *Blackwell handbook of childhood social development*. Oxford: Blackwell.

Herbert, M. (2008). *Typical and atypical development: from conception to adolescence*. Malden, MA: Blackwell.

Hergenhahn, B.R. (2005). *An introduction to the history of psychology*. Belmont, CA: Wadsworth.

Hetherington, E.M., & Stanley-Hagan, M. (1999). Adjustment of children with divorced parents: a risk and resiliency perspective. *Journal of Child Psychology and Psychiatry*, 40, 120–140.

Heuser, J.E., & Reese, T.S. (1973). Evidence for recycling of synaptic vesicle membrane during transmitter release at the frog neuromuscular function. *Journal of Cell Biology*, 57, 315–344.

Hewitt, J.P., & Stokes, R. (1975). Disclaimers. *American Sociological Review*, 40(1), 1–11.

Hewstone, M., Islam, M.R., & Judd, C.M. (1993). Models of crossed categorization and intergroup relations. *Journal of Personality and Social Psychology*, 65(5), 779–793.

Hinsz, V., & Davis, J. (1984). Persuasive arguments theory, group polarization, and choice shifts. *Personality and Social Psychology Bulletin*, 10(2), 260–268.

Hintzman, D.L. (1986). 'Schema abstraction' in a multiple trace memory model. *Psychological Review*, 93, 411–428.

Hobsbaum, A., Peters, S., & Sylva, K. (1996). Scaffolding in reading recovery. *Oxford Review of Education*, 22, 17–35.

Hoerr, T.R. (2000). *Becoming a multiple intelligence school*. Alexandria, VA: Association for Supervision and Curriculum Development.

Hofstadter, R.D., & Dennett, D.C. (1981). *The mind's I: fantasies and reflections on self and soul*. Brighton: Harvester.

Hogg, M.A. (1996). Group polarisation. In A. Manstead & M. Hewstone (Eds), *The Blackwell encyclopaedia of social psychology*. London: Blackwell.

Hogg, M.A. (2006). Social identity theory. In P.J. Burke (Ed.), *Contemporary social psychological theories* (pp. 111–136). Palo Alto, CA: Stanford University Press.

Hogg, M.A., & Vaughan, G.M. (2008). *Social psychology* (5th edn). Harlow: Prentice Hall.

Hollway, W., & Jefferson, T. (2000). *Doing qualitative research differently: free association, narrative and the interview method*. London: Sage.

Hovland, C., & Sears, R.R. (1940). Minor studies in aggression VI: correlation of lynchings with economic indices. *Journal of Psychology*, 9, 301–310.

Huchting, K., Lac, A., & LaBrie, J.W. (2008). An application of the theory of planned behavior to sorority alcohol consumption. *Addictive Behaviours*, 33(4).

Hughes, C., Jaffe, S., Happ, F., Taylor, A., Caspi, A., & Moffitt, T. (2005). Origins of individual differences in theory of mind: from nature to nurture? *Child Development*, 76, 356–370.

Hughes, M., Pinkerton, G., & Plewis, I. (1979). Children's difficulties on starting infant school. *Journal of Child Psychology and Psychiatry, 20,* 187–196.

Hull, D.L., & Van Regenmortel, M.H.V. (2002). Introduction. In M.H.V. Van Regenmortel & D.L. Hull (Eds), *Promises and limits of reductionism in the biomedical sciences.* Chichester: Wiley.

Hulme, C., Hatcher, P.J., Nation, K., Brown, A., Adams, J., & Stuart, G. (2002). Phoneme awareness is a better predictor of early reading skill than onset-rhyme awareness. *Journal of Experimental Child Psychology, 82,* 2–28.

Hunt, E. (2005). Information processing and intelligence: where we are and where we are going. In R.J. Sternberg & J.E. Pretz (Eds), *Cognition and intelligence* (pp. 1–25). Cambridge: Cambridge University Press.

Hussong, A.M. (2000). Distinguishing mean and structural differences in adolescent friendship quality. *Journal of Social and Personal Relationships, 17,* 223–243.

Hyde, J.S. (2005). The gender-similarities hypothesis. *American Psychologist, 60,* 581–592.

Hyde, T.S., & Jenkins, J.J. (1969). Differential effects of incidental tasks on the organization of recall of a list of highly associated words. *Journal of Experimental Psychology, 82,* 472–481.

Imperato-McGinley, J., Peterson, R.E., Gautier, T., & Sturla, E. (1979). Androgen and the evolution of male-gender identity among male pseudohermaphrodites with 5α-reductase deficiency. *New England Journal of Medicine, 300,* 1233–1237.

Ingham, A.G., Levinger, G., Graves, J., & Peckham, V. (1974). The Ringelmann effect: studies of group size and group performance. *Journal of Experimental Social Psychology, 10,* 371–384.

Jackson, J., & Harkins, S.G. (1985). Equity in effort: an explanation of the social loafing effect. *Journal of Personality and Social Psychology, 49,* 1199–1206.

Jackson, J.M., & Latané, B. (1981). All alone in front of all those people: stage fright as a function of number and type of co-performers and audience. *Journal of Personality and Social Psychology, 40,* 73–85.

Jackson, J.W. (1993). Realistic group conflict theory: a review and evaluation of the theoretical and empirical literature. *Psychological Record, 43*(3), 395.

James, W. (1890). *The principles of psychology.* Cambridge, MA: Harvard University Press.

Janis, I.L. (1972). *Victims of groupthink.* Boston: Houghton Mifflin.

Janis, I.L. (1982). *Groupthink: psychological studies of policy decisions and fiascos.* Boston: Houghton Mifflin.

Janis, I.L., & Mann, L. (1977). *Decision making: a psychological analysis of conflict, choice, and commitment.* New York: Free.

Jenkins, J.G., & Dallenbach, K.M. (1924). Obliviscence during sleep and waking. *American Journal of Psychology, 35,* 605–612.

Jensen, A.R. (1993). Why is reaction time correlated with psychometric *g*? *Current Directions in Psychological Science, 2,* 53–56.

Jensen, A.R. (1998). *The g factor: the science of mental ability.* Westport, CT: Praeger.

Jensen, A.R., & Johnson, F.W. (1994). Race and sex differences in head size and IQ. *Intelligence, 18,* 309–333.

Johnson, C., Ironsmith, M., Snow, C.W., & Poteat, G.M. (2000). Peer acceptance and social adjustment in preschool and kindergarten. *Early Childhood Education Journal*, 27: 207–212.

Johnson, F., & Johnson, D.W. (1987). *Joining together: group theory and group skills* (3rd edn). London: Prentice Hall.

Johnson, M.H., & Morton, J. (1991). *Biology and cognitive development: the case of face recognition*. Oxford. Blackwell.

Johnson-Laird, P.N. (1983). *Mental models*. Cambridge: Cambridge University Press.

Johnson-Laird, P.N. (1999). Deductive reasoning. *Annual Review of Psychology*, 50, 109–135.

Johnson-Laird, P.N., & Byrne, R.M.J. (1991). *Deduction*. Hove: Erlbaum.

Johnson-Laird, P.N., Gibbs, G., & de Mowbray, J. (1978). Meaning, amount of processing, and memory for words. *Memory & Cognition*, 6, 372–375.

Johnston, R.S., & Watson, J. (2004). Accelerating the development of reading, spelling and phonemic awareness. *Reading and Writing*, 17, 327–357.

Jonas, E., Schimel, J., Greenberg, J., & Pyszczynski, T. (2002). The Scrooge effect: evidence that mortality salience increases prosocial attitudes and behavior. *Personality and Social Psychology Bulletin*, 28, 1342–1353.

Jones, E.E. (1979). The rocky road from acts to dispositions. *American Psychologist*, 34, 107–117.

Jones, E.E., & Davis, K.E. (1965). From acts to dispositions: the attribution process in person perception. In L. Berkowitz (Ed.), *Advances in experimental social psychology*, 2 (pp. 219–266). New York: Academic.

Jones, E.E., & Harris, V.A. (1967). The attribution of attitudes. *Journal of Experimental Social Psychology*, 3, 1–24.

Jones, E.E., & Nisbett, R.E. (1972). The actor and the observer: divergent perceptions of the causes of behaviour. In E.E. Jones, D.E. Kanouse, H.H. Kelley, R.E. Nisbett, S. Valins, & B. Weiner (Eds), *Attribution: perceiving the causes of behaviour* (pp. 79–94). Morristown, NJ: General Learning Press.

Jones, G. (2003). Testing two cognitive theories of insight. *Journal of Experimental Psychology: Learning, Memory, and Cognition*, 29, 1017–1027.

Jones, J.M. (1991). Psychological models of race: what have they been and what should they be? In J.D. Goodchilds (Ed.), *Psychological perspectives on human diversity in America* (pp. 3–45). Washington: American Psychological Association.

Jones, P.E., & Roelofsma, P.H.M.P. (2000). The potential for social contextual and group biases in team decision-making: biases, conditions and psychological mechanisms. *Ergonomics*, 43(8), 1129–1152.

Jost, A. (1897). Die Assoziations festigkeit in ihrer Abahängigkeit von der Verteilung der Wiederholungen [The strength of associations in their dependence on the distribution of repititions]. *Zeitschrift fur Psychologie und Psysiologie der Sinnesorgane*, 14, 436–472.

Judge, T., Piccolo, R., & Ilies, R. (2004). The forgotten ones? The validity of consideration and initiating structure in leadership research. *Journal of Applied Psychology*, 89 (1), 36–51.

Kagan-Krieger, S. (1998). Women with Turner syndrome: a maturational and developmental perspective. *Journal of Adult Development*, 5, 125–135.

Kahneman, D., & Tversky, A. (1972). Subjective probability: a judgment of representativeness. *Cognitive Psychology, 3*, 430–454.

Kail, R.V. (2007). *Children and their development* (4th edn). New Jersey: Pearson.

Kam, C.L.H., & Newport, E.L. (2005). Regularizing unpredictable variation: the roles of adult and child learners in language formation and change. *Language Learning and Development, 1*(2), 151–195.

Kamin, L.J. (1977). *The science and politics of IQ*. Harmondsworth: Penguin.

Kant, I. (1907/1978). *Anthropology from a pragmatic point of view* (trans. V.L. Dowdell). Carbondale, IL: Southern Illinois University Press. (*Anthropologie in pragmatischer Hindsicht*. Berlin: Reimer.)

Karau, S.J., & Williams, K.D. (1993). Social loafing: a meta-analytic review and theoretical integration. *Journal of Personality and Social Psychology, 65*, 681–706.

Kassin, S., Fein, S., & Markus, H.R. (2008). *Social psychology* (7th edn). Boston: Houghton Mifflin.

Kaye, K., & Brazelton, T.B. (1971). Mother–infant interaction in the organization of sucking. Paper presented to the Society for Research in Child Development, Minneapolis, March.

Kaye, K., & Fogel, A. (1980). The temporal structure of face-to-face communication between mother and infants. *Developmental Psychology, 16*, 454–464.

Kaye, K., & Marcus, J. (1981). Infant imitation: the sensorimotor agenda. *Developmental Psychology, 17*, 258–265.

Kelley, H.H. (1967). Attribution theory in social psychology. Paper presented at the Nebraska Symposium on Motivation, Nebraska.

Kelly, G.A. (1955). *The psychology of personal constructs*, vol. l. New York: Norton.

Kendler, K.S., Thornton, L.M., Gilman, S.E., & Kessler, R.C. (2000). Sexual orientation in a U.S. national sample of twin and non-twin sibling pairs. *The American Journal of Psychiatry, 157*, 1843–1846.

Keppel, G. (1968). Retroactive and proactive inhibition. In T.R. Dixon & D.L. Horton (Eds), *Verbal behavior and general behavior theory* (pp. 172–213). Englewood Cliffs, NJ: Prentice Hall.

Kitzinger, C., & Wilkinson, S. (1996). *Representing the other: a feminism & psychology reader*. London: Sage.

Kline, P. (1991). *Intelligence: the psychometric view*. London: Routledge.

Kline, P. (1993). *The handbook of psychological testing*. London: Routledge.

Knoblich, G., Ohlsson, S., Haider, H., & Rhenius, D. (1999). Constraint relaxation and chunk decomposition in insight problem solving. *Journal of Experimental Psychology: Learning, Memory, and Cognition, 25*, 1534–1555.

Knoblich, G., Ohlsson, S., & Raney, G.E. (2001). An eye movement study of insight problem solving. *Memory and Cognition, 29*, 1000–1009.

Knowles, M., & Gardner, W. (2008). Benefits of membership: the activation and amplification of group identities in response to social rejection. *Personality and Social Psychology Bulletin, 34*(9), 1200–1213.

Kodituwakku, P.W. (2007). Defining the behavioral phenotype in children with fetal alcohol spectrum disorders: a review. *Neuroscience and Biobehavioral Reviews, 31*, 192–201.

Koelega, H.S. (1992). Extraversion and vigilance performance: thirty years of inconsistencies. *Psychological Bulletin, 112,* 239–258.

Kohlberg, L. (1976). Moral stage and moralization: the cognitive-developmental approach. In T. Lickona (Ed.), *Moral development and behaviour: theory, research and social issues* (pp. 84–107). New York: Holt, Rinehart & Winston.

Kohlberg, L., & Power, C. (1981). Moral development, religious thinking and the question of the seventh stage. *Journal of Religion and Science, 16,* 203.

Köhler, W. (1925). *The mentality of apes.* New York: Harcourt Brace & World.

Konczak, J. & Timmann, D. (2007). The effect of damage to the cerebellum on sensorimotor and cognitive function in children and adolescents. *Neuroscience and Biobehavioral Reviews, 31,* 1101–1113.

Korte, C. (1971). Effects of individual responsibility and group communication on help-giving in an emergency. *Human Relations, 24*(2), 149–159.

Kravitz, D.A., & Martin, B. (1986). Ringelmann rediscovered: the original article. *Journal of Personality and Social Psychology, 50,* 936–941.

Krishna, D. (1971). The self-fulfilling prophecy and the nature of society. *American Sociological Review, 36*(6), 1104–1107.

Kruglanski, A.W. (1996). Motivated social cognition: principles of the interface. In E.T. Higgins & A.W. Kruglanski (Eds), *Social psychology: handbook of basic principles* (pp. 493–520). New York: Guilford.

Krull, D.S. (1993). Does the grist change the mill? The effect of the perceiver's inferential goal on the process of social inference. *Personality and Social Psychology Bulletin, 19,* 340–348.

Kuhl, P.K., & Padden, D.M. (1982). Enhanced determinability at the phonetic boundaries for the voicing feature in macaques. *Perception & Psychophysics, 32,* 542–550.

Ladd, G.W., Birch, S.H., & Buhs, E.S. (1999). Children's social and scholastic lives in kindergarten: related spheres of influence? *Child Development, 70,* 1373–1400.

Lamb, S.J., Bibby, P.A., Wood, D.J., & Leyden, G. (1998). An intervention programme for children with moderate learning difficulties. *British Journal of Educational Psychology, 68*(4), 493–504.

Lamme, V.A.F. (2003). Why visual attention and awareness are different. *Trends in Cognitive Sciences, 7,* 12–18.

Lansdale, M.W. (2005). When nothing is 'off the record': exploring the theoretical implications of the continuous recording of cognitive process in memory. *Memory, 13,* 31–50.

Lansdale, M.W., & Baguley, T. (2008). Dilution as a model of long-term forgetting. *Psychological Review, 115*(4), 864–892.

LaPierre, R.T. (1934). Attitudes vs. actions. *Social Forces, 13,* 230–237.

Larkin, J. (1983). The role of problem representation in physics. In D. Gentner & A.L. Gentner (Eds), *Mental models* (pp. 75–98). Hillsdale, NJ: Erlbaum.

Larsen, R.J., & Buss, D.M. (2008). *Personality psychology: domains of knowledge about human nature.* New York: McGraw-Hill.

Lasco, M.S., Jordan, T.J., Edgar, M.A., Petito, C.K., & Byne, W. (2002). A lack of dimorphism of sex or sexual orientation in the human anterior commissure. *Brain Research, 936,* 95–98.

Latané, B., & Darley, J. (1969). Bystander apathy. *American Scientist, 57*(2), 244–268.

Latané, B., & Wolf, S. (1981). The social impact of majorities and minorities. *Psychological Review*, *88*(5), 438–453.

Latané, B., Williams, K.D., & Harkins, S.G. (1979). Many hands make light the work: the causes and consequences of social loafing. *Journal of Personality and Social Psychology*, *37*, 822–832.

Lavie, N. (1995). Perceptual load as a necessary condition for selective attention. *Journal of Experimental Psychology: Human Perception and Performance*, *21*, 451–468.

Lavie, N., & Driver, J. (1996). On the spatial extent of attention in object-based visual selection. *Perception & Psychophysics*, *58*, 1238–1251.

Leahey, T.H. (2004). *A history of psychology: main currents in psychological thought* (6th edn). Englewood Cliffs, NJ: Prentice Hall.

Leana, C.R. (1985). A partial test of Janis's groupthink model: effects of group cohesiveness and leader behaviour on defective decision making. *Journal of Management*, *11*, 5–17.

LeBon, G. (1895). *The crowd: a study of the popular mind* (trans. 1898). London: Transaction, 1995.

Lecanuet, J.-P. (1998). Foetal responses to auditory and speech stimuli. In A. Slater (Ed.), *Perceptual development: visual, auditory and speech perception in infancy*. Hove: Psychology.

Lee, D.N. (1976). A theory of visual control of braking based on information about time-to-collision. *Perception*, *5*, 437–459.

Lee, D.N., Lishman, J.R., & Thomson, J.A. (1982). Regulation of gait in long jumping. *Journal of Experimental Psychology: Human Perception and Performance*, *8*, 448–459.

Leifer, A.D., Leiderman, P.H., Barnett, C.R., & Williams, J.A. (1972). Effects of mother–infant separation on maternal attachment behavior. *Child Development*, *43*(4), 1203–1218.

Lenneberg, E.H. (1967). *Biological foundations of language*. New York: Wiley.

LePine, J.A., & Van Dyne, L. (2001). Voice and cooperative behaviour as contrasting forms of contextual performance: evidence of differential relationships with Big Five personality characteristics and cognitive ability. *Journal of Applied Psychology*, *86*, 326–336.

Lerner, M.J., & Miller, D.T. (1978). Just world research and the attribution process: looking back and ahead. *Psychological Bulletin*, *85*, 1030–1051.

LeVay, S. (1991). A difference in hypothalamic structure between heterosexual and homosexual men. *Science*, *253*, 1034–1037.

Levine, M., & Thompson, K. (2004). Identity, place, and bystander intervention: social categories and helping after natural disasters. *Journal of Social Psychology*, *144*(3), 229–245.

Levine, M., Prosser, A., Evans, D., & Reicher, A. (2005). Identity and emergency intervention: how social group membership and inclusiveness of group boundaries shape helping behavior. *Personality and Social Psychology Bulletin*, *31*(4), 443–453.

Lewis, D. (1966). An argument for the identity theory. *Journal of Philosophy*, *63*, 17–25.

Lewis, M. (2005). The child and its family: the social network model. *Human Development*, *48*, 8–27.

Lewis, M., & Brooks-Gunn, J. (1979). *Social cognition and the acquisition of self*. New York: Plenum.

Lichtenstein, S., Slovic, P., Fischhoff, B., Layman, M., & Combs, B. (1978). Judged frequency of lethal events. *Journal of Experimental Psychology: Human Learning and Memory, 4,* 551–578.

Likert, R. (1932). A technique for the measurement of attitudes. *Archives of Psychology, 140,* 1–55.

Lippmann, W. (1922). *Public opinion.* London: Allen & Unwin.

Loftus, E.F. (1996). *Eyewitness testimony.* Cambridge, MA: Harvard University Press.

Loftus, E.F., & Pickrell, J. (1995). The formation of false memories. *Psychiatric Annals, 25,* 720–725.

Loftus, E.F., Miller, D.G., & Burns, H.J. (1978). Semantic integration of verbal information into a visual memory. *Journal of Experimental Psychology: Human Learning & Memory, 4,* 19–31.

Lohmann, H., Carpenter, M., & Call, J. (2005). Guessing versus choosing – and seeing versus believing – in false belief tasks. *British Journal of Developmental Psychology, 23,* 451–469.

Looren de Jong, H. (2001). Introduction: a symposium on explanatory pluralism. *Theory and Psychology, 11*(6), 731–735.

Lorenz, K. (1981). *The foundation of ethology.* New York: Springer.

Ludman, L., Lansdown, R., & Spitz, L. (1992). Effects of early hospitalization and surgery on the emotional development of 3 year olds: an exploratory study. *European Child and Adolescent Psychiatry, 1*(3), 186–195.

Lynn, R., & Vanhanen, T. (2002). *IQ and the wealth of nations.* Westport, CT: Praeger.

Lyons, A., & Kashima, Y. (2003). How are stereotypes maintained through communication? The influence of stereotype sharedness. *Journal of Personality and Social Psychology, 85*(6), 989–1005.

Maass, A., & Clark, R. (1984). Hidden impact of minorities: fifteen years of minority influence research. *Psychological Bulletin, 95,* 233–243.

Maccoby, E.E. (1988). Gender as a social category. *Developmental Psychology, 24,* 755–765.

Maccoby, E.E. (1990). Gender and relationships: a developmental account. *American Psychologist, 45,* 513–520.

Maccoby, E.E., & Jacklin, C.N. (1974). *The psychology of sex differences.* Stanford, CA: Stanford University Press.

MacCoun, R.J., & Kerr, N.L. (1988). Asymmetric influence in mock jury deliberation: jurors' bias for leniency. *Journal of Personality and Social Psychology, 54,* 21–33.

MacGregor, J.N., Ormerod, T.C., & Chronicle, E.P. (2001). Information processing and insight: a process model of performance on the nine-dot and related problems. *Journal of Experimental Psychology: Learning, Memory, and Cognition, 27,* 176–201.

Maddi, S. (1989). Personality theories: a comparative analysis. Chicago: Dorsey.

Maguire, E.A., Gadian, D.G., Johnsrude, I.S., Good C.D., Ashburner J., Frackowiak, R.S.J. and Frith, C. (2000). Navigation-related structural change in the hippocampi of taxi drivers. *Proceedings of the National Academy of Science, 97,* 4398–4403.

Maier, N.R.F. (1931). Reasoning in humans. II: The solution of a problem and its appearance in consciousness. *Journal of Comparative Psychology, 12,* 181–194.

Main, M., & Solomon, J. (1990). Procedures for identifying infants as disorganised/disoriented during the Ainsworth Strange Situation. In M. Greenberg, D. Cicchetti, &

E. Cummings (Eds), *Attachment in the preschool years* (pp. 121–160). Chicago: University of Chicago Press.

Mandler, G. (1967). Organization and memory. In K.W. Spence & J.T. Spence (Eds), *The psychology of learning and motivation*, vol. 1 (pp. 327–372). New York: Academic.

Maner, J.K., & Gailliot, M.T. (2007). Altruism and egoism: prosocial motivations for helping depend on relationship context. *European Journal of Social Psychology*, 37(2), 347–358.

Manning, R., Levine, M., & Collins, A. (2007). The Kitty Genovese murder and the social psychology of helping: the parable of the 38 witnesses. *American Psychologist*, 62(6), 555–562.

Manstead, A., & Hewstone, M. (1996). *The Blackwell encyclopaedia of social psychology*. London: Blackwell.

Markus, H., & Wurf, E. (1987). The dynamic self concept: a social psychological perspective. *Annual Review of Psychology*, 38, 299–333.

Marschark, M., & Surian, L. (1989). Why does imagery improve memory? *European Journal of Cognitive Psychology*, 1, 251–263.

Martin, J.T., & Nguyen, D.H. (2004). Anthropometric analysis of homosexuals and heterosexuals: implications for early hormone exposure. *Hormones and Behavior*, 45, 31–39.

Matlin, M.W., & Foley, H.J. (1992). *Sensation and perception* (3rd edn). Boston: Allyn & Bacon.

Matthews, G., Jones, D.M., & Chamberlain, A.G. (1989). Interactive effects of extraversion and arousal on attentional task performance: multiple resources or encoding processes? *Journal of Personality and Social Psychology*, 56, 629–639.

Matthews, G., Deary, I.J., & Whiteman, M.C. (2003). *Personality traits*. Cambridge: Cambridge University Press.

McAdams, D.P., & Pals, J.L. (2006). A new Big Five: fundamental principles for an integrative science of personality. *American Psychologist*, 61(3), 204–217.

McCauley, C. (1989). The nature of social influence in groupthink: compliance and internalization. *Journal of Personality and Social Psychology*, 57, 250–260.

McCormick, C.M., & Witelson, S.F. (1991). A cognitive profile of homosexual men compared to heterosexual men and women. *Psychoneuroendocrinology*, 15, 459–473.

McCrae, R.R., & Costa, P.T. (1983). Joint factors in self-reports and ratings: neuroticism, extraversion and openness to experience. *Personality and Individual Differences*, 4, 245–255.

McCrae, R.R. & Costa, P.T. Jr (1997). Personality trait structure as a human universal. *American Psychologist*, 52(5), 509–516.

McGeoch, J.A. (1932). Forgetting and the law of disuse. *Psychological Review*, 39, 352–370.

McGeoch, J.A. (1942). *The psychology of human learning: an introduction*. New York: Longmans.

McGuire, F. (1994). Army alpha and beta tests of intelligence. In R.J. Sternberg (Ed.), *Encyclopedia of intelligence*, vol. 1 (pp. 125–129). New York: Macmillan.

McRae, C.N., Hewstone, M., & Griffiths, R.J. (1993). Processing load and memory for stereotype-based information. *European Journal of Social Psychology*, 23(1), 77–87.

Meadows, M. (2008). *I, avatar*. Berkeley, CA: New Riders.

Meltzoff, A.N., & Moore, M.K. (1977). Imitation of facial and manual gestures by human neonates. *Science*, 198, 74–78.

Meltzoff, A.N., & Moore, M.K. (1983). Newborn infants imitate adult facial gestures. *Child Development*, *54*, 702–709.

Memon, A., Hope, L., & Bull, R.H.C. (2003). Exposure duration: effects on eyewitness accuracy and confidence. *British Journal of Psychology*, *94*, 339–354.

Merton, K. (1957). *Social theory and social structure* (rev. edn). New York: Free.

Meyer-Bahlburg, H.F.L, Dolezal, C., Baker, S.W., & New, M.I. (2008). Sexual orientation in women with classical or non-classical congenital adrenal hyperplasia as a function of degree of prenatal androgen excess. *Archives of Sexual Behavior*, *37*, 85–99.

Meyer-Lindenberg, A., & Weinberger, D.R. (2006). Intermediate phenotypes and genetic mechanisms of psychiatric disorders. *Nature Reviews Neuroscience*, *7*, 818–827.

Miles, T.R. (1957). Contributions to intelligence testing and the theory of intelligence. I: On defining intelligence. *British Journal of Educational Psychology*, *27*, 153–165.

Milgram, S. (1974). *Obedience to authority: an experimental view*. London: Tavistock.

Miller, D.T., & Ross, M. (1975). Self-serving biases in the attribution of causality: fact or fiction? *Psychological Bulletin*, *82*(2), 213–225.

Miller, H., & Arnold, J. (2000). Gender and web home pages. *Computers and Education*, *34*, 335–339.

Miller, H., & Arnold, J. (2001). Breaking away from grounded identity? Women academics on the web. *Cyberpsychology and Behaviour*, *4*(1), 95–108.

Miller, H., & Arnold, J. (2003). Self in web home pages: gender, identity and power in cyberspace. In G. Riva & C. Galimberti (Eds), *Towards cyberpsychology: mind, cognition and society in the internet age* (pp. 74–93). Amsterdam: IOS.

Miller, H., & Arnold, J. (2009). Identity in cyberspace. In S. Wheeler (Ed.), *Connected minds, emerging cultures: cybercultures in online learning* (pp. 53–64). Charlotte, NC: Information Age.

Milner, A.D., & Goodale, M.A. (1995). *The visual brain in action*. Oxford: Oxford University Press.

Milner, P. (1970). *Physiological psychology*. New York: Holt, Rinehart & Winston.

Mischel, W. (1968). *Personality and assessment*. New York: Wiley.

Mohler, E., Parzer, P., Brunner, R., Wiebel, A., & Resch, F. (2006). Emotional stress in pregnancy predicts human infant reactivity. *Early Human Development*, *82*, 731–737.

Money, J. (1975). Ablatio penis: normal male infant sex-assigned as a girl. *Archives of Sexual Behavior*, *4*, 65–71.

Moon, C., Pannenton-Cooper, R.P., & Fifer, W.P. (1993). Two-day-olds prefer their native language. *Infant Behaviour and Development*, *16*, 495–500.

Moore, B.C.J. (2003). *An introduction to the psychology of hearing* (5th edn). San Diego: Elsevier.

Moorhead, G. (1982). Groupthink: hypothesis in need of testing. *Group and Organizational Studies*, *7*, 429–444.

Moorhead, G., & Montanari, J. (1986). An empirical investigation of the groupthink phenomenon. *Human Relations*, *39*, 399–410.

Moray, N. (1959). Attention in dichotic listening: affective cues and the influence of instructions. *Quarterly Journal of Experimental Psychology*, *11*, 56–60.

Morgan, M.J., & Casco, C. (1990). Spatial filtering and spatial primitives in early vision: an explanation of the Zöllner–Judd class of geometrical illusion. *Proceedings of the Royal Society of London Series B, 242*, 1–10.

Morra, S., Gobba, C., Marini, Z., & Sheese, R. (2007). *Cognitive development: a neo-Piagetian perspective*. Mahwah, NJ: Erlbaum.

Morris, C.D., Bransford, J.D., & Franks, J.J. (1977). Levels of processing versus transfer appropriate processing. *Journal of Verbal Learning and Verbal Behaviour, 16*, 519–533.

Morris, J.A., Jordan, C.L., & Breedlove, S.M. (2004). Sexual differentiation of the vertebrate nervous system. *Nature Neuroscience, 7*, 1034–1039.

Morris, M.W., & Peng, K. (1994). Culture and cause: American and Chinese attributions for social and physical events. *Journal of Personality and Social Psychology, 67*, 949–971.

Morton, N., & Browne, K.D. (1998). Theory and observation of attachment and its relation to child maltreatment: a review. *Child Abuse & Neglect, 22*, 1093–1104.

Moscovici, S., & Nemeth, C. (1974). Social influence. II: Minority influence. In C. Nemeth (Ed.), *Social psychology: classic and contemporary readings*. Oxford: Rand-McNally.

Moscovici, S., & Zavalloni, M. (1969). The group as a polarizer of attitudes. *Journal of Personality and Social Psychology, 12*, 125–135.

Muczyk, J., & Reimann, B. (1987). The case for directive leadership. *Academy of Management Review, 16*, 637–647.

Mustanski, B.S., DuPree, M.G., Nievergelt, C.M., Bocklandt, S., Schork, N.J., & Hamer, D. (2005). A genomewide scan of male sexual orientation. *Human Genetics, 116*, 272–278.

Mynatt, C.R., Doherty, M.E., & Tweney, R.D. (1977). Confirmation bias in a simulated research environment. *Quarterly Journal of Experimental Psychology, 29*, 85–95.

Nadder, T.S., Silberg, J.L., Rutter, M., Maes, H., & Eaves, J. (2001). Comparison of multiple measures of ADHD symptomatology: a multivariate of genetic analysis. *Journal of Child Psychology and Psychiatry and Allied Disciplines, 42*, 475–486.

Neath, I., & Suprenant, A.M. (2003). *Human memory: an introduction to research, data, and theory* (2nd edn). Belmont, CA: Wadsworth.

Neck, C.P., & Moorhead, G. (1995). Groupthink remodelled: the importance of leadership, time pressure, and methodical decision-making procedures. *Human Relations, 48*(5), 537–557.

Neisser, U., & Fivush, R. (1994). *The remembering self*. Cambridge: Cambridge University Press.

Neisser, U., & Joplin, D. (Eds) (1997). *The conceptual self in context: culture, experience, self understanding*. New York: Cambridge University Press.

Neisser, U., Boodoo, G., Bouchard, T.J. Jr, Boykin, A.W., Brody, N., Ceci, S.J., Halpern, D.E., Loehlin, J.C., Perloff, R., Sternberg, R.S., & Urbina, S. (1996). Intelligence: knowns and unknowns. *American Psychologist, 51*, 77–101.

Nemeth, C., Swedlund, M., & Kanki, B. (1974). Patterning of the minority's responses and their influence on the majority. *European Journal of Social Psychology, 4*(1), 54–64.

Nettle, D., & Clegg, H. (2006). Schizotypy, creativity and mating success in humans. *Proceedings of the Royal Society Series B, 273*, 611–615.

Newell, A., & Simon, H. (1972). *Human problem solving*. Englewood Cliffs, NJ: Prentice Hall.

Newell, A., Shaw, J.C., & Simon, H.A. (1958). Elements of a theory of human problem solving. *Psychological Review*, 65, 151–166.

Newstead, S.E., Pollard, P., Evans, J. St B. T., & Allen, J.L. (1992). The source of belief bias effects in syllogistic reasoning. *Cognition*, 45, 257–284.

Neylan, T.C. (1999). Frontal lobe function: Mr Phineas Gage's famous injury. *Journal of Neuropsychiatry and Clinical Neuroscience*, 11, 280–281.

Niccols, A. (2007). Fetal alcohol syndrome and the developing socio-emotional brain. *Brain and Cognition*, 65, 135–142.

Nisbett, R.E., & Ross, L. (1980). *Human inference*. Englewood Cliffs, NJ: Prentice Hall.

Norman, W.T. (1963). Toward an adequate taxonomy of personality attributes: replicated factor structure in peer nomination ratings. *Journal of Abnormal and Social Psychology*, 66, 574–583.

Nowakowski, R.S., & Hayes, N.L. (2002). General principles of CNS development. In M.H. Johnson, Y. Munakata, & R.O. Gilmore (Eds), *Brain development and cognition. A reader*. Oxford: Blackwell.

O'Brien, M. (1992). Gender identity and sex roles. In V.B. van Hasslet & M. Hersen (Eds), *Handbook of social development: a lifespan perspective* (pp. 325–345). New York: Plenum.

Oakes, P.J., Haslam, S.A., & Turner, J.C. (1994). *Stereotyping and social reality*. Oxford: Blackwell.

Oates, J. (2005). First relationships. In J. Oates, C. Wood, & A. Grayson (Eds), *Psychological development and early childhood*. Oxford: Open University Press.

Ong, W.J. (1982). *Orality and literacy*. London: Methuen.

Ormerod, T.C., MacGregor, J.N., & Chronicle, E.P. (2002). Dynamics and constraints in insight problem solving. *Journal of Experimental Psychology: Learning, Memory, and Cognition*, 28, 791–799.

Osgood, C.E., Suci, G.J., & Tannenbaum, P.H. (1957). *The measurement of meaning*. Urbana: University of Illinois Press.

Osler, W. (1910). The Lumleian lectures on angina pectoris. *The Lancet*, 175(4517), 839–844.

Otten, C.A., Penner, L.A., & Waugh, G. (1988). What are friends for: the determinants of psychological helping. *Journal of Social and Clinical Psychology*, 7, 34–41.

Pantin, H.M., & Carver, C.S. (1982). Induced competence and the bystander effect. *Journal of Applied Social Psychology*, 12(2), 100–111.

Parsons, T. (1954). *The social system*. Chicago: Chicago University Press.

Pawlby, S. (1977). Imitative interaction. In H.R. Schaffer (Ed.), *Studies in mother–infant interaction*. London: Academic.

Payne, S.J., & Baguley, T. (2006). Memory for the process of constructing an integrated mental model. *Memory & Cognition*, 34, 817–825.

Pena Trevino, R. (1955). Introduction of Dr Henri Laborit from France at the meeting of the Academy on 8 March 1955. *Cirugia y Cirujanos*, 23(4), 181–182.

Penfield, W. (1958). *The excitable cortex in conscious man*. Liverpool: Liverpool University Press.

Penfield, W. (1975). *The mystery of the mind: a critical study of consciousness and the human brain*. Princeton: Princeton University Press.

Penfield, W., & Jasper, H.H. (1954). *Epilepsy and the functional anatomy of the human brain.* Boston: Little, Brown.

Pennington, B.F., Willcutt, E., & Rhee, S.H. (2005). Analyzing comorbidity. In R.V. Kail (Ed.), *Advances in child development and behaviour.* San Diego, CA: Elsevier.

Perner, J., Leekam, S.R., & Wimmer, H. (1987). Three-year-olds' difficulty with false belief: the case for a conceptual deficit. *British Journal of Developmental Psychology, 5,* 125–137.

Perrin, A.J. (2005). National threat and political culture: authoritarianism, antiauthoritarianism, and the September 11 attacks. *Political Psychology, 26*(2), 167–194.

Petitto, L.A., Holowka, S., Sergio, L.E., Levy, B., & Ostry, D.J. (2004). Baby hands that move to the rhythm of language: hearing babies acquiring sign languages babble silently on the hands. *Cognition, 93,* 43–73.

Pettigrew, T.F. (1958). Personality and sociocultural factors in intergroup attitudes: a cross-national comparison. *Conflict Resolution, 2,* 29–42.

Pettigrew, T.F. (1997). Generalised intergroup contact effects on prejudice. *Personality and Social Psychology Bulletin, 23,* 173–185.

Pettigrew, T.F., & Tropp, L.R. (2006). A meta-analytic test of intergroup contact theory. *Journal of Personality and Social Psychology, 90*(5), 751–783.

Pheonix, C.H., Goy, R.W., Gerall, A.A., & Young, W.C. (1959). Organizing action of prenatally administered testosterone propionate on the tissues mediating mating behavior in the female guinea pig. *Endocrinology, 65,* 369–382.

Phillips, A. (1993). *On kissing, tickling & being bored: psychoanalytic essays on the unexamined life.* Cambridge, MA: Harvard University Press.

Phillips, A., & Taylor, B. (2009). *On kindness.* London: Penguin.

Piaget, J. (1952). *The origins of intelligence in children.* International University Press.

Piaget, J. (1963). *The psychology of intelligence.* New York: Routledge.

Piliavin, J.A., Piliavin, I.M., Dovidio, J.F., Gaertner, S.L., & Clark, R.D.I. (1981). *Emergency intervention.* New York: Academic.

Pillsbury, W.B. (1911). *Essentials of psychology.* New York: Macmillan.

Pinker, S. (1995). *The language instinct: the new science of language and mind.* London: Penguin.

Pinker, S. (2002). *The blank slate: the modern denial of human nature.* London: Penguin.

Pinker, S., & Prince, A. (1988). On language and connectionism: analysis of a parallel distributed processing model of language acquisition. *Cognition, 28*(1), 73–193.

Place, U.T. (1956). Is consciousness a brain process? *British Journal of Psychology, 47,* 44–50.

Plomin, R. (1990). The role of inheritance in behaviour. *Science, 248,* 183–188.

Plomin, R., DeFries, J.C., McClearn, G.E., & McGuffin, P. (2005). *Behavioral genetics* (5th edn). New York: Worth.

Polkinghorne, D.E. (1996). Explorations of narrative identity. *Psychological Inquiry, 7*(4), 363–367.

Polkinghorne, D.E. (2000). The unconstructed self. *Culture & Psychology, 6,* 265.

Popper, K.R. (1968). *The logic of scientific discovery.* London: Hutchinson.

Posner, M.I. (1980). Orienting of attention. *Quarterly Journal of Experimental Psychology, 32,* 3–25.

Postman, L., & Philips, L.W. (1965). Short-term temporal changes in free recall. *Quarterly Journal of Experimental Psychology, 17*, 132–138.

Postmes, T., & Spears, R. (1998). Deindividuation and antinormative behavior: a meta-analysis. *Psychological Bulletin, 123*(3), 238–259.

Potter, J., & Wetherell, M. (1987). *Discourse and social psychology: beyond attitudes and behaviour*. London: Sage.

Premack, D., & Woodruff, G. (1978). Does the chimpanzee have a theory of mind? *Behavioral and Brain Sciences, 1*(4), 515–526.

Prentice-Dunn, S., & Rogers, R.W. (1982). Effects of public and private self-awareness of deindividuation and aggression. *Journal of Personality and Social Psychology, 43*, 503–513.

Prigogine, I., & Stengers, I. (1984). *Order out of chaos: man's new dialogue with nature*. London: Heinemann.

Pruden, S., Hirsh-Pasek, K., Golinkoff, R., & Hennon, E. (2006). The birth of words: ten-month-olds learn words through perceptual salience. *Child Development, 77*(2), 266–280.

Pye, C. (1986). Quiche Mayan speech to children. *Journal of Child Language, 13*, 85–100.

Quinlan, P.T., & Wilton, R.N. (1998). Grouping by proximity or similarity? Competition between the Gestalt principles in vision. *Perception, 27*, 417–430.

Quinn, P.C., Westerlund, A., & Nelson, C.A. (2006). Neural markers of categorisation in 6-month-old infants. *Psychological Research, 17*, 59–66.

Radley, A. (1991). *In social relationships*. Milton Keynes: Open University Press.

Radley, A. (1995). The elusory body and social constructionist theory. *Body & Society, 1*(2), 3–23.

Rahman, Q., & Wilson, G.D. (2003). Born gay? The psychobiology of human sexual orientation. *Personality and Individual Differences, 34*, 1337–1382.

Rahman, Q., Abrahams, S., & Wilson, G.D. (2003a). Sexual orientation related differences in verbal fluency. *Neuropsychology, 17*, 240–246.

Rahman, Q., Wilson, G.D., & Abrahams, S. (2003b). Sexual orientation related differences in spatial memory. *Journal of the International Neuropsychological Society, 9*, 376–383.

Rahman, Q., Andersson, D., & Govier, E. (2005). A specific sexual orientation-related difference in navigation strategy. *Behavioral Neuroscience, 119*, 311–316.

Ramachandran, V.S., & Blakeslee, S. (1998). *Phantoms in the brain: probing the mysteries of the human mind*. New York: Morrow.

Ramus, F., Hauser, M.D., Miller, C., Morris, D., & Mehler, J. (2000). Language discrimination by human newborns and by cotton-top Tamarin monkeys. *Science, 288*(5464), 349–351.

Rauschecker, J. P. & Tian, B. (2000). Mechanisms and streams for processing of 'what' and 'where' in auditory cortex. *Proceedings of the National Academy of Sciences, 97*, 11800–11806.

Reicher, S. (2004). The context of social identity: domination, resistance and change. *Political Psychology, 25*(6), 921–945.

Reicher, S., & Haslam, S.A. (2006). Rethinking the psychology of tyranny: the BBC prison study. *British Journal of Social Psychology, 45*, 1–40.

Rensink, R.A. (2002). Change detection. *Annual Review of Psychology, 53*, 245–477.

Rice, G., Anderson, C., Risch, N., & Ebers, G. (1999). Male homosexuality: absence of linkage to microsatellite markers at Xq28. *Science, 284*, 665–667.

Rock, I., & Gutman, D. (1981). Effect of inattention on form perception. *Journal of Experimental Psychology: Human Perception and Performance, 7*, 275–285.

Roediger, H.L. III, & Karpicke, J.D. (2006). Test-enhanced learning: taking memory tests improves long-term retention. *Psychological Science, 17*, 249–255.

Rogoff, B. (1990). Apprenticeship in thinking: cognitive development in social context. New York: Oxford University Press.

Rose, N. (1989). Individualising psychology. In J. Shotter & K.Gergen (Eds), *Texts of identity*. London: Sage.

Rose, S., Kamin, L.J., & Lewontin, R.C. (1984). *Not in our genes*. Harmondsworth: Penguin.

Rosenblith, J. (1992). *In the beginning: development from conception to age two* (2nd edn). Newbury Park, CA: Sage.

Rosenman, R.H., & Friedman, M. (1977). Modifying type A behavior patterns. *Journal of Psychosomatic Research, 21*, 323–331.

Rosenthal, R., & Jacobson, L. (1968). Pygmalion in the classroom. *The Urban Review, 3*(1), 16–20.

Ross, L. (1977). The intuitive psychologist and his shortcomings. In L. Berkowitz (Ed.), *Advances in experimental social psychology 10* (pp. 173–220). San Diego: Academic.

Ross, L., Greene, D., & House, P. (1977). The 'false consensus effect': an egocentric bias in social perception and attribution processes. *Journal of Personality and Social Psychology, 35*, 485–494.

Rubin, M., & Hewstone, M. (2004). Social identity, system justification, and social dominance: commentary on Reicher, Jost et al., and Sidanius et al. *Political Psychology, 25*(6), 823–844.

Ruble, D.N., & Martin, C.L. (1998). Gender development. In W. Damon (Ed.), *Handbook of child psychology. Vol. 3: Social, emotional, and personality development* (5th edn) (pp. 933–1016). New York: Wiley.

Ruble, T.L. (1983). Sex stereotypes: issues of change in the 1970s. *Sex Roles, 9*, 397–402.

Ruffman, T., Slade, L., Rowlandson, K., Rumsey, C., & Garnham, A. (2003). How language relates to belief, desire, and emotion understanding. *Cognitive Development, 18*, 139–158.

Rundus, D. (1971). Analysis of rehearsal processes in free recall. *Journal of Experimental Psychology, 89*, 63–77.

Rushton, J.P., & Campbell, A. (1977). Modeling, vicarious reinforcement and extraversion on blood donating in adults: immediate and long term effects. *European Journal of Social Psychology, 7*, 297–306.

Rushton, J.P., & Jensen, A.R. (2005). Thirty years of research on race differences in cognitive ability. *Psychology, Public Policy, and Law, 11*, 235–294.

Rushton, J.P., Russell, R.J., & Wells, P.A. (1984). Genetic similarity theory: beyond kin selection. *Behavior Genetics, 14*, 179–193.

Sacks, O. (1973). *Awakenings*. New York: Vintage.

Sameroff, A.J., & Chandler, M.J. (1975). Reproductive risk and the continuum of caretaking casualty. In F.D. Horowitz, M. Hetherington, S. Scarr-Salapatek, & G. Siegel (Eds), *Review of Child Development Research*, vol. 4. Chicago: University of Chicago Press.

Sanders, G., & Wright, M. (1997). Sexual orientation differences in cerebral asymmetry and in the performance of sexually dimorphic cognitive and motor tasks. *Archives of Sexual Behavior, 26*, 463–480.

Sanders, G.S., & Baron, R.S. (1977). Is social comparison irrelevant for producing choice shifts? *Journal of Experimental Social Psychology*, 13, 303–314.

Santa Lucia, R.C., Gesten, E., Redina-Gobioff, G., Epstein, M., Kaufmann, D., Salcedo, O., et al. (2000). Children's school adjustment: a developmental transactional systems perspective. *Journal of Applied Developmental Psychology*, 24, 429–446.

Satz, P., Taylor, H.G., Friel, J., & Fletcher, J.M. (1978). Some developmental and predictive precursors of reading disability. In A.L. Benton & D. Pearl (Eds), *Dyslexia: an appraisal of current knowledge* (pp. 457–501). New York: Oxford.

Saudino, K.J., Carter, A.S., Purper-Ouakil, D., & Gorwood, P. (2008). The etiology of behavioral problems and competencies in very young twins. *Journal of Abnormal Psychology*, 117, 48–62.

Schaffer, H.R. (2000). The early experience assumption: past, present, and future. *International Journal of Behavioral Development*, 24(1), 5–14.

Scheerer, M. (1963). Problem solving. *Scientific American*, 208, 118–128.

Schlenker, B.R., Phillips, S.T., Boniecki, K.A., & Schlenker, D.R. (1995). Championship pressures: choking or triumphing in one's territory? *Journal of Personality and Social Psychology*, 68, 632–643.

Schmalhofer, F., & Glavanov, D. (1986). Three components of understanding a programmer's manual: verbatim, propositional and situational representations. *Journal of Memory and Language*, 25, 279–294.

Schwann, T. (1839). *Mikroskopische Untersuchungen über die Uebereinstimmung in der Struker und dem Wachsthum der Thiere und Pflanzen*. Berlin: Reimer. English trans. H. Smith 1845, reprinted New York: Kraus, 1969.

Sergeant, M.J.T., Dickins, T.E., Davies, M.N.O., & Griffiths, M.D. (2006). Aggression, empathy and sexual orientation among males. *Personality and Individual Differences*, 40, 475–486.

Shallice, T. (1982). Specific impairments of planning. *Philosophical Transactions of the Royal Society of London*, 298, 199–209.

Shallice, T., & Warrington, E.K. (1970). Independent functioning of verbal memory stores: a neuropsychological study. *Quarterly Journal of Experimental Psychology*, 22, 261–273.

Sherif, M. (1966). *Group conflict and cooperation: their social psychology*. London: Routledge & Kegan Paul.

Sherrington, C. (1897). In M.A. Foster, *Text-book of physiology*. London: Macmillan.

Shevlin, M., Walker, S., Davies, M.N.O., Banyard, P., & Lewis, C. (2003). Can you judge a book by its cover? Evidence of self–stranger agreement on personality at zero acquaintance. *Personality and Individual Differences*, 35, 1373–1383.

Simons, D.J., & Chabris, C.F. (1999). Gorillas in our midst: sustained inattentional blindness for dynamic events. *Perception*, 28, 1059–1074.

Simons, D.J., & Levin, D.T. (1998). Failure to detect changes to people during a real-world interaction. *Psychonomic Bulletin and Review*, 5, 644–649.

Simpson, S.A., & Harding, A.E. (1993). Predictive testing for Huntington's disease: after the gene. The United Kingdom Huntington's Disease Prediction Consortium. *Journal of Medical Genetics*, 30, 1036–1038.

Singh, I.L. (1989). Personality correlates and perceptual detectability of locomotive drivers. *Personality and Individual Differences*, 10, 1049–1054.

Skinner, B.F. (1948). *Walden two*. Oxford: Macmillan.

Skinner, B.F. (1957). *Verbal behaviour*. New York: Appleton-Century-Crofts.

Skinner, B.F. (1971). *Beyond freedom and dignity*. New York: Knopf/Random House.

Slater, R. (2007). Attachment: theoretical development and critique. *Educational Psychology in Practice*, 23, 205–219.

Slee, P.T., & Rigby, K. (1993). The relationship of Eysenck's personality factors and self-esteem to bully–victim behaviour in Australian schoolboys. *Personality and Individual Differences*, 14, 371–373.

Smart, J.J.C. (1959). Sensations and brain processes. *Philosophical Review*, 68, 141–156.

Smith, J.A. (2004). Reflecting on the development of interpretative phenomenological analysis and its contribution to qualitative research in psychology. *Qualitative Research in Psychology*, 1, 39–54.

Smith, J.A., & Osborn, M. (2007). Pain as an assault on the self: an interpretative phenomenological analysis. *Psychology and Health*, 22, 517–534.

Smith, P.K., Cowie, H., & Blades, M. (2003). *Understanding children's development* (4th edn). Oxford: Blackwell.

Snow, C.E. (1999). Social perspectives on the emergence of language. In B. Macwhinney (Ed.), *The Emergence of Language* (pp. 257–276). London: Erlbaum.

Snow, R.E. (1969). Unfinished Pygmalion. *Contemporary Psychology*, 14, 197–199.

Snowden, R., Thompson, P., & Troscianko, T. (2006). *Basic vision: an introduction to visual perception*. Oxford: Oxford University Press.

Snyder, J., & Miene, P.K. (1994). On the functions of stereotypes and prejudice. In M.P. Zanna & J.M. Olson (Eds), *The psychology of prejudice: the Ontario symposium* (pp. 33–54). Hove: Erlbaum.

Söderfeldt, M., Söderfeldt, B., Ohlson, C.-G., Theorell, T., & Jones, I. (2000). The impact of sense of coherence and high-demand/low-control job environment on self-reported health, burnout and psychophysiological stress indicators. *Work & Stress*, 14(1), 1–15.

Spearman, C. (1904). General intelligence objectively determined and measured. *American Journal of Psychology*, 15, 201–293.

Sperry, R.W. (1964). Problems outstanding in the evolution of brain function. James Arthur Lecture. New York: American Museum of Natural History. Reprinted 1977 in R. Duncan & M. Weston-Smith (Eds), *Encyclopedia of ignorance* (pp. 423–433). Oxford: Pergamon.

Spies, R.A., & Plake, B.S. (2005). *The sixteenth mental measurement yearbook*. Lincoln, NE: Buros Institute of Mental Measurements.

Stangor, C., & Schaller, M. (1996). Stereotypes as individual and collective representations. In C.N. Macrae, M. Hewstone, & C. Stangor (Eds), *Foundations of stereotypes and stereotyping* (pp. 3–37). New York: Guilford.

Staub, E. (2000). Genocide and mass-killing: origins, prevention, healing and reconciliation. *Political Psychology*, 21(2), 367–382.

Steele, C.M. (1997). A threat in the air: how stereotypes shape intellectual identity and performance. *American Psychologist*, 52(6), 613–629.

Steele, C.M., & Aronson, J. (1995). Stereotype threat and the intellectual test performance of African Americans. *Journal of Personality and Social Psychology*, 69(5), 797–811.

Steele, C.M., Spencer, S.J., & Aronson, J. (2002). Contending with bias: the psychology of stereotype and social identity threat. In M.P. Zanna (Ed.), *Advances in experimental social psychology*, vol. 34 (pp. 277–341). San Diego: Academic.

Sternberg, R.J. (1984). Toward a triarchic theory of human intelligence. *The Behavioral and Brain Sciences*, 7, 269–315.

Sternberg, R.J. (2004). The concept of intelligence. In R. Sternberg (Ed.), *Handbook of intelligence* (pp. 3–15). Cambridge: Cambridge University Press.

Sternberg, R.J., Grigorenko, E.L., Ngrosho, D., Tantufuye, E., Mbise, A., Nomes, C., Jukes, M., & Bundy, D.A. (2002). Assessing intellectual potential in rural Tanzanian school children. *Intelligence*, 30, 141–162.

Stevens, J.R., Cushman, F.A., & Hauser, M.D. (2005). Evolving the psychological mechanisms for cooperation. *Annual Review of Ecology, Evolution and Systematics*, 36, 499–518.

Stevens, R. (1996). *Understanding the self*. Milton Keynes: OUP/Sage.

Stevens, R.J., & Slavin, R.E. (1995). The cooperative elementary school: effects on students' achievement, attitudes, and social relations. *American Educational Research Journal*, 32, 321–351.

Stitch, S.P., & Ravenscroft, I. (1994). What is folk psychology? *Cognition*, 50(1–3), 447–468.

Stiles, J., Reilly, J., Paul, B., & Moses, P. (2005). Cognitive development following early brain injury: evidence for neural adaptation. *Trends in Cognitive Sciences*, 9, 136–143.

Storms, M.D., & Thomas, G.C. (1977). Reactions to physical closeness. *Journal of Personality and Social Psychology*, 35, 412–418.

Strack, F., Martin, L.L., & Stepper, S. (1988). Inhibiting and facilitating conditions of facial expressions: a non-obtrusive test of the facial feedback hypothesis. *Journal of Personality and Social Psychology*, 54, 768–777.

Strickland, B. (1989). Internal–external control expectancies: from contingency to creativity. *American Psychologist*, 44, 1–12.

Stuart, M. (1999). Getting ready for reading: early phoneme awareness and phonics teaching improves reading and spelling in inner-city second language learners. *British Journal of Educational Psychology*, 69, 587–605.

Sulmont-Rosse, C., Chabanet, C., Issanchou, S., & Koster, E.P. (2008). Impact of the arousal potential of uncommon drinks on the repeated exposure effect. *Food Quality and Preference*, 19(4), 412–420.

Sumner, W. (1906). *Folkways*. New York: Ginn.

Super, C.M., & Harkness, S. (1977). The infants niche in rural Kenya and metropolitan America. In L.L. Adler (Ed.), *Issues in cross-cultural research*. New York: Academic.

Swaab, D.F., & Hoffman, M.A. (1990). An enlarged suprachiasmatic nucleus in homosexual men. *Brain Research*, 24, 141–148.

Swaab, D.F., Gooren, L.J.G., & Hoffman, M.A. (1995). Brain research, gender and sexual orientation. *Journal of Homosexuality*, 28, 283–301.

Tajfel, H. (1978). *Differentiation between social groups: studies in the social psychology of intergroup relations*. London: Academic.

Tajfel, H. (1981). *Human groups and social categories*. Cambridge: Cambridge University Press.

Tajfel, H. (Ed.) (1982). *Social identity and intergroup relations*. Cambridge: Cambridge University Press.

Tajfel, H., & Turner, J.C. (1979). An integrative theory of intergroup conflict. In W.G. Austin & S. Worchel (Eds), *The social psychology of intergroup relations* (pp. 33–47). Monterey, CA: Brooks/Cole.

Tajfel, H., & Wilkes, A. (1963). Classification and quantitative judgment. *British Journal of Social Psychology*, *54*, 101–114.

Tajfel, H., Billig, M.G., Bundy, R.P., & Flament, C. (1971). Social categorization and intergroup behaviour. *European Journal of Social Psychology*, *1*, 149–177.

Tesser, A., Gatewood, R., & Driver, M. (1968). Some determinants of gratitude. *Journal of Personality and Social Psychology*, *9*, 233–236.

Tetlock, P.E. (1979). Identifying victims of groupthink from public statements of decision makers. *Journal of Personality and Social Psychology*, *37*, 1314–1324.

Thompson, M.M., Zanna, M.P., & Griffin, D.W. (1995). Let's not be indifferent about (attitudinal) ambivalence. In R.E. Petty & J.A. Krosnick (Eds), *Attitude strength: antecedents and consequences* (pp. 361–386). Mahwah, NJ: Erlbaum.

Thompson, P. (1980). Margaret Thatcher: a new illusion. *Perception*, *9*, 483–484.

Thompson, P. (1982). Perceived rate of movement depends on contrast. *Vision Research*, *22*, 377–380.

Thompson, R.A. (2000). The legacy of early attachments. *Child Development*, *71*, 145–152.

Thompson, R.H., Cotnoir-Bichelman, N.M., McKerchar, P.M., Tate, T.L., & Dancho, K.A. (2007). Enhancing early communication through infant sign training. *Journal of Applied Behavior Analysis*, *40*, 15–23.

Thorndike, R.L. (1968). Review of the book *Pygmalion in the classroom*. *American Educational Research Journal*, *5*, 708–711.

Thornton, S. (2008). *Understanding children's development*. London: Palgrave Macmillan.

Tomasello, M. (2000). Do young children have adult syntactic competence? *Cognition*, *74(3)*, 209–253.

Treisman, A.M. (1960). Contextual cues in selective listening. *Quarterly Journal of Experimental Psychology*, *12*, 242–244.

Treisman, A.M. (1964). The effect of irrelevant material on the efficiency of selective listening. *American Journal of Psychology*, *77*, 533–546.

Triplett, N. (1898). The dynamogenic factors in pacemaking and competition. *American Journal of Psychology*, *9*, 507–533.

Tulving, E., & Pearlstone, Z. (1966). Availability versus accessibility of information in memory for words. *Journal of Verbal Learning and Verbal Behavior*, *5*, 381–391.

Tulving, E., & Thomson, D.M. (1973). Encoding specificity and retrieval processes in episodic memory. *Psychological Review*, *80*, 352–373.

Turner, J.C. (1975). Social comparison and social identity: some prospects for intergroup behaviour. *European Journal of Social Psychology*, *5*, 5–34.

Turner, J.C. (1991). *Social influence*. Buckingham: Open University Press.

Turner, J.C. (1996). Henri Tajfel: an introduction. In W.P. Robinson (Ed.), *Social groups and identities: developing the legacy of Henri Tajfel*. London: Routledge.

Tversky, A., & Kahneman, D. (1974). Judgment under uncertainty: heuristics and biases. *Science*, *185*, 1124–1131.

Tversky, A., & Kahneman, D. (1980). Causal schemata in judgments under uncertainty. In M. Fishbein (Ed.), *Progress in social psychology*, vol. 1 (pp. 49–72). Hillsdale, NJ: Erlbaum.

Tversky, A., & Kahneman, D. (1983). Extensional versus intuitive reasoning: the conjunction fallacy in probability judgment. *Psychological Review*, *90*, 293–315.

Tweney, R.D., Doherty, M.E., Worner, W.J., Pliske, D.B., Mynatt, C.R., Gross, K.A., et al. (1980). Strategies for rule discovery in an inference task. *Quarterly Journal of Experimental Psychology*, *32*, 109–123.

Tzeng, O.J.L. (1973). Positive recency effect in a delayed free recall. *Journal of Verbal Learning and Verbal Behavior*, *12*, 436–439.

Umiltà, C. (2001). Mechanisms of attention. In B. Rapp (Ed.), *The handbook of cognitive neuropsychological*. Hove: Psychology.

Underwood, B.J. (1957). Interference and forgetting. *Psychological Review*, *64*, 49–60.

Underwood, B.J., & Ekstrand, B.R. (1967). Effect of distributed practice on paired-associate learning. *Journal of Experimental Psychology, Monograph Supplement 1*, *73*, 1–21.

Underwood, J., Baguley, T.S., Banyard, P., Coyne, E., Farrington-Flint, L., & Selwood, I. (2007a). *Impact 2007: personalising learning with technology. Final report*. Coventry: British Educational Communication and Technology Agency.

Underwood, J., Banyard, P., & Davies, M.N.O. (2007b). Students in digital worlds: lost in Sin City or reaching Treasure Island? British Learning Through Digital Technologies. *BJEP Monograph Series*, *5*, 83–99.

Vainio, S., Heikkilä, M., Kispert, A., Chin, N., & McMahon, A.P. (1999). Female development in mammals is regulated by Wnt–4 signalling. *Nature*, *397*, 405–409.

Valenza, E., Simion, F., Macchi Cassia, V., & Umiltà, C. (1996). Face preference at birth. *Journal of Experimental Psychology: Human Perception and Performance*, *22*, 892–903.

Van der Kolk, B.A., & Fisler, R. (1995). The psychological processing of traumatic memories: review and experimental confirmation. *Journal of Traumatic Stress*, *8*, 505–525.

Van Langenhove, L. (1995). The theoretical foundations of experimental psychology and its alternatives. In J.A. Smith, R. Harré, & L. Van Langenhove (Eds), *Rethinking methods in psychology*. London: Sage.

Vygotsky, L.S. (1978). *Mind and society: the development of higher mental processes*. Cambridge, MA: Harvard University Press.

Walk, R.D., & Gibson, E.J. (1961). A comparative and analytical study of visual depth perception. *Psychological Monographs*, *75*, 15.

Walker, F. (2007). Huntington's disease. *The Lancet*, *369*, 218–228.

Wallace, D. (2004). *Random acts of kindness: 365 ways to make the world a nicer place*. London: Ebury.

Wason, P.C. (1960). On the failure to eliminate hypotheses in a conceptual task. *Quarterly Journal of Experimental Psychology*, *12*, 129–140.

Watson, J.B. (1913). Psychology as the behaviorist views it. *Psychological Review*, *20*, 158–177.

Watson, J.B. (1930). *Behaviourism* (2nd edn). New York: Norton.

Watson, S.E., & Kramer, A.F. (1999). Object-based visual selective attention and perceptual organization. *Perception & Psychophysics, 61*, 31–49.

Waugh, N.C. (1970). Primary and secondary memory in short-term retention. In K.H. Pribram & D.E. Broadbent (Eds), *The biology of memory*. New York: Academic.

Waugh, N.C., & Norman, D.A. (1965). Primary memory. *Psychological Review, 72*, 89–104.

Wechsler, D. (1958). *The measurement and appraisal of adult intelligence* (4th edn). Baltimore: Williams & Wilkins.

Weiskrantz, L., Warrington, E.K., Sanders, M.D., & Marshall, J. (1974). Visual capacity in the hemianopic field following a restricted occipital ablation. *Brain, 97*, 709–728.

Weissenberg, P., & Kavanaugh, M. (1972). The independence of initiating structure and consideration: a review of the evidence. *Personnel Psychology, 25*, 119–130.

Wellman, H.M., Cross, D., & Watson, J. (2001). Meta-analysis of theory-of-mind development: the truth about false belief. *Child Development, 72*, 655–684.

Wentzel, K.R. (1999). Social influences on school adjustment: commentary. *Educational Psychologist, 34*, 59–69.

Wetherell, M., & Edley, N. (1999). Negotiating hegemonic masculinity: imaginary positions and psycho-discursive practices. *Feminism & Psychology, 9*(3), 335–356.

Whittlesea, B.W.A., & Dorken, M.D. (1993). Incidentally, things in general are particularly determined: an episodic account of implicit learning. *Journal of Experimental Psychology: General, 122*, 227–248.

Whitty, M.T. (2008). Revealing the 'real' me; searching for the 'actual' you: presentations of self on an internet dating site. *Computers in Human Behaviour, 24*, 1707–1723.

Wicklund, R.A. (1975). *Objective self-awareness*. New York: Academic.

Wiener, Norbert (1948). *Cybernetics, or control and communication in the animal and the machine*. Cambridge, MA: Technology Press.

Williams, D. (1996). *Autism: an inside-out approach. An innovative look at the 'mechanics' of 'autism' and its developmental 'cousins'*. London: Jessica Kingsley.

Williams, J.E., Paton, C.C., Siegler, I.C., Eigenbrodt, M.L., Nieto, F.J., & Tyroler, H.A. (2000). Anger proneness predicts coronary heart disease risk: prospective analysis from the Artherosclerosis Risk in Communities (ARIC) Study. *Circulation, 101*, 2034–2039.

Williams, K.D., & Karau, S.J. (1991). Social loafing and social compensation: the effects of expectations of co-worker performance. *Journal of Personality and Social Psychology, 61*, 570–581.

Willig, C., & Stainton Rogers, W. (Eds) (2007). *Handbook of qualitative research in psychology*. London: Sage.

Wilson, G., & Rahman, Q. (2005). *Born gay: the psychobiology of sexual orientation*. London: Owen.

Wimmer, H., & Perner, J. (1983). Beliefs about beliefs: representation and constraining function of wrong beliefs in young children's understanding of deception. *Cognition, 13*, 103–128.

Windelband, W. (1894/1998). History and natural science (trans. J.T. Lamiell). *Theory & Psychology, 8*(1), 6–22.

Winnicott, D.W. (1964). *The child, the family, and the outside world*. Harmondsworth: Penguin.

Winter, J.S.D., & Couch, R.M. (1995). Sexual differentiation. In P. Felig, J.D. Baxter, & L.A. Frohman (Eds), *Endocrinology and metabolism* (3rd edn) (pp. 1053–1104). New York: McGraw-Hill.

Witelson, S.F., Beresh, H., & Kigar, D.L. (2006). Intelligence and brain size in 100 postmortem brains: sex, lateralization and age factors. *Brain, 129*, 386–398.

Witelson, S.F., Kigar, D.L., Scamvougeras, A., Kideckel, D.M., Buck, B., Stanchev, P.L., Bronskill, M., & Black, S. (in press). Corpus callosum anatomy in right-handed homosexual and heterosexual men. *Archives of Sexual Behavior*.

Wixted, J.T. (2004a). The psychology and neuroscience of forgetting. *Annual Review of Psychology, 55*, 235–269.

Wixted, J.T. (2004b). On common ground: Jost's (1897) law of forgetting and Ribot's (1881) law of retrograde amnesia. *Psychological Review, 111*, 864–879.

Wixted, J.T. (2005). A theory about why we forget what we once knew. *Current Directions in Psychological Science, 14*, 6–9.

Woldorff, M.G., Gallen, C.C., Hampson, S.R., Hillyard, S.A., Pantev, C., Sobel, D., & Bloom, F.E. (1993). Modulation of early sensory processing in human auditory cortex during auditory selective attention. *Proceedings of the National Academy of Sciences, 90*, 8722–8726.

Wolfberg, P.J., & Schuler, A.L. (1993). Integrated play groups: a model for promoting the social and cognitive dimensions of play in children with autism. *Journal of Autism and Developmental Disorders, 23*(3), 467–489.

Wood, D., Bruner, J., & Ross, G. (1976). The role of tutoring in problem solving. *Journal of Child Psychology and Psychiatry and Allied Disciplines, 17*(2), 89–100.

Woodward, S. (2007). *Why women wear what they wear*. Oxford: Berg.

Worchel, S. (1979). Co-operation and the reduction of intergroup conflict: some determining factors. In W.G. Austin & S. Worchel (Eds), *The social psychology of intergroup relations* (pp. 262–273). Monterey, CA: Brooks/Cole.

Wright, D.B., & Loftus, E.F. (2008). Eyewitness memory. In G. Cohen & M.A. Conway, *Memory in the real world* (3rd edn) (pp. 91–106). Hove: Psychology.

Wright, S.C., Aron, A., McLaughlin-Volpe, T., & Ropp, S.A. (1977). The extended contact effect: knowledge of cross-group friendships and prejudice. *Journal of Personality and Social Psychology, 73*, 73–90.

Wundt, W. (1862). *Beiträge zur Theorie der Sinneswahrnehmung*. Leipzig und Heidelberg: C.F. Winter.

Wundt, W. (1873). *Principles of physiological psychology*. Leipzig: Engelmann.

Yeung, N.C.J., & von Hippel, C. (2008). Stereotype threat increases the likelihood that female drivers in a simulator run over jaywalkers. *Accident Analysis & Prevention, 40*(2), 667–674.

Zaccaro, S.J. (1984). Social loafing: the role of task attractiveness. *Personality and Social Psychology Bulletin, 10*, 99–106.

Zajonc, R.B. (1965). Social facilitation. *Science, 149*, 269–274.

Zajonc, R.B. (1968). Attitudinal effects of mere exposure. *Journal of Personality and Social Psychology, Monograph Supplement 2, Part 2, 9*, 1–27.

Zimbardo, P.G. (1969). The human choice: individuation, reason, and order vs. deindividuation, impulse and chaos. In W.J. Arnold & D. Levine (Eds), *Nebraska Symposium on Motivation* (pp. 237–307). Lincoln: University of Nebraska Press.

INDEX

NOTE: page numbers in **bold** type refer to glossary entries.